"The majority of the enlisted men in the army are simply human driftwood – men who have committed crime elsewhere, and are hiding in the service under assumed names; men who cannot brook the liberties and familiarities of society, and take refuge in military discipline; men who are disappointed, disheartened, and ambitionless, and find the lazy life of a soldier a relief." — A Chicago newspaperman, 1874

"It takes all kinds o' men to make up an army. Officer, o' course, whose doins is writ up in books, but it takes a lot o' common fellows too, like me and Tuttle, and Billy Blake and others – jist privates, men that don't know nothing except what they're told to do, that kills and gits killed, and that the world never hars about. Jist privates we was, jist rough, strong young fellows ready to march all day, tired, hungry, thirsty, to go here, go thar, without understandin' why nothin' except to shoot and shoot to kill. And yet to ourselves we seemed important. Every private's trouble meant jist as much to him as though he'd been a Major. Hundreds of graves scattered over Dakota and Montana of men that's never been missed, never been writ up, but they was good soldiers jist the same, and without 'em thar wouldnt've been no country, maybe." — A 7th Cavalry Trooper

"You felt like you were somebody when you were on a good horse, with a carbine dangling from its small leather socket on your McClellan saddle and a Colt army revolver strapped on your hip. You were a cavalryman of the Seventh Regiment. You were part of a proud outfit that had a fighting reputation." — A 7th Cavalry Trooper

"They aren't forgotten because they haven't died. They're living right out there – Collingwood and the rest – and they'll keep on living as long as the regiment lives. The pay is $13 a month. The diet: beans and eggs – may be horsemeat before this campaign is over. They fight over cards or rot-gut whiskey, but share the last drop in their canteens. The faces may change, names, but they're there. They're the regiment – the Regular Army – now and 50 years from now." — John Wayne in Fort Apache, 1948

"The Government pays you to get shot at." — Frederick Benteen

CUSTER's BEST

THE STORY OF COMPANY M, 7TH CAVALRY AT THE LITTLE BIGHORN

Colonel French L. MacLean

Schiffer Military History
Atglen, PA

Book design by Robert Biondi.

Library of Congress Catalog Number: 2011922742.

Printed in China.
ISBN: 978-0-7643-3757-4

We are always looking for people to write books on new and related subjects. If you have an idea for a book, please contact us at the address below.

Published by Schiffer Publishing Ltd.
4880 Lower Valley Road
Atglen, PA 19310
Phone: (610) 593-1777
FAX: (610) 593-2002
E-mail: Info@schifferbooks.com.
Visit our web site at: www.schifferbooks.com
Please write for a free catalog.
This book may be purchased from the publisher.
Please include $5.00 postage.
Try your bookstore first.

In Europe, Schiffer books are distributed by:
Bushwood Books
6 Marksbury Ave.
Kew Gardens, Surrey TW9 4JF
England
Phone: 44 (0)20 8392-8585
FAX: 44 (0)20 8392-9876
E-mail: info@bushwoodbooks.co.uk
www.bushwoodbooks.co.uk

PREFACE

"The idee of the Seventh gittin' licked never entered our minds."[1]

Twice in my lifetime the United States has experienced a seminal event so shattering that almost everyone who was at least in elementary school at the time can remember exactly where he or she was when they heard about it, and what they were doing. Being born in 1952, the two seminal events for me were the assassination of President John F. Kennedy on November 22, 1963 – when I was eleven – and the terrorist attack on the World Trade Center in New York and the Pentagon in Washington, D.C. on September 11, 2001 – when I was 49. My father can add a third event for his life that is forever etched in his mind – the Japanese attack on Pearl Harbor on December 7, 1941; Dad was just 18 at the time.

The Battle of the Little Bighorn on June 25 and 26, 1876 was probably another of those events for people alive at that time. Unlike the three more-recent examples, communications were not instantaneous back then and most Americans did not hear about the demise of General George Custer – a genuine military hero of the Civil War eleven years previously, nicknamed "Hard Ass" by the enlisted men of the 7th Cavalry – and much of his command until over a week after the battle; many citizens got the news on July 4, 1876, which happened to be the 100th anniversary of American independence. Most people in polite society – that is east of the Mississippi River – did not know where the Little Bighorn was located; it was just part of the northern Great Plains somewhere, for in central and eastern Montana – which was not yet a state – there were no cities or towns, no military bases and no farms or ranches.[2] There was just space – lots of space.

The American public's mood can best be summed up by the initial comment of General William T. Sherman, the commander of the United States Army, on first hearing the news of Custer's demise:[3]

> "I don't believe it, and I don't want to believe it, if I can help it."

Of course, it was hard to believe. Between the end of the Civil War in 1865 and 1890 the United States Army and hostile Indian warriors engaged in 950 fights, all of which resulted in the death of 930 soldiers and the wounding of another 1,060.[4] The Little Bighorn would account for roughly one-fourth of those total deaths in a two-day period; and most of those fatalities occurred in just a few hours.

Pre-Little Bighorn public opinion of Custer ranged from flattering to sublime: the "Boy General," the "Napoleon of the Plains," the "Darling of the Gods," the "Last of the Cavaliers" and the "Murat of the American Army" were just a few of the noble titles bestowed on the cavalry leader. But, occasionally, other epithets were heard: the "Chief of Thieves" and "Glory-Hunter."[5] Yes, he may have been somewhat tactically unimaginative in combat, preferring the all-or-nothing cavalry charge, but that technique worked more often than not. Between 1868 and 1878 there were 18 cavalry attacks on the frontier against Indian villages of 200 or fewer teepees and all of them were successful, and his phenomenal good fortune brought on the epithet "Custer's luck."[6] Why, George Custer had nine lives.

Unfortunately, each of his soldiers had but one. The *New York Times* first ran the story of the Little Bighorn disaster on July 7, 1876, not a nefarious delay in reporting, but reflecting that news traveled much more slowly in those days than it does in our own. That July morning the entire front page was devoted to the account under the headline "The Little Horn Massacre." The following day, July 8, the newspaper again devoted the entire first page to Custer's demise under the banner "The Indian Slaughter." On July 9, the *New York Times* again reserved the bulk of the front page to the battle beneath the proclamation "Custer's Last Fight." But the story then began

The land stirred men's souls for warriors and cavalrymen alike. This photo, taken in mid-May 2010 about ten miles from the battlefield, shows how desolate the terrain was at higher elevation. In order to obtain adequate water and food for their families, the mass of Lakota and Northern Cheyenne warriors had to establish their campsites in the lush river valleys, where sustenance was more plentiful. The U.S. Army knew this and concentrated their search for the Indian villages in these valleys.

to fade; there was a small article on page five of the *New York Times* on July 12 about the Indian Chief Sitting Bull, but it was clear that the *Times* had moved on to other more pressing stories.

The Little Bighorn story resurfaced almost three years later. In 1879, during the army court of inquiry concerning the battle held in Chicago, Illinois, the *Chicago Times* stated about Custer's defeat at the Little Bighorn that "no occurrence of modern times carried such a shock to the American populace." The newspaper went on to compare the event to the 1865 assassination of President Abraham Lincoln.[7] The *New York Herald* described the event this way in its July 12, 1876 edition:[8]

> "Long after this generation has passed away, long after every vestige of merciless Sioux has passed from the continent, long after this Yellowstone country has become a seat of towns and cities and a prosperous civilization, the name of Custer and the story of his deeds will be fresh in men's memories. The story that comes to us today with so much horror, with so much pathos, will become a part of our national life."

Modern historians have continued to attempt to capture the mood of the nation after the battle. One scribe in 1973 – almost 100 years after the battle – tried to get his arms around the nation's mood on hearing of George Custer's defeat:[9]

> "George Armstrong Custer, after four years of resounding success against one of the best armies in American history, had been destroyed with his command by the warriors of a Neolithic culture. Occurring in the centennial year of American independence, the blow came as a rude shock, to a nation proudly surveying its growth and achievements in the face of serious threats to its united existence. The death of five companies of the Seventh Cavalry and of its illustrious leader shook the faith of the country, albeit briefly, in the military leadership that vanquished Lee."

Since that day in 1876, "Custer's Last Stand" not only has become part of our national life, not only entered the lexicon of military history, but also has assumed almost mythic proportions in the saga of America and her love affair with the western frontier. It is strange, then, how many Americans – seemingly in increasing numbers with each passing year – believe that the entire 7th Cavalry Regiment was annihilated along with its commander George Custer at the Little Bighorn. Nothing could be further from the truth. Although there were no proven human survivors of the five cavalry companies (C, E, F, I and L) that went with their regimental commander (Captain Myles Keogh's horse "Comanche" was found and nursed back to health, as was a little gray horse from Company E named "Nap" though) the three companies led by Major Marcus Reno (A, G and M), the three companies led by Captain Frederick Benteen (D, H and K) and Company B – which was escorting the logistical pack train – although hit hard by Sitting Bull's warriors, survived fairly intact.

It is also interesting to assess how much of the post-battle literature over these many years has been Custer-centric. With some notable exceptions, it is quite easy for authors to focus on the commander, unfortunately at the expense of the common soldier, as was illustrated by this quotation concerning Custer in a piece written about the battle in the late 1800s:[10]

> "His candle of life was too soon snuffed out, under circumstances that surround his and his brave men's death with a halo of glory, an appropriate ending to a soldier's career."

The goal of this book is to shed as much historical light as possible on one of these surviving units – Company M – the sergeants and junior soldiers of which performed quite heroically during the two-day battle, who were not interested in an appropriate ending to their military career, and who were a microcosm of the U.S. Army on the frontier – overworked, underpaid, misunderstood, under-appreciated and often just plain forgotten.

This is their story.

Colonel French L. MacLean
United States Army, Retired
Decatur, Illinois

Contents

List of Maps

Acknowledgments

An author, much like a commissioned officer, can never go it alone. Many individuals contributed mightily to this endeavor and need to be recognized.

Sheila Abarr, Public Affairs Specialist of the Armed Forces Retirement Home (Soldiers' Home) in Washington, D.C., for information on this venerable facility.

Hank Adams of Bozeman, MT: of "The Wild Bunch" – we rode the battlefield together; no commander had a more loyal Operations Officer.

Sandy Barnard: an outstanding author of *Custer's First Sergeant John Ryan*, *Digging Into Custer's Last Stand*, and editor of *Ten Years with Custer: A 7th Cavalryman's Memoirs*, who got me interested in First Sergeant John Ryan.

Bob Biondi: my editor at Schiffer who can take my simple document, photos and maps, and format all of it into something wonderful to read.

Ken Real Bird of Garryowen, MT: a descendent of Chief Medicine Crow, who saddled us up on horses and helped us see the Little Bighorn from a unique perspective.

T.G. Bolen: our next-door neighbor, who knows more about everything than anyone I have ever met, who wrote the foreword and ensured this work was logical in thought and sequence.

Dr. John Bradley: our across-the-street neighbor who put up with my ramblings about the Little Bighorn over a beer or wine on too many occasions to remember.

Joanne Codi of Coatesville, PA: for showing me John Ryan's 1922 letter to Thomas Norwood.

Dennis K. "DK" Clark of Fort Leavenworth, KS: my old 3rd Armored Division buddy and excellent author of "Private Roman Rutten: Custer's Tailor," as well as numerous other articles, for providing a wealth of information on Company M; he may be our generation's quintessential expert on command and control at the Little Bighorn.

Bob Connor and Staff Sergeant Edward C. Connor, U.S. Army (Retired): great-grandsons of Private Jean Baptiste Gallenne, for providing detailed information and photos on their great-grandfather; as an example of the "Army Family," Troop D of the 1st Squadron in the 7th Cavalry conducted the reenlistment of Staff Sergeant Ed Connor on April 29, 1999 at Comanche Airfield near Tuzla, Bosnia, in honor of Private Jean B. Gallenne.

Jim Court, former Superintendant of the Little Bighorn National Monument: for giving me permission to walk the terrain at the timber line fight.

Wes Cowan, owner of Cowan's Auctions in Cincinnati: for his interest in the project and our discussions concerning artifacts from the 7th Cavalry and the Little Bighorn; and Linda Gillings of the firm who provided several photographs.

Carlton Dean, Pharmacy Manager, and Molly Ann Wagoner of the Grand Avenue Walgreen's, Decatur, IL: for carefully weighing each artifact shown in the book and asking so many interesting questions; and Melissa Garcia for help in developing photographs.

Marvin Decker at Fort Leavenworth, KS: my West Point classmate, who provided to me tons of cavalry info and moral support from our frigid days patrolling the Czech border in Germany to handing me my retirement saber on Last Stand Hill over two decades later.

Louis DiMarco at Fort Leavenworth, KS: of "The Wild Bunch" – we rode the battlefield together; author of *War Horse*, the preeminent book on cavalry horses throughout history; no commander ever had a finer executive officer.

John A. Doerner, Little Bighorn, MT: Chief Historian of the Little Bighorn Battlefield National Monument – his insight into the battle, derived from twenty years onsite, is unmatched and made this book a lot more complete than it otherwise would have been.

Marianne Driscoll of Oakton, VA: one of our best friends and for the last fifteen years, my editor and proofreader par excellence.

Mike Dykes: another old army-buddy; what he taught me about using terrain during hunting helped reveal what really transpired at the Little Bighorn.

Haim Gottschalk: archivist at the Lilly Library, Indiana University, for helping me navigate through the Walter M. Camp manuscript collection there.

Neal Gray of Selby's Essco in Billings, MT: he provided me with every map of Montana and the Little Bighorn imaginable.

Bev Hackney at the Decatur Public Library: for helping me to find all the pertinent *New York Times* articles.

Dennis Hagen: Archivist, 10th Mountain Division Resource Center; Western History/Genealogy Department; Denver Public Library, for finding the transcript of Charles White's diary.

Dr. Tim Hastings, Decatur, IL: firearms expert, for providing technical expertise on the weapons involved in the battle.

Gary Hendershott in Little Rock, AR: one of the premier dealers of western and firearm artifacts; his expertise of period weapons is unmatched.

Joyce Henderson, Decatur, IL: of Mariná Bridal Shop, an expert, experienced seamstress, for helping to identify the cloth artifact found on the battlefield.

David H. Lowenherz of Lion Heart Autographs in New York: for his expertise on period documents.

David MacLean: my brother, who – when we were assigned together in a cavalry squadron – served as the perfect role model for what a cavalry officer should be – fearless, ornery and imaginative, and with a touch of mischief; a retired colonel, he should have been a cavalry regimental commander.

Myron "Mac" MacLean, Decatur, IL: my father, who asked me every day how I was progressing on the book and encouraged me to keep at it.

Mike Mahon, Alexandria, VA: of "The Wild Bunch" – we rode the battlefield together; a retired Navy Rear Admiral, he should have been the Chief of Naval Operations.

Steven Meadow: owner of *War of the Rebellion*, for providing expert assistance on period Cartes de Visite, cabinet cards and period documents.

Montgomery C. Meigs: as a young lieutenant colonel, encouraged me as an even younger captain to pursue my interest in military history.

Lee Noyes: Editor, Custer Battlefield Historical & Museum Association *Battlefield Dispatch*, for his explanation of the Charles White papers.

Kim Olmsted: my former squadron commander in the 1st Squadron of the 1st Cavalry Regiment; he was the spitting image of George A. Custer in thought, word and deed and gave me an insight into that cavalry leader's soul.

Jack Pattison, Marietta, GA: of "The Wild Bunch" – we rode the battlefield together; my West Point First Captain, he should have been the Chief of Staff of the Army.

Wes Pietsch of Decatur: an accomplished period firearms expert and Little Bighorn aficionado, he reviewed the lengthy draft and provided invaluable expertise on weapons at the battle.

Jason Pitsch of Garryowen, MT: his understanding of the Little Bighorn valley terrain, and the battle artifacts found in the area, is unmatched; he has finally demonstrated where the Reno skirmish line and timber position were located.

Gwenith Podeschi, Reference Librarian, and Dennis E. Suttles, Abraham Lincoln Presidential Library, Springfield, IL: for finding many published books I could locate nowhere else.

Steve Pyle, owner of Landmark Photo Studios in Decatur, IL: for the amazing photo work with the Company M battlefield artifacts.

Larry Sklenar in South Carolina: a superb Little Bighorn author of *To Hell with Honor; Custer and the Little Bighorn*, who provided a copy of Private Jean Gallenne's letter recounting the battle.

Sharon A. Small: Curator; Little Bighorn Battlefield National Monument, for the wonderful photographs and opportunity to visit the battlefield archives.

Bob Snelson in Colorado: an excellent Little Bighorn author of *Death of a Myth: Seventh Cavalry at the Little Bighorn*, who provided the partial transcript of the Thomas H. French court martial.

Brian Spatola, Collections Manager, Anatomical Division, and Michael Rhode, Archivist, Otis Historical Archives, National Museum of Health and Medicine, Armed Forces Institute of Pathology, who provided valuable information concerning the medical aspects of the death of Private Frank Braun of Company M.

Glen Swanson, Agua Dulce, CA: author of the acclaimed *G. A. Custer; His Life and Times*, for providing several photos of Company M troopers that I could find nowhere else.

David Veve, Cohutta, GA: my godson and indefatigable scout for Company M gravesite photos across the country.

Tom Veve: my original Army Buddy who encouraged me never to grow up; a real historian with a PhD, who fights his own never-ending battle to ensure that historically-challenged college students understand how great this country really is.

Karen Weston and Deronica Goldsmith: University Archivist and Archives Assistant at the University of Wisconsin at Whitewater Library, for navigating me through the extensive Dr. Kenneth Hammer collection at UWW.

Alice Younker of DynaGraphics in Decatur: for producing all the preliminary drafts of this work so I could send it out to get "fresh eyes" to find my errors.

Sergeants Adams, Anderson, Boston, Casanova, Cheatham, Ciolino, Clark, Clayton, Cook, Espinoza, Gehrig, Hearns, Horne, Jackson, Johnson, Kubista, Landers, Lemon, Maxwell, McClanahan, Metzler, Mobley, Paxson, Perry, Preston, Rodriguez, Sewell, Taisican, Thompson, White, Williams, wherever you are; and all the others whose names my old age has robbed me of remembering: I couldn't have done it without you.

Olga: my wonderful wife and best friend; to paraphrase General Douglas MacArthur a bit – when I finally cross the river, my thoughts will be about you and you and you.

Any errors in the book come from me alone, usually when I ignored the sage advice of any of the people listed above.

DEDICATION

"The sergeant is the Army."[1]

This book is dedicated to First Sergeant John Ryan and all the other non-commissioned officers in Company M of the 7th Cavalry Regiment at the Little Bighorn.

In my own thirty years of service on active duty in the army, in many infantry and cavalry units, there has been many a sergeant, who salvaged my career in peacetime and – more importantly – saved my life in wartime. Quite simply, without them I would not have been worth a hoot as a commissioned officer.

It is within this personal context that in April 2009, when I had an opportunity to bid on a group of items at auction that had been owned by First Sergeant Ryan, I once again called on my own "First Sergeant," my wife Olga, and asked her permission to try and obtain them. As has happened so often in our three decades of marriage, she supported me to the hilt and several weeks later I was holding John Ryan's army discharge paper issued in December 1876. The document is signed by his company commander, Captain Thomas H. French, who wrote the following characterization concerning the service of his departing senior non-commissioned officer – and very likely his fast friend: "A brave, capable, and trustworthy First Sergeant." I hope that I will provide a good home for First Sergeant Ryan's discharge from the army.

This work is also dedicated to the other tough non-commissioned officers and young enlisted men, who made up Company M – and the other companies of the regiment. The first quotation on the preceding pages, by a Chicago newspaperman, captured the feeling at the time of many civilians toward the soldiers in the army. To many citizens of the day, the men of the 7th Cavalry and every other army unit were "bummers, loafers and foreign paupers." Congress must have agreed with that sentiment, as in 1871 the monthly pay of a trooper was reduced from sixteen to thirteen dollars a month.[2] Elizabeth Custer, the wife of George Custer, once wrote that the 7th Cavalry Regiment was a "city of refuge" for outraged husbands due to the number of domestic difficulties they often recited to her.[3]

But I disagree, and while some troopers may have had their faults – as evidenced by the John Wayne quotation from the motion picture, *Fort Apache* – the junior enlisted soldiers gave their best effort in a difficult set of circumstances. I am not alone in that assessment. As one distinguished author wrote:[4]

> "But in truth, men survived by small, individual acts of ingenuity, bravery, and perseverance and by the selflessness of their comrades – not to mention a fair share of good fortune."

But good fortune only takes you so far when the sun is blazing, your throat is cracking, your heart is pounding, the bullets are flying and the enemy – who outnumbers you four or five to one – is all around; on that razor-sharp precipice between living and dying, whether you are a young private or an old colonel, you had better have a damned-good First Sergeant leading you out.

Above

The "Wild Bunch" at "Last Stand Hill" in August 2004; (l-r) Lou DiMarco, Marv Decker, Mike Mahon, Olga MacLean, Hank Adams, Joyce DiMarco and Jack Pattison. The author, standing behind his wife, Olga, in the center retired at that spot and date. The previous day the group rode the battlefield on horseback thanks to Ken Real Bird, experiencing 100° heat, similar to the temperature on June 25, 1876.

Command Sergeant Major of the Army coin for outstanding service (front and rear views). The author received the prized momento from Command Sergeant of the Army Major Kenneth Preston on the occasion of the author's retirement from active duty in 2004.

INTRODUCTION

"When you fight, you don't fight for abstract values like the flag, or the nation, or democracy. You fight for your buddy. You fight to keep him alive, and he fights to keep you alive, and you go on that way, day after day, battle after battle."[1]

George A. Custer took all 12 companies of the 7th Cavalry Regiment on the 1876 summer campaign that culminated in the Battle of the Little Bighorn. Each company had its own "personality," which was usually formed by the personalities and professionalism of its commander, its commissioned officers, and its sergeants and corporals[2] – in the case of Company M, given the quality of those leaders, that personality was probably along the lines of "Follow Me!" A soldier's primary loyalty on the frontier was to his company and within the 7th Cavalry companies had unique personalities. Company A, a fairly unruly and wild lot, was known throughout the regiment as "the Forty Thieves."[i] Company K, whose members took their white canvas trousers – used for stable duty – and had the company tailor remake them into tight-fitting, cavalry breeches, became known as a well-dressed unit and thus was called "Dude Company."[3] And Company I had a reputation throughout the army as a heavy-drinking unit; its moniker was the "Wild I."[4] After the company exhumed some of the 7th Cavalry dead on the battlefield, a year after the fight, for a more proper burial, Company I received a new nickname – "The Grave Robbers."[5]

The enlisted men in Company M certainly were a wild bunch as well. While they gave as good as they got on the battlefield, Company M troopers often sat on the wrong side of a court martial; swigged more than their fair share of rot-gut whisky; got in a brawl with "Wild Bill" Hickok; did time at the military prison at Fort Leavenworth; went absent, when the mood struck them, to the gold fields in the Black Hills and Alaska; participated in shootouts over poker games; visited "hog ranches," where they came down with a few venereal diseases; mistook a friendly Indian scout for an enemy and shot him; and, on occasion, told officers to "go to Hell." In fact, just two months before deploying on the 1876 Sioux Campaign, Company M erupted into a fist-flying riot that put good order and military discipline into extreme jeopardy.

But in later life, many of the survivors of the Little Bighorn from Company M returned to be "regular guys." One trooper went on to get a law degree, rose to a judgeship and served as a city politician in New York. Another had his mother-in-law move in with his family of seven children. Grandchildren who recalled their grandfathers getting noodles stuck in their moustache, while drinking a cup of soup, or giving the youngsters a small sip of wine, while telling them stories, have a way of transforming even the most hard-bitten cavalry trooper into plain old "Gramps."

No previous works have focused exclusively on Company M, although many books have mentioned the unit and its capabilities. Larry Sklenar, in *To Hell with Honor; Custer and the Little Bighorn*, for example, wrote:[6]

> "With its complement of non-commissioned officers virtually intact, and with [Captain] French in command, M Troop was as formidable as any available to Custer."

Sklenar continued his discussion by describing the regimental organization that would lead Major Marcus Reno to the fight in the valley by stating:[7]

> "Captain French and M Troop were the strongest component in the regiment in terms of leadership, experience, and numbers, and if Reno was to have the advance, he would need the most capable force available."

This author went on in his description of the company with this statement:[8]

> "At the head of the column, after Reno and his staff, [were] Captain French and M Troop. Presumably by design, Custer had given Reno probably the strongest single unit in the regiment and arguably the most courageous company commander."

Company M was certainly not George Custer's favorite company in the regiment. He most certainly reserved that distinction for B, C, E, F, I or L.[9] But in all probability, Custer's preferences were based on his degree of affinity with the company commander, not the overall capability of the unit. And Captain French was clearly not General Custer's favorite.

Many historians do not agree with Custer's assessment. Larry Sklenar had additional high praise for Captain Thomas French:[10]

[i] Regiments had nicknames as well. The 5th Cavalry Regiment was nicknamed the "Dandy Fifth." For a time in the late 19th century, the 12th Cavalry Regiment was named "The Junior Seventh" because so many officers had previous served with the 7th Cavalry.

"For all practical purposes, the only officer who had remained on the [skirmish] line [in the valley] for any length of time, directing Reno's primary attack force, was Captain French."

James Willert, author of *Little Big Horn Diary: Chronicle of the 1876 Indian War*, had this comment about Captain French:[11]

"He was a courageous officer, a calm person under fire, and had a ready sense of humor."

Later, when Captain French had his own problems, several members of the company came to his aid. By then it was too late; French left the army and died alone, a broken man, shortly thereafter. Other men from the unit went on to successful careers; one wayward private – who had accidentally shot a comrade in a hunting accident before the campaign – even became a municipal judge in New York City. His courtroom in the Bronx must certainly have been a far cry from Reno Hill! The last survivor of the battle from Company M lived until 1933; about the time that military theorists were defining the role the tank should assume in future warfare. One of these inter-war mobile warfare experts was George Patton; and it does not take much of an imagination to find some similarities between the two Georges – Custer and Patton. And the last 7th Cavalry Regiment survivor of the battle, Private Charles "Dutchy" Windolph, did not pass away until 1950, just two years before I was born.

While each of the dozen company outfits was also unique in its own experience at that fight, Company M's record of bravery, post-battle personal accounts, omission of gallantry awards and the absence of Company M testimony at the 1879 Major Marcus Reno Inquiry are elements of a fascinating story of what was and what might have been. While many aspects of the fight concerning the other eleven companies have remain veiled from historical sight, because so many Company M troopers survived, and because so many were not shy in later expressing their views of what happened in the encounter, we can piece together a fairly comprehensive history of the company.

This work will not, however, solve the great mystery of the Little Bighorn – what exactly happened to George A. Custer and the five companies of the 7th Cavalry that rode with him on the eastern bluffs of the river to their ultimate fate and Custer and Calhoun Hill. But that is just as well.

If the day ever comes that we do know the final answer to that enigma, the battle will cease to be perhaps the most powerful magnet for intellectual and amateur curiosity in the entire spectrum of military history, an apex position it has held from June 1876 to this day. We will also lose an insight into our own soul, because the Little Bighorn, "Custer's Last Stand," is also a figurative shimmering mirror. What we think about the battle says as much about ourselves as it does about the actual event – and this lends itself to everlasting argument, which often becomes quite heated. This "mirror effect" of the Little Bighorn also reflects within each of us, although we would probably never divulge our thoughts beyond our closest buddies – and certainly never to our spouses – the question of how we would have faced our own final moments had we been there on the valley skirmish line, Reno Hill, Calhoun Ridge, Deep Ravine or Last Stand Hill, when it is just us, our last friends and forever. John A Cockeril, a *New York Herald* reporter of the era, visited the battlefield in 1890 and tried to capture that overwhelming, singular feeling. He wrote in part:[12]

"I tried to form some idea of the awful sensation which must have come to each of these brave fellows as he realized the horror of the situation. That death awaited every man."

• • •

This book contains first-person accounts of many Company M participants in the fight. Perhaps the most controversial "testimony" comes from Sergeant Henry C. Weihe, also known as Charles White. Born in Saxony, Germany in 1847, Weihe enlisted under the name Charles White in 1867 in Company D of the 17th Infantry Regiment. He left the service in late 1870 and became a farmer but re-enlisted in March 1871 in Philadelphia, Pennsylvania and was soon assigned to Company M. In January 1877 Weihe became the first sergeant of Company M after John Ryan left the army.[13]

Over the years Henry Weihe either kept a diary or made contemporaneous notes that he later put together in an account of his army service. There is no indication in what I could find that Weihe attempted to have these remembrances published; it does not appear that he even showed them to anyone outside his family. Henry Weihe died of heart disease on October 23, 1906 at Fort Meade, Sturgis, South Dakota. In 1909 his widow loaned her husband's diary to noted Little Bighorn researcher Walter Mason Camp. It could not have been placed in better hands.

Walter Mason Camp was born at Camptown, Pennsylvania on April 21, 1867. At age 16 he took his first railroad job walking track; in 1891 he graduated from Pennsylvania State College with a degree in civil engineering. Over the next several years, Walter Camp moved to California and became a draftsman for the Southern Pacific Company, a superintendent for the Rainier Avenue Electric Railway, and a foreman for the Seattle Lake Shore and Eastern Railway. In 1897 he became the engineering editor for the *Railway and Engineering Review* (later renamed *The Railway Review*); this occupation apparently conserved enough time for Camp to begin researching the Little Bighorn in particular and the American West in general. The well-informed Camp began a multi-year task of interviewing (or at least corresponding with) as many survivors of the battle still living; he found over 200 cavalrymen and warriors to record their input, and visited 41 western battle sites.[14] Camp was able to question many of the 200 by himself; for others he dispatched a representative with a pre-written questionnaire to interview the battle veterans.[15]

Walter Camp had hoped one day to publish his findings in a book titled *History of the 7th U.S. Cavalry*, but this was not to be. His health began to fail and he died at his home in Kankakee, Illinois on August 3, 1925 at age 58. After his death, Camp's extensive papers initially made their way into private collections until most were later consolidated at three locations: the Lilly Library at the University of Indiana, the Harold B. Lee Library at Brigham Young University and the Denver Public Library.[16]

For Walter Camp, the Little Bighorn battle was a mystical event. In his field notes, now at the Lilly Library, Camp wrote of the field:[17]

"This battlefield site is the shrine of all the West. The fact that the Indian life of the Plains has passed, or is passing, away makes it all the more so. This landmark belongs to the heroic."

Walter Camp did not have the opportunity to actually interview Henry Weihe, but he did type up several pages of Weihe's document so that the researcher would have Weihe's observations after the diary was returned to the family. Despite numerous efforts, this study has been unable to locate the complete original document. Camp's transcript of a portion of the diary is in the Denver Public Library, but archivists there say that there is no original diary present, nor is there any evidence that the original was ever in their control. The Lilly Library at the University of Indiana does not have the original diary either, nor does the Harold B. Lee Library at Brigham Young.

Eminent Little Bighorn historian Sandy Barnard, author of *Custer's First Sergeant John Ryan* and editor of *Ten Years with Custer: A 7th Cavalryman's Memoirs*, does not know of the diary's resting place, nor does Jim Donovan, author of the widely-acclaimed *A Terrible Glory: Custer and the Little Bighorn – the Last Great Battle of the American West*. Valley expert Lee Noyes, author of "The Valley Fight: The Enlisted Man's Perspective," has made an extensive search for the document but does not know its whereabouts. If these true experts cannot find it, the elusive manuscript may be lost to history.

We are thus left with Camp's transcript. His notes at first appear to be a verbatim transcript of Weihe's recollections, but upon closer review one can see numerous cross-outs and pencil annotations, most likely added by Walter Camp. In some areas the typewritten document discusses Henry Weihe; clearly these are Camp-authored statements. Thus, we face a conundrum of determining just exactly what part of Walter Camp's notes are faithful transcripts of Weihe's writings and which portions are Camp's inferences of what he believed Weihe was trying to communicate. Lee Noyes believes the "diary" does not appear to be contemporaneous, but rather a document based on the original and later expanded, updated and perhaps "corrected."

Researching difficulties do not end there. As the reader will later note, many of Weihe's assertions are extremely controversial, dealing with officer intoxication and cowardice. Walter Camp was unable to "cross-examine" Sergeant Weihe about these conclusions. My own experience over 30 years of Regular Army service has led me to almost always trust information provided by non-commissioned officers, but there have undoubtedly been occasions when sergeants have stretched the truth or told outright fabrications – as have commissioned officers.

Other factors contribute to analyzing testimony concerning a battle. With the passing of time, memories of many participants can become faulty. Inexperience under fire can cause a witness to use exaggeration in describing violent events, which seasoned soldiers might view as the normal course of battlefield events. Chaos and confusion, which seem to have been present in many parts of the Little Bighorn fight, can affect witnesses. Terrain in the valley of the Little Bighorn has changed significantly over the last 130-plus years, both with respect to the shifting channel of the river, to the agricultural and transportation developments over the years. Thus, when a witness discusses where he was in relation to the river may not be the same distance today even though the points on the ground are exactly the same. Some individuals are simply bad historical witnesses; either because they are ignorant of events surrounding them, non-observant or untrustworthy. Finally, personal animosities between individuals sometimes continue for many years after a significant event – the Custer saga is replete with officer animosities of this nature.[18]

To evaluate the veracity of Sergeant Weihe's writing, let us now turn to one of the most well-read, knowledgeable men I have ever known, Attorney-at-Law T.G. Bolen, who is not only a fifty-plus-year veteran of the Illinois bar, a founding partner in Bolen, Robinson and Ellis Law, and a well-respected local historian, but also my next-door neighbor and one of my best friends.

But before we do that, I must add one small piece of information about Mr. Bolen – a small but important nugget that I sometimes think about when we discuss history over a hot, steaming cup of coffee, in front of a roaring fire in the hearth on a cold, crisp Illinois afternoon in the late fall. In the 1930s, T.G. was a young boy in the tiny Illinois farming village of Maroa, some 15 miles north of Decatur. As neighbors often do in central Illinois, a very old man, who had been a lawyer in his own youth, saw something in young T.G. and spent time telling the precocious child stories and parables of life, well before the young lad attended Maroa's one-room schoolhouse, which sat next to one of Illinois' innumerable cornfields. The old man undoubtedly happily relived part of his own youth as he sat down with his young pupil during the Depression in rural Illinois, as many things seemingly had not changed that much since his own pre-school years back in the 1850s.

Back then – before the Little Bighorn and even the Civil War – another lawyer had taught T.G.'s later teacher some homespun stories to improve his vocabulary and keep him interested in obtaining an education. That first lawyer was a tall, gangly man who had taught himself how to read many years before, about the time his mother Nancy Hanks passed away. Abraham Lincoln loved telling stories throughout his life.

Sometimes you can read history and sometimes, if you are really fortunate, you can feel history around you, as the fire dances on the logs, listening to stories about the past.

Opposite

***Top left*: Cavalry company barracks.** Reconstructed barracks is at Fort Abraham Lincoln, just south of Mandan, ND. Pairs of bunks were pushed together to maximize space; this led to the term "bunkies." The company was the basic social group for soldiers on the frontier. Photo taken in 2010.

***Top right*: Non-commissioned officer area in cavalry company barracks.** Sergeants and corporals slept at the end of the barracks, closer to the dining area and heating stoves. The company first sergeant usually had his own room. Photo taken in 2010.

***Bottom left*: A coveted heating stove area in the barracks.** Bunks in the vicinity were prime locations as temperatures in the Dakotas frequently dipped below zero at night. Photo taken in 2010.

***Bottom right*: Dining area in the barracks.** For some new troopers it was the first time in their lives that they ate on a regular basis. Food on frontier posts was generally better than in recruit depots as company cooks at forts had to come back to their units at some point and face their comrades. This exhibit shows china plates; standard tableware was a tin cup and tin plate. Photo taken in 2010.

A cavalryman's first duty was to his horse. Reconstructed stable is at Fort Abraham Lincoln, just south of Mandan, ND. This is one of the horse stalls. Horses ate hay, corn and oats in garrison; much of the trooper's day was spent caring for his mount. Photo taken in 2010.

Reconstructed stable. Compact size of the building helped retain heat in the frigid northern plains' winters. Photo taken in 2010.

Fort Meade, Dakota Territory, in 1882. Company M was stationed here for many years after the Little Bighorn. *Photo courtesy of the Little Bighorn Battlefield National Monument.*

FOREWORD

In the reconstruction of any event, the prime way of determining what happened is by examining the testimony of the witnesses to the affair. The obvious problem that occurs is that when witnesses testify in opposition to each other, some way must be found to determine which witness is telling the truth. Further, it is not always a question of 100 percent truth on one side and 100 percent falsehoods on the other, but rather there are shades in the testimony of both sides which might impel a jurist one way or the other.

Over human existence a number of methods have been tried to determine the truth of the testimony of a witness ranging from making the witness walk over red hot coals, to drowning them in a pool of water to see if they float, to torturing them to the limit of human endurance to see if their testimony changes.

The Anglo-American system has arrived at a different method of determining the truth. The truth is weighed by citizens of the community who serve as jurors and determine what actually happened with respect to the event in question. This normally leads to disagreements among the members of the jury, sometimes advancing to threats or even physical assault.

In the American system, there are basically two different types of trials. The first is a criminal trial in which the result is the defendant being found either guilty or not guilty with some sort of punishment being dealt out to a defendant found guilty. In a civil case, two parties litigate a matter which is of difference to them, with the result generally being that a successful plaintiff is awarded financial damages from the defendant.

The way to weigh testimony can be illustrated by the difference in these two types of trials. The judge in either type of adjudication will instruct the jury at the end of the case as to the law they must follow. In a criminal case he will advise them that they must find the defendant guilty beyond all reasonable doubt. In a civil case the judge will instruct the jury that the standard is not beyond a reasonable doubt, but instead is determined by the preponderance of the evidence, which presumably means that the jurors will reach at least a 51 percent conclusion with respect to the believability of one side.

When the court, however, attempts to tell the jury what "reasonable doubt" means, one finds the difficulty in the entire system of weighing testimony. Courts over the years have tried to define "reasonable doubt" and have basically given up in the attempt. They have tried to say it must exclude every reasonable conclusion which a reasonable man would reach in regard to whether or not a defendant is guilty or not guilty. The courts have abandoned all such attempts and simply say to the jury that the standard is reasonable doubt, leaving the jury to determine what that means, which means that it means absolutely nothing.

The Jury will deliberate, presumably weighing the evidence, but frequently using what the law assumes is the common sense of a jury, which is simply that these everyday people will reach a common sense conclusion about whether or not a witness appears to them to be believable or not. Obviously this leaves a lot of room for extraneous standards to be introduced in the deliberations.

Assessing testimony is difficult to accomplish when you hear and see the witness testify in person. It clearly becomes much more difficult when you attempt to determine the weight to give testimony with respect to an occurrence that occurred over a century ago.

The purpose of this foreword, after this lengthy preamble, is to provide the reader a set of scales by which he or she may weigh the historical testimony throughout this book. Everyone knows the result of the Battle of the Little Bighorn of June 1876. This work sets forth a detailed description of what happened during the course of the battle and how the final result occurred through the eyes of one-twelfth of the regiment, a single company. To my knowledge, this is the first detailed description of the actions of Company M of the 7th Cavalry as detailed by the men who fought there, augmented by the further analysis of maps, artifacts, and the use of procedures not available at the time the original accounts were written.

Many articles and books have been written about the Custer engagement, but this particular work is unique in two regards. First, it details the men of Company M and their actions throughout the course of two days with illustrations of the tactics employed and the affect of their actions. The reader will be educated not only by the depth of the research but by the fact that the author is a senior officer of over thirty years experience in the United States Army and who has seen actual combat and commanded troops, but perhaps more importantly knows what makes soldiers tick.

Numerous of the previous written constructions of the event have been done by very talented writers who spent months, if not years or decades, assembling the details of their account. However, like any written account, it is viewed through the lens of the writer's personal experiences. Bruce Catton and Shelby Foote have given us brilliant analysis of the Battle of Gettysburg, the other seminal event of the American 19th Century. But as excellent as their accounts are, they may view the engagement from a different perspective than Pershing or Eisenhower, whose profession was military operations. So in this respect, what Colonel MacLean has done may be seen to be much more akin to the accounts given in the decades following the battle by Edward S. Godfrey, Luther R. Hare or Winfield S. Edgerly, with the exception that he does not have a dog in the fight in the same way that these actual veterans of the battle certainly did.

In reviewing this testimony, the reader must take into account the same test in that the recollections of the men involved may vary according to their own remembrances of the military itself, as well as the men and officers who fought with them. The testimony is divided into three specific classes. First is the testimony of the two surviving commissioned officers of Company M, Captain Thomas H. French and First Lieutenant Edward G. Mathey – although Mathey was with the pack train at the beginning of the fighting; secondly is the testimony of the sergeants and corporals; and lastly is the testimony of the large group of individual soldiers – the junior enlisted men – who formed what was Company M of the 7th Cavalry.

Next, the testimony can also be divided into three categories by its origin. The first category is testimony given at an official inquiry or at courts martial, which seem to have occurred with unbelievable frequency to the twenty-first century reader! The second class of testimony is written accounts made reasonably contemporary with the occurrence, the chief of these being the diary written by Sergeant Henry C. Weihe and that written by First Sergeant John Ryan; and the third being small recollections, either written or oral, occurring close to the time of the occurrence or over the life of the men who participated in the battle.

In weighing the testimony of the commissioned officers – both in Company M and in the other elements of the regiment – one has to keep in mind that their view of the battle and that of their fellow officers' performance must necessarily be influenced by the fact that their roles would be reviewed as they bore the responsibility for the success or failure of the unit. The testimony of the sergeants and corporals should be considered, knowing that they were closer to the officers than the junior soldiers, and the non-commissioned officers frequently had a relationship which, if not personal, was at least based on mutual respect. Their writings, like the officers', must be viewed with an understanding what interests they may have in the record.

Particular attention is given to the diary of Sergeant Henry Weihe. The reader should weigh it taking into account what he believes to have been the sergeant's motives in writing the same, as well as the important fact that apparently the sergeant never revealed his writings to anyone during his lifetime, and it is particularly good fortune that a transcript of this record even exists – and would be a bonanza if the entire original document could ever be found!

The reader will have to decide whether these entries are Sergeant Weihe's best memories recorded without fear of favor or influence, or whether they bear some slight course correction based on Sergeant Weihe's relationship with his fellow non-commissioned officers and particularly the commissioned officers engaged in the battle. Sergeants would have had a particular feeling of respect or even gratitude to some of the commissioned officers whose competence and intelligence would be responsible for the life or death of the men under their command. With the sergeants, as well as the other enlisted men, their memories of an officer's performance in the battle may be colored by their respect for that officer based on his previous treatment of the men and their abilities. When you consider the line between the privates in the company and the commissioned officers, it is well to remember that the distance was more like a gulf than a line. Therefore, these men may have been willing to ascribe dereliction of duty more quickly to an officer for whom they had little regard prior to the battle.

When the reader considers the overall conduct of the battle with respect to the performance of Company M, his overall review of the battle itself can be bounded by two extremes. On the one hand, the reader may feel that the battle led to the destruction that it did because the entire regiment was led by recklessness, with a gross under-estimation of Indian strength and motivation, compounded by a significant portion of the regiment being incompletely prepared for battle. At the other extreme, the reader may feel that the 7th Cavalry was a force of brave, capable men who met with a series of bad luck at the Little Bighorn, which Ernest Hemingway captured in a line in his work *For Whom the Bell Tolls*:

> "'[George Custer] just had a great ability to get himself in and out of trouble,' his grandfather went on, 'and on the Little Big Horn he got into it but he couldn't get out.'"

Was it recklessness or bad fortune as the 7th Cavalry marched toward the Little Bighorn? Did any reasonable military officer of the time need to assume that the topography of much of the potential battlefield would not be suitable for army cavalry? Would a reasonable senior officer have assumed that his battle plan would not be faithfully and competently executed by his subordinates? Could any veteran of Indian fighting have assumed that the regiment was going to meet the largest and most capable Indian armed force that ever existed on the Plains, and that these exquisitely lethal warriors would not only stand and fight, but go over to the offensive and attempt to annihilate an entire army cavalry regiment?

Between these two extremes, the reader should weigh the material contained herein, understanding that for all these men, this was the greatest experience of their life and probably the one occurrence which colored the remainder of their existence as they looked back on the memories of the Little Bighorn, General Custer and their loyalties to the only bonding group they ever knew – their fellow soldiers of Company M.

T.G. Bolen
Decatur, Illinois

CHAPTER ONE

Company M History

"From the bottom to the top of the army's chain of command, the Indian campaigns were viewed as isolated events of fleeting duration, with each incident viewed as being the last."[1]

1866

The United States Army organized the 7th Cavalry Regiment on September 10, 1866 at Fort Riley, Kansas as part of the expansion of the Regular Army, after the massive demobilization of the predominantly volunteer Union Army of the Civil War. In May 1865 there had been 1,034,000 volunteers in service; by November of 1865 that number had decreased by 800,000; and by the end of 1865 only 38,545 men were left.[2] Even the biggest "doves" realized that figure was too small for the nation's needs. In 1865 there were approximately 270,000 Indians spread across the western half of North America; the army estimated that about 100,000 were hostile to white men. The primary mission of the frontier army – the small Regular Army, not the mass conscripts or volunteers, characteristic of the Civil War – was to control and subdue those 100,000.[3]

The authorized strength, established by Congress, of the Regular Army was 54,000 men in 1866; but Congress would see fit to actually decrease the end strength of the army to 37,000 in 1870 and reduced the army's overall strength again in 1874 to a paltry 25,000.[4] Concerning senior officer positions, at the conclusion of the Civil War, there was one General of the Army (Ulysses Grant), one Lieutenant General (William Sherman), five Major Generals and 19 Brigadier Generals.[5] But those numbers also decreased and soon thereafter, there were only 11 general officer positions in this smaller army, with the competition to obtain even a colonelcy extremely "fierce."[6]

On paper a cavalry regiment was to have 888 troopers (including 43 officers), with each of the 12 line companies to have three officers and 70 enlisted men.[7] That was on paper, and the frontier wasn't guarded by paper; like every other regiment, the 7th Cavalry was chronically under strength. The regiment initially was under the command of Major John W. Davidson[i] until November 25, 1866, when Colonel Andrew J. "Whiskey" Smith assumed command. Second-in-command of the regiment was Lieutenant Colonel George A. "Jack" Custer.[ii] The mission of the regiment was to protect railroad construction crews as they built the tracks for the "Iron Horse" across the central plains to tie the industrial East with California; at the tactical level, the 7th Cavalry would deal with the tribes along the Republican and Smokey Hill rivers.[8]

Company M was organized on September 17, 1866; like the rest of the regiment, the company was initially staffed by officers of the 2nd Cavalry Regiment. Second Lieutenant William W. Cooke was assigned to Company M on December 4 and became the temporary regimental adjutant four days later. First Lieutenant Owen Hale arrived at Company M on December 29, 1866, and became the acting commander.[9]

Some 365 enlisted recruits assembled at Carlisle Barracks, Pennsylvania in August 1866; all were slated to go to the 7th Cavalry. They departed two months later for Fort Riley, Kansas.[10] On September 1, 1866, 198 recruits for the 7th Cavalry arrived at Jefferson Barracks, Missouri (just south of St. Louis); the men departed for Fort Riley on September 5. Another 200 recruits for the regiment arrived at Jefferson Barracks on September 7 and left for Fort Riley on September 9.[11] By the end of the year, the regiment had 15 commissioned officers and 963 enlisted men assigned, but in what would be a festering trend in the organization, in just these first four months of the regiment's existence, some 80 men deserted.[12] On December 13, 1866, First Sergeant Joseph Bates assumed duties as Company M's senior non-commissioned officer. Thomas Norwood served as another sergeant in the company as did a George Stoll and Charles Miligan.[13]

1867

The 7th Cavalry remained under the command of Colonel Andrew J. Smith until February 26, 1867, when he was placed on detached service from the regiment and commanded the Department of the

---

[i] John W. "Black Jack" Davidson was born in Fairfax County, Virginia on August 14, 1825. An 1845 graduate of West Point, he saw action in the Mexican War at the Battle of San Pasqual and the Battle of Rio San Gabriel. On March 30, 1854, while serving with the 1st Regiment of Dragoons (later renamed the 1st Cavalry Regiment), he fought against the Jicarilla Apaches at the Battle of Cieneguilla, near present day Pilar, New Mexico. During the fight, Lieutenant Davidson lost 22 killed and 36 wounded (including himself) of his force of 60 troopers. Davidson fought primarily in the West in the Civil War, capturing Little Rock, Arkansas; he also commanded the 3rd Brigade of the 2nd Division of the 4th Corps during the Peninsula Campaign in Virginia in 1862. After brief service in the 7th Cavalry, Davidson assumed command of the 10th Cavalry Regiment, which consisted of black soldiers; it was in this position that he acquired his nickname of "Black Jack." He commanded the 10th Cavalry (later known as the Buffalo Soldiers) until March 1875. On March 20, 1879 Davidson was made colonel and commander of the 2nd Cavalry Regiment. John W. Davidson died at St. Paul, Minnesota on June 26, 1881 after in serious accident four months previously when his horse slipped on ice and fell on top of him. He is buried at Arlington National Cemetery, Section L in Lot 1199.

[ii] Close associates called Custer "Jack," derived from his initialed luggage – "G.A.C." Many troops called him – obviously behind his back – "Iron Ass."

Upper Missouri.[iii] Lieutenant Colonel George A. Custer assumed command. Second Lieutenant William W. Cooke was replaced by First Lieutenant Myles Moylan as adjutant. Company M had Captain Lewis M. Dayton assigned to be the company commander; however, Dayton was not present with the company, but rather was on the staff of General William T. Sherman.[iv] Company M remained at Fort Riley until March 26, 1867 when it went with Companies A, D and H as a detachment under Lieutenant Colonel Custer from Fort Riley as part of Major General Winfield S. Hancock's expedition to central Kansas. First Lieutenant Owen Hale was in command of Company M; Second Lieutenant James T. Leavy[v] assisted him after he arrived in May.[14] First Sergeant George Stoll assumed duty as the senior non-commissioned officer of the company that summer.[15] On February 24, 1867 Adjutant William Cooke transferred from Company M to Company A.[16] The muster roll listed 20 men in Company M as deserters on February 28, 1867.[17]

The unit arrived at Fort Harker on April 1 and continued to Fort Larned, which it reached on April 7, 1867. Hancock then turned north, and after failing to bring several Cheyenne and Lakota chiefs to a council, pursued the Indian bands for almost 300 miles.[vi] The 7th Cavalry reached camp outside Fort Hays, Kansas on April 19; Company M's muster roll listed 20 men as deserters on April 30, 1867.[18] From June 1 to 10, Company M and four other companies – all under Lieutenant Colonel Custer – marched toward the Platte River and arrived at Fort McPherson, Nebraska on June 10.[19] One 7th Cavalry officer summed up the expedition quite succinctly in a letter to his wife:[20]

> "I have no idea where we are going!"

The command then moved toward the north fork of the Republican River, arriving at its destination on June 22. One week later the regiment moved toward the Platte River and subsequently arrived at Fort Wallace – in far western Kansas – on July 14. Company M listed 16 deserters as of June 30, 1867.[21] The fort was effectively under siege by Indians; it was short of ammunition, food and medical supplies, with many soldiers wracked with illness. The arriving regiment found cholera in some men, but escaped an epidemic. The march had been so demanding that men "deserted in droves" and Custer issued orders to shoot them on sight – four troopers were, in fact, shot by officers sent to chase them down and apprehend them – the group of officers included Major Joel Elliott, First Lieutenant Thomas Custer and First Lieutenant William W. Cooke; one of the apprehended deserters died[vii] On July 15, Lieutenant Colonel George Custer left the command – without proper authority – and rode back to Fort Riley.[22]

The army, which sometimes overlooked eccentric behavior on the part of former war heroes, had now had enough of Custer's behavior, and Major General Winfield S. Hancock urged Colonel Andrew J. Smith to bring charges against his unruly subordinate, which Smith finally did. On August 7, 1867, General in Chief of the United States Army, Ulysses S. Grant, ordered that a General Court Martial be convened the following month at Fort Leavenworth, Kansas to try Lieutenant Colonel Custer. The prosecution brought two charges against George A. Custer at the court martial – Charge I: Absent without leave from his command; and Charge II: Conduct prejudicial to good order and military discipline, which primarily pertained to his treatment of regimental deserters, abandoning the two men killed by Indians and for marching his troops for excessive distances. There were eight individual specifications included in the two charges. The trial lasted from September 15 to October 11, 1867.

The panel, which was headed by Colonel William Hoffman – an infantryman – and that included two distinguished cavalry colonels, John W. Davidson and Benjamin H. Grierson, convicted Custer of five of the specifications and sentenced him to be suspended from rank and command for one year, forfeiting his pay for that time. The sentence became effective on November 20, 1867. Custer spent the next several months at Major General Philip Sheridan's personal quarters at Fort Leavenworth and then returned home to Monroe, Michigan in June 1868 to spend the remainder of his enforced absence.

Company M continued local operations in Kansas and returned to Fort Harker, Kansas, where it took up winter quarters.[23] The August 31, 1867 muster roll showed 21 deserters, and stated two men had died of cholera; the roll dated October 31, 1867 reflected two deserters; and the roll for December 31, 1867 showed 10 deserters and two men who had drowned in a flood. By the end of the year the company first sergeant was Charles Miligan.[24]

1868

The regiment remained at Fort Leavenworth until August 18, 1868, when it moved by rail and horse to Fort Dodge, Kansas. Perhaps sensing imminent large-scale operations, the officers of the 7th Cavalry appealed to Major General Philip H. Sheridan to terminate Custer's year-long enforced absence and return him to command the regiment (which was then under command of Major Alfred Gibbs)[viii] in the field.

[iii] Andrew J. "Whiskey" Smith was born on April 28, 1815 in Bucks County, Pennsylvania. He graduated from West Point in 1838 and subsequently fought in the Mexican War and on the frontier in the Southwest. During the Civil War, Smith saw action in the Vicksburg Campaign, Red River Campaign, Price's Raid, the Battle of Tupelo (where he defeated Nathan Bedford Forrest), and the Battle of Nashville. This last action earned him a promotion to brevet major general. Smith earned his nickname "Whiskey" for supposedly ordering – while drunk – that the captured Confederate town of Oxford, Mississippi be burned in August 1864. Also known as "Old A.J.," in April 1869 Smith retired from military service and became the postmaster of St. Louis, Missouri, which fitted with his preference for administrative duties. Andrew Jackson Smith died in St. Louis on January 30, 1897. He is buried there.

[iv] Lewis M. Dayton was born in Albany, New York on June 20, 1835. A civil engineer by education, during the Civil War he was an aide-de-camp for William T. Sherman. After the war, he was assigned to the 7th Cavalry Regiment on November 26, 1867. Dayton served as the military secretary to General Sherman from March 8, 1869 to December 31, 1870, when Dayton was discharged from the army. He served no time in the field while assigned to Company M. Lewis Dayton was appointed in 1890, as a colonel, to be a member of the Board of Visitors of the United States Military Academy. Lewis M. Dayton died in Cincinnati, Ohio on May 18, 1891.

[v] James T. Leavy was born in Lexington, Kentucky on February 4, 1840; he served in the Civil War in the 3rd Kentucky Cavalry Regiment, fighting at Shiloh and the capture of Savannah and receiving two brevet promotions to first lieutenant and captain. He was appointed a Second Lieutenant in Company M on January 22, 1867 and joined the regiment at Fort Hays in May 1867 but did not stay long; the following year a retirement board found him incapacitated by reason of insanity and retired him on July 31, 1868. He was subsequently confined in the Government Hospital of the Insane, until his wife secured his release in October 1868. In 1872 Leavy enlisted under an assumed name in the 4th U.S. Artillery and served in the Modoc War. He returned to the retired list in 1878. James T. Leavy died on July 8, 1893 near Harper's Ferry, West Virginia; he is buried at Arlington National Cemetery in Section West in Section 1, in Grave 83-B.

[vi] Winfield S. "Hancock the Superb" Hancock was born on February 14, 1824 in Montgomeryville, Pennsylvania. He graduated from West Point 18th in his class of 44 in 1844; during the Mexican War, Hancock fought at the Battles of Contreras, Churubusco and Molino del Ray. At the beginning of the Civil War, Hancock commanded a brigade but was rapidly promoted and commanded the 1st Division of the 2nd Corps at the Battle of Antietam, Fredericksburg and Chancellorsville. At Gettysburg, upon the death of Major General John F. Reynolds, Hancock took temporary command of the Union forces in the field before the arrival of Major General Meade, and organized the defenses that would ultimately lead to the Union victory. He was wounded in the fighting and after a partial recuperation was given command of the 2nd Corps; he played a pivotal role in the Battle of the Wilderness, shattering the Confederate defenses at the Mule Shoe position. He later fought at the Siege of Petersburg; at the end of the war, he supervised the execution of the Lincoln assassination conspirators in Washington, D.C. In 1866 Hancock assumed command of the Military Department of the Missouri; he was the convening authority for the General Court Martial of George Custer. Hancock ran for president in 1880 and narrowly lost the election. He died of an infected carbuncle – complicated by diabetes – at Governors Island, New York on February 9, 1886. He is buried at the Montgomery Cemetery in Norristown, Pennsylvania.

[vii] Troopers of the day called desertion "The Grand Bounce" and "Taking French Leave." Despite the frivolity of the word choices, the problem was huge for the army. Between 1867 and 1891, some 88,475 soldiers went absent without official leave of the 255,712 men recruited, a rate of over 34 percent. Source: Alexander Rose, *American Rifle: A Biography*, New York: Delacorte Press, 2008, 211.

[viii] Alfred "General Etiquette" Gibbs was born on April 22, 1823 in Astoria, Long Island, New York. He graduated from West Point in 1846 (ranked 42 of 59 cadets); previously he had attended Dartmouth

Major General Sheridan devised a three-prong assault to attack the tribes south of the Arkansas River. One column, commanded by Major Eugene A. Carr, focused on the area southeast of Fort Lyon, Colorado. The second formation, under Major Andrew W. Evans, would depart from Fort Bascom in the New Mexico Territory. The third – and major – column would advance south from Kansas; this formation would be led by Brigadier General Alfred Sully, and would feature George Custer and the 7th Cavalry.[25]

The officers' premonitions proved correct; the regiment departed Fort Dodge (five miles east of present Dodge City, Kansas) on September 1, 1868. Events initially did not go well; on September 7, a party of warriors swooped into camp and took two men from Company F – part of the rear guard of the column – prisoner, later killing one. A new commander was needed, and even Captain Frederick Benteen was approached about taking command, but he declined.[26] Sheridan[ix] sent the following telegram on September 24, 1868 to General (his Civil War brevet grade)[x] G.A. Custer, who was at his home in Monroe, Michigan:[27]

> "General Sherman, Sully[xi] and myself, and nearly all the officers of your Regiment have asked for you, and I hope the application will be successful. Can you come at once? Eleven companies of your Regiment will move about the first of October against hostile Indians from Medicine Lodge and towards the Wachita Mountains."

Later, George Custer would state that General Sheridan was even more effusive in his praise of the wayward lieutenant colonel, when he told the 7th Cavalry's commander:[28]

> "I rely on you in everything, and shall send you on the expedition without orders, leaving you to act entirely on your own judgment."

Custer arrived at Fort Hays by September 30, and returned to the regiment in the field at Bluff Creek (not far from Fort Dodge) on October 6.[29] The command remained at this location until October 9, when it marched down the Arkansas River – including Company M – and rode to Bluff Creek. On October 12, Company M and the regiment began a reconnaissance of more of the Arkansas River and engaged the Indians in a skirmish; with rations running short, the 7th Cavalry marched to Camp Sandy Forsyth, arriving there on October 28, 1868. The regiment – minus Company L – crossed the ice-covered Arkansas River on November 12, 1868 and headed toward the Washita Mountains. Custer tinkered with the unit's organization, creating a temporary company of about forty sharpshooters – under the command of First Lieutenant William W. Cooke, an excellent marksman in his own right – from the rest of the regiment. Custer also instituted a short but efficient program of drill and target practice to whip the command into shape for the upcoming fight; he demanded and received adequate ammunition to do this.

The regiment's route of advance took it to Beaver Creek (North Canadian River), where it helped establish Camp Supply, which would be its logistical base for the upcoming operation. On November 23, 1868 Custer and the regiment departed Camp Supply – along with a small 36-wagon supply train – and at daybreak on November 27, 1868 charged into Cheyenne Chief Black Kettle's village on the Washita River. For the fight, Company M was assigned to the three-company battalion, along with Companies G and H, commanded by Major Joel Elliott. Their mission was to move around the left of the village and occupy a position as close as possible to the rear of the village. Other elements of the command were given separate missions; it would not be the last time that Lieutenant Colonel Custer would divide his regiment into four pieces for a concentric attack.[30]

In command of Company M was First Lieutenant Owen "Holy Owen" Hale;[xii] he was assisted by Second Lieutenant Thomas J. March[xiii] Captain Lewis Dayton was still the commander on paper, but he was on detached duty to St. Louis with General Sherman. Second Lieutenant Donald McIntosh was also assigned to the company but was on sick leave.[31] The senior non-commissioned officer was First Sergeant Daniel Duane. The fight initially went well for the cavalry, who had achieved surprise over the unsuspecting village. However, some of the warriors escaped downstream, and Major Elliott, without

for a year. He had a distinguished record in the Mexican War, where he was severely wounded once and brevetted twice. Gibbs served in the 2nd Cavalry Regiment. In 1857 he campaigned against Apaches in New Mexico, where he received a serious lance wound in his side. At the beginning of the Civil War he was captured by Texan troops on July 27, 1861 and not exchanged for over one year. During the final stages of the Civil War, he commanded the 3rd Brigade of the 1st Division in Sheridan's Cavalry Corps. He ended the conflict as a brevet major general. Gibbs served as a major in the 7th Cavalry Regiment from its formation to December 26, 1868. Alfred Gibbs died suddenly of congestion of the brain at Fort Leavenworth, Kansas on December 26, 1868. He is buried at the Saint Mary's Episcopal Churchyard in Portsmouth, Rhode Island.

[ix] Philip H. "Little Phil" Sheridan claimed to have been born in Albany, New York, in 1831, but some historians believe that he was born in County Cavan, Ireland or on a ship sailing from Liverpool, England to the United States. Growing up in Somerset, Ohio, Sheridan attended West Point, but took an extra year to graduate after a twelve-month suspension for assaulting a fellow cadet with a bayonet; he graduated 34th of 52 cadets in his class in July 1853. Commissioned in the infantry, Sheridan gained his fame in the Civil War. He served as chief quartermaster and chief commissary of Subsistence, Army of Southwest Missouri, Department of the Missouri (1862); commander, 2nd Michigan Cavalry (1862); commander, 2nd Brigade, Cavalry Division, Army of the Mississippi (1862); commander, 11th Division, Army of the Ohio (1862); commander, 3rd Division, Right Wing, 14th Corps, Army of the Cumberland (1862-1863); commander, 2nd Division, 4th Corps, Army of the Cumberland (1863-1864); commander, Cavalry Corps, Army of the Potomac (1864); commander, Army of the Shenandoah (1864-1865); and commander, Sheridan's Cavalry Command (March-April 1865). Weighing in at 115 pounds, he resembled a jockey, which resulted in his nickname of "Little Phil," an affectionate moniker given to him by his troops. He was also foul-mouthed and hard drinking, which may have resulted in his being a bachelor until relatively late in life. After the war, as military governor of Texas and Louisiana, he ran afoul of President Andrew Johnson and was removed from command. In 1869 Sheridan succeeded William T. Sherman as the commander of the Division of the Missouri, with his headquarters in Chicago. In October 1871, Sheridan brought army troops into Chicago during the Great Chicago Fire to stop looting; he also helped direct firefighting and reconstruction of the city. "Little Phil" had the reputation as "a good drinker" and much champagne was consumed when he made the rounds visiting posts. Sheridan became the Commanding General of the United States Army in 1884 and held that position until his death; Congress awarded him a fourth star shortly before he passed away. Philip Sheridan died on August 5, 1888 in Nosquitt, Massachusetts. He is buried in Section 2, Site S-1, at Arlington National Cemetery.

[x] Brevet promotions authorized a commissioned officer to temporarily hold a higher rank; sometimes the officer concerned received the pay of that higher grade, but most often they did not, although in either case the officer would wear the insignia of that higher grade. The brevet promotion would be noted in the officer's title and later, after the officer reverted to his Regular Army grade, he would still be referred to by his higher brevet grade. Brevet promotions were often confusing when it came to determining which officer was senior to another. The practice was widespread in the Civil War era; officers could receive brevet promotions (often several) for acts of heroism or battlefield achievement. In the modern era, brevetting occurs on rare occasions, when officers are selected for promotion to a higher grade, but have yet to reach their effective date of promotion. It has nothing to do with battlefield bravery or achievement. In 1996 I was "brevetted" (the term then was "frocked") to colonel from lieutenant colonel at the Pentagon so I could better engage in significant Army Force Modernization issues (bringing in new equipment and changing organizations) that my position called for me to do. This work generally presents Regular Army grades for officers (i.e., Lieutenant Colonel Custer instead of Brevet Major General Custer).

[xi] Alfred Sully was born in Philadelphia, Pennsylvania on May 22, 1821. He graduated from West Point in 1841. Prior to the Civil War, Sully fought in the Seminole War in Florida, the Mexican War, and in California. During the conflict he was promoted to colonel and placed in command of the 1st Minnesota Volunteer Infantry Regiment in 1862, fighting at the Battle of Fredericksburg, before advancing to brevet brigadier general and various commands in the Dakota Territory. Alfred Sully died on April 27, 1879 at Fort Vancouver in the Washington Territory. He is buried at the Laurel Hill Cemetery in Philadelphia, Pennsylvania.

[xii] Owen "Holy Owen" Hale, a descendant of American Revolutionary War patriot Nathan Hale, was born in Troy, New York on July 23, 1843. During the Civil War, he first served as a sergeant major in two New York cavalry units; on May 8, 1863 he was commissioned a second lieutenant in the 7th New York Cavalry Regiment. Promoted to first lieutenant on March 13, 1864, he was brevetted to captain on March 13, 1865. After the war, Hale was in Denver, where he was appointed a first lieutenant in the 7th Cavalry in 1866. He received his nickname of "Holy Owen" due to his reputation as an ideal army officer. Hale was promoted to captain in the regiment on March 1, 1869. He also participated in the 1873 Yellowstone campaign. Prior to the 1876 campaign, he was placed on detached service at Jefferson Barracks, Missouri and missed the fight at the Little Bighorn. But "Holy Owen" Hale got into the fight at Snake Canyon in September 1877 and on September 30 was killed leading a cavalry charge. He is buried in Troy, New York.

[xiii] Thomas J. March was born in Pennsylvania in April 1844. March graduated from West Point in 1868, ranking 46 in a class of 54; but he was at the very bottom of his class in cavalry tactics! He joined the 7th Cavalry as a second lieutenant on June 15, 1868 and resigned on March 10, 1872. Thomas March died in Pennsylvania on February 8, 1909.

Custer's knowledge, took 19 troops and pursued them. What neither Elliott nor Custer knew was that several miles downstream were three sizable Indian camps. As Elliott, who was extremely popular in the regiment, passed Hale on his galloping horse, he yelled to the Company M commander: "Here goes for a brevet [promotion] or a coffin."[32]

But, it would be coffins for all of Elliott's small command, which included seven men from Company M. Custer secured the village and captured many non-combatants but later that morning some 1,500 warriors from the other villages in the area – the existence of which appear to have been unknown before the attack – began to ring the bluffs around the regiment. Custer, sensing that the tide had turned, ordered the regiment to advance – with the non-combatants – toward the other villages along the river, with the regimental band loudly playing "Ain't I Glad to Get Out of the Wilderness," the combined effect of which caused the warriors to withdraw to protect their families. But Custer had no intention of sticking his neck out further, and under cover of approaching darkness counter-marched the regiment away from the villages toward Camp Supply. During the battle, Custer dispatched Captain Edward Myers to look for Elliott, but the officer could not find him. Custer would later claim that he had to put the interests of the regiment ahead of Elliott's detachment (by assuming that Elliott had simply become lost and would find his own way back to Camp Supply), but some officers in the regiment – notably Captain Frederick W. Benteen[xiv] – would later allege that Custer had abandoned Elliott and his men.[33] The incident would split the regiment's officers into two factions, the Custerphiles and the Custerphobes.[34]

During the fighting, Private John Ryan – who would later be the company first sergeant at the Little Bighorn – had a close call:[35]

> "I was riding around the foot of a small bluff, when all of a sudden I came upon an Indian warrior about to shoot one of our men down. This man was dismounted, his horse having been shot. This Indian fired at him once and missed him, and was about to fire at him a second time. I was so close to this Indian that it was impossible for me to check my horse, so it flashed through my mind in an instant the best thing to do, as it meant death for one or the other of us. I put spurs to my horse and tried to run over him. As I went by, I fired and dropped him with the first shot. My horse was going so fast that he shot by him quite a distance before I could check him. I wheeled around and put two more bullets from my Spencer into him and then emptied my Colt six-shooter into him."

Ryan scalped the fallen foe but quickly discarded the bloody trophy, as it had left blood on his overcoat.[36]

The regiment arrived at Camp Supply two days later; Elliott and his men were nowhere to be found. On December 7, Custer and his command left Camp Supply and marched toward Fort Cobb, Indian Territory. On December 11, 1868 the regiment camped some six miles from the site of the Washita fight and again took up the search for Major Elliott and his troopers. General Sheridan, Lieutenant Colonel Custer and a detail found the mutilated, frozen bodies – that had also been chewed on by wolves – of Elliott and his men. Company M soldiers had received terrible desecrations: Farrier Thomas Fitzpatrick had his head and both arms cut off; Private John Myers had been scalped, had his throat cut and had 19 bullet holes in him; Private Cal Sharpe had his throat cut and had numerous bullet and arrow wounds.[37] It was a scene the regiment would never forget.

The 7th Cavalry finally arrived at Fort Cobb on December 18, 1868.[38] John Ryan recalled the condition of Company M at the conclusion of the winter campaign:[39]

> "[We were] almost destitute of clothing, our trousers being patched with seamless meal bags. A large number of hats belonging to the men were made of the same material. The legs of our cavalry boots were pretty scorched and burned from standing around camp fires, and as substitutes we used leggings made from pieces of tents. A number of men had to use woolen blankets in place of overcoats."

That type of clothing – and the weather – contributed to illness as well. From 1866 to 1868 the 7th Cavalry Regiment lost fifty-one men who perished from cholera.[40]

It was an up and down 1868 for Company M as well. In February, former sergeant George Stoll was charged with killing Private James Smith (the charges may have been later dropped for lack of evidence); five men also deserted that month. Major Joel Elliott inspected the company and found it "good" in discipline, military appearance, arms, accoutrements and clothing, but determined the unit was "middling" in instruction. William Doherty assumed duties as company first sergeant for several months; five men deserted in June, fifteen in August and six in October. First Sergeant Daniel Duane took over as the senior non-commissioned officer on July 8, 1868. He was replaced at the end of the year by First Sergeant David Gordon.[41]

1869

The entire army had a busy year, so much so that General William Sherman remarked:[42]

> "At this moment, we have not a single regiment that may be said to be in reserve."

Company M began the year at Fort Cobb (in current Oklahoma), but left there on January 6, when it left with the entire regiment to go south to the Washita Mountains; the regiment established camp on Medicine Bluff Creek. It remained there until March 2, when it departed for the north fork of the Red River. First Lieutenant Owen Hale departed Company M on March 1; First Lieutenant Thomas W. Custer assumed command. On June 7, 1869 thirty men of Company M departed camp near Fort Hays and accompanied detachments of Company A and Company D to scout along the Saline River. They then moved along the Smokey Hill River and finally returned to camp on June 19. On July 21, 1869 Company M escorted a herd of domestic animals to Fort Dodge, arriving there on July 21. The company returned to camp on August 5. For the next two months the unit conducted local scouting and escort duties until October 25, when it returned to Fort

[xiv] Frederick W. "Fred" Benteen was born in Petersburg, Virginia on August 24, 1834. After his mother died, Benteen moved with the family to Missouri. He joined the Union Army in the 1st Missouri Volunteer Cavalry Regiment. He fought at Wilson's Creek, Pea Ridge, Vicksburg, Mine Creek, Columbus and Westport and was brevetted twice – to major and lieutenant colonel. In 1864 he was appointed commander of the 10th Missouri Cavalry Regiment. Immediately after the conflict, Benteen commanded the 138th U.S. Colored Volunteer Regiment, a unit of black soldiers. He later joined the 7th Cavalry Regiment as a captain, and command of Company H. Benteen fought in all major engagements with the regiment, including the Washita River – where he was critical of Custer's handling of the fight. At the Little Bighorn, Benteen rode a horse named "Old Dick." After the Little Bighorn, Benteen fought in the Nez Percé Campaign of 1877; he was brevetted to brigadier general in 1890 for his actions at the Canyon Creek fight of the campaign. Called "White Bird" by the Indians, Benteen was promoted to major in the 9th Cavalry in 1882. He was court-martialed in 1887 for drunk and disorderly conduct; the original punishment was dismissal from the army but President Grover Cleveland reduced the sentence to a one-year suspension. On July 7, 1888 Benteen retired; he died in Atlanta, Georgia on June 22, 1898. Originally buried at the Westview Cemetery in Savannah, Georgia, his remains were interred in 1902 at Arlington National Cemetery, Section 3 in Site 1351.

Leavenworth, Kansas. Beginning in 1869, Colonel Samuel D. Sturgis[xv] assumed formal command of the regiment, but was uninterested in frontier service and managed to be on detached service most of the time, leaving George Custer as the *de facto* commander.[43]

• • •

The army's command and control structure for the Plains was fairly straightforward, based on geographic considerations. In overall command was the Military Division of the Missouri. With its headquarters in Chicago, and commanded from 1869 to 1883 by General Philip Sheridan, the division extended from Illinois to Utah, and from the border with Canada to the border with Mexico. Business was brisk in the Military Division of the Missouri; from 1867 to 1884 troopers from this division fought 619 engagements with western Plains Indian tribes.[44]

Subordinate to the division were four departments. In the northern tier stood the Department of Dakota, which comprised Minnesota, and what would become North Dakota, South Dakota and Montana.[xvi] This department was headquartered in St. Paul and commanded by General Winfield S. Hancock from 1869 to 1872 and subsequently by General Alfred Terry from 1872 to 1886. To the south was the Department of the Platte. Headquartered in Omaha, it comprised Iowa, Nebraska and what would become Wyoming and Utah. General Christopher Augur commanded the department from 1869 to 1872; General Edward Ord commanded from 1872 to 1875; and General George Crook commanded from 1875 to 1882.[45]

Still further south was the Department of the Missouri, with its headquarters at Fort Leavenworth, Kansas. This department included Illinois, Missouri, Kansas, the northern tip of the Texas panhandle, and what would become Colorado, New Mexico and the northern half of Oklahoma. The department was commanded by General John Pope from 1870 to 1883. The southernmost department was the Department of Texas. With its headquarters in San Antonio, the department consisted of the bulk of Texas and what would become the southern half of Oklahoma. General Joseph Reynolds commanded the department from 1870 to 1872; General Christopher Augur was in command from 1872 to 1875; and General Edward Ord from 1875 to 1880. With the general elimination of all significant military threats to the Plains by the beginning of the last decade of the 1800s, the army would finally disband the Military Division of the Missouri and its four subordinate departments, in the 1891 to 1892 timeframe.[46]

• • •

For much of the year, First Lieutenant Thomas W. Custer served as the commander of Company M. First Sergeant David "Harry" Gordon served as the senior non commissioned officer until his death from an accidental gunshot.[47] Desertions continued to plague the unit. Company M reported 10 deserters on the April 30 muster roll, eight deserters on the June 30 muster roll, three deserters on the August 31 muster roll, four deserters on the October 31 muster roll and two deserters on the December 31 muster roll.[48]

1870

Company M began the year stationed at Fort Leavenworth, Kansas. John Ryan temporarily assumed duties as company first sergeant on February 1, 1870 and held the position until First Sergeant Frederick Thies transferred to the unit on April 4, 1870. On May 2, 1870 the company left Fort Leavenworth with Lieutenant Colonel Custer and three other companies for Camp Sturgis, which was located near Fort Hays, Kansas. This detachment arrived at Camp Sturgis on May 18. Forty men from the company – five sergeants, four corporals and 31 men – departed on June 1, as part of a detachment under Captain George Yates, to protect settlers along the Solomon and Saline Rivers in central-western Kansas. The element returned to Camp Sturgis on June 9. Two days later, First Lieutenant Tom Custer and First Lieutenant Donald McIntosh of the company took 33 men and joined a detachment under Captain Myles Keogh to protect the railroad going east from the camp.[xvii] They returned to the company on June 13. The entire company scouted along the Saline, Solomon and Republican Rivers beginning August 8; the men returned to camp on August 23; during this month John Ryan served as acting first sergeant, when Thies was absent. The company marched to the Solomon River and arrived there on October 12. It remained in the field until October 23, 1870, when it returned to Fort Hays for winter quarters.[49] The unit reported 23 deserters on the April 30 muster roll, 10 deserters on the June 30 muster roll, 12 deserters on the October 31 muster roll and two deserters on the December 31 muster roll.[50] Even day-to-day life in the cavalry could be brutal. On November 17, 1870, Sergeant David Gordon was accidentally shot in the leg. The bullet shattered so much of the interior of the limb that an amputation was finally ordered and conducted on December 14. Gordon died of shock two days later at Fort Larned, an event that ended the year for the company on a down note. First Sergeant Frederick Thies re-assumed duties as the senior non-commissioned officer of Company M after Gordon's death.[51]

• • •

A couple of men from Company M got a little too close for comfort to national notoriety while at Fort Hays. The pair walked into Drum's Saloon at Hays City on the Kansas moonlit summer evening of July 17, 1870. According to a later first sergeant of Company M, there at the bar stood James Butler "Wild Bill" Hickok, who was also the city

[xv] Samuel D. Sturgis was born on June 11, 1822 in Shippensburg, Pennsylvania. He graduated from West Point in 1846 (ranked 30 of 59 cadets) and was appointed a second lieutenant in the 2nd Dragoon Regiment. He was captured by the enemy near Buena Vista in the Mexican War – and held for eight days – while serving with the 1st Regiment of Dragoons (later the 1st Cavalry Regiment). In 1861 he fought at the Battle of Wilson's Creek; he later commanded the 2nd Division of the 9th Corps at South Mountain, Antietam and Fredericksburg. In June 1864, Nathan Bedford Forrest defeated Sturgis at Brice's Crossroads, Mississippi, after which Sturgis did not play a significant role in the war effort. Brevetted a major general for his role at Fredericksburg, he reverted to his Regular Army rank of lieutenant colonel after the war and initially commanded the 6th Cavalry Regiment before assuming command of the 7th Cavalry. He advised his son James G. Sturgis not to join the cavalry, but the younger Sturgis did not heed his father's advice, joined the 7th Cavalry, and was killed at the Little Bighorn. Colonel Sturgis later served as Governor of the Soldiers' Home before retiring from active service at Fort Meade, Dakota Territory, in 1886. Samuel D. Sturgis died after a brief illness at St. Paul, Minnesota on September 28, 1889. He is buried at Arlington National Cemetery in Site 1042.

[xvi] Colorado was admitted to the Union in 1876. North Dakota, South Dakota and Montana were admitted in 1889. Wyoming was admitted in 1890, with Utah entering in 1896, Oklahoma in 1907 and New Mexico in 1912.

[xvii] Myles Keogh was born on March 25, 1840 in Orchard House, Leighlinbridge, in County Carlow, Ireland. In 1860 he joined Papal military forces in Italy and later became a member of the Vatican Guard, in the Company of Saint Patrick. He immigrated to New York, arriving on April 1, 1862. During the Civil War, he served on the staff of Brigadier General John Buford, the commander of the 1st Cavalry Division, fighting at Brandy Station and Gettysburg. Buford's role at Gettysburg was significant in the Union victory and Keogh received a brevet promotion to major. After John Buford died of typhoid in December 1863 – with Myles Keogh at his deathbed – Keogh was appointed aide de camp to General George Stoneman. Both were captured in Georgia and held for several months as prisoners of war. By the end of the conflict, Keogh was promoted to brevet lieutenant colonel. Myles Keogh joined the 7th Cavalry Regiment in 1866. Keogh had two horses on the 1876 campaign, the famous "Comanche" and the officer's favorite horse "Paddy." He was killed in action on Calhoun Ridge on June 25, 1876 at the battle of the Little Bighorn.

marshal."[xviii] The famous gunfighter and lawman was having a chat with the bartender at Drum's Saloon, minding his own business, when the two troopers jumped on top of him and wrestled him to the floor. They had picked the wrong man for a fight. Gunfire broke out. In the ensuing melee, "Wild Bill" shot and killed one of the cavalrymen – who had tried to fire point-blank at Hickok only to have the percussion cap misfire – and seriously wounded the other, who was hit in the wrist and knee. Several other Company M troopers thought discretion was the better part of valor and raced out of the tavern. Hickok apparently thought the same and believing that the pair may have had reinforcements he jumped through a window, shattering glass on the walkway outside and ran to his rented room to grab his Winchester repeater and 100 rounds of carbine ammunition. "Wild Bill" then laid up in a cemetery just outside of town, where he could ensure no one would sneak up on him.[52]

"Wild Bill's" hunch was correct and more Company M troopers, including Sergeant John Ryan, returned to town. The "blue-bellies" were in a vengeful mood, but they were unable to pick up the scent of "Wild Bill" and returned to camp. The next morning Hickok rode to Big Creek Station, some eight miles out of Hays City, and hopped a Kansas Pacific train to get out of town until passions cooled down. The dodge worked and "Wild Bill" went on to become an American legend, cementing his legacy two months after the Little Bighorn, when he was shot and killed during a poker game at a saloon in Deadwood, Dakota Territory.[53]

• • •

1871

First Lieutenant William W. Cooke returned to the regiment and assumed duties as the adjutant. Company M began the year stationed at Fort Hays, Kansas. On February 15, 1871 Captain Thomas Henry French assumed command of the company. Prior to Captain French, Company M was commanded by the aforementioned First Lieutenant Owen Hale and First Lieutenant Tom Custer – the General's younger brother. First Lieutenant Donald "Tosh" McIntosh was also with the company and very likely was the senior commissioned officer present in the company on many days, making him the *de facto* commander[xix] From March 16 to 28, Company M conducted reconnaissance operations on the north and south branches of the Solomon River.

The next month, from April 13 to 29, the company scouted between the Solomon and Republican Rivers in northern Kansas and southern Nebraska. It remained at Fort Hays until May 23, 1871, when the company transferred by rail for Louisville, Kentucky to begin what would be a two-year stint of Reconstruction duty. It arrived in the Bluegrass State on May 28 but stayed only three days before continuing by train to Darlington, South Carolina – arriving there on June 14. Company M remained in Darlington until October 18, when it left on a four-day march to Spartanburg, South Carolina. On November 7, 1871 Company M marched to Unionville, South Carolina.[54]

Meanwhile, Lieutenant Colonel Custer was granted a four-month leave during the year; unhappy with the assignment of the 7th Cavalry to Reconstruction duties in the south, he went to New York City during his furlough to examine post-army employment prospects. Not finding any to his liking, Custer concluded that he would remain in the service and returned to the regimental headquarters, then in Kentucky.[55]

One man in Company M was reported as dying of disease on the June 30 muster roll, but desertions were significantly reduced – just two men were classified as deserters on the June 30 muster roll and two others listed the same on the December 31 muster roll. August was a bad month, however, with six Company M men listed as deserters.[56]

1872

Company M continued its law enforcement duties in Unionville, South Carolina. It was difficult duty from the standpoint of public perception. To southerners, the cavalrymen were generally despised as being vestiges of the "Yankee" invasion of the south; in the North, the troopers were often shunned and viewed as simple national policemen, not the hometown heroes of the Civil War, who had temporarily put down their plowshares to defend the union in a noble undertaking. As the regiment was greatly dispersed from Kentucky to South Carolina, there were no regimental operations at all during the year. On December 24, 1872 the company left the Palmetto State by rail for a new assignment at Oxford, Mississippi.[57]

Two troopers in Company M died in February, while another two deserted. Two more men died in April, while desertions increased to 12. Seven men were listed as deserters in the Company M muster roll on June 30. On the August 31 report one man had died of typhoid fever and three troopers had deserted. Two men were listed on October 31 as deserters and another two in late December.[58]

Meanwhile, the regimental commander had a new set of challenges and opportunities. In January 1872, General Sheridan requested that Custer accompany Russian Grand Duke Alexei Alexandrovich, the son of Czar Alexander II, on a Great Plains hunting trip as a goodwill gesture.[xx] Custer did, and the pair was quite successful in their hunting adventures. Accompanied by Sheridan and William Frederick "Buffalo Bill" Cody – and two companies of infantry, two companies of cavalry, a cavalry regiment band and assorted cooks and servants – Duke Alexei was given the high honor of using "Lucretia," "Buffalo Bill's" famed hunting rifle that had reportedly brought down 4,200 buffalo over the years. After the expedition, Duke Alexis travelled to St. Louis, Missouri and subsequently to Louisville, Kentucky, where George and Elizabeth Custer then accepted an invitation from the duke to sail by steamboat down the Ohio and Mississippi to New Orleans; George Custer continued the escort of the duke to Florida. Duke Alexei set sail from Pensacola on February 22, 1872. Custer then raced to Monroe, Michigan for the wedding of his sister Margaret "Maggie" to Lieutenant James "Jimmy" Calhoun on March 7. The 7th Cavalry's commander then returned to Elizabeth, Kentucky for the remainder of the year.[59]

[xviii] James Butler "Wild Bill" Hickok was a gunfighter, scout, buffalo hunter, professional gambler and sometimes lawman in the Old West. He was born on May 27, 1837 in Homer (now named Troy Grove), Illinois. In 1855 he moved to the Kansas Territory. He was originally nicknamed "Duck Bill" because of a protruding upper lip and thus grew a mustache to get rid of the moniker. He was involved in a deadly shootout with the McCanles Gang in Nebraska in 1861. During the Civil War he served in the Union Army in Kansas and Missouri. In 1865 he killed another man in a gunfight in Springfield, Missouri. In 1869 he was elected city marshal in Hays, Kansas and killed two more men in gunfights. Hickok moved to Abilene, Kansas in 1871 and became marshal there. On October 5, 1871 he killed another man in a gunfight, but then accidentally shot and killed a special deputy marshal, an event that haunted him for the rest of his life. He was diagnosed with glaucoma in 1876 and then went further west, trying his hand in the gold fields of the Dakota Territory. On August 2, 1876, while playing poker at Nuttal and Mann's Saloon No. 10 in Deadwood, he was shot in the back of the head and killed, holding a pair of black aces and black eights, which became known as the "dead man's hand." He is buried at the Mount Moriah Cemetery in Deadwood, South Dakota.

[xix] Donald "Tosh" McIntosh was born in Montreal, Canada on September 4, 1838. The son of a Hudson Bay Company trapper, who was killed when Donald was 14, and an Indian mother, who was the direct descendant of Chief Red Jacket of the Six Nations, McIntosh was a chief clerk to Brigadier General Daniel Rucker during the Civil War. He was appointed a second lieutenant in the 7th Cavalry on August 17, 1867 and was promoted to first lieutenant on March 22, 1870. For the 1876 campaign, Custer appointed him to command Company G. Killed at the Little Bighorn in the valley, where he has a stone marker near the timber line position, McIntosh is buried in Section 1, Site 107-D at Arlington National Cemetery. His wife Mary is buried with him; she died on May 12, 1910.

[xx] In his book *My Life on the Plains*, George Custer called much of the Great Plains "the Great American Desert."

1873

Company M began the year moving by train from Unionville, South Carolina to Oxford, Mississippi. The company remained in Oxford until March 16, when Company M marched to Memphis, Tennessee; on April 2, 1873, the company moved by the steamboat *Pauline Carroll* up the Mississippi River to Cairo, Illinois. At Cairo, Company M was delayed a few days to deal with diseased and disabled horses and to arrange for the burial for a soldier from Company E. The trooper had been sleeping on the deck of the steamboat *Emma C. Elliott* enroute to Cairo, when a poisonous spider bit him on the neck; he died a few hours later.[60] Company M then moved by rail to the Dakota Territory, arriving at Yankton on about April 11, 1873. Three days later a tremendous blizzard struck the region and delayed further movement until May 7.

On that day, the regiment – with Company M in tow – departed the Yankton area for Fort Randall, which they arrived at one week later. The command finally reached Fort Rice on June 10, 1873. Ten days later, on June 20, 1873, the 7th Cavalry began an expedition to the Yellowstone. Custer crossed the Little Missouri River, called the Forked River by the Arikara, on July 11; the command reached the Yellowstone River, called the Elk River by the Arikara, on July 15 and crossed the river on July 24. The 7th Cavalry, still including Company M, camped near the mouth of the Powder River on July 31, 1873. Company M was commanded by Captain Thomas French; First Lieutenant Thomas Custer was second in command and Second Lieutenant Richard H.L. Alexander[xxi] was also assigned to the company, but was detached to Company D.[61]

• • •

Fort Rice served as the home for Company M from 1873 to 1877. General Alfred Sully established the facility in 1864 to supply his campaign against the Sioux and also to protect river traffic on the Missouri River. The Secretary of War named the fort in honor of Brigadier General James Clay Rice, who had been killed in action in May 1864 in Virginia. Troopers from the 30th Wisconsin Infantry Regiment did the original construction of the wooden buildings that had sod roofs. In 1868 the original buildings were torn down and new ones built. The small fort measured 864 feet by 544 feet, and was surrounded by a 10-foot stockade. By 1875 Fort Rice had four company barracks, seven buildings for officers, five storehouses, a post hospital, a bakery, an ammunition bunker and a guardhouse. Outside the stockade were facilities for the horses and livestock. In July 1865 Sitting Bull and 400 warriors attempted to attack and destroy the camp, but were repulsed.

• • •

On August 2, the command marched up the Yellowstone. On August 4, part of the regiment had a tough fight with about 300 Indians. The Lakota attempted to decoy the cavalry into a trap, but Custer saw the ruse at the last minute and foiled it. Custer got on the trail of a large Indian camp; on August 11 about 900 Lakota attacked the cavalry; it took three hours to break up the attack, and Company M then pursued the fleeing Indians for almost eight miles.[xxii] The expedition left the Yellowstone River's course at Pompey's Pillar and marched to the Mussel Shell River, where they arrived on August 19 and departed on August 27. Two days later, the commander of the expedition instructed the 7th Cavalry to return to Fort Abraham Lincoln; they arrived on September 21, 1873, having marched over 1,500 miles since leaving Yankton in May.[62]

Company M reached Fort Rice on September 28. Lieutenant Colonel Custer later wrote of Company M and its commander during the August 11 engagement:[63]

> "Captain French commanding the right wing [Companies A, B, G and M] was directed to watch the parties crossing [the Yellowstone] below...Captain French, who was engaged with the Indians who were attacking us from below, succeeded by a shot from his rifle in shooting a warrior from his saddle...The appearance of the main command in sight, down the valley, enabled me to relieve Captain French's command below us, and he was ordered to join in the pursuit..."

The Leavenworth Times would later amplify Captain French's participation in the fight:[64]

> "Captain French was one of the best and most unerring shots in the army, and dismounting he crawled through the grass to a clump of trees standing on the bank [of the Yellowstone] just opposite where the red devils were hooting and yelling and making all kinds of offensive demonstrations. Coolly singling out a brave, who was making himself more conspicuous than the rest, the sharp crack of the captain's rifle broke in upon the demoniacal yells across the river. There was a splash in the water and a riderless horse galloped wildly away."

Fort Rice would remain the home of Company M, when they were not on campaign. It was no garden spot, although better than many smaller posts in the west. The barracks at the fort were frame buildings of wood. On the inside, the troopers made walls of bricks made out of prairie sod; once the bricks were in place, the soldiers whitewashed them. Each barrack was one story tall and could hold 100 men. At the end of the building, the first sergeant had an office and a separate bedroom. Officers had their own quarters.[65]

Company M's commander then went on leave on October 2, 1873; First Lieutenant Edward Mathey assumed temporary command of the company for the remainder of the year.[66] On October 28, 1873 First Sergeant Frederick Thies[xxiii] was discharged in order to accept an appointment as a second lieutenant in another unit; Sergeant John Ryan was elevated to the first sergeant position three days later.[67] Seven men were listed as deserters on the February 28 muster roll and 13 appeared on the April 30 report. Nine deserters were listed on the June 30 muster roll; this figured was reduced to just two on the October 31 report.[68]

[xxi] Richard H.L. "Lee" Alexander was born in Louisville, Kentucky on February 15, 1851. Alexander's father was an infantry colonel and close personal friend of Ulysses Grant. "Lee" was assigned to the 7th Cavalry Regiment on December 12, 1872; he reported to the regiment in February 1873. Never in the best of health, Alexander went on sick leave in 1874 and never returned to duty. Richard Alexander died on February 9, 1875 at Sacramento, CA of tuberculosis, still assigned to the regiment on paper.

[xxii] This work primarily uses Lakota, although that is not generally what the troopers of Company M, and the 7th Cavalry, knew their foe by, Sioux. The tribes of the day certainly would have preferred the term Lakota, as they disliked the bastardized French word Sioux. Source: James Donovan, *A Terrible Glory: Custer and the Little Bighorn – the Last Great Battle of the American West*, New York: Little, Brown and Company, 2008, 19.

[xxiii] Frederick Thies was born in Germany. Prior to serving in the 7th Cavalry Regiment, Thies was assigned to the 37th Infantry Regiment. He joined Company M of the 7th Cavalry as a private on July 7, 1870 and was promoted to corporal on August 8, 1870. On November 1, 1870 he was made the first sergeant of Company M. He became a second lieutenant in the 3rd Infantry Regiment after leaving Company M and was promoted to first lieutenant on April 14, 1884. Frederick Thies died on January 20, 1888 at Fort Shaw, Montana Territory; he was the regimental quartermaster of the 3rd Infantry at the time of his death.

1874

Captain Thomas French remained on leave until the beginning of the year when he was placed on an unspecified temporary duty at Fort Abercrombie, Dakota Territory until March 18, 1874 when he returned to Fort Rice.[69] On May 31, 1874 Captain French took 31 troopers of Company M from Fort Rice, Dakota Territory as part of a detachment that was scouting for a band of Indians threatening the Berthold Indian Agency near Fort Stevenson. The mission proved fruitless, and Company M returned to Fort Rice on June 3. The company moved into camp two miles from Fort Abraham Lincoln on June 20, 1874 in preparation for the Black Hills Expedition. First Lieutenant Edward G. Mathey was still assigned to the company as was Second Lieutenant Richard H.L. Alexander, who was on detached service at Fort Abraham Lincoln.[70]

On June 8, 1874 Brigadier General Terry ordered Custer to organize and lead a reconnaissance of the Black Hills. The regiment was short of officers and Custer wrote to Major Joseph G. Tilford, assigned to the 7th Cavalry, but in command of Fort Rice, asking him to join the regiment's expedition; Custer wrote:[71]

> "As the services of another field officer are greatly required by the cavalry of the expedition and as you had previously announced your readiness to take the field, while the medical officer reports you physically qualified, I have decided it best to give the expedition the benefit of your services and in so doing I am sure the interests of the service will be promoted, since personally I will be extremely gratified."

Major Tilford accepted the offer. Much-needed equipment was arriving as well. On July 1, 1874 First Lieutenant James Calhoun, the Acting Assistant Adjutant General of the regiment, noted:[72]

> "The new Springfield arms and ammunition were issued to the command today. They seem to give great satisfaction."

The expedition, with Company M included, began its mission on July 2 and marched 416 miles southwest of Fort Abraham Lincoln, escorting a scientific party attempting to gather information on the character of the land and potential routes of communication through the region.[xxiv] In what would prove to be a difficult problem, a miner in the command – Horatio Nelson Ross – also discovered gold in the Black Hills area that had been reserved for the Lakota Indians in the Treaty of 1868, which granted the Lakota most of what would become South Dakota and 22,000,000 additional acres to the west and north.[73] On the morning of August 2, 1874 gold was discovered and Custer ordered government scout "Lonesome Charley" Reynolds to ride through hostile territory for some 90 miles to deliver the news to Fort Laramie. He would have to travel alone, riding by night and hiding by day.[74] Reynolds got his gear together and found that James Calhoun had marked his canvas dispatch bag with:

> *Black Hills Express Charley Reynolds, Manager Connecting with All Points East, West, North, South Cheap Rates, Quick Transit; Safe Passage; We are protected by the Seventh Cavalry!*

Private "Dan" Newell, an experienced blacksmith, from Company M described his role in the event:[75]

> "Charley had to go horseback, travelling nights and sleeping hidden during the daytime. The owners of that country didn't want people trespassing on their grass and scaring their buffaloes. And every precaution had to be taken in order to fool them. So before starting out I was called on to shoe his horse. I placed the shoes on backward. It was some job to do this in such a way as not to interfere with the animal's gait and still leave a track going the wrong way and one that the Indians wouldn't get onto. However, the trick was done and Charley made the trip without any great trouble. Trouble enough came of that gold discovery afterwards, however."

Indeed it did, and it can be argued that the discovery would lead to the battle of the Little Bighorn two years later. There were significant events inside Company M as well. On July 22, 1874 Private George Turner and Private William Roller got into an argument. The quarrel escalated and Roller shot Turner, fatally wounding him in the liver; Turner died later that day. The same evening the regiment assembled and Private George Turner was buried on a little knoll with full military honors, another lonely cavalry grave on the frontier.[76]

The regiment returned to Fort Abraham Lincoln on August 30, 1874. On November 14, 1874 Company M left for Fort Rice; days later they assisted the U.S. Marshal in arresting several Indians at the Standing Rock Indian Agency. The weather was brutal as two privates in the company were seen by a doctor on November 17 for frostbite, and a third trooper was afflicted by the cold a day later. On December 13, 1874, Captain French took 25 men as part of a detail under Captain George Yates that returned to the Standing Rock Agency and arrested several Indians, including Rain in the Face, suspected of murder.[xxv] The detachment was recalled to the agency, once again, on December 19 to protect it against Indians there, who were showing signs of violence based on those recent arrests, and it remained there until December 24, 1874.[77]

Desertions remained a problem during the year in Company M. One man was listed as a deserter at the end of February, eight in April, five in June, one in August and two in October.[78]

1875

Company M remained at Fort Rice for much of the year. On February 9, 1875, Captain French and 25 men of Company M marched to the Standing Rock Agency to apprehend two army soldiers of Company D of the 17th Infantry Regiment, who were charged with killing an Indian the previous day. The detail returned to Fort Rice on February 11. The winter remained brutal and on February 12, 1875 three Company M troopers – who were probably part of Captain French's detail – were all treated for frostbitten toes. On March 17, 1875, a 17-man detachment from Company M assisted in the capture of an escaped Indian prisoner at the Standing Rock Agency, returning to Fort Rice on March 19. Captain Thomas French assumed acting command of Fort Rice in June, while Major Joseph Tilford was away.[79] On August 25, 1875 a 12-man detachment from Company M – under command of First Sergeant John

[xxiv] It is apparent that the expedition believed they would find gold before they even started the mission, as two experienced gold prospectors accompanied the column. The Lakota had taken the Black Hills from the Cheyenne, who had taken the area from the Comanches and Kiowas, who had taken the region from the Crows. Source: James Donovan, *A Terrible Glory: Custer and the Little Bighorn – the Last Great Battle of the American West*, New York: Little, Brown and Company, 2008, 82.

[xxv] George W. Yates was born on February 26, 1843 in Albany, New York. An early close personal friend of George Custer's, Yates served as a second lieutenant in the 4th Michigan Cavalry during the Civil War. Yates fought at the First Battle of Manassas, Antietam, Fredericksburg and Gettysburg. On June 12, 1867 he was appointed a captain in the 7th Cavalry; he reported to the unit at Fort Leavenworth on November 20, 1867 and given command of Company F. He was one of Custer's "inner-circle" in the 7th Cavalry. Killed at the Little Bighorn, George W. Yates was reinterred at Fort Leavenworth National Cemetery.

Ryan – went after a band of Indians that had stolen 30 army mules near the Cannon Ball River, the detachment returned to camp two days later empty-handed. Custer went on leave in September and remained away from the regiment for the rest of the year.[80] There was an early winter that year; the wife of Lieutenant Francis Gibson recalled that the first snow at Fort Rice was in September and on October 7, 1875 the snow was knee-deep.[81] Much of the duty would now turn dull; for example, on October 6, Captain French was ordered by the post commander to inspect a sick horse and mule to ensure they did not have any communicable animal diseases.[82] Concerning good news, Company M received five new horses on September 5, 1875 and 14 sets of maps of Montana and Dakota on November 20, 1875.[83]

But these inspections were necessary. On October 17, 1875 Captain French requested that a board of officers convene to ascertain the nature of damage he had found to four Springfield carbines in his company. No results are recorded, but the request is evidence that French understood what was important in his command and proper weapon function was one of them.[84]

Company M was ordered to report to Fort Abraham Lincoln on October 19, 1875 and spent a short period of time there.[85] They had returned to Fort Rice by November 18, as on that date Captain French and First Lieutenant Mathey were assigned to a board of officers meeting to audit the books of the post treasurer.[86]

Meanwhile, the troopers in Company M continued their own routine. A Fort Rice garrison circular from November 15, 1875 published the daily schedule to be followed:[87]

Daylight – Reveille
6:30 a.m. – Breakfast
7:30 a.m. – Sick Call
7:45 a.m. – Fatigue Formation
9:00 a.m. – Guard Mount
10:45 a.m. – Stables
Noon – Dinner
4:00 p.m. – Stables
9:00 p.m. – Taps

1876

The year would see the regiment transform from one of the army's most-colorful formations to one of its most legendary. However, during the first part of the year, several key leaders were absent from the preparations for the upcoming Little Bighorn expedition. George Custer, for example, had been on leave for five months; his approved absence terminated on February 15, 1876. But Custer would have to leave again; he ordered his subordinates to prepare for the upcoming campaign in the same manner as he had directed in 1874 for the Black Hills Expedition; however, they would fall short.[88]

The weather was brutal in the spring of 1876, and supplies and provisions did not begin to arrive at Fort Abraham Lincoln until the latter half of April. With Custer in Washington, D.C. at that time, local supervision of logistical preparations fell on the shoulders of Major Marcus Reno.[89] Major Marcus Reno telegraphed his departmental headquarters on February 9, 1876 stating that they needed horses at Fort Lincoln, but the required number never arrived.[90]

If those responsibilities were not enough, Major Reno had to deal with a substantial brawl down in Company M! Or maybe it was a riot.

It all started on March 18, 1876. Sergeant Patrick Carey was supervising the company stable guard, and Private John Whisten decided he would drink during his guard and became drunk. That was enough for Sergeant Carey to attempt to take Whisten to the guardhouse, but apparently the private was reluctant to follow. Carey got reinforcements in the form of First Sergeant John Ryan. But as Ryan approached the scene of the fracas, Whisten shouted:[91]

> "Ryan, you God-damned son-of-a-bitch; I'll kill you as soon as I get out of the guard house."

With that, Private Bernhard Golden tried to assist his fellow private by grabbing First Sergeant Ryan by the throat. Private Henry Gordon, who had also been drinking, decided at this moment to enter the fray and assaulted Sergeant Carey. Carey and Ryan, although outnumbered, were not going down without a fight. Fists flew and when the dust settled five days later, a General Court Martial attempted to determine the sequence of events and who deserved what punishment for the various infractions. John Whisten, who started the melee, was hammered the hardest; he was fined $13 and confined for a month. Additionally, whenever he was not working during confinement, or eating at his two authorized 30-minute meal sessions, Whisten was sentenced to carry a log weighing not less than 30 pounds. Bernhard Golden, by some twist of justice and perhaps a few failed memories, was acquitted; Gordon was convicted for his part in the scuffle and sentenced to a $10 fine and 20 days at hard labor.[92] Less than 60 days before the start of the campaign, it seemed that the troopers of Company M were more eager to fight each other than to get to grips with the Lakota and Northern Cheyenne.

• • •

To assemble the regiment, several companies had to march from outlying bases to Custer's headquarters. Company M, along with Company H, arrived at Fort Lincoln, Dakota Territory on May 5 – after riding some 20 miles from their home station at Fort Rice. Captain Thomas French was in command of the company. First Sergeant John Ryan had served as the senior non-commissioned officer in the unit until April 16, 1876 when he was court-martialed for abusing a soldier. Sergeant William G. Capes, who had been acting quartermaster sergeant of the company, became acting first sergeant and held this position until May 9, 1876 when Ryan was restored to his former rank and reinstated to the position of senior non-commissioned officer in the company.[93]

The regiment, as well as Company M, was now prepared to head west, but it would become a march through hell for many of the cavalry troopers.

• • •

Despite some later popular claims to the contrary, George Armstrong Custer did not start the war against the Lakota in 1876, nor did he conspire to exterminate the Lakota tribes during that period. (One current Native-American journalist continually refers to Custer as the "Adolf Hitler of the Plains.") But the issue was far greater than one man; George Custer's role was simply to find and fight the tribes.[94] In fact, in 1874 Custer wrote in *Life on the Plains*:[95]

> "Yet there are those who would have the public believe that the army is at all times clamorous for an Indian war. I have yet to meet the officer or man belonging to the army, who, when the

> question of war or peace with the Indians was being agitated, did not cast the weight of his influence, the prayers of his heart, in behalf of peace."

After the Civil War, government experts estimated that there were about 270,000 Indians – divided into 125 tribal groups – in the huge area known as the American West.[96] The country was expanding and political leaders believed that one culture would have to be subjugated by the other; and it was not going to be the white man who held the short stick at the end of the day. General William T. Sherman, a man who seemed never to be bothered by what others thought of his opinions or public exclamations, characterized the struggle as:[97]

> "...the great battle of civilization with barbarism."

But in private conversation in 1868, Sherman synthesized what this grandiose language really meant:[98]

> "The more we can kill this year, the less will have to be killed in the next war, for the more I see of these Indians, the more convinced I am that they all have to be killed or be maintained as a species of paupers. Their attempts at civilization are simply ridiculous."

This was not the original view of President Ulysses Grant. When he came into office in 1868, after much analysis, including input from the Quakers, Grant placed his friend Ely Parker, a full-blooded Seneca, as Commissioner of Indian Affairs. Grant needed a program as well and soon described his intentions to craft:[99]

> "An Indian policy founded on peace and Christianity, rather than force of arms."

Ensuing official government policy, less bloody than General Sherman envisioned, but not as benign as President Grant had hoped, could be boiled down to a simple plan: convince or coerce the Indians to move into reservations[xxvi] which would not impede westward expansion of European-settler travel lanes; establish a Bureau of Indian Affairs to oversee the native peoples; teach the Indians on these reservations how to cultivate land; Christianize as many inhabitants as possible; and gradually wean the reservation dwellers off their traditional ways – all with the goal that perhaps one day the grandchildren of these people could leave the reservations and join the white civilization in some undetermined manner.[100]

Whatever orderly timeline that Washington D.C. bureaucrats envisioned, it was soon overtaken by events. White emigration to this area of the Plains had increased like a tidal wave since the end of the Civil War in 1865. First came the wagon trails; the railways followed shortly after – both drove off the buffalo herds, the foundation of the Indian economy; an average Lakota adult consumed six buffalo a year. The Union Pacific Railroad was following the Platte River bound for California. The Northern Pacific Railroad, which would cross the initial flatlands from Duluth, Minnesota and later through the mountains to the mouth of the Columbia River on the Pacific, would in the middle of its trace parallel the Yellowstone River deep into Montana – Indian country.[101]

In addition, President Ulysses Grant was in a dilemma. Since gold was discovered in 1874, more and more prospectors had infiltrated the Black Hills region, in violation of previous treaties with the Lakota. Within a year of the announcement of gold in the area, there were 15,000 prospectors in the Black Hills; by 1876 that number had jumped to 25,000 and the tide of gold-seekers showed no sign of abating.[102]

Grant needed a solution and settled on military action. The army was simply too small to keep the prospectors out. But if they could not quarantine the area, the army could deal with the Indians, if only they could find them. Many of the Lakota lived on government reservations, but an increasing number of Indians were becoming roamers, hunting and living in unceded territory not within reservation boundaries. Some of these roamers only left the reservation during good weather in the summer, but a large number were now winter roamers, meaning that they lived off the reservation almost completely. Grant ordered the army to pursue these groups of roamers and drive them back to the reservation. A tough campaign against them would either cause a majority of reservation Indians to sign away their ownership of the Black Hills, or failing that the government could seize the Black Hills outright after the conflict as spoils of war. In either case, the region would open up to the masses of whites pouring west in search of gold; such a move would also expedite the expansion of the railroads west.[103]

President Ulysses Grant probably made his decision to go to war on November 3, 1875. On that date General Phil Sheridan, General George Crook and the new Secretary of the Interior Zachariah Chandler met with President Grant in the White House. For some time, General of the Army William Sherman and Lieutenant General Philip Sheridan had advocated all-out war against the Indians; now President Grant would move in that direction by allowing miners into the Black Hills – a decision that would almost certainly provoke the roving Lakota bands into war.[104]

On December 6, 1875 Commissioner of Indian Affairs E.P. Smith[xxvii] directed the Indian agents at the major Lakota Indian reservations to communicate with Lakota Chief Sitting Bull and the other Indian leaders that they and their winter-roaming bands were to surrender at their agencies no later than January 31, 1876 or be driven in by military force.[105] But Sitting Bull would have none of it. A complex, extremely intelligent leader, the Lakota chief once remarked:[106]

> "I have killed, robbed, and injured too many white men to believe in a good peace. They are medicine, and I would eventually die a lingering death. I had rather die on the field of battle."

January 31, 1876 came and went without any winter-roaming Lakota bands returning to the reservations. That month George Custer, still on leave away from Fort Abraham Lincoln, sensed that action would imminently come, as he wrote in a letter to his brother Tom:[107]

> "I think the 7th Cavalry may have its greatest campaign ahead."

[xxvi] A reservation was defined as an area of land set aside by the government for the exclusive use of a single Indian tribe, or sometimes a group of tribes. An agency was the government administrative seat for a particular area; at this location, Indians were registered on government rolls and government agents issued rations and supplies. Some reservations were served by a single agency, while very large reservations might have several agencies. Source: Charles M. Robinson, *A Good Year to Die: The Story of the Great Sioux War*, New York: Random House, 1995, x.

[xxvii] Edward Parmalee Smith was born in South Britain, Connecticut in June 1827. He was educated at Dartmouth and Yale Colleges and later graduated from the Theological Seminary at New-Haven. Smith served as the Commissioner of Indian Affairs from 1873 to 1875. After leaving his post as Commissioner of Indian Affairs, he died on July 27, 1876 on Sheroro Island near Accra on the west coast of Africa of a fever, while part of an American Missionary Association visit. He had been selected to be the president of Howard University in Washington, D.C. before his death.

On February 8, 1876 General Sheridan sent a confidential telegram to General Alfred Terry and General George Crook alerting them that the War Department had ordered operations against hostile Indians (defined as those who would not return to the reservations). Both generals were to make plans to that end. George Custer finished his lengthy leave on February 15 and reported to General Terry's headquarters in St. Paul, Minnesota. Terry and Custer began planning; Custer would lead the entire expedition out of Fort Abraham Lincoln, which would include the 7th Cavalry, as well as a contingent of infantry – which were called "Walks-a-Heap" by Indians. The next day Terry requested that General Sherman release the three cavalry companies in the 7th, currently assigned to the Department of the Gulf, to return to the regiment in the Dakota Territory. The request was batted back and forth in Washington; the three companies finally arrived in Bismarck on May 1.[108]

George Custer contacted the Adjutant General on February 19 to request the transfer of a lieutenant in Company E out of the regiment;[xxviii] he also requested that the regiment receive 70 new enlisted recruits to replace those soldiers scheduled for discharge before May 1. Sixty-three recruits finally reported to the regiment on May 1 (although only after Custer personally took this request to Sherman), but unfortunately there were no horses for them. Terry outlined the plan that he and Custer had drafted to General Sheridan on February 21; initially the plan called for Custer to begin operations about April 15. As Terry would summarize to Sheridan:[109]

> "I think my only plan will be to give Custer a secure base well up on the Yellowstone from which he can operate, at which he can find supplies, and to which he can retire at any time the Indians gather in too great numbers for the small force he will have."

How little General Terry understood of his subordinate; the word "retire" was not in George Custer's vocabulary. And finding the Indians might have deserved special attention; the Lakota and Northern Cheyenne could be anywhere in an area of 90,000 square miles.[110]

Custer left St. Paul and arrived in Fargo, Dakota Territory, where he boarded a special train fitted with two snowplows and three locomotives to cut through the heavy snow. It left Fargo on March 6, but the brutal winter weather delayed his arrival. Sixty-five miles from Bismarck the massive train could go no further and Custer completed the trip by mule-drawn sleigh. He arrived at Fort Abraham Lincoln on March 13, when he immediately saw that the timetable for the campaign was too optimistic.[111]

Custer saw that the command was a mess. Reno had failed to recruit any Indian scouts, and that supplies for the campaign were almost non-existent.[112] Knowing that he soon would be called to the nation's capital, Custer gave instructions to Major Reno at Fort Abraham Lincoln and Captain Benteen at Fort Rice to put their garrisons in "efficient condition for prolonged service in the field." Reno responded by ordering four to six weeks of training that concentrated on company and battalion drill but did not include much horsemanship and no individual combat training – learning how to fight warriors in close quarters. Reno originally ordered that the regiment conduct daily hour-long target practice, but reduced this to only 30 minutes per day on April 6.[113]

At just 30 minutes, only a few men could be supervised firing every day by more senior non-commissioned officers; additionally it is not certain that the marksmanship training was even carried out, regardless of what was ordered.[114] That was due, in part, to the weather that winter and spring, which was brutal. The rudimentary buildings occupied by the 7th Cavalry had no space to conduct indoor training.[115] Reno was not alone in his decision-making; the military's primary function on the frontier was to construct and maintain the government posts it occupied, and the forts were always in need of this fix or that.[116] But the ammunition was there. In a February 25, 1876 letter from Fort Rice to the Department of Dakota some 35,350 rounds of Springfield carbine ammunition and 12,589 rounds of .45 pistol ammunition were reported on hand.[117]

Custer then entered the maelstrom of Washington politics that almost derailed his participation in the campaign and certainly adversely affected the unity of effort needed to get the regiment prepared for action. The *New York Herald* had previously published a series of articles suggesting that the Secretary of War William W. Belknap[xxix] was up to his elbows in graft and corruption concerning the management of trading posts at the Indian agencies and army posts along the frontier. Seeing the handwriting on the wall, Belknap resigned on March 2, and President Grant replaced him with Alonso Taft six days later.[118]

Congress called Custer to depart Fort Abraham Lincoln on March 21 to travel to the capital to testify in a particularly nasty hearing concerning Belknap, now out of office, which expanded to include accusations against the president's brother. Custer arrived in Washington on March 29 and began testifying the following day. Custer had not been fond of the secretary. In late summer of 1875, Belknap visited Fort Abraham Lincoln. The post trader, Robert C. Seip, had been demanding unreasonable prices for his goods, and Custer had sent the regiment's officers to Bismarck to buy them at a cheaper price. Seip was furious and complained to Washington, D.C. Belknap ordered Custer to stop interfering. As a result, several months later, when Belknap again visited the post, Custer avoided meeting him – a personal snub of the Secretary of War that fueled the bad blood between the two men. During his Congressional testimony, Custer also discredited Major Lewis Merrill for accepting cash from state governments and accepting bribes. Merrill was assigned on paper to the regiment, but for the last eight years had been on detached service.[119]

Custer finished testifying and initially departed Washington on April 20, but was recalled on April 24 by a Board of Managers involved in impeachment proceedings against the departed Belknap. Custer rambled in this second round of testimony and included generalized accusations against Orvil L. Grant, the President's younger brother. But Belknap had his supporters; Grant reportedly came to the conclusion that it may have been Custer who had been involved in graft, and more importantly, who certainly had slandered "poor old" Orvil Grant.[120]

Days later President Grant apparently discussed his displeasure with Custer's latest testimony and through the War Department and army leadership on April 28 relieved Custer of command and directed that Terry place someone other than the flamboyant cavalryman in command of the upcoming expedition.[121] Terry, perhaps knowing his

---

[xxviii] Transfer of an officer outside of the regiment was a difficult process, as the officer personnel system assumed that most officers would spend most of their careers in the same regiment. Promotions for an officer in the regiment could only come when a vacancy occurred higher, such as a senior officer retiring or dying. Thus an officer could spend many years at the same rank even though he had already mastered the skills associated with that post. To bring a new officer into a regiment would cause those less senior to fall even further behind on the date of rank list, which could lead to bad blood between officers and poor morale within the unit.

[xxix] William W. Belknap was born in Newburgh, New York on September 22, 1829. He graduated from Princeton and Georgetown Universities, became a lawyer and served in the Iowa House of Representatives. During the Civil War, Belknap was promoted to brigadier general and placed in command of the 4th Division of the 17th Corps in General Sherman's operations in Georgia. He became the Secretary of War on October 25, 1869. Belknap resigned the position on March 2, 1876, but the House of Representatives impeached him anyway; the Senate did not confirm the articles of impeachment. William W. Belknap died of a heart attack in Washington, D.C. on October 13, 1890. He is buried at Arlington National Cemetery in Section 1, Lot 132.

own limitations, dragged his heels on the decision, including when Major Marcus Reno – behind Custer's back – petitioned him for command of the regiment.[122]

George Custer left Washington – after an unsuccessful attempt to personally see President Grant on May 1, during which he cooled his heels all day at a White House waiting room – and arrived on May 4 in Chicago, where he was promptly placed under temporary military arrest. Over the next few days, after much wailing, gnashing of teeth and humble beseeching, George Custer maintained command of the 7th Cavalry, but would not be given overall command of the Fort Abraham Lincoln column. Brigadier General Alfred Terry would be in overall command of that entity, while Lieutenant Colonel Custer would clearly be in a subordinate position. The two officers reached Fort Abraham Lincoln on May 10; General Terry assumed formal command of the expedition on May 14.[123]

But all that Washington intrigue was above the interest of the troopers in Company M. They were concerned with the important matters at company level – issues that could directly affect life or death.

George A. Custer, shown seated, with Indian scouts and Private John Burkman, his orderly, standing in the upper right. Scout kneeling on the right is Bloody Knife, who was killed in the timberline near Company M on June 25, 1876. Some versions of this photo have the image reversed. *Photo courtesy of the Little Bighorn Battlefield National Monument.*

"Grant stood by me when I was crazy, and I stood by him when he was drunk, and now we stand by each other." Original 1862 *Carte de Visite* of William T. "Uncle Billy" Sherman in which Sherman does look a bit deranged! Reverse of the CDV says it was taken at *Morse's Gallery of the Cumberland* in Nashville, TN.

Lieutenant General Phil Sheridan. Photo taken after 1880.

General Philip H. Sheridan; foul-mouthed and short-tempered, "Little Phil" more than any other superior officer allowed Custer to use his independence and initiative in command. Photo shows Sheridan as a major general during the Civil War in 1864. *Photo courtesy of the Little Bighorn Battlefield National Monument.*

Captain Thomas W. Custer as a first lieutenant in 1870. During this time he was the commander of Company M. Note his two Medals of Honor from the Civil War. *Photo courtesy of the Little Bighorn Battlefield National Monument.*

Captain Frederick W. Benteen; what he did and did not do on June 25, 1876 has contributed to the mystique of the Little Bighorn ever since. What is more certain is that Company M's charge on Reno Hill on June 26, 1876 helped save Benteen's company. *Photo courtesy of the Little Bighorn Battlefield National Monument.*

Major Marcus A. Reno about 1875. Excoriated after the battle; later court-martialed for conduct unbecoming an officer; died in disgrace; granted a posthumous honorable discharge, he will probably never be forgiven by history for, at least, partial culpability in the disaster on the Little Bighorn. *Photo courtesy of the Little Bighorn Battlefield National Monument.*

***Left*: Major Joseph G. Tilford about 1876.** He served as the commander of Fort Rice for many years that Company M was stationed there. In 1874 he participated in the Black Hills Expedition, but was not present at the Little Bighorn two years later. *Photo courtesy of the Little Bighorn Battlefield National Monument.*

Opposite

***Top*: Group photograph of officers, wives and children at Fort Rice, Dakota Territory; photo was taken in the spring of 1874.** Several officers can be identified: standing in the middle row on the far right with white hair is Captain Frederick W. Benteen; standing in the bottom row on the far left with his left hand on his saber hilt is First Lieutenant Charles C. "Count No-Account" DeRudio; standing in the top row just right of center with his hand on his sabre is Major Joseph G. Tilford (not at LBH); standing just to the left of Tilford is First Lieutenant John Aspinwall (not at LBH); standing left of Aspinwall is First Lieutenant Edward G. "Bible Thumper" Mathey wearing kepi; standing on the porch left of the door is Captain Thomas H. "Tucker" French; seated in the front row third from the left with a blond-headed child on his lap is First Lieutenant Edward S. Godfrey; seated in the center front row with saber tip touching the ground is Captain Owen "Holy Owen" Hale (not at LBH); finally Captain Verling Hart (not at LBH) seated above children in left center with helmet in his lap. *Photo courtesy of the Little Bighorn Battlefield National Monument.*

***Bottom*: "Lonesome Charlie" Reynolds: renowned scout, guide and hunter.** Reynolds is seated in the chair in the front row looking left. Most of the other men are labelled as Lakota (Sioux). *Photo courtesy of National Anthropological Archives, Smithsonian Institution.*

Bust of James Butler "Wild Bill" Hickok at his birthplace in Troy Grove, (formerly Homer) Illinois.

Dedication plaque for "Wild Bill" Hickok monument in Troy Grove. The information does not include his confrontation with troopers from Company M in a saloon in Kansas in 1870.

"Wild Bill" Hickok. *Photo courtesy of John Doerner.*

CHAPTER TWO

Company Organization and Leadership

"And I reckon they ain't no regiment in the hull world made a better showin' than we did on parade, horses feelin' their oats and prancin', colors flyin', band playin', every damned thing about us spic and span and clean down to the horses' hoofs. Them was great days."[1]

Before getting too far ahead in the Company M saga on the march from Fort Abraham Lincoln to the ensuing fight at the Little Bighorn, it would be prudent to review the organization and leadership of the unit. The 7th Cavalry Regiment fielded twelve companies; there were no formal battalion organizations, although battalions – renamed squadrons seven years after the Little Bighorn – did exist, with Companies A-B-C-D forming 1st Battalion, Companies E-F-G-H assigned to 2nd Battalion and Companies I-K-L-M assigned to 3rd Battalion. There was no company designated J in the regiment.

The company lay at the heart of the 7th Cavalry; in fact, the company lay at the heart of the entire U.S. frontier army in the West, as typical encounters with Indians usually occurred at the company level. Each cavalry company[i] fielded two cavalry platoons; in theory, each platoon would be led by a commissioned officer, but due to officer shortages throughout the West this was hardly ever the case. If a company was short-handed in the field, the two platoons were sometimes combined into one. Platoons were generally the smallest tactical maneuver element in a cavalry formation. Each platoon had two subordinate elements – known as sections – that were authorized to be led by a sergeant. Each section had two subordinate elements called squads. Each squad was designed to be led by a corporal and have seven privates. Thus a squad had eight cavalrymen; a section had 17 troopers; a platoon – with the platoon leader – had 35.

In addition to the two platoon leaders working directly for the company commander, a first sergeant did as well. The company first sergeant handled all matters of discipline and the assignment of enlisted men.[2] That was a huge responsibility because troopers in those days could be a rowdy lot; in fact, they could get far worse than just rowdy. During a 10-month period in 1875-1876, for the entire army, the following number of court martial convictions were recorded: six – becoming violent to a superior officer; 10 – assault with intent to kill; 140 – selling, losing or wasting government property; 142 – larceny; 214 – assault and battery; 289 – disrespect toward a superior; 347 – desertion; 526 – disobedience of orders; 705 – drunkenness on duty; and 1,568 – drunkenness (not on duty).[3] Those 3,947 convictions must also be taken into consideration with respect to the total strength of the army which was about 25,000.[ii] Thus, about one of every six troopers in the army was court-martialed in that year alone, with another one of every sixteen successfully deserting.

Working directly for the first sergeant was a company clerk and two trumpeters. Another sergeant handled logistics; under this non-commissioned officer were a saddler, two farriers/blacksmiths, a wagoner and the quartermaster sergeant. The farrier served as the company veterinarian and was responsible for the treatment, food and medicine for the horses.[4] In the field, the farrier also helped determine where the horses would be picketed each evening. That was important as many of the troopers were novices who needed direction on how to live in the field.

Recruits arriving at the regiment had previously received only three or four weeks of training at the depot at Jefferson Barracks, Missouri – the collection point for all recruits entering mounted units. Recruit depots, during this era, were not intended to serve as training centers for the new soldiers; company veterans would have to teach many recruits how to ride a horse and the basics of cavalry tactics. Life at the recruit depot was unpleasant; the depot appeared to most new soldiers as cold and impersonal. The new soldiers, who at this point were only paid half the salary of a private, were issued uniforms, some of which were of poor quality or leftovers from the Civil War.

Additionally, many of the uniforms were labeled with sizes larger than they actually were; this was no chance mistake as many unscrupulous contractors intentionally defrauded the government by mislabeling and thus realizing profits through the savings in cloth not used. Some necessities, such as a cleaning kit, were not included in the issue and had to be privately purchased on credit from the post sutler.[5] Army-issue hats were terrible, especially when they became wet. Company C, E and L in the 7th Cavalry bought civilian white hats to wear on campaign. Company M troopers wore black hats as did most of the regiment.[6] Socks were the worst, and for soldiers protecting one's feet was always of paramount importance. One lieutenant colonel described these government-issue socks:[7]

> "The poorest articles issued to the troops…A great many of the men do not wear them at all, preferring to buy a better

[i] Cavalry companies were officially renamed cavalry troops in September 1883.

[ii] From June 30, 1875 to June 30, 1876, the army reported 1,832 desertions. Source: Thomas B. Marquis, *Keep the Last Bullet for Yourself*, Algonac, MI: Reference Publications, 1985, 48.

article off dealers. Thirty days is about their maximum duration in garrison. On campaigns they will not last over ten days. They are very uncomfortable to march in owing to the lumpy character of the seams."

Food at the depots was probably the worst in the army. For breakfast – which was sometimes put on the tables the night before and occasionally had begun to spoil – the recruits were treated salt pork, thin stew or fried mush, accompanied by strong black coffee. At dinner the recruits were presented with slumgullion stew (a thin stew of meat and vegetables) with dry bread and the black coffee chaser; cooks sometimes substituted cold corn bread, sopped with a hot water and flour gravy. Supper may not have been highly anticipated, unless the new soldier liked dry bread and still more black coffee, with an occasional highlight of three prunes. Army rations of the day did not include eggs, butter or milk. To add insult to injury, serving portions of every meal were too small.[8]

Years later, *The Republic* newspaper of St. Louis described the food at nearby Jefferson Barracks, through which many 7th Cavalry recruits passed on their way to the frontier. Perhaps with tongue in cheek, the reporter penned:[9]

> "The fare served in the general mess may not be of sufficient variety of delicacy to tempt a disciple of Epicurus to enter the army, but what there is of it is well cooked and palatable, and no one need complain of having 'dined with Duke Humphrey' after rising from a mess-room table."[iii]

Most cavalry troopers, if asked, would probably not have listed either Epicurus or Duke Humphrey as close personal friends. Creature comforts did not apply to life in the barracks either. A recruit's bunk consisted of an iron headpiece and foot with wooden slats running across the frame stringers. On top of the slats was a cotton cloth bedsack, which the recruit filled once a month – if he was there that long – with fresh straw; this filling was nicknamed "prairie feathers." But sometimes the straw was not fresh, and worse, when no straw was available, hay from the horse stables was used as substitute filler; when done, this gave the barracks a gamey aroma.[10]

As recruit life was spent doing fatigue details and non-technical construction projects, it was no wonder that they relished the day when they shipped out, usually by train, to the west and regimental duty. First, they began to receive full pay, some $13 a month, although according to a soldier song of the period:[11]

> "A dollar a day is damn poor pay, but thirteen a month is less!"[iv]

Soldiers were required to wash their hands and faces at least once a day and their feet at least twice a week. This did not always happen. Men often bathed in streams, but in winter they could go weeks without a bath.[12]

But memories of the recruit barracks could later grow fond.[v] Some of the old sergeants, who were instructors, were almost legendary. Private William Slaper of Company M recalled:[13]

> "We were taught how to groom a horse in regulation style, by a crusty old sergeant named 'Bully' Welch, a character whom all old cavalrymen of that day will remember."

Once at the regiment, recruits became acclimated to army life and made friends. Pairs of men would commonly pool blankets and slept together in the field; these pairs were known as "bunkies." "Bunkies" shared more than just blankets; they shared secrets about their backgrounds (more than ten percent of the men in the 7th Cavalry had enlisted under an alias) to what happened to them when they visited off-post saloons and brothels (known as "hog ranches"),[vi] or went on a "whiskey soak",[vii] and often became best friends.[14]

Two pairs of men formed together in a system of "fours," which was the smallest-size fighting unit in the cavalry; there were two "fours" per squad. A "four" generally did not deploy independently. "Fours" became close friends as well. Columns marched in fours; when the troopers dismounted, one of the four men would become a horse-holder – called Number Four – who would hold the reins of all four horses a short way behind the other three men, who would form as skirmishers on foot.[15] The Number Four in each quartet, who would be on the left of the quartet when on line, was sometimes the oldest and most-experienced trooper of the group, but one soldier recalled that each morning the companies would conduct a "Count Off" and so determine the positions by chance, allowing the quartets to change.[16] While this tactical system was old hat to seasoned troopers, it took a while for the new recruits to get acclimated.

According to the 1874 army *Cavalry Tactics* manual, horsemanship training was not a quick process. The manual concluded that to make a trooper a good horseman, it required about one hour of riding every day for at least two months.[17] It was a rough process, beginning with the basic ability to maintain a proper military seat in the saddle; as might be expected, the infantrymen on a cavalry post frequently called the horse-soldiers "sore-asses."[18]

This required training was for both rider and mount. Almost half of the horses in the regiment were new to the organization and were unaccustomed to actual combat or even gunfire in general. This inexperience of the horses further decreased the regiment's potential combat effectiveness and would lead to some mounts riding out of control at the Little Bighorn with fatal results for a few of their riders.[19]

By 1876 each trooper in the regiment was armed with a .45-caliber Model 1873 Springfield Carbine (a single-shot trapdoor-style breechloader) and a six-shot .45-caliber Colt Single Action Army revolver, nicknamed the "Peacemaker," although in Company M a few troopers carried the .45-caliber Smith & Wesson Schofield revolver.[20]

[iii] To "dine with Duke Humphrey" was a common phrase of English Elizabethan literature that equated to not eating at all; it was said to have originated from the practice of the poor gentry who spent their entire dinner hour by a promenade near the tomb of Humphrey, the Duke of Gloucester, in Old Saint Paul's cathedral in London, and thus not eating.

[iv] During the Civil War a private's pay had been $16 a month. Congress lowered pay in 1870 for the enlisted troops as follows: private ($13), saddler ($15), farrier/blacksmith ($15), corporal ($15), sergeant ($17), first sergeant ($22) and sergeant major ($23).

[v] Despite the tough conditions of recruits in any year in the post-Civil War era, there were many times more applicants than openings in the army. One reason for this was that the majority of enlisted men left the army at the end of the first enlistment period.

[vi] Bismarck's seediest district of "hog ranches" and saloons was Fourth Street. Just to the south of town – opposite Fort Abraham Lincoln – was an area known as "Whiskey Point," which consisted of rum shops and gambling halls. These dark dens of iniquity were rampant with disease and often cost an unsophisticated trooper not only money but also "a case of the clap." In addition to being a generic term, there actually was a bordello at Point Pleasant at Bismarck named "The Hog Ranch." More "refined" troopers referred to a prostitute as a "Nymph du Prairie." Unfortunately venereal disease (VD) was one of the top two reasons for medical discharge every year in the army from 1877 to 1889. Troopers referred to VD as "the pox," "old dog," gambler's rot," "the gleet," and "the French disease."

[vii] A "whiskey soak" was period army slang for a heavy drinking session or an extremely heavy drinker. Whiskey was frequently referred to as "coffin varnish," a "Little Drop of the Creature" and "Sheepherder's delight"; cheap whiskey was called "Bug Juice" and "Taos Lightning." At least one source asserted that purveyors of the drink on the Plains cut the base liquor with various additives to increase the volume, with the mixture having the additional effect of making it "the meanest whiskey on earth."

For safety reasons, most of the soldiers loaded the cylinder of the pistol with only five bullets instead of six; this would preclude an unintended discharge, as the hammer rested on an empty chamber.[21]

In perfect conditions, a trained soldier firing the infantry rifle model of the 1873 Springfield could place 16 of 20 shots into a target 27 inches in diameter at a range of 800 yards.[22] But this statistic was misleading. First, cavalry carbines fired less powerful rounds – backed by 55 grains of black powder versus the 70 grains in the rounds for the rifle; the cavalry round had less muzzle velocity as a result, which decreased accuracy, due in part to an increase in trajectory.[viii] Second, the carbine barrel was shorter than the barrel of the infantry rifle, which lessened accuracy further. For the carbine, the point-blank distance – the distance at which sighting was accomplished by simply looking directly down the top of the barrel – was 100 yards.[23] Historian Gregory Michno has concluded that the effective range of the carbine was less than 300 yards.[24] Finally, many cavalry troopers were simply not as well-trained in rifle marksmanship as their infantry brothers-in-arms.

Since 1876 there have been many assertions concerning the degree of carbine marksmanship training conducted in the regiment prior to the Little Bighorn campaign. According to the 1874 *Cavalry Tactics* manual, published by the army, soldiers in a unit were first trained in range estimation. According to the manual, soldiers with normal eyesight would first be able to distinguish the movement of arms and legs of an enemy at a range of 800 yards – further than that, this movement could not be distinguished. At a range of 600 yards, the soldier marksman could distinguish the upper part of the target's body, while at 500 yards he could distinguish the target's head. At closer ranges, the marksman could first distinguish the target's face at 300 yards, the eyes at 80 yards and the white of the eyes at 30 yards. There were two other identification points concerning what could be seen on an enemy's uniform but in Indian fighting these two were not applicable. In short, what a soldier could and could not distinguish about the enemy he was engaging would tell him generally how far the target was from his firing position.[25]

These standards were somewhat misleading as well. To qualify for enlistment a recruit had to be free of disease and able to see a black circle of three feet in diameter against a white background at a distance of 600 yards. For a trooper who barely could determine this large black circle at this distance, it was probably very difficult for him to see a man's head at 500 yards or a man's face at 300 yards, the aforementioned range estimation standards.[26]

To practice dismounted shooting at these various ranges, soldiers constructed wooden targets in standardized sizes as directed in the manual. All practice targets were directed to be six feet tall, a somewhat generous height for a typical man of that time. For targets placed at ranges of 100 to 200 yards, the width of the target was specified at 22 inches. For targets at 250 to 300 yards, the targets were constructed with a width of 44 inches. For those targets to be fired on at ranges of 350 to 400 yards, the width was specified to be 66 inches. For targets greater than 400 yards, the target width was proscribed to be 44 additional inches in width for every 100 yards distance past 400. From the manual's description, it thus appears that the army intended that there would be targets at four different groupings of range for marksmanship training.[27]

The manual then described the allocation of training ammunition per soldier for each year, stating:[28]

> "Each man will be allowed to fire annually ten rounds at each target up to 400 yards and five rounds at each target above 400 to 800 yards…two of the ten shots, at 400 yards and under, will be fired at a rest, two kneeling and six standing."

Colonel Richard I. Dodge, once an aide-de-camp to General William Sherman, commented on the sad state of training resources during the period:[29]

> "Compared with the white hunter of the plains, the Indian is a wretched shot. He is about equal to the United States soldier, being deficient for the same reason – lack of practice. The Government and the Indian are each too poor to afford to waste more than ten cartridges a month on drill, and no man ever became an expert marksman on that allowance."

In September 1875 this monthly allocation was increased to 15 rounds per month.[30] But the increase came with a caveat in the form of General Order 83 from the War Department, which read:[31]

> "This number [15] is to be divided between the carbine and revolver at the discretion of the commanding officer. No greater allowance can be authorized on account of the insufficiency of the appropriations for the manufacture of metallic ammunition."

The actions of the men in Washington would later hang the men in the Dakotas out to dry.

Depending on how the non-commissioned officers read the actual army manual (it is doubtful that all sergeants actually read the later General Order) could determine the aggregate number of training rounds for each man. If the company sergeants understood that they would place one target at the 100-200 yard range, a second target at the 250-300 yard range, a third target at the 350-400 yard range, and one target somewhere further than 400 yards, the trooper would have fired between 35 and 180 carbine rounds each year for training; if the sergeants did not see the requirement that way, the targets and numbers of rounds fired would be different – it did not make for standardized training.

Firing while mounted was not preferred, as only very few men could hit a target with their carbine fire from the back of a horse; additionally, mounted men made easier targets for enemy fire.[32] The cavalry manual prescribed that mounted carbine firing would be practiced at ranges of 50 to 200 yards, while pistol firing would be practiced at ranges of 10 to 50 yards. There were no ammunition allocations for mounted marksmanship training.[33]

There is one other requirement for marksmanship training, although it was listed as a general rule – which places some degree of uncertainty on it concerning the 7th Cavalry in 1876. This final requirement stated:[34]

> "Before every campaign, the troops will be required to expend at least sixty rounds per man at target practice; this is particularly necessary with raw troops, to give them confidence in their arms, and prepare them for the noise of battle."

[viii] First Sergeant John Ryan later stated that he occasionally traded some of his 55-grain cartridges for 70-grain cartridges when he wanted to do long-range shooting. It is not known how many other cavalrymen made these exchanges as well, or if any Company M men at the Little Bighorn, other than Ryan, had the more powerful cartridges. Source: Sandy Barnard, editor, *Ten Years with Custer: A 7th Cavalryman's Memoirs*, Terre Haute, IN: AST Press, 2001, 257.

But the breech-loaded metallic ammunition was expensive and often in short supply. In some instances, commanding officers were afraid that they personally might have to pay for using too much ammunition for training.[35] That would have been expensive as the cost of 1,000 .45/70 Springfield rounds was $35.[36]

Nineteen troopers in Company M joined the army in 1875 in their first enlistment, and for them this was their first campaign against an enemy. A key question is: did any of them and the more-veteran soldiers in the company receive the opportunity to fire these additional 60 rounds? By the official manual, it could be argued that each man on the expedition should have fired a minimum of 95 carbine rounds in training in the months prior to departing Fort Rice (35 in annual marksmanship training and 60 in pre-expedition firing); in reality some may have fired far less.[ix] The degree of marksmanship training in Company M in 1876 is additionally complicated by the fact that First Sergeant John Ryan was not the senior non-commissioned officer in the company for three weeks leading up to the Little Bighorn expedition, and it is quite possible – even probable – that his replacement did not conduct this pre-expedition marksmanship training either.

Some historians have postulated that the companies intended to have the new soldiers practice marksmanship during the march west by hunting wild game to supplement army rations, but this is counter-intuitive. If the goal is to shoot antelope for food along the flanks of the march, it will be the best shots in the unit who are detailed to this task, not the least experienced. Additionally, there is scout testimony that they were paid when they provided fresh meat.

Intuition aside, respected historian Edgar I. Stewart, author of *Custer's Luck*, has written that Major Marcus Reno held no target practice, while he was in temporary command of the regiment, during the time Custer was in Washington, D.C.[37]

There was one additional issue concerning the 1873 Springfield. This model of the firearm had two hammer positions only – full cock and half cock. On half cock, it was possible for the trapdoor to be jolted open, which would allow dirt to enter the breech – an unsatisfactory condition.[38] However, on full cock, with a round in the chamber, serious accidents and unintentional discharges could occur; thus in 1876 troopers actually loaded their carbines only under orders of an officer or by the senior man present in an emergency, who subsequently would bear responsibility for any mishap.[x]

What was not an issue was the stopping power of the 1873 Springfield. Firing a 405-grain bullet, the lead slug was fondly referred to as the "ounce of lead" as it rumbled toward its target. At 100 yards the Springfield's bullet could penetrate 10 inches of pine – twice what a Winchester repeater could do – and even out at 700 yards the rifle version of the round could penetrate 7.3 inches of pine boards.[39] Warriors and ponies alike did not fare well when struck at any range.

Company M went through a series of weapons from its formation in 1866 to its participation in the Little Bighorn 10 years later. The company undoubtedly began its service armed with M1865 Spencer caliber .50 carbines from the Civil War. Reports from the fourth quarter of 1870 indicated that Company M had 51 Sharps caliber .50 carbines and eight caliber .44 Remington New Model Army pistols. Unit small arms' reports show that Company M at Fort Hays, Kansas had 61 Sharps caliber .50 carbines on hand during the first quarter of 1871. The unit reported the same number in the second quarter of 1872. In Unionville, South Carolina in the fourth quarter of 1871, Company M was credited with having 68 Sharps caliber .50 carbines and 11 caliber .44 Remington pistols. In the fourth quarter of 1872 in Oxford, Mississippi, Captain French's command owned 67 Sharps caliber .50 carbines. In the first quarter of 1873, Company M reported from Memphis, Tennessee that it owned 54 Sharps caliber .50 carbines.[40]

Then the unit began to transition to the newer carbine and pistol models. The second quarter of 1874 arms' report indicates that Company M had 35 Sharps caliber .50 carbines and 70 of the new Colt Model 1873 caliber .45 pistols. In the third quarter 1874 report, Company M had 83 Springfield Model 1873 caliber .45 carbines and 68 Colt Model 1873s. In the fourth quarter of 1874, the company reported possessing 79 Springfield Model 1873 carbines, 64 Colt Model 1873 pistols and one Sharps caliber .50 carbine. In both the first and second quarters of 1875, Captain French reported that his unit had the same numbers as the previous reporting period.[41]

Before the expedition the 7th Cavalry commander ordered that cavalry sabers would not be taken on the operation, out of concern that the noise of sabers rattling during mounted operations would reduce stealth, which would be crucial to catching the Indian encampment off guard.

Supplemental food sources were important, as enlisted rations in the field on campaign were only slightly better than those provided to the recruits in depots. The regiment often took a small heard of beef cattle with it for butchering in the field. But the range beef was tough and of poor quality and was mostly sliced or cubed for use in hash and stew. The ever-present salt pork sometimes became rancid in the field. If the young soldiers thought they had escaped beans, rice, hardtack and black coffee, they would be sadly mistaken. When the possibility of enemy contact was low, company commanders would detail troops to a 10-day stint of cooking; apparently the soldier's previous experience at such a task did not enter in to the selection process. As an added insult, the soldier's 10-day tour in the field kitchen often ruined his uniform with grease and food spills; hopefully the soiled trooper had an extra set of trousers and shirt, but that was not always the case, which meant in the summer he would be a fly-magnet for the remainder of the campaign.[42] And issue coffee in the field was not roasted or ground. The troopers received green coffee beans, which they then roasted as best they could in a Dutch oven or a frying pan; the cavalrymen then ground the beans by placing them in a cloth and pounding them with a carbine butt or a large stone.[43] A trooper in Company M later described the ever-present hardtack, also known as "Petrified Crackers":[44]

> "Did you ever attempt to eat a hard-tack? If not, try to bite a piece out of an old fire-brick. I do not wonder the Government examines a man's teeth so carefully before he is enlisted; it should provide steel teeth and a file with which to sharpen them."

Sometimes a lack of food variety plagued the officers as well. After Captain Thomas French rode up to Fort Abraham Lincoln after spending several months at Fort Rice, he remarked at a meal:[45]

> "Gosh-a-Mighty, we haven't seen an onion in six months."

That observation may have been true, but the men did have access to vegetables. In October 1875 the Fort Rice post surgeon inspected the company dining facilities and found that each trooper of Company M received an average of 15-17 ounces per day of potatoes, onions, beans

[ix] Peter Thompson of Company C later told his daughter that he was scared "spitless" of his Springfield carbine because he scarcely knew how to shoot it.

[x] This design oversight was corrected in later models of the Springfield that had a three-position hammer, which allowed a cartridge to be safely chambered in the weapon.

or cabbage; although this was slightly lower that month than what the other companies, stationed at Fort Rice, received.[46]

Company M had a present-for-duty strength of 56 on the morning of June 25, 1876 – significantly under authorization (70 enlisted.) The company was authorized one captain and, of course, was fine there with Captain Thomas French. The unit was authorized two lieutenants and although First Lieutenant Edward Mathey and Second Lieutenant James G. "Jack" Sturgis[xi] were assigned on paper, they were not with Company M, but rather served on the campaign as the commander of the pack train and as second in command of Company E, respectively. Thus, Captain French was the only commissioned officer actually with the company the day of battle.

The unit was authorized one first sergeant, and in Company M that was filled by First Sergeant John "Paddy" Ryan.[47] But the company was authorized five other sergeants and had but four present at the battle (80 percent). Concerning corporals, four were authorized and three were on hand (75 percent). Non-commissioned officers were extremely important and ran the company in a tough manner. Unless first talked to by a commissioned officer, a soldier had to get the first sergeant's permission to even speak to an officer. Officers left the enforcement of discipline in the company to the non-commissioned officers, especial the first sergeant. In fact, most company officers – even the ultra-conscientious – left the actual work of running the company to their first sergeants.[48] To a young soldier, the company sergeants may not have been the Almighty, but they were certainly on speaking terms with that higher authority.[49]

French's unit was authorized two trumpeters and had two – important positions, as in the din of battle in that era of technology, orders were transmitted by various trumpet calls that had to be heard by every soldier. Trumpeters were also expected to serve as messengers. Therefore, to qualify for the position a prospective trumpeter had to demonstrate the capacity to repeat a 20-word message verbatim.[50] According to a later Company M trumpeter, when in combat situations one trumpeter in each company was detailed to stay with the company commander, while the second would accompany the company first sergeant.[51]

And the company had both authorized blacksmiths/farriers, which would help keep the horses shod over a long campaign – they also did rudimentary veterinarian duties for the animals.[52] One of these men was Farrier George "Cully" Weaver. Born in 1842 in Philadelphia, Pennsylvania, "Cully" was 5'7" tall, had brown eyes, brown hair and a florid complexion; his previous work experience had been with the railroad. He was also illiterate. Weaver first enlisted in the army on August 11, 1869 in Philadelphia and was assigned to Company G of the 7th Infantry Regiment. "Cully" reported sick for a boil on December 9, 1874.[53] He reenlisted in Pittsburgh on May 1, 1875 – joining Company M on October 21, 1875 at Fort Rice, Dakota Territory.[54]

Additionally, Company M had men who had learned the blacksmith trade and could assist in this key task: Private John Sivertsen was a blacksmith in civilian life as was Private Dan Newell.

Company M had one wagoner authorized and one assigned, but he was not present at the fight. The company was at full authorized strength of one saddler, but it was at the rank of private that the unit most felt the pinch of being under-strength. Like every company in the 7th Cavalry, Company M was authorized 70 privates – the men who actually did the bulk of fighting. On the morning of June 25, Company M had 48 privates assigned, but only 42 were present-for-duty, just 78 percent of those authorized (54). Thus, Captain French would have to try to compensate with quality instead of quantity.

Excellent leadership in Company M started right at the top beginning with the company commander Captain Thomas H. French. Born in Baltimore, Maryland on March 5, 1843, he was baptized in Baltimore's St. Paul the Apostle Church. Young Thomas, a Catholic, became a "day scholar" and attended Georgetown College in Washington, D.C. between the ages of 10 and 14. Thomas's father died in 1858 and he was adopted by his mother's brother, Colonel Martin Burke, a Regular Army officer.[xii] Burke wanted his nephew to attend West Point, trying for several years to gain his admittance, but could not secure an appointment. Colonel Burke then went to Secretary of War Edwin M. Stanton to seek a commission. Stanton interviewed Thomas French on January 6, 1864 and told him that after enlisting if he proved himself he would receive a commission. French duly enlisted at Fort Lafayette, New York Harbor, on January 13, 1864 in the 10th Infantry Regiment. Records show that he was 5'81/2" tall, with brown hair and hazel eyes. Events progressed very quickly; Colonel Burke was the commanding officer of the post, and assigned his nephew to a clerical position. Within weeks, several officers requested that Private French be commissioned at the soonest opportunity. On March 21, 1864 an officer examining board in Washington reviewed French's application for commission and found him to be qualified for selection.[55]

Thomas H. French received his commission to second lieutenant in the 10th Infantry Regiment on May 18, 1864; barely one month later he was promoted to first lieutenant. French fought at the siege of Petersburg and the battle of the Weldon Railroad. For this latter action he was brevetted to captain in the volunteers. He also fought at Chapel House, Virginia, where he was wounded in action. French later wrote of his experience:[56]

> "In the battles on the Weldon Railroad August 18th, 19th and 21st 1864, I commanded the 10th Infantry and was rewarded with the brevet of Captain...At the battle of Chapel House... [On] October 1st, I received a severe and extremely painful wound – also a slight one – in the left leg. I was the only officer of the regiment there and the only one of those present who was not brevetted for the engagement."

In November 1866 the army offered Thomas French the grade of permanent captain in the 44th Infantry Regiment of the Veteran Reserve Corps. He declined the promotion, probably as he wished to remain in a Regular Army regiment. His time finally came and on March 26, 1868 Thomas French was promoted to captain in the 10th Infantry Regiment at Fort Ripley, Minnesota. However, a year later Congress

[xi] James G. "Jack" Sturgis was born on January 24, 1854 in Albuquerque. He graduated from West Point in 1875 ranking 29th of 43 in his class. His father, who was commander of the 7th Cavalry, advised him not to join the cavalry, but the younger Sturgis did anyway. After graduation from the Academy, Sturgis was detailed to serve for several months on court martial duty at St. Louis. Sturgis was initially assigned to Company M on October 21, 1875. From March 1 to May 2, 1876 he served as the Fort Rice post signal officer. He was attached to Company E on May 12 as second in command. Sturgis is reported to have been a popular officer with the troopers, a characteristic that seems to have been somewhat rare in the regiment. "Jack" Sturgis was killed on June 25, 1876 with George Custer's element; there has been uncertainty concerning his remains that has lasted to this day, and he has no official grave.

[xii] Martin Burke was commissioned as a second lieutenant in the 8th Infantry Regiment on January 28, 1820. During the War with Mexico, he was promoted to brevet major for gallantry and meritorious conduct at the Battles of Contreras and Churubusco on August 20, 1847. He received a promotion to brevet lieutenant colonel on September 8, 1847 for meritorious conduct during the Battle of Molino del Ray. During the Civil War, Martin Burke was promoted to colonel and to brigadier general on March 13, 1865; he commanded several military prisons that held Confederate prisoners and sympathizers. Martin Burke died on April 24, 1882. He well was known throughout the army as a man who would follow orders. General Winfield Scott, initial Commander of the Union Army in the Civil War, once said of him: "Colonel Martin Burke is famous for his unquestioning obedience to orders. He was with me in Mexico, and, if I had told him at any time to take out one of my aides-de-camp and shoot him before breakfast, the aide's execution would have been duly reported."

reduced the size of the army and Captain French was in limbo again due to his lack of seniority in grade. In May 1869 he was ordered to duty with a military commission convened at Austin, Texas and for the next 18 months he and his uncle marshaled support for assignment to another regiment, where the chances of remaining in the service were higher. On November 9, 1870 Brigadier General Alfred Terry[xiii] joined Thomas French's corner and wrote the following to the Army Adjutant General:[57]

> "[Captain French] bore the reputation of an intelligent, well-conducted and faithful officer."

Four days later, Colonel Alvan C. Gillem,[xiv] commander of the 11th Infantry Regiment, also wrote the Adjutant General and included this summary:[58]

> "It is not inconsistent with the interests of the service that I earnestly recommend that Captain French may be assigned to my Regiment – 11th U.S. Infantry…Captain French is young, energetic, temperate, and has great taste for the military profession."

Something finally worked in Washington – probably after the commander of the army General William T. Sherman[xv] assured Colonel Burke that he would "provide" for his nephew – and on January 1, 1871 Captain Thomas French was ordered to report to the 7th Cavalry at Fort Hays, Kansas. He assumed command of Company M on February 15, 1871. French participated in the Yellowstone Campaign in 1873 and the Black Hills Expedition in 1874. Captain French distinguished himself on August 11, 1873 in temporary command of a battalion of two companies that prevented the Lakota from crossing the Yellowstone River and engaging the main body of the regiment.[59]

Along with the regimental adjutant, First Lieutenant William W. Cooke, French was thought to be the best shot in the regiment. First Sergeant John Ryan said of this ability:[60]

> "The captain of my company, Thomas H. French, was considered a dead shot."

On expeditions, unlike all his soldiers who carried .45-caliber weapons, Captain French carried a .50-caliber Model 1870 Springfield rifle, known as a "Long Tom," or a "Big Fifty."[61] The weapon fired a 425-grain bullet using 70 grains of black powder, and apparently in Captain French's hands – "Buffalo Bill" Cody also used the caliber to hunt buffalo – it was a lethal combination.[xvi] But Captain Thomas French was probably not the fastest runner in the unit; a former enlisted man later said that in 1876, French – nicknamed "Tucker" by the enlisted men for unknown reasons – was "a fat man with a falsetto voice."[62]

Captain Thomas French also had a dark side and was experiencing problems with alcohol consumption. In August 1875 he was unable to lead a detachment into the field; a non-commissioned officer then had to fulfill that duty. Major Joseph G. Tilford,[xvii] the commander of Fort Rice, stated in a letter to regimental headquarters at that time that French was honoring a pledge made to him to abstain from the use of alcohol.[63] It was not effective; on most photographs of officers during this period, Captain French is conspicuous in his absence, even though the photographs appear to have been taken in mid-day.

• • •

But French's pledge of abstinence had unfortunate second order effects. French had given this word of honor to Major Joseph Tilford, the post commander at Fort Rice. However, George Custer – stationed at nearby Fort Abraham Lincoln and French's tactical superior – believed he could weigh in on the issue as the regimental commander and wrote to the Department of Dakota himself. He opined that French had already broken his promise of sobriety and that several officers could testify to that fact. Tilford, when queried by the Assistant Adjutant General of the Department of Dakota, became irate and wrote back to St. Paul, Minnesota stating that Custer had no business butting in to a situation involving Fort Rice and should provide the names of those officers posthaste, who had eyewitness testimony describing Captain French's condition, and whom Tilford could ostensibly interview.[64] This does not appear to have happened and was just one more example of the officers of the 7th Cavalry Regiment lining up against each other on an issue and added to the atmosphere of mistrust in the unit.

• • •

[xiii] Alfred H. Terry was born in Hartford, Connecticut on November 10, 1827 and as a young man attended Yale Law School. A lawyer by trade, when the Civil War started, Terry raised and led a regiment of Connecticut volunteers and was appointed a colonel. He fought at First Bull Run, Fort Wagner, Petersburg, New Market Heights and Charleston Harbor. Terry's greatest achievement in the conflict came when he was placed in command of the Fort Fisher Expeditionary Corps in 1865. After heavy fighting, Union troops took the fort and Terry was promoted to brigadier general in the Regular Army. He was generally considered one of the most capable Union generals, with no previous military training or experience, to emerge from the war. Nicknamed "One Star" by the Arikaras and "Morning Star" by the Crow, Terry served as the Military Commander of the Dakota Territory from 1866 to 1869, and again from 1872 to 1886. Terry, a bachelor, lived in St. Paul with his mother and four sisters. Alfred H. Terry died on December 16, 1890 at New Haven, Connecticut; he is buried at the Grove Street Cemetery there.

[xiv] Alvan C. Gillem was born on July 29, 1830 in Gainesboro, Tennessee. In 1851 he graduated from West Point and was commissioned an artilleryman. Gillem fought in Florida the following year in the Second Seminole War. Prior to the Civil War, Gillem served in Texas. During the Civil War he served in various campaigns in his home state (including the Battles of Shiloh, Morristown and Bull's Gap), ending the war as a brevet major general. In 1866 he left the volunteer army and was commissioned as a colonel in the Regular Army. He later fought against the Modoc Indians and participated in the Battle of the Lava Beds in 1873. Ten days later, on April 26, 1873, his forces suffered a setback at Sand Butte; he was relieved of command shortly afterward. Alvan C. Gillem died on December 2, 1875 outside of Nashville, Tennessee. He is buried at the Mount Olivet Cemetery in Nashville.

[xv] William T. "Uncle Billy" Sherman was born in Lancaster, Ohio on February 8, 1820. He graduated from West Point in 1840, ranking sixth of 42. Missing action in the Mexican War, Sherman resigned his commission in 1853 and tried banking and a streetcar company in St. Louis, where he was living at the outbreak of the Civil War. Sherman was commissioned a colonel in the 13th U.S. Infantry Regiment, but soon became the commander of the Department of the Cumberland. Sherman later commanded the 5th Division and subsequently the Army of the Tennessee. He later commanded three armies in his march through Georgia fulfilling his promise to "make Georgia howl." Shortly after the war ended, Sherman assumed duties as the commander of the Military Division of the Missouri. On July 25, 1866, Congress promoted Sherman, who was also nicknamed "Cump," to lieutenant general. When Grant became president in 1869, Sherman was appointed as Commanding General of the United States Army, receiving a fourth star. Sherman retired from the army on February 8, 1884. William Tecumseh Sherman died on February 14, 1891 in New York City. He is buried in St. Louis, Missouri at Calvary Cemetery in Section 17, Lot 8.

[xvi] The Model 1870 had a 32.5 inch barrel with three lands and grooves. The rear sight had an adjustable leaf graduated to 900 yards. Source: Douglas C. McChristian, *The U.S. Army in the West: 1870-1880*, Norman, OK: University of Oklahoma Press, 1995, 125-126.

[xvii] Joseph G. Tilford was born in Georgetown, Kentucky on November 26, 1828. He entered the United States Military Academy by appointment from Kentucky on July 1, 1847. On July 1, 1851, Tilford graduated from West Point – ranking 40 of 42 – and was appointed a Brevet Second Lieutenant in the Mounted Rifles. He was commissioned a Second Lieutenant on January 27, 1853; he was promoted to First Lieutenant on June 14, 1858, and to Captain on July 31, 1861. Tilford served at the Cavalry School and on frontier duty from 1851 to 1862. During the Civil War, he was engaged in actions from New Mexico to Tennessee, where he was in the campaign at Chattanooga. Tilford received the brevet rank of Major on February 21, 1862, for his gallant and meritorious services in the battle of Valverde, New Mexico; he was promoted to brevet Lieutenant Colonel on March 13, 1865, for his faithful and meritorious services during the Civil War. Tilford was appointed a Major in the 7th Cavalry on November 27, 1867 (with an effective date of rank to major of November 14, 1867), and served with the regiment until September 22, 1883; during that time he constantly seemed to be in ill health. He was on a leave of absence during the 1876 Sioux Campaign. Tilford continued in command of Fort Meade and later commanded Fort Sill, Indian Territory. On April 11, 1889 he assumed command of the 9th Cavalry Regiment. Joseph Tilford was married to Cornelia Van Ness; the couple had several children including Nina Dean Tilford (1864) and James Dean Tilford (1877), who went on to be a colonel in the army. Tilford retired on July 1, 1891 and was promoted to Brigadier General on the retired list on April 23, 1904. Joseph G. Tilford died February 24, 1911 in Washington, D.C. He is buried in Section 2, Grave 1205, at Arlington National Cemetery. His wife died in 1923.

By 1874 Thomas French's health began to fail in many areas. On May 12, 1874 he reported sick with acute diarrhea. He was diagnosed with acute dyspepsia – severe indigestion – on March 9, 1875 and June 1, 1875.[65] Both instances could have been alcohol induced.[66] French was diagnosed on July 17, 1875 and August 20, 1875 with epilepsy, which could have actually been alcoholic seizures. On this last episode, he did not return to duty until September 5. Captain French reported ill with stomach flu on December 11, 1875 as well.[67] Although he was absent much of the time, he made an effort and attended the wedding of Lieutenant Francis Gibson in 1875.[68] Because of his condition, much of the company duties would fall to the senior non-commissioned officer to perform.

First Sergeant John "Paddy" Ryan was the "rock" of Company M. Born in West Newton, Massachusetts on August 25, 1845, he was the son of Edward Ryan and Hannora Lynch Ryan of Tipperary, Ireland. Ryan entered service as a 16-year-old volunteer in Company C of the 28th Massachusetts Infantry and fought in the major bloody battles at Second Manassas, Fredericksburg, Chancellorsville, Gettysburg and Petersburg and numerous smaller, but deadly fights such as Fort Lamar and Reams Station – he was wounded twice during the conflict.[69]

Not satisfied with civilian life immediately following the war, John Ryan – also nicknamed "Jack" – enlisted in Company M in 1866; he participated in the Battle of the Washita River in 1868 and also took part in the Yellowstone Campaign of 1873 and the Black Hills Expedition of 1874. Ryan was promoted to corporal on November 23, 1866 and to sergeant on January 1, 1869. He was elevated to first sergeant in February 1870 and held the position until April of that year. Ryan became the first sergeant again in late October 1873. He was a feisty non-commissioned officer; 5' 61/2" tall, he had gray eyes, auburn hair and a ruddy complexion. Ryan was a carpenter by trade and sometimes was called on to perform that skill; for example, from October 17 to October 30, 1875 Ryan was detailed to serve as the carpenter in the quartermaster department at Fort Rice – at a time when he certainly had more than enough to do as a company first sergeant, especially given his commanding officer's medical condition.[70]

But cavalry life was tough, especially for first sergeants. Records show that Ryan was treated for a sprain on January 28, 1867 and for acute diarrhea on September 23, 1869. On January 5, 1870 he reported on sick call with a boil. A doctor diagnosed him with an ulcer on March 13, 1870; he was treated for another boil on July 23, 1870. On September 4, 1870 Ryan reported on sick call with some type of lacerated wound. On October 1, 1870 Ryan was treated for erysipelas, a type of skin infection similar to cellulitis. He was treated for a fever on August 30, 1871 and September 20, 1871. Ryan had a bad cut that required treatment on January 3, 1873. He was treated for hemorrhoids on March 31, 1875 and for consumption on January 12, 1876.[71] And these were just the maladies that he reported on sick call; there undoubtedly were many instances when the first sergeant just "gutted it out" and did not seek medical attention.

Ryan took part in the arrest of Chief Rain-in-the-Face at the Standing Rock Agency, Dakota Territory, in December 1874. A tough disciplinarian, Ryan ran afoul of the army's judicial system in 1876. On April 11, 1876 he caught Private Charles Kavanaugh cutting a government horse bridle. For this destruction of government property, Ryan had Kavanaugh tied up to a tree, suspended off the ground by his wrists, as punishment. Kavanaugh complained to a doctor, and the post commander at Fort Rice ordered that a Garrison Court Martial be held. The results included:[72]

> "Before a Garrison Court Martial which convened at this Post pursuant to Post Orders No.39 from these headquarters, and which Captain T.H. French, 7th Cavalry, is President, was arraigned and tried: 1st Sergeant John Ryan, Company M, 7th Cavalry.
>
> Charge: Violation of the 62nd Article of War.
>
> Specification: In that he, 1st Sergeant John Ryan, Company M, 7th Cavalry, did illegally cause to be tied up and suspended by the arms for punishment, Private Charles Kavanaugh, Company M, 7th Cavalry; this to the prejudice of good order and military discipline. All this [happened] at Fort Rice, Dakota Territory on or about the 11th day of April, 1876, during morning stables.
>
> Pleading: Guilty
> Finding: Guilty
> Sentence: To be reduced to the rank of a Private Soldier
>
> The Proceedings, Finding and Sentence in the foregoing case of 1st Sergeant John Ryan, Company M, 7th Cavalry, are approved. The sentence is confirmed and will be duly executed.
>
> The Garrison Court Martial of which Captain T.H. French, 7th Cavalry, is President is hereby dissolved."

First Lieutenant Charles C. DeRudio was the judge advocate. The board found Ryan guilty, but recommended clemency. Captain Frederick Benteen, who was serving as the acting commander of Fort Rice at the time, upheld the guilty verdict but declined to apply clemency. Ryan then became the acting quartermaster sergeant for the company. However, on May 9, 1876 – just before the Little Bighorn expedition began – the regiment published the following special order:[73]

> "Upon the recommendation of the Company Commander the following appointment is hereby made in Company M, this regiment, to date from May 9, 1876: Private John Ryan to be 1st Sergeant, vice reduced. He will be obeyed and respected accordingly.
>
> By order of Major M.A. Reno
> W.W. Cooke
> 1st Lieutenant and Adjutant
> 7th Cavalry"

There may have been some grumbling by a few of the troopers at Ryan's restoration as first sergeant – especially those who had been in the March riot – but most of them knew they needed a tough veteran like "Paddy" when push came to shove in combat. Ryan not only knew how to shove, he knew how to shoot. On the Little Bighorn campaign, First Sergeant Ryan carried a .45-caliber heavy barrel Model 1874 Sharps telescopic rifle that had been specially made for him in Bismarck at the cost of $100. The weapon, which was probably provided by Bismarck gun-dealer and gunsmith O.H. Beal, fired the same ammunition that the infantry version of the 1873 Springfield did – .45/70; Ryan traded some of the cavalry rounds to First Sergeant William Bolton of Company G in the 17th Infantry Regiment before the expedition in return for the more powerful infantry rounds.[74]

The weapon possibly had a tube sight, the forerunner to the scope, a long metal tube that rested above the barrel. Using standard-type iron sights inside the tube, it thus provided no magnification but did block out superfluous light. Given the cost of the weapon, however, it is more likely that the sight was indeed a telescopic sight, perhaps a thirty-inch-long William Malcolm three-power version, which were made in Syracuse and considered the finest of the day.[xviii] Malcolm's scopes featured achromatic lenses that provided a much better definition of the target, with a flatter field of view and a clear definition at the edge of any target. His telescopes also had precise windage and elevation adjustments. The action was a falling block, breech-loading, single-shot. Triggers on the model could be single or double set; either would have allowed for a greatly reduced trigger pull that is beneficial to accuracy. Given Ryan's particular weapon had a heavy barrel, it was probably thirty-two inches long and octagonal.[75] Thus, it is quite possible that First Sergeant Ryan had the most accurate long-range rifle in the entire 7th Cavalry.

• • •

Many of the other sergeants in the company had a direct European connection. Sergeant Patrick Carey was born in Tipperary, Ireland on April 14, 1828. A bachelor, Carey enlisted on September 14, 1866 in Company I of the 36th Infantry Regiment; enlistment records show he was 5' 71/2" tall, with gray eyes, gray hair with a light complexion. After completing his initial enlistment, Carey, who was nicknamed "Patsy," enlisted on March 4, 1870 with Company M of the 7th Cavalry at Fort Leavenworth. He completed this enlistment as well and re-enlisted in Company M on March 22, 1875. He was promoted to corporal on August 15, 1873 and to sergeant on December 10, 1874.[76] Carey was close with First Sergeant Ryan; it had been Ryan for whom he had called when in trouble during the opening stages of the company riot in March.

Sergeant John McGlone hailed from Sligo, Ireland, where he was born in 1844. Another bachelor, he enlisted in Philadelphia, Pennsylvania on December 18, 1872. Records show he had been a laborer and was 5' 91/2" tall, with brown eyes, dark hair and a ruddy complexion. He joined Company M on February 9, 1873. McGlone was appointed to the rank of corporal on February 10, 1875 and sergeant on June 17, 1876.[77]

Sergeant Miles F. O'Hara was born in September 1851 in Alton, Ohio. A laborer in civilian life, he first enlisted in Columbus, Ohio on October 30, 1872; he joined Company M at Unionville, South Carolina on December 9, 1872. O'Hara was 5' 81/2" in height with gray eyes, light hair and a ruddy complexion. His wife was a company laundress[xix] at Fort Abraham Lincoln; the couple had a young daughter.[78]

Born in Saxony, Germany on September 16, 1847, Sergeant Henry C. Weihe actually enlisted under the name Charles White, on November 6, 1867 in Company D of the 17th Infantry Regiment, due to a clerk's inability to spell his given name. He left the service in late 1870 and became a farmer but re-enlisted on March 8, 1871 in Philadelphia, Pennsylvania and was assigned to Company M on May 30, 1871 in Louisville, Kentucky. Weihe fractured his right thigh on June 19, 1873.[79] He was promoted to corporal on January 25, 1873, and was promoted to sergeant on December 1, 1873. Weihe was 5' 31/2" tall, had gray eyes, brown hair and a fair complexion. On March 8, 1876 Weihe was discharged as a sergeant with excellent character, and immediately re-enlisted for a term of five years. At the time of the Little Bighorn, Henry Weihe held the position as first duty sergeant of Company M.[80] He was also close with First Sergeant Ryan.

Corporal Henry M. Cody enlisted in Boston, Massachusetts on September 24, 1873 under the name of Henry M. Scollin; he arrived at Company M on October 21, 1873. Previously a painter, Cody was 5'7" tall, with blue eyes, dark hair and a medium complexion. He was born in Nashua, New Hampshire in 1851. On April 3, 1874 he fell off his horse and was treated for a sprain. He then spent time detailed as the company cook. For several months in 1875 Cody served as the company wagoner. Henry Cody was promoted to corporal on August 2, 1875.[81] Cody's best friend in the company was Private "Dan" Newell.

Corporal William Lalor was also from the Isle of Saint Patrick, having been born in County Queens in January 1839. He first enlisted in Detroit, Michigan for three years in Company E, U.S. Engineers on May 22, 1866; his previous occupation was a tinsmith. Lalor was 5'8" tall and had blue eyes, brown hair and a fair complexion. Lalor was discharged at West Point, New York on May 22, 1869. He then spent five years as a civilian before enlisting again at St. Louis, Missouri on September 29, 1875. He joined Company M at Fort Rice, Dakota Territory on October 21, 1875. He reported sick at the Fort Abraham Lincoln Post Hospital on May 6, 1876 with a boil; he was returned to duty five days later. William Lalor was appointed to the rank of corporal on June 17, 1876.[82]

Corporal Frederick Stressinger was born Frederick Streing on June 24, 1852 in Ripley County, Indiana. A laborer by trade, he enlisted at Louisville, Kentucky on October 19, 1872; he was listed as 5' 51/2" tall, with gray eyes, light hair and a fair complexion. He joined Company M in Unionville, South Carolina on December 9, 1872. In April 1873 he was diagnosed with acute bronchitis and was on the steamer *Western* as the company travelled from Yankton to Fort Rice in April and May 1873. He was detailed as the company cook in August 1873 and served as the company carpenter from April to June 1875. He also appears as the company blacksmith in July 1875. A Fort Rice Garrison Court Martial convicted Stressinger on February 5, 1875 for refusing to perform the duties of the company cook and fined him $5.[83] He was acquitted by another Garrison Court Martial on April 13, 1875 of the charge of being absent at the retreat formation. Frederick Stressinger was promoted to corporal on June 17, 1876.[84]

Two other men also had definite Civil War experience, while another one or two probably did. Private Joseph "Joe" Bates, who enlisted as Joseph C. Murphy on March 29, 1858 in Buffalo, New York, served in Company I, 1st Massachusetts Cavalry during the Civil War, rising to First Sergeant and later was commissioned as a company commander.[85] His unit fought at Charleston and helped capture Jacksonville, Florida. Bates hailed from Providence, Rhode Island, where he was born in 1837. He stood 5'10" tall, with blue eyes, brown hair and a fair complexion. Bates joined Company M on December 10, 1866 and was appointed the company first sergeant three days later. But in 1867 he was absent without permission and placed in arrest at Fort Hays in June 1867. Bates was reduced to private on August 9, 1867. Absent without leave from February 27 to March 27, 1869 and discharged, he reenlisted on July 18, 1870 at Carlisle Barracks, Pennsylvania. Joining Company F, he again began to rise through the ranks and was promoted to corporal on February 1, 1872 and to sergeant on February 5, 1872. But he deserted on May 11, 1872.

[xviii] William Malcolm built scopes that were three to twenty power, but the greater the magnification the narrower the field of vision. Higher power magnification is good for target shooting but the lower power models would have been more advantageous in combat for finding potential targets.

[xix] Two company laundresses for Company M during this time were Mrs. Norris and Mrs. McLaughlin. Source: Letter, Post Surgeon, Fort Rice, Dakota Territory to Post Adjutant, dated October 31, 1875, Records Group 393, Records of U.S. Army Continental Commands, 1821-1920, Part V, Military Installations, Fort Rice, South Dakota, Entry 4.

Bates was apprehended on December 19, 1873 by the 16th Infantry Regiment in Lebanon, Kentucky and remained in confinement for five months. About this time he fractured his right arm. Bates transferred back to Company M on January 4, 1875. On August 2, 1875 he was again promoted to corporal, but he was reduced to private on November 6, 1875, when a Garrison Court Martial convicted him of being drunk on stable guard.[86]

Private Henry H. "Harrison" Davis served in Company A of the 193rd Pennsylvania Volunteers in 1864, but his regiment participated in no large actions, primarily guarding bridges in Pennsylvania. Davis was either born in Bellvernon, Virginia on January 20, 1846 or in Fayette City, Pennsylvania on January 19, 1846; his civilian occupation was a miner. After the Civil War ended, Davis waited about eighteen months before enlisting again – this time with the 7th Cavalry – on December 21, 1866; he joined Company M on January 22, 1867. On October 16, 1868 he was diagnosed with acute diarrhea; he returned to duty a month later. "Harrison" Davis stood 5' 61/2" tall, had brown eyes, sandy hair and a fair complexion.[87] Private Davis had his share of spills in Company M; he was diagnosed at Camp Sturgis on July 6, 1870 with a contusion. On May 3, 1874 a doctor treated him for a lacerated finger.[88] A Fort Rice Garrison Court Martial convicted Davis of going absent without official permission from his guard duty; it then fined him $12 and sentenced him to one month confinement. Records indicate that he was illiterate, but he was a veteran cavalryman. First Sergeant John Ryan would later state that Davis was one of the best shots in Company M.[89]

Private Charles Kavanaugh may have fought in the Civil War. In April 1876 he told a physician at Fort Rice that he had been wounded in the shoulder during the war, but this study has found no paper trail to support his assertion.[90]

In 1878 Private Henry C. Weaver made a statement at his own court martial that he initially joined the army in 1861, but his assertion may have been made as an attempt to gain sympathy.[91]

• • •

It may be appropriate at this point to briefly discuss the U.S. Army court martial system in place during this period, as so many Company M troopers seem to have gone through various military judicial proceedings during their careers. Although on the books there were five types of legal court proceedings (General Court Martial, Regiment Court Martial, Garrison Court Martial, Field Officer's Court and Summary Court), the army usually used just two types of courts martial on the frontier – and everywhere else for that matter – the General Court Martial and the Garrison Court Martial. The more serious of the two, a General Court Martial, was ordered to be empanelled ("convened") by a general officer (brigadier general, etc.), was to consist of 13 members (commissioned officers) – although in difficult circumstances this could be reduced to five officers – and could sentence a defendant to any punishment authorized for a particular crime to include significant prison sentences and the death penalty for some cases. Prior to 1874 a convicted soldier could be flogged, branded or tattooed; after that date, those punishments were prohibited.[92] In theory, therefore, a General Court Martial was designed to handle more serious offenses; this often included larceny from fellow soldiers, aggravated instances of drunkenness on duty and absence without leave.[93] A General Court Martial usually lasted one or two days. Because of the approval procedures and distances involved, a General Court-Martial often took place several weeks or a few months after the alleged incident took place.[xx] Accused enlisted soldiers were often held in confinement until their court convened.[94]

The senior officer on a court martial was termed the President of the Court. The other officers were called Members of the Court. A Judge Advocate was also appointed, but this officer was neither a judge nor an advocate, but a prosecuting officer with the added duties of legal advisor to the court and recorder for the court. A judge advocate was usually not higher than a major.[95] It does not appear that most judge advocates had been lawyers in civilian life. Additionally the judge advocate set up the court-room, summoned witnesses and, in general, organized the entire proceedings.

"Every court martial shall keep a complete and accurate record of its proceedings," stated Paragraph 914 of *Army Regulations*.[96] The Judge Advocate did this task and then was required to transmit the proceedings to the officer having the authority to confirm the sentence. For General Courts Martial in the Department of Dakota, that was Brigadier General Alfred Terry in St. Paul. For Garrison Courts Martial, the post commander generally had the authority to confirm the sentence.

A Garrison Court Martial would be convened at the discretion of the garrison, or post, commander, an officer usually with the grade of major, lieutenant colonel or colonel, although any line commissioned officer – who was also a post commander – could convene one. The post commander could not, however, assign himself to serve on his own garrison proceedings. Originally a Garrison Court Martial consisted of a five-officer panel; this was later reduced to three officers.[97] It appears that this usually meant that the court consisted of one captain and two lieutenants. Results of this type of court martial did not include the death penalty; it could not try capital offenses. In fact, a Garrison Court Martial did not impose penalties of more than one month at hard labor or more than a one-month forfeiture of pay.[98] It was a speedier venue, often conducted its proceedings within just a few days of the offense. Defendants could have counsel to assist them at courts martial and could present matters in defense, call witnesses and cross-examine prosecution witnesses. Until 1880 there was no Judge Advocate in a Garrison Court Martial. The junior officer on the court acted as the court recorder.[99]

A provision of military law, dated March 3, 1877, directed that all trial records of non-General Courts Martial would:[100]

> "After having been acted upon, be retained and filed in the judge advocate's office at the headquarters of the department commander in whose department the courts were held, for two years, at the end of which time they may be destroyed."[xxi]

This procedure came about because the Bureau of Military Justice had become overwhelmed by the vast number of such records. Therefore, regimental and garrison commanders, after having finally reviewed the proceedings and sentences of the courts ordered by them, transmitted the records to department headquarters "to be disposed of as prescribed."[101]

[xx] The records for army General Courts Martial for the period can be found at the National Archives and Records Administration, Records Group 153, Records of the Office of the Judge Advocate General – Army, Court Martial Case Files, 1809-1894.

[xxi] The effect of this directive has presented problems for historians. While this study could find special orders listing that a Garrison Court Martial had occurred, who had been members of the court, the detailed description of the offense and the details concerning the sentence, it could find no additional court details – such as the names of witnesses called, statements from the accused, etc., for any Garrison Courts Martial for Company M soldiers.

• • •

It appears that 19 soldiers in Company M, over a third of the force, were in their first year of military service; on the other hand, 30 percent had over five years of military service.[102] Late in his life, First Sergeant John Ryan commented on the experience level of the soldiers in Company M:[103]

> "You must recollect that the 7th Cavalry of 1876 was not the 7th of 1868 as in 1868 the majority of men were Civil War veterans and a great many served under Custer in the Civil War. We had a lot of recruits in that [1876] regiment and some of those men never fired a shot mounted up to this battle and some of them were never on a cavalry horse. Now I know that for a fact for some of them joined my company at Fort Lincoln before the expedition started out in the field."

Second Lieutenant Luther Hare confirmed Ryan's opinion and later told Walter Camp in an interview that many of the soldiers in the regiment had little marksmanship training.[104] Many of the recruits who enlisted in the fall of 1875 did not arrive at the regiment until the winter months of late 1875 and early 1876.[105]

Typical of these new soldiers was Private Morris Cain, who claimed his age was 22. Born on April 29, 1857 in Pittsfield, Massachusetts, Cain enlisted on September 16, 1875 in Boston, Massachusetts – at an actual age of 18. He arrived at Company M on October 21, 1875. A farmer by trade, Cain – who spelled his first name Maurice while in the army – stood 5'7", with brown eyes, black hair and a dark complexion. In April 1876 Cain was detailed for duties with the regimental quartermaster.[106]

But men who had longer service were not necessarily combat veterans. Between 1866 and 1876, although Company M participated in several small skirmishes, it could count only two significant fights that were of such magnitude that they could be considered giving the troopers involved combat experience fighting warriors. These were the battle at the Washita in November 1868 and the fighting along the Yellowstone River in August 1873. In the entire regiment, according to historian James Donovan, only 172 men could be considered to have fought Indians before the Little Bighorn.[107]

Examining the careers of the Company M troopers at the Little Bighorn, it appears that only First Lieutenant Edward G. Mathey, First Sergeant John Ryan and Private Henry "Harrison" Davis fought at both the Washita and the Yellowstone.[xxii] Captain Thomas French, Sergeant Patrick Carey, Saddler John "Jack" Donahoe, Private Roman Rutten, Sergeant Henry C. Weihe (Charles White), Private Henry "Tom" Gordon, Private George Lorentz, Sergeant John McGlone, Private William D. "Tinker Bill" Meyer, Private Hugh Moore, Corporal Frederick Stressinger, Private Henry "Jim" Turley, Private John "Big Fritz" Sivertsen and Private James W. "Crazy Jim" Severs appear to have fought on the Yellowstone River in 1873. Thus 17 men in the company had some combat experience against the Plains Indians, but only three had seen significant combat.

Private Charles Kavanaugh, who was assigned to the company during the period, but was not present at the Washita, was an interesting trooper. One source states that Kavanaugh was born in Pittsburgh, Pennsylvania in 1840, although his gravestone shows that he hailed from Missouri. He had been a tobacconist in civilian life, when on August 7, 1867 he enlisted in St. Louis, Missouri; it is quite possible that he had earlier served in the Civil War and was even wounded in that conflict. Kavanaugh spent his first term of enlistment in Company G of the 7th Cavalry, spending some time as the company cook. He deserted during the first part of this enlistment, but was apprehended on December 8, 1867.[108] Discharged on August 7, 1872, it appears that Charles Kavanaugh then went to New York City; he enlisted there some three years later on September 13, 1875 and was assigned to Company M on October 21, 1875 at Fort Rice. Kavanaugh was 5' 81/2" tall and had gray eyes, fair hair and a dark complexion.[109] Kavanaugh had a checkered career. He was reported as being absent without official leave on January 14, 1876, but a Garrison Court Martial at Fort Rice acquitted him of the charge.[110] And on April 11, 1876 he was involved in the halter-cutting incident with First Sergeant Ryan.[111]

• • •

Charles Kavanaugh could have possibly been a "Galvanized Yankee," a term used to refer to former Confederate prisoners of war who later swore allegiance to the Union during the conflict in order to be released from prison camps. Due to lingering doubts about their loyalties, these 6,000 new Union soldiers were formed into separate units and sent to garrison forts far from the battlefield; they also were posted to the frontier to fight Indians. The 1st U.S. Volunteer Regiment, for example, was composed of "Galvanized Yankees." Formed at Point Lookout, Maryland in 1864, it served along the Virginia coast until August when it moved to St. Louis, Missouri. Six companies then traveled from St. Louis to Fort Rice, Dakota Territory, arriving there October 17. The unit returned to St. Louis and was mustered out on November 27, 1865. First Sergeant John Ryan believed that Kavanaugh had served in the Confederate army.[112] While we cannot be certain that Kavanaugh was in this – or any other – "Galvanized Yankee" unit, this scenario would have placed him in St. Louis shortly before he enlisted in 1867 and could have served as a basis for the home state later noted on his tombstone.[xxiii] There were several "Galvanized Yankees" believed to have served in the 7th Cavalry; the mood in the unit appears to have been to let bygones be bygones.[xxiv]

• • •

Based on existing excellent research by John M. Carroll and Ronald H. Nichols, we can determine some demographical data about the men of Company M. The company had a definite northeastern U.S. flavor; seven troopers hailed from Pennsylvania, six men were born in New York, four men came from Massachusetts, two were born in New Hampshire and one man each was raised in Rhode Island and Maine. While we do not know the previous civilian occupation for each man, we can determine that there were at least: three blacksmiths, a broker, a carpenter, two clerks, six farmers, 12 laborers, a machinist, a miner, four painters, a printer, a sail-maker, a safe-maker, a salesman, a shoe-

[xxii] At the Washita, Edward G. Mathey claimed he had snow-blindness and switched positions with Captain Louis M. Hamilton; he thus became the commander of the supply train. Hamilton went with the fighting force and was killed in action. Source: Ernest L. Reedstrom, *Bugles, Banners & War Bonnets*, Caldwell, ID: The Caxton Printers, 1977, 53.

[xxiii] In his memoir, John Ryan wrote that when he first joined Company M in 1866 there were 17 soldiers in the company that earlier had served in the Confederate Army during the Civil War, including Charley Boren of Texas and John C. "Old Tar Heel" Pickens. Source: Letter from John Ryan to Thomas S. Norwood, Littlestown, PA, dated January 19, 1922. (Letter is in the possession of Joanne Codi of Coatesville, PA [cyclist@verizon.net])

[xxiv] Although the army looked the other way in allowing former Confederates to serve in the enlisted ranks, former Confederate officers were prohibited by law from holding a U.S. Army officer commission.

maker, a tailor, two teamsters, a tinsmith and a tobacconist among the trades represented.

Most troopers appear to have been bachelors. Dr. Kenneth Hammer has researched that the regiment had 38 widows after the battle.[113] Given that an accepted figure of fatalities in the regiment for the fight was 268, that would indicate that in the aggregate, 14.2 percent of the men in the regiment were married; in Company M, this would extrapolate to nine married men. There is a reason why the numbers are so few. Colonel Edward M. Offley, who early in his career served with several officers that had been at the Little Bighorn, has written that during this era, an enlisted soldier required special permission from his regimental commander before he could re-enlist, if he had taken a wife during his service.[114] This undoubtedly fell under the category, "If the army wanted you to have a wife, it would have issued you one!"

Walking through Company M would have treated a visitor to a variety of foreign languages when the men were off duty. Many men were immigrants: at least eight soldiers in Captain Thomas French's command were born in Ireland and another eight emigrated from areas that would later form Germany, while two came from Switzerland and two from England. Canada, France and Norway each contributed one son to Company M. An obvious question could not be answered in the scope of this study: we do not know the language proficiency for these immigrant-soldiers. One source has stated that large numbers of Germans enlisted in the army as one of the quickest and easiest ways of learning English.[115] Another source states that there were men in the army "without the least knowledge of the English language.[116] However, as previously mentioned, three of the four sergeants present were foreign-born, as was one of the three corporals; and these non-commissioned officers could not have achieved those ranks without close to fluency in English. An example of this fractured English can be found in the following description that a trooper gave a surgeon one morning to explain how he was sick:[117]

> "Der matter ish, ich habe pains in mein pelly und der copn und der brust und back so ever ash I eat anytings, und ich can eat notings und nicht schlafen deese dree nachts, und bin ich so krank ich nicht bin fit fur dooty, und der sarchint he say gottam ven I tells him so."

Communication with soldiers having this level of English would be a hit and miss operation, with plenty of hand signals, unless a German-born corporal or sergeant was in the area to fully translate both question and answer – and in combat that might not be possible.

Recruits attempting to enlist in the army could join on their own volition at age 21. Those young men between 18 and 21 needed parental or guardian consent, but given a wide variety of factors consent was often difficult to prove. On the other hand it was difficult for army recruiters to quickly and easily verify information given to them by these would-be soldiers. As one expert succinctly summarized:[118]

> "In a period when birth records were likely to consist of nothing more than a note in the family Bible or church baptism records, any teenager old enough to shave stood a good chance of passing himself off as twenty-one."

The youngest soldier in Company M was Private Rollins L. Thorpe of New York City. Born there on November 6, 1859, he enlisted on September 7, 1875 in Chicago, Illinois and gave a fraudulent age of 21, instead of his actual age which was 15. Thorpe stood 5' 71/2" tall, with gray eyes, dark brown hair and a dark complexion, which may have made him look older. A hostler by trade, he joined Company M on October 21, 1875; he was often called "Robert." On November 19, 1875 Rollins reported ill and was diagnosed with whitlow, an infection of the tip of a finger.[119] Two weeks after the battle he was discharged as a minor; his age discrepancy actually had been discovered in May, but army bureaucracy took two months to take final action! The oldest soldier in Company M was Sergeant Patrick Carey, who was 48 at the time of the battle.[120]

Concerning the size of the troopers, one will note that they appear to be much smaller than modern-day young soldiers. Army regulations of the day mandated that the minimum height for an enlisted man in the cavalry was 5'5". The maximum height for a horse-soldier was set at 5'10". There was no minimum weight for a cavalryman (other branches set a lower limit of 128 pounds though); the maximum weight for a cavalryman was set at 165 pounds – dictated, no doubt in part to the fact that a trooper's cavalry horse would have to carry both him and his equipment. That gear included a McClellan saddle of about twenty pounds, blue saddle blanket, the seven-pound carbine, small carbine socket, full canteen (3.84 pounds), ammunition (5.4 pounds), overcoat (5.25 pounds), blanket (5.13 pounds), ground cloth (3 pounds), extra clothes (2-4 pounds), five days rations (8.75 pounds), 10 to 15 pounds of oats for the horse, a spare set of horseshoes and nails for his mount (as well as a currycomb and brush for grooming his horse), pots and pans (every man was expected to prepare his own food in the field and thus his mess kit consisted of a folding-handle frying pan and a shallow plate), and a leather or canvas cartridge belt (most companies in the regiment had them in 1876) or a leather cartridge pouch – all of which could be almost 80 pounds, plus the weight of the trooper. The Model 1859 saddlebags that most men had were universally condemned as being too small, but added to the overall weight the horse had to carry nonetheless.[121]

• • •

The incident concerning Private Kavanaugh cutting a halter strap, for which he was punished for destroying government property, sheds light on another interesting facet concerning these cartridge belts. During the post-Civil War era, troopers were issued leather ammunition pouches or boxes in which to carry their carbine and pistol ammunition. But the pouches were disliked by the soldiers as they were cumbersome to open and allowed for damage to cartridges as they bounced around inside or picked up corrosion from the leather container. Troopers on the frontier solved the problem by making or buying what were called prairie, thimble, "Fairweather Christian" or loop belts, which were cartridge belts, buckled around the waist, with loops holding individual rounds for easy access. Captain Otho Michaelis, who was detailed from the Ordnance Department to observe the use of equipment in General Terry's column during the 1876 expedition, noted in his after-action report:[122]

> "I was very favorably impressed by a pattern of the loop belt worn by some companies of the 7th Cavalry. I understand that it is the invention of one of the company saddlers. This belt has a pendant looped arc on the left side for revolver cartridges. I would advise the issue of a number for trial."[xxv]

[xxv] Captain Otho Michaelis experienced a rude awakening on the subject. Dismayed at seeing so many cavalrymen with the homemade prairie belts, Michaelis initially chastised several company

Colonel Nelson Miles of the 5th Infantry Regiment noted that some soldiers were so anxious to make a belt of this type that they used their trouser suspenders to make them. Other popular materials were horse bridles and halters. It is quite possible that Private Kavanaugh was not cutting a halter strap for simple malicious amusement, but rather to use the leather for the construction of his own prairie belt. And given the high regard that Company M's John "Jack" Donahoe had as the best saddler in the regiment, it is possible that he could have been the "inventor" of the 7th Cavalry version of the prairie belt.

• • •

Army records of the period do not list weights, but they do list a soldier's height on enlistment.

Bearing in mind that some – if not a goodly number – of the men continued to get somewhat taller after they enlisted, the following is the height distribution for every enlisted man in Company M who fought at the Little Bighorn.

Height	**Number of Troopers**
5'3" to 5' 31/2"	2
5'4" to 5' 41/2"	2
5'5" to 5' 51/2"	9
5'6" to 5' 61/2"	11
5'7" to 5' 71/2"	13
5'8" to 5' 81/2"	8
5'9" to 5' 91/2"	7
5'10" to 5' 101/2"	3

From this distribution it would appear that the army waved the height requirement for at least four incoming enlisted men. But many, including the aforementioned Sergeant Henry C. Weihe (known as Charles White), were a lot tougher in a fight than their height might first indicate!

They would need that martial characteristic. Artist George Catlin visited the Minneconjou tribe in the 1830s. He estimated that of the 8,000 to 10,000 warriors he saw during his extensive period with the Lakota, at least half were six feet tall or greater.[123] Crazy Horse was believed to have been 5'7" and Sitting Bull stood 5'10".[124] George Custer was 5'11", while Second Lieutenant Winfield S. Edgerly was a towering 6'4".[125]

• • •

Another characteristic of the unit needs to be addressed at this time, as the environment of the army in 1876 was much different than it is today. The "Old Army" of a decade after the Civil War was a drinking man's army; it was a rare soldier who did not imbibe at all; heavy drinkers sometimes achieved legendary status if they could still perform their official duties after a prolonged binge; army doctors prescribed whiskey as medicine and as a substitute for pain-killers; and officers fully permitted post sutlers to sell alcohol on paydays and other times when the troopers had money.[126] In fact, an examination of the ledgers of sutlers John W. Smith and the Leighton brothers, who were on the Yellowstone River with the army in the summer of 1876, reveals that the 7th Cavalry Regiment out-drank every other unit in the field![127]

Among the officers of the 7th Cavalry, George Custer had forsaken alcohol years before (as well as tobacco), but most of the other officers were far from teetotalers and several imbibed fairly often. Major Marcus Reno[xxvi] was well-known as a heavy drinker. Captain Frederick Benteen (Company H) liked his whiskey and although was not considered a heavy drinker, was obnoxious and aggressive after downing too many drinks at one sitting. Captain Thomas Weir (Company D) was a steady imbiber. On one occasion Marcus Reno brought charges against Weir for insubordination while drinking, but the matter was dropped. Captain Thomas French may have consumed the most and would have alcohol problems until the day he died. Captain Tom Custer, who was called "Wounded Face" by the Arikaras, was described by one historian as having a "wretched drinking habit." Captain Myles Keogh was "seldom sober" and often "hopelessly boozy." Major Joseph Tilford, who commanded the post at Fort Rice, where Company M was stationed, was a heavy drinker as well.[128]

First Sergeant John Ryan commented on the situation in a newspaper series of articles in the *Newton Circuit* in "Ten Years with General Custer among the Indians," in the twenty-fourth installment on June 4, 1909:[129]

> "There were a number of officers who liked their liquor pretty well, and when not under its influence were, probably, as fine and gallant officers as there were in the regiment."

However, the manner in which the army treated officer intoxication versus enlisted drunkenness was different according to First Sergeant Ryan, who also wrote in his memoirs:[130]

> "If an officer imbibed more liquor than was good for him at this fort, he could go to his quarters and sleep it off, and if he was unfit for duty the next morning, he could be placed on the sick roll and that ended the matter, whereas if an enlisted man got in the same position and was not able to report for duty the next morning he found himself suddenly transferred from his comfortable quarters to the guard house, and would most likely be found the next morning walking up and down in front of the guard house with a log on his shoulder."

Officers were regarded as gentlemen and many spent exorbitant amounts of money to portray themselves as true upper class gentility.[131]

---

commanders for allowing their soldiers to violate army equipment regulations. He finally spotted a sergeant with an issue cartridge box on his belt and yelled out, "Here, my man! I see you know how to carry your ammunition; let us see your box." The veteran trooper handed over the cartridge box, which was found to contain not .45/55 carbine rounds but two pounds of salt pork!

[xxvi] Marcus A. Reno was born on November 15, 1834 in Carrollton, Illinois; his father died when Marcus was eleven; his mother died three years later. The area of his youth was deeply split in opinion on slavery and states' rights. Reno graduated from West Point in 1857 ranked 20 of 38 cadets and was commissioned in the cavalry. At West Point one of his best friends was James A. Whistler who dropped out of the academy but went on to be a famous painter. During the Civil War Reno was brevetted to major, lieutenant colonel, colonel and brigadier general for service, serving in the Peninsula campaign and Antietam. Reno was wounded during the fighting at Kellysville, Virginia in March 1863. He was appointed a major in the Regular Army in 1868 and assigned to the 7th Cavalry. Reno's wife died in 1874; he missed both the Yellowstone and Black Hills expeditions, but was on the Small Arms Board in 1872-73 that helped select weapons for the army. From October 1874 to October 1875 Reno took a leave of absence from the regiment and travelled to Europe. After the battle, on July 24, 1876, Reno was placed under arrest for an unspecified incident. He had additional problems that fall and was placed in command of Fort Abercrombie, perhaps to keep him away. In February 1877 Reno was court-martialed and suspended from pay and grade for two years; the sentence was mitigated a few months later. Reno was court-martialed again on November 24, 1879 at Fort Meade, Dakota Territory for conduct unbecoming an officer, which included accusations of being a "peeping Tom" and peering through the bedroom window of the regimental commander's teenage daughter and was dismissed from the service on April 1, 1880 with a dishonorable discharge. He died on March 30, 1889 at Providence Hospital in Washington, D.C., following surgery for tongue and throat cancer. Originally buried in Mount Olivet Cemetery in the District, his body was later re-interred in the Custer Battlefield National Cemetery. On May 31, 1967 his military record was changed to reflect honorable service.

Enlisted men were often viewed as drunken bums, who would do anything for a drink versus an officer who, if intoxicated, merely had temporarily succumbed to the pressures of his office. But there was another insidious aspect to alcohol use: it was generally accepted that if an officer and a commander drank, his troopers would drink as well.[132]

The 7th Cavalry Regiment was not alone in its fondness for drink; but it may have achieved a singular status as to the effects of liquor in a most unfavorable way, as events on the Little Bighorn would later reveal.

Captain Thomas H. "Tucker" French, Company Commander of Company M, 7th Cavalry Regiment. French was one of the best officers in the regiment; he was a Civil War veteran and a deadly shot. Photo appears to be from 1876. *Photo courtesy of the Little Bighorn Battlefield National Monument.*

First Lieutenant Edward G. "Bible-Thumper" Mathey. Assigned to Company M, he may have been the most profane man in the regiment. *Photo courtesy of Glen Swanson.*

Edward Mathey in later years as a captain. *Photo courtesy of the Little Bighorn Battlefield National Monument.*

The "Rock" of Company M; First Sergeant John Ryan of Company M, 7th Cavalry Regiment taken in 1906, thirty years after he retired. He is wearing a Grand Army of the Republic veteran's hat and his military medals, as well as his military belt. *Photo courtesy of the Little Bighorn Battlefield National Monument.*

First Sergeant John "Paddy" Ryan (left) and Sergeant William Capes (seated) about 1875. Sergeant Capes remained at the Powder River Camp to supervise the five other Company M soldiers who remained there. *Photo courtesy of Glen Swanson.*

John Ryan about 1871. *Photo courtesy of Glen Swanson.*

Sergeant Miles F. O'Hara of Company M. Shown here as a corporal, and born in Alton, Ohio, the 24-year-old had a wife – who was a company laundress – and a young daughter. He would be hit while fighting on the skirmish line in the valley, but may have made it to Reno Hill before he died. *Photo courtesy of the Little Bighorn Battlefield National Monument.*

Trumpeter Charles "Bounce" Fischer. Born in Breslau, Germany, prior to joining the 7th Cavalry, Fischer deserted and was later confined to a military prison. One source identifies this photo as being of Sergeant John Vickory, who was killed with Custer. *Photo courtesy of Glen Swanson.*

Private Henry Klotzbucher. Klotzbucher was the "striker" or orderly for Captain French and was born in Baden, Germany. *Photo courtesy of Glen Swanson.*

Private George Lorentz. Born in Holstein, Germany, Lorentz was a painter by trade. He also served in 1875 as a cook at the post hospital. *Photo courtesy of Glen Swanson.*

Private William E. "Bill" Morris. Although he fought well at the Little Bighorn, Morris later told his first sergeant to stick a written order up his "arse," broke his arm in a fight and was discharged as a soldier of "worthless" character. Morris later became a municipal judge in New York and served as a New York City Alderman. This photo is from 1926. *Photo courtesy of Glen Swanson.*

Private Daniel "Dan" Newell. During the Black Hills expedition, Newell put horseshoes on "Lonesome Charlie" Reynolds' horse backwards, so enemy warriors could not track his route as he rode to deliver the news of gold in the area. This photo is from 1926. *Photo courtesy of Glen Swanson.*

Wagoner Joseph Ricketts. Ricketts remained at the Powder River Camp during the battle as part of Company M's support detail. *Photo courtesy of Glen Swanson.*

Top view of kepi belonging to First Sergeant Ryan. Leather brim is cracked by age.

Kepi belonging to First Sergeant John "Paddy" Ryan. It was probably privately purchased by John Ryan after his military career ended in December 1876 and later worn by him to various veterans' functions – as the two side buttons have the Grand Army of the Republic insignia. In the field, troopers rarely wore the kepi as it gave little protection against the elements; old soldiers instead sometimes used the kepi as a feedbag for their horses!

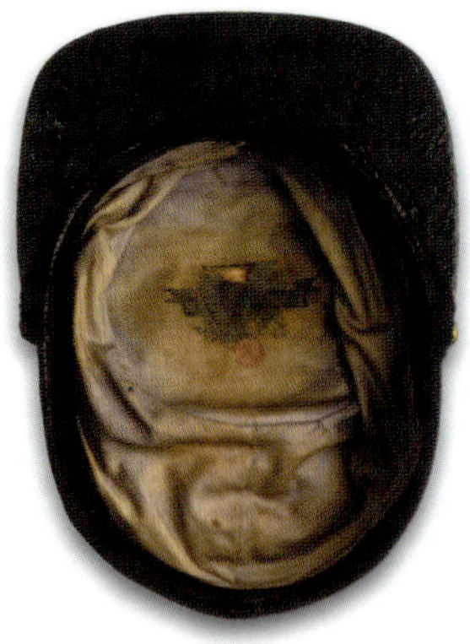

Inside view of First Sergeant Ryan's kepi. This was a private purchase cap, not issued to Ryan by the army.

Side view of First Sergeant Ryan's kepi. Side button is that of the Grand Army of the Republic, which was formed after the Civil War of Union Army veterans.

***Left*: Belt buckle found at the Company M position in the timberline (45° 31' 23.077" N, 107° 24' 19.277" W); brass buckle measures 1.59" by 1".** Buckle is not Army-issue; it appears to be from a privately-acquired prairie belt, also known as a fair-weather belt. These belts were later Army-produced and issued to troopers; they had cartridge loops sewn in them which proved a far superior method of carrying carbine ammunition than did the cumbersome cartridge box. There has been an ongoing argument on the extent that the 7th Cavalry had these belts at the Little Bighorn; this is one small piece of evidence that Company M may indeed have had some of these belts. ***Right*: Reverse side of brass belt buckle.** Corrosion in the middle of the buckle could be from an iron prong.

***Left*: Thimble found in the horse-holder area of the timberline in the valley of the Little Bighorn (45° 31' 26.917" N, 107° 24' 18.005" W).** Horse-holders led their horses to this location as they began to engage the warriors early in the fight. Reno's men later withdrew to this position, mounted their horses and wildly retreated. Private Roman Rutten of Company M survived the battle and reported that his ride out of the timber was a rugged one, including bone-jarring jumps over fallen trees and tree stumps. Rutten was the company tailor and carried thimbles, thread, sewing needles, extra buttons, cloth patches, pins and other sewing items with him, probably in his saddlebag. It is interesting to contemplate if this thimble possibly belonged to Rutten and if it bounced out of his saddlebag during his wild ride. Thimble measures 0.83" high and 0.70" in diameter at the base. ***Right*: Top view of thimble found in the horse-holder area.** The thimble was possibly made of tin or other alloy that resisted corrosion.

***Left*: Cavalry saddle with saddle blanket and bed roll.** Photo taken at a display at the Little Bighorn Battlefield National Monument in 2009.

Opposite

***Top*: Field layout of clothing typically taken on campaign by a cavalryman.** Photo taken at a display at the Little Bighorn Battlefield National Monument in 2009.

***Bottom*: Variety of equipment carried on campaign;** chain with two leather straps is to hobble the trooper's horse in camp at night so it would not wander away. Canteen held three pints of water. Photo taken at a display at the Little Bighorn Battlefield National Monument in 2009.

Demon drink. A bottle of whiskey was the undoing of many an officer and sergeant in the frontier army. Photo was taken at a cavalry re-enactment, where bottle was for display purposes only!

Civil War era army surgeons saw used for battlefield amputations. This particular saw was not present at the Little Bighorn. However, a regimental surgeon amputated a soldier's leg at Reno Hill with similar equipment.

Jefferson Barracks, Missouri. This stable was built in 1851 to house four horses and two spring wagons used to haul the munitions produced at the St. Louis Arsenal to the various ordnance magazines in Jefferson Barracks.

Period advertisement for Bismarck, Dakota Territory gunsmith O. H. Beal. First Sergeant John Ryan bought a custom-made caliber .45/70 Sharps rifle from a Bismarck gunsmith; Beal could have been this gun dealer, as he was well regarded in the territory. *Photo courtesy of John Doerner.*

***Below*: Sharps Heavy 16 Pound Barrel Buffalo Rifle with a Long Range Telescope attributed to J. B. H. (James Butler Hickok, more famously known as "Wild Bill".)** The rifle is fitted with a full-length, long-range telescope. It was offered for sale in 2009 by one of the premier dealers of antique firearms in the United States, Gary Hendershott. *Photo courtesy of Gary Hendershott Collections, Little Rock, Arkansas.*

***Bottom*: Close-up view of the receiver of the same Sharps Heavy 16 Pound Barrel Buffalo Rifle with a Long Range Telescope.** Firing a .45 caliber round that measured 2.875" in length, this particular weapon was made by a frontier gunsmith in Kansas or Iowa using a Sharps Civil War carbine action. From the description provided by First Sergeant John Ryan, it appears that he carried a similar Sharps weapon at the Little Bighorn. First Sergeant Ryan's rifle was made in Bismarck, Dakota Territory and cost $100 – equivalent to $1,800 in today's currency. *Photo courtesy of Gary Hendershott Collections, Little Rock, Arkansas.*

CHAPTER THREE

THE MARCH FROM HELL

"...Maybe it ain't what you'd properly put into a book but its sich things that makes army life. Fightin' ain't so hard. You git all excited and kinda like it but jist endurin' this and that, day in day out, mile after mile, seein' horses droppin' in their tracks, petered out, shootin' 'em and goin' on, that what takes guts. One time one o' the horses broke its leg scramblin' down a steep place and had to be shot. The fellow that owned him broke down and cried like a baby."[1]

The thirty-eight day march over roughly five hundred miles from Fort Abraham Lincoln to the valley of the Little Bighorn severely weakened components of the regiment for the upcoming fight.[2] In military theory terms, this extended trek over rough terrain, in bad weather conditions, with troops and horses alike feeding on insufficient rations, caused the 7th Cavalry Regiment to come dangerously close to reaching its culminating point – that time when an attacking force (e.g., one on the offensive) can no longer continue its advance because of a diminution of its strength, be that due to supply limitations, personnel and/or equipment losses, the need for rest, or an unfavorable correlation of forces with respect to the enemy (e.g., the defender is now stronger than the attacker). A day-by-day review will show the effects of terrain, weather and supply to the fighting power of the 7th Cavalry.[i]

May 17, 1876 – Fort Lincoln to Little Heart River

The expedition had been scheduled to depart on May 15, but a rainstorm delayed the event. Before departing, Company M left two men behind, who would not go on the expedition: Farrier William W. Wood, a veteran with over four years service remained to take care of company property; Private John Zametzer, with almost nine years of service, was sick in the post hospital.[3]

Several days before departing, Custer organized the regiment into marching formation. The regiment would be composed of two equal wings, a left wing – with six companies under Captain Frederick Benteen – and a right wing of six companies under Major Marcus Reno. Each wing in turn was composed of two battalions; Benteen was in command of the 2nd and 4th Battalions; Reno led the 1st and 3rd Battalions. Each battalion had three companies assigned. Company M was detailed to the 4th Battalion; Captain Thomas French assumed command of the battalion as the senior officer present.[4]

On May 17, buglers (often referred to by the troopers as "wind jammers") awakened the 7th Cavalry Regiment at 4:00 a.m. The previous night had been rainy and the valley was enveloped in a cold heavy fog as the troopers rose off the damp ground under their A-shape field tents. The wetness precluded the men finding useable firewood, so there would be no hot coffee; the men's breakfast consisted of hardtack washed down with muddy water. At 5:00 a.m. another bugle call sounded and the troops, many still in damp clothes, socks and boots, took down their tents, rolled their blankets and packed their saddles. Sunrise occurred at 5:05 a.m. local time; the moon was still visible in the twilight sky.[5] By 6:00 a.m., the wagon train was on the road, escorted by marching infantrymen. The column was in heavy marching order, as it would be a long campaign and, at least at the start, there was no danger of an imminent enemy attack.[6]

It was a lengthy formation, although the forty Arikara scouts rode on the flanks and front, making it seem wider than it actually was.[7] Tromping along were 752 mules, 32 quartermaster horses, 695 government horses, 26 battery horses (for the Gatling gun battery), 95 private horses (many owned by the officers) and 74 hired horses (used to haul supplies.)[8] Most of the 114 large wagons, each pulled by six mules, were filled with grain forage for the horses, often a load of between 3,000 and 5,000 pounds; First Sergeant John Ryan later said that the wagons could be loaded with up to 6,800 pounds. The six mules pulling each wagon were driven in three pairs: the two mules up front were called leaders and were generally smaller in size; the pair in the middle were known as swings and were a little bigger in size and strength; the rear two mules were called wheelers and were strong, heavy mules. The teamster, who drove the mules, sat on the left hand ("nigh") wheeler and controlled the team with a jerk-line. Lighter wagons, pulled by a pair of mules, carried much of the camp equipage and ammunition; their loads varied from 1,500 to 2,000 pounds. The large wagons were government-owned, while the smaller ones were civilian-owned and contracted to the government.[9]

Company M had its own smaller wagon that carried five days of rations for the troops, some forage for the horses, ammunition and mess equipment. It also carried a 10-day supply for the officers. Captain French may have had his own wagon as well, probably carrying his tent, extra clothes, a cot, chairs, small writing table, a Sibley stove, a cooking stove, a Dutch oven, a camp kettle, mess-ware for four persons and his orderly.[10]

The column also appeared to resemble a small cattle drive. Private Walter Sterland, a Company M trooper, had been detailed to serve as

[i] The concept of culminating point was first succinctly explained by Prussian military thinker Carl Clausewitz in the 1820s. While it is doubtful that Lieutenant Colonel George Custer or Brigadier General Alfred Terry knew of the theory in terms of Clausewitz's thinking, they certainly saw the effects of culmination during the Civil War, as the Confederacy became progressively weaker at the strategic level, and – for example – when General Robert E. Lee's forces hit their tactical culminating point at the Battle of Gettysburg during "Pickett's Charge."

a quartermaster butcher at regimental headquarters. Sterland later told researcher Walter Camp that there were 77 head of cattle at the start of the campaign; some would be killed and butchered along the route to provide fresh meat for the officers and men.[11]

Most of the troopers anticipated that the campaign would take four to six weeks; the latest information from the scouts was that Chief Sitting Bull was some 150 miles to the west along the Little Missouri River with a force of 3,000 warriors.[12] The troopers from Company M apparently sensed that the expedition would be a long one. After the Civil War, regulations allowed that each enlisted man in the army was authorized tobacco rations – up tó one pound a month. According to ration records of the 7th Cavalry, of the 64 soldiers in Company M in the May-June 1876 timeframe, 59 (91.7 percent) drew their tobacco ration. Given use rates in 1880 – which were probably similar to rates in 1876 – some 55 percent of tobacco use came in the form of plugs (chewing) with 18 percent cut tobacco (for pipes), 24 percent cigars, two percent snuff and just one percent cigarettes.[13] The amount of tobacco spit by the troopers on the campaign must have cut the tail dust down as the regiment marched to its destiny!

Even with the hundreds of beasts, the regiment was short of horses and 78 recruits had to begin the expedition on foot, in the hope that additional horses would be procured at the Yellowstone River – which was 318 miles away![14] First Lieutenant Edward Mathey, of Company M, commanded this dismounted detachment. These men carried only carbines and 50 rounds of carbine ammunition apiece. They marched in the rear of the column and guarded the wagon train.[15] These recruits had high-heeled cavalry boots, which were not made for continuous marching on foot; some troopers thought the boots were so bad that they preferred to walk barefooted. One of the unit surgeons wrote about the boots worn by the cavalrymen:[16]

> "Shoes of cavalry boots were manufactured at Fort Leavenworth Military Prison and were of poor quality. One soldier reported to the medical department that the shoes were very course leather; the uppers were fastened to the sole by brass screws. These were very uncomfortable, but he solved the matter by walking through a creek until the uppers were thoroughly soaked, then walked the whole day in them, and so got a foot form comfort. Soldiers generally rubbed soap on their feet and socks to avoid blisters when wearing newly issued shoes."

The regiment marched 13.5 miles that day and established a camp site at a bend in the Little Heart River about 2:30 p.m.[17] However, there was a problem according to one of the troopers:[18]

> "Before the troops were even able to think of setting up camp, they were obliged to eliminate one serious menace. The whole flat was infested with rattlesnakes. The eradication of this deadly viper was, however, routine with the soldiers, and their method was simple. They formed a skirmish line across the width of the camp area, secured heavy sticks, rocks, their sabers, revolvers, and proceeded to fire and slash and beat into the tall grass and sage, and kill every rattler they came upon, until they had traversed thoroughly the entire ground. Not only were these venomous creatures numerous, but sizable as well, several measuring two-and-a-half feet in length, and the thickness of a child's forearm."

• • •

At one point during the march toward the Little Bighorn, a trooper was bitten by a rattlesnake. He was given a lot of whiskey to dull his senses and then his wound was cauterized. Captain Thomas French came along the scene, observed the stupefaction of the victim and commented that a whole lot of good whiskey was going to waste![19]

• • •

Once in camp, the soldiers unbridled and tied their horses to picket pins. They then wiped the outside of saddles and bridles and sponged the eyes and nostrils of their mounts. They then picked stones out of their horses' hooves and fed the animals a little hay or oats. After the horses cooled down, the troopers removed the saddles, watered, groomed and fed the animals. They then examined their horses' backs for signs of inflammation. Only then did the cavalry trooper really think about himself. The call to extinguish lights usually sounded at 8:30 p.m., after which loud talking was prohibited so the horses could rest.[20]

Private Daniel Newell of Company M summarized the day's activities:[21]

> "After dragging along through the mud all that day we finally got into camp but it was so wet we couldn't make the campfires although details were sent out and returned with plenty of wood which wouldn't burn."

There was one other task to be completed that initial day of the march. The troopers had not been paid their monthly salary before leaving Fort Lincoln. The source of that decision remains unclear; some authors believe that Brigadier General Terry made the decision, while others believe that George Custer was the source of the order. In either case, the motivation was the same; both commanders knew that the fleshpots of Bismarck would cause desertion, disease and debauchery if the troopers had received their money a day or two before the expedition began.[22]

May 18, 1876 – Little Heart River to Sweet Briar Creek

During the night, a prairie fire started near the camp and the buglers woke the entire command. The troopers spent over two hours of work combating the blaze before it was extinguished and they tried to return to sleep. Private William Slaper of Company M described the scene:[23]

> "The prairie all about us was on fire, and we were kept busy fighting the flames to prevent their spreading through the camp."

At 2:40 a.m. the buglers sounded "Reveille." The men then had 20 minutes to wash up and make for the field latrine before they began the process of feeding their horses. They then cooked some hardtack and bacon. The march began shortly thereafter. This was well before sunrise, which occurred at 5:04 a.m. local time.[24] After riding some 10.8 miles the regiment made camp at 1:45 p.m. near Sweet Briar Creek. The wagons would not arrive for four more hours. The men had no more than set up their pup tents when a heavy rain struck at 3:00 p.m. The rain subsided but there was little dry kindling then available for cooking fires, so some of the men ate raw bacon and hardtack soaked in water. Brigadier General Terry, on the other hand, dining in his tent and warmed by a fire, ate a supper of roast beef, mashed potatoes, warm biscuits and a raw onion salad with vinegar![25]

May 19, 1876 – Sweet Briar Creek to Crow's Nest Butte

Buglers awakened the men at 4:20 a.m.; it had been a wet night and many of the men had slept with their clothes and boots on. The column commenced its march at 6:30 a.m. and began to encounter rougher terrain complete with ravines and rocky ground. The cavalry passed through a prairie dog village, where the men took care that their horses did not step in a burrow hole. About noon a vicious thunderstorm struck; high winds and hail pelted the men and horses. Brigadier General Terry provided a description of the weather:[26]

> "The storm terrified the drenched and bawling herd of beef cattle into a wild stampede! Man and beast alike sustained bruises from this untoward assault from the skies. The drovers tried to keep the heard as contained as possible, to prevent stampede, for the hailstones could be observed literally dancing from the exposed backs of the frightened beasts. Hailstones ripped into the muddied white canvas covers of the wagons like white mini-balls. The cavalry mounts, struck repeatedly, whinnied and snorted in wild-eyed fright and uncertainty, and their riders had to hold tight rein to prevent bolting. As the hailstones developed, the infantry men took cover beneath wagons, and the cavalrymen brought their horses in close to the wagons for protection. The mules fought their harness, and pelted teamsters had to crack their heavy bull-snake lashes repeatedly to maintain their teams under control…"

The hailstones were as large as hickory nuts.[27] After 12.5 miles, the column went into camp at the Crow's Nest Butte. With no dry kindling, and the "buffalo chips" – also known as "prairie coal" or "Dakota soft coal" – too wet to make a fire with, the men again ate raw bacon and hardtack.[28]

May 20, 1876 – Crow's Nest Butte to Hail Stone Creek

The men suffered through another night of hard rain; the buglers wakened the troops at 5:00 a.m. The campsite was nearly a sea of mud and breakfast once again was a cold one. The march for the day covered 9.5 miles, halting at Hail Stone Creek. Lightning strikes stampeded some of the animals; the soldiers had another cold supper. One of the troops recalled his situation:[29]

> "We have no change of [dry] clothing now so will have to get dry as best we can, and the best way is to roll up in your saddle blanket and sweat it out, all the time getting full benefit of the aroma that arises from the sweat of your horse's sides and back, as it creeps up out of the blanket."

May 21, 1876 – Hail Stone Creek to Hay Creek

Once again, during the night, the heavens opened up and showered the men continuously. "Reville" sounded early at 3:00 a.m.; there was no hot breakfast except for the officers, whose wagons carried drying kindling under the canvas for an emergency. The column began to move at 6:00 a.m. Three of the recruits on foot were deemed disabled – one had accidentally shot himself in the foot – and all were placed in the ambulance wagon. The weather finally turned nice and the men began to gather "buffalo chips," which would be used for later camp fires. After 13.25 miles the command established camp; the troopers had a hot meal and hot coffee that night.[30] This evening, as happened most other evenings, the Arikara scouts camped near Custer's headquarters so they would be available for quick missions.[31]

May 22, 1876 – Hay Creek to Knife Creek

The troops again awoke at 3:00 a.m. to the sounds of the bugler. In Company M, Private David Summers reported ill with a sore throat.[32] The soldiers consumed a hot breakfast and cup of coffee after feeding their horses; at 4:40 a.m. the column was on the march. By noon, the advance elements of the column had made 15.5 miles; Brigadier General Terry decided to halt for the day, and a camp was made at Knife Creek. That evening the troops again had a hot meal; for dessert, some of the troopers fried hardtack in fat and covered it with sugar. But much of the water in the area had a high level of alkaline, which acted as a laxative. The soldiers called the effect of drinking this questionable water "The Dakota Quick Step." Custer decided that the evening deserved a concert and had the 7th Cavalry Band play for the encampment after supper.[33]

One of the favorite songs for the troopers in the regiment was "Captain Jinks" which made fun of a cavalry captain who was not cut out for army service, but who was quite proficient at wining, dining and dancing with teenage girls. One of the verses in this ballad, written in 1869, would prove eerily prophetic for some:[34]

> "I joined the Corps when twenty-one,
> Of course I thought it capital fun,
> When the enemy comes, of course I run,
> For I'm not cut out for the Army."

But the band could also play more serious music such as "The Blue Danube."[35] A 7th Cavalry song that was composed by the regimental band leader Felix Vinatieri was entitled "The Mosquitoes of Dakota Waltz."

But just over a month later the fun and songs would end.

May 23, 1876 – Knife Creek to Young Man's Butte

The troops awoke, took care of their horses, ate breakfast and broke camp at 5:00 a.m. In Company M, Private David Summers again reported ill with a sore throat.[36] After just 7.75 miles, Brigadier General ordered a halt near Young Man's Butte; the troops would get rest this day. For most of the daily camps the command formed a rectangle, or parallelogram, a half-mile-wide, with the two longest sides formed by cavalry wings and the shorter ends occupied by infantry and headquarters. The wagon train would be located in the center of the rectangle, but horses and mules initially grazed outside the enclosure until nighttime, when the animals were brought inside for protection.[37]

During the evening, however, troopers saw a party of Indians moving along a ridgeline three miles away; Custer ordered that the guard force around the camp be increased and that mounted outposts be placed on surrounding hills; the men on this duty did not get their anticipated full night's sleep as a result, but security came first.[38] As one descriptive writer of the day noted:[39]

> "The moon – that nocturnal artist – with its inimitable brush, catering to our excited imaginations, transformed the rocks on the hillsides, and the bushes by the gullies, and the trees in the woods, into painted savages ready with a war whoop to pounce on us."

May 24, 1876 – Young Man's Butte to Green River

The troopers awoke early, left camp by 4:15 a.m., and made 19 miles on the march. Once again, in Company M, Private David Summers reported ill with a sore throat.[40] Temperatures rose about noon. Terry halted the command at 2:00 p.m. at the Green River. The camp was almost ideal, having good bathing, plenty of fish in the streams, good wood and water and an ample area for grazing for the horses. Many troopers caught crawfish along the banks of the stream, which they cooked that evening. After supper, many soldiers soaked their aching feet in the cool, clear water of the Green River that evening.[41] The river must have been a lifesaver for the dismounted detachment, which had walked all day.

May 25, 1876 – Green River to Crow's Ridge

Buglers awakened the soldiers earlier than normal, and by 4:00 a.m. the column was on the march. As was becoming usual, in Company M Private David Summers reported ill with a sore throat.[42] George "Cully" Weaver was diagnosed with a contusion on the right knee.[43] The weather was mild and clear; the column traveled 20 miles. An hour before sunset – as on all days – the buglers sounded "Stable Call" and the cavalrymen marched their horses to a watering place and then back to the company area, at which they groomed and fed their mounts. The cooks then announced that supper was ready and the men received a hot meal. Dr. James M. DeWolf,[ii] one of the regimental surgeons, wrote a letter home saying that the sun that day was strong enough to cause sunburn of his ears.[44]

May 26, 1876 – Crow's Ridge to Heart River

The column was on the march by 5:30 a.m. In Company M, Private David Summers again reported ill with a sore throat.[45] Private Charles Wiedman was diagnosed as suffering from a boil.[46] The troopers marched 12 miles in hot and dry weather; underfoot the ground was literally covered with young grasshoppers, while in the air multitudes of mosquitoes bothered troopers and horses alike. After reaching the Heart River, the column halted at 2:30 p.m.; unfortunately there were thousands of mosquitoes in the air.[47] The scheme of maneuver during much of the march was for the regiment to be deployed in a large elongated diamond, with a battalion in the front, a battalion on each flank and a battalion in the rear – with the infantry and wagons protected in the middle from any surprise attack. Indian scouts roamed miles ahead of the main formation in an advanced security role.[48]

May 27, 1876 – Heart River to Davis Creek

The march began this day at 5:00 a.m.; the weather was warm and clear, after an early morning fog burned off after an early morning shower ended. As expected, in Company M, Private David Summers again reported ill with a sore throat.[49] The cavalrymen traveled 18 miles and now encountered the desolate badlands.[50] As General Sully had exclaimed earlier on his first sight of the region:[51]

> "Gentlemen, it looks like the bottom of Hell, with the fires out."

At the day's end campsite, which was reached at 2:15 p.m. at Davis Creek, the men found plenty of firewood, but the water was alkaline and the grass was poor for grazing.[52]

[ii] Dr. James M. DeWolf was born on January 14, 1843 at Mehoopany, Wyoming County, Pennsylvania. Prior to the Civil War he was a farmer, but enlisted at age 17 in the 1st Pennsylvania Artillery and saw combat at the First Battle of Manassas. The following year he was severely wounded in the arm. After the conflict, DeWolf attended Harvard Medical School, graduating in June 1875. He became a contract surgeon to the army later in the year and reported to Fort Abraham Lincoln in the Dakota Territory. Assigned to Major Reno's battalion, he was killed in the retreat to Reno Hill. James M. DeWolf is buried at the Woodlawn Cemetery in Norwalk, Ohio.

May 28, 1876 – Davis Creek to Davis Creek

In tough terrain, the troopers began a march through the Davis Creek canyon at 4:25 a.m. For the seventh straight day, Private David Summers again reported ill with a sore throat.[53] The weather turned warmer and by 12:30 p.m. Brigadier General Terry called a halt to the march and the command established a new camp along the creek; the 7th Cavalry had only traveled 4.5 miles. The men found wood and the grass was better, but the water was too alkaline to drink.[54] Company M constructed two small bridges to facilitate the movement of the column the next day.[55]

May 29, 1876 – Davis Creek to the Little Missouri River

At 3:00 a.m. the buglers awoke the men; after a quick breakfast, the column began to move at 4:45 a.m. Like clockwork, in Company M Private David Summers reported ill with a sore throat.[56] The troops began to expect an Indian attack, but one never materialized. By now many soldiers were experiencing sunburn. The column made eight miles before Brigadier General Terry called a halt for the day on the Little Missouri River, which was called the "Thick Timber River" by the Lakota because of the many groves of elm, pine and cottonwood trees.[57] Dr. James DeWolfe reported that he had several patients due to injuries. The troops, some of whom had lice – known as "graybacks" – took a bath in the Little Missouri River.[58] Private Daniel Newell of Company M explained what happened to him:[59]

> "Just what day it was I am not sure, that we camped about three miles from the Little Missouri. I was cutting into a cottonwood log to make firewood when my captain, Tom French, came along and after watching me for a while said, 'Say a beaver could do better work than that. Let me show you how to do that.' So I gave him the axe and after he had made a few strokes and commenced to sweat he offered me the axe saying, 'There, that's the way to do it.' 'Stick to it, captain,' I told him, 'You are doing fine.' He grinned but I had to cut up that log after all."

Meanwhile, back at Sheridan's headquarters, "Little Phil" wrote a letter to General William Sherman describing how he saw the campaign unfolding:[60]

> "As no very accurate information can be obtained as to the location of the hostile Indians, and as there would be no telling how long they would stay at any one place, if it was known, I have given no instructions to Generals Crook or Terry, preferring that they should do the best they can under the circumstances and under what they may develop, as I think it would be unwise to make any combinations in such country as they will have to operate in. As hostile Indians in any great numbers cannot keep the field as a body for a week, or at most ten days, I therefore consider – and so do Terry and Crook – that each column will be able to take care of itself and of chastising the Indians should it have the opportunity.
>
> The organization of these commands and what they can expect to accomplish has been as yet left to the Department Commanders. I presume the following will occur: General Terry will drive the Indians toward the Big Horn Valley, and General Crook will drive them back toward Terry, Colonel Gibbon moving down on the north side of the Yellowstone to intercept, if possible, such as may want to go north of the Missouri to the Milk River."

"Little Phil" was a better fighter than a prognosticator as events would soon show. The three columns could not expeditiously communicate with one another. Riders were out of the question; they would in all probability never find their moving recipient – assuming they survived on their own in this hostile territory. In 1876 there was no telegraphic communication between Bozeman in the west and Bismarck in the east from which Colonel John Gibbon and General Alfred Terry were advancing, respectively. In the south, from whence General Crook[iii] was advancing, the nearest telegraph line was at Fort Laramie – Sheridan could only hope they would coordinate their actions.[61]

May 30, 1876 – Little Missouri River (Custer's Reconnaissance)
After "Reveille" sounded at 3:30 a.m., Lieutenant Colonel Custer began to assemble four companies of the 7th Cavalry, along with some Arikara scouts and five pack mules, for a special reconnaissance to the south to determine possible Lakota locations.[iv] At 4:00 a.m. these companies ate breakfast, and were in the saddle by 5:00 a.m. Some sources have stated that Custer picked his favorite companies; in any case, Company C, D, F and M headed up the river valley with their regimental commander. Private David Summers did not accompany them as again he reported ill with a sore throat.[62] The remainder of the regiment remained in camp on the Little Missouri; leaders posted security pickets, while many of the men in camp went fishing. At 6:00 p.m. Custer and his element returned to camp, having covered 55 miles. Later that evening a heavy thundershower struck the camp.[63]

May 31, 1876 – Little Missouri River to Andres Creek
The troopers awoke after a wet night; with no dry kindling, the men had a cold breakfast of hardtack, raw bacon and muddy drinking water from the Little Missouri. Because much of the tentage was wet, the column did not start moving until 8:00 a.m. Despite the late start, Private David Summers in Company M again reported ill with a sore throat.[64] The trail was through very rough terrain and Brigadier General Terry ordered a halt at 2:00 p.m., after the column had covered 12.9 miles and reached a branch of Andres Creek. The weather turned colder that afternoon, the herald of a cold front moving in; a chilling rain began at 7:00 p.m.; the men did not get much sleep.[65]

June 1, 1876 – Andres Creek (The Snow Camp)
Sometime during the night it began to sleet and then to snow, which continued all day – just less than three inches of snow fell during the day. Reveille occurred at 3:00 a.m. as the men continued to huddle together, teeth chattering, around sporadic camp fires, except Private David Summers who walked over to the medical tent and again reported ill with a sore throat.[66] By 7:00 a.m. it was snowing harder. Due to the absence of firewood, some men stole spare parts off the supply wagons to burn for fuel. Brigadier General Terry decided that the column would remain in camp at Andres Creek and not continue the march this day.[67]

June 2, 1876 – Andres Creek (The Snow Camp)
The blizzard continued and the expedition remained in camp all day. On the open plain, snow drifted halfway to the top on many tents.[68] Dr. DeWolf reported that he had two new patients, one with an abscess on his hand and the other with serious congestion in a lung. He also had an old patient: Private David Summers and his sore throat.[69] Brigadier General Terry directed that all the 10-gallon kegs tied to the sides of the wagons that contained emergency water that was alkaline be emptied and filled with fresh water from melting snow. Some of the smaller tents had snowdrifts over halfway to the top; inside many of the tents water actually froze in canteens and containers. When the men bridled their horses, they first had to dip the bridle bits in warm water to avoid them freezing in the mouths of the horses.[70]

June 3, 1876 – Andres Creek to Beaver Creek
The column departed Andres Creek at 5:15 a.m., after the troopers had another cold breakfast. The sun was bright, but snow remained on the hills and the wind was cold. In Company M, Private David Summers reported ill with a sore throat.[71] Later in the day the weather improved. At 4:25 p.m. the column reached camp at Beaver Creek – a distance of 25 miles. At the campsite, Beaver Creek (which was a major tributary of the Little Missouri River) was 35 feet wide and one to six feet deep, with cold and clear water, good grazing land and plenty of firewood. That evening, however, mosquitoes were thick and made sleeping difficult.[72]

Private John Burkman later described the torment caused by these blood-sucking pests:[73]

> "And then nights, when we was all tired out, horses and men, they was the damned mosquitoes to fight. It all comes back to me, the nights so dark and still, no sound except men cursin' and moanin' and slappin' whilst they lay sprawled on the ground, tryin' to sleep, and horses picketed out to graze, fidgetin' and stompin' and shiverin' off the mosquitoes, and the crunch of night guards' feet on dry grass, and their call, regular, 'All's well!' or maybe, occasional, a sharp: 'Who's thar?' when they seen a shadow movin' from behind a tree or rock, which more'n likely was a scout creepin' in to camp."

June 4, 1876 – Beaver Creek to Beaver Creek
During the night two mules died of exhaustion. Private David Summers was more fortunate, but he did again report sick with a sore throat.[74] At 4:55 a.m. the column began moving along the east bank of Beaver Creek in a southerly direction. The column now passed through rolling grasslands, where plenty of wild game was visible. The regiment marched 18 miles and reached camp on the left bank of Beaver Creek by 2:35 p.m. The campsite was next to cold and clear water from the creek; firewood was plentiful from the trees along the banks; as always, when firewood was plentiful the men tied some up in bundles and tied the bundles from both sides of the wagons for use later in areas where there was no wood.[75]

[iii] George Crook, called "Gray Fox" by the Apache and the "Granddaddy of the Pack Mule" by his own soldiers, was born on September 8, 1828 in Taylorsville, Ohio. He graduated from West Point in 1852, ranking 38 of 43 cadets in his class. He then was assigned as a second lieutenant to the 4th Infantry Regiment and fought for several years in California and Oregon against several Indian tribes. In 1857 he was severely wounded by a warrior arrow in the hip. During the Civil War, Crook commanded the 36th Ohio Volunteer Infantry Regiment. Rising through the ranks, Crook fought at Antietam, Chickamauga, Cedar Creek, Five Forks, Sailor's Creek and Appomattox. A brevet major general at the end of the conflict, Crook reverted to a regular rank of lieutenant colonel and commanded the 23rd Infantry Regiment in the Pacific Northwest. He then moved to the Arizona Territory and helped subdue Cochise and Apache bands, which earned him a promotion to brigadier general and an additional nickname of "Arizona." After the 1876 Sioux campaign, in which Crook was hit hard at the Rosebud a week before the Little Bighorn, Crook commanded the Department of the Platte and later returned to Arizona. His favorite mode of transportation on campaign was a mule named "Apache." Crook retired in 1888 as a major general. George Crook died in Chicago, Illinois on March 21, 1890. He is buried at Arlington National Cemetery in Section 2.

[iv] The Arikaras, often called Rees, were blood enemies of the Lakota. These scouts were paid $16 a month, and earned an extra $12 for each pony they furnished. The Arikaras were sometimes called the Corn Indians as they partially subsisted on agricultural pursuits, a trait the Lakota despised. The Arikaras had once been a large and powerful tribe that disease had decimated, but their warriors were tough and brave.

June 5, 1876 – Beaver Creek to Pennel Creek

The column began the march at 5:00 a.m.; the troopers probably had a hot breakfast beforehand. We do not know if Private Summers ate before or after he reported sick with his habitual sore throat.[76] After three hours the trail turned ugly; the lush grasslands turned to more badlands filled with sagebrush, prickly pear and cactus growing in dry, dusty alkaline soil. Some surface veins of coal had caught fire and were billowing smoke, making for a surreal scene.[77] The columns of horses churned up clouds of dust, while the hot sun beat down on the marching soldiers. Those cavalrymen who had no horses suffered the most, as the terrain prohibited them from walking without wearing their boots. Some of the horses had their fetlocks bloodied from the numerous prickly pears. The regiment traveled 20.5 miles before halting for the day at Pennel Creek. The only water found at the campsite was in small pools – it proved alkaline.[78]

June 6, 1876 – Pennel Creek to O'Fallon Creek

The regiment began the march at 4:35 a.m. During the morning, Chief of Scouts and guide "Lonesome Charley" Reynolds, who earlier that spring had told Custer that Sitting Bull and his warriors were amassing Winchester repeating rifles and ammunition, found that he had gone astray and the regiment had to retrace its steps. The mules had to work hard pulling the wagons through broken terrain. The column finally made 18 miles before stopping for the day at O'Fallon Creek. Although wood was plentiful, Brigadier General Terry had to order the use of the snow water that had been collected, as the water along the march was too alkaline to drink. A private from Company H accidentally discharged his revolver and shot himself in the foot. Early in the evening an electrical storm hit the camp accompanied by strong wind and heavy rain. There was a full moon that night, which undoubtedly added to the macabre atmosphere.[79]

June 7, 1876 – O'Fallon Creek to the Powder River

The troopers awoke at 3:00 a.m. The column began to move early in the morning at 4:44 a.m.; at one point Brigadier General Terry thought that the terrain was so rough that the wagons might have to be abandoned, but after 32 miles the intact expedition made camp at the Powder River, some twenty miles from its junction with the Yellowstone. The regiment pulled into camp at 6:55 p.m.; it would be 9:00 p.m. before all the wagons arrived. Several horses were too weak to carry their riders by the march's end and had to be led bareback. At 10:00 p.m. Brigadier General Terry sent a small group of Arikara scouts to make contact with the river steamer *Far West* – called the "fireboat" by the Indians – and advise the boat's captain, Grant Marsh, of the command's location.[v] The troopers worked until midnight, feeding and grooming their horses before getting their own supper.[80]

Private John Burkman, Custer's striker, sensed the mood had changed as the regiment moved ever westward:[81]

> "After we got aways into Montana the band didn't play nights no more and we was mighty careful about campfires, boilin' coffee quick and puttin' out the fires instant, lest the smoke give the enemy inklin' of our whereabouts. And nights we lay on the ground, not settin' up no tents except for the officers, each trooper by his horse, and we kept the horses saddled and bridled ready to mount instant at command."

June 8, 1876 – The Powder River

The soldiers built small fire pits and ate a hot breakfast with hot coffee. After skipping a day, Private David Summers again reported ill with a sore throat.[82] The morning's weather was cloudy with the portent of rain. The soldiers washed their clothes in the Powder River. At 12:30 p.m. Brigadier General Terry departed with Company A and Company I as escorts for the mouth of the Powder River (where it joined the Yellowstone River). Before he left, Terry gave a warning order to Major Reno that in a few days Reno would lead a large reconnaissance up the Powder River. At 4:00 p.m. it started to rain; the downpour continued all night.[83]

June 9, 1876 – Powder River

Farriers and blacksmiths worked all day shodding horses and mules in preparation for the next march. Meanwhile, in Company M, Private David Summers reported ill with his habitually sore throat.[84] At about 4:00 p.m. the rain returned and lasted all night.[85] There were still no signs of the enemy. English poet Alexander Pope had written a piece over a century earlier – entitled "Essay on Man" – a part of which lamented the trials and tribulations of the Indians in America. It began with:[86]

> "Lo, the poor Indian! Whose untutor'd mind, Sees God in clouds, or hears him in the wind."

Most troopers, having seen their adversary at close-range, simply dropped "the poor Indian" and referred to their foe as "Lo," "Poor Lo," or "Mr. Lo."[87] And at this point on the Powder River, "Lo" was nowhere to be found.

June 10, 1876 – Powder River

That morning Brigadier General Terry held a meeting with the senior officers of the regiment. During the gathering – as promised – Terry ordered Major Reno to take six companies of the 7th Cavalry and scout up the Powder River; Custer was not pleased with the decision. Company M remained with Custer and the main body, while Reno moved south. In Company M, Private David Summers again reported ill with a sore throat, but it was the last time on the expedition he would do so.[88]

Reno's orders were to take Company B, C, E, F, I and L and go south down the Powder River to the mouth of the Little Powder River. From there he was to cross to the headwaters of Mizpah Creek and follow it to its junction with the Powder River. From there he was to cross to Pumpkin Creek and the Tongue River – called by the Indians the "Talking River" because voices echoed off its steep rock bluffs – and finally to follow the Tongue to its junction with the Yellowstone River.[89] In addition to the cavalry, Reno took 70 pack mules and a Gatling gun battery; he was to take supplies for a 12-day march. Reno departed the Powder River camp at 3:30 p.m.[90]

[v] Grant Marsh was born on May 11, 1834 in Chautauqua County, New York. As a young man, he worked on the Mississippi River as a deckhand; he was the first mate on the steamer *A.B. Chambers No.2* along with Samuel Clemens (Mark Twain) who was the second mate. Clemens later said of Marsh: "A mighty good fellow, and smart too." During the Civil War he worked with riverboats of the Union fleet on the lower Mississippi. During the Montana Gold Rush in 1866, Marsh skippered the steamer *Luella*; on one run from Fort Benton, Montana Territory to St. Louis, Missouri, carrying 2.5 tons of gold dust, the richest cargo ever to be transported down the Missouri River. For the 1876 Sioux Campaign, the army leased the riverboat *Far West* for $360 a day. During his career, Marsh was regarded as the finest steamboat captain on the upper Missouri River and one of the best in all of America. Grant Marsh died at home in Bismarck, North Dakota on January 2, 1916. He is buried there in St. Mary's Cemetery.

June 11, 1876 – Powder River to the Junction of the Powder and Yellowstone Rivers

Buglers woke the troopers still in camp at 3:00 a.m. At 5:00 a.m., the command began their march north to the junction of the Powder River and the Yellowstone River. After arriving later that day at about 6:15 p.m. – a journey of 20 miles – Custer and the six companies in the main body camped about one and one-half miles up the Powder River from its mouth in a large open prairie. After taking care of their horses, the men settled down, and according to one source there was some gambling and drinking as the troopers spent some of their pay they had recently acquired. Meanwhile, blacksmiths continued to re-shoe the horses. Private William Slaper of Company M remembered:[91]

> "At [the] Powder River [and Yellowstone] our wagons were all sent back. Our sabers were also here boxed and returned. No one, not even an officer, retain [retained] his. The regimental band also was sent back.[vi] Thereafter, pack mules carried the rations and ammunition and supplies of whatever nature were taken along…"

First Sergeant John Ryan was one trooper who was not sad to see the sabers left behind. He later wrote:[92]

> "Sabers, I might as well say here, would be about as much good as a broom stick fighting Indians in an engagement with them, as a great many of the Indians, in addition to those [fire] arms, carried a lance."

By this time in the expedition the regiment had traveled 318.2 miles, with an average day's march of 15.9 miles.[93]

June 12, 1876 – Junction of the Powder and Yellowstone Rivers

The troopers took care of their horses and then themselves. A sutler had set up his store at the large camp and the men bought food and small uniform items from him. Some soldiers were detailed to help unload the supplies for the regiment from the steamers *Far West* and *Josephine*. The command referred to this campsite as the Supply Camp. One man from Company D on a work detail drowned in the Yellowstone. That evening some of the troopers purchased dollar-a-pint whiskey from sutlers John Smith and James Coleman – who had arrived with their wares on the *Far West* – and got "gloriously drunk."[94] The pair sold the whiskey at one dollar a pint and each trooper's canteen held three pints![95] Other soldiers drank a few Jamaica Gingers, a strong ginger-based drink.[96]

• • •

The *Far West* was one of those uniquely American marvelous designs that helped win the American West – in this case, brave the monumental rivers of the American heartland that seemed to have a penchant for crushing river traffic sent against them. Built in 1870 in Pittsburgh, she was 190 feet long, with a beam of 33 and-a-half feet. Unloaded, her draft was only an incredible 20 inches; fully loaded at her capacity of 200 tons of freight, her draft increased to just 30 inches. In visual terms this meant that Company M's shortest cavalryman, standing in water up to his waist, was standing in a river the *Far West* – fully loaded – could navigate. Two 15-inch diameter engines, powering pistons with a stroke of five feet, served as her propulsion unit; additionally on each side of the bow was a steam-powered capstan designed to assist in navigating shallow places in the river as well as rapids.[97]

How the *Far West* accomplished this special navigation was a true marvel. Upon encountering a sand bar, the crew of the *Far West* would swing two spars out ahead of the bow and drive the telegraph pole-looking columns into the river bottom mud. They then engaged the two mighty capstans, which pulled thick ropes, which were connected to the bow, through block and tackle at the top of the pair of spars. This maneuver would actually hoist the bow out of the river, suspending half of the ship in mid-air. Then the stern paddlewheel, displacing tons of water with each turn, would powerfully drive the craft forward and over the offending sandbar to adequate-depth water beyond. While there may have been technical terms that described this motion in terms of torque and moment arms, the crew – and any onlookers – simply referred to it as "grasshoppering."[98]

• • •

June 13, 1876 – Junction of the Powder and Yellowstone Rivers

The command spent the day shifting supplies from the wagons to the pack mules.[99] By this time the 7th Cavalry horses and mules may have been suffering from effects of the mineral selenium. According to equine nutritionist Harold Hintz at Cornell University, the area that the expedition traveled through was rich in the mineral, which manifested itself in local plants including the two-grooved milkvetch plant and other prairie grasses. Selenium, in combination with vitamin A, helps build strong muscles, unless too much is ingested. When that occurs, the mammal can experience hoof deterioration and lameness. This cause and effect was not known at the time; it is also speculation to conclude that the deterioration experienced by any of the animals on the march came because of this one reason, but later – at the valley fight – every step of quickness could prove to be a matter of life and death for a trooper riding a less-than-perfect mount.[100]

June 14, 1876 – Junction of the Powder and Yellowstone Rivers

The command continued to prepare to depart Supply Camp and move to the Tongue River, where they were to rendezvous with Major Reno's scouting mission.[101] That night, Captain French and First Sergeant Ryan determined which soldiers would remain at Supply Camp to do logistical work, while the rest of the company went forward with the regiment to find and engage the enemy. Company M left six men: Sergeant William Capes, a trooper with over three years service to look after company property; Wagoner Joseph Ricketts, another veteran, to watch over company mules; Private James McCormick, who was with the regimental band; Private Walter S. Sterland,[vii] a three-year veteran, to serve as a butcher; Private Ferdinand Widmayer, a two-and-a-half-year veteran; and Private John Dolan.[102] Dolan had engaged Captain French that day in a fist-fight and had just been court-martialed.[103]

• • •

[vi] The regimental band was led by noted composer Felix Vinatieri. Born in Turin, Italy in 1834, he had previously been the bandleader of the Queen's Guard of Spagnis in Italy before immigrating to the U.S. in 1859. Two years later he enlisted in the 16th Infantry Regiment in Massachusetts as a musician. In 1873, Vinatieri enlisted as the Bandleader of the Seventh Cavalry; he was discharged at Fort Abraham Lincoln on December 18, 1876. A prolific composer, Felix Vinatieri served as the leader of the Yankton Band (Yankton, South Dakota) until he died on December 5, 1891. Felix Vinatieri's great-great-grandson is Adam Vinatieri, an outstanding placekicker in the National Football League for many years.

[vii] John Ryan, in a 1910 letter to researcher Walter Camp, stated that Walter Sterland was present with Company M during the fight, but it appears that Ryan was in error.

The eight men of Company M (two that remained at Fort Rice and six at the Supply Camp) who did not go to the Little Bighorn may have initially been relieved not to continue the march, or they may have felt left out of an upcoming battle shoulder-to-shoulder with their buddies, we can never really know their true emotions. What is clear is that most of these men disappeared from history – no different than tens of thousands of other enlisted men who toiled on the frontier from just after the Civil War to 1890.

Sergeant William Capes, who remained at the Powder River Camp, was born in Portland, Maine about 1848. He enlisted on December 30, 1872 in New York City for the 7th Cavalry and joined Company M in Oxford, Mississippi on February 9, 1873. A good soldier, he was promoted to corporal on June 12, 1873 and to sergeant on August 18, 1873. Capes stood 5' 91/2" tall and had gray eyes, black hair and a ruddy complexion. He served on the Black Hills Expedition in 1874. The following year he served as acting quartermaster sergeant and in charge of the company kitchen. After the Little Bighorn, Capes fought against the Nez Percé and was cited for gallantry in action on September 13, 1877. He was discharged from the army on December 30, 1877 at Fort Abraham Lincoln as a sergeant of good character. Capes moved to Pittsburgh, Pennsylvania, where he died on April 10, 1900.[104] In his later years, William Capes collected a number of items about the 7th Cavalry at the Little Bighorn including many Cartes de Visite; many of these artifacts were sold by Cowan's Auctions in 2009.

Private John Dolan, another trooper who remained at the Powder River Camp, was born on April 14, 1843 in Dublin, Ireland. After arriving in the United States, he enlisted in the 4th New York Volunteer Cavalry on October 4, 1861, giving his prior occupation as a laborer. After serving in the entire Civil War, Dolan enlisted in the 1st Cavalry Regiment, before deserting on June 10, 1871 in California. He enlisted in the 7th Cavalry under the name of Thomas Brown on October 1, 1873 and joined Company M on October 21; this time he gave his birthplace as New York City and his occupation as a machinist. The following month he admitted his earlier desertion, but avoided a court martial. Dolan was promoted to corporal on December 10, 1874 and to sergeant on August 2, 1875. In the months leading up to the 1876 Sioux Campaign he was detailed to serve as the quartermaster in charge of the corral. On the recommendation of Captain French – with whom he reportedly had a fistfight on June 14 – Dolan remained at the Powder River Camp.[105]

Dolan was discharged on July 3, 1876; he re-enlisted on August 2, 1876 in St. Louis, Missouri and joined Company B of the 7th Cavalry. He was 5'9" tall with hazel eyes, brown hair and a ruddy complexion; he was married and had two children. Enlistment papers showed that he had gunshot wound scars on the back of his head and on his lower left leg; how he received them is unknown. Dolan remained in the regiment until April 10, 1896 at Fort Grant, Arizona Territory, when he received his final discharge as a sergeant; his character was described as very good. Now deaf in both ears, John Dolan died on March 31, 1922 at Fort Myer, Virginia.[106] He is buried at Arlington National Cemetery.

Private James McCormick was probably left at the Powder River Camp because he was a troublesome soldier. He originally enlisted on August 26, 1861 and served in the Civil War in the west. On March 19, 1868 in enlisted in the Regular Army at Fort Leavenworth, Kansas and joined Company A of the 7th Cavalry; enlistment records show that he was 5' 61/2" tall with dark eyes, dark hair and a sallow complexion. McCormick was in confinement from October 1870 to February 1871 and again in February 1875. After the Little Bighorn, he deserted on July 12, 1878. He was apprehended on June 12, 1879, dishonorably discharged on September 4, 1879 and sentenced to two years confinement in a military prison. On July 2, 1880 he was released from prison in part because of ill health and disappeared from history.[107]

Wagoner Joseph Ricketts, on the other hand, was an excellent soldier, but was left at the Powder River Camp because his skills were needed there. Ricketts was born near Morrow, Ohio on February 27, 1850 and enlisted on January 16, 1873 in Cincinnati, Ohio. Standing 5'9" tall, with blue eyes, black hair and a ruddy complexion, Ricketts was a farmer by trade. He joined Company M in Oxford, Mississippi on February 9, 1873. Because of his background, Ricketts often was assigned as a teamster in the cavalry; he was also a sawyer and was made wagoner on July 14, 1875. On June 15, 1876 he was detailed to be in charge of the mules remaining at the Supply Camp. After the Little Bighorn, Ricketts became the farrier for Company M from January 11, 1877 to January 16, 1878, when he was discharged. He later re-enlisted in Company H. On May 17, 1882 his leg was broken when a horse kicked him. Ricketts received his final discharge from the army on February 6, 1883. Joseph Ricketts died in Dayton, Ohio on February 26, 1909.[108]

Private Walter Sterland, who remained at the Powder River Camp, was another excellent soldier. Born in Sheffield, England on April 16, 1851, he enlisted on November 18, 1872 in Pittsburgh, Pennsylvania. A teamster by trade, Sterland stood 5' 51/2" tall and had blue eyes, light hair and a fair complexion. Sterland joined Company M at Unionville, South Carolina on December 9, 1872. Over the next three years he was frequently detailed to serve as a herder, butcher and cook; he became the Fort Rice post butcher on October 30, 1875. After the Little Bighorn, he served as the acting quartermaster sergeant for the company; he was promoted to corporal on October 18, 1876. He was discharged from the army at Fort Rice on November 18, 1877 as a corporal of good character. After his army days, Sterland owned a confectionary and news depot in Bismarck in 1882. He appears to have later been a city justice of the peace for Dickinson, North Dakota. Walter Sterland died on August 27, 1922 at Dickinson. His wife continued to receive his pension. Sterland is buried at the Dickinson Cemetery in Block P, Lot 8 in Grave 2.[109]

Private Ferdinand Widmayer was the final Company M trooper who remained at the Powder River Supply Camp. Born in Württemberg, Germany on February 18, 1849 he immigrated to Pennsylvania, where the 1870 census shows he resided in Philadelphia. Widmayer enlisted on September 26, 1873 at that city and stood 5'5" tall, had blue eyes, brown hair and a fair complexion. He joined Company M on October 21, 1873 at Fort Rice. During his first few years with the company, Private Widmayer sometimes served as a teamster and laborer. On December 5, 1874 a Fort Rice Garrison Court Martial found him guilty of neglect of duty while a watchman at the post quartermaster department and fined him $3. After the Little Bighorn, Widmayer was the company cook in 1877 and a quartermaster teamster in 1878. Married, Widmayer served the next 25 years from the Arizona Territory to Puerto Rico and the Philippine Islands. He retired on November 4, 1902 as a color sergeant. Ferdinand Widmayer died at Palmyra, New Jersey on September 18, 1913.[110] His grandson later remembered that when he was young, his grandfather told him stories about the cavalry that included being ambushed by Indians and being hit in the leg by a tomahawk. The grandson also remembered that the old horse-soldier wore wire-rim glasses, had a "soup-strainer's moustache" and:[111]

"When he would eat noodle soup, he'd have half of the noodles hanging on his moustache."

Ferdinand Widmayer is buried at the Epworth Methodist Church Cemetery in Palmyra, Burlington County, New Jersey.[112]

Farrier William Wood had already remained at Fort Rice. Born in Grafton, New York, he enlisted in Troy, New York on January 11, 1872. Wood was a farmer, stood 5' 101/2" tall, with blue eyes, red hair and a fair complexion. Wood joined Company M in Unionville, South Carolina on February 14, 1872. He served as a quartermaster teamster before being appointed a company farrier on August 1, 1873. He was left at Fort Rice on May 5, 1876 to oversee company property when the company departed for Fort Abraham Lincoln in preparation for the 1876 Sioux Campaign. A Garrison Court Martial convicted him of drunkenness in July 1876 and sentenced him to pay a $3 fine. Wood was discharged on January 11, 1877 at Fort Rice and then went east. He re-enlisted on November 12, 1881 in Albany, New York in the 15th Infantry Regiment, but deserted this unit at Fort Lewis, Colorado on May 28, 1882. Wood then moved to Chicago, assumed the name of Jason White, and worked as a teamster for a Chicago coal dealer. William Wood was killed in an accident in December 1885 in Chicago.[113]

Private John Zametzer was the second trooper from Company M to remain at Fort Rice. Born in Bavaria, Germany about 1835, he immigrated to the United States and enlisted on August 12, 1867 in New York City. A laborer, he stood 5' 91/2" tall and had gray eyes, brown hair and a fair complexion. Zametzer joined Company M at Fort Harker, Kansas on September 8, 1867. He was promoted to corporal on February 14, 1870 and to sergeant on August 1, 1871. He was discharged on August 12, 1872 and went north to Boston. Zametzer re-enlisted in Boston on December 23, 1874 and was assigned to Company A of the 7th Cavalry. He transferred to Company M on March 1, 1876, but was diagnosed with influenza of the lungs on April 22, 1876 and remained in the post hospital at Fort Rice for three months. Zametzer was promoted to corporal on October 18, 1876. On February 26, 1877 he once again became quite ill with pulmonary consumption and remained in the hospital until August 19, 1877 when he was discharged from the army as disabled. He was characterized as a corporal of excellent character. But his days were numbered and John Zametzer died at the Soldier's Home in Washington, DC on September 24, 1877. He is buried in the cemetery there.[114]

• • •

June 15, 1876 – Junction of the Powder and Yellowstone Rivers to Yellowstone River

At 6:00 a.m. the main body, under the command of Captain Frederick Benteen, moved out of the Yellowstone River supply depot toward the mouth of the Tongue River. One hour later, George Custer departed camp to catch up with the column, after meeting again with Brigadier General Terry. Terry ordered that Custer leave the regimental band at the Yellowstone, a decision that perturbed the cavalry commander. Private James Wilber Darcy (known as James Wilber) of Company M later recalled in an interview with researcher Walter Camp:[115]

"Custer wanted to take the band beyond Powder River, but Terry would not consent to it."

Custer reluctantly complied with his commander's directive and used the seventeen horses belonging to the band members as mounts for some recruits who had no horses, but well over one hundred 7th Cavalry troopers remained on the Yellowstone. The column, now with Custer present, travelled 25 miles and halted in the afternoon along the Yellowstone River. To the troopers' delight, sutler John Smith and his whiskey accompanied the move![116]

June 16, 1876 – Yellowstone River to Old Indian Camp (Two miles from the Tongue River)

The march began early in the morning. Two miles short of the Tongue River the regiment discovered an old Lakota camp that had been occupied months earlier; Custer decided to halt for the day and camp on the same site the Indians had used. It was a macabre scene; later First Lieutenant Edward S. Godfrey[viii] described what transpired:[117]

"A number of their [Lakota] dead, placed upon scaffolds, or tied to the branches of trees, were disturbed and robbed of their trinkets. Several persons rode about exhibiting their trinkets with as much gusto as if they were trophies of valor, and showed no more concern for their desecration than if they had won them at a raffle."

Worse, however, the abandoned Indian camp was undoubtedly dirty. In addition to the decaying bodies, hundreds of people and ponies had defecated in the area; lice and fleas very probably remained after the Indian ponies had departed. Isaiah Dorman, one of Custer's interpreters, was ordered to unwrap one of the dead; he did so and threw the body into the river, from which men were refilling their canteens. The regiment would have been better served to have encamped some distance away and to have left the remnants of death alone.[118]

June 17, 1876 – Old Indian Camp to Mouth of the Tongue River

During the night it rained. The buglers woke the troops at 4:00 a.m. Some of the troopers had fish for breakfast that they had caught the evening before. Captain Benteen led the column out of camp at 6:00 a.m. for the short two-mile march to the mouth of the Tongue River. The regiment arrived at this new location at 8:30 a.m. Unknown to Terry, Custer or any other officer in the command, some ninety miles to the southwest General George Crook, the commander of another prong in Sheridan's attack plan, was being attacked by almost 2,000 warriors on Rosebud Creek. Crook had 1,100 officers and men, augmented by approximately 300 Crow and Shoshone Indian scouts, but the ferocity of the attack caused Crook to withdraw to a previous Goose Creek supply bivouac (near present day Sheridan, Wyoming) which provided Sitting Bull's warriors with several dozen abandoned army firearms. Crook suffered nine killed and 23 wounded; his Indian scouts lost another eight casualties. Custer's men, meanwhile, selected a heavily timbered area for their newest campsite.[119]

[viii] Edward S. Godfrey was born in Kalida, Ohio on October 9, 1843. After serving as a private in the 21st Ohio Volunteer Infantry Regiment at the beginning of the Civil War, Godfrey entered West Point and graduated in 1867 (ranked 53 of 63 cadets). He was commissioned a second lieutenant in the 7th Cavalry Regiment on June 17, 1867 and was assigned to Company K. He served in combat at both the Washita and on the Yellowstone expedition. He served as the assistant engineer on the Black Hills expedition in 1874. Godfrey, who was deaf in one ear, later testified at the Reno Inquiry in 1879 and served on the staff at West Point. Godfrey was brevetted to major on February 27, 1890 and awarded the Medal of Honor for his actions at Bear Paw Mountain against the Nez Percé Indians on September 30, 1877. He also was at Wounded Knee. He was promoted to brigadier general on January 17, 1907; he retired on October 9, 1907. Edward Godfrey died on April 1, 1932 in Cookstown, New Jersey. He is buried at Arlington National Cemetery in Section 3 in site 4175-E.

June 18, 1876 – Mouth of the Tongue River

The men generally rested, bathing in the river and fishing after they took care of their horses.[120] This close to potential fighting, the troopers did not use their firearms and so the Arikara scouts did not hunt and provide fresh meat. During the march the scouts had sold this game to the troopers for two dollars for a deer hind quarters and one dollar for either a front quarter, back cut or saddle cut of meat.[121]

June 19, 1876 – Mouth of the Tongue River

The day's activities were much the same as on June 18. Meanwhile, Major Marcus Reno and his wing of the regiment marched 33 miles to try and close on Custer's and Terry's encampment, but at 4:00 p.m. Reno called a halt. The men with Reno were near collapse and the horses were extremely tired; during the scout Reno had rationed the animals to only two pounds of oats per day – one-sixth of their normal allowance. Additionally, one of the pack mules fell into a creek and the rations it carried were spoiled, further reducing rations.[122] Reno's location was now only eight miles away from the rest of the regiment; he sent a message to Brigadier General Terry, which read in part:[123]

> "My animals are leg weary and need shoeing. We have marched near to 250 miles."

June 20, 1876 – Mouth of the Tongue River to the Yellowstone River

Brigadier General Terry envisioned that Reno's reconnaissance would last six days; Reno took eight. He did not follow Terry's orders and instead followed an Indian trail all the way to Rosebud Creek. Reno's six companies thus had many more miles on their mounts than the rest of the regiment, which may have later contributed to the Little Bighorn defeat – as all five companies that fell with Lieutenant Colonel Custer had been on Reno's lengthy Rosebud sojourn. Terry was not happy that Reno's detachment had exceeded his orders and that many of the men and horses were now worn out.[124]

To complicate matters, as Reno had stated, all the horses in his detachment now needed to be re-shod. The *Cavalry Tactics* manual called for horses to be shod at least once a month, and the campaign had commenced on May 17. The farriers had to check the length of each hoof – a time-consuming process – as hoof condition, rather than the wear on the shoe, determined when a horse needed to be re-shod.[125]

Custer departed the camp at the mouth of the Tongue River at 8:00 a.m. to get to Reno's encampment before General Terry could arrive on the *Far West* on the Yellowstone River. Both Custer and Terry were irate at Reno's conduct on the reconnaissance. Custer wished to chastise Reno first, before Terry could arrive. Custer arrived at Reno's camp at 11:30 a.m., but Reno was already down at the Yellowstone awaiting Terry, who would arrive on the *Far West* at 12:30 p.m. After the three officers discussed the operation, the regiment began another march at 4:00 p.m. and marched 14 miles along the Yellowstone, halting at 8:30 p.m. The sun had set at 8:02 p.m. local time, so it was quickly getting dark. The waning crescent of the moon had set at 7:28 p.m. local time.[126] However, the regimental rearguard did not pull into camp until 11:00 p.m. It had been a very long day.[127]

June 21, 1876 – Yellowstone River to the Mouth of Rosebud Creek

Sunrise on June 21 was 4:14 a.m. local time.[128] The regiment marched to the mouth of Rosebud Creek, approaching at about 9:30 a.m.; by noon the regiment had established its bivouac site. Custer joined General Terry and Colonel John Gibbon aboard the *Far West* at about 1:00 p.m. for a detailed discussion of the upcoming operation. The trio discussed where they thought the large Indian village might be, but they could only be fairly certain that it was west of the Rosebud, north of the Big Horn Mountains, possible near the Big Horn River. Terry took a sensible approach. He ordered Custer to take the 7th Cavalry Regiment – the most mobile of the expedition's formations – to move upstream in a southerly direction along the Rosebud and directed that Gibbon – with his slower infantry element – to move upstream along the Big Horn. Custer would then cross the ridge separating the Rosebud from the valley of the Little Bighorn and ride downstream on the Little Bighorn to meet Gibbon – hopefully trapping the Indians between the two forces.[129] No one seemed overly concerned that the Lakota and Northern Cheyenne would stand and fight. During the afternoon, Custer rejected a suggestion that he take elements of the 2nd Cavalry Regiment; he initially accepted the idea of taking Second Lieutenant William H. Low's Gatling gun battery, but later nixed the suggestion. Interpreter Frederic F. Gerard later described the conversation:[130]

> "I had a conversation with Custer one night before we reached the Yellowstone. Custer said he would have some Gatlings along, and if he got within range of a village he would make short work of it. I told him, 'General, don't you be deceived in believing you can get Indians to stand while you grind out shots with a Gatling. I would advise [to] you to leave [the] Gatlings behind and take a twelve-pounder that will throw shells. Then if you get within a mile or two of an Indian camp, you can make them scatter pretty lively."

Scatter is exactly what George Custer did not want the Indians to do. He needed to be bold to prevent that from happening. As he once wrote:[131]

> "Faint heart never won fair lady, neither did it ever pursue and overtake an Indian village."

This leader discussion took all day; it was not until 9:00 p.m. that Custer departed the *Far West*. Custer and Terry than walked together to Custer's tent for a few final words; Terry then returned to the *Far West*, leaving his subordinate to issue his own orders to the regiment.[132]

The sun had set at 8:02 p.m. local time; the moon had set shortly thereafter, but it had been a new moon, so it wouldn't have added to the ambient light anyway.[133] Custer subsequently called his officers together and briefed them on the events to follow. They were told to load the pack mules the following morning, June 22, with 15 days of rations of hardtack, coffee and sugar (and 12 days of bacon) for the men; each soldier would carry 12 pounds of oats to be rationed to the horses. Custer reminded his commanders that each company would have a dozen pack mules; the strongest animals would split the 24,000 rounds of reserve ammunition, while each trooper would carry 100 rounds of carbine ammunition and 24 rounds of revolver ammunition. He then dismissed the officers, but First Lieutenant Edward Godfrey and Captain Myles Moylan remained with him to voice their concerns about the pack mules that were in a weakened condition due to Reno's long reconnaissance. Custer grew impatient and snapped:[134]

> "You had better carry along an extra supply of salt; we may have to live on horse meat before we get through."

That was no idle threat. Many troops found horsemeat "stringy," "leathery," with an "ominous odor" and often "nauseating." Mule meat, often fatty, was characterized as "offensive in smell and taste."[135] The best cut of meat – of the otherwise tough mule – was the upper lip, called by the soldiers a "Jenny Lind Steak."[136] But living off mule or horsemeat was an unpleasant thought in any condition.

The soldiers wrote letters home, repacked their belongings and talked; some played poker far into the night in nervous apprehension.[137] According to the chief historian of the Little Bighorn Battlefield National Monument, John Doerner, some of the officers and men in the regiment probably filled their three-pint canteens with whiskey in preparation for departure.[138] The wind whistled through the trees and a light rain fell; it would get heavier and be accompanied by hail after midnight. Later that evening, Second Lieutenant Winfield Edgerly[ix] stopped by Custer's tent for a dose of confidence. Custer told him that the regiment would be victorious, saying:[139]

> "It all depends on you young officers. We can't get Indians without hard riding and plenty of it."

There would be much hard riding over the next few days and Winfield Edgerly would remember it for the next fifty-one years.

[ix] Winfield S. Edgerly was born on May 29, 1846 in Farmington, New Hampshire. The son of a farmer, he graduated from West Point in 1870, ranking 50 of 58 cadets and was commissioned in the cavalry. He joined Company D of the regiment at Fort Leavenworth on September 28, 1870. After the Little Bighorn, Edgerly transferred to Company L to help reform that unit. The following year he again transferred, this time to Company C. In 1890 Edgerly fought at Wounded Knee Creek. In 1902 as a colonel he was appointed to command the 2nd Cavalry Regiment; he went to both Cuba and the Philippines with this unit. Edgerly was promoted to brigadier general on June 28, 1905; he later commanded the Department Dakota before retiring on December 29, 1909 due to ill health. Winfield S. Edgerly died at Farmington, New Hampshire on September 10, 1927 of chronic nephritis. He is buried at Arlington National Cemetery in Section 3 in Grave 3886A.

Mouth of the Tongue River where it meets the Yellowstone River. The 1876 campaign was a maneuver from river to river – by the Lakota and Northern Cheyenne to find adequate food and water for their people, and by the U.S. Army trying to find the large Indian villages in likely locations. Photo taken in May 2010.

Rosebud Creek about one-half mile from its mouth on the Yellowstone River. Photo taken in May 2010.

Powder River near its mouth where it meets the Yellowstone River. General Terry's Powder River Supply base was not far from this location. Photo taken in May 2010.

Bighorn River, about five miles below the mouth of the Little Bighorn River. View is looking south. River captain Grant Marsh was able to maneuver his steamer *Far West* to the Little Bighorn, which greatly aided in evacuating wounded cavalrymen after the battle. Photo taken in May 2010.

"Gentlemen, it looks like the bottom of Hell, with the fires out." The Badlands; photo taken in June 2009.

CHAPTER FOUR

COMPANY M AT THE LITTLE BIGHORN BATTLE SUMMARY

"Mount your horse my boy and stick to him. You are fighting Indians now!"[1]

The following is a chronological summary of Company M's role in the two-day fight; the summary actually starts on June 22, as the final lead-up to the battle greatly influenced the events that would follow. While this study is confident of the general sequencing of events concerning Company M for this time period, it is not so certain of the exact time of day that each occurred. The times are derived, in part, on the computations postulated by Jack Pennington (which he based – in part – on his belief that the Reno Inquiry deliberately falsified the timeline) and John Gray's comprehensive studies (which accepted the Reno Inquiry's version of event times).[i]

At noon on June 22, 1876 Company M and the rest of the 7th Cavalry rode out of camp at the junction of the Yellowstone and Rosebud Rivers to begin the attempt to locate the Lakota camp. The command got up at 4:00 a.m. and drew supplies. Sunrise occurred at 4:15 a.m. local time.[2] There had been a lengthy rain that night and the fields were muddy. As planned, Custer left the wagons at the river as well. Supplies would be carried on the mules, loaded on the "leaders" and "swings." The larger "wheel" mules were left behind.[3]

To carry the supplies, the mules were saddled with a crossbuck supply saddle that looked like a small A-frame contraption, whose double girth straps caused the mules to be even more unruly than was their normal cantankerousness. It would take a full three companies of the regiment to initially control the beasts, many of which stuck in the mud with their heavy loads or bucked off any improperly-tied item of gear. Company M probably had 13 mules, as did each other company; they should each have had 14, but Reno's earlier reconnaissance had made a dozen of the mules lame.[4] Company M had one officer and 54 enlisted men in the company proper. One other officer (First Lieutenant Edward Mathey) was assigned to the pack train to command that gaggle of men and animals, while another officer, assigned on paper (Second Lieutenant James Sturgis), was on detached service with Company E. Private William Robinson of the company was detailed as an assistant to Dr. Henry Porter, an acting assistant surgeon, in a regimental order dated May 16.[5]

The regiment departed about noon. Frederic Gerard later claimed he overheard General Terry make the following remark after Custer departed:[6]

> "Custer is happy now, off with a roving command of fifteen days. I told him if he found the Indians not to do as Reno did, but if he thought he could whip them to do so."

The column made about twelve miles by 4:00 p.m. before bedding down for the night.[7] Not all the available men made this final part of the journey; each company had left a few men at the Yellowstone supply base to guard company stores, and some men later said that a few troopers feigned illness so they would not have to continue, although there is no evidence found by this study to indicate that occurred in Company M.[8]

• • •

In October 1868 Custer had "colored the horses," somewhat standardizing the colors of the cavalry mounts by company, so that from a distance it was easier to identify each company. This was done by giving the senior-most company commander his pick of color, followed by the second in seniority and so forth. At the conclusion of this reshuffling, the command had the following patterns:[9]

Company A – dark bays (generally dark mahogany)
Company B – light bays (various shades of red-brown from tan to mahogany)
Company C – sorrels (light yellow-brown to light red-brown)
Company D – blacks
Company E – grays
Company F – light bays
Company G – mixed colors
Company H – light bays
Company I – light bays
Company K – sorrels
Company L – light bays
Company M – mixed colors (black, sorrel and light sorrels)

[i] Part of the rationale for believing the timeline was altered came from Major Reno's letter of July 5, 1876 to Captain E.W. Smith, Acting Assistant Adjutant General at the 7th Cavalry Headquarters, in which Reno gave the following timeline for June 25: the command crossed the divide about 8:00 a.m.; the command approached the Lone Teepee about 11:00 a.m.; Reno received orders to move against the village at 12:30 p.m.; Reno had completed the valley fight and had moved to the vicinity of the hill defensive position, meeting Captain Benteen at 2:30 p.m. Source: Jack Pennington, *The Battle of the Little Bighorn: A Comprehensive Study*, El Segundo, CA: Upton & Sons, Publishers, 2001, 40. Another problem was time standardization. The U.S. did not standardize time-zones until 1883.

Company M, when on duty in the south, had received as many as 45 black horses; many remained in the outfit three years later.[10] Officers could have whatever color horse they wanted. According to Private Charles "Dutchy" Windolph, the last survivor of the battle, company horses, ridden by the enlisted men, were all geldings.[11] It appears that the regimental band, trumpeters and non-commissioned officers all had grays. Each horse was branded on the hip with the number of the regiment and the letter of the company. Enlisted men were not supposed to exchange horses.[12] By the time of the 1876 campaign, Company M was the only element in the regiment that had mixed colors.[13] Concerning the size of the mounts, we have scant information. A letter from Captain French in January 1876 discussed one company horse standing 15 1/2 hands high.[14]

Captain Thomas French had two horses on the campaign. One was named "Pete," while the other horse, which was gray and quite distinguishable in a company formation, was named "Big-Head" and was a lot to handle according to one of the men:[15]

> "'Big-Head' gave him a great deal of trouble and, as a matter of course, riled him. Oh, what a horse that was. He would go along all right for a while, and then the first thing you knew he would take it into his head to walk on the other side of the company; and, not being particular where he went, or how he got there, he would take a side carom on the company, and through [it] he would go knocking the men out of line, in spite of all that the Captain could do to try and stop him. I have seen the other officers laugh at the antics of that sorrel. The Captain said that it was the only horse he ever mounted that he could not handle, but that he had to give beat on that one."

• • •

Custer had two horses and routinely changed mounts every three hours.[16] Custer's orderly, Private John W. Burkman,[ii] later recalled the mood of the troopers that morning:[17]

> "I can't say as any o' the Seventh felt specially glum that morning except maybe some that'd lost in poker the night afore. We knowed we was goin into a big fight and that out o' the six hundred of us thar was some wouldn't come back, but that sort o' thing a soldier takes for granted. Jist afore we started they was a lots squattin' on their haunches scribblin' letters to send on the boat that was goin' down river. For most o' them they was the last letters they ever writ. But the feelin' in general was that we was proud as hell 'cause it was the Seventh bein' sent out to git the Indians 'stead o' Gibbon's men or Terry's."

Not everyone shared Private Burkman's enthusiasm. One soldier from Company M, who had severe misgivings of the upcoming fight, was Private Jean Baptiste Desire Gallenne, who wrote in his daily journal that evening:[18]

> "I am sick since three days, I feel so unhappy, so sad, that I wish God had called me away from this life."

"Frenchy" Gallenne was an interesting soldier. Born at the street Rue de Revolution, in Lorient, France on February 19, 1849, he was the only child of Jean Baptiste and Marie Eugenie Dagorne; when he was young his father was killed at sea. Possibly spurred by his mother, who did not want him conscripted during France's war with Prussia, young Jean immigrated to New York; he was a student there on September 30, 1873 when he enlisted in the army. Records show that Private Gallenne stood 5' 51/2" tall, with blue eyes, black hair and a dark complexion. He joined Company M at Fort Rice on October 21, 1873.[19] Private Gallenne was diagnosed with a fever on January 21, 1874 and went on sick call for catarrh on April 24, 1876.[20] That fall he was detailed as a herder for the post cattle. On April 29, 1875 a Garrison Court Martial at Fort Rice convicted Private Gallenne of giving a soldier 2 1/2 loaves of bread, while Gallenne was serving as a company cook. He was fined $5 for this offense.[21]

Gallenne was probably not the only soldier to feel the itch to be somewhere else. A soldier from another company in the regiment on the campaign later said that it had been impossible to maintain personal cleanliness during the march and that many of the dirty and unshaven soldiers were infected with lice.[iii] As he said:[22]

> "We had cooties then, just as the army today."

While the young man from France was bemoaning his condition, and "bunkies" were cursing each other for having lice, Custer ordered an officers' call that evening. He told his subordinate officers that the rest of the advance would be in easy 25-30-miles-per-day stages to conserve the horses and synchronize the regiment's advance with that of Colonel John Gibbon's infantry column, closing from the north on the anticipated location of the Indian village.[iv] Gibbon's column was small, however; he had only 300 infantry soldiers and 150 troopers from the 2nd Cavalry Regiment.[23] Custer also informed the officers there would be no bugle calls; cooking fires would be kept small to just heat coffee for the men and put immediately out afterward. The soldiers would have to prepare their food, primarily salt pork (known as "Cincinnati chicken") and hardtack (called by the soldiers "angel cake," "Uncle Sam's seed cakes" and "worm castles") as best they could.[24]

Custer went on to explain why he had decided not to bring the Gatling gun battery on the march and why he refused the offers of a battalion from the 2nd Cavalry Regiment. Finally, Custer expressed confidence in his officers and requested that any suggestions they thought appropriate be submitted through the chain of command.[25] The officers were stunned. This was not the headstrong commander they had

---

[ii] Private John M. "Old Neutriment" Burkman was reported born on January 10, 1839, probably in Allegheny County, Pennsylvania; however, late in life he told a friend that he was actually born in Germany. Illiterate, Burkman served in the Civil War; he enlisted in the 7th Cavalry in 1870 and served in Company A and L. Before the battle, Custer told him to stay with the pack train, a decision that saved Burkman's life. He was discharged from the service in 1879 for physical disability after falling off a horse, but his experience on the campaign permanently scarred his mind. "Old Neutriment" never married, worked for some years as a teamster and lived in a small shack, subsisting on a meager pension of six dollars a month. Sporting a long, white beard that made him look like a hermit, John M. Burkman committed suicide by shooting himself on November 6, 1925 in Billings, Montana – his body was found with a pistol in one hand and a bag of candy in the other. According to the *New York Times*, Burkman had almost a total loss of sight and hearing and had attempted to enter the Soldiers' Home at Sawtelle, California but was denied and returned to Billings. John Burkman is buried at the Custer Battlefield National Cemetery. Source: "Custer Trooper a Suicide," *New York Times*, November 8, 1925, E2.

[iii] Some of the men in Colonel Gibbon's column came down with scurvy as well.

[iv] Brigadier General John O. Gibbon was born on April 20, 1827 in Holmesburg, Pennsylvania (now located in Philadelphia); he graduated from West Point in 1847, and was commissioned in the artillery. Gibbon fought in the Mexican War and in Florida against the Seminole Indians before becoming a tactics instructor at West Point, a position he held from 1853 to 1859. During the Civil War, Gibbon commanded the "Iron Brigade" and later was wounded at both the battle of Fredericksburg and Gettysburg; in this latter battle, Gibbon's troops helped repulse the rebel attack that became known as "Pickett's Charge." During the conflict three of Gibbon's brothers served in the Confederate army. He ended the war a brevet major general and the commander of the Union 2nd Corps. Called "No Hip" by the Crows, he was wounded again in 1877 during the fighting against the Nez Percé Indians. Promoted to brigadier general in 1885, he retired in 1891. John Gibbon died in Baltimore, Maryland on February 6, 1896 of pneumonia. He is buried at Arlington National Cemetery in Lot 986.

grown to love or hate – depending on the individual officer. Previously, Custer had mostly been abrupt with his subordinates and seemed disinclined to consider their suggestions; it was a style of leadership they had not witnessed before in their commander. The officers then synchronized their watches; they were operating on Chicago time, which was one and a half hours ahead of local time.[26] Sunset occurred at 8:02 p.m. local time. The moon was just a sliver and provided only one percent illumination; it set at 9:33 p.m.[27]

On June 23, Company M and the rest of the command rose early and crossed the Rosebud.

The stable guard woke the men, as Custer had suspended bugle calls for fear of alerting hostile warriors within sound range. Sunrise was at 4:15 a.m. local time.[28] The march began at 5:00 a.m.; with the Crows riding ahead and the Arikaras on the flanks, the scouts soon found a large Indian trail. That afternoon they crossed Greenleaf Creek and discovered at least three recently-occupied Lakota camps.[29] Custer called Second Lieutenant Charles Varnum[v] forward and gave an indicator of things to come:[30]

> "Here's where Reno [on his earlier reconnaissance] made the mistake of his life. He had six troops of cavalry and rations enough for a number of days. He'd have made a name for himself if he'd pushed on after them."

Indeed Reno would have made a name, but not in the manner that Custer believed; that honor would be his alone in two days' time. With the excited Custer pressing them onward, the 7th Cavalry travelled 33 miles that day in search of the Indians.[31]

• • •

The 7th Cavalry, in 1876, operated under the manual of United States Army *Cavalry Tactics* by Colonel Emory Upton, who wrote the manual while he served as the Commandant of Cadets at West Point.[vi] The doctrine was published in 1874. In theory, a cavalry regiment did not just saddle-up in the morning and ride all day. Instead, the formation would march initially for one hour, at which point the column would halt for 10 to 15 minutes to adjust tack (saddle, bridle, saddle girth, etc.). The troopers would then remount and the column would resume the march for another hour. After the second hour, the troopers did not rest, but rather dismounted and led their horses for 20 minutes. The cavalrymen then re-mounted and the column moved forward at the trot (a rate of speed of seven to eight miles an hour) for 20 minutes. The column then slowed – but stayed mounted – to a walk (three and three-quarters miles per hour). At the end of this third hour – and at the end of each succeeding hour – the column would halt for five minutes. This pattern of dismounted walk, trot and walk was maintained, along with short gallops to allow the horses to stretch (nine to eleven miles per hour), was designed to conduct a march of six hours per day, during which the column would cover 25 miles.[32] However, as the 1874 *Cavalry Tactics* manual warned:[33]

> "The gallop very soon breaks down horses, and is the exceptional gait at drill and in campaign; on all other occasions it is strictly prohibited."

Climbing hills and descending slopes was also tiring.[34] First Sergeant John Ryan later explained how the cavalry minimized the impact of going uphill:[35]

> "A cavalry command marching on a campaign in approaching a hill would always dismount. The company in advance would dismount first and all the others in [the] rear [would] follow suit, then lead the horses up the hills. After travelling over the hills we would mount up again, as it saves the horses a great deal."

The manual also stated that the best time to feed grain to the horses – and army horses could not just solely be turned loose to feed on prairie grasses – was in the morning and in the evening, after the day's march.[36] Under normal circumstances, a cavalry horse was a prodigious eater, consuming 14 pounds of hay and 12 pounds of grain each day![37]

Many of the recruits had never ridden 20 total miles on a horse in their entire lives.[38] Now, their lives depended on their mounts holding up over a long, grueling campaign. So, the troopers developed a rhyme to remember these critical rules of horsemanship:[39]

> "Up the hill, gallop me not
> Down the hill, trot me not
> On the plain, spare me not
> In the stable, forget me not."

• • •

By the close of June 23, considering that the 7th Cavalry had travelled all the way from Bismarck, Dakota Territory, the horses were getting pretty tired; the column probably traveled at least 400 miles since leaving Fort Abraham Lincoln (250 more for those who had ridden with Reno on the additional scout mission), much of that over very difficult terrain. In fact, noted twentieth century cavalryman and equine health expert Colonel Elwood Nye came to the conclusion that the regiment began the Battle of the Little Bighorn on exhausted mounts.[40] Whether that assessment was accurate for the horses in Company M, we do not know.

[v] Charles A. "Crazy Horse" Varnum, an 1872 graduate of West Point, was born on June 21, 1849 in Troy, New York. Upon graduation, Varnum joined the 7th Cavalry, initially serving with Company A and C and participated in the Yellowstone and Black Hills campaigns. He took over command of the regiment's Detachment of Indian Scouts in May 1876 from First Lieutenant William W. Cooke. After the Battle of the Little Bighorn, Varnum, who was also called "Peaked Face" by the scouts, transferred to Company C and hence to command Company I. The following year he fought in the Nez Percé Campaign at Canyon Creek and Snake Creek. Court-martialed in April 1886, Varnum fought at White Clay Creek and Wounded Knee Creek as the commander of Troop B; he received the Medal of Honor on September 22, 1897 for the former fight. Charles Varnum retired on October 31, 1907 for disability; he was subsequently promoted to colonel. Charles A. Varnum died in Letterman General Hospital in San Francisco on February 26, 1936. He is buried in the San Francisco National Cemetery at the Presidio; Section OS, Grave 3-3-A. He was the last surviving officer of the Little Bighorn and was frequently asked his opinions of the battle; researcher Walter Camp extensively interviewed him.

[vi] Emory Upton was born on August 27, 1839 near Batavia, New York. He graduated from West Point on May 6, 1861, a classmate of George A. Custer. Unlike Custer, who graduated 45 out of 45 in the class, Upton was an academic and graduated eighth. Commissioned in the artillery, Upton served as an aide-de-camp to Brigadier General Daniel Tyler and was wounded in the arm and side on July 21, 1861 at the First Battle of Bull Run. Fifteen months later Upton was appointed a colonel and the commander of the 121st New York Volunteer Infantry Regiment; he led this regiment at the Battle of Fredericksburg and then commanded another regiment at Gettysburg. Cited for gallantry at Rappahannock Station, Upton earned a promotion to brevet major in the Regular Army. At Spotsylvania Courthouse in 1864 he introduced a tactic to successfully assault dug–in defenders by massing infantry to attack only a small section of the defenses, without pausing to trade fire. Upton was wounded in the attack; he finished the war as a cavalry commander. Major General James H. Wilson said of Upton, "He was incontestably the best tactician of either army." From 1870 to 1875, Emory Upton served as the Commandant of Cadets at West Point; he also served as a tactics instructor for the cadets and rewrote several army tactics manuals. In 1881 Upton, who was now a colonel, served as the commander of the 4th Artillery Regiment at the Presidio of San Francisco. Probably suffering from a brain tumor that caused him terrible headaches, Emory Upton shot himself in the head and died on March 15, 1881 at the Presidio. He is buried in the Fort Hill Cemetery at Auburn, New York in Section 74 in the Throop-Martin plot.

There was a certain resignation in the troopers; that we do know. Second Lieutenant "Jack" Sturgis probably received a copy of the will of his company commander Captain Thomas French to hold for safekeeping before the day was out.[41]

The 7th Cavalry continued the march on June 24.
The command began to move early in the morning, breaking into two columns to reduce the size of the dust clouds kicked up by the horses. A brisk headwind blew from the south.[42] Sunrise was at 4:21 a.m. local time.[43] The day grew uncomfortably warm and this alkaline, chalky, beige dust stuck to the sweat of trooper and horse.[44] Company F served as the pack escort for the day. Company M began the day as the rear guard for the column.[45] At 1:00 p.m., Custer called a halt and directed the scouts to investigate several areas along the route of advance. They did, and returned at 4:00 p.m. with news that a fresh Indian campsite was 12 miles ahead.[46] The regiment resumed moving at 5:00 p.m. After a total of 12 miles, the command camped at Busby, two miles below the mouth of Davis Creek at about 7:45 p.m. It was a good campsite, with a cool, clear running stream, wild rosebushes in full bloom and occasional low willows; there was plenty of lush grass on which the horse could graze.[47] The animals needed the energy; they had marched 28 total miles that day. Additionally, the animals had been under saddle for almost 15 hours and on the alert for most of that time.[48] Unknown to George Custer or any of the troopers, the camp site was just 18 miles distant from the site of General Crook's defeat the prior week.[49]

Sunset occurred at 8:04 p.m. local time.[50] The soldiers believed they would get a good night's sleep, but according to Sergeant Weihe at about 9:00 or 10:00 p.m. Captain French and the other officers received orders that they would be advancing soon.[51] It was about midnight when the column moved out. For the troopers this was disturbing news; most considered a night ride worse than a full week's worth of day marches, as horses stumbled and fell in the darkness and even smooth riding was fatiguing for the soldiers. The moon had been at 12 percent illumination, but had set at 10:44 p.m. so it was no help to the tired troopers on the march.[52] By this point in the expedition, many troopers had long, shaggy hair; most were unshaven and a few had beards and needed a bath. Private Daniel Newell remembered the hours just prior to the move:[53]

> "I took a bunch of canteens and went down to the Rosebud and had a swim. Just as I was getting into my clothes, the order came to pack up right away and be prepared to march. We were not looking for this and the men and horses were all tired out, but there was nothing to do but go. While I was down swimming, my Bunkie Scollin had been sleeping, but when I got back he was writing in his diary and he read to me what he had written. I said to him, 'what in the hell are you thinking about; you don't count on dying, do you?' He said, 'Dan, if anything happens to me, notify my sister, Mary, who lives in Gardiner, Massachusetts. My name is Henry Cody, and the name Henry Scollin is assumed'…I think he had a premonition of what was in store for him…"

Post-battle historical analysis has generally postulated that each of the 12 companies detailed four to six men each for duty with the pack train, which brought up the rear of the column. Prior to late June 24, a senior captain and three companies provided security for the pack train as shown in a regimental order that was promulgated earlier at the mouth of the Rosebud.

Company M's First Lieutenant Edward G. Mathey was detached from company duties on June 22 and served as Custer's direct representative at the mule train; each night he reported to the regimental commander how well the companies performed their duties with respect to the pack train.[54] At this point in the march, Custer ordered the companies to provide a small detail each. Perhaps because Company M had already provided First Lieutenant Mathey, Custer let them off the hook for additional support, but in any case the number of Company M troopers with the pack train has remained an uncertain quantity to this day.[55]

Edward G. Mathey was born in Besancon, France on October 27, 1837, immigrating to the United States in 1846, when he was just nine years old and settling in Corydon, Indian. An only child, whose parents had aspirations that he enter the priesthood, in April 1861 he enlisted as a private in Company C of the 17th Indiana Infantry Regiment. He was appointed first sergeant of the company on May 31, 1861 and was promoted to second lieutenant 11 months later. He resigned his commission in the 17th Indiana in August 1862 and was appointed a second lieutenant in the 81st Indiana Infantry Regiment; he fought with the regiment at Stone River, Tunnel Hill, Buzzard Roost, Liberty Gap and Chickamauga, seeing heavy fighting. Mathey was promoted to first lieutenant on March 21, 1863 and to captain on November 8, 1863. He later fought at Kennesaw Mountain, Marietta and the siege of Atlanta. Edward Mathey was promoted to major on September 12, 1864; he temporarily commanded the entire regiment at the battles of Franklin and Nashville.[56]

After the Civil War ended, Edward Mathey left the army, returned to Indiana, and became a store clerk, but two years later – on September 24, 1867 – he was re-appointed a second lieutenant and joined the 7th Cavalry. Three months later Mathey joined Company I. He participated in the Washita Campaign in 1868 and was promoted to first lieutenant on May 10, 1870.[57]

During this period, Edward Mathey was not a well man. On June 22, 1868 he reported sick with acute diarrhea at Camp Gibbs, Kansas. He went on sick call for a fever on January 4, 1869. On January 26, 1869 he reported suffering from constipation. He complained of headaches on June 3, 1869. On January 18, 1870 Mathey was diagnosed with frostbite. He again reported acute diarrhea on March 20, 1870. His medical files show that he also reported ill on March 19, 1874 with rheumatism.[58] Mathey, who was also called "Gus," had brown eyes.[59]

On August 18, 1870 Colonel Sturgis recommended that Mathey appear before a disciplinary board in Washington, D.C., as a "chronic gambler…an insecure man." But George Custer begged to differ and wrote a letter praising Mathey; Custer's influence worked and First Lieutenant Mathey remained in the service. Recent photo analysis by James V. Schneider has identified Edward Mathey on the 1873 Yellowstone Campaign; he also participated in the Black Hills Expedition in 1874. Nicknamed "Bible-Thumper" because of his tendency to be profane, Mathey – who may have become an agnostic in rebellion against his parents – transferred from Company I to Company M on November 1, 1873.[60] Like all cavalry officers, Mathey caught his share of onerous duty. On October 12, 1875, for example, he received orders to inspect incoming oats being delivered to Fort Rice by a contractor and eleven days later conducted a similar inspection of incoming hay.[61]

On the 1876 Sioux Campaign, First Lieutenant Mathey rode a horse named "Blue Skin."[62] He apparently had his saber on the campaign, because he was frequently called to use it to dispatch rattlesnakes at the campsites.[63] Later, Charles Varnum said that Edward Mathey was not a "literary great" and did not like to write letters for fear his poor grammar would be criticized.[64]

Sometime on June 24, George Custer decided that Second Lieutenant Charles Varnum could use some assistance running the Detachment of Indian Scouts for the regiment. The regimental commander tabbed Second Lieutenant Luther R. Hare[vii] of Company K with the mission; Varnum subsequently assigned Hare to oversee some of the Arikara scouts. At 9:00 p.m., Varnum took the Crow scouts and a few Arikaras to move toward the Crow's Nest from which they believed they might be able to see the Indian village the next morning.[65] The moon was in its crescent phase that night and set at 11:49 p.m., making the night seem even darker.[66]

•••

Unknown to the 7th Cavalry, there was not just one single Indian village somewhere ahead of them. In what would play a pivotal role – and would confuse historians for over a century – there were several small villages that were generally moving west to link up with the large Indian village along the Little Bighorn River, the next waterway to the west. Each of these rivers flowed between hills and broken ridges in its own slender valley; travel between the valleys was difficult over these divides. One of these small villages, containing perhaps 20 to 30 teepees, with 50 to 100 warriors, was located on June 24 near what would become known as the "Lone Teepee." The next day they would sense the advancing "pony soldiers" and begin to move northwest toward the large village.[67]

•••

Early on the morning of June 25 Custer spotted the Little Bighorn Indian camp with the aid of his scouts located at the Crow's Nest.

The command had stopped between 2:00 a.m. and 3:00 a.m. at Davis Creek; the men were ordered to make some coffee and then tried to get some sleep. George Custer did not partake of either, knowing that he had to quickly determine the enemy's strength and location more fully.[68] It had been a difficult march in the darkness; no torch lights were permitted and often troopers in the rear of the column only knew they were on the trail if they could smell the dust created by the horses in front of them. Troopers at the rear of a company formation sometimes pounded their tin drinking cups on the horns of their saddles so the company behind them could follow more accurately.[69]

First Sergeant Ryan later recalled the night march:[70]

> "We marched very rapidly and some of the packs became loosened, so we cut the ropes and let them go, the pack belonging to my company was among them. The Indians probably got them afterwards. We halted in a ravine and went temporarily into camp, without unsaddling our horses. We just simply dropped down, threw the bridle reins over our arms and went to sleep, which was not an uncommon thing for a cavalryman to do on a campaign...We ate a hearty breakfast; for our bill of fare in this particular instance we had some raw bacon, hardtack, and cold water, which we relished very much."

Sunrise was at 4:22 a.m.[71] Per Custer's order, each company was permitted to have only one small fire and that was to cook coffee only.[72] Private William Slaper, of Company M, later wrote:[73]

> "As I recall, it was about daylight when we halted and made coffee. I remember this very distinctly, because I did not get any of the coffee, having dropped down under a tree and fallen asleep, holding to the bridle-rein of my horse, and I did not awaken until called to fall in line. We did not unsaddle at this halt so the animals [were] secured but [got] little rest."

William Slaper was born in Cincinnati, Ohio in November 23, 1854. His father and one of his uncles were killed while serving in the Union Army in the Civil War. A safe-maker by trade, after becoming unemployed, Slaper enlisted in the army in Cincinnati on September 10, 1875 – much to his mother's dismay. The 19-year-old was sent to Jefferson Barracks, St. Louis for six weeks, where he was instructed in dismounted drill and training at stables in horse care and grooming. From there he took a troop train to Bismarck, Dakota Territory, and hence to Fort Lincoln.[74] He had an interesting experience enroute. As the train stopped at Fargo, an Irish sergeant told the young soldiers to go to a certain saloon, trade their firearms for liquor and bring the liquor back to the train. Slaper and his mates did as they were told, at which point the sergeant:[75]

> "...then took a squad of recruits, armed them as guards and marched them [back] over to the saloon. Here he threatened the proprietor for buying government arms, and immediately confiscated the pawned weapons! He thus secured plenty of whiskey at no expense."

William Slaper joined Company M at Fort Rice on October 21, 1875. Records show that he was 5' 81/2" tall, with blue eyes, brown hair and a fair complexion.[76] His nickname in the unit was "Bill."[77]

Lieutenant Charles Varnum reached the Crow's Nest and sent a note to Custer at 5:00 a.m. Recent theory indicates that Custer may have visited the Crow's Nest twice that morning. Sometime after the second trip to that observation point, Company M's Private Daniel Newell recalled:[78]

> "General Custer ordered halt and fires, and coffee. I was so tired...unsaddled my horse and made a pillow of saddle...was soon asleep...Orderly call but too late for coffee...all gone...my Bunkie and I took a good [drink] of water...All I know is that neither of us got any coffee or anything else and Henry was mad about it. Henry also was sore about losing his sleep."

Private "Dan" Newell later overheard Custer tell Captain Thomas French:[79]

> "It will all be over in a couple of hours. I was at their camp last night and they have only ten or twelve tepees."

[vii] Luther R. Hare was born on August 24, 1851 in Noblesville, Indiana; his family then moved to Sherman, Texas. Hare's father fought for the Confederate cause, but that did not stop Hare from graduating from West Point in 1874, ranked 25th in his class of 41 cadets. Joining Company K after graduation, his effective date of promotion to first lieutenant was June 25, 1876, to fill losses of the regiment at the Little Bighorn. Hare commanded Company L after the Little Bighorn and fought in the Nez Percé Campaign in 1877. He led the 33rd U.S. Volunteer Infantry Regiment in the Spanish American War, winning two Silver Stars for gallantry in the Philippines. Hare retired as a colonel on July 9, 1916. Luther R. Hare died on December 29, 1929 of throat cancer at Walter Reed Hospital in Washington, D.C. He is buried in Arlington National Cemetery at Section S in Lot 3933.

Custer was probably referring to the area now described as the Lone Teepee, believing that he saw several Indian lodgings at that site. First Sergeant John Ryan of Company M supported that theory, when he came to the conclusion that:[80]

> "I think Custer had preparations made to charge that camp, thinking it was an Indian camp."

Officers from other companies were not so sure about Custer's intent, but Captain French and First Sergeant Ryan had served with Custer for many years and probably had a good read of their commander's intentions. On the other hand, Frederic F. Gerard, who was an experienced "Indian-hand," later stated that he told Custer there were probably 1,500 to 2,000 warriors facing the regiment; such a force certainly would take more than a few hours to defeat.[81]

George Custer had originally planned to rest the command on June 25 and attack the camp in the morning of June 26. The regiment would move forward so as to be able to dash to the village the next morning. Captain Thomas M. McDougall,[viii] commander of Company B, had overslept and thus was penalized by Custer and ordered that his company be the regimental rear guard and protect the pack train. The decision may have spared McDougall's life, although he did not realize it at the time; "Captain Mac" was disappointed that he would have to play a subordinate role in the upcoming attack.[82]

As the campsite was stirring, Custer spoke with Private John Burkman and told him to saddle "Vic" for the advance. He then told his striker to take Custer's other horse, "Dandy," and to ride with the pack train. The officer put his hand on his orderly's shoulder and said:[83]

> "You're tired out. But if we have to send for more ammunition you can come in on the home stretch."

Burkman would wonder the rest of his life if Custer somehow knew then that he was sparing his loyal subordinate from the fate he would meet hours later; that tortured thought would lead to John Burkman's suicide many years later. But the private would obey the order as he always did. One soldier in Company A recalled that before moving out his company conducted a "Count Off" to determine the makeup of each "four" and which positions inside that element would be skirmishers and who would be the horse-holder.[84] It is not clear if Company M conducted a similar drill or if the chain of command used some other method to designate the composition of each "four."

Company M and the rest of the regiment began moving again from their final rest area (8:45 a.m.).

The command began to move toward the Indian camp, which was still about fifteen miles away. On the left front were Varnum and the Arikara scouts; to the right front were Hare and the Crow scouts. The cavalrymen were tired and hungry, as sleep the previous night had been short and fitful. As the ground was very dry, to cut down on the dust, the command moved in a column of fours, with 50 feet between each company.[85] First Sergeant Ryan recalled that each company was instructed to ride a little to the right or left of the company in front of them so as not to raise large dust clouds that would warn the Indians of their approach. At this point, George Custer was still away in the vicinity of the Crow's Nest observation point; the main body of the regiment was under temporary control of Major Reno.

The regiment halted at Davis Creek to conceal itself and await the return of the regimental commander (10:00 a.m.).

Custer arrived shortly thereafter at Davis Creek, which was about four miles from the previous night's halt on the same creek. The commander then reiterated to his officers that he believed the Indians knew of the regiment's presence, and therefore they would have to attack the village later this day, rather than wait for the following morning, when surprise would have been greater. Captain French probably conducted one last inspection of Company M during this halt, along with First Sergeant Ryan. At this time Custer ordered each company commander to select one non-commissioned officer and six enlisted men to go to the pack train and help lead the company mules.[86]

• • •

A mystery exists concerning the identities of those Company M troopers who accompanied the pack train on the morning of June 25, 1876. Private William Morris stated that 10 troopers from the company, whom he defined as "old guard" veterans, assisted leading the mules in the train. First Sergeant John Ryan gave the figure as six soldiers. Both men disagreed on the total number of pack mules allocated to the company: Ryan stated there were 12 mules and Morris thought it a smaller total, at six to eight. In either case, the mules each carried up to 300 pounds of supplies.[87] Ronald H. Nichols and Dr. Kenneth Hammer, *Men with Custer: Biographies of the 7th Cavalry*, did not delineate which Company M troopers were with the pack train; instead they listed all Company M troops as having participated in the valley fight, which occurred well before the pack train arrived on Reno Hill. Roger L. Williams, author of the 2009-published *Military Register of Custer's Last Command*, perhaps the most comprehensive biographical source to date for 7th Cavalry troopers in 1876, identified only two men – Private Henry Davis and Private William Morris – of Company M's pack train detail; although Williams did write that each company provided one non-commissioned officer and six privates to accompany the pack mules – each trooper leading two mules.[88]

But the ambiguity continues. Little Bighorn expert Dennis K. Clark, at Fort Leavenworth, has postulated that the pack train details may have been even larger than required. As he points out, the mules indeed carried ammunition and forage, but there are numerous examples that they also carried personal items, such as whiskey, comfort items, etc. This dual-use of the mules was the reason why there was such animosity about losing packs and finding "skulkers" in the pack train, as both situations often resulted in loss or theft of valuable personal items. Therefore, the first sergeants may have provided a larger detail than tasked. In addition, as the march progressed, cavalry horses "played out" and the riders would join their company's mules in the pack train and then close up with their unit at the end of the day. However, there is no mention of this gravitation to the pack train happening to Company M on June 25.[89]

[viii] Thomas M. McDougall was born on May 21, 1845 in Prairie du Chien, Wisconsin. The son of a brevet brigadier general and army surgeon, at age 18 he was appointed a second lieutenant in the 10th Louisiana Volunteers of African Descent (re-designated the 48th U.S. Colored Infantry Regiment). McDougall fought at the siege of Mobile, Alabama; at the fighting at Lakeville, Mississippi he was severely wounded. After being mustered out of the service at the end of the Civil War, McDougall received a Regular Army commission in the infantry; on December 31, 1870 he transferred to the 7th Cavalry Regiment at Fort Leavenworth. He was promoted to captain on December 15, 1875 and assumed command of Company B the same day. McDougall testified at the Reno Inquiry in January 1879. McDougall remained in the 7th Cavalry until July 22, 1890, when he was retired as a major for disability, brought on by malaria. Known as "Captain Mac," McDougall was said to be Frederick Benteen's best friend in the regiment. Thomas M. McDougall died on July 3, 1909 at Brandon, Vermont. He is buried at the Arlington National Cemetery in Section 1, Grave 412-B.

To add to the debate is Larry Sklenar, author of the acclaimed *To Hell with Honor; Custer and the Little Bighorn*. His analysis has led to a conclusion that the companies on the right wing with Custer provided the bulk of the troopers with the pack train on June 25. Thus the pack train was composed of troopers as follows from the right wing: Company L – 12; Company E – 10; Company C – eight; Company I – eight; and Company F – six. Sklenar posited that the left wing of Major Marcus Reno and Captain Frederick Benteen provided the following pack train support: Company G – 3; Company A – 2; Company K – 2; Company H – 1; Company D – 0; and Company M – 0. He concluded:[90]

> "As it turned out, a few troopers from the left wing did remain with the packs, but only because they had either shown exceptional proficiency in managing the mules or were detailed to perform some special duty, such as leading an officer's second horse."

This study concludes that Sergeant John McGlone was the non-commissioned officer who led Company M's pack train detail. This conclusion derives from the fact that every other sergeant in Company M has been identified in the valley fight; there is also no mention of McGlone in the valley fighting. It also seems certain that Private Henry "Harrison" Davis was also part of the detail; he would have fit the pattern as an "old guard" veteran. Roger Williams places him with the pack train and there are no recollections of Davis in the valley combat. I believe that Private William Morris probably started the early morning in the pack train, but by noon had moved forward, as witnesses placed him with First Sergeant Ryan scouting along the Little Bighorn during the valley advance.

It is quite possible that Saddler John Donahoe was also on the pack train detail. John "Jack" Donahoe was born in 1848 in Galway, Ireland. He joined the army by enlisting in 1866; his second enlistment occurred at Chicago, Illinois on October 20, 1871. He arrived at Company M as a saddler on December 22, 1871 in Unionville, South Carolina. Donahoe stood 5'3", with hazel eyes, brown hair and a light complexion; he was also nicknamed "Little Donahoe" and was regarded as the best saddler in the regiment. On November 17, 1874 he was treated by a doctor for frostbite.[91] Donahoe was convicted by a Garrison Court Martial on June 12, 1875 for being drunk and disobeying orders and fined him $7.[92] Another Garrison Court Martial at Fort Rice convicted John Donahoe of being drunk during stable call and then going absent without official leave on January 11, 1876 and sentenced him to a fine of $7.[93] Donahoe was one of the "old guard." He was an expert at saddles and would have been invaluable at ensuring that the mules were properly packed; he could have also quickly fixed any piece of tack equipment that broke. Finally, there are no recollections by Company M troopers that Donahoe was in the valley fight.

There may have been more Company M troopers back with the packs. Captain French had a second horse; his two orderlies were near him in the valley fight, so someone would have had to take care of this second horse back with the pack train. Finally, First Sergeant John Ryan was truly a veteran and would have probably wanted to ensure that he had some savvy veterans with the packs to take care of Company M's interests. By a process of elimination, we can at least present possible additional men who could have been with the pack train. Once we eliminate those men who later stated they were in the valley fighting – which would preclude them from being with the packs – and eliminating all recent recruits, the following troopers are possible pack-train candidates: Corporal William Lalor, Private Joseph Bates, Private Bernard Golden, Private George Heid, Private Charles Kavanaugh, Private Henry Voight, Private John Whisten and Private Charles Williams. But these eight men are only possible candidates; the study has found no sources to indicate that any actually were with the pack train.

• • •

The regiment resumed the march toward the Indian village (11:30 a.m.).

The column then traveled about a mile to the divide, a ridge in the Wolf Mountains, which separated the Rosebud and Little Bighorn Valleys. The cavalry was in its usual column of fours; the interval between companies was about sixty feet. Custer had previously ordered that the pack train, and Company B escorting that supply element, would not begin moving until twenty minutes after the main body moved out in order to maintain proper spacing and keep the dust cloud down on the approach.[94]

Custer halted the command (12:05 p.m.) to task organize the formation.

On the opposite side of the divide, Custer halted again and discussed how the regiment would be formed with First Lieutenant William W. Cooke, the regimental adjutant. The two men pulled their horses to the side of the formation and made notations on a piece of paper for a few minutes.[95]

George Custer would keep Companies C, E, F, I and L with him – the same companies whose horses were probably more tired than the rest of the regiment, as they had gone on the eight-day scout mission with Major Reno. Companies D, H and K would be assigned under the command of Captain Frederick Benteen. Company A, G and M would fall under the command of Major Marcus Reno. Company B would stay in the rear of the column with the supply pack train to protect that slow-moving element against any Indians that might infiltrate from the rear – Company B had also gone on the scout mission with Reno, and the slower pace of the pack train was probably good therapy for these horses. While we cannot know with certainty what Custer's tactical plan was, several eminent historians have summarized a logical scheme of the commander: Major Reno was to attack the southern end of the village; Captain Benteen was to sweep to the west and attack the village from the left; Lieutenant Colonel Custer would take the main effort and attack the village from the east (right); and Company B would guard the pack train against any small band of warriors that might stumble into this valuable logistical tail. Ideally the three attacks would be near-simultaneous in timing.[96]

According to Second Lieutenant Hare, in addition to the carbine ammunition that the troops carried with them – each man with 100 rounds – each company had one mule in the pack train that was packed with two boxes of carbine ammunition (1,000 rounds in each box) for a total of 2,000 additional rounds per company.[97] Some of the mules lost their packs during the morning, including one mule carrying Company M supplies.[98] Shortly afterward the command started moving again, but with Captain Benteen's battalion moving to the left to scout several ridges a few miles southwest of Custer's route of march to ensure that no Indians were lurking to that flank, waiting to hit the regiment in the rear, or attempting to flee if the Indian camp on the Little Bighorn did not contain all the Indian groups. Benteen immediately put First Lieutenant Francis Gibson in charge of a 10-man advance guard for this mission and began to move.[99] Custer's battalion was on the right, or north, side of Reno Creek,[ix] while Reno's battalion was moving on the left (south) side of the creek.[100] As the battalions separated, the temperature was already reaching one hundred degrees; it would soon get even hotter.[101]

Custer and the main body of the regiment approached the Lone Teepee area (1:35 p.m.)

One mile after Custer's battalion took the right side of Reno Creek and Reno took the left, the formation reached the Lone Teepee area, but found no Indians, a fact that disappointed the regimental commander, as he may have hoped to capture some non-combatants in the area. Now, having a separate direction of travel, Major Reno apparently formed an advance guard of Company M for his battalion. In front of Company M were the Indian scouts, who led out only after being on the receiving end of Custer's wrath for advancing too slow and not following his orders.[102] Private Jean Gallenne, riding with Company M in the front of Reno's column, later observed:[103]

> "…a wigwam of war and a large column of dust about ten [*sic*] miles ahead. We believed it to be the Indians retreating."

There apparently had been some Sans Arc at the Lone Teepee area until just minutes before, and they were now retreating. But this group had remained too long, was now much closer to the regiment and was in jeopardy of being captured by the cavalrymen. Company M's Private William Morris recalled seeing about 100 Indians fleeing away from the cavalry.[104] They were from a smaller village, in the area of the Lone Teepee that was en route to the large Indian village along the Little Bighorn. The regiment probably remained at the Lone Teepee area for about thirty minutes, long enough to set it on fire and check out the immediate surroundings for hiding Indians. The command resumed moving about 2:05 p.m.

Reno and his battalion moved along the right side of Reno Creek to the "flat," where he received his attack orders through the regimental adjutant, First Lieutenant William W. Cooke (2:35 p.m.).

Reno's march west from the Lone Teepee took about 30 minutes until he arrived at a tongue of level bottomland between Reno Creek and the gradually approaching North Fork, which as its name suggests, was angling toward Reno Creek from the northeast. This tongue of bottomland has been termed "the flat" in recent histories. Reno's route was following an Indian trail and at this location he received his orders to attack.[105]

Adjutant Cooke informed Reno that he was to move his three-company element rapidly toward the Indian village and then to charge. He added that the entire regiment would support the attack; however, at this point, nothing had been heard from Captain Benteen and his three companies that had gone left.[106] How Reno interpreted those instructions has been a significant bone of contention ever since the battle. Reno and his detachment, led by Company M, moved out at a trot in a column of twos at about the time that Varnum returned to Custer and told him that only a few teepees were visible but the whole Little Bighorn valley was full of Indians.[107]

Private William E. Morris of Company M recalled speaking with his half-brother, Private Byron Tarbox of Company L (in Custer's battalion) as the columns began to disperse; Tarbox yelled:[108]

> "Look out for your scalp, Bill. The Indians don't like red-headed fellows."

"Bill" Morris did not have time to respond. According to First Lieutenant George Wallace, in a letter nine days after the battle, after receiving his orders Reno ordered his column forward at a gallop, which they maintained for another mile and a half.[109]

Major Reno and his battalion arrived at the Little Bighorn River (2:40 p.m.).

To accomplish his mission, Major Reno and his command had to cross the Little Bighorn to advance into the valley. But first they had to cross to the left side of Reno Creek in order to descend to the Little Bighorn. Somewhere during this period, Major Reno pulled the advance guard back to the battalion. Sergeant Henry Weihe's diary presented an interesting observation:[110]

> "When we arrived at the first teepee [Lone Teepee] we found the Indians gone. Then a brisk trot was ordered and a detachment was sent to the front as a kind of advance guard. Lieutenant Hare was in charge of this party, which consisted of Sergeants White [Weihe], and O'Hara, Corporal Scollin [Cody], Blacksmith Newell and Privates Meier, Gordon, Turley, Gallenne, Braun and Thorpe. These ten men moved forward until the Indians were sighted, and then Major Reno directed that we should join our company. We had now arrived at the Little Horn River and we at once proceeded to cross."[x]

Only Braun and Thorpe could be considered new troops, the other eight had been on some type of operation before. One period source stated that companies frequently put seasoned troops into the first "set of fours" in column because the commander had confidence in their shooting abilities.[111] It is thus possible that this advance guard – sometimes referred to as vedettes – which had two "fours" in it, would have been pretty competent and be able to fight well ahead of the rest of the column. Daniel Newell would later clarify several aspects of this advance guard and state that it was under the command of Sergeant Charles White (Henry Weihe).[112] Newell also later said that Hare was told to take ten men from Company M and draw the Indians out from under cover – and that Newell was the first man called to go.[113] Researcher Walter M. Camp noted that "Frank" Neely was also part of the advance guard.[114]

This study believes that Major Reno may have recalled the advance guard at "the flat" to inform them of his new orders, but then pushed another advance guard, possibly some of the same troopers, out forward. Several other sources have stated that Major Reno was very concerned that during his entire march the Indians were attempting to lure his command into a large ambush, a tactic they had employed before successfully on the frontier, when Indians used decoy warriors to lure cavalry forces forward or totally concealed all the warriors.[115]

[ix] Reno Creek was obviously not named that in 1876. Troopers in interviews simply called it "the creek." The Crows referred to it as "Ash Creek." It was later called "Sundance Creek" and finally "Reno Creek."

[x] Newell actually was not officially selected to be a blacksmith until after the company returned to Fort Rice.

Arikara scouts – known as "wolves for the Bluecoats" by the Plains Indians – were out front, about a half-mile ahead, looking for the Indian ponies.[116] Behind them the advance guard – probably 500-600 yards ahead of Reno and his main body – was ensuring that no enemy trap was set, while Reno and the other officers, including Captain French, checked potential fording sites at the Little Bighorn River. Given doctrinal deployment, the advance guard would have arrived at the Little Bighorn crossing site when the main body was still 400 yards away.[117]

Reno's battalion moved out smartly from "the flat" and crossed to the left bank of Reno Creek about five minutes later. Reno's command then moved three-quarters of a mile to the Little Bighorn.

Beginning at about 2:40 p.m. Company M crossed the Little Bighorn first at what would later be called Ford A – followed by Company A and Company G – in a column of twos. The men watered their horses at this point, but Captain French was a veteran commander and knew the momentum of the advance had to be maintained. Therefore, he positioned a non-commissioned officer in the middle of the Little Bighorn to keep the company well closed-up.[118] First Sergeant Ryan recalled the events:[119]

> "We arrived at the bank of the Little Bighorn and waded to the other side, and here was a very strong current and there was quicksand about 3 feet deep. On the other side of the river we made a short halt, dismounted, tightened our saddle girths, and then swung into the saddle."

Company M's Private Edward Pigford had his own recollections of the events:[120]

> "When we were riding down to the ford before the first fight on the day before, I didn't feel afraid, but several times I wondered how it felt to get shot."

Pigford was about to find out.

The immediate path to the Little Bighorn passed to the left of a small knoll near the bank. Although there was a larger trail around the right, Reno picked the left path and the column entered the water. About 50 feet wide, with water up to the bottom of the troopers' stirrups, the column had difficulty maintaining close order as horses – parched from hours of riding since last quenching their thirst – began to drink from the cool, refreshing river. It was a hot day and almost windless.[121] Troopers leaned down from their saddles as well, filling their near-empty canteens, all of which added to some confusion and congestion at the crossing site.[122]

• • •

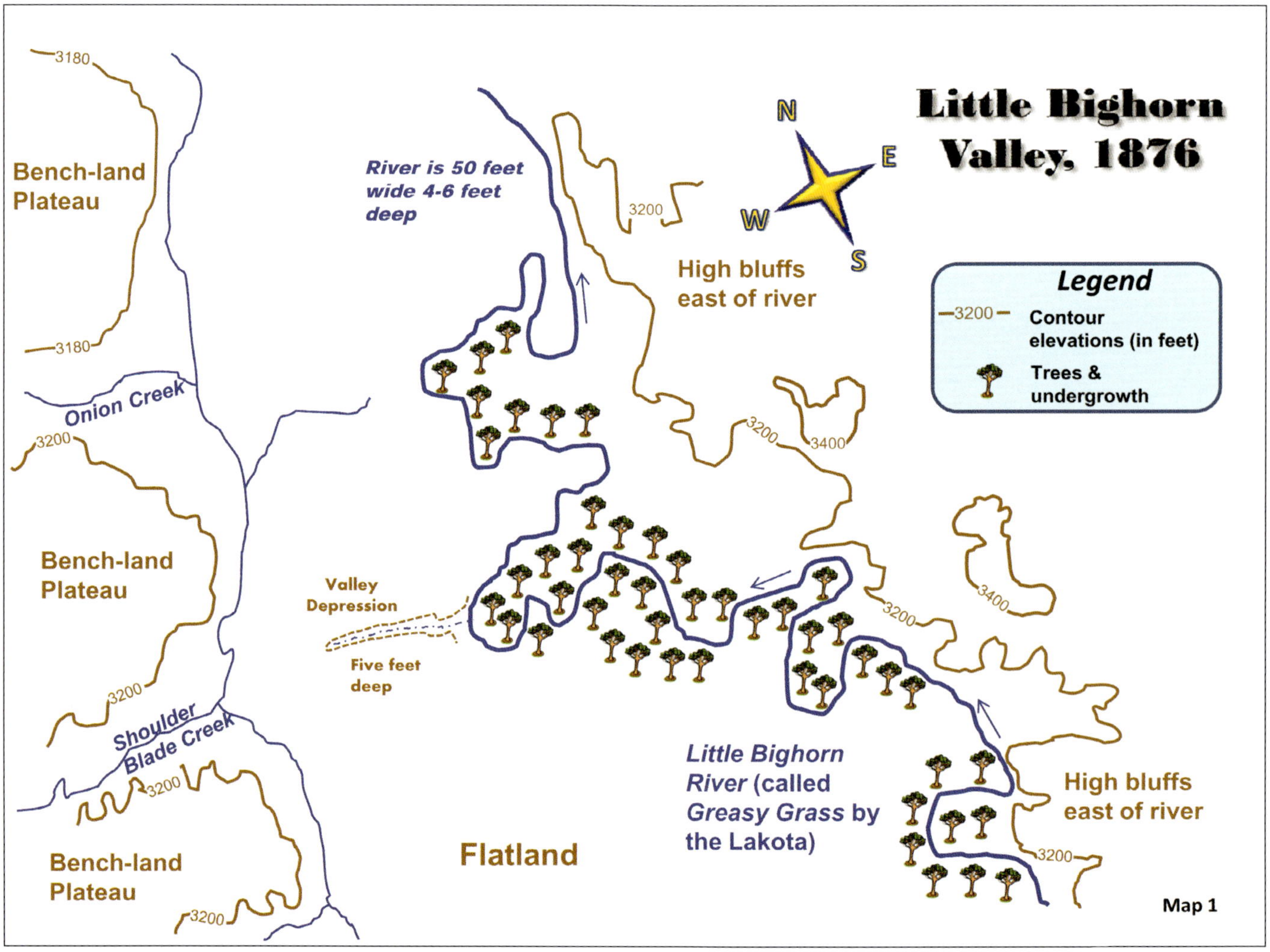

The Little Bighorn River, called the Greasy Grass by the Lakota, and the Little Goat River by the Arikara, obviously played a major role in the events that transpired on June 25, 1876.[123] At this point in the river's course – which flowed from south to north – the waterway was generally from 20 to 40 yards wide, and at ordinary stages from two to five feet in depth. Without taking into account the banks of the river, a horse could generally wade across most locations as the river bottom is predominantly flat; in other places, the widening river reduced current speed and increased depth to where a horse could swim across. In the summer of 1876, however, the summer came late, with snows melting later than usual and producing deeper water, which was clear and icy cold that June. The banks of the river were – and are – steep, resembling tiny, muddy cliffs; this acute gradient limits entrance and exit points for fording; in fact the stream is only fordable by horses at certain limited locations – often hundreds of yards apart.[124] At this time of year, big black mosquitoes were especially blood-thirsty along the river.[125]

Along much of the riverbanks, cottonwood trees grew thickly, mixed in with some box elder and ash trees. The underbrush consisted of small willows, dogwood and roses – much of it a thorny mess, and providing some limited concealment for small game avoiding predators. Sometimes these green vegetation belts were over 100 yards wide, at other points they were only one-tree deep. Significant bluffs – ash-gray in color – often rise immediately along the eastern side of the river; these cliffs can feature shear drops of 100 to 200 feet from their crowns to the valley floor below. As at the river banks – but on a larger scale – there are limited pathways down the bluffs; these rugged coulees, looking like painful, giant, brown gashes in the earth, twist and turn as they gouge downward from the rolling ground above. To the west of the river, the prairie undulates steadily higher until it meets flat-topped, elevated bench lands rising a half mile away.[126]

The floor of the valley in those days was generally flat and open; scant remnants of oat grass, wild rye and barley survived the previous grazing of Indian ponies. Sage and bull-berry bushes sprouted in small clumps here and there, with prickly pears – a type of small cactus – and prairie dog villages dotting the landscape.[127] Because of the recent Indian migration, much of the valley floor was covered with three to four inches of fine dust.[128]

In the general vicinity of the great Indian village and the ensuing battle, there were four fords – areas which could be fairly easily crossed by cavalry – provided, and this is an extremely important caveat, that the cavalry was not under enemy fire while attempting to cross. The southernmost ford, just above the mouth of Reno Creek, was where Reno's detachment first crossed the Little Bighorn River, and became known later as Reno Ford or Ford A. The next ford, approximately at the foot of Medicine Tail Coulee, was named Minneconjou Ford. It received this name after the battle, as it was located opposite the Minneconjou circle of wigwams in the village; Minneconjou Ford is sometimes referred to as Ford B. The third ford became known as Cheyenne Ford (also known as Ford C) and was about one mile north of Minneconjou Ford, somewhat north of the Northern Cheyenne (*Sahiyela*) circle of lodges in the village.[129] Recently a fourth ford has entered the discussion of the Little Bighorn battle. Known as Ford D, this crossing site was north of the Indian village and northwest of "Last Stand Hill," and may have been approached by part of Custer's force near the end of that portion of the battle.

What was not a proper ford was a location along the Little Bighorn River that was two miles downriver from Reno Ford and one mile south of the Indian village. With steep banks and some buffalo trails cutting gashes in the earth around it, this location could be physically crossed but only under great peril. It would later become known as the Retreat Ford.[130]

• • •

The company finished crossing the Little Bighorn (2:50 p.m.) and Captain French began moving through a timbered area on the Indian side of Ford A.

A myriad of actions occurred at this time. Once the horses finally crossed the stream and got out of the way of follow-on companies, Company M troopers probably dismounted and adjusted equipment including saddles, saddle blankets and all tack. This took a few minutes; undoubtedly some of the troopers were so nervous about their upcoming baptism of fire that they had to relieve themselves, which added a minute here and there. Then Captain Thomas French moved his unit through the timber on the western side of Ford A – which was later reported to be anywhere from 50 to 200 yards wide – at a slow pace, which may have taken another five minutes.[131]

Once free of this constricting terrain, the detachment went into a column of fours formation, with Company M in the lead, Company A second in the order of march and Company G bringing up the rear; as Reno would not have given the order to advance down the valley until all three companies were ready to do so, this order probably did not come until about 3:05 p.m., at the earliest. Some minutes later, Reno ordered the lead two companies brought on line with Company M on the right, and Company A on the left, with the command "Advance in columns of four, left front, into line." Company G was trailing the other two.[132] Sergeant Henry Weihe reported that the order to draw pistols was given at this time. It was probably about 3:10 p.m.

• • •

Cavalry troopers usually carried their revolvers on the right hip, with the butt forward and muzzle pointing behind. As most men were right-handed, most troopers drew their pistol with their right hand by turning their wrist and hand inward, grasping the butt of the revolver and drawing it clear of the leather holster with a twisting movement, which became known as the "cavalry draw."[133]

• • •

Down the valley some two miles from the formation was a place where the Little Bighorn swung west out into the prairie – it had no name then but would later be called the Garryowen Loop. To the west, Weihe could have seen that the plain extended west to some low bluffs; the open distance from river to bench land was about one-half mile wide. Over the previous five weeks, Company M had ridden 500 difficult miles; these last two would be the hardest of all. That would be made clear in an instant when, at this moment, Frederic Gerard[xi], an interpreter who had been with the Crow scouts, rode up to give his observations to Major Reno:[134]

> "Major, the Indians are coming up the valley to meet us."

[xi] Frederic F. Gerard was born in St. Louis on November 14, 1829. He attended Xavier College and made his first trip up the Missouri River in September 1848, and later married an Arikara woman with whom he had three children. In 1864 Gerard served as a scout for General Sully's expedition against the Sioux. On July 6, 1872 he was hired as the post interpreter at Fort Abraham Lincoln; he remained in this position until 1883. He was later employed with the Pillsbury flour mills. Frederic Gerard died in St. Cloud, Minnesota of arteriosclerosis on January 30, 1913; he is buried in the cemetery at St. Benedict's Covent at St. Joseph, Minnesota.

At this point, Reno's detachment looked like an accordion going down the valley; units sped up, slowed down and then sped up again to maintain proper intervals. In the lead was Second Lieutenant Luther Hare with his advance guard of troopers and a few Arikara and Crow scouts. The element was galloping down the valley and Private Jean "Frenchy" Gallenne was complaining that they were riding too fast, and that Captain French had not ordered them to move at that quick a pace. Hearing the complaint, Private Dan Newell yelled at the trooper:[135]

> "Shut up! What's the odds whether you gallop or walk? If you are going to be hit, you will be hit anyway."

The two troopers were in the same "four;" Newell was the Number One, while Gallenne was the Number Four.[136] After all the miles put on the horses throughout the campaign, exacerbated by the last day's advance, it was probably a slow gallop at best.

In addition to advance guard duties, the Indian scouts were attempting to capture some of the Lakota and Northern Cheyenne pony herds west and southwest of the Indian village. At least two hundred yards behind them – sometimes more, sometimes less, the change in distance resembling an accordion – was Major Reno and his small command group of a bugler, perhaps two messengers and one or two others, possibly his adjutant as well. Hare and the advance guard were probably taking hand and arm instructions as well as verbal orders from Major Reno and Second Lieutenant Hodgson, which was causing some confusion.[xii] Behind Reno another 100 yards were his three companies, Company M on the right, Company A on the left and Company G following the two.[137] Again the distances between the companies were probably always changing, causing the troopers to sometimes ride faster, sometimes slower.

In addition to the scouts on the left, other Arikaras were searching for Lakota ponies along the Little Bighorn riverbed. After crossing the Little Bighorn, six scouts (Boy Chief, Red Star, Strikes Two, Little Sioux, One Feather and Buffalo Ancestor) turned right along the river and rode north.[138]

Second Lieutenant Luther Hare began to veer left, heading for Shoulder Blade Creek; Reno, his command group and Company A

[xii] Benjamin H. "Benny" Hodgson was born on June 30, 1848 in Philadelphia, Pennsylvania. He graduated from West Point in 1870, ranking 45 of 58 cadets in his class. After graduation he was appointed a second lieutenant and assigned to Company B of the 7th Cavalry. After serving on the Black Hills expedition in 1874, Hodgson went on detached service at Shreveport, Louisiana. By this time Hodgson was in a bad frame of mind and had decided to leave the service. According to Douglas Paul Westfall, *Letters from the Field: Wallace at the Little Big Horn*, during his return to Fort Rice, while in St. Louis, Second Lieutenant Hodgson threatened to shoot a soldier and had to be restrained by First Lieutenant Donald McIntosh, who later placed Hodgson under arrest at Austin, Minnesota on April 24, 1876. The Sioux expedition began before any potential court-martial proceedings could be started. Second Lieutenant Benjamin Hodgson was killed in action close to the Little Bighorn River during the fighting in the valley on June 25, 1876. "Benny" Hodgson is buried at Laurel Hill Cemetery – Section 10, Lot 126 – in Philadelphia.

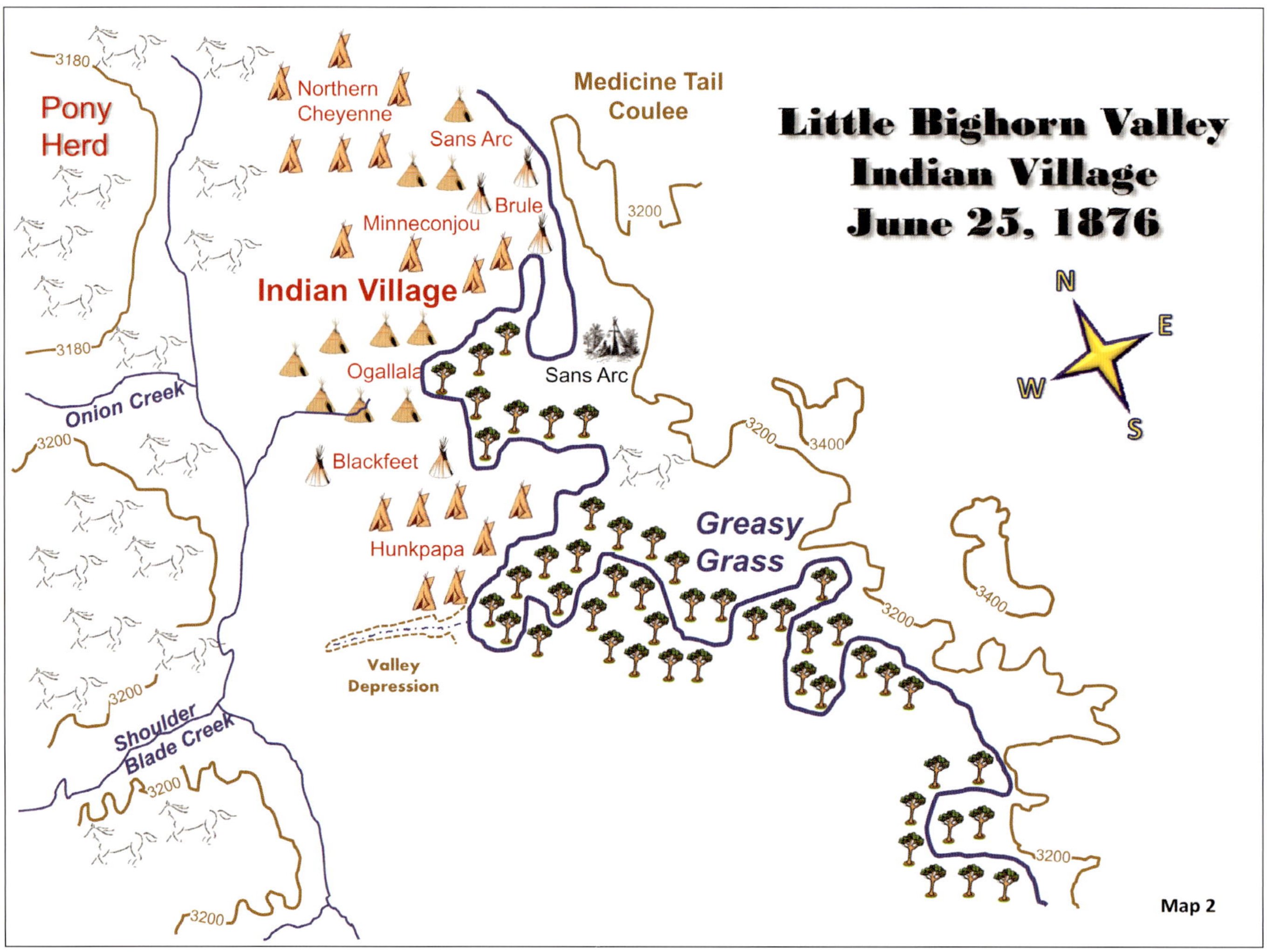

began to veer as well. But Company M probably hugged the Little Bighorn to the right; French could not be sure what was in there; in any case a gap started to develop between Company M and Company A. Wanting to address this developing vacant space, Major Reno ordered Company G forward from its rear position to form on-line between the forward two companies.[139]

The forty to fifty warriors, seen by Frederic Gerard, were protecting their withdrawing village from the Lone Teepee area, not the immense main encampment stretching almost two more miles downstream and spilling westward for one mile toward some low hills where the immense pony herd was grazing. The lead elements of Reno's column could see some of the ponies at this point but only guess at the size of this new village. However, Gerard knew the real truth.[140]

• • •

The big village was immense. Closest to the cavalry was a circle of Hunkpapa lodges. Following Indian custom, a circle of lodges belonged to one tribe; each circle generally was always located in the same place relative to the other circles. The Hunkpapa this day were led by Sitting Bull, Crow King, Gall and Black Moon. To the north of the Hunkpapa was a circle of Minneconjou lodges; this tribe's leaders were Hump, Lame Deer and Fast Bull. To the north came the Sans Arc tribe, led by Spotted Eagle and Fast Bear. Further north, under the leadership of Crazy Horse, were the Oglala. Smaller groups of Brulé, Blackfeet Lakota, Two Kettle, Santee, Yankton and Yanktonai rounded out the Lakota. Still further north were the Northern Cheyenne, with Two Moon, Little Horse, White Bull and Lame White Man. Around the edges of each tribe were temporary campsites of unmarried warriors and married men who had left their families at the reservations. The Lakota had been at the site for a few days; according to Northern Cheyenne warrior Soldier Wolf, the Cheyenne had only been there one night.[141]

Each tribe normally had three or four warrior societies (*akicitas*), which constituted the tribe's military forces. The Lakota societies included the Kit Foxes (*Tokalas*), Badgers (*Irukas*), Plain Lance Owners (*Sotka Yuhas*), Brave Hearts (*Cante Tinzas*), White-Marked Ones (*Wicinskas*) and Crow Owners (*Kangi Yuhas*).[142] Cheyenne warriors identified with the society they belonged to; Lakota warriors were more likely to be identified by their tribes.[143]

Membership in warrior societies was by invitation; some members were volunteers such as the suicide boys who pledged to fight to the death in certain engagements. [i] Each warrior society elected its own leading chief and up to nine "little chiefs." Dr. Thomas B. Marquis estimated that at the battle there may have been 20 leading chiefs and up to 180 subordinate chiefs.[144] Northern Cheyenne warrior Wooden Leg recalled the following *akicitas* among his tribe:[145]

- Elk warriors: leading chief – Lame White Man; little chiefs – Left-Handed Shooter, Pig, Goes After Other Buffalo, Plenty Bears, Wolf Medicine, Broken Jaw, A Crow Cut His Nose, White Hawk and Tall White Man.

- Crazy Dog warriors: leading chief – Old Man Coyote; little chiefs – Black Knife, Beaver Claws, Iron Shirt, Little Creek, Snow Bird, Crazy Mule, Strong Left Arm, Red Owl and Crow Necklace.

- Fox warriors: leading chief – Last Bull; little chiefs – Wrapped Braids, Plenty of Buffalo Bull Meat, Little Horse, Sits Beside His Medicine, Two Moons, Bears Walk on a Ridge, Mosquito, Rattlesnake Nose and Weasel Bear.

Above the warrior societies were the leadership societies, composed of patriarchs past their prime, famous older hunters and warriors and distinguished spiritual leaders. Their function was to serve as a brake against the more impetuous youth, who wanted to solve every problem with fighting. Lakota leadership societies included Big Bellies (*Naca Ominicias*), Tall Ones (*Miwatanis*), Owl Feather Headdresses (*Iyuptalas*) and White Horse Owners (*Ska Yuhas*).[146]

All-in-all it was the largest known gathering of Plains Indians ever assembled on the North American continent. Just considering the pony herds, there were from 12,000 to 15,000 horses. Between the tribes, the 1,200 lodges contained a minimum of 7,000 people of which at least 2,000 were warriors, although some historians have estimated the figure at several times that.[147] Two thousand warriors led by 20 premier warrior-leaders – and up to 180 up-and-coming combat leaders – would be a formidable force.

• • •

George Custer had 575 to 580 troopers riding under the colors of the 7th Cavalry.[148] And he had perhaps half the number of truly reliable senior leaders as the Lakota and Northern Cheyenne.

Major Marcus Reno, in a later estimate, had 112 of those cavalrymen riding with him; other sources would place his command at 134 officers and men, and 16 Indian scouts, while at the high end historian John Gray postulated 140 troopers and 35 Indian scouts.[149] A Company M veteran – Private Jean Gallenne – however, later wrote that each of the companies was between 30 and 60 men strong, with Company M having only 35 troopers.[150] Reno was not one of those reliable leaders as events would prove, although at this point in the advance he rode at the front of his main body, the best position from which to exert personal leadership; this would be his first real taste of Indian warfare. The Lakota had known of the approximate location of the regiment, but only Box Elder, an old blind Cheyenne, had a vision of the enemy arriving so soon.[151] Most of the others, if they contemplated time-distance factors, would have guessed that the earliest any action would occur would have been the following dawn – certainly not at mid-day.[xiv] But they knew something was out there; Crow Indian Scout White-Man-Runs-Him would later say that Lakota scouting parties had Custer's command under surveillance from the time it left camp at the mouth of Rosebud Creek.[152] Tracking the regiment would not have been that difficult according to Private Charles Windolph, a later Medal of Honor winner:[153]

> "Shod cavalry horses, you know, cut up the grass so a half-blind man could follow them."

Many years later Private William Morris of Company M described what happened as the command pursued the warriors fleeing from the first village discovered by the Lone Teepee:[154]

[xiii] Northern Cheyenne suicide boys who fought at the battle included: Little Whirlwind, Cut Belly, Closed Hand and Noisy Walking.

[xiv] Henry Weibert, local expert on the battle and historian in his own right, vehemently disagreed that the tribes did not know the cavalry was coming. He maintained in his book *Sixty-six Years in Custer's Shadow* that they did and even positioned warriors on the flank at Shoulder Blade Creek to ambush Reno's advance.

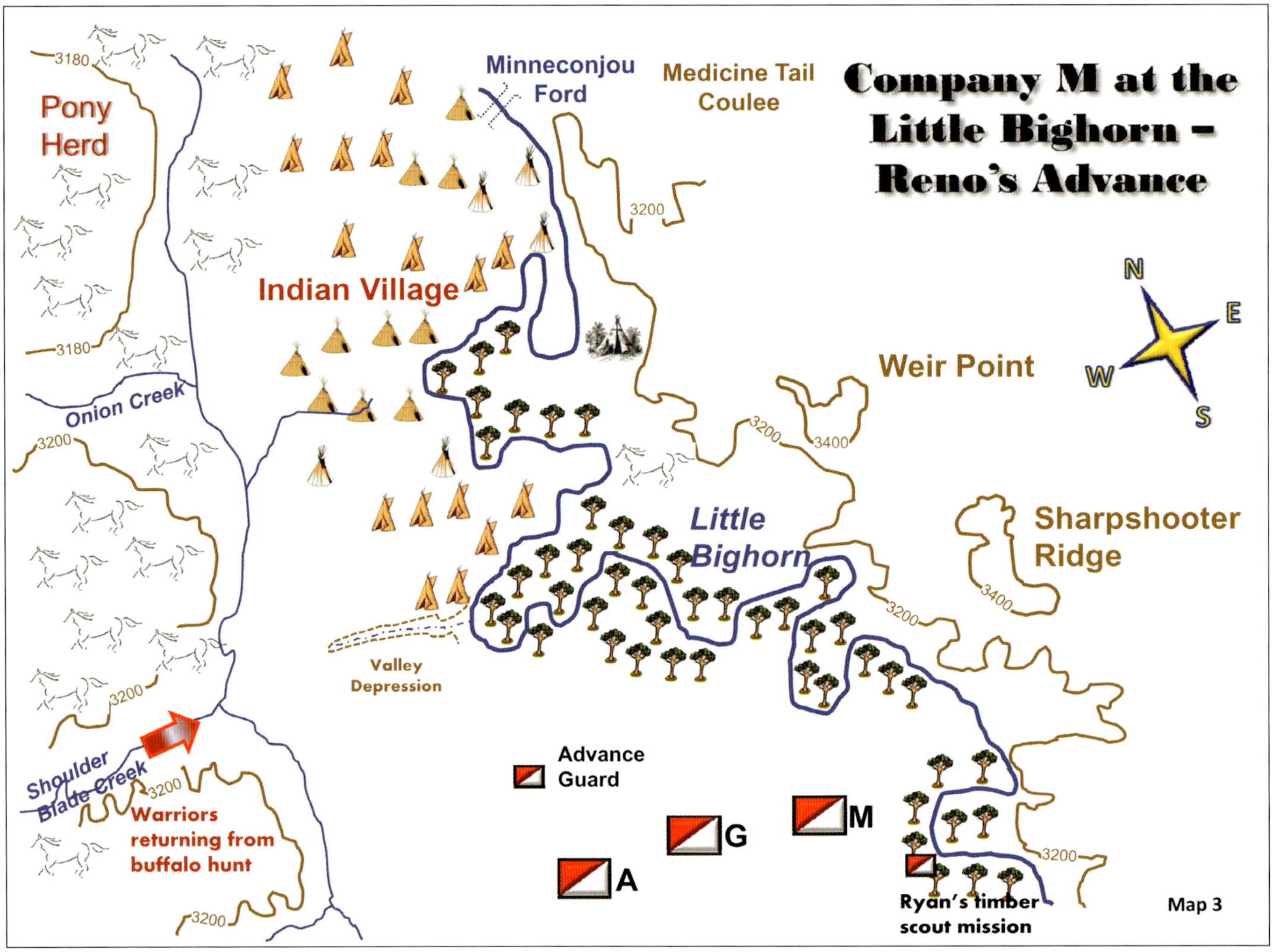

"We saw a party of about one hundred Indians before we reached the river; we pursued them across the Little Horn and down the valley. As soon as we forded, Reno gave the command, 'Left into line, gallop — forward, guide, center,' and away we went faster than I had ever ridden before. The Indians rode as fast as they could, and the battalion in line of battle after them. A body of at least two thousand came up the valley to meet the one hundred or more we were pursuing. They immediately made a flank movement to our left and a stand, [and] opened a galling fire…"

As Captain French advanced, he perceived that there were upward of 40 warriors from the first village, originally spotted fleeing from the Lone Teepee area, paralleling his formation, moving through the timber along the Little Bighorn to his right front, possibly firing intermittently at his unit. It is likely that the 40 warriors that Captain French saw were the same 40 that Frederic Gerard observed.

Captain Thomas French was a cagey, veteran commander and would have wanted a flank guard – under his command – to screen his exposed right flank, both to prevent these warriors from remaining along the Little Bighorn and also to prevent them from getting behind his company, as he advanced. He, therefore, ordered First Sergeant Ryan to explore the woods contiguous to the Little Bighorn.[155]

It is unknown whether Ryan received the order to recon the right flank before Reno's command to move up the valley because French anticipated a problem, or whether the order came during the advance. Based on post-battle statements by various men, it appears that Private Roman Rutten, Private James W. Darcy, Private Hobart Ryder and Private William E. Morris constituted part of this scout force.[156] Ryan later said that Captain French told him to take 10 men on the mission; for tactical cohesion the first sergeant probably took two "fours" and possibly an additional sergeant; they did not intend to go in advance of Captain French – the advance guard was doing that mission – but probably attempted to remain abreast of him to his right. Private James W. Darcy remembered that this detachment advanced as far as the first teepees of the Indian village.[157] This detachment thus went several hundred yards further than where the skirmish line would be established and would have to move from that exposed position south to link up with Captain French and the rest of Company M.

Reno's command did not make their veer in a completely straight line, but rather in a slight curve that paralleled the Little Bighorn. He was guided by an old, unused Indian trail, not the recent main Indian trail a few hundred yards to the west.[158] The ground was fairly flat and quite open, with only some sagebrush sticking up, as the grass had earlier been trampled flat by thousands of Indian ponies over the last several days. Reno's men would have seen sheer rugged cliffs some two to three hundred feet high on the right bank of the Little Bighorn. Impossible to climb by either horse or man – except at a few deep ravines and coulees that slashed down from the heights to the water's edge – the cliffs concealed the village from sight for anyone approaching from the east until they reached the edge of the bluffs.[159]

Meanwhile, Second Lieutenant Hare, seeing that the Indians had indeed been drawn from cover, told his advance guard – and Private Daniel Newell:[160]

> "Men, join your troop. In place of us drawing the Indians, they are drawing us."

Major Reno then yelled "Charge!" One soldier from Company A later recalled that he was near the major and Second Lieutenant "Benny" Hodgson at the time; he observed both men take a hefty swig from a half-full flask of whiskey.[161] Part way down the valley, about a half mile from Garryowen Loop, Reno probably dispatched his striker, Private Archibald McIlhargey – who rode a fast horse – at this point to go to Custer to report that the Indians were advancing, not retreating.[162]

The dust was thick, made more so by a group of about 50 warriors riding back and forth ahead of the cavalry intentionally creating the temporary visual imparity; at least one historian wrote that some of the warriors set intentional fires to create smoke in the valley as well. He also observed that warriors often raced their ponies back and forth before a fight to give them their second wind.[163] The dust and smoke was not so thick, however, to prevent the advance guard cavalrymen from seeing a shallow ravine ahead of the advance – some five feet deep and 10 feet wide – that had once been part of the river's bed and was now a small unnamed intermittent tributary; Reno would have to halt the command before reaching it.[164]

Had Reno been more experienced, or more resolute, he might have veered the command around the obstacle and continued the attack into the village – which either would have won the day or led to his own destruction, but Reno chose not to do so.[xv] The warriors from the village were at least 500 yards away at this time. Most were not mounted; it was customary for warriors to picket their best horses near their lodges at night, ready for instant action. In the morning, and June 25 was no exception, young men would lead these horses first to water – in this case the Little Bighorn – and then to the area of the large horse herds for grazing. Most of the horses this day were in the large pony herd hundreds of yards away. Northern Cheyenne warrior Wooden Leg later said that tribal herds were kept separate from each other.[165]

But there was a wild card. According to one source, an unknown number of warriors, perhaps up to 200, had been hunting buffalo earlier in the day to the west of the big village and the pony herds. By this time, these hunters were returning home with meat for the village inhabitants, generally following Shoulder Blade Creek, which the Lakota called Muskrat Creek. As the warriors approached the village from the southwest, they saw the advancing cavalry to their right front, somewhat lower in elevation, as outliers of this warrior party were on the high ground south of Shoulder Blade Creek. This chance encounter, although local historian Henry Weibert postulated that these warriors were waiting in ambush for Reno, meant that even at the moment of attack, Reno's detachment was in jeopardy of being flanked to the west by mounted warriors.[166]

Captain French undoubtedly led his company in the advance. Riding close to him would have been Private Frank W. Sniffin, who carried the Company M colors during the fight in the valley, and Trumpeters Charles Fischer and Henry C. Weaver, who would have translated French's verbal orders into bugle calls that could be heard by every soldier.[167]

Private Frank W. Sniffin was born in New York City on September 12, 1857. He enlisted in the 7th Cavalry Regiment on September 1, 1875 in St. Louis, Missouri and joined Company M at Fort Rice on October 21, 1875. Previously a laborer, Frank Sniffin stood 5'7" tall, had blue eyes, light hair and a fair complexion.[168]

Trumpeter Charles Fischer hailed from Breslau, Germany, where he was born in 1844. He appears to have first enlisted on February 9, 1867 in Brooklyn, New York under the name of Charles Hanke, serving in Company G of the 1st Artillery Regiment. He was discharged after his term of service, but re-enlisted the same day on February 9, 1870. A hunter in civilian life, Fischer deserted on October 5, 1871; he surrendered to authorities on March 11, 1872 at Rock Island Arsenal, Illinois, and was sentenced to two years imprisonment at a military prison. His sentence was remitted on January 4, 1873 and he was transferred to Company I of the 5th Infantry Regiment as a trumpeter; he was discharged on July 15, 1875 at Fort Leavenworth for "intemperate habits" and for not being a band musician, which he had earlier claimed at enlistment. He enlisted as Charles Fischer on September 14, 1875 in St. Louis, Missouri; he arrived at Company M at Fort Rice on October 21, 1875. Almost immediately, Fischer got in trouble. On November 6, 1875 a Fort Rice Garrison Court Martial convicted him of being drunk and fined him $5.[169] A second Garrison Court Martial convicted Fischer of being drunk during stable call on January 31, 1876 and fined him $2.[170] Charles Fischer was 5' 41/2" tall, had gray eyes, dark brown hair and a fair complexion; he was nicknamed "Bounce."[171] At the Little Bighorn "Bounce" carried a .45 Colt pistol, with a serial number of 16341.[172]

Trumpeter Henry C. Weaver was born in Philadelphia, Pennsylvania in 1842 and was a hat-maker. Papers show that Weaver's initial enlistment in the army was on August 11, 1869. However, at a later court martial he testified that he had first joined the army in 1861, making him a Civil War veteran. Weaver served with Company G of the 7th Infantry Regiment and was discharged at Fort Shaw, Montana Territory on August 11, 1874. Weaver re-enlisted in Pittsburgh, Pennsylvania on May 1, 1875. He joined Company M on October 21, 1875 as a trumpeter. Weaver was listed as 5'5" tall, with gray eyes, dark hair and a ruddy complexion. Both trumpeters Weaver and Fischer were experienced soldiers, which was critical for performing their duties.[173]

First Sergeant John Ryan later described the advance:[174]

> "We started down on a trot and then at a slow gallop. Between the right of my company and the river bank, there was quite a little underbrush and bull-berry bushes. Captain French gave me orders to take ten men off the right of my Company M, and form a skirmish line, so as to cover the brush from our line to the riverbank, as Indians might be lurking there. We advanced in that formation from 1 1/2 to 2 miles until we came to a piece of heavy timber...When we got to the timber we rode down an embankment into the timber and dismounted. This was where the channel of the river had changed and was probably 20 feet lower than the level of the prairie."

[xv] The exact location of this depression has flummoxed historians since the battle. Some believe that it was a dry or intermittent creek bed that fed into the Little Bighorn and has since disappeared. At least one other expert feels that the depression was an extension of Should Blade Creek slightly to the west – this study has chosen the latter for the maps.

Part-way down the valley, Private Daniel Newell of Company M saw Custer's battle flag on the high bluffs east of the Little Bighorn.[175] It appeared that the commander's overall plan was going well, with parallel columns ready to strike the Indian village at different points. But the plan of attack began to break down almost immediately according to Company M's Private William Slaper:[176]

> "Our horses were scenting danger before we dismounted, and several at this point became unmanageable and headed straight for the opening among the Indians, carrying their helpless riders with them. One of the boys, a young fellow named Smith [Private George E. Smith] of Boston, we never saw again, dead or alive."

According to early Little Bighorn historian Dr. Thomas Marquis, Indian odor always excited horses familiar only with white men and Indian ponies were always frightened by the scent of white men.[177] It appears that Company M may have had some of the least-skilled horsemen or the most unruly horses of Reno's detachment.[178] Private George E. Smith, for example, had been in the cavalry less than one year; he arrived at Company M at Fort Rice on October 21, 1875. Prior to his enlistment he had been a shoemaker in Boston, Massachusetts. He was born in 1850 in Kennebunk, Maine; his enlistment papers indicate that Smith was 5' 61/2" tall, had gray eyes, brown hair and a fair complexion.[179] On January 14, 1876 George Smith was outside his barracks after taps and got into a disturbance with another trooper. A Garrison Court Martial at Fort Rice two days later convicted Smith of "committing a nuisance" during the commotion and fined him $2.[180] Smith's lack of experience as a horseman and his aggressive nature probably contributed to his demise.[xvi]

Major Reno's detachment halted in the valley and began to form a skirmish line (3:25 p.m.).

Deciding not to continue the attack into the village, Reno ordered the command to halt and form a skirmish line, the formation of choice in many Indian fights from Montana to the Rio Grande.[181] The skirmish line extended several hundred yards in length; Company M would have somehow moved to a position on the far left (west) flank of the line toward some bluffs – probably doing this on foot after dismounting; some of the 7th Cavalry Indian scouts were on the left; to the right of Company M was Company A; to the right of Company A was Company

[xvi] John G. Bourke, *On the Border with Crook*, has asserted that when Reno's detachment charged the village, Chief Crazy Horse was dismounted, but seeing a single soldier riding into the village from the south, ran up to the mounted trooper and struck him in the head with his stone war-club, killing him. Crazy Horse then mounted the fallen trooper's horse; it is possible that the cavalry trooper was Private George Smith of Company M who lost control of his mount in the village.

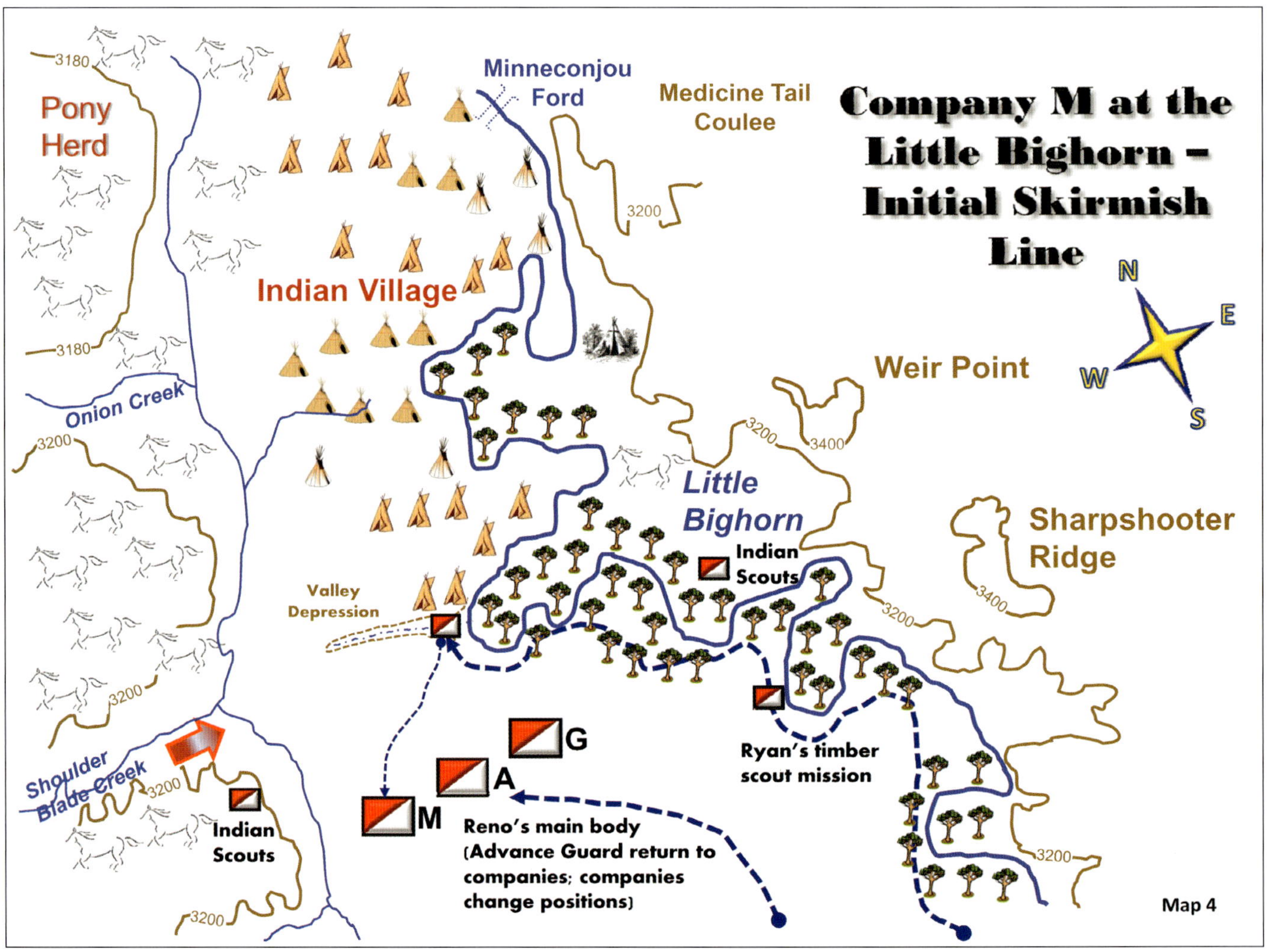

G.[182] On the far right, Reno's line rested on a dry, wooded creek bed.[183] The *Cavalry Tactics* manual specified that the habitual interval between skirmishers was five yards, with intervals of 15 yards between squads, and there is no reason to conclude that this was not the case – at least at the beginning of skirmish line operations.[184]

According to Second Lieutenant Luther Hare, about 300 yards in front of the skirmish line was a coulee which concealed many of the Indians from the cavalrymen until the Indians emerged toward Reno's units; Reno's attack had struck the Hunkpapa and Blackfeet circle of lodges; the bulk of which were about 900 yards away. The distance to the closest lodges is difficult to ascertain. Some survivors stated these near teepees were 400 yards from the skirmish line, but Second Lieutenant George Wallace observed that the dismounted skirmishes halted just 70 yards away from the nearest lodge. Other Indians in the timber to the right front of the skirmish line also fired at the cavalrymen from an oblique direction, which made seeing them more difficult.[185] About this time First Sergeant Ryan signaled Captain French that the river bank was clear of warriors. Ryan's men may have been even closer than 70 yards away at this point. This would have triggered the orders for all Number Fours on the skirmish line to gather the horses to make for the timber. Colonel Edward M. Offley, a veteran cavalryman – who served some years after the battle with three of the 7th Cavalry officers who had been at the battle – explained how this happened:[186]

> "This was normal, routine drill training. At the command, 'Fight on foot,' Numbers One, Two and Three from each set of four would dismount, link their horses together with the 'skirmish link,' a strap with a snap hook, and Number Three would pass his reins to Number Four, who would remain mounted. The 'guidon-sergeant' would then take the led-horses off to any available cover."

If Company M followed this procedure to the letter, Private Frank Sniffin, the guidon-bearer, may have left the skirmish line and led all the Number Fours to the timber line.

Actions at this time probably also triggered Major Reno to send a second messenger, Private John Mitchell, with a report that Reno had halted to form the skirmish line; Mitchell's body was later found with Custer's command, so it is logical to assume that he passed that information to Custer or Cooke.[187]

On the right, in the area previously cleared by First Sergeant Ryan and his detachment, some of Custer's six Arikara scouts, who had gone in this direction, began to shoot at a few Lakota women and children on the flats to the east of the Little Bighorn River.[188] Because of old hatreds, the scouts wanted to kill these Lakota non-combatants; Custer, on the other hand – as he had successfully done several years before – understood that by capturing non-combatants alive, he could possibly leverage the Lakota warriors into giving up the fight. Northern Cheyenne warrior Tall Bull said in an interview two years after the fight that some of Reno's troops set a few of the village dwellings on fire; this possibly could have been Ryan's men or the six Arikara scouts.[189]

• • •

In 1866 Congress authorized the army to recruit up to 1,000 Indian scouts to serve on the frontier. Scouts frequently enlisted for periods of up to six months and were authorized to re-enlist again and again; some Indian scouts in the cavalry enlisted for longer periods. Indian scouts, as opposed to civilian scouts, were allocated by military district, which then assigned a certain number of scouts per fort. The purpose of Indians as scouts in the army on the frontier was not to conduct line fighting. Instead, their three primary missions were to trail and locate the enemy, skirmish the enemy to gain time, and either run off or capture enemy pony herds to reduce the warriors' mobility.[190]

Such an independent set of missions sometimes proved hazardous to the friendly scouts, who at times were fired on by the cavalrymen, who mistakenly believed they were the enemy; this would happen at the Little Bighorn. The army attempted to better identify friend from foe by having the scouts wear distinctive brass insignia on their headgear that showed a pair of crossed arrows with the initials "USS" (United States Scout) above it. But the device only measured one-and-a-half by two-inches and was thus not able to be distinguished at any substantial distance. Moreover, the insignia was not used in the 7th Cavalry at the Little Bighorn. At this point in the battle the scouts had indeed located the bulk of the warriors and now began to attempt to capture part of the huge Lakota pony herd to the west. The pony herd would be guarded by a few of the older boys, but with so many ponies, the Arikaras would be able to grab several each.[191]

• • •

The Number Four in each group of four cavalrymen remained mounted and led the three other horses into these woods using the snap rings on their bridle straps.[192] Orderlies road their own horses and led the horses of the officers to the woods as well. Chief Historian John Doerner believes that one trumpeter from each company would have gone with the horse-holders as well.[193] Somewhat later, once they had reached the woods, the Number Fours walked the horses a little further to an old riverbed in the middle of the woods. It appears that the Number Fours were led by Lieutenant Hare as they left the skirmish line for the woods with their charges.[194] Private Jean Gallenne was one of the horse-holders in the timber and later reported:[195]

> "I am mounted and hold six frightened horses. The bullets, and the branches of trees cut off by them, fall like hail around me."

That is an interesting observation and indicates that this particular Number Four was in control of seven animals, instead of the customary four. If Gallenne was not an exception, it may indicate that Captain French – understanding his lack of relative numerical strength – attempted to make up for it by having fewer horse-holders, thus increasing his firepower on the company skirmish line.

Private Jean Gallenne may not have noticed that bullets were not the only missiles to be falling in through the trees – after all, he may never have seen a bow and arrow before. From behind cover, dismounted Lakota warriors used a "rainbow" trajectory to fire high-arcing, iron-tipped arrows into timber areas where cavalrymen and horses bunched. These hissing, plunging arrows further added to the confusion and chaos of the situation.[196]

Another trooper who lost control of his horse was Private Roman Rutten. His excited mount began to circle around the three advancing companies soon after the column crossed Ford A, as Rutten held on for dear life; he appears to have gotten further into the village than any other trooper who survived. Some of his fellow troopers found his predicament amusing at this point; they would soon change their tune.[197] As First Sergeant Ryan and his detachment withdrew to join Company M on the skirmish line, Rutten's horse lunged ahead of the detachment, rode through part of the Hunkpapa circle of teepees and disappeared in the dust.[198] Rutten later told Walter Camp that he finally got the horse to begin to circle to the right and he rode through the timber to safety.[199] Private John "Snopsy" Meier had a similar harrowing adventure, but successfully shot his way out with his Colt .45.[200] Private Daniel Newell recalled the incident:[201]

> "Snopsy Meyer's [Meier's] horse got away from him and bolted through the Indians' line on our right, but he got back to us, shooting his way out with his six-gun. How he did it is a mystery."

Captain Thomas French very likely had some 47 to 52 troopers riding with him in the company, once the outriding security details returned to his control – the spread of potential troopers being the result of how many men were with the pack detail. As Company M set up the skirmish line, First Sergeant John Ryan observed:[202]

> "Private [Henry] James Turley of my troop, when we arrived at the timber and had orders to halt, could not control his horse which carried him towards the Indian camp. That was the last we saw of him."

"Jim" Turley – just as George Smith before him – was carried by his horse into the Hunkpapa village, but First Sergeant Ryan may have been incorrect about his fate. Unlike Private Smith, Henry Turley had been a cavalryman for almost four years and was an experienced rider. Born in Troy, New York in March 1851, he enlisted in the army on October 29, 1872 at Troy, New York and joined Company M on December 9, 1872 at Unionville, South Carolina. Previously a laborer, Henry Turley was 5' 41/2" tall, had brown eyes, black hair and a dark complexion. "Jim" seemed accident-prone. In April 1874 a horse stepped on his left foot, resulting in Turley spending seventeen days on quarters. On May 24, 1874 Private Turley was accidentally shot in the right forefinger and right thigh and spent two months in the hospital. For a time there was some doubt that he would recover complete use of his right thumb, but "Jim" finally recuperated and was pronounced fit for duty. He then spent six months detailed to herd cattle on post that were used to feed the troopers.[203] On July 28, 1875 a Fort Rice Garrison Court Martial convicted private Turley of four specifications[xvii] of conduct prejudicial to good order and military discipline and sentenced him to a fine of $10 and hard labor for one month.[204] "Jim" Turley was killed at the Little Bighorn, but probably later in the fight.

According to Private John Sivertsen:[205]

> "We rode [in the valley] until we got pretty close to the Indian camp. By this time we saw Indians on every side, the bluffs on the left being crowded with them. The command was given, 'Dismount and fight on foot!' and we did so, forming a skirmish line, five feet apart."

Sivertsen's description of "bluffs on the left" appears to refer to the bench-land plateaus on either side of Shoulder Blade Creek across the valley to the west; this area was part of the grazing ground for the vast Indian pony herds and undoubtedly the cavalrymen would have seen increasing numbers of warriors run to this area to retrieve their mounts for combat. Sivertsen continued the description of the early action:[206]

> "The Indians were shooting at us from all sides. Then we went into a clump of timber. I was the tallest man in the troop – they called me 'Big Fritz' – and I was Number One in the line. When we dismounted in the timber I gave my horse to Number Four, who held it [by the reins, using the snap rings] with his own and two others."

John Sivertsen, nicknamed "Big Fritz," was born on December 10, 1841 in either Jensen or Frondorm, Norway. He came to the United States in 1870. A blacksmith by trade, Sivertsen enlisted on June 19, 1873 into the 7th Cavalry with Captain Thomas French, joining Company M the same day. "Big Fritz" was one of the taller men in the company at 5'10"; he had blue eyes, sandy hair and a fair complexion. He had participated in the 1873 Yellowstone Campaign and the 1874 Black Hills Expedition. He was also nicknamed "Big Swede." Sivertsen helped take care of livestock in the regiment from November 1874 to April 1875 and later spent six months running the post sawmill, ending that duty in April 1876. At the Little Bighorn on the morning of June 25, 1876, "Big Fritz" was designated the Number One in his "four."[207]

Private William Morris provided this view of the skirmish line fight:[208]

> "We had entire confidence in our officers and in ourselves, and went to work smiling and as cool as if we were at target practice. In less time than it takes to relate it, the Indians were on three sides of us. We were ordered to lie down, and every man that I could see, except Reno and French, were fighting lying down. Reno walked along the line giving instructions to the men, while French was calling his men's attention to his own marksmanship with an infantry long-tom that he carried.
>
> While in this position, the man next on my right, Sergeant O'Hara, was killed. The smoke obscured the line, but bullets were taking effect all along it. We were perfectly cool, determined, and doing good execution and expected to hear Custer attack. We had been fighting lying down about fifteen minutes when one of our men came from the timber and reported that they were killing our horses in the rear. Every troop had, at this time, suffered loss and the enemy was closing in, despite our steady and deadly fire."

Morris later said that his own carbine jammed after he fired some 30 rounds in it.[209] First Sergeant John Ryan, whose security detachment may have gotten the word late to form a skirmish line, based on their positioning to the flank during the advance, added additional detail concerning the skirmish line:[210]

> "Some of the men laid [*sic*] down and others knelt down. At this particular place, there was a large prairie dog town and we used the mounds for temporary breastworks. We got the skirmish line formed and here the Indians made their first charge. There were 500 of them coming from the direction of their village. They were well mounted and well armed. They tried to cut through our skirmish line. We poured volleys into them, repulsing their charge (my troop being on the extreme [left] end of the line) and emptying a number of their saddles."

[xvii] There is no mention of the actual crimes committed which is unusual. The punishment also seems pretty severe, considering other punishments that Fort Rice Garrison Courts Martial routinely handed down for even more serious offenses. The Garrison Court Martial also convicted Private John McArthur of Company F, 6th Infantry Regiment of the same charges that day.

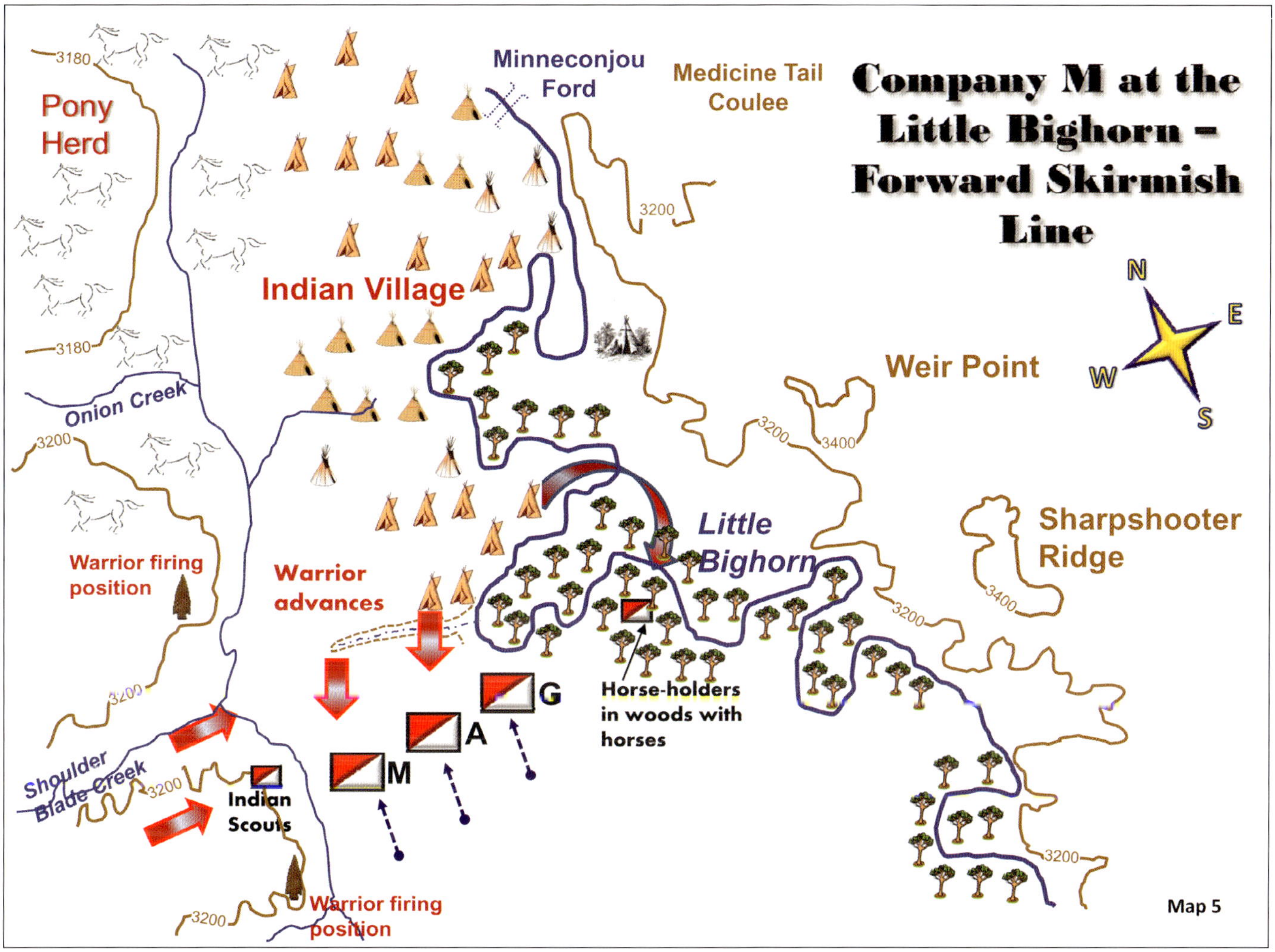

The troopers would have fired their initial rounds on command, reloaded and then continued to fire until given the cease-fire command.[211] After firing a few rounds from this initial skirmish position, the troops received orders to advance from Major Reno. The cavalrymen's targets were at extremely long range. Aiming was uncertain as at this great range – far more than the 800 yards, according to the manual – at which soldiers with normal eyesight would first be able to distinguish the movement of arms and legs. As the men could not distinguish this movement at the range the warriors were now, they had no way of knowing if the distance was 900 or 1,200 yards. That was important information as the 1873 Springfield Carbine sight had graduations stamped on the side for ranges of 100 to 500 yards; at greater ranges the rear leaf sight was used, which had settings up to 1,200 yards.[212] But the rear sight system did not have the ability to be set to account for different windage (lateral movements that would affect the strike of the round left or right of the target). Those soldiers who did not already understand these intricacies of their weapon were not going to learn them in a crash course on the skirmish line, when return fire showed them they had missed!

The men paced forward (north) some 75 to 100 yards, where many troopers assumed the prone firing position to have some sort of remote chance to engage the warriors who were now advancing across a wide front.[213] The left end of the entire line – immediately to the left of Company M – was anchored by the leader of the Arikara scouts, Bobtail Bull.[xviii] With Bobtail Bull on the left were scouts Bloody Knife, Forked Horn, Goose, Little Brave, Red Bear, Red Foolish Bear, Young Hawk, Half-Yellow-Face and White Swan.[214] It appears that Isaiah Dorman and Billy Jackson were on the skirmish line toward the left as well.[215] But there were problems.[216] Sergeant Henry C. Weihe (Charles White) later stated about Company M:[217]

> "[Captain French] was the first officer to get his Company out on the line of skirmishers. I was wounded as soon as I took my place on the line and was ordered to the timber, where I had the opportunity to see what was going on. The Captain told some of the men to take notice [of] that Indian on the gray horse to see if he'd fall after he fired; he fired and shortly after the Indian reeled out of his saddle and was dragged off into the bush."

Captain Thomas French later wrote that he believed that Reno's detachment, and by conclusion his own company, should have continued the charge into the village proper:[218]

[xviii] Bobtail Bull was later killed at the river crossing by a Cheyenne warrior; the two fired at each other simultaneously and both died. But another historian, Henry Weibert, believed that Bobtail Bull was killed at the start of the fighting on the left flank near Shoulder Blade Creek.

> "What made him [Reno] halt and dismount when he did is a matter in regard to which I am equally ignorant. It was not the kind of warfare to which I had been accustomed – and that was this – to be watchful, and prudent and never to take less than an even chance, but when once in do as is said to be the custom of the Donnybrook Fair – 'if you see a head, hit it.' I thought we were to charge headlong through them all – that was the only chance."

Captain French acted as though he was right in the midst of the brawling at that annual Irish fair near Dublin. Private Hobart Ryder recalled the actions of his commander:[219]

> "Captain French ordered the Company to deploy as skirmishers. We did so. Captain French stood within a very few feet of me. I saw him kill one Indian [riding a gray horse] I supposed and wound another."

One historian has postulated that Lakota warrior Good Bear Boy and Sitting Bull's favorite horse – which was injured just after Sitting Bull mounted him – were both wounded by Captain French's or First Sergeant Ryan's accurate long-range fire.[220]

Private Hobart Ryder had been born in New York City in 1846. A laborer by trade, he moved to Chicago, Illinois and enlisted on September 15, 1873; he stood 5' 71/2" tall, had gray eyes, dark brown hair and a fair complexion. Ryder joined Company M on October 21, 1873; he served as the company cook for a month a year later. On April 24, 1875 a Garrison Court Martial acquitted him of the charge of absent without official leave. He was court-martialed on January 20, 1876 and sentenced to confinement at hard labor for three months and a forfeiture of $10/month for three months; he was released from confinement in April 1876. Ryder's horse was named "Kaiser."[221]

Private William E. "Bill" Morris, who was also fighting close to his first sergeant and commander, later credited both Ryan and French with hitting several advancing Indians; the two were clearly the best shots in the company. Morris was born on May 1, 1854 in Boston, Massachusetts. A salesman by trade, Morris first enlisted in the army in his hometown on September 22, 1875, along with his half-brother Byron Tarbox who would end up in Company L. William Morris joined Company M on October 21, 1875.[222] He was 5' 71/2" tall, had brown eyes, auburn hair and a fair complexion. Morris was one of those wild young troopers who thought he could take on the world – he would be given that opportunity on this day.[223] In March 1876, Morris and another private left Fort Rice without authority and went a few miles up-river to hunt some wild game. While crawling toward some prairie chickens, roosting on a tree limb, the men had a hunting accident in which Morris accidentally shot his comrade through both knees. Doctors later had to amputate one of the trooper's legs, but Morris did not receive a court martial for the incident.[224] However, in early April 1876 a Garrison Court Martial determined that Private Morris had been insubordinate to Corporal McGlone and sentenced Morris to a $5 fine.[225] At the Little Bighorn "Bill" Morris rode a horse named "Stumbling Bear."[226]

• • •

To the left of Company M, on the westernmost tip of Reno's skirmish line, was "Lonesome Charley" Reynolds – Custer's Chief of Scouts and superlative guide, who had been ordered to accompany Reno for this phase of the fight. Reynolds was a legend; born in Warren County, Illinois on March 20, 1842, his father was a physician. Before moving to Pardee, Kansas in 1859, Reynolds attended Abington College. During the Civil War, Reynolds served with the 10th Kansas Regiment. After the war, he tried his hand as a trader and hunter, but kept to himself and earned the nickname "Lonesome Charley." One legend maintains that in 1867, when Reynolds was a buffalo hunter, he got into a fight with an army officer at Fort McPherson in which the military man lost an arm. Among warriors across the Plains, Reynolds was known as "Lucky Man" and "Hunter-Who-Never-Goes-Out-For-Nothing." Standing 5'8" tall, with gray eyes, Reynolds was often shy and soft-spoken. In 1876, he signed on with the 7th Cavalry for $100 a month for the expedition. But during the march from Fort Abraham Lincoln he developed an infected abscess on a hand, which severely limited his dexterity by the time of the fight. His friend, Grant Marsh, the skipper of the *Far West*, urged him to stay on the steamer for treatment but Reynolds refused, saying he would rather be dead than miss the upcoming fight.[227]

Reynolds would acquit himself well. Second Lieutenant Luther Hare would later write of the soft-spoken guide:[228]

> "I saw him several times during the fight in the bottom and, of course, noticed and was impressed by his wonderful coolness and apparent indifference to the warm fire that was being poured on us."

• • •

At this early point in the fighting, the men were in good spirits, talking and laughing – unaware of the exact danger that was preparing to fall on them.[229] Some leaders – especially Second Lieutenant "Benny" Hodgson, according to First Sergeant Ryan – were telling the troopers to fire low; this would have made it at least a little easier to adjust fire, based on seeing the strike of the round, and also because wounds to an enemy's thighs or abdomen were likely to be fatal with the big soft-lead slugs from the Springfield.[230] But other officers – and this may have included Captain French – seemed more concerned with personally shooting at and hitting enemy targets, to the detriment of exercising effective command and control of the fire of their subordinates.[231]

Historian Edgar I. Stewart, in his work *Custer's Luck*, stated that during the skirmish line fighting an order was issued for every other trooper on the line to go back to the horses and retrieve additional ammunition from his saddlebags, but post-battle testimony from Company M soldiers never mentioned this order. Guide George Herendeen later told researcher Walter Camp that he was on the extreme left of the skirmish line – which would have allowed him to initially observe Company M – just behind the line in a small swale; "Lonesome Charley" Reynolds and "Fred" Gerard were with him, he said. But Gerard seems to have told Camp that he and Herendeen tied their horses in the timber and took a spot to the rear of the skirmish line "where it rested on the timber," which would have been behind Company G, not Company M. At that time, Gerard said, there were no warriors within effective range, but he observed some warriors sitting on their ponies on the bluffs to his left.[232]

• • •

What should have transpired, concerning fire control, was for an officer or experienced non-commissioned officer to estimate the range to the target, either by using range estimations previously discussed or by setting his sights for a given range, firing and then observing the results. Once the leader had accurately assessed the range, he would communicate that distance to the troopers who would then set their sights to it for their own weapons and begin firing. As the enemy came closer or moved farther away, the leader would signal changes to the range and the soldiers would reset their sights accordingly. These subsequent adjustments were important. Because of the relatively low muzzle velocity of the carbine, the trajectory of the round was a high arc. Thus, if the sergeant called for the range to be set at 500 yards, but did not communicate any subsequent adjustments, by the time the warriors had advanced to a distance of 300 yards, the troopers' rounds would be sailing 12 feet over their heads![233] The sergeants would have to pull the load on fire control; First Lieutenant Edward Mathey was back in the pack train and Second Lieutenant "Jack" Sturgis was riding with another company, leaving Captain French as the only commissioned officer present.

• • •

Private Edward D. Pigford recalled that he personally fired only four or five rounds while on the skirmish line and said that the skirmish line was no sooner formed than it "broke up."[234] Dan Newell, showing how a mind under the stress of combat can have tricks played on it, thought that the company was on the skirmish line for two hours.[235]

The first Company M man to be observed to fall was Sergeant Miles F. O'Hara, who was killed either on the skirmish line or 50 yards from the timber – another example of the confusion in the fight – shot through the chest.[xix] According to Private Edward Pigford, O'Hara, lying in the sagebrush and amid the prairie dog mounds – which were along the skirmish line and behind which some troopers sought limited cover – did not immediately expire, but cried out for help as his comrades withdrew.[236] The fighting on the skirmish line continued for a few more minutes, but the Lakota began to flank Reno's skirmish line to the west, which extended only to a point half way to the low hills in the west. The Arikara scouts were on some of this rising ground, but they soon began to withdraw when the Lakota presence frustrated any attempt to capture grazing Indian ponies.[237] Examining Gregory F. Michno's *Lakota Noon: The Indian Narrative of Custer's Defeat*, it appears that his excellent analysis locates He Dog as one of the warriors on the flanking position. A member of the Oglala, He Dog was a veteran of the March 1876 Powder River fight and also had fought Crook's forces at the Rosebud just a week earlier.[238]

• • •

What the untested troopers in Company M and the rest of Reno's detachment were beginning to experience was the Lakota and Northern Cheyenne way of war. Based on experiences in animal hunting and inter-tribal strife, almost every warrior on the field of battle that day was a veteran. Their preferred manner of fighting cavalry was to: lure small numbers to advance and then spring an ambush or an attack from an unexpected direction; pressure the cavalry to retreat or attempt to move to a perceived more-advantageous position; swoop in on the flanks and rear of the moving column; and start eliminating the most-exposed elements first – all the while performing feats of tribal bravery as individual warriors.

Ten years earlier – armed primarily with bows, spears and a few firearm weapons – this style of warfare had met its match against the carbines and rifles of army forces. But by the time of the Little Bighorn, a large portion of the warrior force had firearms, many high quality, lever-action repeating arms such as Henrys and Winchesters. These weapons were accurate out to 200 or 300 yards and could fire many shots per minute, although George Custer once wrote that the Winchester was a good weapon up to 150 yards, beyond which its effectiveness diminished quickly.[239] But that rapidity of fire had its negative impact; weapons-developers found that they needed to keep calibers small and use less powder to avoid fragmenting the bullet in the barrel due to the enormous heat and stress generated by rapid fire.[240] Archaeological evidence has provided evidence that over 40 types of firearms were in Indian hands; some were older – flintlocks and percussion – but deadly nonetheless, while others were Civil War vintage Spencers and Sharps. The Model 1860 Spencer carbine fired a caliber .56/56 round, while the Model 1865 Spencer was in caliber .56/50 and had a seven-shot magazine – although the effective range was less than 200 yards.[241]

Additionally, some warriors were actually armed with captured .45 Springfield carbines, taken on the Rosebud battlefield a week before from Crook's forces (an engagement of which Custer was unaware). Recent statistical analysis of spent cartridges and bullets found on the battlefield postulate that the Lakota/Northern Cheyenne force may have mustered 597 to 697 individual firearms. One historian has indicated that it was an exception for a warrior to possess both a rifle and a pistol.[242]

Those warriors who did not have firearms had bows, which were still deadly in the right terrain – and the terrain, especially to the east of the Little Bighorn, was suitable for archery engagements due to the plethora of small ravines and gulches that allowed dismounted warriors to closely approach troopers from concealed positions. Although Plains Indian bows were capable of shooting an arrow a considerable distance, warrior accuracy with the weapon was developed primarily under 40 yards. In some instances, the warriors fired arrows in a high arc into positions they knew were concealing cavalry horses; any animal struck in the back by the sharp projectile was likely to stampede.[243] Earlier stone arrowheads had frequently been replaced by iron and steel arrowheads purchased from white traders, or made by imaginative warriors from iron wagon-wheel hoops, iron frying pans and steel barrel hoops.[244]

For close combat, many of the warriors carried six-to-seven foot lances with metal tipped heads. Most had knives, and many had either stone-headed clubs – that could inflict lethal blunt force trauma – or clubs with knife blades protruding at the end; some warriors even carried captured cavalry sabers obtained in earlier battles, as at the Little Bighorn the 7th Cavalry did not carry this weapon.[245]

Whether armed with firearm, bow, lance or club, the warriors' preferred approach to their quarry – beast or man – was from the right side, circling their targets in a counter-clockwise direction, so that arrows and bullets could be shot toward the left or close combat weapons struck in that direction, a natural motion that provided greater accuracy and control, rather than twisting on the horse to the right and then firing in that direction.[246] This maneuver was precisely that employed by the warriors against the skirmish line, passing around the left-hand side of the troopers!

• • •

[xix] It is possible that O'Hara did not die in the valley, but was assisted up to Reno Hill badly wounded, where he subsequently expired – based on much later forensic evidence, although no Company M survivor claimed to have done this.

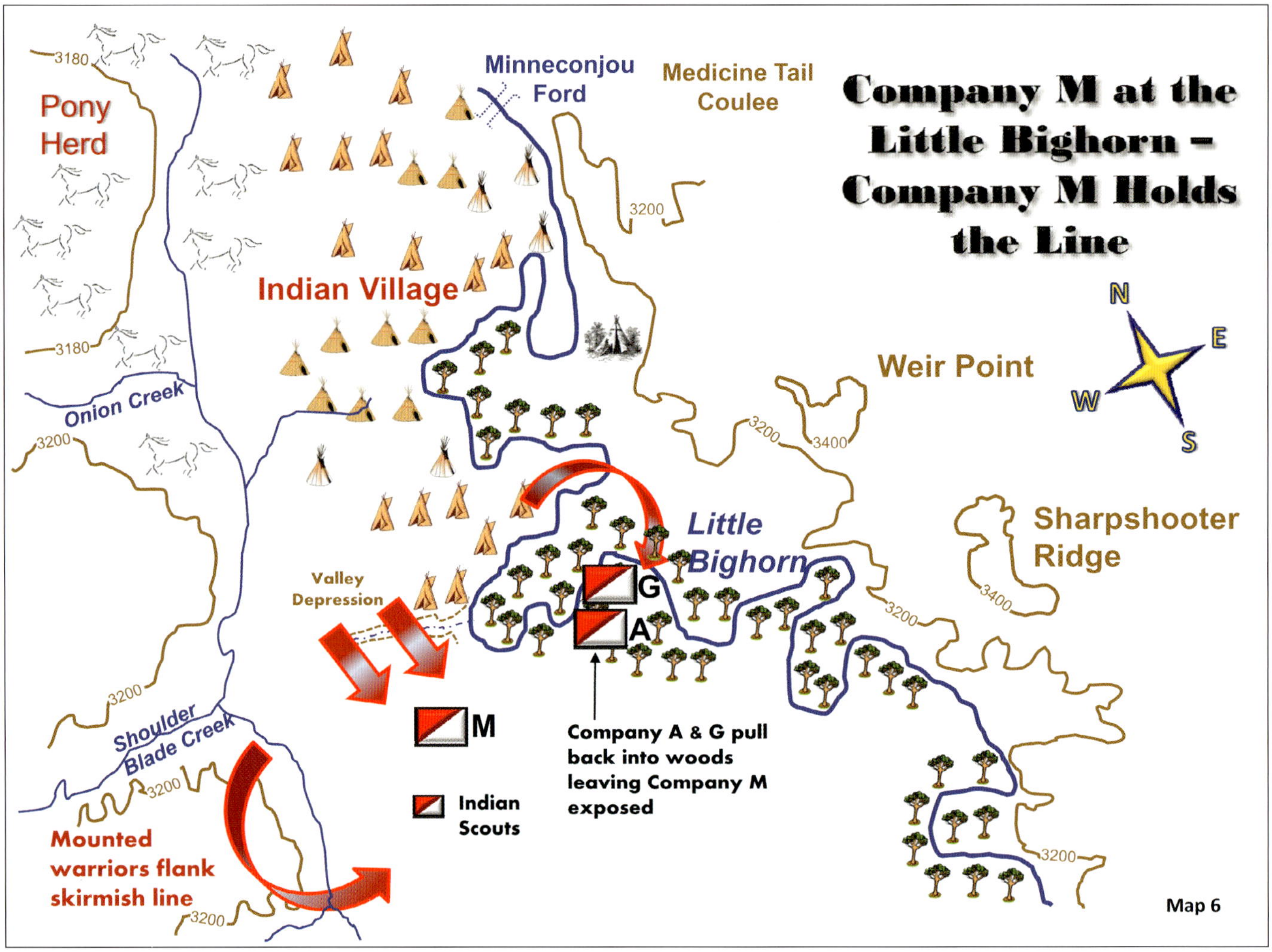

Major Reno's detachment began to withdraw from the skirmish line to a timbered area (3:40 p.m.).

The total time Reno's detachment spent on the skirmish line – the initial and advanced positions combined – was perhaps 15 to 20 minutes.[247] During this time, as some troopers ran low on ammunition, they were ordered to go back to their horses, grab their pasteboard boxes containing twenty rounds of additional carbine ammunition from their saddlebags and return to their firing positions – actions that would have taken them away from non-commissioned officer control and leadership for several minutes.[248] It appears that Reno, fearing for the safety of the detachment's horses, ordered Company G to the timber first, which left the skirmish line too thinly dispersed to be effective, but Larry Sklenar, in *To Hell with Honor; Custer and the Little Bighorn*, says that Reno and the officers of Company A and G were motivated to abandon the field to seek safer positions for themselves, and the men subsequently followed their leaders. In any case, the Company G troopers moved into the bottomland in the woods and took up hasty positions in the woods and along the banks of the Little Bighorn to protect the valuable horses from warriors attempting to infiltrate into the position from the north and the northeast – the warriors were now on both sides of the Little Bighorn.[249]

The skirmish line was shrinking and Company M, which in effect had been left hanging on an exposed flank, had to bend around to the south and also close east as Company G and A pulled out, heading for the horse-holders in the timber. By this time French's men were probably covering 200 yards of skirmish line and the distances between each man were getting perilously greater, thus dispersing fire, not concentrating it – a bad situation. At least 200 warriors had turned the left flank and were heading east across the valley.[250] Finally, Captain French ordered the company to withdraw, saying:[251]

> "Steady there men; I will shoot the first man that turns his back on the enemy – fall back slowly; keep up a continual fire, you damned fools!"

Private Hugh Moore later recalled the situation:[252]

> "When the Sioux charged our line I saw the Captain shoot one Indian himself and the Recruits that came the fall before [i.e., 1875] started to run, some few, the Captain called them back saying – 'I want every man to stand; the first man that runs I'll shoot him;' they all came back."

Private Hugh N. Moore was born in 1842 in Dorchester County, Maryland. A sail-maker, he enlisted in the army on August 24, 1872 in Louisville, Kentucky. Moore reported for duty at Company M on

September 1, 1872 in Unionville, South Carolina. Records indicate that Private Moore was 5' 71/2" tall, with gray eyes, brown hair and a fair complexion. They also indicate that Moore was an alcoholic. On February 12, 1875 Private Hugh Moore was treated for frostbitten toes. In June 1875 he served as the company cook. Moore served as a herder for post cattle in February 1876.[253]

We do not know who the men were who possibly considered running, but many of the recruits clearly had not been adequately trained before the campaign. Captain French did not have to shoot any of his men. As Daniel Newell later said of obeying his company commander:[254]

> "We went like a bunch of sheep."

Private Newell also heard First Sergeant John Ryan take charge and yell to his men:[255]

> "For God's sake, don't run! Fight as you retreat or not one of us will ever get out."

French and Ryan saved the unit. The troopers, firing as they went, crossed over 300 yards of open ground – and negotiated down a four-foot embankment that was part of the old river channel that had been carved away by river erosion – now in the concealed area in the timber. French's wheeling maneuver put Company M on the left of the new line formed by Reno's detachment, set up on the edge of the timberline. The men took positions behind the old riverbank, facing west; standing on the edge of the four-foot depression, Company M troopers for the first time that day had some protection from enemy fire.[256] The last men in Company M's line had to sprint for their lives, but Captain French and First Sergeant Ryan remained with the men, maintaining unit cohesion to the last, and the entire Reno detachment had closed in the timber by 3:45 p.m.[257] The warriors did not close at this point, but remained several hundred yards away; the warriors also did not increase their rate of fire.[258]

However, the troopers' problems were not over; ammunition was running low and the troopers continued to take turns going back to their horses to get additional rounds.[259] That now proved an even more difficult, time-consuming task as some of the horse-holders had released the animals in their charge during the chaos.[260]

The timber position was along an old dry-cut bank of the Little Bighorn, some three hundred yards to the east of the original skirmish line. The position faced west and southwest. In the confusion, the defensive line in the timber was not longer than 150 yards. Company G was on the right flank, close to a dry bed of the river; Company A held the center of the line; Company M held the left flank.[261]

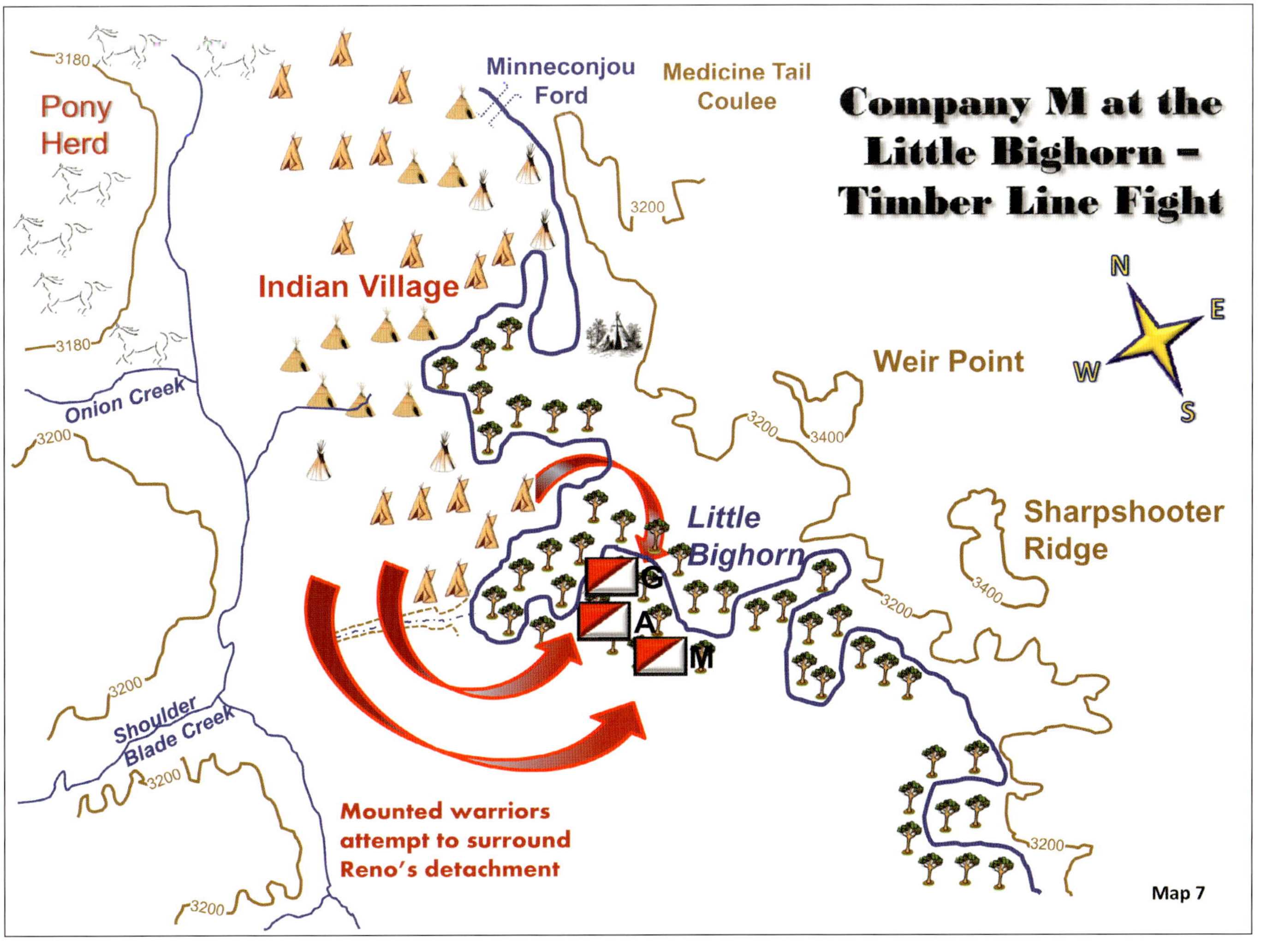

"Big Fritz" Sivertsen described the fighting in the woods:[262]

> "The fight in here [the timber] was very hot and men were falling fast. We could not see the Indians, but they were signaling all the time to each other with their little bone whistles, and they seemed to be on all sides."

Sergeant Henry C. Weihe (Charles White) picked up the action, indicating that the stay in the timber did not amount to a great deal of time:[263]

> "The column then commenced a retreat and retreated towards the timber and there they mounted and retreated out. The Captain [French] waited until all his men got out of the timber then followed up in the rear."

The timber area itself was a fairly effective defensive position due to the density of trees behind which the troopers could take cover and because of the thick underbrush which made it difficult for mounted Indians to quickly close with the cavalrymen. The ground could certainly be crossed by individual warriors, but it was not suited to a mass-charge from any one side, not that the warriors at this point had given any indications they would attempt that type of tactic. In the center of the timber was a relatively open area 50 yards wide and 100 yards long, where many of the horse-holders had led their mounts. The ground throughout, which in high water was flooded by the Little Bighorn, was quite gravelly; to the east of the Little Bighorn was bottomland lower than Reno's position and consisting of brush and fallen trees; to the north was the double-loop bend in the river (Garryowen Loop) that had to be traversed by the Indians attacking from that direction. As it also would now have to be crossed by Reno to get at the village, any thought he may have had of continuing the attack north was gone.

By this time hundreds of warriors had roughly surrounded the timbered loop of the Little Bighorn, where the cavalrymen were defending. In an attempt to drive Reno's men out of the woods the warriors set fire to the thick grass near the river, but the moist vegetation limited the spread of the blaze, producing thick, dense smoke instead.[264] Private Daniel Newell, who later said that the fighting sounded like "one continuous roar," described the warrior tactics at this point:[265]

> "The Sioux would gallop in bunches and deliver their fire and then retreat, their places to be filled instantly by another bunch."

By now, Major Reno had no intention of continuing the attack, soon decided the timber position was untenable and ordered that the command to move back to the Little Bighorn to cross to the east and higher terrain. However, instead of ordering the trumpeters to sound the appropriate bugle call – which would have been repeated by each company trumpeter and thus heard by all the soldiers – he gave the order verbally. Reno later stated that he sent Second Lieutenant Benjamin Hodgson with the order to leave the woods, but it is not clear that this actually occurred.[266]

Some of the men heard the order and mounted their horses; others did not, being too distant to hear his command. Confusion began to increase and the troopers' fire slackened, which permitted many Indians to advance to close range, where their fire became more effective. First Sergeant John Ryan described this situation in the timber just before his unit began their withdrawal toward the east side of the Little Bighorn:[267]

> "As we mounted, I looked in the rear in the direction of the river and saw the Indians completing the circle riding through the brush. I mentioned it to Captain French, say: 'Captain, the Indians are in our rear.' He made the reply, 'Oh, no, those are Custer's men.' Just on the moment one of those Indians fired and Private George Lorentz of my company, who was number one of the first set of fours on my left, was shot, the bullet striking him in the back of the neck, coming out of his mouth. He dropped tip forward out of his saddle. Just then, the Indians fired into us in good shape. I said to Captain French, 'Captain, the best thing we can do is cut right through them.' By this time they had us surrounded. They were on higher ground than we were."

Captain French requested that several men try and bring the wounded man along with them. Private William Morris responded to Captain French's request and attempted to help the mortally-wounded Lorentz, but the dying man said:[268]

> "Go on; you cannot do me any good."

George Lorentz had been born on September 30, 1851 in Holstein, Germany. He enlisted in St. Louis, Missouri on November 13, 1872. Lorentz was assigned to Company M on December 9, 1872 at Unionville, South Carolina. Previously a painter, Lorentz stood 5' 61/2" tall, had gray eyes, dark brown hair and a fair complexion. From October 1874 to May 1875 he served as a cook at the post hospital.[269] On February 6, 1876 he was detailed to serve a week as a nurse in the same hospital.[270]

Historian John S. Gray believed that Dr. Henry Porter then came along and attempted to treat Private Lorentz.[271] Dr. Porter picks up the description in his own words:[272]

> "A soldier was shot in the little clump of trees where I was. I dismounted and found him mortally wounded. Reno ordered the troops to mount and "charge." A running fight ensued. My horse was rearing and plunging, and I had all I could do to hold him. The Indians, in their mad pursuit of our troops, did not notice me in the timber. They were passing within ten feet of where I was. I placed laudanum on the wound of the soldier and bandaged it as best I could, and again mounted my frightened horse. As I was leaving the poor soldier said: 'For God's sake, Doctor, don't leave me to be tortured by those fiends.' Bullets were flying thick and fast, and I turned my horse loose and caught up with our troops, who had gotten half a mile away."

But Lorentz had previously told his comrades to leave him, whereas fatally wounded Sergeant Miles O'Hara had begged them not to depart his side. Could it be possible that Dr. Porter gave the laudanum not to Lorentz, but instead to Sergeant O'Hara, who then managed to mount a horse and get to Reno Hill before he died? That possibility would explain the location of O'Hara's remains, which appear to have been found on Reno Hill years later.

Private William Slaper described how difficult it was to hear in the timber:[273]

> "I could hear nothing but the continual roar of Indian rifles, the sharp resonant bang-bang of cavalry carbines mingled with the whoops of the savages and the shouts of my comrades."

The confusion increased and reached a crescendo when a warrior – who could have been part of a group that crept close to Company M's positions – shot Bloody Knife, Custer's favorite scout who was on his horse next to Major Reno. With Bloody Knife's blood and brains all over Reno's body, the major panicked, ordered the command to dismount and then to remount; then Major Reno put his spurs to his horse and dashed for the river in an "every man for himself" moment. Captain French was more in control; but even he was getting confused. French later stated:[274]

> "When he [Reno] started to that hill he had told me, not one minute before that he was going to fight."

But the veteran Captain French quickly reacted to Reno's change in plans. Almost three years after the valley fight, Private Hobart Ryder recalled:[275]

> "After leaving the skirmish line we went to the woods where we left our horses. I heard Captain French give the order 'M Company, follow me.' I supposed that we were going to make a charge. We started to move out of the woods."

But the reaction of the captain may not have been quick enough. During these moments a group of warriors snuck through one of the dry riverbeds to a position 30 to 90 feet from Company M's line. As Company M troopers began to pull back to get their horses, the warriors, who one source said were mounted, fired a "shower" of bullets – likely from repeating rifles that were quite accurate at this short range – that wounded Private Daniel Newell, Private Frank Braun and Private Henry Klotzbucher.[276] It is possible that the volley also hit Bloody Knife. "Lonesome Charley" Reynolds was hit in the chest about this time as well.[277] Newell, hit in the left thigh, called out to his first sergeant:[278]

> "I am hit."

Either Sergeant Patrick Carey or First Sergeant John Ryan replied:[279]

> "Mount your horse my boy and stick to him. You are fighting Indians now."

In the turmoil it is very difficult to determine exactly who shot the troopers. However, historian Gregory Michno says that Cheyenne warriors Crooked Nose, Old Man and Turkey Leg fired a volley about this time and may well have targeted Newell, Braun and Klotzbucher.[280]

Private Frank Braun had been wounded in the face and left hip, which would later prove fatal. At the time he was hit, Braun was apparently squatting on the ground, when he was probably hit by a .44 round from a Henry or Winchester repeater.[281] Braun hailed from Berne, Switzerland, where he was born in 1848. A laborer, he enlisted in the army on September 23, 1875 in Louisville, Kentucky and joined Company M on October 21, 1875. Private Braun was 5' 61/2" tall, with hazel eyes, fair hair and a fair complexion. On February 10, 1876 he reported sick at the Fort Rice Post Hospital with catarrh, a respiratory infection.[282]

Private William Slaper, also of Company M, described what he saw during this close-range firing by the warriors that hit Klotzbucher:[283]

> "When I got my horse, there were not many of us left in the timber that I could see. Soon after, Private Klotzbucher, who was 'striker' for Captain French, was shot through the stomach, just as he was in the act of mounting his horse. He fell to the ground and I saw Private Francis Neely dismount to help him. I thereupon got off my horse and helped Neely drag the wounded trooper into a clump of heavy underbrush, where we thought he might not be found by Indians. William E. Morris, another comrade, came up at this juncture and helped us care for Klotzbucher. We saw he was probably mortally wounded, so we left him a canteen of water and hurriedly mounted again, dashing toward the river in the wake of our flying trooper comrades."

The last to leave Klotzbucher's side was Private "Bill" Morris. Henry urged his comrade to leave, but Morris would have none of it saying:[284]

> "Captain told me to take care of you."

Henry again told Morris to leave, and he finally did. Don Rickey, Jr., author of *Forty Miles a Day on Beans and Hay*, later surmised that Klotzbucher had been shot in the stomach by an arrow.[285] Private Henry Klotzbucher was born in Baden, Germany in 1848. He enlisted in Philadelphia, Pennsylvania on October 4, 1873 and joined Company M on October 21, 1873 at Fort Rice. A cooper (barrel maker) by trade, Klotzbucher served as the company clerk – which indicates he was proficient in English – and also was the "striker" (which was unofficially termed "dog-robber" by the other troopers, the joke being that an orderly would even steal scraps of food from the family dog) for Captain French. In this capacity he helped put up the commander's tent, helped cook his food, care for his horse and helped him pack out his gear. Henry also served stints as the post gardener, company cook and post hospital nurse. Klotzbucher was 5' 61/2" tall, had brown eyes, brown hair and a ruddy complexion.[286] Henry Klotzbucher got in a fight on October 29, 1874 and reported on sick call for contusions of his hand; he was returned to duty 10 days later. He was finding that the "Wild West" was a dangerous place and may have wanted a bit tamer work as in January 1876, he applied for an appointment as a hospital steward.[287] He held that position until March 31, 1876.[288]

• • •

In 1992 Jason Pitsch was searching on his ranch with a metal detector, part of a 10-year effort to discover artifacts of the valley fighting. Although Mr. Pitsch was not a professional archaeologist, he meticulously plotted every find on detailed maps and overhead photographs of the area. As a result of his painstaking work, he was able to accurately plot company locations on the skirmish line and the timberline and has been recognized for his efforts by many historians. On this particular day, Jason Pitsch made a startling find in the timber. In one small area, he found a dark-blue piece of a cavalry uniform, a pressed tin, four-hole uniform button and a pile of expended .45/55 cartridges – all of which are shown later in this book. This study has concluded that this pattern of artifacts closely resembles the remains of a hasty gravesite for one of the cavalrymen.

If that conclusion is correct, given that Pitsch has shown that this location was at the Company M timber position, we can use the process of elimination to determine who fought (the expended rounds) and probably died (the presence of a uniform) here. Private Frank Braun was fatally wounded in the timber, but he did not die of his wounds until October 1876 at Fort Abraham Lincoln, so this was not his position. Sergeant Miles O'Hara was fatally wounded in this vicinity, but modern forensic techniques indicate that O'Hara was buried up on Reno Hill; we can rule him out. That leaves Private George Lorentz and Private Henry Klotzbucher.

Private George Lorentz was shot through the back of his neck, with the bullet exiting his mouth. The force of the wound knocked him out of his saddle and on the ground. Assuming that the wound did not paralyze him, Lorentz would have been bleeding so badly that this and the fall would have severely limited him from putting up an effective defense – there probably would not have been a pile of expended cartridges where he lay. But it is possible that he did fight. Klotzbucher was wounded in the stomach, possibly by an arrow; such a wound would be fatal, but not for some time; until he collapsed from loss of blood he could have put up a fight. Klotzbucher, as did Lorentz, urged his friends to continue on without him; that act shows that either was mentally prepared to help his friends as best he could; in this case it would be covering fire for his buddies. Before his comrades left, they pulled him to a pile of dense undergrowth to hopefully conceal him from the foe. But Henry, or George, may have gone down fighting, not hiding, and these remnants found by Jason Pitsch mark their own personal "Last Stand."

• • •

Henry Klotzbucher's would-be rescuer, Private Francis "Frank" Neely hailed from Collinsville, Ohio, where he was born in 1850. He stood 5'10" tall, had gray eyes, light hair and a fair complexion. A painter in civilian life, "Frank" Neely enlisted in the 7th Cavalry on April 8, 1871 at Louisville, Kentucky, and was assigned to Company M at Unionville, South Carolina on May 30, 1871. He reported sick with a fever on September 19, 1871.[289] First Sergeant John Ryan would later credit Private Neely as being one of the best marksmen in the company; he was obviously a veteran cavalryman. But Private Neely was quick to head to greener pastures and deserted on June 20, 1873 at Fort Rice.[290] Six months later he returned to the army and got into cavalry operations in full swing. Winter was cold on the prairie and on November 18, 1874 Neely was seen by a doctor for a frostbitten ear; he would return to duty eight days later. In February 1875 he served as the company cook.[291]

Major Reno's detachment began to retreat upstream on the west side of the Little Bighorn from the timber area (3:50 p.m.).
The three companies remained in the timber for a very short period of time, perhaps 10 minutes. Later archaeological finds of roughly 500 expended cavalry-weapon rounds in their timber positions indicates that

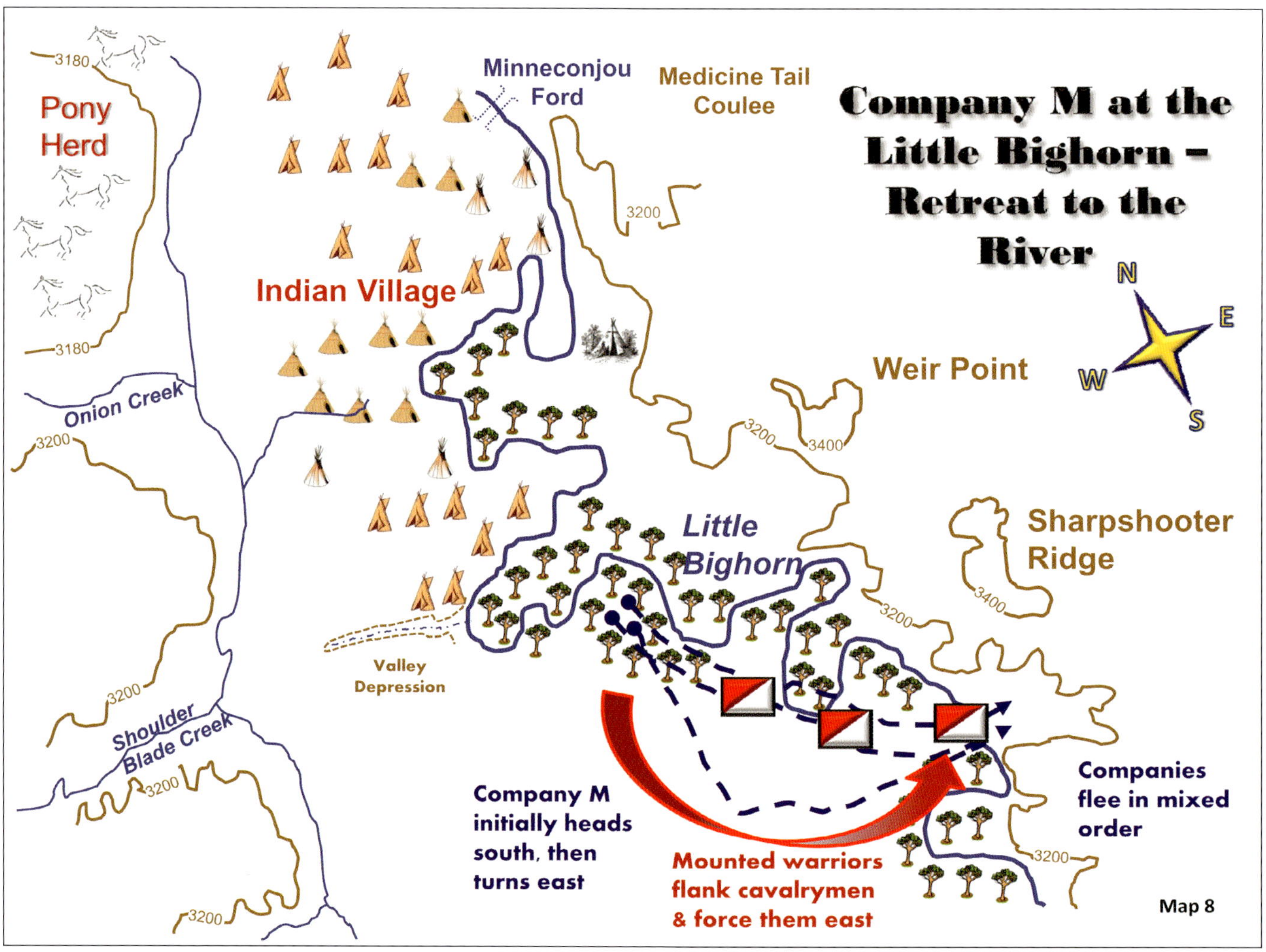

each man averaged firing about five rounds each – which clearly could have been accomplished in just a few minutes.[292] The river was about three-quarters of a mile away and the terrain was generally open – a potential death trap for the cavalrymen, who would be outmaneuvered by their pursuing warrior foes. It would be a 17-minute ride out of *Dante's Inferno*. Although many accounts indicate that Company G – with Lieutenant George Wallace in the lead – was the first element out of the timber, the three companies essentially rode intermixed; it appears, however, that Captain Thomas French brought up the rear of the mass of Company M – riding a little to the right of his men and acting as a one-man rear guard.[293] White Bull, a Minneconjou, who was already a famous warrior and a nephew of Sitting Bull, appears to have attempted to bring Captain French down, but could not hit the man riding a gray horse.[294] Black Elk may have also seen Captain French during the retreat. The 13-year-old Oglala saw a Lakota charge a man and try and grab his horse. The cavalryman took aim with his revolver and shot the Lakota warrior off his horse. An instant later Black Elk watched the same soldier drop two more warriors with what appeared to be cool, well-aimed shots.[295]

On June 16, 1880, Captain Thomas French wrote a letter to Mrs. Angelina Augusta Cooke, mother of the deceased adjutant of the 7th Cavalry William W. Cooke.[xx] In it, Captain French described his role in the retreat:[296]

> "…when all had gone for safety was when I sought death – and tried to fight the battle alone – and did so for nearly a mile… [Concerning the Indians he fought] and there is no mistake in this – I saw them fall – all eighteen of his [Red Horse's] men who rode up to a few yards of me – tumbled off as I fired, and their ponies ran loose. How many were dead I don't know and did not stop to see. Just before I had killed one with my rifle and on crossing the creek two more…"[xxi]

At least one historian, Larry Sklenar, concluded that during the "mad run" for the river probably few of the soldiers – with the exception of Captain French and perhaps a few men on foot – hit any of the Indians with the fire.[297] On the other side, Wooden Leg, who stood 6'2" tall and weighed 235 pounds, said he fired four shots with has cap-and-ball six shooter but did not know if any of his bullets did any harm.[298] Private Hobart Ryder confirmed that the Company M commander put the safety of his men first:[299]

> "After leaving the woods, Captain French was in the rear of the Company with a drawn pistol and I did not see him ahead of the company."

Sergeant Henry Weihe (Charles White) also observed the actions of his commander:[300]

> "The Captain waited until all his men got out of the timber then followed up in the rear; he drew his revolver and firing at the Indians as they were riding alongside of him some twenty yards on each side of him. The Captain had barely [a] chance to get to the ford and the Indians were so thick that you could hardly see what was going on until the Captain got on the other side of the river; he then dismounted from his horse, took his rifle and fired on the Indians standing on the river bank. I saw that he killed two there."

At the start of the retreat, the movement surprised the warriors who thought the cavalrymen were actually charging. As a result there were soon no warriors directly in front of the fleeing troopers, but as the soldiers headed toward the river the warriors soon closed in on the sides and rear to a distance of about 50 yards; occasionally they moved closer, sensing weakness. Distances were deceiving, however, as heavy dust made it difficult to see more than 50 feet.[301] Once again, the warriors were able to approach their quarry from the right side, circling many of the cavalrymen in a counter-clockwise direction that was their lethal trademark.

Against these tactics, even the intrepid French could not save all his men; many of those later killed straggled out of the timber after Captain French and the main body had gone – numerous warriors appear to have anticipated this straggling and swooped in. Private Daniel Newell of Company M, who later estimated that he only fired five shots in the timber fight, related what happened to his bunkmate on the scramble from the timber to the Little Bighorn River:[302]

> "Soon after we started with [First] Sergeant Ryan on retreat, I saw my Bunkie, Scollin [Henry C. Cody] fall. He was on ahead and when I got there I saw his horse had fallen in some sort of wallow and thrown him out of the saddle. He had been shot but was still alive when I got to him. I couldn't help him and he was beyond help anyway. All he could say was 'Goodbye boys.'"

Private William Morris, who claimed that he was the last man to leave the timber other than Lieutenant Luther Hare, saw Scollin's demise a little differently. He later told Walter Camp that Scollin's horse was shot and went down in the first depression after leaving the timber toward the river. The ground was soft; Scollin took his carbine from the fallen horse and looked for a way out. Troopers flew by as Scollin, according to Morris, cried out:[303]

> "For God's sake boys, don't leave me here."

All of a sudden, Private "Robert" Thorpe rode up and helped Scollin jump on the back of his horse. Away they rode until they reached a second hollow, where it was Thorpe's horse that was hit. Down they went. Private Thorpe jumped up, saw an Indian pony without a rider, somehow grabbed him and jumped up on his back.[xxii] In all the confusion Thorpe rode pell-mell for the river, while Scollin remained in the hollow.[304]

Private "Dan" Newell was more fortunate; he had only been wounded in the left thigh from the warrior close-range volley. At this point, Newell also thought that the company was attempting to go back to the initial fording site across the Little Bighorn.[305] He had finally

[xx] William W. "The Queen's Own" Cooke came from a wealthy Canadian family. He was born in Mount Pleasant, Ontario, Canada on May 29, 1846. He immigrated to the U.S. in 1860. In 1863 he joined the 24th New York Volunteer Cavalry. Promoted to second lieutenant in 1864 and first lieutenant at the end of that year, Cooke was wounded at the Battle of Petersburg; he also fought at the Wilderness and Spotsylvania. Also called "Cookie," he joined the 7th Cavalry in 1866 as a second lieutenant and was promoted to first lieutenant on July 31, 1867. He received three post-Civil War brevet promotions (for Sayler's Creek, Dinwiddie Courthouse and Petersburg), the last to brevet lieutenant colonel. Cooke served as the commander of the regiment's Detachment of Indian Scouts until May 1, 1876. To his friends he was also nicknamed "Willie"; the Arikara called him "the Handsome Man." At the battle, Cooke rode the thoroughbred mare "Malita"; she was killed during the fighting along with William Cooke. He is buried at the Christ Church Section of Hamilton Cemetery, Hamilton, Ontario, in Plot 63.

[xxi] One source presents that French wrote that he killed 18 warriors, while another source states he only claimed eight Indians dispatched. This study believes seven may be more accurate.

[xxii] William Morris later thought that the Indian pony was a sorrel-colored mule.

mounted "Pete," his horse and the two rode toward the crossing site.[xxiii] As they approached the river, "Pete" was hit by an Indian bullet, but did not go down. Shortly after crossing the Little Bighorn, the gallant "Pete" was hit again and finally fell, having been struck by bullets three times during the fighting.[306] Newell, who later thought he may have been the last trooper out of the river, finally hid in some brush on the bluff hillside with Private Hobart Ryder until the warriors left the area to pursue Custer's force; the two then crawled up the hill toward friendly positions.[307] At some point they met "Frenchy" Gallenne, who had his own close encounter:[308]

> "Headed by Reno, we charge the enemy at full speed out of the woods. The Indians, about 1,800 in number, come over us, reach us, pass us, surround us! We arrive on the river, and recross it. My horse falls under me, but the valiant animal rises and reaches the opposite bank exhausted. I give to Newell, whose horse has been killed, a fresh one I have held all this while. Now I can use my arms. We want to ascend to the flats above the river. The Indians shoot us from everywhere, but we succeed."

Private Jean Gallenne may have mis-characterized the charge and over-estimated the number of warriors, but he probably did lead at least one extra horse out and did give that mount to Private Newell at some point; the act may have saved Newell's life. Daniel Newell hailed from Ballinough, County Roscommon, Ireland, where he was born on March 17, 1847. He learned the trade of blacksmith in London, England before immigrating to the United States in 1870. Newell enlisted in Philadelphia, Pennsylvania on October 8, 1873; he was assigned to Company M on October 21, 1873. One of 13 children, Daniel Newell stood 5' 71/2" tall, had gray eyes, brown hair and a dark complexion. He reported sick on April 21, 1874 with a boil.[309] Newell was a veteran of the Black Hills Expedition of 1874.[310] It was a rough year and Private Newell was treated for frostbite on November 17, 1874; he returned to duty on December 4, 1874. He actively assisted as a blacksmith in the company in 1875 and 1876.[311] But Daniel Newell had a wild side as well. He was acquitted by a Fort Rice Garrison Court Martial on June 6, 1875 of being drunk and disobedient and then going absent without official leave.[312] But, on June 12, 1875 a Garrison Court Martial convicted him of being drunk and disobedient, fining him $5.[313]

It was a rough ride for Private Daniel Mahoney as well. During the wild retreat from the valley, Mahoney ruptured his right testicle when he was thrown off his saddle and his groin hit the saddle pommel.[314] Private Mahoney hailed from Cork, Ireland, where he was born in 1852. A laborer, he enlisted on September 28, 1875 in Boston, Massachusetts. He arrived at Company M at Fort Rice on October 21, 1875. Mahoney stood 5' 91/2" tall, with gray eyes, brown hair and a fair complexion, and was a bachelor. Daniel was one of the three Mahoney brothers who served in the 7th Cavalry Regiment. Private Bartholomew Mahoney served in Company L, while Private John J. Mahoney was assigned to Company C.[315]

As the retreat began, Corporal Fred Stressinger (also known as Frederick Streing) was killed just outside the edge of the timber, as was Private David "Sandy" Summers, the brand-new cavalryman with the perpetually sore throat. Summers, born in 1848 in Pettis County, Missouri, had previously served as an infantryman (enlisting on April 24, 1871 at Garlington, Kansas) in Company I of the 6th Infantry Regiment. He was discharged from that unit on April 24, 1876 at Fort Abraham Lincoln and enlisted in Company M on May 13, 1876 – just days before the expedition began. Summers stood 5' 81/2" tall, had blue eyes, sandy hair (which may have been the reason for his nickname) and a ruddy complexion. While "Sandy" very probably was a good shot – given his infantry background – his experience in the saddle must have been as miserable as his throat usually felt. This double torment may have prompted him to report sick during the march, as after that, "Sandy" rode in the sick wagon until June 12.[316]

Second Lieutenant Luther Hare observed that during the retreat from the timber Company M initially made a straight line toward their original crossing point at Ford A, but then – perhaps realizing they could not get that far unscathed – veered left and forded where the other companies did. During the confusion, Hare reported, Captain French became separated from his command, with three or four Indians engaging him in close combat.[317] The company was not massed but intermingled in groups with the other units. Just outside the timber was another prairie dog village, which made footing difficult for the spooked horses.[318]

Respected historian Bruce Liddic has postulated that the retreat column initially made for Ford A – where Reno had originally crossed the Little Bighorn during his initial advance. However, mounted warriors on the right flank of the retreating troopers forced the column to veer left instead, along a small buffalo trail that led easterly to what would later be known as Retreat Ford. Additionally, Liddic has demonstrated that recent research shows that a group of twenty troopers chose another path that led directly southeast and crossed the loops of the Little Bighorn three times before arriving at Retreat Ford at the same time the rest of Reno's detachment did.[319]

Sergeant Henry Weihe, Sergeant Patrick Carey, Private George Weaver and Private John Sivertsen became separated from Company M in the timber and formed a small group of defenders – all without horses – with five troopers from Company G and George Herendeen,[xxiv] a guide.[320]

Private William Morris saw the men and later related:[321]

> "[I was the] last man to leave the timber, with the command, with the exception of Lieutenant Hare, who passed me in the bottom. Sergeant Charles White was wounded in the arm and his horse killed. He was left in the woods, as was also 'Big Fritz,' a Norwegian, whose surname I do not remember, but whose horse was killed. 'A' and 'G' had men left in the timber also, and they all reached the command on the hill during the night with De Rudio, or about the same time."

Private John Sivertsen later described what he did next:[322]

> "It [the water] looked rather deep and as I was the tallest man there, I was ordered to cross first and show the way. Sergeant

[xxiii] Ken Real Bird, who raises horses along the Little Bighorn, told me that for some mysterious reason a horse often takes on the characteristics of the name it is given. For example, a horse named "Thunder" or "Lightning" would be very strong-headed and difficult to control, while a horse named "Sleepy" or "Pillow" would be more suitable for less-experienced riders. If his observation is true, "Pete" must have been a good, solid, reliable horse based on his name. Two other horses in Company M were named "Old Sugar" and "Hog."

[xxiv] George Herendeen was born on November 28, 1846 in Parkman Township, Geauga County, Ohio. An orphan at thirteen, he later served in the Civil War and headed west in 1868. He worked various jobs in what would become New Mexico to Montana. In the spring of 1876 he hired on with Colonel John Gibbon's Montana Column in the expedition against the Lakota; he was detached to serve with Custer's forces on June 22 and was subsequently temporarily detached to Marcus Reno's element. In 1877 Herendeen served as a scout during the Nez Percé Campaign. In January 1879 he testified at the Reno Inquiry in Chicago, Illinois. A year later, he worked as a guide at Yellowstone Park. Herendeen later resided in Bozeman and Great Falls, Montana and finally was employed at the Fort Belknap Indian Reservation. George Herendeen died of pneumonia on June 17, 1918 at Havre, Montana and is buried at the Harlem Cemetery.

> White, who was done out, asked me to take his gun, which I did, and waded the stream carrying two guns and two canteens. I got over all right and was the first to reach the other shore."

Herendeen had his own account and praised the conduct of a wounded sergeant, who was undoubtedly Sergeant White (Walter Camp also concluded this):[323]

> "Once in awhile while in the timber, I would go to the edge and look, and finally seeing only a few Indians, I told the men we would go out and that we must walk and not run and go across the open flat. There was a wounded corporal or sergeant. On the way out of the timber only one shot was exchanged with these Indians. I told the men not to shoot unless necessary, that I did not wish to stir up a general engagement with them – not to run but to go in skirmish order, take it cool, and we would get out. I told them I had been in just such scrapes before and knew we could get out if we kept cool. I told them I could get out alone, and if they would do what I told them I could get them out also. The wounded sergeant then spoke up and said: 'They will do what you want, for I will compel them to obey. I will shoot the first man who starts to run or to disobey orders.' This wounded sergeant helped me out in good shape. When we got to the river, the water was rather deep [chest high] where we forded. This sergeant and I remained on the west bank while the balance forded, and we told them when they would get over to protect us while we forded, and they did so.

The group had forded the river downstream from where the rest of Reno's detachment did. Then they climbed the bluffs, which were also further north; in fact, Herendeen and Sergeant White retreated even further north than the spot where Dr. DeWolf was killed.[324]

Private John H. Meier was wounded in the back of the neck during the fight in the valley; Private Edward D. Pigford was wounded in the right hip – it did not hurt as bad as he had earlier feared. Nicknamed "Snopsy," John Meier was born January 26, 1846 in Hanover, Germany, and was 5'5" tall, had blue eyes, red hair and a light complexion. A varnisher by trade, he enlisted on September 6, 1866 in Company K of the 7th Cavalry, but deserted at some point during this initial enlistment. Meier was one of the few enlisted men in the company who was married; he and his wife Mary had four children under the age of six, with another child on the way. At some time John Meier made his way to Boston, Massachusetts, where he enlisted on September 3, 1873, just before his third child was born.[325] He joined Company M on October 21, 1873. Cavalry life was a rough business; on July 7, 1875 Meier went on sick call for rheumatism, while on August 4, 1875 "Snopsy" was treated for a lacerated hand. Meier was also nicknamed "Smokey."[326]

Private Edward D. Pigford was born on June 11, 1856 in West Elizabeth, Pennsylvania. He enlisted on September 13, 1875 in Pittsburgh, Pennsylvania; his enlistment papers show that he was 5' 61/2" tall, with gray eyes, auburn hair and a light complexion. Pigford was a coal miner by trade. He was first sent to Jefferson Barracks in St. Louis, Missouri and then to Fort Abraham Lincoln, Dakota Territory; he joined Company M on October 21, 1875 at Fort Rice, where he spent the winter.[327] Pigford later described the scene at the retreat crossing:[328]

> "My horse was killed just after we crossed the river, but I afterward caught an officer's horse."

Private Roman Rutten, who had survived his earlier wild ride through the Hunkpapa camp, later estimated that a group of 200 Indians were on the right flank of the cavalrymen as they retreated from the timber. The warriors generally remained 50 yards away from the retreating troopers, unless they saw a wounded trooper or identified that a horse went down with its rider.[329] In those cases – much like on a buffalo hunt – the warriors quickly gathered, swarmed over the weakened target and finished it off. The dust in the air, caused by hundreds of galloping cavalry horses and Indian ponies, made it difficult to see. Rutten saw his friend, interpreter Isaiah Dorman – whose horse had been killed and who was making a stand firing his sporting rifle – go down:[330]

> "Isaiah and I were intimate acquaintances, and as I passed him he looked up at me and cried out, 'Goodbye Rutten.'"

Private Roman Rutten also saw First Lieutenant Donald McIntosh of Company G trying to urge his horse to continue, but the animal faltered. The last Rutten saw, 20 to 30 Indians had surrounded the officer and pulled him to the ground, and as the tailor knew, with few exceptions, the Plains Indians took no combatant prisoners.[331] Rutten was probably riding alone at this point – perhaps parallel to the retreating mass of cavalry – and may have been thinking he could be the next to fall. He also recalled that many of the warriors riding along the side of the cavalry withdrawal did not fire their weapons but instead yelled and screamed at the troopers.[332] Private William Morris, who had earlier been forced to threaten another trooper – who tried to take his horse – with shooting the man, saw McIntosh on his horse facing death as well, a short distance from the river:[333]

> "…sitting as calm as a deacon at service."

Roman Rutten was born on August 13, 1846 in Waldürn, Baden in Germany. His original name was probably Roman Ruttenauer. He first entered military service in about 1863, mobilizing in Karlsruhe with a Baden brigade of the German Federal Corps for the impending war between Prussia and Denmark. In June 1866 he mobilized again in Karlsruhe for the Austro-Prussian War, but again did not see combat. This was enough for Rutten who left shortly afterward for a new life in the United States.[334]

A tailor by trade, Rutten enlisted in the 8th Cavalry on November 7, 1866, which was stationed at San Francisco, California. He was 5' 61/2" tall, had brown eyes, light brown hair and a ruddy complexion; Rutten's nickname was "Henry." After his five-year enlistment, Rutten left the army and moved to Philadelphia, Pennsylvania, where he attempted to start a tailor shop. Probably in 1871 he married an 18-year-old Pennsylvania girl named Catherine. The tailor business did not work out and Rutten re-enlisted on July 17, 1872 in Philadelphia and joined Company M of the 7th Cavalry on September 1, 1872 at Unionville, South Carolina. "Henry" Rutten continued to be an excellent tailor and when off-duty made uniforms for the officers and men; as such, he got to know more men throughout the regiment then most junior enlisted soldiers did. His wife "Kate," who followed him from post to post, also cooked for the soldiers. She was not the only army wife to follow her husband to a frontier post. Many others did as well, and their quarters where they did laundry and cooking quickly became known as "Suds Row." He reported sick with a fever on April 22, 1873 and rode on the steamer *Western* from Yankton to Fort Rice.[335] Rutten was detailed as the company tailor as an additional duty.[336] While the position did not call for extra pay from the army, each tailor received payment from the soldiers for each job.[337]

But Roman Rutten was not thinking about money at that moment. Rutten jumped his horse over fallen timber and tree stumps, galloping for the river and possible safety. Spotting the high, steep entrance bank and the mob of men and horses already in the water, Roman felt momentary dismay until:[338]

> "When I reached the river, the water ahead of me was full of horses and men struggling to get across. I thought I had better keep out of the muddle and so turned my horse downstream. The opposite bank was high and steep, and men were riding both upstream and downstream trying to find some place to get up. Finally the mob of horsemen made for a narrow trail cut by buffalo in going for water…"

In most places of the river crossing the near bank was five or six feet above the water, while on the far side the bank jutted eight feet above the water. Some troopers had to dismount and grab the tails of their horses and hang on for dear life as the mounts scrambled up.[339]

Later, when Colonel John Gibbon's column arrived at the battlefield, Captain Walter Clifford of the 7th Infantry Regiment examined the positions and the river banks and remarked that the true marvel of the retreat from the timberline was that with that many warriors around[xxv] so many of the cavalrymen were able to escape.[340] Private William Morris expressed similar sentiments twenty-eight years later:[341]

> "I say we were sent into that valley and caught in an ambush like rats in a trap. That if we had remained ten minutes longer, there would not have been one left to tell the tale."

Reno's companies began to cross the Little Bighorn at what would become known as the Retreat Ford (4:00 p.m.); they then scrambled up the bluffs and hastily reformed on Reno Hill (4:10 p.m.).

Private James W. Darcy was another Company M soldier who barely survived; he described the flight of Company M:[342]

[xxv] Valley expert, historian C. Lee Noyes, has estimated that only about seven warriors were killed in the valley fighting. Source: C. Lee Noyes, "Was There A Timber Fight?" Indianapolis, IN: Indianapolis Little Bighorn Symposium, September 12, 2009.

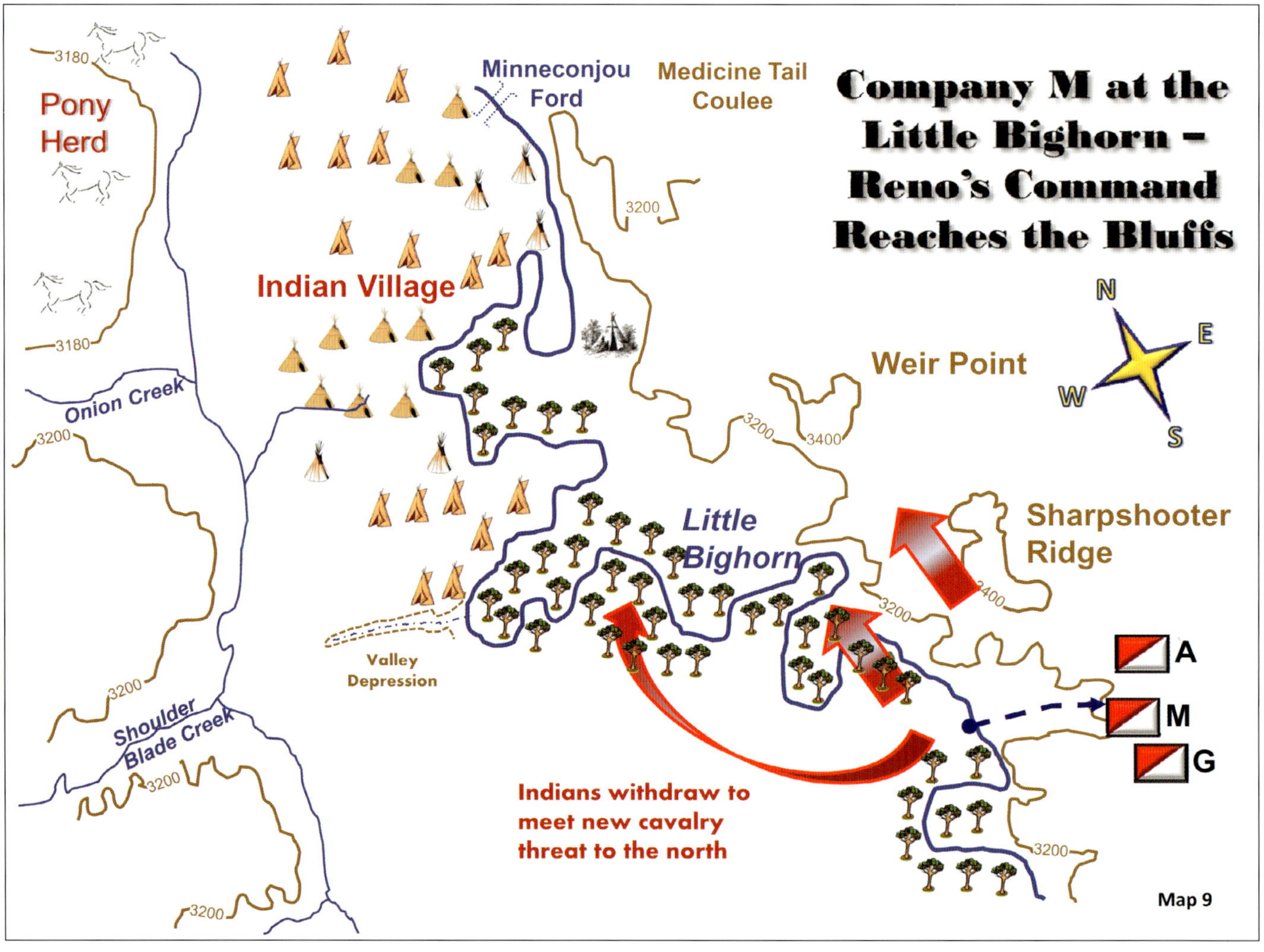

"When we left the woods to cross the Little Big Horn and reach the bluffs on the other side, I was lucky enough to get my horse. It was a wild rush for the river with the Indians on all sides yelling like devils, shooting into our ranks, and even trying to drag men from their horses. One big Sioux rode alongside of me as we went along full gallop, and tried to pull me from the saddle. He had been shot in the shoulder, and every jerk he made at me the blood gushed from the wound and stained my shirt and trousers. He was a determined devil and hung on to me until we almost reached the river. Right at the Little Big Horn a trooper was shot down in front of me and Lieutenant Hodgson got his first wound. My horse stumbled over Hodgson and went over the bluff into the stream, but got to his feet again and carried me across and up the hill. Lieutenant Hodgson hung on to the stirrup of Bugler Myers and got over the river and part way up the hill, but received another wound there and was killed."

The banks on the western side of the river, where the cavalrymen entered the water, were steep and high – some five feet higher than the water. Some cavalrymen must have hesitated at the thought of jumping their horses that far down into the stream. But they did not have long to contemplate their precarious situation as those who hesitated even for an instant had their horses pushed from behind by other cavalry mounts urged on by their riders whose sole intent was on saving themselves. At many points, the water's depth was up to a dismounted man's shoulders.[343]

It would get much worse, as the banks on the other side of the Little Bighorn made these western banks look tame in comparison. Some of the eastern banks were eight feet higher than the water level.[344] To make matters worse, exiting the river was also an exercise in defeating gravity which had been no problem going into the water. A few troopers understood this added impediment, dismounted behind their horses in the water, grabbed their tails and attempted to have the horses pull them behind up the steep slope. This all occurred in the maelstrom of combat that found some of the braver warriors riding into the river as well – attempting to get at their retreating foe with sharp tomahawks and bone-crushing stone-head clubs. The warriors knew that they could kill many more soldiers in hand-to-hand fighting than they could by attempting to shoot them from a distance – the same formula used in a buffalo hunt.[345]

Private Darcy may have been mistaken as Company M did not have a trumpeter named Myers. However, Private John H. "Snopsy" Meier was present, having returned from his harrowing ride through the Indian village. In the confusion, Darcy may have confused Meier with one of the trumpeters. In any case, Private James Wilber Darcy, also known as James Wilber, was a good man. He was born on August 2, 1849 in Laurel, Maryland, and prior to serving in the army did a stint in the United States Navy on the *USS Allegheny*, an iron-hulled steamship. He enlisted in the army on September 8, 1875 in Chicago, Illinois; Darcy arrived at Company M at Fort Rice on October 21, 1875. Records show he was 5' 81/2" tall, had hazel eyes, light hair and a fair complexion.[346]

Private William Morris, who later wrote that at this point in the fighting "The bullets were flying like hailstones," was swept along out of the timber:[347]

"Corporal Scollen and Private Sommers fell in the charge from the timber to the ford. It was a charge and not a retreat, and it was led by Reno. Every man that I saw used his revolver at close range. I was at least twenty yards behind the rear of the command. The Indians closed in, so I was compelled to jump my horse off the bank, at least fifty yards below the ford, and while in the river had an excellent view of the struggle. It was hand-to-hand, and McIntosh was certainly there at the ford and sold his life as dearly as he possibly could.

When I reached the cut in [the] bank, I found Turley and Rye mounted and Lieutenant Hodgson wounded and dismounted. He was waist-deep in the water. He grasped my off stirrup strap with both hands. Rye let Turley go ahead through the cut, and he was killed as he reached the top; Rye followed without receiving a scratch."

This was where Private Turley actually perished, not in the Hunkpapa village as thought by First Sergeant Ryan. Private David Summers, on the other hand, was Number Four in his set of "fours," and thus was a horse-holder.[348] Private William W. Rye was born in Pike County, Georgia in 1849. A farmer, he enlisted on October 9, 1875 at Jefferson Barracks, Missouri. On January 25, 1876 a Garrison Court Martial at Fort Rice convicted Private Rye of selling parts of his uniform a few days earlier. The court sentenced Rye to a $6 fine and also sentenced him to 10 days in confinement.[349] Records show that Rye was 5' 81/2" tall, with gray eyes, brown hair and a fair complexion.[350]

Private William Slaper added this account, and also contributed to the subsequent confusion as to exactly who tried to save Second Lieutenant "Benny" Hodgson, who was serving as the adjutant for Reno's detachment:[351]

"As I glanced about me, the first thing that engaged my attention was Trumpeter Henry Fisher of M Troop riding in the river some distance up with Lieutenant "Benny" Hodgson hanging to one stirrup."

Hodgson appeared to have been shot in both legs.[352] He had no horse, although cavalry protocol allowed an officer who was dismounted in an engagement by the loss of his horse could temporarily take an enlisted trooper's horse.[353] It is possible that Private Pigford later recovered Hodgson's horse immediately after he crossed the river.[354]

The confusion over Lieutenant Hodgson's attempted escape continued with Private Daniel Newell's recall of the incident:[355]

"As 'Snopsy' got to the river his horse was shot from under him and he started for the river afoot. I saw him and 'Benny' Hodgson – we called him the 'Jack of Clubs' – starting for the same horse. 'Snopsy' got the horse and Hodgson hung on to the stirrup, was dragged to the other side and was hit by a bullet [in the head] and killed just as he got across."

Some of the warriors dismounted, hid in the bushes by the river and set up ambushes.[356]

Private William D. Meyer was shot in the eye and killed, while climbing the bluffs – where the bluffs steepened and the men slowed their ascent – during the retreat from the valley fight. According to one witness, a mounted warrior had followed Meyer to the east side of the river and was the one who shot him as he slowed.[357] Private Edward Pigford remembered the event:[358]

"I was close behind Bill Myers [Meyer] of Pittsburgh. As we were going up he turned to me and said, 'Pigford, this is damned hot.' 'Go on: we'll talk about this later,' I replied. The next instant a bullet hit Myers [Meyer] and his blood spurted in my face. I turned and saw the Indian who had shot him. I fired and disabled him or hit his gun. I do not know which, but he disappeared almighty quick."

Private William D. Meyer was nicknamed "Tinker Bill." He hailed from Pittsburgh, Pennsylvania, where he was born in May 1850. A laborer by trade, "Tinker Bill" enlisted on December 16, 1872 in Pittsburgh; enlistment papers show that he was 5' 91/2" tall, with blue eyes, light hair and a fair complexion. One period source states that Meyer served as a maintenance man in the old Pittsburgh Opera House before entering the military. Meyer joined Company M at Oxford, Mississippi on February 9, 1873. First Sergeant John Ryan later stated that Meyer was a company farrier. "Tinker Bill" had acute rheumatism and was unfit to march with the regiment to the Dakota Territory on May 4, 1873; he travelled instead on the steamer *Katie P. Kountz* to Yankton. A Garrison Court Martial convicted "Tinker Bill" of being absent without official leave on January 14, 1876 and sentenced him to a $1 fine.[359] Private William Meyer had an additional duty from February 1875 to May 1876 of regimental tin-smith due to his metalworking skill; it is probably the source of his nickname as well. First Sergeant Ryan would also write that Meyer made knives for the men in the company, shaping old files for the blades and using deer and elk horns for the handles.[360] This must have made him popular with his fellow troopers.

• • •

The point on the bluffs to which Reno took his three-company detachment was 400 yards from the river-crossing site, and if any terrain could have been more hellish than the riverbanks this was it. The slopes upward were irregular and prevented any movement uphill in an organized unit fashion, not that the three companies were organized at this point in the rout. The slopes of the overall funnel-shaped ravine ranged from 30° to 60°, depending on whether the climber took one of the smaller interior gullies or managed to stay on top of the sloping ridges between these crevasses.[361] In either case, the ascent proved so steep that most men had to dismount and lead their horses on foot, which greatly added to the ascent time that may have been 10 minutes.[362] But these smaller gullies often had dense tangles of small trees and shrubs, which further impeded progress. Some men had to stop for a few minutes to catch their second wind; sometimes they had to stop more than once.[363] However, this was a deadly choice, as some warriors had already gained the heights above and were shooting down on the climbing troopers, in some cases turning their ascent of the bluffs into an ascent to the hereafter.

• • •

Private William E. Morris, who had reloaded his pistol while crossing the Little Bighorn moments before and who had just adjusted his saddle, was wounded in the left chest climbing the bluffs as well.[364] Morris, who could see a trail of bodies of horses and men from the timber to the water, and then observe those dead troopers floating down the Little Bighorn, remembered the chaos halfway up the bluff:[365]

"I remember saying to Tom Gordon, 'It was pretty hot down there!' He answered, 'You'll get used to it, shavetail [recruit.]' As he spoke, there came a rain of bullets…Gordon fell dead with a bullet in the brain. Bill the Tinker was shot through the throat and fell from his horse. I was shot through the left breast, by a big Indian close to me, but managed to stay on my horse and reach the top of the bluff."

Not just the troopers were sustaining casualties that day. All three horses in Morris' group were shot as well.[366]

Born in Chatham, England in 1851, Henry Gordon must have been in shock as to what was happening that hot Montana afternoon. With two nicknames, "Tom" and "Dave," he had enlisted in Boston, Massachusetts on December 5, 1872; records show that he had been a laborer, was 5'6" tall, with brown eyes, brown hair and a fair complexion. Gordon joined Company M on February 9, 1873. He served as the company cook in April 1875.[367] While Morris said that Gordon was felled by a bullet to the brain, another source maintained that Gordon was hit with a shot that passed through his windpipe.[368] In any case, the wound was fatal.

Private "Frank" Neely was one of those riding up the ravine after crossing the river when he ran into Private William O. Taylor of Company A. Taylor had been assigned to Company M for several years until the previous winter when he was re-assigned, so "Frank" knew him well. Because he was a latecomer to Company A, Taylor was assigned a broken-winded horse by the name of "Steamboat" – the name based on the sound the animal made when he breathed. After crossing the river at Retreat Ford, "Steamboat" refused to go further, leaving Taylor without a horse. After a short time, Private Neely, who was mounted, overtook Taylor; fortunately, "Frank" was leading another horse named "Old Dutch," offered him to his former company-mate, after which they both made it up the hill.[369]

By this time Captain French had made it to Reno Hill. Seeing that the last of Reno's troopers were crossing the Little Bighorn under heavy enemy pressure, a sergeant from another company, seeking any kind of leadership, went to Captain French on the bluff and asked him if he would organize covering fire to give the stragglers a fighting chance to make it up the bluffs. French responded:[370]

"I'll try – I'll try."

But French did not organize any covering volleys, other than fire his own weapon, when he apparently dropped a few more warriors. Discipline was gone; only individual fighters were responding now, much as what was later surmised to have occurred on Custer and Calhoun Hills.

The dean of Little Bighorn historians, Walter M. Camp, had his own view of the retreat from the timber, to across the river and up to Reno Hill:[371]

"In this [retreat] there was neither order nor semblance of discipline – each man who could do so got himself up on his horse and fled."

As William Slaper of Company M later wrote:[372]

"Death seemed to ride on every hand, and yet a kind Providence must have been watching over me, for I crossed the stream unscathed."

General Charles A. Woodruff[xxvi] later called the retreat a "horse race."[373] Historian Bill Yenne concluded that in the hour from the moment the attack began through their retreat across the Little Bighorn, Reno's element suffered a 44 percent casualty rate, one of the worst such rates for a one-hour fight in U.S. Army history.[374] But perhaps the best description came from an actual participant in the fight. As Second Lieutenant Luther Hare would later relate to his friend First Lieutenant Edward Godfrey:[375]

> "[We] had a big fight in the bottom and got whipped like hell."

Company M, with the rest of Reno's command, augmented by Benteen's force and the pack train defended what would later be called Reno Hill.

Sometime shortly after the bulk of the survivors of Reno's command reached the hill (about 4:10 p.m.), Benteen's element and the pack train closed on Reno Hill some ten minutes later. During the final part of Benteen's advance, he saw the last few dismounted troopers of Reno's command near the Little Bighorn battling with at least 900 Indians. First Sergeant Ryan would have been in charge of making a list of those present and those still missing, in addition to accounting for government property.[376] Company M had lost eight killed and two wounded, but Captain French probably was not sure about the fate of many of the men.[377] Then big Private John Sivertsen and his group of stragglers finally made it up – better late than never:[378]

> "Captain French shook my hand said, 'Fritz, I'm glad to see you. You are on the list of the dead, and here you are back to life again. You're wet from fording the river. Go to the sergeant and get a blanket and sit down by the camp fire.' So I found my troop [company], got a blanket and some food, partly dried my clothes and got straightened out a little."

The last few minutes had been especially harrowing for "Big Fritz:"[379]

> "A short distance up the hill I came across the body of an Indian. He was lying on his back with a carbine in one hand and a whip in the other. I felt his head and found that he had been scalped, so I suppose he was one of the Crow scouts that had joined us some days before."

Sivertsen's assumption seems to have been incorrect; historian Richard Hardorff has concluded that the dead warrior was White Eagle of the Oglala.[380] But the dead were beyond caring.

Sivertsen and the other survivors could see what one historian has described as "The pale bodies of the soldiers floated like dead fish."[381] Some of the wounded men were already crying out for water as a few Indians continued to fire at them from nearby high ground. Someone in the company chain of command ordered three men, including Private Jean Gallenne, to go for water. The warriors had left and the trio brought back some full canteens; it would be the last water for a while.[382]

Reno's entire command had lost more than 30 dead and dying, with another 15 to 20 men hiding out in the woods and in the Little Bighorn along her overgrown banks.[383] On the hill, Major Reno initially told Captain French to search for the body of Second Lieutenant Hodgson, and French began to depart in the direction of the river. However, in short order Reno recalled French to the top of the hill, and Reno began to search for his missing adjutant himself.[384] Then Captain French, after the arrival of the pack train, saw to the resupply of ammunition to his depleted company.[385]

• • •

The geographical feature that later became known as Reno Hill looked less defensible than it really was – just the opposite of the terrain to the north in which George Custer and his five companies would be defeated. The area is actually two roughly parallel crests, not one hill, that run from east to west. In the middle of these two ridges is a small swale – or valley. But the crests are not truly parallel; the hill appears almost triangular with the northern base of the form about 175 yards in width and a length of 350 yards to its apex. Then a narrow ridge extends southeasterly, long and narrow on its crest, just 30 feet wide on the top, but having steep slopes. This ridge, or tail, is the highest point on the hill and projects 500 feet southward from the rest of Reno Hill. The position is roughly 100 feet above the elevation of the river. Along the tail ridge sits the head of a small ravine that plunges southwest downward to the Little Bighorn. The gully would later be named "Water Carrier's Ravine."[386] There are no trees or large bushes on the crest of the hill to provide concealment.

• • •

At some point, three groups of troops, including Company M, advanced to Weir Point. The timing of the advance remains one of the most-debated aspects of the battle to this day. The advance was precipitated by many of the officers hearing gunfire coming from the direction in which Custer and his detachment had earlier ridden. Edward S. Godfrey later told Walter Camp that the wind was blowing from the north at the time, which may have aided in hearing the distant sounds from that same direction. The timing of this gunfire remains uncertain; it probably occurred between 4:25 p.m. and 4:45 p.m.[387]

The order in which the companies advanced is also uncertain. According to Second Lieutenant Winfield S. Edgerly of Company D in a later interview, Company D led the way – following their company commander, Captain Thomas Weir, as he rode the ridgeline.[388] Company M, probably after leaving their wounded on Reno Hill, led the second group of companies toward Weir Point, with Captain French in the lead – the unit was the only one of Reno's detachment to advance; Company M was followed by Company K and Company H – both these companies had previously been with Captain Frederick Benteen.[389] These three units may have ridden closer to the edge of the bluffs as they moved north.[390] One source says that Captain Benteen ordered Captain French to form a company skirmish line behind Company D.[391]

On Weir Point, some of the men observed Indians about three miles away – either in the final stages of the fight against George Custer's battalion or shortly after the last cavalryman in that group had been killed. According to Private Edward Pigford, Captain French told him and two other troopers to head north to see how Custer was faring. Pigford said the three men went far forward – perhaps even one to two miles north, where Edward Pigford later recalled seeing the Indians firing from a big circle, which then became a large black mass on the

---

[xxvi] Charles Albert Woodruff was born in Burke, Vermont on April 26, 1845. A veteran of the Civil War, in which he was wounded several times, Woodruff entered West Point in 1867; he graduated on June 12, 1871, ranking 11th in his class. Commissioned in the Infantry, he was then assigned as a second lieutenant in the 7th Infantry Regiment. In that unit he was with Colonel Gibbon's command that arrived at the Little Bighorn shortly after the battle. Woodruff was wounded three times at the Battle of Big Hole on August 9, 1877. He then was assigned to numerous commissary positions and was the assistant to the Commissary General in 1894. He made the remark in a speech in 1912 during his tenure as the Commandant of the California Veterans Retirement Home. Brigadier General Charles Woodruff died in California on August 13, 1920.

side of the hill toward the river. Pigford, sometimes remembered as an old veteran with a fanciful tale to tell, recalled that an overwhelming mass of warriors then chased the trio back to Company M's lines, where he breathlessly told his company commander:[392]

> "Captain, there ain't a man left; they're all butchered."

How far forward Pigford and his two cohorts went will always be open to speculation. Wherever he went – if he indeed went forward at all – this observation was probably done between 5:40 p.m. and 6:00 p.m.[393]

• • •

When the men of Company M were observing the last stages of Custer's fight, many of the wives of the regimental officers and troopers were gathered at one of the officer quarters at Fort Abraham Lincoln hundreds of miles away as the crow flies, but perhaps occupying the same space as the human spirit flutters. At about 5:00 p.m. the ladies began singing: "Nearer My God to Thee."[394]

• • •

Company D deployed on the eastern-most projection of the elevation. Company M was finally positioned to the west of Company D and a little to the south. Company K deployed to the left flank of Company M. Later the remnants of Company G arrived forward and filled in immediately left of Company D. Captain Benteen led Company H to the two peaks that paralleled the river; Benteen personally then went to the northernmost point for a better view.[395]

The companies were thus strung out in this position with no ability – based on the terrain – to defend for any length of time. Second Lieutenant Winfield S. Edgerly later stated that the command remained on Weir Point for two hours, but he may be incorrect in his memory.[396] At some point, several hundred Indians began to move once again toward Reno's troops and although Weir's and French's companies initially opened fire on the advancing Indians, the situation became precarious. Company H withdrew first and Company K began to mount up and join them. Seeing this, but receiving no orders, Captain French ordered Company M to mount and discussed the situation briefly with the acting commander of Company D.[397] Then French's company hastily withdrew from Weir Point to Reno Hill, with Company M almost out of control at a gallop as it crossed Sharpshooter Ridge. According to some witnesses, the company was out of control. Edgerly continued his recollection of the event:[398]

"Near the close of the two hours, Captain French, who was holding a crest very close to mine, called out to me, 'Edgerly! Major Reno has given orders for us to fall back.'"

The situation was confusing and it is not clear what Major Marcus Reno did or did not do. But after Company M departed, Company D and Company G followed suit. It is likely that Company M was only at Weir Point for a few minutes, not two hours. That was long enough for First Sergeant John Ryan to observe a .45 caliber bullet strike the right side of the pommel of his saddle.[399]

Once the companies returned from Weir Point, Major Reno formed a defensive perimeter on the hill that would later bear his name, with Company M facing west toward the steep gullies leading from the hill to the Little Bighorn River. Actually, Captain Benteen picked the defensive positions and Major Reno approved of the plan.[400] In the aggregate, the 7th Cavalry perimeter was a thin oblong some 500 yards long by only 17 yards wide. It was impossible to find significant cover or concealment, and casualties began to rise from the effects of Indian sharpshooters firing as far away as 900 yards – on Sharpshooter's Ridge – to as close as just a stone's throw, although most warrior firing points seemed to be from 200 to 500 yards distant. Post-battle analysis by Henry Weibert found that there were a minimum of 13 warrior group positions around Reno Hill.[401] In general, the surrounding country was rough and broken, "bad lands" in the truest sense of the word, with small hills and ridges falling away to little ravines that could conceal warriors from the troopers. The troopers who had horses there began to unsaddle them, while others unpacked the mules. Then most of the animals were picketed in a rough hollow square around what was becoming a field hospital.[402]

Most sources seem to indicate that Indian fire probably began about 7:00 p.m. However, in an interview with Walter Camp, Edward Mathey stated that the warriors began firing even before he was able to get the pack train corralled on Reno Hill.[403] Inside the perimeter it must have seemed a confusing mess, with the at least 150 pack mules and several hundred horses in various stages of physical condition, many already panicked by the noise and violence, with more than a few already wounded.

The troopers had only three shovels with which to dig in.[404] The tools were not enough to dig adequate parapets, as the warriors were now armed with 200 additional Springfield carbines.[405] An analysis by historian Don Weibert of his father's research on warrior-fired cartridge casings found around Reno Hill indicated that 29 percent were caliber .44 – fired by Henrys or Winchesters. Nine percent were .50/70s and two percent of the cartridges had been fired in Spencer repeating carbines. By far, however, the greatest percentage, 59 percent, were .45/55 cartridges. That compared to Weibert's research of the Custer

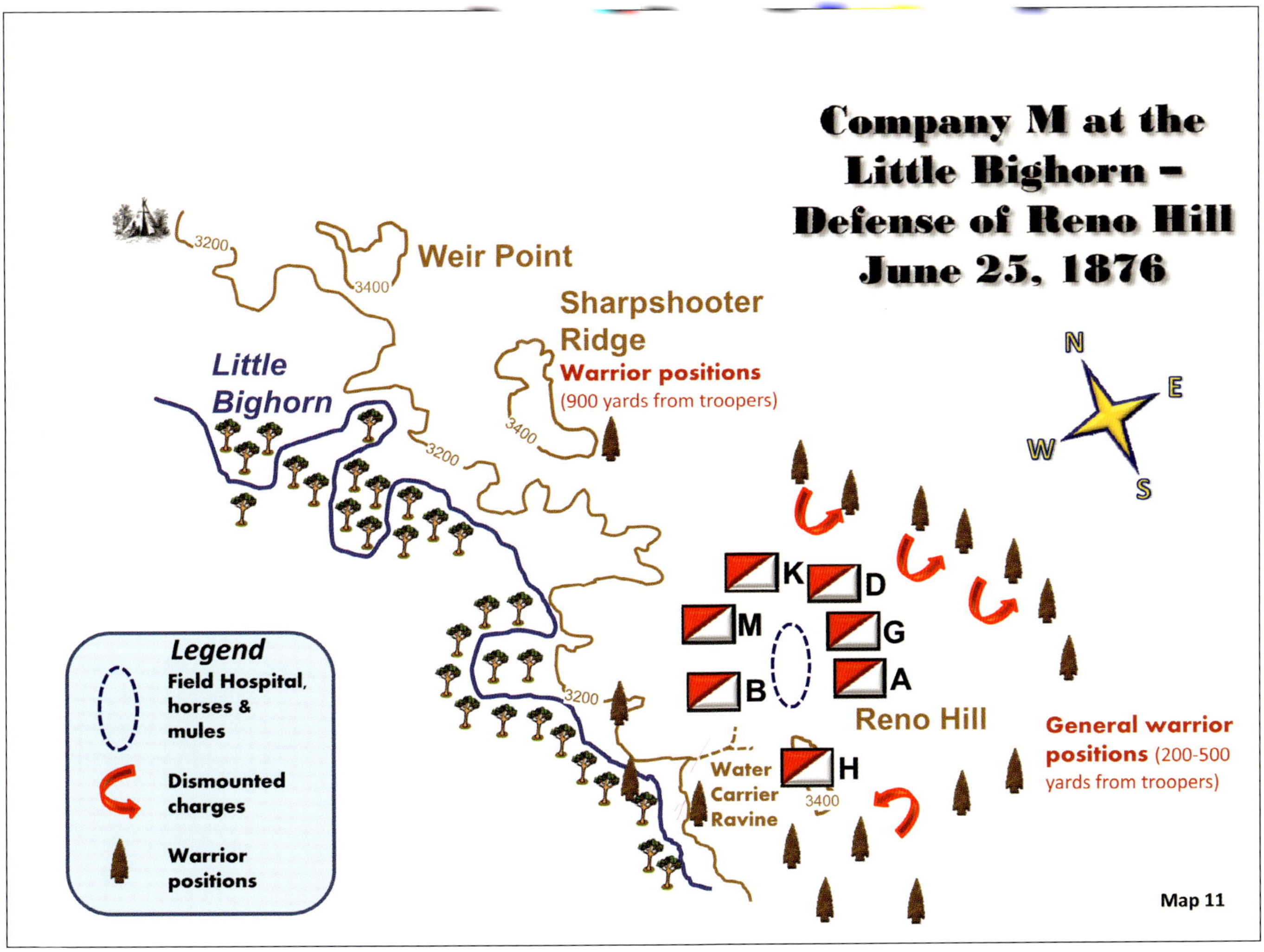

fight (on Custer and Calhoun Hills) that showed that 62 percent of the warrior cartridges there were .44, 23 percent were .50/70, five percent came from Spencers and 10 percent were .45/55.[406]

Later, Captain French, First Sergeant Ryan and six men charged toward an Indian marksman and probably killed him. Sergeant Henry Weihe, although wounded himself, tended to the men, according to Private Daniel Newell:[407]

> "Sergeant White [Weihe], though badly wounded in the elbow, stayed on his feet and did everything he could to relieve the suffering. He had a glassful of jelly in his bags and each wounded man got a small spoonful of that."

But Sergeant White was having a problem. Due to his wound, he could not use his carbine, but his holster was too tightly fixed to his belt, making it difficult to draw and holster his pistol. He could also not slide off the cartridge holder attached to the belt. Finally, White gave his carbine, pistol, belt knife and belt to Trumpeter Charles Fischer and was given Fischer's belt and pistol in return. Months later the switch would almost get "Bounce" Fischer court-martialed, but on Reno Hill men thought of their lives in terms of minutes, not months.[408]

Private William E. Robinson of Company M had been detailed to be a medical assistant to Dr. Henry Porter[xxviii] for the expedition, and the pair tended to the wounded on Reno Hill, placing them in the deepest part of the swale and covering them with a fly tent – but bullets would rip through the canvas every so often.[409] Robinson was born on April 12, 1842 in Down, Ireland, although researcher Walter M. Camp believed he was born in 1847 in Madison County, Kentucky. Robinson enlisted in the army on September 30, 1873 in Philadelphia, Pennsylvania, and was assigned to Company M on October 21, 1873. He was 5'9" tall, with blue eyes, dark brown hair and a fair complexion; Robinson had been a cloth finisher in civilian life. He served as the company cook from April to June 1875. On November 13, 1875 Robinson became a nurse at the post hospital and remained in this position until May 4, 1876.[410]

There were too many wounded to handle on the hill. At some point, the chain of command detailed Hobart Ryder to assist Dr. Porter at the field hospital. Ryder would remain in this role for the remainder of the fighting.[411]

On the hill, Private Roman Rutten had two bullets pass through the crown of his hat before receiving a severe flesh wound in the right shoulder; Private Thomas Varner was wounded in the right ear, and Private Charles Wiedman was wounded in the left leg.[412] Thomas Varner, nicknamed "Happy Jack," was born in Franklin County, Missouri in 1853. He enlisted in Louisville, Kentucky – he listed his civilian occupation as a farmer – on August 24, 1875 and arrived at Company M on October 21, 1875. Varner was 5' 81/2" tall, with blue eyes, brown hair and a fair complexion. He got his nickname based on his always happy disposition.[413] Varner reported sick with acute bronchitis on February 21, March 28 and April 9, 1876 but by April 21 was able to return to duty.[414]

Private Charles T. Wiedman had been born in Boston, Massachusetts on May 28, 1856. A machinist by trade, Wiedman enlisted in Boston on September 23, 1875 – he too was a new soldier. Wiedman was listed as 5' 91/2" tall, with gray eyes, brown hair and a dark complexion. On November 6, November 21 and December 9, 1875 he reported on sick call with boils.[415]

First Sergeant John Ryan described a more serious casualty on the hill:[416]

> "There was a gray horse belonging in my company that was ridden by Captain French, and he was the best buffalo horse in the command. He was among the horses near the wounded, and an Indian shot him through the head. He was staggering among the other horses, and Private Henry C. Voyt [Voight] of my company took hold of him to lead him out of the way of the other horses, and Voyt, at the same instant had his brains blown out."

Another trooper added that Voight had been trying to untangle several horses that had become frightened by the noise and commotion; in all some 46 horses and mules were killed on Reno Hill. Several men yelled at him to get lower, so he would not expose himself to enemy fire, but at that instant he was hit in the head.[417] Private Henry C. Voight was born in Hanover, Germany on June 24, 1855. A baker by trade, he enlisted in Philadelphia, Pennsylvania on October 1, 1873. He joined Company M on October 21, 1873. Voight was single, stood 5' 51/2" tall, with blue eyes, brown hair and a fair complexion. He was detailed as the post baker in December 1873, and again from December 1874 to August 1875. Voight contracted syphilis and was in the hospital from June 4 to July 27, 1874.[418] He was later assigned as the Fort Rice post baker on December 11, 1875 and held this position until April 16, 1876.[419]

Some of the other men began to waiver, which called for tough action on the part of the non-commissioned officers. First Sergeant John Ryan described what happened with one trooper:[420]

> "[Private] Kavanaugh showed the white feather on the skirmish line and immediately broke from the skirmish line, skipped down among the pack mules and horses, where our wounded were. One of the men called my attention to it. I got my gun and immediately started after him. There I found him. I ordered him up on the skirmish line, saying, 'Kavanaugh, you better get back on the skirmish line. You may as well get shot there as here because if you don't, I will shoot you here.' Kavanaugh immediately went back on to the skirmish line."

But other men seemed unaffected by the firing. Second Lieutenant Winfield Edgerly observed:[421]

> "A man of M Troop was walking from one part of the line to another when a bullet hit his carbine splintering the stock. Without changing his gait, he looked towards the Indians and angrily shouted at them, 'Damn you! You will have to shoot better than that to get me!'"

Private Edward Pigford later mentioned that an Indian bullet had hit the stock of his carbine and filled his face with splinters, but the Pennsylvania coal miner never mentioned shouting at the warriors, so perhaps the close call happened to another soldier.[422]

[xxviii] Henry R. Porter was born on February 13, 1848 in Lee Centre, New York. He graduated from the Georgetown University School of Medicine in 1872, and soon became a contract acting assistant surgeon with the 5th Cavalry Regiment in the Arizona Territory. He then became the post surgeon at Camp Grant, before moving to San Francisco, but then volunteered to serve at Camp Hancock, Dakota Territory. In May 1876 he signed a three-month contract to accompany the 7th Cavalry in the Sioux campaign. After the campaign he lived in Bismarck and later toured around the world. Dr. Henry Porter died of heart disease at the Hotel Metropole in Agra, India on March 3, 1903. He is buried there in the Cantonment Cemetery.

During the evening's fight, at least one mule with an ammunition pack ran away from the position and reached the river, only to have the warriors capture its valuable cargo. The heavy firing by the Indians ended about sunset (8:04 p.m. local time) on June 25.[423] The *New York Times* later characterized the fighting:[424]

> "They [the Indians] gained higher ground than Reno occupied, and as their arms were longer range and better than the cavalry's, they kept up a galling fire until nightfall."

The men tried to dig in as best they could with the few tools they had during the night and constructed very simple breastworks. Scattered survivors of the valley fight made their way in the darkness to the friendly positions on the hill. The night turned cool and there was a brief rain shower that night but not enough rainfall fell to collect and drink. Some of the men who could find their horses, unstrapped their greatcoats from behind their saddles and put them on to cut the chill.[425] At about 10:00 p.m., the companies posted picket positions up to 300 yards in front of the main defensive line to warn them of night attacks; the men took two hour turns in these forward outposts.[426] The moon, at 21 percent illumination, provided a little light, but it set at 11:07 p.m. local time.[427]

At the field hospital on Reno Hill, Private William Morris received treatment for his wound, lying close to Arikara scout Goose,[xxviii] who had been wounded in the right hand during the valley fight. Morris struck up a conversation with surprising results:[428]

> "A Ree Indian, one of our scouts, about seventeen or eighteen years of age, was sitting at the foot of my blanket with a bandage on his arm. I said to him, 'How cooler?' He held up his hand, pointing to me and pointing to his arm and smiled, accusing me in the sign language of shooting him in the wrist. I then recognized him as one of the two Indians that I was shooting at while crossing the bottom."

During the night, the companies tried to dig in except for Company H, who tried to get some rest. The warriors were also busy; Walter Camp later concluded that they built at least five small heaps of stones at different firing positions overlooking Reno Hill.[429] Indian firing began anew about 3:00 a.m.[430] Arrows flew in from unseen positions in those small gullies near the perimeter. Nearly all the arrows had arrowheads cut from sheet iron and the missiles produced deadly wounds; deep penetrating arrows of the trunk of a cavalryman were commonly fatal due to loss of blood. They were hard to remove, as when they struck a bone almost always bent over, making them difficult to extract. Those that hit the abdomen could easily cause peritonitis, which would kill before a trooper reached a garrison hospital.[431]

Sunrise occurred at 4:22 a.m. local time.[432] Captain Frederick Benteen ordered the trumpeters to sound reveille.[433] Private Edward Pigford recalled that at one point the Indians stuffed a buckskin uniform to look like a man, tied it on top of a pony and then set the pony loose, perhaps hoping to draw fire that could be observed by Indian marksmen.[434] Pigford also recalled a warrior who would rise up from his firing position every so often and shoot at a trooper. Pigford soon figured out the warrior's timing and when his opponent exposed too much of his upper body, the cavalryman shot and killed him.[435] Richard Hardorff, in his acclaimed *Hokahey! A Good Day to Die; The Indian Casualties of the Custer Fight,* has concluded that the warrior Pigford shot was Long Road[xxix] of the Sans Arc.[436]

Private Pigford, who received a second wound in the right forearm, described the defensive position:[437]

> "All that saved us was that hill. They [the warriors] couldn't get at us like they did Custer. We had pretty fair trenches by daylight, and they had to do their fighting at long range. Indians have no stomach to charge up a steep hill on foot in the face of heavy fire; but just the same the fighting was desperate."

Meanwhile, inside the perimeter the men fought as best they could, often improvising in the dire conditions. As numerous horses and mules were killed by Indian fire, their legs were used as horse pickets to more securely tether those animals still unwounded but clearly scared.[438] One survivor recalled that the defenders dragged the bodies of a few dead horses to the front of several firing positions.[439] George Wylie of Company D later said that manning Captain Benteen's defensive position on Reno Hill was not only Benteen's Company H, but also men from the other companies drawn from the pack train detail who had arrived on the hill.[440]

The stoic "Big Fritz" Sivertsen settled in to his own defensive position:[441]

> "I was put on the firing line. With my butcher knife I dug a little hole behind sagebrush and fought from there. The bush wasn't two foot high and I was the biggest man in the troop, but somehow that bush seemed to be a protection."

• • •

On the morning of June 26 on Reno Hill, Captain French redeployed his company a little to the south to better support Captain Benteen's position on the southern tip of the perimeter; Company M would assist that morning in Benteen's counterattack against close-in Indian positions, one of which was a low bluff only 100 yards away. During the night, Second Lieutenant Varnum had moved over to the small trench that Captain French had built and stayed there for two or three hours. Private Daniel Newell described early action on Reno Hill that morning:[442]

> "Early in the morning of the 26th the Sioux got to pressing close to Benteen's company which was guarding the south side of the hill. Benteen decided to charge and M Company came over from the north to reinforce him. They charged and drove the enemy back but Tanner [Private Jacob Henry Gebhart, who enlisted as James J. Tanner] of my company was badly wounded in the charge. He was carried back to the hospital and I said to him, 'Poor old Tanner they got you.' 'No,' he gasped, 'but they will in a few minutes.'"

Tanner was wounded a short way down from the crest of the hill.[443] The slug penetrated his chest and left lung. Private Jacob Gebhart was

---

[xxviii] Goose, an Arikara scout, was born in 1855. Earlier he had worked for the army during the Yellowstone expedition in 1873 and the Black Hills expedition in 1874. He enlisted in the Indian Scouts for the fifth time on April 26, 1876 and helped recruit other Arikara scouts as well. He was severely wounded in the hand during the valley fight; he rode on the *Far West* with the other wounded until he reached his home at Fort Berthold on the Missouri River. Goose is buried at the Indian Scout Cemetery. His tombstone bears the inscription, "Goose, Indian Scout, USA."

[xxix] Pigford did not scalp Long Road. Hardorff reports that interpreter Frederic F. Gerard scalped the fallen Sans Arc warrior. Several years later Gerard claimed that he gave the scalp to a newspaper man in Chicago at the Reno Court of Inquiry in January 1879.

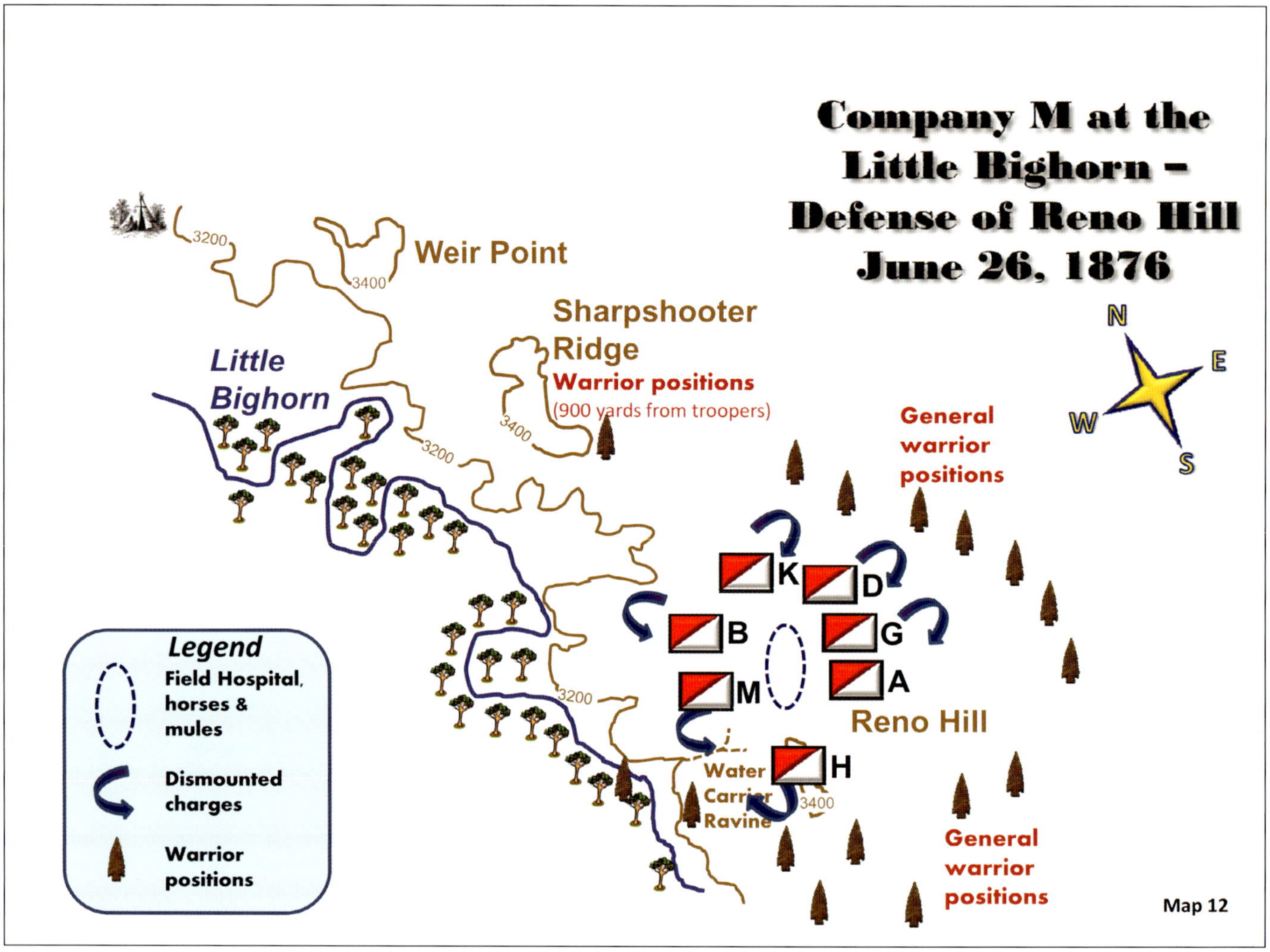

born on June 6, 1848 in Altoona, Pennsylvania; another source states he was born in Ligonier. His father was killed in action during the Civil War. Ten years after that conflict, after trying his hand as a fireman, working at a paper mill and putting up lightning rods, Gebhart enlisted in the army at Chicago, Illinois on September 18, 1875, using the alias of James J. Tanner. He arrived at Company M at Fort Rice on October 21, 1875. By the next summer he was one of the most popular soldiers in the company. Gebhart stood 5' 71/2" tall and had brown eyes, black hair and a dark complexion.[444]

Benteen's company, in the vernacular of the day, was "having a regular monkey and parrot time of it" that morning fighting the warriors.[445] Private Roman Rutten later added his observations concerning this critical part of the defensive struggle on Reno Hill:[446]

> "Benteen came over and told [Reno] how rapidly he was losing his men and that if he did not get assistance soon, he could not hold his hill, and he quietly remarked that if his hill was carried by Indians the remaining six companies would not last long. Benteen discussed the matter with Reno, who finally said he might take one of the companies on that [western] side, and Benteen, without discussing which one he was to have, said: 'All right, I will take French.' French was informed about this and immediately went along the line and told his men to be still but ready, when he would give the word, to jump up and run for Benteen's line. Benteen's line, being on the highest ground in the vicinity, the men going to his assistance would clearly be exposed for some 100 yards while going up the slope. At French's word all the men present, but not all the available men in the company, leaped to their feet, scattered, and started up the hill. In this run Wilbur [Wilber] was wounded."[xxx]

Private Hugh Moore added some additional details about the battle that morning:[447]

> "Captain French ordered the company over [to support Company H], and said, 'I want every man to go. When I say go, I want every man to go.' The company went over at the time. In going over was where we lost the most men. Soon as we got over we had four or five men shot as we were going over, and four or five men were shot as soon as Captain French formed the line. Shortly after the line was formed the Indians charged the line, and when Captain French said I want every man to stand

[xxx] Rutten was talking about James Wilber (James W. Darcy), but it is not clear if Darcy was wounded at this point or shortly later when he was going to get water for the wounded.

the company did stand. That was the only thing that stopped the Indians coming in because that was the strongest point, or where the Indians made the strongest attack."

The charge by Company H and part of Company M occurred at 9:00 a.m. Private Roman Rutten estimated that the company ran toward the warriors for at least 100 yards. Some of the Company M troopers grumbled that the reason Company H was in this predicament (that required a charge) was that Company H had failed the night before to extend and fortify their positions.[448]

Private James W. Darcy was wounded on the second day of the fight, as he went for water for the wounded men; the wound fractured his tibia and left him partially immobile.[449] Out of water since the previous day, Dr. Henry Porter informed Major Reno that some of the wounded would die if they did not get fluids soon; several men volunteered to brave Indian fire and scamper down the gullies to the Little Bighorn, where they filled canteens and returned with them to the perimeter.[450] By noon the temperature had risen to almost 100°.[451] It was a dangerous journey, a full 100 yards across open ground just to get to the head of the ravine, where they then had to work their way down to the river.[452] At least three Company M troopers carried water under enemy fire to wounded comrades.

Private Edward Pigford provided long-range covering fire for the water carriers. In one instance he put up his rear sight and fired at a warrior perched in a tree on the west side of the Little Bighorn – several hundred yards away. The target fell, and after the battle troopers found the body; the warrior had fallen out of the tree and likely broken his neck.[453] The thirst was terrible; Private Edward Pigford later stated:[454]

> "I'd have given all the money I ever expected to have for just one big swig of good licker."

Some of the troopers tried to assuage their hunger by trying to eat some raw bacon and hardtack, but as Private John Burkman said, that was:[455]

> "…like hay scratchin' down our dry throats."

Others took more drastic action. Northern Cheyenne oral history maintains that some troopers drank the urine of their horses, but this has not been substantiated by cavalry sources.[456]

The fighting lessened somewhat toward evening, but was still deadly. First Sergeant Ryan described a long-range action:[457]

> "Along towards evening, the firing on the part of the Indians slackened, with exceptions on one point of the bluff …Here the Indians put in a number of well-directed shots, which laid a number of our men low…Captain French of my company asked me if I thought I could do anything with those Indians, as they were out of range of the cavalry carbines. I told the captain I would try it, as I had a seventeen-pound Sharps Telescope Rifle, which I had made in Bismarck before the expedition started out. This rifle cost me one hundred dollars. I fired a couple of shots until I got the range of that group of Indians, and then I put in a half dozen well-directed shots in rapid succession into that group, and the Indians soon scampered away from that point of the bluff and that ended the firing from the Indians…"

Private John Burkman recalled First Sergeant Ryan's shooting abilities:[458]

> "All durin' the twenty-fifth and sixth whilst the Indians down below was firin' up at us they was a fellow on a hill overlookin' ours that kept poppin' down at us with a long range buffalo gun. He was a good shot. We couldn't see him every time his gun popped down dropped one o' our men or a horse or a mule. That Indian did more to pester us than all the bunch [of warriors] down below. Toward the last Captain Ryan got him with a long range gun. After the fight I went over the hill and seen him layin' thar, the buffalo gun still in his hand, back o' some boulder he'd piled up for breastworks."[xxxi]

Local battlefield expert Henry Weibert believed that at least one of these accurate long-range shooters on Sharpshooter Ridge was a renegade white man, perhaps a deserter, who was an accomplished marksman, but no evidence has been found to substantiate this theory.[xxxii] During another incident, a warrior continued to ride in front of the defenses on Reno Hill, holding a cavalry guidon. First Sergeant Ryan and an unnamed other trooper with a long-range rifle (possibly Captain French) fired at the Indian repeatedly and finally dropped him off his horse. That evening, Ryan crept out to the dead warrior's location and retrieved the colors.[459]

However, ammunition on the hill was running short and some officers observed that many young soldiers – certainly this did not include Ryan – could not hit the enemy. As a result the officers ordered troops not to fire unless they had permission.[460] Four recruits certainly fell into the category of new soldiers, who may have required an officer's or sergeant's permission before they fired.

Private John Seamans was born in 1854 in New London, New Hampshire. A clerk in civilian life, Seamans enlisted on September 21, 1875 at Boston, Massachusetts. He arrived at Fort Rice and Company M on October 21, 1875. Seamans was 5'9" tall, with blue eyes, brown hair and a fair complexion.[461] On January 16, 1876 a Fort Rice Garrison Court Martial convicted John Seamans of "committing a nuisance" for being outside his barracks room door after taps with Private George Smith and getting into a disturbance. Seamans was fined $2 for the event.[462] On Reno Hill Seamans would need to be more than a "nuisance" toward the attacking warriors if he expected to survive.

Private Robert Senn hailed from Zurich, Switzerland, where he was born in 1848. A farmer, he enlisted in Louisville, Kentucky on September 23, 1875. Private Senn was 5' 71/2" tall, with blue eyes, brown hair and a fair complexion. Senn was detailed as a clerk in the adjutant's office in December 1875. He was further detailed as the post librarian in February 1876.[463] Both jobs would have severely limited any training that Private Senn needed to obtain. He was diagnosed with catarrh, a respiratory infection, on April 25, 1876 and with a general fever on May 13, 1876.[464] But he was able to go on the campaign a few days later.

Private Frank Stratton was born in Nottingham County, England in 1848. He enlisted at St. Louis, Missouri on September 18, 1875 and arrived at Company M at Fort Rice on October 21, 1875. A printer

[xxxi] Burkman used Ryan's later police rank of captain in his recollection, rather than his army rank of first sergeant. There were no officers in the 7th Cavalry with the name Ryan.

[xxxii] These white men who lived with Indians were often derogatorily called "Squaw-Men." This came from the fact that many of these non-Native Americans were married (either in a formal or informal sense) to a woman of the tribe. A study to ascertain the role of white renegades at the Little Bighorn would be fascinating but probably extremely difficult to accomplish.

by trade, Stratton stood 5' 51/2" and had hazel eyes, brown hair and a fair complexion.[465]

Private Levi Madison Thornberry hailed from Marietta, Ohio, where he was born on February 3, 1853. Thornberry, a teamster, enlisted in Cincinnati, Ohio on September 20, 1875. He was 5' 61/2" in height, with blue eyes, brown hair and a dark complexion. Thornberry arrived at Fort Rice on October 21, 1875 and joined Company M. He reported on sick call at the Fort Rice Post Hospital for a boil on February 9, 1876.[466]

But overall the men remained calm, and the Indians decided not to press the attack now that they were losing men to accurate fire. Because interspersed with those recruits were four additional veteran troops who knew how to handle a weapon and who liked to mix it up in a fight.

Private Bernard Golden hailed from Cavan, Ireland, where he was born in 1842. He first enlisted in the army on September 8, 1870 in St. Louis, Missouri. Golden was 5'7" tall, with gray eyes, brown hair and a ruddy complexion. He first served with Company F of the 8th Cavalry Regiment; he was discharged at Fort Garland, Colorado on September 8, 1875. Golden then travelled to St. Louis, where he re-enlisted on October 5, 1875; he joined Company M at Fort Rice on October 21, 1875. Nicknamed "Barney," on February 12, 1875 Golden was treated for frostbitten toes.[467] On January 1, 1876 "Barney" smashed a window at the Fort Rice post trader's store and attempted to enter it. He was apprehended and four days later a Garrison Court Martial convicted him of the crime and sentenced him to a fine of $5 and 14 days on confinement.[468] It had been Golden who had grabbed First Sergeant Ryan by the throat during the Company M riot on March 23, 1876. Now "Barney" had the opportunity to come to grips with the enemy.

Private George Heid was born in Bavaria, Germany in 1842. He enlisted in the army first in July 1865 just after the Civil War. Heid re-enlisted in Cincinnati, Ohio on June 17, 1870 and joined Company M on June 29, 1870 at Fort Hays, Kansas. A farmer by trade, Heid was 5' 6 1/2" and had gray eyes, dark hair and a ruddy complexion. In South Carolina, George Heid reported sick with a fever on September 16, 1871. Cavalry life was rough and George Heid deserted on February 8, 1872. Changing his name to George Hyed, he enlisted in the Marine Corps on November 27, 1872 in Philadelphia, Pennsylvania. That service did not seem to suit him either, and George Heid surrendered to authorities on November 6, 1873 at Norfolk Barracks, Virginia. Heid was transferred to Fort Snelling, Minnesota and re-joined the 7th Cavalry on May 19, 1874. On March 4, 1875 Heid created a disturbance at the Fort Rice post trader's store by engaging in a fight. A Garrison Court Martial found him guilty of the offense and sentenced him to a fine of $5. On April 14, 1876 he received a contusion to his right foot when a wagon rolled over it.[469]

Private John Valentine Whisten was born on February 14, 1852 in New York City, the son of Irish parents; it would appear he received his middle name based on the date of his birth, a fact that might have provided his army buddies great mirth. On September 22, 1873 Whisten enlisted in New York; he joined Company M on October 21, 1873 at Fort Rice. A laborer by trade, Private Whisten stood 5' 51/2" tall and had blue eyes, light hair and a fair complexion.[470] Any man who would threaten to kill his own first sergeant, as Whisten had done during the Company M riot on March 23, 1876, was probably not afraid of a few warriors – as long as his carbine worked and he had plenty of ammunition.

Private Charles H. Williams hailed from Delaware County, Pennsylvania, where he was born in 1849. He first enlisted in Philadelphia, Pennsylvania on July 15, 1870 in Company C of the 22nd Infantry Regiment and remained in that unit until July 15, 1875, when he was discharged at Fort Brady, Michigan. During that enlistment, in June 1871 he had been court-martialed. Seeking a job where he could ride instead of walk, Private Williams enlisted in Baltimore, Maryland on August 3, 1875 and found his way to Company M, arriving on October 21, 1875. He was 5'5" tall and had blue eyes, brown hair and a fair complexion.[471] On February 14, 1876 Charles Williams was diagnosed with catarrh, but recovered quickly from this respiratory infection.[472] As a former infantryman, he was probably a decent marksman.

After a fusillade of rifle fire by the warriors at about 2:00 p.m., Indian fire markedly slackened during the afternoon of June 26, as warriors began leaving the Reno Hill battle just after noon.[473] Sometime that evening the village packed up, and in the darkness of the second night the Lakota and Northern Cheyenne disappeared toward the mountains. Company cooks built cooking fires and prepared the first real meal the soldiers had consumed in over two days. The troopers watered their horses and the regiment moved slightly closer to the river to give them better visibility of the valley and to get away from stench emanating from the scores of dead animals and men at their former positions. In total, 18 cavalrymen had been killed on Reno Hill, with a further 52 wounded; some of the seriously wounded would later die of their wounds before reaching Fort Abraham Lincoln.[474] First Lieutenant Edward Godfrey recalled in his field diary that during the evening he had a cup of coffee with Captain French.[475] Sunset occurred at 8:04 p.m. local time. The moon was at 31 percent illumination, but it set at 11:26 p.m. local time.[476]

At 3:00 a.m. on June 27, First Lieutenant Charles DeRudio appeared on Reno Hill from the valley and called out to the sentries. According to the lieutenant, he had been narrowly escaping the Indians in the valley for the last thirty-six hours. Captain Frederick Benteen and Captain Thomas French, both of whom had always categorized DeRudio as a braggart, walked away from him in disgust.[477] DeRudio would not soon forget the insult.

Shortly after sunrise, which occurred at 4:22 a.m., the men ate breakfast.[478] Early that morning Private Jacob H. Gebhart (James Tanner) died of his wounds. With no shooting around, some of the men were able to eat a meal of hardtack, bacon and coffee.[479] Dr. Henry Porter began operating on several wounded cavalrymen, but the chloroform he was using to put the patients under also caused two of his assistants to faint.[480] One of those affected by the fumes was probably Private William Robinson.

Later on the morning of June 27, General Alfred Terry's column, advancing from the north, swept through the Indian village – which had been abandoned by the Lakota and Northern Cheyenne the previous afternoon as they moved toward the Big Horn Mountains – and arrived at Reno Hill. As Private Edward Pigford of Company M later remarked:[481]

> "I never saw anything in all my life that looked as good to me as Terry's men."

But those feelings of relief were not shared by those arriving at the terrible scene. According to an eyewitness, General Alfred Terry:[482]

> "...saw the slaughter and cried."

• • •

The battle was over; the troopers of Company M would share in one more duty, helping to bury the 7th Cavalry dead. The command divided the battlefield into five sectors and assigned responsibilities to each company to bury those corpses in their sector, as well as keep a count of the deceased and identify those that they could. Company B scoured the sector closest to the Little Bighorn; Companies D and H were assigned the area furthest from the river. In the middle, Companies M, G and K were assigned these duties for "Last Stand Hill."[483]

As part of the detail to take care of the dead on June 28, First Sergeant John Ryan, Private "Crazy Jim" Severs and Private "Harrison" Davis reportedly buried George Custer on "Last Stand Hill" along with many others of that lost command.[484] Ryan stated that Private "Frank" Neely also helped the detail to bury four other commissioned officers and 42 enlisted men.[xxxiii] During the process, Ryan directed "Crazy Jim" to remove a lock of hair from Custer's head, while he collected five or six spent cartridges from under the commander's body; all these mementos were later sent to Elizabeth Custer.[485] It was a sickening business as most of the putrescent corpses were bloated, mutilated, bloody and fly-infested; some of the men vomited during the task. Private William Slaper described the process as:[486]

> "…remove a little dirt in a low place, roll in a body and cover it with dirt."

The dead horses looked like great gray and brown mounds, bloated and stinking, with mouths open and tongues dangling in some last search for a drink of water they would never taste. Private Edward Pigford later – probably honestly – told a journalist that, as the heads of some of the soldiers had been cut off and when the burial detail did its work, they were not certain that they placed the "right head with the proper body."[487] Hands, feet, arms and legs had been roughly severed and scattered about the area. At one point during the burial details, Captain Thomas French became overwhelmed, according to Major Reno:[488]

> "The stench was sickening. Captain French came to me and said, 'Have you got any whisky?' I answered that I had a little, and he said, 'Give me a drink for I am sick at the stomach,' and I did so."

John Ryan, who later stated that his detail buried about 45 bodies, came across the body of Captain Thomas Custer and could only identify him based on the India ink letters tattooed on his arm: T.W.C. The general's younger brother had been disemboweled and had his head smashed flat.[489] Ryan also observed what he thought were 18 to 20 troopers from Company E in a ravine, where it appeared they had tried unsuccessfully to get out and were shot in the back. "Bill" Slaper also recalled the bodies of Company E:[490]

> "These bodies were on the line nearest to the river, making it appear that they were halted by an overwhelming force, which closed in on them so rapidly and in such superior numbers that they were given but little chance to put up a fight."

The troopers from Company M found Henry Cody's horse, which had died halfway between the timber and the retreat crossing site of the Little Bighorn. In his saddlebag was Henry's prayer book, *The Key of Heaven*. Private Daniel Newell later mailed it to Cody's sister; she then wrote back asking if her brother had been mutilated – "Dan" Newell lied in his response, because by then they had also found Henry Cody.[491] First Sergeant Ryan buried Cody in the bottom land halfway from the timber to "Retreat Ford." Ryan said they identified the body because of the corporal stripes.[492]

They found "Jim" Turley's body; his hunting knife had been driven to the hilt through his right eye into his brain.[493] They found the body of "Tom" Gordon; he had been mutilated. They found "Sandy" Summers' body; he had been mutilated. They found the body of "Tinker Bill" Meyer; he had been mutilated.[494] They found "Lonesome Charley" Reynolds. The quiet scout's body had been stripped, with his head cut off. And the Company M boys, who had grown into men over the previous two days, started the legend that there were 60 spent cartridges around "Lonesome Charley's" body.[495]

They also found Private Henry Klotzbucher's body; it was not mutilated and had probably not been found by the Indians.[496] They buried two of their own, Henry Voight and James Tanner (Private Jakob Gebhardt) in a single grave in the center swale on Reno Hill, where the horses, mules and field hospital had been located. For a headstone the troopers used the lid of a hardtack box on which they wrote the two men's names in pencil.[497] First Sergeant John Ryan later said he could not find Sergeant O'Hara's body, but thought that the Indians probably threw it into the river.[498]

The same day a detail of troopers[xxxiv] shot and killed some 20 cavalry horses – that were wounded and could not be saved – which were still located in the timber, by the river and at the bottom of the bluffs.[499] It was the last act of kindness they could give to their four-legged comrades.

• • •

The remnants of the regiment carried the wounded to the steamer *Far West*, which was at the mouth of the Little Bighorn. Captain Grant Marsh directed his crew to construct an improvised field hospital on the stern deck of the steamer. The medical column reached the boat at 2:00 a.m. on June 28, 1876 and the men were placed aboard for their 710-mile journey back to Fort Abraham Lincoln. Marsh pulled out all the stops and made the voyage in an astonishing 54 hours.[500] Just before the *Far West* departed, Brigadier General Terry gave Marsh his guidance:[501]

> "Captain, you have on board the most precious cargo a boat ever carried. Every soldier here who is suffering with wounds is the victim of a blunder, a sad and terrible blunder."

It had been a harrowing experience for the men of Company M. Most had survived, but their experiences on those hot days on the eastern Montana plains would haunt them for the rest of their lives.

[xxxiii] Troopers from Company G also later claimed that they buried Custer and some other officers. It may have been that many men participated in small ways in the task, or were so close while watching that they considered that they were part of the effort, not just observers.

[xxxiv] Walter Camp noted that some troopers – he did not mention the company – also found the body of a bearded white man in Indian garb buried up in a tree in the valley. The white man had been shot five or six times, and the troopers concluded – or at least Camp concluded – that he had been engaged near Reno Hill. Perhaps this was Weibert's marksman. Source: Walter M. Camp, "Field Notes," Lilly Library, Indiana University, Bloomington, IN., Box 2, Folder 10 – Little Bighorn, Part 2.

Opposite
***Top*: 7th Cavalry Regiment Rosebud Creek campsite on June 23, 1876.**

***Bottom*: East side of Little Bighorn River below Weir Point.** A small part of the village was on the east side of the river. While most of the pony herd was on the table ground to the west of the village, some of the ponies were on the flat ground show here just below small hills. Six Arikara scouts attempted to steal ponies from this location.

***Right*: Company M's right flank point on the initial skirmish line; view looks west.** The company's left flank position was between house and railroad track, neither of which was present in 1876. Artifact finds by Jason Pitsch support identification of this position.

***Below*: Company M's right flank point on the initial skirmish line; view looks east.** Company A's left flank would have begun here and extended toward light colored bushes; Weir Point is in the far background on the left. Artifact finds by Jason Pitsch support identification of this position.

***Bottom right*: Company M's left flank point on the initial skirmish line; view looks east.** This position was exposed to warriors flanking to the west. Artifact finds by Jason Pitsch support identification of this position.

***Above*: Warrior initial position at the pony herd to the left front of Reno's initial skirmish line.** Distance from this position to the middle of Company M's initial skirmish line is 985 yards. Artifact finds by Jason Pitsch support identification of this position. Fort is a former museum, obviously not present in 1876. Photo taken in May 2010.

***Below*: Warrior flanking position on high ground west/southwest of Company M's skirmish line positions.** The warriors moved to the flat-top hillock just right of the white trailer in attempt to get behind the cavalry. At this point, they are 300 yards from the left end of Company M's skirmish line. Artifact finds by Jason Pitsch support identification of this position. Photo taken in May 2010.

***Above*: Side view of this flanking hillock showing its elevation.** Warriors on top would have been firing to the left. Just this increase in elevation allowed the warriors to see the entire width of Reno's skirmish line; conversely troopers in the valley had no idea whether or not more warriors were behind the hill. Artifact finds by Jason Pitsch support identification of this position. Photo taken in May 2010.

***Below*: View from the top of this flanking hillock position, looking northeast.** Road and red-roofed museum fort would not have been present in 1876. Reno's advance skirmish line would have been just to the left of where the museum is. Wooded area in the far distance on the left side of the horizon is the current national cemetery; the straight-line distance from the hillock to the cemetery is 3.83 miles. Artifact finds by Jason Pitsch support identification of this position. Photo taken in May 2010.

***Above*: View from the top of the flanking warrior hillock position; view looks east.** Reno's initial skirmish line began between the red-roofed museum and the blue house, neither of which were there in 1876. High ground on the left skyline is Weir Point. Artifact finds by Jason Pitsch support identification of this position. Photo taken in May 2010.

***Below*: Second warrior flanking position on high ground southwest of Company M's skirmish line positions.** Position is on the brown mound midway up the ridge in the center of the photo. Artifact finds by Jason Pitsch support identification of this position. Photo taken in May 2010.

***Right*: Company M's right flank point of advanced position on the skirmish line; view looks west.** The left flank of Company M was on the other side of the road, which was not present in 1876. Artifact finds by Jason Pitsch support identification of this position.

***Below*: Company M's right flank point of advanced position on the skirmish line; view looks east.** The troopers at this point would have seen Company A and G soldiers running from the open field to the front of the timberline on the right. Artifact finds by Jason Pitsch support identification of this position.

***Bottom right*: Company M's left flank point of advanced position on the skirmish line; view looks east.** Artifact finds by Jason Pitsch support identification of this position.

Above: **West side of timberline position to which Company M withdrew from the skirmish line.** View is from the south. Remnants of an old riverbed exist. Company M troopers used the channel wall of this riverbed for cover. Photo taken in May 2010; trees were much thicker in 1876. Artifact finds by Jason Pitsch support identification of this position.

Below: **South side of Company M's timberline position.** Old channel wall of the riverbed is just behind the bare trees. Warriors would have approached this position from where this photographer stood. Photo taken in May 2010. Artifact finds by Jason Pitsch support identification of this position.

***Above*: Company M's position on Reno Hill; view looks west and shows part of the Little Bighorn River across which troopers fled.** Soldiers then climbed the ravine leading to this position. Those who scaled the bluffs to the right were killed by waiting warriors.

***Below*: Company M's position on Reno Hill; view looks southwest.** Parts of the Little Bighorn River can be seen, although the river's trace has changed since 1876.

Above: **Company M's position on Reno Hill; view looks northwest.** The high ground to the right is part of Sharpshooters' Ridge.

Below: **Water Carriers' Ravine on the right; view looks west/southwest into the Little Bighorn valley.** Company M's Private James W. Darcy (also known as James Wilber), Private William C. Slaper and Private James Weeks braved enemy fire to run down the ravine to the front right to get river water for the wounded. Some warriors took positions in the trees to the other side of the river and sniped at the cavalry troopers.

***Above*: Sharpshooters' Ridge; the view is of the highest point on the ridge from Reno Hill.** Company M's First Sergeant John Ryan fired accurate long-range shots against Indian sharpshooters in this vicinity with his specially-made Sharps hunting rifle.

***Below*: View of Custer Hill from Company M position on Weir Ridge.** Subtle ridges along the line of sight obscure Calhoun Hill, while "Last Stand Hill" marker can be faintly seen to the right of the large group of pine trees. Those trees, which frame the national cemetery, were not there in 1876. Exact actions on Custer Hill would have been difficult to identify for anyone on Weir Ridge without binoculars as straight-line distance from this point to the monument is 3.00 miles. Photo taken in May 2010.

For want of a nail, the shoe was lost; For want of a shoe, the horse was lost; For want of a horse, the rider was lost; For want of a rider, the battle was lost; For want of a battle, the kingdom was lost; And all for the want of a nail. The cavalry used a link strap (side view) to control their horses while the dismounted owner moved on foot or fought on a skirmish line. The link strap buckled to the horse's halter which was worn under the bridle. The snap hook on the opposite end was snapped to one of the lower rings of the curb bit. When ordered to form a skirmish line, the Number One, Number Two and Number Three troopers would unsnap the link from his horse's bit and snap it to the horse next to him and then dismount, the Number Four trooper remaining mounted so that he could lead the now attached three horses of his comrades, "daisy-chained" to his horse, to a more secure position behind the dismounted troopers.

Link strap (top view). On the Reno skirmish line, the Number Fours took the horses to the right flank and an open area inside the timberline. This artifact, found at that location is a metal snap hook previously affixed to a horse-holder strap. Missing is a thin piece of metal that acted as a spring closure for the device's opening. It was hooked to the end of the snap hook opposite of the curved hook, and adjacent to where the leather strap was affixed. The base of the spring closure was held secure to the clasp by a small iron band. For maximum holding strength, this small iron band should have been affixed to the snap hook with its ends on the side of the clasp opposite of the spring closure device. On this artifact, as seen from above, the small iron band is on backwards, with its open ends securing what would have been the thin spring closure device, which has since corroded away. This flaw in the M1874 link strap could have been in the design, or this example could have had the thin band put on incorrectly at the arsenal. In either case, made this way, the snap hook would have been weaker than expected.

A link strap held by a young trooper at a modern cavalry reenactment.

Link strap (bottom view). Private Jean Gallenne of Company M was a Number Four and recalled that he was ordered to secure eight horses instead of the usual four at the skirmish line. This modification would have provided Captain French with additional skirmishers to fire their weapons, but would also have put more stress on the horse-holder straps, with twice as many frantic animals pulling in different directions; the combination of more horses per Number Four and a poor design/construction of the snap hook **could** have led to equipment failures and a loss of control of a number of horses by the horse-holders at the Little Bighorn.

CHAPTER FIVE

Accounts of Bravery in Company M at the Little Bighorn

"Captain French was as brave an officer as ever served in the 7th Cavalry."[1]

Every 7th Cavalry company had its share of bravery at the Little Bighorn and Company M was no exception. Some of the incidents of heroism can be inferred, such as non-commissioned officers leading from the front. While we cannot know with certainty where each sergeant and corporal was during the fight, we do know that three of five Company M sergeants who fought at the battle were killed or wounded (60 percent), while two of three corporals (66 percent) present became casualties.

Other courageous acts were more than just inferred. Private James W. Darcy, for example, was wounded in the left leg while carrying water to his wounded comrades on June 26.[2] Private William Slaper described another water-carrier act of heroism, that of Private James Weeks:[3]

> "I had made the trip for water with a young comrade named Jim Weeks. On our way back Jim was hailed by Captain Moylan [Company A], requesting a drink. I was surprised to hear Jim blurt out, 'You go to hell and get your own water; this is for the wounded.'"[i]

Private James Weeks was born in June 1854 in Halifax, Nova Scotia, Canada. He enlisted in Boston, Massachusetts on August 23, 1875 and joined Company M on October 21, 1875. A laborer by trade, Weeks stood 5' 91/2" tall, with blue eyes, brown hair and a fair complexion. He was nicknamed "Jim."[4]

Private James W. Severs performed his own act of bravery that Private Daniel Newell later described:[5]

> "While the fighting was the thickest one of the pack mules with its load on its back started to leave. He had gone maybe a hundred yards when he was overtaken by a man we called 'Crazy Jim' Seivers [Severs] who brought him back. He was exposed to the fire of the Sioux from the minute he started until he got back. I saw this and it was a mighty brave deed but Sievers [Severs] never got any Medal of Honor for that I know of. Sergeant Hanly [Richard Hanley, of Company C, who was originally with the pack train] got a medal for doing practically the same thing on the retreat back to the hill and well deserved it."

Private James W. Severs, nicknamed "Crazy Jim," was born in October 1851 in Lyons, Wayne County, New York. A teamster by trade, he enlisted at Chicago, Illinois on November 12, 1872; he arrived at Company M on December 9, 1872 at Unionville, South Carolina. Records indicate that "Crazy Jim" was single and illiterate; he stood 5' 51/2" tall, with blue eyes, light brown hair and a fair complexion. Prior to the Little Bighorn, Severs was often detailed to work as a teamster in the regiment. He earned his unusual nickname after earlier in his army career being seen by his comrades killing, skinning and eating a rattlesnake[ii] – an act his army buddies thought was quite crazy. "Crazy Jim" thought the snake meat tasted like eels after frying them. As a result, none of the other troopers would borrow his frying pan. Severs stuffed the skin of the dead snakes with grass and wore them around his neck like a scarf![6] A Garrison Court Martial convicted him of stealing a whip from the post corral on September 15, 1874; he paid a fine of $5. On November 3, 1874 a Fort Rice Garrison Court Martial convicted "Crazy Jim" of sleeping on guard duty and fined him $1.[7]

Another soldier who showed bravery was Private Frank Sniffin, the 18-year-old guidon-bearer for Company M. After the remnants of the company reached the top of Reno Hill, Captain French, by this time in a foul mood, noticed that Sniffin did not have the prized colors and hollered:[8]

---

[i] Myles Moylan was born in Amesbury, Massachusetts on December 17, 1838. He enlisted in the 2nd Dragoon Regiment in 1857, serving in Nebraska and Utah. He fought with the unit – now known as the 2nd Cavalry Regiment – at Wilson's Creek, Fort Henry, Fort Donelson, Shiloh and Corinth, before being commissioned a second lieutenant. He was court-martialed in 1863 for taking an unauthorized absence and was cashiered out of the army, but enlisted under an assumed name in the 4th Massachusetts Cavalry Regiment and soon was elevated to first lieutenant and then captain. After the war Moylan joined the 7th Cavalry as the sergeant major; George Custer encouraged him to apply for a commission and after an unsuccessful first attempt to do so, Moylan was finally appointed a lieutenant; he was promoted to captain on March 1, 1872. Moylan was not well-liked in the regiment and was roundly condemned by the enlisted men after the battle. One source stated that Moylan was a bit vulgar and not fit for civilized company. Private John Burkman, Custer's "striker," later said that Moylan was called "Aparejo Mickie" (Aparejo being a Spanish term for a pack-saddle) because he never left the protection of the mule packs that provided some cover for his company on Reno Hill. Other men nicknamed Moylan "hardtack Mick" because he remained hidden behind the bacon and hardtack boxes for the first day of the defensive fighting. On October 22, 1872 Myles Moylan married Charlotte Calhoun, the 19-year-old sister of Lieutenant James Calhoun. Despite his conduct in 1876, in 1894 Moylan was awarded a Medal of Honor for his performance at the Snake Creek (Bear Paw Mountain) fight, in which he was wounded in the thigh, in September 1877. Myles Moylan died of stomach cancer in San Diego on December 11, 1909; he is buried at the Greenwood Memorial Park in the city. Charlotte "Lottie" Moylan died on March 29, 1916.

[ii] Captain Tom Custer was also known to catch rattlesnakes. First Sergeant John Ryan wrote in his memoir, "Tom Custer was a great man for catching rattlesnakes and carrying them along in a nose bag and keeping them alive in camp." Source: Sandy Barnard, editor, *Ten Years with Custer: A 7th Cavalryman's Memoirs*, Terre Haute, IN: AST Press, 2001, 203.

"You damned fool, where are your colors?"

The captain need not have been concerned. During the valley fight, Sniffin had torn the guidon from its staff and crammed it under his shirt to prevent the flag's capture – the other two companies under Reno lost their colors. Sniffin reached under his shirt and showed the precious unit symbol to his commander.[9] Rescuing the colors was no mean feat. In the army of that era (which also included the Civil War) a unit placed the utmost importance on the colors during every battle; these flags were usually relinquished only on the death of the color bearer.[10]

Despite his frequent tirades, Captain Thomas French conducted himself in a brave manner throughout the battle. Private Daniel Newell recalled his company commander on Reno Hill:[11]

> "During all this fighting I was near Captain French helping get the guns loaded whenever an empty shell would stick, and this happened to most of the guns as soon as they got hot. Captain French was a crack shot and always carried a 'Long Tom' infantry rifle. This gun had a ramrod carried under the barrel and I think it was the only ramrod in the outfit. Whenever a shell would stick, he would recover the gun and either pick it out with his knife, or I would push it out with his ramrod. We would then load the gun and return it to its owner. In doing this Captain French was exposed most of the time but was perfectly cool and for some reason or other escaped unhurt."

Private Daniel Newell was not the only one to observe Captain French's bravery. Chief Red Horse was a head chief among the Lakota council, and fought both at the valley and later against Custer's detachment across the Little Bighorn; he subsequently created many well-known ledger drawings of the events of the battle. In 1881 at the Cheyenne River Agency, Red Horse related his version of events to an acting assistant surgeon in the U.S. Army, Dr. Charles E. McChesney, who was also a United States Indian Agent:[12]

> "Among the soldiers was an officer who rode a horse with four white feet. The Sioux have for a long time fought many brave men of different people, but the Sioux say this officer was the bravest man they had ever fought. I don't know whether this was General Custer or not. Many of the Sioux men that I hear talking tell me it was. I saw this officer in the fight many times, but did not see his body. It has been told me that he was killed by a Santee Indian, who took his horse. This officer wore a large-brimmed hat and a deerskin coat. This officer saved the lives of many soldiers by turning his horse and covering the retreat. Sioux say this officer was the bravest man they ever fought."

Chief Red Horse may not have known the name of the officer, but Dr. McChesney was certain that it was Captain Thomas French.[13] While some recent historians have concluded that Red Horse was mistaken in his identification, it is probably one of those mysteries of the battle that will never be definitively resolved. Sometime during the battle on Reno Hill an enemy bullet passed through Captain French's hat, narrowly missing his head. According to Private John Sivertsen, French drolly remarked:[14]

> "Boys, that's a pretty close shave, and I guess it's about time I should make a move."

Three years after the battle, Sergeant Henry C. Weihe (Charles White) recalled his company commander in the valley fight:[15]

> "[After leaving the timber] he drew his revolver and firing at the Indians as they were riding alongside of him some twenty yards on each side of him. The Captain had barely chances to get to the ford and the Indians were so thick that you could hardly see what was going on until the Captain got on the other side of the river. He then dismounted from his horse, took his rifle and fired on the Indians standing on the river bank. I saw that he killed two there."

First Sergeant John Ryan, who probably was somewhat biased toward his company commander, nevertheless later had this to say about his commander:[16]

> "Captain French was as brave an officer as ever served in the 7th Cavalry."

Captain Frederick Benteen paid a grudging compliment to Captain French several years later. In correspondence with another battle survivor, Benteen discussed officer leadership in the valley:[17]

> "They were all a pack of cowards, Captain French excluded."

Perhaps Private William Slaper summed up his company commander best:[18]

> "Captain French was as 'cool as a cucumber' throughout the entire battle, and although I searched his face carefully for any sign of fear, it was not there. He had such perfect self-control that I had to admire his courage and bravery, and was indeed glad to be under his leadership."

First Sergeant John Ryan also demonstrated courage in action. On the morning of June 26 a Company M soldier was badly wounded during a charge of Captain Benteen's and Captain French's companies against the Indians pressing the perimeter on Reno Hill. First Sergeant Ryan described the event:[19]

> "Private James Tanner of Company M was shot in this charge and his body lay on the side of the bluff in an exposed position. There was a call for volunteers to bring him down, and I with three others grabbed a blanket, rushed to his assistance, laid the blanket on the ground, and rolled him on to it. We made quick time getting him from the side of the bluff down to where the balance of our wounded lay. Very fortunately, none of the rescuing party received any more than some balls through their clothes. After being placed with the rest of the wounded, he died in about five minutes."

Wounded Sergeant Henry Weihe (Charles White) was also commended for his bravery. In 1879, Captain Thomas French testified to Sergeant White's conduct at the Little Bighorn:[20]

> "The sergeant [White] not withstanding his wounds, made his way across the river from the brush, where we were compelled to leave him and others, and joined Major Reno's command

and did good service in saving company property and with his unwounded arm, bringing ammunition to the line."

The enlisted men of Company M, from the youngest private to their tough first sergeant, certainly had displayed bravery throughout the fight; what only remained was how the army might reward that gallantry.

Captain Thomas H. French. Many Company M troopers later said that their company commander was quite heroic during the fighting; photo was taken at Fort Abraham Lincoln in 1873. *Photo courtesy of the Little Bighorn Battlefield National Monument.*

Chief Gall of the Hunkpapa; his bravery at the Little Bighorn was legendary. Gall is shown here in about 1881, with buffalo robe, and bow and arrows. *Photo courtesy of the Little Bighorn Battlefield National Monument.*

Northern Cheyenne warrior Wooden Leg. He initially fought in the valley armed with an 1860 Colt cap-and-ball revolver. Photo was taken in 1927 showing Wooden Leg holding Springfield carbine he captured during the fighting. *Photo courtesy of the Little Bighorn Battlefield National Monument.*

White Bull, a famous Minneconjou warrior. He appears to have attempted to shoot Captain Thomas French during the retreat from the timber, but could not hit him. *Photo courtesy of Wes Cowan Auctions.*

Ledger book drawing by Wooden Leg. Scene shows how he captured a Springfield carbine during the cavalry retreat from the timberline to Retreat Crossing of the Little Bighorn River. *Photo courtesy of the Little Bighorn Battlefield National Monument.*

***Right*: Rain in the Face**. Photo taken in 1886 at Standing Rock, Dakota Territory; earlier, after he was arrested by Captain Tom Custer and a group of Company M troopers, he swore eternal revenge. *Photo courtesy of Wes Cowan Auctions.*

Water Carriers Ravine. Seventeen 7th Cavalry troopers later received the Medal of Honor for actions concerning this area and gathering water for the wounded. Photo taken in 2010.

CHAPTER SIX

Company M's Exclusion from Bravery Awards

"All or none."[1]

Established during the Civil War, the Congressional Medal of Honor was the only national award for heroism in the country until well after the Indian Wars. The Army Adjutant General later summarized that during the Indian Wars the Medal of Honor was awarded for:[2]

> "Showing combat initiative and rescuing wounded men under intense close-range fire; securing water for the wounded, outside the lines; showing conspicuous gallantry as a sharpshooter; bring a body through hostile lines; bringing up reserve ammunition, and rallying soldiers in exposed positions; declining to leave the line after being wounded, and continuing to fight bravely; capturing war parties, of Sioux, larger than the capturing detachment; and carrying dispatches alone for long distances through hostile territory."

The army awarded twenty-four soldiers of the 7th Cavalry the Medal of Honor for their actions at the Little Bighorn. None were officers; six men were sergeants, two men were blacksmith/farriers and 16 were regular privates. The following companies were represented in the medal count: Company A – three, Company B – six, Company C – three, Company D – seven, Company G – one and Company H – four. Company M had no recipients. Private William Morris heard a rumor of why the company was excluded:[3]

> "It was rumored, subsequently, that French recommended his First Sergeant, John Ryan, a sharpshooter, and some other men for medals, and that Benteen refused to indorse the recommendation as to Ryan, because he failed immediately to order the men out of their pits at his end of the line at his (Benteen's) order. It was claimed that French thereupon withdrew his list. Ryan was in charge of the ten men that Reno sent to skirmish the woods."

It is believed that Captain French indeed submitted a list of Company M soldiers some time after the battle through Captain Benteen and Major Reno and on this list was First Sergeant John Ryan. Per one account, when asked to clarify the nominations for medals, French replied:[4]

> "All or none."

Whatever subsequently happened between the three men, Captain French withdrew his entire list from consideration, and thus no Company M troopers received awards. Some sources have stated that Benteen indeed refused to approve the medal for First Sergeant Ryan because he believed that Ryan had not ordered his men fast enough to support the June 26 charge of Company H and Company M, after Benteen ordered the advance.[5]

For some reason, the regiment's company commanders did not formally submit their lists of nominees for awards to 7th Cavalry headquarters until May 1877. At some point after this date, the regiment forwarded these lists to the Department of Dakota headquarters in St. Paul, Minnesota. Eight months later, Brigadier General Terry – still in command of the department – returned the lists to the regiment for review and revision. During this period it is possible that some names were added, while others were removed. The revised final list was then submitted to a board of officers; historian Larry Sklenar postulates that the president of the board could have been Major Lewis Merrill of the 7th Cavalry; he was definitely on the panel. The board began their deliberations on June 23, 1878. Major Joseph Tilford was also on the panel, and as he was senior to Merrill in time in grade as a major, he could have been the president of the board.[6] Based on the board's final decision, the army awarded the medals, officially issuing them on October 5, 1878.[7]

As Larry Sklenar noted, Captain Thomas French refused to nominate anyone, although he believes that it is difficult to determine whether French meant the names he submitted or the whole company – a likely scenario if Captain French was attempting to secure a unit citation for the company. Private Roman Rutten later stated he believed that this was his commander's intent. However, Private William Morris disagreed and later asserted that Captain French turned in a shorter list, which included First Sergeant John Ryan. Then when Captain Frederick Benteen refused to endorse Ryan's inclusion, French withdrew his entire list.[8]

Based on these standards at that time, enumerated above, for the award of the Medal of Honor and given many similarities of acts of bravery between some of the troopers in Company M and those men in other companies who did receive the Medal of Honor for heroism during the Little Bighorn fight, I believe the following ten men should have been seriously considered for this decoration:

Individual: Qualifying Action

Captain Thomas H. French: led his unit to safety from the valley fight through hostile lines; conducted a counterattack on Reno Hill; moved exposed to defensive positions to fix weapons under enemy fire.

First Sergeant John Ryan: rescued a wounded soldier under enemy fire; showed conspicuous gallantry as a sharpshooter.

Sergeant Charles Weihe (Charles White): led surrounded troopers out of the timber.

Private James W. Severs: recovered a supply mule under enemy fire.

Private James W. Darcy (James Wilber): carried water under enemy fire to wounded comrades.

Private William C. Slaper: carried water under enemy fire to wounded comrades.

Private James Weeks: carried water under enemy fire to wounded comrades.

Private Frank Sniffin: saved the company colors.

Private John H. Meier: attempted to rescue Second Lieutenant Benjamin Hodgson.

Private Rollins Thorpe: attempted to rescue Corporal Henry Cody.

Company H's Private Charles Windolph, who received the Medal of Honor for his role in the fighting, later wrote that he believed that James Severs, Dan Newell and William Slaper deserved "the highest of decorations."[9] First Sergeant Ryan, in a letter to Elizabeth Custer dated September 6, 1909, certainly believed he was cheated out of a Medal of Honor by Major Reno and Captain Benteen.[10] In Benteen's battalion, Sergeant Richard Hanley received a Medal of Honor for chasing and recovering a mule named "Barnum," which had broken loose shortly after Benteen arrived on Reno Hill and was headed toward Indian positions with his valuable cargo of ammunition.[11] But "Crazy Jim" Severs recovered another mule in similar circumstances and received nothing.

There could have been more award winners. Private Jean Gallenne was an early water-carrier; depending on the level of warrior opposition when "Frenchy" went for the life-saving water could warrant a Medal of Honor for him as well.

William Slaper also had a complaint after he learned that Peter Thompson had received a Medal of Honor for carrying water, a feat that "Bill" Slaper accomplished as well. In a letter to Charles Windolph of Company H on October 20, 1930, Slaper wrote:[12]

> "I never got one [Medal of Honor] for my share because I never knew they were issued until many years later and heard it too late to get it. So I have been losing the ten dollars per month ever since…"

A good old Company M trooper; "Bill" Slaper's main concern was about not receiving the monthly stipend associated with the award of the medal!

Medals of Honor awarded to troopers at the Little Bighorn. Awardees shown here were James Pym, Charles Windolph and Henry Meckin; no troopers from Company M received the award although ten men should have. Photo was taken at the Little Bighorn National Monument Museum.

Private William C. Slaper standing at Water Carriers' Ravine in 1926 at the 50th Anniversary of the Battle of the Little Bighorn. Slaper braved enemy fire of June 26, 1876 to get water from the wounded; he was not awarded a Medal of Honor, but should have been. *Photo courtesy of the Little Bighorn Battlefield National Monument.*

Private William C. Slaper standing at the Little Bighorn River where he repeatedly filled canteens under enemy fire on June 26, 1876. Photo was taken in 1926 at the 50th Anniversary of the Battle of the Little Bighorn. *Photo courtesy of the Little Bighorn Battlefield National Monument.*

Frederick Benteen. Picture shows him wearing the insignia of a lieutenant colonel. Benteen did not approve Captain French's recommendations for awards to be given to Company M troopers after the campaign. *Photo courtesy of the Library of Congress.*

CHAPTER SEVEN

COMPANY M'S ABSENCE AT THE 1879 MARCUS RENO INQUIRY

"...there suddenly sprang up among the Seventh Cavalry Officers an understanding and resolve about that affair which would reflect in any way upon the honor of their regiment or regimental esprit, even if they had to sacrifice their own individual opinions concerning the plan of the campaign or the conduct of the battle, either by Reno or Custer."[1]

On January 13, 1879 a court of inquiry ordered by the President of the United States convened at Chicago, Illinois. It began in a smallish room on the second floor of the prestigious Palmer House Hotel, but on the second day, with space at a premium, the proceedings were moved to the third floor and remained there. Colonel John H. King, Commander of the 9th Infantry Regiment, served as the president of the court.[i] Colonel Wesley Merritt, Commander of the 5th Cavalry Regiment, and Colonel William B. Royall, Commander of the 3rd Cavalry Regiment, completed the board.[2]

Major Marcus Reno, who since the battle had endured many informal charges of cowardice and incompetence, finally could take no more. These taunts began in 1876 at the officers' club at Fort Abraham Lincoln. The officers were enjoying a good meal and some drinks after their extended campaign, when Lieutenant John Manley of the 22nd Infantry Regiment crossed the line. According to First Lieutenant William Craycroft, who had been on detached service during the 1876 expedition, but was back at the regiment:[3]

> "Reno did by his malicious and insulting remarks to a brother officer, provoke a personal encounter and did engage in fisticuffs and rough and tumble fight."

Nothing good can come from a major fighting a lieutenant; after three years Reno figured out his reputation would never recover unless he requested the court to meet to investigate his conduct at the Battle of the Little Bighorn. At the court of inquiry every officer of the 7th Cavalry – who had participated in the fight – still living, with the exception of Captain Thomas French of Company M and First Lieutenant Francis M. "Gibby" Gibson of Company H, was called as a witness. Captain French had been scheduled to testify; it is not clear who made the decision for him not to do so, but that may have been understandable as French was in a unique situation at the time, being court-martialed on an unrelated incident.[4] We do not know why Gibson was not called. However, given several accounts concerning his conduct on Reno Hill during the fight, in which he was observed to show cowardly actions, the army may not have wanted to expose him to the court.

The same day that the Reno court of inquiry opened proceedings, an army General Court Martial in the Dakota Territory convicted Captain Thomas French on a variety of charges, including drinking on duty and violating his terms of close arrest at Camp Ruhlen. Author Jack Pennington goes so far to say that the French court martial charges were "more than likely initiated because of his known views concerning Reno, and the military's desire to prevent him from testifying."[5]

The recorder for the inquiry was First Lieutenant Jesse M. Lee, who was the Adjutant of the 9th Infantry Regiment. Lee was not a career prosecutor but he was experienced in Indian affairs, having served in 1877 as the acting Indian Agent at the Spotted Tail Agency in northwestern Nebraska.[ii] But he did not have to be a prosecutor; the Articles of War in 1879 specifically stated that the recorder was a finder of facts:[6]

> "...since the investigation is not a trial, nor will he [the recorder] properly assume the role or manner of a prosecutor."

Lee's objective was to demonstrate if there was significant evidence to support an accusation that Major Marcus Reno had engaged in conduct unbecoming an officer. Specifically, First Lieutenant Lee pressed to prove that Major Reno did not follow the orders of his superior – Lieutenant Colonel George Custer – and because of this failure, Custer and the five companies that accompanied him were wiped out. Lee's logic in support of this assertion was that had Reno attacked the village, or at the least held his position in the timber, his detachment would have tied down a large part of the enemy. However, because Reno retreated from the timber, his action permitted the warriors to temporarily leave Reno's front and mass against Custer, defeating him in detail.[7]

[i] John H. King was born in Michigan on February 19, 1820. He was appointed a second lieutenant in the 1st Infantry Regiment in the Regular Army on December 2, 1837. King was stationed in Florida and the western frontier until 1846; during that time he was promoted to first lieutenant on March 2, 1839 and to captain on October 31, 1846. He fought at Vera Cruz during the Mexican War. During the Civil War, John King – who had been promoted to major on May 14, 1861 – fought at the Battle of Shiloh, the advance on Corinth and the Battle of Murfreesboro. He was commissioned a brigadier general of volunteers on November 29, 1862. King later commanded a brigade of regular troops until the end of the war, seeing action at Chickamauga, Resaca, New Hope Church, Kennesaw Mountain, and Peach Tree and Utoy Creeks. He was appointed a colonel of the 9th Infantry Regiment in December 1866. Colonel King retired from active service on February 6, 1882. John H. King died in Washington, D.C. on April 7, 1888. He is buried at Arlington National Cemetery in Section 1.

[ii] Born in 1843 in Indiana, Jesse M. Lee served in the Civil War as a private in the 59th Indiana Volunteer Infantry Regiment; he was commissioned a second lieutenant in the infantry on July 28, 1866 and over the next thirteen years served in the 39th Infantry Regiment, the 25th Infantry Regiment and the 9th Infantry Regiment. He also served as the agent at the Spotted Tail Indian agency from 1877 to 1879. He was elevated to captain on May 1, 1879 and to major on April 26, 1898. Lee was promoted to brevet brigadier general on June 17, 1902 and retired as a major general. Jesse M. Lee died in 1926.

Secondarily, First Lieutenant Lee attempted to demonstrate that leaving the timber was not only evidence that Major Reno had disobeyed orders, but also that this action was proof of cowardly conduct. Lee would also suggest that Major Reno was inebriated during the action, another indicator of conduct unbecoming an officer.[8]

During the twenty-six day inquiry, the court called twenty-three witnesses.[9] Daily sessions seldom lasted more than three hours. The panel did not meet on Sundays.[10] The Reno court adjourned on February 11, 1879. The members of the court knew where Captain Thomas French was located, and although Company M's former first sergeant, John Ryan, had been discharged in December 1876, they could have easily found Ryan as a police officer in West Newton, Massachusetts and brought both men to Chicago. That the court called neither to testify was a conscious decision on the part of someone in the army – a decision that probably has impaired historical efforts concerning what happened at the valley and hill-top fight ever since.

Sergeant Henry Weihe (Charles White) of Company M was also not called to testify; had he been in the witness chair in Chicago, it is quite likely that the court would have erupted into pandemonium. Weihe kept a diary – or at least contemporaneous notes – of his time in the cavalry and showed this to no one outside his family during his lifetime. He died in 1906; three years later his widow loaned the document to Little Bighorn researcher Walter Camp. Camp made a typed copy of part of the document and added marginal notes to these typed pages for his own files. Ignoring Camp's notes, Weihe's private observations at one point discuss Reno's detachment moving down the valley:[11]

> "We moved with our right resting in rear of a belt of timber, and 15 men in charge of Company M were at once directed to deploy to the right as mounted skirmishes and to move through the timber. The first sergeant of Company M directed me to go one way and one of the drunken officers another. I am writing this not without proper proof. With my own eyes I saw these officers open a bottle of whisky and drink enough to make any ordinary man drunk. I then witnessed the greatest excitement among intoxicated officers I ever saw. The only officer who maintained self-control and acted like an officer should do was Captain T.H. French. When the order was given to dismount and fight on foot he led his company out.
>
> Lieutenant Wallace[iii] was then with his company, Lieutenant Varnum was with his company, but Colonel Reno, Captain Moylan, Lieutenant Hodgson and Lieutenant McIntosh were under the shelter of the timber. The form of Captain French could be seen towering above all the rest of the line, and I then formed my estimate of him as a brave and fearless officer brave as a lion and it was not whisky that made him fearless. Two company commanders, the battalion commander and his adjutant were in the timber. Captain Moylan was keeping himself very close."

Assuming Weihe did not lie to himself in his diary, based on his account a conservative estimate concerning intoxicated officers would be that Major Reno, Captain Moylan, Second Lieutenant Hodgson and First Lieutenant McIntosh had been imbibing for some time; Weihe could not have observed Lieutenant Varnum in the thick woods as the chief of scouts was with the other scouts on the other end of the timber position. But another source said that Varnum and scouts Frederic Gerard and Charley Reynolds were observed drinking from a whiskey flask there.[12] We do not know which officer gave Weihe a conflicting order from that he received from First Sergeant Ryan; two likely candidates were Reno[iv] or Hodgson, who was acting as Reno's adjutant.

Depending on how much the officers actually consumed, their problem-solving abilities would have been impaired. That could have contributed to the deaths of "Benny" Hodgson and "Tosh" McIntosh during Reno's retreat from the timber to the other side of the Little Bighorn. He does not say that Captain French did not consume any whiskey; his phrase "maintain self-control" may indicate that French drank on other occasions (which we know he did from other sources) but not this one, or that he did drink on this day but that in Weihe's opinion that level of consumption of alcohol did not adversely affect him.

Had Weihe testified in this manner, his glowing comments concerning Captain French might have caused the court to order that French report to Chicago to testify himself. Then, if the army publically chose not to recall French because of his alcohol-related offenses for which he was then being court-martialed out west, the newsmen present at Reno's proceedings could have made their own inferences concerning officer use of alcohol in the regiment, which – in turn – could have opened up Pandora's Box concerning widespread alcohol use within the regiment, officer intoxication, and its effects on the unit's performance in the battle.[v] If several officers with Major Reno were intoxicated, the line of reasoning might develop: were officers with Benteen's three companies, or even with Custer's detachment also impaired by drink during the fight?

During the Reno inquiry, Captain Thomas French did talk with a reporter at Fort Lincoln. His remarks were later picked up by the *Bismarck Tribune* and the *New York Times*, but never brought up at the court; the *New York Times* front page article read:[13]

> "Captain French, of the Seventh Cavalry, who is credited with great bravery at the Battle of the Little Big Horn, and a coming witness before the Reno court in Chicago, stated today that he saw nothing of Major Reno from the evening of the June 25th until noon of June 26th; that Reno was out of sight and that he [French] could not find anyone who did see him; in other words, that Reno slunk away in a hole and left the command to Benteen."

That article should have perked the interest of the Reno inquiry, but it would be left to others to tell the story in Chicago. Weihe continued in his diary, taking Reno to task for his tactics in the valley fight:[14]

[iii] George D. "Nick" Wallace was born in York County, South Carolina on June 29, 1849. He graduated from West Point in 1872 ranked ninth in his class of 57; he was initially assigned to Company G of the 7th Cavalry. Wallace participated in the 1873 Yellowstone expedition and the 1874 Black Hills campaign – where he commanded the regiment's Indian Scouts. He then was on detached service in New Orleans for two years, returning a month before the regiment departed Fort Abraham Lincoln in 1876. He was appointed first lieutenant effective June 25, 1876 and became the regimental adjutant in August. In 1877 Wallace fought in the Nez Percé Campaign. He later commanded Company L and Company K of the 7th Cavalry. Wallace presented key testimony at the Reno Inquiry at Chicago in January 1879. He also served as an instructor at the Cavalry School at Fort Leavenworth and on recruiting duty at Jefferson Barracks. George D. Wallace, also nicknamed "Tony Soldier," was killed in action at Wounded Knee on December 29, 1890. He is buried at the family plot in the Rose Hill Cemetery in Yorkville, South Carolina.

[iv] Weihe's assertion concerning Reno's drinking is partially supported by sutler records. Between August 1 and August 23, 1876, Reno purchased seven gallons of whiskey at a trader's store. Source: James Donovan, *A Terrible Glory: Custer and the Little Bighorn – the Last Great Battle of the American West*, New York: Little, Brown and Company, 2008, 328.

[v] Warriors later reported finding canteens filled with whiskey after the battle among the dead with Custer, according to John Doerner, Chief Historian at the Little Bighorn Battlefield National Monument. Source: Lorna Thackeray, "Haunted by history: Tragedy followed Bighorn battle survivors," *Billings Gazette*, Billings, MT: June 21, 2009.

"Up to this time we had been expecting reinforcements and two men had been wounded, but Major Reno appeared on the bank of the timber and ordered the men to fall into the timber, mount their horses and cut their way out. In this move Major Reno lost his men, for the soldiers were not instructed as to the movement to be executed before starting. The men rode pell mell through the timber and as soon as they got outside of it they were met by the Indians and shot down like buffalo.

In my own mind I have no doubt of the result of fighting Indians from cover of timber, and I have also enquired of some noted Indian fighters whether it was not a good advantage to fight Indians from timber as shelter, and they all tell me that timber is the best shelter white troops can get into when they are outnumbered by Indians. It is my firm belief that had Major Reno held the timber in which his men were well formed, and near the village, those Indians who attacked us first would certainly have been compelled to remain there and instead of going to the assistance of Crazy Horse, who was ordered by Sitting Bull to cut Custer off, and which he did, and with the combined forces accomplished Custer's defeat. Had Reno held to the timber, we could have moved into the village and set it on fire very quickly in event of their leaving our front as they did do when we retreated across the river."

The court of inquiry may well have taken Weihe's tactical observations with a grain of salt, given his enlisted rank. Officers were officers and were responsible for tactics. Non-commissioned officers, on the other hand, were not considered tactical experts and their opinions on tactics were only that. On the other hand, after the retirement of First Sergeant Ryan in December 1876, Sergeant Henry Weihe was elevated to the position of Company M's first sergeant just a month later, a personnel move that indicates that the company and regimental leadership thought highly of his military and leadership skills.

But Weihe's diary continued and in addition to intoxication, the specter of officer cowardice raised its ugly head:[15]

"When I got back to the command [on Reno Hill] I went to the hospital [the central area of the defensive position where Dr. Porter was treating casualties] and received medical assistance for my wound and went to bed. Our position had then been selected by Colonel Benteen. He was the only officer present whom we could rely upon and he behaved well. During the engagement on the hill on the 26th he was constantly where the bullets were the thickest, encouraging the men. Lieutenant E.G. Mathey went to the hospital during the fighting in the afternoon on the 25th and up to 10 a.m. on the 26th, when he got ashamed of himself and took a carbine and joined Captain Moylan, who lay behind some dead mules that had been shot during the engagement. The most cowardly officers I ever saw were there and some of the bravest whom I have ever seen.

The men lost from my company in retreating out of the bottom were Sergeant O'Hara, Corporal Scollin, Corporal Stringer, Privates Gordon, Klotzbucher, Lorenz, Smith, Summers and Turley. Privates Tanner and Voight were killed on the hill. The ten men killed in the valley were only wounded when they fell from their horses and were finished up by about fifty Indian arrows when the Indians were making for Custer's column.

Sergeant Thomas McLaughlin, of Company H told Major Reno that there should be someone sent to rescue the wounded, and Reno remarked that the Sergeant might get a detail and rescue them himself, if he wanted to. The poor wounded were butchered in sight of the seven companies, and there was no officer brave enough to go to help them. This had a discouraging effect on the men. If Colonel Benteen had been in command there would have been a different tale to tell."

The purpose of the court of inquiry was to determine the appropriateness of Major Reno's actions, not those of the entire officer corps of the 7th Cavalry. Weihe clearly and directly damned First Lieutenant Edward Mathey, Captain Myles Moylan and Major Marcus Reno for acts of cowardice. While Captain Benteen might have been pleased with Weihe's potential testimony on personal bravery – or lack thereof – it is clear that the army would not have been so inclined; neither Philip Sheridan nor William Sherman wished for the entire 7th Cavalry Regiment to be so damned – nor the entire army for that matter.

But damned it could have been if Weihe had been in the witness chair and had continued in a manner consistent with his chronicle observations, as it would have opened the door for other observations concerning the officers. Next, in Henry Weihe's diary he commented on George Custer himself. Weihe wrote:[16]

"On the morning of the 27th General Gibbon's column came in sight, as agreed to by General Terry. Custer and Gibbon were expected to communicate with each other by couriers, but General Custer, being insane, we did not expect anything better from him than disobedience of orders which he received from his superior officer."

Researcher Walter Camp annotated the notes to opine that because Weihe was German-born and not well-acquainted with the English language, he probably intended to say that Custer was "rash," not insane. We obviously do not know the answer concerning what Sergeant Weihe intended to connote. If Weihe did mean insane, his characterization of his regimental commander is an entirely new level of how at least one enlisted man in the regiment viewed George Custer. Most viewed him as vain and a "hard-ass"[vi] for imposing harsh discipline and tough, demanding standards. However, many commanders throughout the country's military history have been "hard asses"; in fact some degree of maintaining standards is desirable. But insanity has never been considered an endearing army leadership trait. Had the public started to conclude that perhaps Custer did go insane out on the Plains, a logical subsequent question to ask would have been: why did the army leadership (read Sheridan and Sherman) select and maintain in command a man who might be deranged? This is especially critical as Lieutenant General Sheridan had already "put the word out" that he wanted no disclosures at Chicago that would reflect poorly on the United States Army.[17]

In the best case, Weihe's phrase, "We did not expect anything better from him than disobedience of orders which he received from his superior officer," is not much more flattering. An army exists by leaders at every level following instructions by their superiors. Sooner or later, soldiers who see their leaders disobeying orders will start disobeying orders themselves, an intolerable situation. Much of the court of inquiry was devoted to what degree Major Reno followed

[vi] Once, when some regimental officers were getting late in awaking on an expedition, George Custer had their tents set on fire! Source: James Donovan, *A Terrible Glory: Custer and the Little Bighorn – the Last Great Battle of the American West*, New York: Little, Brown and Company, 2008, 62. "Hard ass" also referred to Custer's ability to ride all day.

orders. While the court may have been inclined to let some of the blame for the defeat rest with a dead hero (Custer), it was another matter altogether to infer that this hero was a serial disobedient of orders from his own superiors.

Finally, Weihe talked about compassion from the commissioned officers toward the soldiers. While compassion may not have been a word understood by many of the soldiers on the frontier, considering the conditions in which they toiled on a daily basis, the public perhaps would not liked to have heard:[18]

> "On the 29th we were landed safely on the boat [the *Far West*], where we took as comfortable places as we could find. The officers of the other regiments were very kind to us, but our own officers kept their distance, with the exception of Colonel Weir[vii] – he was very kind and considerate toward the wounded, and they all remembered him for it."

Thomas French, John Ryan and Henry Weihe from Company M could have shed considerable light on the events in the valley and the hill during the battle at the Little Bighorn. It was unfortunate that none were called to testify; at the very least it would have made the inquiry board investigate far more diligently the events surrounding those confusing two days in June 1876, and provided information that would have made possible a more rigorous examination of those other witnesses who were called to the stand.

Or perhaps it would not have mattered. Walter Camp noted that on October 27, 1912 Jesse Lee, the former recorder of the Reno Inquiry, told him that at the conclusion of the inquiry Colonel Wesley Merritt made a telling comment.[viii] Merritt, one of the colonels on the panel and almost as famous as George Custer before the Little Bighorn, told the group in advance of the public concluding session:[19]

> "We have politely cursed him [Reno] and whitewashed it over."

[vii] Thomas B. Weir was born on September 28, 1838 in Nashville, Ohio. A three-year student at the University of Michigan, he left after graduating to enlist in the 3rd Michigan Cavalry in 1861. He soon was commissioned and was promoted several times being finally brevetted to lieutenant colonel. Weir fought at the battles at Corinth and was a prisoner of war for six months. On July 28, 1866 Weir was appointed a first lieutenant in the 7th Cavalry Regiment; he was promoted to captain on July 31, 1867. Weir participated in the Washita battle and was later given command of Company A; he subsequently became the commander of Company D. At the Little Bighorn he rode a horse named "Jake." Weir was an extremely heavy drinker; he was also rumored to have had a long-term affair with "Libbie" Custer – but this has never been proven. During the reduction of officers in the army in 1869, a board recommended that he be discharged (undoubtedly in part due to his drinking), but a reprieve issued by superiors saved his career. Thomas B. Weir died of congestion of the brain – brought on by acute alcoholism – on December 9, 1876, while on recruiting duty in New York City. Weir was buried on Governors Island and later re-interred in Cypress Hills National Cemetery.

[viii] Wesley Merritt was born in New York on June 16, 1834. He graduated from West Point in 1860, a year ahead of Custer, ranking 22nd of 41 graduates. He was initially assigned to the 2nd U.S. Dragoons at Fort Crittenden in what later became Utah. He led the 2nd Cavalry Regiment at Brandy Station, the largest cavalry battle of the war. Promoted to brevet brigadier general, Merritt commanded the Reserve Brigade of General Buford's 1st Cavalry Division at Gettysburg. After Buford died in December 1863, Merritt was given command of the division, and later was General Sheridan's second in command during the Appomattox Campaign. He fought at Yellow Tavern and Cedar Creek. After the Civil War, Merritt reverted to a Regular Army rank of lieutenant colonel. He then commanded the 9th Cavalry Regiment "Buffalo Soldiers" and on July 1, 1876 became commander of the 5th Cavalry Regiment. He later served as the superintendent at West Point. During the Spanish-American War, Merritt commanded the VIII Corps and landed in the Philippines. He retired as a major general in 1900. Wesley Merritt died at Natural Bridge, Virginia on December 3, 1910. He is buried at West Point.

Postcard of the Palmer House Hotel in Chicago. The Reno Inquiry was conducted in this spacious hotel in early 1879.

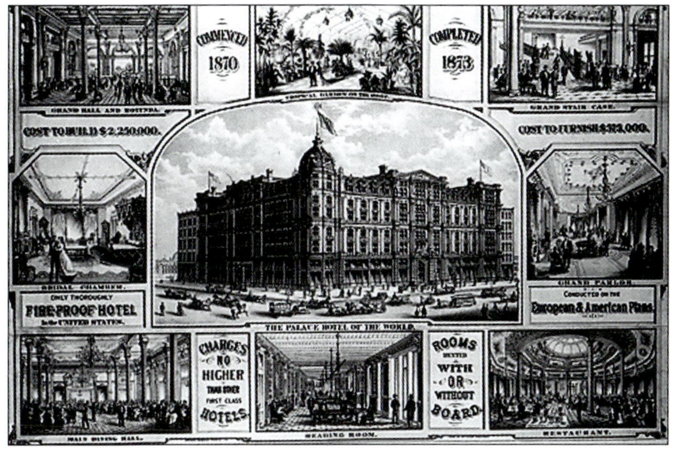

Advertisement for the Palmer House Hotel. The facility was one of the most luxurious in the country.

Sergeant Charles White. White's diary, given to researcher Walter Camp after the trooper's death, indicated that many of the officers in the valley, including Major Marcus Reno, were intoxicated and behaved cowardly. White did not testify at the Reno Inquiry. *Photo courtesy of the Little Bighorn Battlefield National Monument.*

Grave of Colonel John H. King, who served as the president of the court during the Reno Inquiry. He did not call anyone from Company M as a witness; nor did he call First Lieutenant Francis M. Gibson to testify. Colonel King is buried in Section 1 of the Arlington National Cemetery.

Grave of Francis M. Gibson of Company H. Along with Captain French, Gibson was the only commissioned officer of the 7th Cavalry alive in 1879 who was not called to testify. He later served many years as Company M's commander. Gibson is buried in Section 1 of the Arlington National Cemetery.

Grave of First Lieutenant Donald "Tosh" McIntosh of Company G. Killed in the valley, his remains were later re-buried in Section 1 of the Arlington National Cemetery next to the grave of Francis M. Gibson. McIntosh's wife, Mollie, was the sister of Francis Gibson's wife. Many of the officers in the 7th Cavalry were related by marriage.

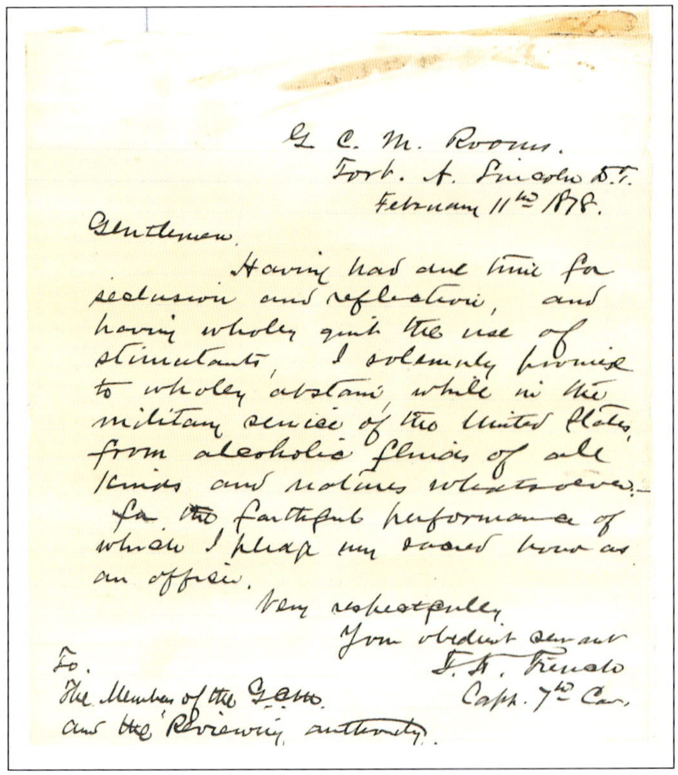

G. C. M. Rooms.
Fort. A. Lincoln D.T.
February 11th 1878.

Gentlemen,

Having had due time for seclusion and reflection, and having wholly quit the use of stimulants, I solemnly promise to wholly abstain while in the military service of the United States, from alcoholic fluids of all kinds and natures whatsoever. For the faithful performance of which I pledge my sacred honor as an officer.

Very respectfully
Your obedient servant
T. H. French
Capt. 7th Cav.

To.
The Members of the G.C.M.
and the Reviewing authority.

Captain French's Letter of Contrition presented at his General Court-Martial in 1879. The original letter is in his court-martial file at the National Archives in Washington, DC. *Photo courtesy of the National Archives.*

CHAPTER EIGHT

POST-BATTLE ACCOUNTS OF COMPANY M PARTICIPANTS AT THE LITTLE BIGHORN

"I think I understand what military fame is; to be killed on the field of battle and have your name misspelled in the newspapers."[1] – General William T. Sherman

Unlike the memoirs of Sergeant Henry Weihe, which were intended to remain private – at least through the lifetime of its author – many veterans of Company M left a wealth of post-Little Bighorn accounts, which have proven to be a boon for Custer and Little Bighorn scholars ever since. One of the first to go public was Private Jean Baptiste "Frenchy" Gallenne, whose account of the battle appeared in the *St. Paul and Minneapolis Pioneer Press* on January 16, 1879. A year after the Little Bighorn, Private Gallenne fought in the campaign against Chief Joseph's band of Nez Percé Indians, and at the battle of Snake Creek on September 30, 1877 he was wounded so severely in the left leg that it had to be amputated. Private Gallenne was discharged at Fort Rice, Dakota Territory, on April 27, 1878 for disability as a private of good character and gave his account nine months later to the newspaper.[2]

First Sergeant John Ryan was a prolific witness to the battle. Some of his recollections appeared in various Newton, Massachusetts newspapers, including the *Allen Megaphone*, the *West Newton Weekly*, the *Newton Town Crier* and the *Newton Circuit* in 1908 and 1909; in 1922 he wrote a piece on Rain in the Face for the *National Tribune*. In June 1923 he published his experiences in both the *Hardin (Montana) Tribune* and *Billings (Montana) Gazette*.[3] But the mother-lode of his experiences – first mentioned in a 1908 letter from Ryan to researcher Walter Mason Camp – remained undiscovered for many decades; it was one of many letters that John Ryan wrote Camp in his later years.[4] Sandy Barnard, the historical community's expert on Ryan, finally tracked down these unpublished memoirs of First Sergeant Ryan in 2000 and published them the following year as *Ten Years with Custer: A 7th Cavalryman's Memoirs*.

Walter Camp interviewed Private James W. Darcy (James Wilber); the account is found in Kenneth Hammer (editor), *Custer in '76: Walter Camp's Notes on the Custer Fight* (1990). Darcy was also featured in "His Story of the Little Big Horn," in *The Tepee Book* (1916), which was reprinted in Colonel Henry Hall's "Reminiscences," *The Tepee Book* (1974). Private John Sivertsen's story was also featured in the same three publications. Camp also interviewed Private William E. Morris; this interview is summarized in *Custer in '76: Walter Camp's Notes on the Custer Fight* (1990) as is Camp's interview of Private John Sivertsen. There is also at least one letter from "Bill" Morris to Walter Camp dated from 1908.[5] Morris also wrote a letter in 1904 to Dr. Cyrus Brady that appears in Brady's *Indian Fights and Fighters* and a letter in 1928 to Robert Bruce that is in the Fred Dustin collection of papers.[6] Sivertsen was also interviewed in 1915 by Colonel Henry Hall; the colonel had intended to publish the account in his own book, *Reminiscences*.[7]

Private Frank Sniffin met with Walter Camp on October 16, 1913 and discussed the battle.[8] The encounter is discussed in *Camp on Custer; Transcribing the Custer Myth* (1995), edited by Bruce Liddic and Paul Harbaugh. Private Ferdinand Widmayer, who remained at the Yellowstone supply depot and did not take part in the ensuing battle, met with Walter Camp on October 7, 1910. His account is summarized in *Custer in '76: Walter Camp's Notes on the Custer Fight* (1990).

Private William C. Slaper had his story, entitled "A Trooper with Custer: The Thrilling Experience of Trooper William C. Slaper, M Company, Seventh Cavalry, in the Battle of the Little Bighorn," in *Hunter-Trader-Trapper Magazine* in 1924. "Bill" Slaper's story is also presented by Earle Alonzo Brininstool, but it is not clear how much of the content was Slaper's and how much was added by Brininstool.[9]

Private Daniel Newell told his story to John P. Everett; it appeared as "The Story of the Bighorn Campaign of 1876" in *The Sunshine Magazine*, a South Dakota publication, in September 1930. Private John Dolan, who also remained at the Yellowstone supply depot, got his discharge there and rode on the *Far West*, arriving at St. Louis on July 13, 1876. His accounts appeared in the *St. Paul and Minneapolis Pioneer Press* on July 16, 1876. Another article, appearing in the *New York Herald*, was entitled "The Dead Hero, Private Dolan's story." It ran on July 23, 1876.[10]

Captain Thomas French did not submit any articles for publication, nor did he record the events of his career in a memoir, as he died just six years after the battle. However, he did write at least four revealing letters to the mother of regimental adjutant, First Lieutenant William W. Cooke, who was killed with Custer on Last Stand Hill. French's February 2, 1880 letter to her contained the following:[11]

> "The fight was not at all in accordance with my ideas. The so-called charge from the valley was almost a rout. I became sick and disheartened with what was going on. It seemed to me that some appalling disaster was being suffered somewhere else – and it was then that I tried to win the combat – or rather turn the tide

– with my single right hand. I hope that you will not regard me as vain or guilty of boastfulness for enclosing this clipping from a newspaper [separated from the letter], because I believe myself to be in the presence of death, and worldly pride – for which I strove so hardily – no longer charms me."

French would be dead in only two years after this letter was written and was now fully haunted by the demons of alcohol, but the writing reveals how wracked he was – sober or intoxicated – with the memories of the battle.

Walter Camp also interviewed Private Edward D. Pigford; several battlefield historians, however, recommend caution when assessing Pigford's accounts.[12] Pigford's story also was published in serial form in the Washington, Pennsylvania *Morning Observer*, October 3-19, 1932, shortly before his death.[13] Camp interviewed Edward Mathey on January 19, 1910.[14]

In the aggregate, Company M troopers provided a large amount of post-battle information for historians to savor for over 130 years. With the exception of a few letters by Captain French, these accounts were entirely an enlisted perspective and which have presented an important facet of cavalry life – and death.

West side of Retreat Crossing of the Little Bighorn River as seen at the 10th Anniversary of the battle in 1886. Original photograph taken by D.F. Barry. *Photo courtesy of the Little Bighorn Battlefield National Monument.*

Opposite

***Top*: East side of Retreat Crossing as seen at the 10th Anniversary of the battle in 1886.** Troopers at the battle then had to scale the high ground to the rear of these horsemen. Original photograph taken by D.F. Barry. *Photo courtesy of the Little Bighorn Battlefield National Monument.*

***Bottom*: Visitors at the 10th Anniversary of the battle in 1886 stand at the northern end of the Reno Hill defenses, where Company M was located on the first day.** Marker to the right is no longer present. *Photo courtesy of the Little Bighorn Battlefield National Monument.*

***Above*: Reno Hill, East End at the 10th Anniversary of the battle in 1886.** View shows depression, or swale, where Captain Benteen established a field hospital. Dozens of small white objects are horse and mule bones; animals were placed on the perimeter of the hospital to serve as shields against enemy fire. *Photo courtesy of the Little Bighorn Battlefield National Monument.*

***Right*: Reno Hill; photo is undated, but was probably taken between 1886 and 1910.** Horse and mule bones are still very visible at the site. *Photo courtesy of the Little Bighorn Battlefield National Monument.*

***Right*: Private William C. Slaper, standing at the left, and Private Daniel Newell, on right, at the 50th Anniversary of the Little Bighorn, 1926**. The two are standing at the monument at the top of Custer Hill; both were interviewed several times by historians. *Photo courtesy of the Little Bighorn Battlefield National Monument.*

***Below*: Private John "Big Fritz" Sivertsen in his older years.** He was later interviewed by Walter Camp. *Photo courtesy of the Little Bighorn Battlefield National Monument.*

***Bottom right*: Private William C. Slaper, in white shirt, with author E.A. Brininstool, at the marker where Dr. DeWolf was killed attempting to climb the bluffs to Reno Hill.** Photo was taken at the 50th Anniversary of the battle in 1926. *Photo courtesy of the Little Bighorn Battlefield National Monument.*

Old Soldiers Never Die; They Just Fade Away

"Shattered and broken with wounds received in serving his country, his last few years were full of pain and suffering."[1]

On November 28, 1876 a board of officers was convened at Fort Rice to dispose of the effects for those troopers assigned to Company M who died at the Little Bighorn. That action took care of the dead, but some of the living might later come to believe that the fallen had been the lucky ones in the fight.[2]

• • •

Toward the end of the Indian Wars in 1891, Secretary of War Stephen Benton Elkins[i] recommended that enlisted men be able to retire from the Regular Army after 20 or 25 years instead of 30 years, which had been the requirement earlier, saying that continuous duty in the West sapped the strongest men in just 10 or 15 years. Secretary of War Elkins said of these old soldiers:[3]

> "They are neither saints nor demi-gods. They are men, often rough in body, ignorant of books, and sometimes deficient in the minor morals, but strong in the sturdy virtues of obedience, truthfulness and fidelity. Prevented from forming family ties, they are friendless in the social world...as guileless and as helpless as children in the sharp competition of civil life."

In many respects, Benton Elkins could have been talking about the men of Company M who survived the battle. While some moved on to a successful life in the civilian world, others languished on the fringes of society, sometimes clearly forgotten by a nation that had moved past the events of the Little Bighorn. Historian Gregory Michno has written one hypothesis that nearly all of Reno's detachment at the battle suffered from "almost every major symptom of combat stress."[4] And he might be correct. Military physicians at the time were one hundred years too early to understand that and post-combat-stress-disorder, which very likely afflicted many survivors of Company M. But the effects of combat were there, both physical and mental, and would haunt many of the troopers in their later years.

[i] Stephen Benton Elkins served as the Secretary of War from 1891 to 1893; during his tenure he improved intelligence functions in the army and improved conditions for enlisted men. Born on September 26, 1841 in New Lexington, Ohio, Elkins also served as a Delegate from the Territory of New Mexico in the early 1870s and as a Senator from West Virginia. He died on January 4, 1911 in Washington, D.C. Senator Stephen Benton Elkins is buried at the Maplewood Cemetery in Elkins, West Virginia.

• • •

Private Frank Braun, who had been wounded in the face and thigh, was transported back to Fort Abraham Lincoln on the steamer *Far West*. But his wounds would not heal; the bullet had burrowed a "tortuous" path through the upper femur into the hip joint. Over the next several months doctors conducted several probes to remove the bullet but were unsuccessful. On September 13, 1876 at Fort Lincoln, Dr. J.V.D. Middleton – the post surgeon – operated on him, enlarging the wound site; the doctor found that elements of Braun's trousers and shirt had been driven into the wound by the bullet. By September 29, Private Braun had symptoms of pyemia, a deadly infection. "Frank" Braun died of this infection early on October 4, 1876.[ii] He originally was buried at Fort Abraham Lincoln, but his body was reinterred in the Custer Battlefield National Cemetery on March 6, 1905 in Grave A-571 (listed as Brown).[5]

• • •

Private James "Jim" Weeks' army career went downhill after the Little Bighorn. He deserted the army on February 3, 1877, but was apprehended by authorities on February 20 in Bismarck and returned to his unit, where he spent time in confinement. On August 24, 1877 Weeks got into an argument with Private "Barney" Golden at Montana Bill's Ranch at the Crow Agency, Montana Territory over a poker game. The exchange grew heated; Golden pulled a pistol and shot "Jim" Weeks in the left hip. Weeks died two days later.[6]

• • •

Captain Thomas H. French had perhaps the most dramatic decline of anyone in Company M after the battle. He bought a new horse – iron-gray in color and $110 in cost – while in camp on Rosebud Creek on August 6, 1876; perhaps this new one was easier to manage than his previous mount.[7] One source states that during the rest of the campaign French consumed only a gallon and a half of brandy but

[ii] Parts of Private Frank Braun's hip are now in the wound trauma collection of the National Museum of Health and Medicine in Washington, D.C., sent there by Dr. J. V. D. Middleton.

was also regularly consuming opium.[8] After attempting to pursue the Indians for the rest of the summer, Company M returned to Fort Rice on November 10 to go into winter quarters.

Again, Captain French was sick. On October 10, 1876 he had been diagnosed with constipation. He was diagnosed with catarrh on November 25, 1876 and January 19, 1877. On April 15, 1877 he complained of chills.[9] In 1877 the regiment again went to the field; Frederick Benteen mentioned on June 9, 1877 in a letter to his wife:[10]

> "French was quite ill, as usual after drunks – and hasn't gotten off his 'toot' as yet. He'll get dropped the 1st thing he knows."

Later in the month, Benteen again wrote his wife, mentioning his fellow captain:[11]

> "I believe French expects to marry in the autumn. He was in arrest for being drunk a few days ago. He won't do to bet a cent on anyway."

Thomas French did not get married, but did continue his tragic decline. Later in 1919, General Hugh L. Scott wrote Colonel Luther R. Hare recalling an incident in 1877 that involved Captain French:[12]

> "At the time we were camped north of the Yellowstone and French took that overdose of opium he stole from the farrier and fell down in front of our tent. He turned blue and I thought he was dead and raised a ruction so the Doctor got him over it."[iii]

But Captain French could still soldier on at times. During the Nez Percé campaign, on June 22, 1877, a soldier noted in his diary French's proficiency with his saber against rattlesnakes:[13]

> "While lying down on the ground today to take a nap, Captain French heard a slight rustle in the sage brush near his head, and he was not slow in getting up either. On investigating with sabre he found a fine rattler, and soon transported its spirit to the happy hunting grounds."

Later in 1877 French was slightly wounded in the left hand on September 13 during the battle of Canyon Creek. Company M went into winter quarters at Fort Lincoln on October 5, 1877; French went on leave for most of December and the first few days of January 1878. But he was even more ill now; he was diagnosed with alcoholism on January 14, 1878 and remained sick in quarters for two weeks. He again reported sick on February 9, 1878 and was diagnosed with acute alcoholism; he remained in quarters for most of the month of February. On May 1, 1878 he reported sick with contusions on his face and hands, most likely the result of a fall when he was intoxicated. On May 10, 1878 he was again diagnosed with chronic alcoholism.[14]

His condition became so bad that soldiers of the company frequently were asked to go to his quarters to help take care of him; this study was unable to confirm if the troopers actually were of benefit or if they went over to drink with their commander to make him feel better – in either case, this relationship between commissioned officer and enlisted was unusual.[15]

In August 1878 the army built a new post, named Camp Ruhlen, four miles south of Bear Butte. Designed for two companies of the 7th Cavalry (Company E and M) and two companies of the 1st Infantry Regiment, it was under the command of Major Henry M. Lazelle of the 1st Infantry.[iv] French apparently reported to Major Lavelle intoxicated, although nothing was said about his condition at the time. In September French went on leave and returned in November. On November 7, 1878 he reported to Major Lazelle as the new Officer of the Day, and again was inebriated. Lazelle put the intoxicated Captain French on four days leave, but First Lieutenant Charles De Rudio,[v] who was a 7th Cavalry Little Bighorn veteran, lodged an official complaint against his superior.[16] French's insult of DeRudio on Reno Hill was about to come full circle.

Major Lazelle was faced with bringing court martial charges against one of the heroes of the Little Bighorn; the four charges and nine specifications included being drunk on duty four times, breaching arrest, making a false statement and drinking with female laundresses; several instances of his conduct on his trip from Fort Abraham Lincoln to Camp Ruhlen in October were entered into the proceedings. French pleaded "Not Guilty" to all counts in the accusation. The General Court Martial at Fort Abraham Lincoln convened on January 6, 1879 and on three different days French absented himself from the proceedings due to illness – most likely being too intoxicated to appear. The trial lasted sixteen days.[vi] Lieutenant John Garland of the 6th Infantry Regiment served as Captain French's counsel. In its final stages, First Sergeant Henry Weihe (Charles White), Sergeant Hugh N. Moore and Corporal Hobart Ryder presented testimony concerning French's sterling performance at the Little Bighorn, to little avail. Realizing that he would be convicted unless something extremely dramatic occurred, Captain Thomas French submitted the following written statement to the court:[17]

[iii] Hugh L. Scott served as the superintendent of West Point from 1906 to 1910 and the Chief of Staff of the United States Army from 1914 to 1917. Born on September 22, 1853, in Danville, Kentucky, he graduated from West Point on June 14, 1876, but did not make it to his initial assignment in the 7th Cavalry Regiment in time for the 1876 campaign; in fact, he had been slated initially to join the 9th Cavalry Regiment before officer shortages caused by losses at the Little Bighorn caused a shift in his assignment. Scott served in the 7th Cavalry for approximately 15 years. Given his considerable talents, Scott probably had a good memory of the event concerning Captain French; General Scott was regarded as the army's most knowledgeable officer on Indian sign language. Hugh L. Scott died in Washington, D.C. on April 30, 1934. He is buried in Section 2 of Arlington National Cemetery.

[iv] Henry M. Lazelle was born in Massachusetts in 1833; he graduated from West Point in 1855, ranking 30th of 34 cadets. While at the academy, he was once the roommate of future artist James McNeil Whistler (who did not graduate). During the Civil War, Lazelle commanded the 16th New York Volunteer Cavalry Regiment. Lazelle later commanded Fort Sully and then Camp Ruhlen (which became Fort Meade) in the Dakota Territory. He became the Commandant of Cadets at West Point in May 1879, and held this position until 1882. Colonel Lazelle later commanded the 18th Infantry Regiment and the post of Fort Bliss, Texas. He was retired for disability in 1894 and subsequently was promoted to brigadier general. Henry M. Lazelle died on July 21, 1917 in Quebec, Canada.

[v] Charles C. "Count No-Account" DeRudio was born on August 26, 1832 in Belluno, Italy. An Italian aristocrat, he attended an Austrian military academy before departing to join a group of Italian patriots during the uprising in 1848. On January 14, 1858 DeRudio was part of an attempt to assassinate Emperor Louis Napoleon (Napoleon III). He was caught and sentenced to life imprisonment on Devil's Island. DeRudio escaped and immigrated to New York City in 1860. He enlisted in the 79th New York Volunteer Regiment and fought at the Siege of Petersburg. On November 11, 1864 Charles DeRudio was commissioned a second lieutenant in the 2nd U.S. Colored Infantry Regiment. After the war he was an unassigned officer until July 14, 1869 when he was assigned as a second lieutenant to Company H of the 7th Cavalry. On December 15, 1875 he was promoted to first lieutenant and assumed command of Company E. For the 1876 campaign, however, Custer placed First Lieutenant Algernon Smith in command of Company E and assigned DeRudio in Company A. After the Little Bighorn, DeRudio commanded a newly-formed Company E during the Nez Percé War in 1877. Stationed at Fort Meade, Dakota Territory, he was promoted to captain on December 17, 1882. DeRudio retired in the grade of major on August 26, 1896. He died on November 1, 1910 in Pasadena, California of acute enteritis and bronchial catarrh. He is buried at the San Francisco National Cemetery.

[vi] The members of the court were: Lieutenant Colonel Charles C. Gilbert (7th Infantry), *President*; Captain John S. Poland (6th Infantry), *Judge Advocate*; Captain Edward P. Pearson (17th Infantry); Captain William A. Elderkin (Subsistence Department); Captain Louis H. Sanger (17th Infantry); Captain Jeremiah P. Schindel (6th Infantry); and Captain Henry Jackson (7th Cavalry).

General Court Martial Room
Fort Abraham Lincoln, Dakota Territory
February 11, 1879

Gentlemen,
Having had due time for seclusion and reflection, and having wholly quit the use of stimulants, I solemnly promise to wholly abstain, while in the military service of the United States, from alcoholic fluids of all kinds and natures whatsoever, for the faithful performance of which I pledge my sacred honor as an officer.

Very respectfully,
Your obedient servant
T.H. FRENCH
Captain, 7th Cavalry

The letter did not win sympathy and the jury found Captain French guilty on four specifications, but after the court martial sentenced French to dismissal from the service, President Rutherford B. Hayes commuted the sentence to suspension of rank and reduction to half pay for one year. Part of the suspension of punishment may have come from a letter written by Brigadier General Alfred H. Terry, approving the results of the court martial on February 26, 1879:[18]

> "I have known Captain French for many years, and, notwithstanding the unfortunate habits into which he has fallen, I have still high respect and regard for him...He has excellent capacity and chivalric courage. There is no stain upon his moral character except this one of intemperance. If he can keep the pledge which he has given, he will be an ornament to the army – an officer whom the service cannot afford to lose. My doubt is whether he has the power, even with the best intentions, to adhere to his resolution.
>
> On the whole, however, I am inclined to think that it would be best to give him this one opportunity for reformation, and I therefore join in the recommendation to mercy."

Terry's approval and recommendation then went to General William T. Sherman. On March 14, 1879 Sherman wrote the following short letter and attached it to the packet, which would go to President Hayes:[19]

> "The proceedings and findings of the General Court Martial in the foregoing case of Captain French, 7th Cavalry, [are] approved, and the record is respectively forwarded to the Honorable Secretary of War for the action of the President. **Attention is respectively invited to the endorsement of General Terry hereon.**" (*Author's emphasis*)

President Hayes understood the chain of command's desire for leniency. On March 22, 1879, he commuted the sentence to suspension of rank on half pay for one year.[20] During this suspension, French stayed at Fort Meade, Dakota Territory for the bulk of 1879. He was replaced as company commander by Second Lieutenant Baldwin D. Spilman[vii] Several visiting officers noted that his problem with alcohol was continuing and the decision was made to initiate retirement proceedings for him. Colonel Samuel D. Sturgis, again in command of the 7th Cavalry Regiment, wrote the following to army officials: [21]

> "But Captain French is useless to the service now and in my judgment will be so for the future, and in his present partially (if not wholly) imbecile condition he is little more responsible for his acts than an infant would be."

Captain Thomas French was ordered to appear before a Retiring Board that was empanelled at Fort Leavenworth, Kansas. By this time, French had been in residence at the Inebriate Asylum. The board found him permanently incapacitated for active service by reason of intemperance, not service-caused. This could have precluded a pension, but in consideration of wounds and service, again President Rutherford B. Hayes intervened and directed that Captain French be placed on the retired list; Captain Thomas H. French retired from the army on February 5, 1880.[22]

Just five days later French reported sick to the post hospital at Leavenworth. Two weeks later a mysterious fire destroyed his home in Bismarck. Sinking deeper into alcoholism, French moved into a hotel in downtown Leavenworth, Kansas, but nothing could stop – or even slow – his descent. On June 16, 1880 he wrote the following to Mrs. Cooke, mother of deceased First Lieutenant William W. Cooke, from the St. John's Hospital at Leavenworth, Kansas:[23]

> "The hotel was a bad place for me. I became worse there, and the rheumatic pains which had been confined to my knees and the joints of the feet extended to my shoulder and hand, on the right side."

On August 6, 1880, an embittered man, he wrote another letter to Mrs. Cooke in which he railed against his accuser Charles DeRudio calling him a:[24]

> "black-faced, and black-hearted Italian scoundrel...[who] could not tell the truth if he tried...I acknowledge that I hate him...That thing knows no more of the [Little Bighorn] fight than any washer-woman in Chicago. He was not in it. Before the first shot was fired he was in the bushes, and stayed there."

Most sources state that Thomas H. French died of apoplexy in his room – Room 11 – in the Planters' House Hotel at Leavenworth on March 27, 1882 at 12:30 p.m. However, author Dennis K. "DK" Clark, who has extensively studied frontier cavalry in general and the 7th Cavalry Regiment in particular, postulates that Captain French may have died of acute lead poisoning, caused by the long-term effects of drinking alcohol from a water canteen that had a lead solder seal.[viii] Such a combination of elements might allow the alcohol to leach the lead found in the solder, after which the poisonous substance would be inadvertently consumed over several years. The conditions described in French's June 16, 1880 letter to Mrs. Cooke lend weight to this conclusion. Thomas French was originally buried with full military honors at the Fort Leavenworth National Cemetery, but his body was reinterred on March 4, 1891 at the Holy Rood Cemetery in Washington, D.C., in Section 23, Lot 257.[25]

[vii] Baldwin D. Spilman was born in Virginia on July 15, 1878. He graduated from West Point in 1878 ranking 28th in his class. He reported to the 7th Cavalry Regiment at Fort Abraham Lincoln on September 29, 1878. Spilman resigned his commission from the Regular Army on September 1, 1887. He then commanded the West Virginia National Guard. Baldwin D. Spilman died at Warrenton, Virginia in 1926.

[viii] "DK" Clark also posits that Captain Thomas B. Weir, commander of Company D, earlier may have died of the same cause in December 1876.

The Leavenworth Times published an obituary on March 28, 1882, which read in part:[26]

> "Those who know Captain French best will bear witness that no truer words were ever written that he was one of the bravest men ever in the service."
>
> "In the army, as before stated, none had a brighter record for bravery than Captain French. He never commanded his men to go where he feared to lead them; and all under him respected him as a true friend in every emergency. Shattered and broken with wounds received in serving his country, his last few years were full of pain and suffering."
>
> "He had his faults; but as he now lies in his coffin, one arm folded on his breast, the other by his side, so quiet and peaceful that he seems only to sleep, and shrouded in the uniform he had never dishonored by cowardice, we only remember that a brave man has been placed on the retired list forever."

• • •

Unfortunately, Private Daniel Mahoney's brother Bartholomew, of Company L, was killed in the battle, but Daniel and his other brother John survived the battle. But Daniel was not a well man and spent from April 19 to November 25, 1877 sick at Fort Rice. Private Daniel Mahoney was discharged for medical reasons at Fort Abraham Lincoln on April 14, 1878 as a private of good character. He received a pension of four dollars/month for an inguinal hernia disability. In December 1883 Mahoney moved to Washington, D.C. Daniel Mahoney died at the Barnes Hospital, U.S. Soldiers' Home, Washington, D.C. on August 7, 1885 of phthisis pulmonalis (tuberculosis), diarrhea and exhaustion. He is buried there at Section K, in Grave 6564; over the years his gravestone has become almost unreadable. His mother received his pension after his death.[27]

• • •

From the mid-1830s, General Winfield Scott fought to establish a soldiers' home for disabled veterans. At the conclusion of the Mexican War, Scott – now a national hero – returned to Washington and offered Congress thousands of dollars for the project. The United States government finally established the Soldiers' Home in 1851 in Washington, D.C. to serve as an asylum for old and disabled veterans.[ix] During this period, soldiers who were amputees, chronically ill, or were classified as mentally deranged could elect to enter the Soldiers' Home. Initially the government purchased a cottage and surrounding farmland to use for the facility at a price of $58,000; the cottage had been constructed in 1843 as the home of banker George W. Riggs – who went on to found the famous Riggs Bank in Washington. Located on the highest point of land in the city, it was regarded at the time as second only to the White House as a mansion in the capital city; it was the first house in the city to have natural gas as a replacement for kerosene in the lamps for illumination.[28]

Inmates first lived at the Early Gothic Revival style cottage – which soon became known as the Anderson Cottage (later renamed the Lincoln Cottage) named for Major Robert Anderson who commanded Fort Sumter in 1861 – for about five years and then moved to Scott Dormitory, just to the east of the cottage. Inmates lived in eight-man squad rooms; almost every room had a large open fireplace; troopers could enter the home even if they were married provided that their spouse lived somewhere else. The home expanded with the addition of a facility medical building, the Barnes Hospital, named for Colonel Joseph K. Barnes, who had been the Army's Surgeon General in the Civil War. The grounds of the home increased over the years to a final size of 320 acres, which included a cemetery. A permanent trust fund – fed by monthly deductions from active duty soldiers' pay, as well as fines imposed by courts martial – provided resources for the operation of the facility.[29]

• • •

Private Charles Kavanaugh transferred to Company E on October 19, 1876 as the regiment reformed those companies that had been wiped out in the battle. Records show that he was in confinement in December 1876. He was discharged on September 12, 1880 at Fort Meade, Dakota Territory as a private of excellent character. Kavanaugh returned to New York, but on June 7, 1881 the call of the army became too strong and Charles enlisted in Battery G of the 3rd Artillery at Fort Schuyler, New York. On June 10, 1882 he was diagnosed with dyspepsia. He was discharged for total disability at Fort McHenry, Baltimore, Maryland for consumption (tuberculosis.) He later received a $24/month pension for disability for a heart ailment, lung consumption and a venereal disease.[x] Charles Kavanaugh died at the U.S. Soldiers' Home, Washington, D.C. on February 14, 1886 of phthisis pulmonalis (tuberculosis). Kavanaugh is buried there at Section K, in Grave 6462.[30]

• • •

Private George "Cully" Weaver remained in Company M after the battle. He reported ill with acute bronchitis on February 23, 1881. He re-enlisted on March 15, 1881 at Fort Meade, Dakota Territory. On September 11, 1881 he was diagnosed with contusions on his face, the result of participation in a brawl. On July 23, 1883 he was thrown from a horse and sustained contusions on his left ankle and side – such was the life of the company farrier.[31] On September 30, 1886 "Cully" Weaver reported ill on sick call and was diagnosed with lumbago. But it wasn't lumbago and he was admitted on October 13 with terrible pain in his bowels. It was peritonitis and he died the next day.[32] The long-time company farrier is buried in the Post Cemetery there, Section 4, Row 6, in Grave 184.[33]

• • •

Private George Heid remained in the 7th Cavalry, but changed companies inside the regiment several times. He was discharged on March 15, 1877, but re-enlisted four days later at Fort Abraham Lincoln for Company G. Sometime later, George Heid transferred to Company I. He served as a hospital nurse for four months and a company tailor in 1881. He was discharged on March 18, 1882 and re-enlisted one additional time six days later at Fort Totten, Dakota Territory. During this final enlistment, George Heid was again a company tailor, cut wood for the post and stacked hay. Private George Heid died at Fort

[ix] The facility later became known as the Old Soldiers' Home and later the U.S. Soldiers' and Airmen's Home.

[x] Mercury, often in the form of calomel, was used to treat venereal diseases at the time. Highly toxic, it could lead to mercury poisoning, which could lead to disintegration of the teeth and gums, loss of memory and shaking of the limbs – often called "mercuric trembling."

Totten on February 1, 1887. He was originally buried there, but his body was re-interred at the Custer Battlefield National Cemetery, Section A, in Grave 97.[34]

• • •

Private Joseph Bates (also known as Joseph C. Murphy) was discharged on February 28, 1877 at Fort Rice, Dakota Territory, but re-enlisted the same day, switching to Company H. Yet alcoholism was claiming another cavalryman. Bates was discharged on February 19, 1878 for disability as a private. The post surgeon that day noted Bates' condition, which included:[35]

> "[He has] constant contamination of his blood with alcohol. He is useless as a soldier and unfit for that profession."

Bates became a civilian teamster (possibly in Arizona), but his troubles continued. On May 13, 1880 he was dragged on the ground by a mule, an accident that resulted in a fractured jaw, loss of teeth; one of the wheels also cut off his left ear in the mishap. Never married, on April 29, 1891 Bates began to receive a $10/month pension for heart disease and rheumatism, but became more and more despondent. "Joe" Bates committed suicide on September 13, 1893 in Sturgis, South Dakota, supposedly by drinking "Paris Green," an insecticide that was also used as a colorant in fireworks. He is buried at the Sturgis-Bear Butte Cemetery, Section 2, Row 2, in Grave 43.[36]

• • •

Sergeant Patrick Carey was transported back to Fort Abraham Lincoln on the *Far West* and then spent five weeks in the hospital. He was court-martialed in January 1878 for being absent without authority (but was acquitted) and again in November 1879. This second trial, a General Court Martial, happened after he was placed in charge of the stable guard for the company at Fort Meade, Dakota Territory on October 12, 1879 and became drunk on duty. Carey immediately went absent without authority for three days before he was arrested at Sturgis City on October 17. The court martial was held on November 11, 1879. Major Marcus Reno was assigned as the President of the Court but as he was under arrest, this position fell to Captain Frederick Benteen. Sergeant Carey pled guilty; during the trial both Major Reno and Captain Benteen testified for the defense concerning Carey's character. Benteen stated: "Outside of his disposition for liquor, I think he is a good soldier."[37]

At the trial a statement was submitted on behalf of Sergeant Carey's company commander, Captain Thomas French. The statement, dated November 11, 1879, read:[38]

> "Sir,
> I am, and have been for several days quite ill, and am unable to leave my room. I am therefore compelled to send a communication instead of appearing in person; my signature can be readily identified.
>
> I have known you since 1871. Your character, except for occasional intemperance, is good. You carried the guidon beside the Commanding Officer in the fight on the Yellowstone River in August 11, 1873, and your conduct was then admirable. You were with, and near me, in the battle on the Little Big Horn on June 25 and 26, 1876, were severely wounded, and behaved exceedingly well.
>
> Very respectfully,
> Your obedient servant
> T. H. French
> Captain, 7th Cavalry"

Patrick Carey submitted his own statement as well, which read:[39]

> "To the Honorable Gentlemen and members of the General Court Martial now in session at this Post:
>
> Gentlemen,
> I have the honor to state in regard to the charges for which I am being tried that I entered a plea of Guilty for the following reasons.
>
> In regard to the 1st Charge and its specifications in violation of the 38th Article of War I entered a plea of Guilty for the reason that I was partially under the influence of liquor, but not so much so, as to be unable to properly perform the duties of a soldier or take charge of my guard. I had been suffering all day with severe griping pains in my stomach caused by indigestion which I am subject to very often, and on several occasions have relieved myself of the pain by taking a small amount of Brandy and a peppermint, and resorted to this mode of cure in this instance, and the first preparation did not relieve me. I repeated it twice, and not being in the habit of drinking intoxicating liquor and my stomach being out of order, the liquor slightly deranged my mental faculties, but not to such an extent as would naturally be supposed as alleged in the charges. In regard to leaving my guard for one hour, I will say I had to leave to attend a call of nature, and from there went to the Post Hospital to get some medicine, but could not find the Steward, so I returned to my guard whereupon I was relieved for being drunk on duty.
>
> I am sure there had been any grounds to show willful intent to leave my guard the charges would be framed under the 40th Article of War instead of the 38th. I was released from arrest by my company commander for this offense (if there was any committed) and returned to duty and upon the committal of the offense alleged in the 2nd Charge and its specifications my company commander ignored the reprieve he had granted me and has me arraigned. Before this court under the charges you see before you, in regard to the 2nd Charge and its specifications I have little to say. I acknowledge I committed a breach of discipline and I expect to be punished accordingly.
>
> I would also state that I have served ten years in the Seventh Cavalry and three years in the Seventh Infantry and of this time have been a non-commissioned officer for four years. The court has seen my discharges and the character they bear and with one exception (and I was acquitted) I have never been arraigned before a General Court Martial before in all my service, and as I have only a short time to serve (about 4 months) to complete this enlistment. I hope the court may take into consideration the facts of the case as I have stated and be as lenient as possible with me.
>
> I am Gentlemen
> Very Respectfully
> Your obedient servant
> Patrick Carey
> Sergeant, Company M 7th Cavalry"

Neither Captain French's nor Sergeant Carey's letter did the trick. Carey was convicted of all charges and reduced to the rank of private. He also was sentenced to a fine of $10 a month for four months.

Private Carey re-enlisted on April 19, 1880 in Troop L of the 7th Cavalry and re-enlisted again on April 19, 1885 in Troop E of the 7th Cavalry, but was never promoted past private again. On July 1, 1887 Carey was discharged for disability with chronic rheumatism. He later received a monthly pension of eight dollars for eye disease. Late in life "Patsy" Carey resided at the U.S. Soldiers' Home in Washington, D.C.; he died at Barnes Hospital there on October 3, 1893 of senile debility and exhaustion. He is buried at the Soldiers' Home National Cemetery in Section K, in Grave 6659.[40]

• • •

Private Hugh Moore was appointed corporal on August 1, 1876 to fill a vacancy caused by Company M's losses at the Little Bighorn and was promoted to sergeant on December 1, 1876. He was discharged from the army as a "brave, trustworthy and faithful soldier" on August 24, 1877 on the Yellowstone River, Montana Territory, but re-enlisted the same day. He was then made the acting quartermaster sergeant for the company, but got into trouble and was placed in arrest from December 1877 to January 12, 1878. Sergeant Hugh Moore was then brought before a General Court Martial on the charge that he was drunk on duty on December 8, 1877. Major Lewis Merrill of the 7th Cavalry was the President of the Court. Moore pleaded guilty but attempted to have the sentence be lenient by submitting a statement from his company commander. Captain Thomas French wrote the following statement – dated January 12, 1878 – on Moore's behalf, which was accepted into evidence by the court:[41]

> "Sir,
>
> You tell me that you are to be tried today before a General Court Martial and you ask for recommendation from me. I do not know what the charges against you are, but I do not hesitate to comply with your request.
>
> Since you have been in my company, and you are now in the first year of your second reenlistment. Your conduct has been excellent, excepting that, at rare intervals I am sure not more than once in any one year, you drank too much, but the occasions have been overlooked by me on account of your value as a soldier in the field.
>
> In the fight at the mouth of the Big Horn River, August 11, 1873, I noticed you and you did well. In the terrible battle of June 25 and 26, 1876 of the Little Big Horn, you did all that any man could do, and I had frequently to check you when I thought that you were needlessly exposing yourself. You contributed in a great part to our success in repelling the charge made on our line by the Sioux on June 26.
>
> In the fight against Joseph's men, September 13 last, you again proved yourself – a brave, true, soldier.
>
> Very respectfully
Your obedient servant
T. H. French
7th Cavalry
Captain of Co. M"

The court was not merciful and reduced Sergeant Hugh Moore to private, put him on hard labor for 30 days (the first seven days were on bread and water) and sentenced him to forfeit five dollars a month for three months.[42]

In February 1879 Hugh Moore testified as a character witness in the court martial of Captain Thomas H. French. He is shown on the company rolls as a private in June 1879 and was detailed as the company cook in October 1879.[43]

Moore again began to rise through the ranks and was promoted to corporal on May 10, 1881 and to sergeant on October 25, 1881. But then disaster struck, and he was court-martialed again on December 28, 1881 and reduced to private. This time he was found drunk while in charge of the company stable guard on November 20, 1881 at Fort Meade, Dakota Territory. He also left his post without authority and went to the Soldiers' Bar Room, which was against the orders of his company commander, now Captain Francis M. Gibson.[xi] Moore pled guilty and was reduced to private, sentenced to hard labor for six months and fined $10 a month for six months.[44]

Moore was discharged as a private on August 12, 1882 and re-enlisted the same day. Once again, he began to soldier again and made corporal on February 14, 1883, but success was temporary. A General Court Martial on October 6, 1883 reduced him to private and sentenced him to two months confinement and fined him $10 a month for two months. This time Moore was drunk on duty at drill at Fort Meade, Dakota Territory on September 20, 1883. Captain Gibson testified that Moore was unable to do the carbine manual of arms because of his condition. Moore tried to defend himself by saying that he had been out on pass the night before and had not slept.[45]

After serving as a target repairer and post librarian, Moore made corporal on May 16, 1885 and sergeant on February 14, 1887. In the meantime, he was diagnosed on March 2, 1885 with intercostal rheumatism.[46] But then disaster struck. Moore reported sick on June 19, 1887 with a headache, a shadow of upcoming events. He was diagnosed on June 23, 1887 with inebriation and kept in quarters until July 13. Moore was reduced to private on July 18, 1887. His condition did not improve and on July 29, 1887 he was once again diagnosed with inebriation; on this occasion he remained in quarters for 16 days. Hugh Moore was discharged at Fort Meade, Dakota Territory on August 23, 1887.[47]

Moore took two weeks to think over what he wanted to do next. But despite his ups and downs, he knew the army was his home and he re-enlisted on September 7, 1887 with Company K. That company promptly transferred him to Company F on September 27, 1887. But some things never changed. While on guard duty on November 25, 1887, at Fort Meade, Dakota Territory, Private Hugh Moore was accused of being drunk on duty. A General Court Martial convened and Moore pled guilty. The court found him guilty, but changed the charge to conduct prejudicial to good order and military discipline. They sentenced him to confinement at hard labor for two months and to forfeit $10 a month for two months.[48]

[xi] Francis M. "Gibby" Gibson was born in Philadelphia, Pennsylvania on December 14, 1847. Also nicknamed "Frank" and "Gib," he was commissioned a second lieutenant in the 7th Cavalry Regiment on October 5, 1867, initially assigned to Company A. He fought at the Washita and later at the 1873 Yellowstone Campaign and 1874 Black Hills Expedition. He was viewed as one of the inner circle of Custer associates in the regiment. Gibson rode a horse named "Blue Streak." During the Little Bighorn fight, he temporarily commanded Company G after Donald McIntosh – his brother-in-law – was killed. Gibson was promoted to first lieutenant on July 11, 1871 and to captain on February 5, 1880. Francis M. Gibson retired from the army on disability on December 3, 1891. He died in New York City on January 17, 1919 and is buried at Arlington National Cemetery in Section 1 – right next to his brother-in-law Donald McIntosh.

In February and March 1888, Moore served as an assistant post librarian.[49] Moore appears to have ended his military service on August 19, 1889 at Fort Sill, Indian Territory; he was discharged as a private of good character "when sober," a chronic alcoholic. He later resided at the U.S. Soldiers' Home in Washington, D.C. Moore applied for a pension but was rejected. Hugh Moore died at the Soldiers' Home on September 3, 1900 of mitral insufficiency. He is buried at the cemetery at the U.S. Soldiers' Home, Section J, in Grave 6825.[50]

• • •

After the Little Bighorn, Private Levi M. Thornberry continued serving in Company M. He suffered a compound fractured nose on March 2, 1878 and did not return to duty for 19 days.[51] By then he had caught gold fever. He deserted on June 7, 1878 with Private "Happy Jack" Varner and went to the Black Hills and subsequently to Alaska to mine gold. Apparently he was quite successful, and with his stake he purchased a farm in Watertown Township, Washington County, Ohio. He got married on July 11, 1899 and had one son, born in 1901, whose name appears to have been Gordon. Levi Thornberry died on May 27, 1902 at Watertown, Ohio. He is buried in the Watertown Cemetery, Watertown Township, Ohio, Section 5, Row S, in Grave 22.[52] Levi has two tombstones; one is a typical stone of the period, while the other has the inscription:

Levi Madison Thornberry
US 7th Cavalry
Veteran Indian Wars

Levi's wife, Linnie, who was born in 1873, died January 6, 1960 and is buried with him.

• • •

Private Henry "Harrison" Davis was appointed to the rank of corporal on August 1, 1876 after the Little Bighorn, but was reduced to private on October 16, 1876 and was discharged from the army on December 21, 1876 as a private of good character. He then spent two years as a civilian; he re-enlisted on January 4, 1879 in Company H, but transferred back to Company M, where he became the company gardener. Davis sprained his left shoulder at Fort Meade on October 23, 1881 when he fell off a porch. On February 4, 1883 he was diagnosed with neuralgia, a type of nerve pain. On April 13, 1883 he reported sick at Fort Meade with a boil.[53]

Davis was discharged on January 3, 1884 at Fort Meade, Dakota Territory, but re-enlisted four days later and was assigned to Company E. For much of this enlistment Davis served as a quartermaster teamster. He was finally discharged from the service on January 6, 1889 at Fort Sill, Indian Territory as a private of excellent character. For a time, he resided near Standing Rock Agency, Dakota Territory. He applied for a pension on July 9, 1890. Henry "Harrison" Davis was reported to have frozen to death in the winter of 1905, but recent research indicates that he may have died in Monessen, Pennsylvania on May 21, 1918. His widow then received his pension.[54]

• • •

Saddler John "Jack" Donahoe was discharged from his second enlistment on October 20, 1876, but re-enlisted the following day. Donahoe got into some difficulties and was placed in confinement in December 1877. He was discharged on October 19, 1881 at Fort Meade, Dakota Territory and re-enlisted immediately. But his career was about to go downhill. Donahoe reported sick on February 14, 1884 and was diagnosed with inebriation. On July 13, 1884 doctors diagnosed him with chronic alcoholism. They made the same determination on November 30, 1884. He then went into confinement and was diagnosed in the guardhouse to be suffering from chronic alcoholism on January 3, 1885.[55]

In February 1885 he was again in confinement and served in confinement once again in June 1885. He was diagnosed three more times that year with either inebriation or chronic alcoholism: July 25, October 8 and November 21. In 1886 he was diagnosed with chronic alcoholism on March 23, June 1 and August 8.[56]

He completed his fourth enlistment on October 20, 1886. Once again, "Jack" Donahoe re-enlisted in Company M. His drinking continued and on November 5 and December 2, 1886 he was diagnosed with inebriation. The following year proved no better. On May 3, 1887 Donahoe went on sick call for alcoholism.[57] Donahoe was transferred to Company G on September 9, 1890. Two months later, the saddler transferred to Company E. He was discharged on October 19, 1891 at Fort Riley, Kansas, and re-enlisted in Company E. Saddler Donahoe was discharged from this enlistment on October 19, 1896 at Fort Grant in the Arizona Territory. He re-enlisted three weeks later at this location. "Jack" retired from the army on November 11, 1896 at Fort Grant, amassing an incredible 30 years of service. John Donahoe died on November 16, 1905 at San Francisco, California of heart failure.[58]

• • •

Private Morris Cain was discharged from the army as a private of excellent character on July 4, 1877 in Sunday Creek, Montana Territory. He remained in the west and was married at Fort Keogh, Montana Territory on January 2, 1881. As a civilian, Morris Cain ran a paint shop, was a wheelwright and operated a blacksmith shop in Glendive, Montana. He also was the first man to carry the mail from Bismarck to Fort Keogh (today Miles City.) Morris Cain died on August 13, 1906 in Colville, Washington. His widow applied for his pension.[59]

• • •

Sergeant Henry C. Weihe (Charles White) was transported to Fort Lincoln on the *Far West*. He recuperated from his wounds and returned to duty on July 20, 1876.[60] Weihe was appointed first sergeant of Company M on January 1, 1877, after First Sergeant Ryan was discharged from the army. He also won Ryan's custom-made Sharps rifle in a raffle.[61] On April 16, 1878 he reported sick suffering from the chills. He was reported as suffering from a fever on August 10, 1877, which developed into acute bronchitis. He did not return to duty until October 29, 1977. On January 15, 1878 he was diagnosed as suffering from catarrh. Doctors confirmed on February 9, 1878 that he had tonsillitis; he remained in quarters for 11 days. On April 14, 1878 he was treated for a boil, while on June 21, 1878 he was diagnosed with acute rheumatism. He reported ill with constipation on July 23, 1878. He ended the year with a sprained left leg after being kicked by a horse on December 20, 1878.[62]

In February 1879 Henry Weihe testified as a character witness in the court martial of Captain Thomas H. French. He reported ill with constipation on July 6, 1879 and remained in his quarters, sick for 20 days.[63]

On September 1, 1879 First Sergeant Charles White received a General Court Martial. A year earlier Company M had a problem soldier, Private William C. Orr. Not only was Orr a problem; he was a thief and had stolen money from his fellow soldiers. Major Marcus Reno served as the President of the Court; Captain Frederick Benteen and Myles Moylan were on the panel as well. White was charged with threatening to "sling-belt out" Private Orr out of the army after learning of his conduct. This was an unauthorized punishment, and was generally understood to mean that the accused would be beaten up with clubs and belts (such as carbine slings) so badly that he would desert. White pled not guilty, but the prosecution brought in several witnesses, including Little Bighorn veterans William Lalor and Robert Senn, who claimed they heard White talk about it. But Orr was never "sling-belted" as he deserted on May 19, 1878. (When he returned he was court-martialed and as a result charges were brought against First Sergeant White.) The defense countered with testimony by Captain Thomas French, who was no longer the company commander. French testified that White had always been truthful, but that Orr was a self-confessed thief and pickpocket. He also stated that in 1877 Private Thomas "Happy Jack" Varner had severely beaten Private Orr after catching Orr stealing $30 from him. Toward the end of the trial, First Sergeant White was sworn in and gave the following testimony:[64]

> "On the 20th day of May 1878, while stationed at Fort Abraham Lincoln, Dakota Territory, as 1st Sergeant of Company M, 7th Cavalry, it was reported to me that Private Orr had stolen $30 from Corporal Lasco. The corporal was at my house at the time he reported it. We started right away to the company kitchen, where Orr was. He denied about stealing the money at first. In the morning about 7 or 8 o'clock he came into the orderly room and said he would sign a receipt for the $30, if Lasco would say nothing further about it. I then went and saw Lasco and he said as long as he got the money back that was all he wanted. The receipt was signed promising to pay Lasco next pay day, for value received and witnessed by myself and sent to Captain French for his approval. During this time a great deal of talk was going on in the company, calling him, Orr, everything they could think of and said he ought to be kicked out and the men were pretty hot about it, and were going to beat him out.
>
> I told them they should not touch him, as he was going to pay the money back. I heard nothing about sling-belting him out of the company. Lasco came in to the orderly room and said: 'Orr has deserted.' This was at noon on May 21, 1878. I asked 'When did he go?' He said: 'I just found it out.' I then sent the corporal after him. I did not use any such conversation to anybody as Private Kane or Lalor testified to. After his, Orr's trial, he came out of the court room and said: 'I am alright, don't you give me away.'"

White's statement apparently did no good. French's testimony did not help. The court found White guilty and sentenced him to be reduced to private, given a dishonorable discharge, ordered to forfeit all pay and allowances and ordered to be confined for six months.[65]

Weihe was dishonorably discharged as a private on October 5, 1879 and began his six months confinement, but the sentence was remitted a month later. First Sergeant Louis E. Hull took over as first sergeant for Company M at this time. Weihe indicated at the conclusion of his court martial that he would try and get the witnesses against him charged with perjury but there is no further record of this action.[66]

Weihe enlisted again on March 16, 1881 in Troop H of the 7th Cavalry. He suffered an ankle contusion when a log fell on him on December 3, 1882 and was diagnosed with acute bronchitis on April 2, 1883.[67] Weihe married Sarah Wells – the widow of Farrier Benjamin Wells, who was killed as a member of Company G in the valley fight at the Little Bighorn – on September 14, 1884; she died three years later. He was in charge of the post garden from March 1885 to January 1886. He was discharged on March 15, 1886 at Fort Meade, Dakota Territory and re-enlisted in Company K. An abscess caused him to be hospitalized from November 1886 to January 1887. After returning to health he again was in charge of the post garden from March to July 1887.[68]

Weihe was court-martialed once again on August 13, 1887 and discharged on November 15, 1887 at Fort Meade. After leaving the army he became a farmer; he remarried on July 29, 1889. Later in life Weihe received a pension of $17 a month as compensation for gunshot wounds, rheumatism and heart disease. Henry C. Weihe passed away of heart disease on October 29, 1906 at Fort Meade, Sturgis, South Dakota. He is buried at the post cemetery there under the name Charles White, in Section 4, Row 6, in Grave 191. Three years after his death his contemporaneous notes of his army career were made available to a Little Bighorn researcher by his widow.[69]

• • •

Private "Frank" Neely continued his checkered career after the Little Bighorn. Promoted to corporal on August 1, 1876, he was discharged on September 9, 1876. Later that day, he re-enlisted, but was reduced to private on October 16, 1876. Neely served several times as the company cook and also ran the company garden. He went on sick call on May 3, 1879 with conjunctivitis. "Frank" Neely suffered a laceration on his left foot, when a wagon ran over it on July 5, 1879; that injury kept him from duty for 13 days. On April 17, 1880 he was diagnosed with tonsillitis.[70]

He finished his term of enlistment and was discharged on September 8, 1881. Neely bummed around Milwaukee for a few months and re-enlisted there on March 20, 1882. He was assigned to Troop K of the 6th Cavalry two months later. By April 17, 1883 he had been promoted to corporal once again; he was promoted to sergeant on April 20, 1884. But his health was not good. On January 11, 1884 at Fort Lowell, Arizona Territory, he was diagnosed with another venereal disease characterized by ulcers and phimosis of his penis. The following day he underwent an extremely painful incision in the area and was returned to duty.[71]

Trouble struck again and "Frank" Neely was reduced to private on January 9, 1886. Three months later he transferred to Troop D in the same regiment and became the troop cook. He re-enlisted the following year and was promoted, yet again, to corporal on August 27, 1888 and to sergeant on February 6, 1890. But disaster walloped Neely once more, and on April 29, 1890 he was busted to private; Neely was discharged from the army a final time on September 23, 1890 at Fort Stanton (in what would become New Mexico) – his up-and-down career indicates the strong possibility that he was an alcoholic. Neely was later reported as living in the Arizona Territory, in San Francisco and near Sheridan, Wyoming. He applied for a pension on November 27, 1896, but abandoned the effort.[72] One source believes that "Frank" Neely may have died on October 24, 1907.[73]

• • •

Private Jean Baptiste Gallenne was diagnosed as suffering from pleurisy at the conclusion of the battle and placed under medical care. He contracted typhoid fever on August 6, 1876 and did not return to duty until November 21, 1876. Gallenne later became a Hospital Steward Second Class. On September 30, 1877, during the Nez Percé Campaign, Gallenne was assisting the surgeons on the battlefield, when he was wounded in the left ankle while getting additional medical supplies. An army surgeon later described the incident:[74]

> "Some time before the [afternoon] charge was made on the village, 1st Lt. Romeyn of the Infantry made an appeal to me to visit some of his men who were in urgent need of attention. They were behind a hill, but separated from the balance of the wounded by a depression which was under fire from the village...I directed the Steward [Gallenne] to accompany me and we all three ran across without receiving any salute from the Indians. Upon opening the medicine case, I saw that the dressings were used up, and directed him [Gallenne] to return to the supplies, fill the case and come back to me. He deliberately walked over. I called to him to run, but he replied, 'Oh, they won't hit me.' He got across safely; but in returning in the same way he was shot through the left ankle, and it was some time before he could be brought out. He crawled some distance and when the attention of the Indians was occupied in another direction, two men helped him to the Hospital."

Oral history in the Gallenne family indicates that Private Jean Gallenne believed he had been accidently shot by an officer's pistol.[75] In the confusion of a firefight, this could have easily happened. Doctors had to amputate Gallenne's left leg on October 14 on the riverboat *Silver City*, effectively ending his army career; before he departed the service he was treated for catarrh on December 11, 1876.[76]

After his army service, Jean Gallenne moved to New Orleans, where he became a druggist and lived at 433 Marais Street. He applied for his military disability pension on May 16, 1878; after his leg had been amputated, Jean had a wooden leg. Life was looking up and on December 9, 1878 he married Josephine Joly – who was born on January 6, 1859 in New Orleans, but whose father had come to New Orleans from Haiti – at St. Joseph's church in Gretna, Louisiana. In 1892 Jean moved to Washington, D.C. – where he lived at 814 6th Street NE – and raised seven children with his wife; it appears that his mother-in-law lived with them. Jean Gallenne later became a watchman in the Department of the Interior; his dark bushy moustache and silver hair gave him a formidable appearance, as he walked the halls with his cane tapping. In later life, Jean's moustache and hair turned white as he became a portly grandfather, sometimes offering a grandchild a sip of wine. Possibly at work, Jean stood on a chair to light a gas lamp – according to family history – and part of the wooden leg snapped and penetrated his leg; the ensuing infection could have hastened his death.[77]

Jean "Frenchy" Gallenne died in Washington, D.C. of a cerebral hemorrhage on February 12, 1911. He is buried at Washington, D.C.'s Mount Olivet Cemetery, North Site, Section 18B, in Lot 218. Josephine received his pension of $30/month until she died on November 21, 1940.[78] Their children included: Rita Marie (born October 20, 1879), Jeanne Gabriel (born July 20, 1883), Jean Baptiste (born December 8, 1884), Genevieve Eugenie (born September 2, 1886), Reine Isabelle (born February 5, 1889), Joseph Michael (who died in early childhood), Jean Baptiste Hector (born June 24, 1891) and Louise (born on March 3, 1901).[79]

• • •

Private James "Crazy Jim" Severs was discharged on November 12, 1877 at Fort Rice, Dakota Territory but re-enlisted the same day. He became the company farrier in January 1878. He also did telegraph line repairing and carpentry. James Severs left the army for good on November 11, 1882 at Fort Meade, Dakota Territory. He later received a six dollars/month pension and resided in Saratoga, Wyoming. But "Crazy Jim" was convicted of grand larceny and sentenced to incarceration at the Wyoming State Prison in 1896; he was granted a full pardon on April 17, 1903. His health began to fail and he was sent to the State Hospital for the Insane at Rock Springs, Wyoming. Private James Severs is believed to have died in the facility of an accident in late 1912.[80]

• • •

Private John Valentine Whisten – the instigator of the Company M riot on March 23, 1876 – was court-martialed again in December 1876; Captain Frederick Benteen served as the President of the Court and Captain Thomas French sat on the jury. Whisten was charged with going to the billiard room at the post trader's store on November 15, 1876, after being ordered not to by his company commander. He pled guilty and offered in defense that he misunderstood his commander's order. The court found him guilty and sentenced him to confinement at hard labor for 15 days and to receive no pay for one month.[81]

Whisten received a second General Court Martial in almost record time. While he was on confinement as a result of the first conviction, he was disrespectful toward Second Lieutenant John Gresham[xii] in the guard house and also gave a false name, when asked his identity. He pled guilty, was convicted by the same sitting General Court Martial board and was sentenced to hard labor and confinement for two months and fined $10 a month for four months.[82]

This double-barrel hit was apparently no impediment to Whisten's career, or was a lacerated wound to his hand he suffered on January 2, 1878.[83] He was discharged as a private of excellent character at Camp Ruhlen, Dakota Territory on September 22, 1878. After a brief break in service, he enlisted in the 3rd Artillery Regiment in 1879, and re-enlisted in the unit in 1884. In 1889 he decided to try his luck in a third branch and enlisted in Company D of the 11th Infantry Regiment. From September 8, 1889 to September 19, 1902, John Whisten served in the 28th and 70th Coast Artillery. During that time he fought in the Spanish-American War in the Philippines, and in China in the Boxer Rebellion. About this time he married and began raising a family of two boys. Now a sergeant, John Whisten retired after 30 years of army service at Fort Point, Presidio, at San Francisco, California on September 19, 1902. John Valentine Whisten died on November 12, 1912 in Oakland, California. The causes of death were chronic nephritis and chronic endocarditis. He is buried at St. Mary's Cemetery in Oakland, Section K, Area 3, Row 3, in Grave 3. His widow received Whisten's pension.[84]

[xii] John C. Gresham was born on September 25, 1851 in Lancaster, Virginia. He graduated from West Point in 1876, 33rd of 48 cadets. Initially designated for assignment to the 3rd Cavalry Regiment, he was re-assigned to Company M to replace Lieutenant Sturgis; on November 27, 1876 he was acting commander of Company M. He was promoted to first lieutenant on June 28, 1878. He fought at the battle of Wounded Knee on December 29, 1890 and received the Medal of Honor for his action. Gresham was promoted to captain on May 8, 1892 and major September 17, 1901. Gresham also served in the Philippines and advanced to the grade of colonel. Colonel John C. Gresham died in San Diego, California on September 2, 1926. He is buried at the San Francisco National Cemetery at the Presidio in Section OS, Row 4-A, in Site 5.

• • •

First Lieutenant Edward G. Mathey was deeply affected by the battle and took leave from October 25, 1876 to September 10, 1877. He was appointed to captain on September 30, 1877 and assumed command of Company K.[85] "Gus" Mathey then went through another period of ill health. On May 29, 1879 he reported ill with rheumatism. He was diagnosed with cholera on July 1, 1879 and on July 18, 1879 reported sick with rheumatism. He was diagnosed with tonsillitis on May 2, 1880. Mathey then was in an accident and was diagnosed with a simple fracture on June 15, 1880. His medical files also show he reported sick with catarrh on April 21, 1883.[86]

Mathey rose to the grade of major and retired for disability on December 11, 1896. He was married to Meda Jones; the couple had one daughter, Julia. Mathey later spent two years as a Professor of Military Science at Baylor University. The army, perhaps sensing that his career was more than the sum of its parts, appointed Mathey to the grade of colonel on the retired list on April 23, 1904. Edward Mathey died on July 17, 1915 at Mercy Hospital in Denver, Colorado. The causes of death were listed as intestinal paresis and renal congestion; one source states that he died after a prostate operation. Edward G. Mathey is buried at Arlington National Cemetery, Section 3, in Grave 2089. His wife died on February 19, 1917; prior to her death she received a $40 per month pension.[87]

• • •

Private "Snopsy" Meier remained in the army for many years after the Little Bighorn. Because of his wound, he was transported on the steamer *Far West* back to Fort Abraham Lincoln. A Garrison Court Martial convicted him in July 1876 of being drunk and disorderly and for fighting a private from Company B of the 1st Infantry Regiment behind the barracks. Perhaps taking his recent trauma in consideration, the panel imposed a fine of just $3.[88]

John Meier was in confinement in April 1878. He was discharged on September 3, 1878 at Camp Ruhlen, Dakota Territory, but re-enlisted two weeks later. Meier was promoted to corporal on August 9, 1883; he was discharged on September 16, 1883 at Fort Meade, Dakota Territory. He re-enlisted and was promoted to sergeant. However, on September 6, 1885 his progress came to an end; on that date he was diagnosed with inebriation at Fort Meade.[89] On December 18, 1886 "Snopsy" was the non-commissioned officer in charge of the stable guard for his company at Fort Meade, Dakota Territory. And "Snopsy" was drunk. Captain Francis Gibson, Meier's company commander, testified at the General Court Martial:[90]

> "I have known the accused for a little over six years. He has been a very good soldier and non-commissioned officer. Often he has been drinking entirely too much to suit me and has utterly ignored the words of warning I have given him on that score – hence his present behavior."

The court found Sergeant John Meier guilty and sentenced him to be reduced to the rank of private, confinement at hard labor for three months and a fine of $10 per month for three months.[91] Meier was court-martialed again on February 17, 1887. Meier bruised his left foot on May 10, 1887 when a wagon ran over it.[92]

"Snopsy" Meier was promoted to corporal on December 1, 1887 and to sergeant on April 10, 1888. He was discharged at Fort Riley, Kansas on September 16, 1888. Meier re-enlisted again and spent a few months drilling recruits, but got into trouble again and was reduced to private at a court martial on August 26, 1889. Apparently, on August 7, 1889 at Fort Riley, Kansas Private Meier was at mounted drill with his unit. And "Snopsy" was drunk. A General Court Martial was convened and Meier pled guilty, offering the following statement in his defense:[93]

> "I was drinking the night before and felt stupid that morning, and I happened to make a few mistakes, which very seldom happens to me. When the drill was over the First Sergeant had us confined."

The court agreed that "Snopsy" had been stupid, found him guilty and sentenced him to one month at hard labor.[94] On April 2, 1890 he was promoted one more time to corporal, but was court-martialed on August 25, 1890 and reduced to private.[95]

On September 10, 1890, when Company M was "skeletonized" and inactivated, Meier was transferred to Company A. He became a corporal on June 1, 1891 and was promoted to sergeant on November 1, 1891. On September 16, 1893, however, he ran afoul of another court martial and was reduced to private and discharged the same day at Fort Riley, the discharge mentioning a weakness for drink. Despite this discharge, Meier was allowed to re-enlist just one week later on September 23, 1893 in Company I. He made corporal once again on July 6, 1894 and sewed on his sergeant's stripes on August 29, 1896. But his army days were numbered and on December 22, 1896 at Fort Huachuca, Arizona Territory he was discharged again. Not to be denied, Meier went east and re-enlisted on March 16, 1897 in New York with Company C of the 5th Artillery Regiment. He supposedly fell down a staircase, fractured his skull and died on February 22, 1899. However, other sources state that after he left the service, Meier became a farmer and moved to Washougal, Washington, where he died of chronic nephritis on July 12, 1917. Those sources state that John H. Meier is buried in Washougal Cemetery, Block 100F, Section B, in Lot 99.[96]

• • •

Private James Wilber Darcy was evacuated to Fort Abraham Lincoln after the battle on the steamer *Far West* due to his serious wound in the left leg, which fractured his tibia. He was discharged at the fort on November 1, 1876 for medical disability as a private of good character. Darcy was admitted to the U.S. Soldiers' Home on December 2, 1877. His gravestone notes that he served in the Spanish-American War. Darcy began to receive a pension in 1917. James Wilber Darcy (James Wilber) died of a cerebral hemorrhage and arteriosclerosis at Barnes Hospital, U.S. Soldiers' Home, Washington, D.C. on July 13, 1920. He is buried there in Section K, Grave 8301. His wife, Martha, received a pension after his death of six dollars/month.[97]

• • •

Sergeant John McGlone was discharged on December 17, 1877 at Fort Abraham Lincoln as a sergeant of excellent character. McGlone then went east to Columbus, Ohio; on December 27, 1877 enlisted with Company F of the 5th Infantry Regiment. McGlone was discharged from that enlistment on December 26, 1882 at Fort Keogh (in what later became Montana). Again he travelled east and re-enlisted in New York on May 1, 1883 with Company C of the 12th Infantry Regiment.[98]

On September 5, 1883 he was on his way with another corporal to attend the Creedmore rifle competition at Creedmore, Long Island – when the two stopped in a New York City saloon for some refreshment. Corporal McGlone consumed too much and somehow lost his weapon and equipment, as well as the other corporal. McGlone panicked and deserted until March 9, 1885, when he surrendered to authorities in Memphis, Tennessee. He was subsequently court-martialed and pled guilty. Originally sentenced to four years confinement at the military prison at Fort Leavenworth, he served three years confinement after the sentence was reduced.[99]

Reportedly John McGlone later lived in San Juan, Puerto Rico for a few years, before moving to the U.S. Soldiers' Home, Washington, D.C. John McGlone died at Barnes Hospital on August 28, 1920 of pulmonary edema, chronic myocarditis and mitral regurgitation. He is buried at the Soldiers' Home National Cemetery. His marker was found and identified to the cemetery superintendent by researcher David Veve in October 8, 2009.[100]

• • •

Private Charles T. Wiedman remained with the company despite his wound and returned to Fort Abraham Lincoln. He was the company cook from December 1876 to February 1877. But 1877 was a terrible year health-wise for the trooper. He was kicked by a horse and suffered a lacerated left leg on July 24. On July 29 Wiedman was diagnosed with gonorrhea. A hospital orderly found that Wiedman was suffering from a toothache on August 1. He was reported as sick with gonorrhea on August 12. His gonorrhea flared up again on August 31; he remained in the hospital until October 6. On October 30 the symptoms of gonorrhea came back. Wiedman was kicked by a mule on November 15. He reported suffering from a boil on December 10. The year ended with Wiedman diagnosed on December 20 with chronic rheumatism.[101]

The next year started out poorly; on January 9, 1878 he was diagnosed with syphilis. Wiedman was discharged for medical disability – due to wounds received at the battle – at Fort Abraham Lincoln on March 20, 1878; he was also listed on the discharge as having syphilis. After becoming a civilian, he next became a mining promoter. Married twice, Wiedman lived in Montana and later Arizona. On November 14, 1918 he began to receive a $20/month pension for gunshot wounds and Bright's disease (acute nephritis). Charles Wiedman died at Oatman, Arizona on May 15, 1921 of heart failure. He is buried in Kingman, Arizona at Mountain View Cemetery, Section 7, Lot 20, in Grave 3. His widow received his pension after his death.[102]

• • •

Private Roman "Henry" Rutten was evacuated on the steamer *Far West* to Fort Abraham Lincoln due to his wounds received in the battle; he returned to duty on August 25, 1876. He then suffered a sprain on September 2, 1876 and did not return to duty until October 11, 1876.[103]

Rutten was discharged as a private of very good character at Fort Rice, Dakota Territory on July 17, 1877 and immediately re-enlisted. He reported sick with chronic rheumatism on August 14, 1879 and again on February 18, 1883.[104]

Rutten continued his exemplary service in the regiment, serving at Camp Ruhlen and Fort Meade in the Dakota Territory, and at Fort Riley and Fort Leavenworth, Kansas. He was diagnosed with influenza on February 1, 1885 and with acute diarrhea on August 30, 1886. On October 15, 1886 Roman was diagnosed with sub-acute rheumatism and did not return to duty for one month. He was diagnosed with chronic rheumatism in both legs on April 29, 1887 and remained sick in his quarters for two months.[105]

At this point, Company M was inactivated in the general downsizing of army cavalry regiments, and Rutten faced reassignment to Troop B at Fort Riley – with expected deployment to the Arizona Territory. Roman Rutten had done his share and instead of accepting that move, admitted himself to the Wadsworth Soldiers' Hospital (at Fort Leavenworth) for wounds sustained at the Little Bighorn and remained there until September 21, 1890, when he was retired for disability. His final duty position had been as tailor for the Army Staff School at Fort Leavenworth, the precursor to today's Army Command and General Staff College, where he had tailored uniforms for such luminaries as Brigadier General Wesley Merritt and Arthur MacArthur. At that point Rutten was credited with 34 years of service, but this was in error; he served 24, which was an admirable total in its own right.[106]

Roman Rutten lived at the U.S. Soldiers' Home for two years and then moved back to Leavenworth, Kansas, where he received a $16/month pension for heart disease, deafness and rheumatism – apparently receiving no compensation for his shoulder wounds acquired at the Little Bighorn. He and "Kate" raised their four children to adulthood, but his daughter Verena passed away in 1914. "Henry" Rutten died on April 16, 1925 in Leavenworth, Kansas of lobar pneumonia and senility. He is buried at the Fort Leavenworth National Cemetery, Plot F, in Grave A-252.[107]

• • •

Private John Sivertsen later fought in the 1877 Nez Percé Campaign, including the fight at Canyon Creek. He was discharged at Fort Abraham Lincoln on June 19, 1878, but re-enlisted a week later at Fort McHenry, Maryland in Battery D, 2nd Artillery. In 1881 "Big Fritz" helped guard Charles J. Guiteau, who had shot President James Garfield. He was finally discharged from the army on June 24, 1883 at Camp Washington, at Gaithersburg, Maryland. Over the next twenty years he was married to Anna Olsen, raised a son, Sigward Oliver, and farmed near Lake Nebagamon, Wisconsin; he was awarded a $24/month pension for total disability. He attended the 40th anniversary of the battle on June 25, 1916. John "Big Fritz" Sivertsen was admitted to the U.S. Soldiers' Home on August 6, 1925; he died of cardiovascular-renal disease and arteriosclerosis at Barnes Hospital, U.S. Soldiers' Home, Washington, D.C. on August 30, 1926. He is buried there in Section L, in Grave 8799.[108]

• • •

First Sergeant John Ryan left the army on December 21, 1876. On his discharge paper his company commander, Captain Thomas French, characterized him as "A brave, capable, and trustworthy First Sergeant." Gregory Michno, *The Mystery of E Troop: Custer's Gray Horse Company at the Little Bighorn*, concluded that Ryan left the army because of Captain Frederick Benteen's enmity toward him and the roadblock that would be on future promotion.[109] But Ryan had seen a lot of killing, killing of his fellow comrades, from the Civil War to the Indian campaigns and that almost certainly weighed on his mind as well.

Ryan returned to his home at West Newton, Massachusetts, joined the police force and raised a family of four children. Soon after becoming a civilian in 1877, he filed for invalid status from the army based on the wounds he had received and the general wear and tear on his body. He rose to the rank of police captain, which he achieved on March 16, 1903. John Ryan retired from the police force on January 21, 1913. He was active in his later years in veterans' reunions and maintaining contact with 7th Cavalry veterans. On August 25, 1915 John Ryan was awarded a pension of $24/month for his service as a private in Company C of the 28th Regiment Massachusetts Infantry; this was increased to $30/month on August 25, 1920. This was later increased to $50/month, and on March 19, 1924 this pension was increased to $72/month for the old veteran. But Ryan's health began to deteriorate and that year he suffered a stroke. Earlier on January 19, 1922 Ryan sent a letter to his "old Comrade" Thomas Norwood, thanking Norwood for encouraging Ryan to accept the position of corporal back in his early days in the 7th Cavalry.

John Ryan died at his home in West Newton on October 14, 1926 at age 81 of myocarditis and arteriosclerosis. He is buried at the Calvary Cemetery there in Section 7, in Lot 673.[110]

• • •

Private William E. Robinson, who had done noble service as a medical assistant for Dr. Henry Porter during the fighting on Reno Hill, later served as a hospital attendant and as a cook at the post hospital. He was diagnosed with acute rheumatism on January 12, 1877 and was kicked in the left foot by a horse on July 27, 1877.[111]

Robinson was discharged from the army on September 30, 1878 at Camp Ruhlen, Dakota Territory. His discharge stated he had been a private of excellent character. In later life, he began to receive a pension on June 5, 1917. William E. Robinson died on February 4, 1928 in Seattle, Washington. He is buried in the Evergreen/Washelli Cemetery (East Side), in the old section 210 in Grave 3.[112]

• • •

Private Frank W. Sniffin, the trooper who saved Company M's colors, was promoted to corporal on April 26, 1877. He reported sick with tonsillitis on January 24, 1878. Sniffin was reduced to private in March 1878. He served as the company cook in June 1878 and was a telegraph line repairman in 1880. He was discharged on August 31, 1880 at Fort Meade, Dakota Territory, but re-enlisted on September 21, 1880.[113] Sniffin then had some really rough years; he was court-martialed twice in nine months. On August 15, 1881 at Fort Meade, Dakota Territory, Corporal Sniffin was insubordinate toward First Sergeant Hobart Ryder. Sniffin pled not guilty but the General Court Martial did not agree and after finding him guilty, sentenced Sniffin to be reduced to private, confined to hard labor for six months and fined $10 per month for six months. However, the convening authority, Brigadier General Alfred Terry, did not agree. Perhaps recalling the valor that Sniffin displayed at the Little Bighorn, and having some issues with Ryder's conduct during the confrontation, General Terry reduced the sentence to just a fine of $10 for one month.[114]

Sniffin was promoted to sergeant within the next year, but ran into more trouble. Late on the night of May 17, 1882 he assisted Corporal Charles M. Clark in assaulting Sergeant Frank Kurtz of Company M in the barracks at Fort Meade, Dakota Territory. It was an open and shut case and Sniffin pled guilty to the charge. The General Court Martial sentenced him to reduction to private, confinement at hard labor for one year and a fine of $10 a month for 12 months. Again Brigadier General Terry intervened; for this case he reduced the confinement to three months and the fine for the same period.[115]

Almost as soon as his sentence was over, Sniffin was promoted back to corporal on November 1, 1882 and to sergeant on August 9, 1883. He had reported sick with catarrh, a respiratory infection, on July 23, 1883.[116] But he had a nose for trouble, especially when it came to trouble with First Sergeant Hobart Ryder. At mounted drill on May 7, 1884, Ryder ordered Sniffin to wear a trial pair of Wallins-type spurs as part of an equipment test. Ryder refused and a General Court Martial followed. He pled not guilty, but the court found him guilty. Perhaps sensing the tension between the two non-commissioned officers, the court sentenced Sniffin to a $10 fine.[117]

Frank Sniffin and Kate Salmon, age 16, became parents on March 4, 1885 at Fort Meade, Dakota Territory, when Kate gave birth to a daughter, Jeanette Francis.[118] Sniffin was discharged on September 21, 1885 as a sergeant of excellent character and immediately re-enlisted. In 1890 Sniffin was at Fort Riley, where he was reduced to private. On December 20, 1892 he transferred to Company E; he was promoted to corporal on January 20, 1893 and to sergeant on March 20, 1893.[119]

"Frank" Sniffin seemed uncomfortable as a non-commissioned officer. On March 2, 1895 Sniffin requested to be reduced to private. He was discharged at Fort Grant, Arizona Territory, on August 3, 1895 and immediately re-enlisted. He became the company clerk for a year and a half and was promoted to corporal on January 26, 1898. After re-enlisting that August, Sniffin was promoted to sergeant. He finally retired as the first sergeant of Company E of the 7th Cavalry on October 24, 1905, having also served in the Spanish-American War in Cuba. He was divorced from his first wife in 1902; on August 8, 1910 Sniffin married Margaret McCarthy, who had been recently divorced. He later lived in Hamilton, Tennessee, and also resided at the Elk's Home in Chattanooga. Frank W. Sniffin died at Fort Oglethorpe, Georgia of a cerebral apoplexy on April 17, 1931; Margaret began receiving "Frank's" pension the following month; she died on March 24, 1959. He is buried, with his wife, at the Chattanooga National Cemetery, Section T, in Grave 13675.[120]

• • •

The thanks that Private Edward D. Pigford received for the Little Bighorn was to be discharged on October 15, 1876 at Fort Abraham Lincoln for concealing the fact that he was underage when he first joined the army. On the reverse of the discharge Captain Thomas French wrote:[121]

> "This soldier was engaged in the Battle of the Little Big Horn, June 25, 1876."

Pigford returned to Allegheny County, Pennsylvania, resumed coal mining and was married in 1880; his first wife died – Edward Pigford and his second wife, Phobe Haire, had three children: Joseph, Charley and Sadie. Pigford received a $30/month pension beginning on March 17, 1917. Edward D. Pigford died at Lock Three, Allegheny County, Pennsylvania of septicemia on December 16, 1932. He is buried at Dravosburg, Pennsylvania in Richland Cemetery, Section C, Lot 568, in Grave 3.[122] Someone has placed a nice metal memorial plaque at his grave stating that he was in Troop M of the 7th Cavalry; there do not appear to be any close relatives buried near him.

• • •

Private Daniel Newell became a farrier/blacksmith for Company M after returning to Fort Abraham Lincoln on the *Far West*. In early September 1876 he got into an argument with a corporal from Company H. Tempers flared and Newell called the non-commissioned officer "a snotty-nosed son of a bitch," and then struck the unfortunate corporal and refused to go to the guardhouse. A Garrison Court Martial found Newell guilty and sentenced him to a $2 fine.[123]

On May 30, 1877 he was diagnosed with diarrhea, while on August 9, 1877 medical personnel said he had colic.[124] Newell fought in the 1877 Nez Percé Campaign. He was kicked in the hand, probably by a horse, and suffered a contusion on February 10, 1878; on February 21 he fell and sprained his left shoulder.[125]

Private Newell was discharged from the army on October 8, 1878 at Camp Ruhlen, Dakota Territory, but became a civilian blacksmith for five years at Fort Meade, Dakota Territory, and later claimed that he had put the last set of horseshoes on the famed 7th Cavalry horse "Comanche."[126] Newell married Mary Harlow on July 9, 1882 and became a city councilman in Sturgis, South Dakota. He later received a $50/month pension for gunshot wounds. Daniel Newell died of gangrene of the right foot, a fracture of the right femur and general senility on September 23, 1933 in Hot Springs, South Dakota at the National Military Home. Newell is buried at the Bear Butte Cemetery, Lot 120, Section 1, in Row 5 at Sturgis, South Dakota. Mary survived him by four years and received his pension during that time.[127]

• • •

After the battle, it appears that "Bill" Slaper became the orderly for Captain Thomas French, as he later recalled cooking for him, and discussing what went on during the battle. Private William C. Slaper later became the Fort Rice hospital cook from December 1878 to February 1879. He then did a stint as the company cook. He was appointed a corporal on October 29, 1879 and became acting company quartermaster sergeant from December 1879 to April 1880. He was discharged from the army on September 9, 1880 at Fort Meade, Dakota Territory as a corporal of good character and initially went back to Cincinnati; his mother – who had not wanted him to join the army – died within three months of his return. William was later a salesman. Slaper's wife died in 1914 – the couple had no children; he received a $75.33/month pension beginning in 1917. When his story was published in 1924, Private William C. Slaper lived in Los Angeles, California. "Bill" Slaper attended the 50th Anniversary Ceremony of the battle in 1926. He died on November 13, 1931 in the National Military Home in Sawtelle, California of advanced myocarditis, arteriosclerosis and senility. He is buried in the Los Angeles National Cemetery, Section 79, in Grave 8.[128]

• • •

Private William E. Morris continued his wild ways after the battle, but only after hearing some tragic news. His half-brother, Private Byron Tarbox of Company L, had been killed with Custer less than three hours after the siblings had parted good-naturedly on the trail.[129]

Morris recovered from his wounds and returned to duty on July 31, 1876. He reported sick with catarrh on January 12, 1877.[130] Later that month Morris was court-martialed and sentenced to fifteen days hard labor and forfeiture of one month's pay for conduct prejudicial to good order and military discipline, after he told his first sergeant he could take a written order and "stick it into your arse."[131] He reported a contusion of the leg on February 20, 1877 and went on sick call for acute diarrhea on July 22, 1877.[132]

On August 24, 1877 Morris broke his left forearm in a drunken brawl with "Jim" Weeks – when Weeks struck him in the forearm with the butt of a pistol, but served during the 1877 Nez Percé Campaign the following month.[133] Morris was discharged from the army on December 11, 1877 at Fort Abraham Lincoln for disability – his company commander termed Morris' character as "worthless." Because the injured arm did not heal properly, his left arm was an inch and a half shorter than his right.[134]

Morris' life then underwent a sea-change. He moved to New York and got a job as a waiter in a Bowery restaurant, studying law at night. He married Sarah Abbie on December 7, 1879 at Calvary Baptist Church and gained admission to the bar; the couple later had a son. Some years later, Morris joined the New York National Guard and became a captain in the 69th Infantry Regiment, serving in Mexico. After forming a criminal defense firm, William Morris was elected in 1911 as a municipal judge in the 2nd District, Bronx, New York City. Beginning on September 23, 1923 he received a $20/month pension for disability (gunshot wounds and rheumatism). He also found time to enter politics and served one term in the New York State Assembly and two terms as an Alderman. William Morris attended the 50th Anniversary Ceremony of the battle in 1926. Judge William E. Morris died on November 26, 1933 at his home in the Bronx in New York City of lobar pneumonia and arteriosclerosis. He is buried in Valhalla, New York at Kenisco Cemetery, Section 178, Lot 7471, in Grave 1.[135]

• • •

Other men just disappeared into the recesses of history. Corporal William Lalor was promoted to sergeant on August 1, 1876 and then ran the post sawmill. He was the acting company quartermaster sergeant in December 1877, but was reduced to private on January 18, 1878. The following month he served as the company cook; he served again as the cook from October 1878 and February 1879. Lalor later tended the company garden. On September 1, 1879, he testified in a General Court Martial against First Sergeant Henry Weihe (Charles White). Private William Lalor was discharged on September 28, 1880 at Fort Meade, Dakota Territory as a private of good character. Later in life, Lalor applied for a pension, but this was denied. He is believed to have returned to Knockannia, Montrath, in County Queens, Ireland and died there sometime after 1912.[136]

• • •

Private Rollins L. "Robert" Thorpe, the young man who lied about his age to get in the army and then was discharged for being a minor, left camp at the mouth of the Big Horn River on the steamer *Durfee* and went to Bismarck. He later married Annie E. Smith in Bismarck, Dakota Territory on December 14, 1879.[137] Rollins Thorpe has not been traced since.

• • •

Bernard Golden remained in Company M after the battle. He was diagnosed with an abrasion on December 12, 1876. At Fort Rice on March 18, 1877 he reported on sick call with chills. After shooting and killing Private James "Jim" Weeks at the Crow Agency, Montana Territory on August 24, 1877, Private Bernard Golden did not stay in the army for long. The unit confined him to the guardhouse after the incident, but he was cut on his left cheek by a knife during a brawl in the field on November 15, 1877. Golden was transferred to the hospital at Fort Stevenson, Dakota Territory and returned to duty on December 6, 1877.[138]

On December 18, 1877 Golden deserted at Fort Abraham Lincoln, Dakota Territory and never appeared again in history. Before he departed the fort, he gave Roman Rutten a "nice lump of money" but never contacted the company tailor to collect it.[139]

• • •

Trumpeter Charles "Bounce" Fischer was court-martialed in December 1876 for losing his .45 army revolver and for being absent without leave from October 7 to October 10, 1876. He pled not guilty. Concerning the charge concerning his weapon, Fischer brought up that he had given his issue pistol to Sergeant Charles White during the fighting at the Little Bighorn, and later obtained another pistol, which was why he did not have his issue .45. Fischer was acquitted of the weapon's charge, but found guilty of being absent and fined eight dollars a month for a two-month period.[140]

He was sick in hospital from February 22 to March 20, 1878 for chronic alcoholism. Fischer was discharged on June 16, 1878 for chronic alcoholism at Fort Abraham Lincoln. Fischer joined the army again on May 15, 1880 at Fort Garland, Colorado and joined Company A of the 6th Cavalry Regiment, but he was discharged on September 20, 1880 in Gunnison, Colorado for fraudulent enlistment. The next five years of his life remain in the shadows. From February 1885 to May 1885 he was in and out of a hospital in St. Louis; he was finally released at his own request. Fischer applied for a pension on October 31, 1885, but his request was rejected. He later worked for Walter Sterland – a former private in Company M who had been on detached duty during the Little Bighorn fight – in Bismarck, North Dakota. Charles "Bounce" Fischer may have later lived in Baltimore, Maryland.[141]

• • •

Private Charles H. Williams was promoted to corporal on May 25, 1877; he then was in charge of the company kitchen in December 1877. He was reduced to private on January 18, 1878 and was placed in confinement; in August that year he was detailed the company cook. In June 1879 Williams again was placed in confinement. He was discharged at Fort Meade, Dakota Territory on August 3, 1880 as a private of good character. He returned to civilian life for nine months; on May 29, 1881 Williams enlisted in Company G of the 7th Cavalry at Fort Keogh, Montana Territory. Williams served as the company gardener in October 1881; in 1884 he was assigned as a quartermaster carpenter and a quartermaster storekeeper. He was discharged from the army and 7th Cavalry Regiment on May 28, 1886 at Fort Keogh.[142]

From 1877 to 1880, Charles Williams' medical records show how tough life could be for a cavalryman on the frontier. On February 18, 1877 he went on sick call with tonsillitis. He was diagnosed with neuralgia on April 7, 1877. He received some type of puncture wound on January 23, 1878. On November 16, 1878, Charles was kicked by a horse and suffered a leg contusion. He was ill with bronchitis on January 14, February 8 and February 13, 1879. On March 5, 1879 he reported sick with a fever. He had constipation on June 1, 1879, and on July 27, 1879 he was diagnosed with acute diarrhea. Williams suffered from influenza beginning on January 29, 1880. Finally on February 25, 1880 he was diagnosed with catarrh.[143]

On June 10, 1886 Charles Williams enlisted for duty with the Provost Guard at Fort Leavenworth, Kansas and remained in this organization until he was discharged on September 7, 1890, when his commander deemed that his service was no longer desirable. According to a 1911 letter from Roman Rutten to John Ryan, Williams then drove for a banker at Leavenworth, Kansas, but in 1898 supposedly departed the city as a teamster in the Army Quartermaster Corps and went to Cuba in the Spanish-American War. Williams applied for a pension on April 8, 1898, but the effort was abandoned.[144]

• • •

Trumpeter Henry C. Weaver ran into trouble after the Little Bighorn, but first served as a company cook in August 1877. But on February 21, 1878 he quit his post on guard at Fort Abraham Lincoln without authority and remained absent for a day. When his General Court Martial met, he found that Captain Thomas French sat on the court. Weaver pled guilty; Captain French testified on behalf of the soldier:[145]

> "He is a very good soldier. He has always been ready for duty when called upon. I don't remember any offense before this. He was in the battle of Little Big Horn June 25 and 26, 1876 and behaved very well and was also in battle 13th September 1877 and behaved equally well."

The court sentenced Henry Weaver to two months hard labor and $10 a month for two months. In his closing statement, Weaver mentioned that he had been in the army since 1861. Weaver was on that confinement until June 1878. He then went on detached service to Camp Ruhlen, Dakota Territory in October 1878. Weaver was court-martialed in November 1878; Captain Thomas French sat on the court, but was not the president. On November 11, 1878 Weaver had gone absent without authority from stable duties at Camp Ruhlen, Dakota Territory. He compounded that by refusing to carry hay to help feed the horses when ordered to do so by the first sergeant. Then Weaver stated he wanted to go to the sutler's store to get a drink. When First Sergeant Charles White told him no, Weaver hit White in the face with his fist.[146]

This was a significant offense and in combat might have earned Weaver a bullet in the head from the first sergeant. He tried to explain his situation to the court:[147]

> "On the 11th day of November 1878 I was so much under the influence of intoxication liquor as to be unable to perform my stable duties properly in the afternoon of the day above specified."

The excuse did not work and Weaver was found guilty and sentenced to be dishonorably discharged. Weaver was discharged from the army on February 4, 1879 at Fort Meade, Dakota Territory, but nothing is documented about his later life.[148]

• • •

Private Thomas B. "Happy Jack" Varner returned to Fort Abraham Lincoln on the steamer *Far West* due to his wounds; he returned to duty on July 20, 1876. He served as a quartermaster laborer and company cook in 1877, but spent December of that year in confinement. This was possibly related to a fight he had with another private after "Happy Jack" severely beat the man for stealing money from him.[149] "Happy Jack" reported sick on January 23, 1878 and was diagnosed with tonsillitis. Varner deserted the army on June 7, 1878, along with Levi Thornberry. Thornberry then went to find his fortune in the gold fields of the Black Hills and Alaska, but we do not know if "Happy Jack" had gold fever as well. Later reports indicated that Thomas Varner may have resided in Poseyville, Indiana, but details of his later life remain unknown.[150]

• • •

Scant post-Little Bighorn details exist on Private William W. Rye as well. He deserted Company M near Bismarck, Dakota Territory on October 26, 1876. He surrendered to military authorities on June 8, 1877, but escaped confinement on September 14, 1877 at Fort Abraham Lincoln and was never documented again.[151]

• • •

In the same category was Private John Seamans. In December 1876 Seamans worked in the subsistence department of the regimental quartermaster. He was in the hospital at Fort Rice for pneumonia from February 1 to April 21, 1877.[152] On May 3, 1877 he was assigned duties in the post commissary department. John Seamans deserted the army at Fort Rice on May 12, 1877.[153]

• • •

Private Frank Stratton also voted with his feet. On October 19, 1876 Stratton went absent without authorization at Fort Rice. He took his army horse, which was theft, and shortly after departing, he shot and killed his horse. Stratton pled guilty at the General Court Martial; Captain Frederick Benteen served as President of the Court, while Captain Thomas French sat on the jury. Stratton submitted a statement that explained why he shot his horse during the incident:[154]

> "The horse was running away with me, and ever since the fight he was wounded in the head at the fight there at the Little Big Horn, he has always been crazy, and he used to frequently run away last Spring, when we were out exercising and he started and ran away from me on the 19th of October, this side of the bridge and I let him run as long as he kept to the open prairie I didn't care how much he ran.
>
> He ran about six hundred or seven hundred yards, then struck across and ran towards the river this side of the boat shack, and I saw the only resource I had was to kill him.
>
> The curb strap broke and after that I couldn't do anything with him.
>
> There is a great many of them old horses that take the bit in the mouth and run away with anybody."

The court found him guilty on the first two charges but agreed with Stratton and found him not guilty of killing his horse. He was sentenced to hard labor for four months and fined $10 a month for four months.[155] Captain Thomas French recommended a remission of part of his sentence, but Stratton deserted the army anyway at Fort Abraham Lincoln on July 28, 1877.[156]

• • •

Private Hobart Ryder accompanied the wounded to the *Far West* after the battle and per a verbal order served as a field hospital nurse from July 1 to September 14, 1876, riding on the *Far West*, assisting the wounded. He was promoted to corporal on March 1, 1877, but was reduced to private on May 25, 1877. Ryder then kept his nose clean and again made corporal on January 21, 1878. He was discharged on September 15, 1878 at Camp Ruhlen, Dakota Territory as a corporal; he was deemed to be of excellent character. He later re-enlisted. In January 1879 Hobart Ryder testified as a character witness in the General Court Martial of Captain Thomas H. French.[157]

Ryder received a General Court Martial himself on September 10, 1879. On July 2, 1879 Ryder had been part of a fatigue detail at Fort Meade, Dakota Territory. He left his post without proper authority and went to the trader's store. Later in the day, Ryder left his barracks and wandered into the officer quarters of First Lieutenant Matthew Markland and his family without knocking. Ryder stated that he thought the quarters belonged to his company commander, Captain Thomas French, and submitted an interesting statement to the court which read:[158]

> "Gentlemen,
>
> I was duly detailed for Quartermaster Fatigue to take charge of 8 men to load two wagons of dirt; the distance was such that it took one half hour for the wagons to make the return trip. During that time there was nothing for the men to do. In the same time there was members of the party got my permission to go to the Traderstore. I seen the wagons returning and the men not back I went to the store to tell them to return when the Adjutant who was at the store asked me if I was not on fatigue. I told him I was, he then asked me what I was doing there. I started to explain the reason for my being there when he told me to shut up and join my fatigue party which I did.
>
> I will also state that in reference of my going to Lieutenant Markland's house that it was through a mistake supposing it to be Captain French's home. Captain French had sent word to me to call to his house that evening. I started to go as I was bid and went into Lieutenant Markland's house when I found that I was wrong I was completely taken by surprise and started to leave, when Spilman saw me and told me to go into my quarters in arrest which I did. I will state that it is a custom now and has been ever since Captain French has been sick, for men of his company to go to his home and set up with him as it is impossible for the man who is waiting on him to be up every night. It is also understood that the man will go in without knocking or making any noise. The first sergeant will certify to this as being true in every particular. I went next morning and apologized to Lieutenant Markland for my mistake, he told me he did not blame me and also told me that as he had always known me as a good Non-commissioned officer he wished me to tell Lieutenant Spilman that he wanted no charges preferred against me. I had no chance to see Lieutenant Spilman until late in the afternoon. I then told him what Lieutenant Markland had stated. Lieutenant Spilman told me that he was very sorry to see anyone in trouble but that the charges had already gone off.
>
> It was my intention to have the matter investigated before the charges went off, but found I was too late. To disabuse the

minds of the gentlemen of the court that I must to have been intoxicated to make such a mistake I will kindly refer them to the case of Private Rutten who being sent for by Captain French made the mistake of going into Captain Moylan's house. Now this man has been very near 15 years in the service and has never been known to take a drink of liquor during that time. Hoping the court will look into my case in a favorable light I remain most respectfully.

Your obedient servant
Hobart Ryder
Corporal, Company M
7th Cavalry"

The court found Hobart Ryder guilty, but did not reduce him in rank. He was fined $10 for one month.[159] But Ryder reversed his bad fortune and was promoted to sergeant on October 6, 1879. He was elevated to be the first sergeant of Company M on January 1, 1881. Ryder was treated for acute bronchitis on April 27, 1883.[160] He was discharged on September 14, 1883 at Fort Meade, Dakota Territory as a first sergeant of excellent character. He immediately re-enlisted and went on detached service at Fort Snelling, Minnesota. On October 1, 1883 he was awarded a six-month furlough, during which he travelled to Europe. He was discharged on September 14, 1888 at Fort Riley, Kansas with an excellent character rating. He promptly re-enlisted and was assigned to Company C on September 9, 1890 when Company M was inactivated, but he spent the period October 4, 1890 to January 5, 1891 in a hospital in Hot Springs, Arkansas for dyspepsia and neuralgia. He then served on recruiting duty. Hobart Ryder received his final discharge from the army on September 14, 1893 as a sergeant of excellent character at Knoxville, Tennessee. Private Roman Rutten later stated in correspondence that Ryder committed suicide in Wheeling, West Virginia.[161]

• • •

Private Robert Senn was detailed to be the post school teacher from December 1876 to March 1877. On February 15, 1877 he reported ill with acute rheumatism. He suffered from chills on April 15, 1877 and from acute bronchitis on September 28, 1877.[162] Senn then served as the company clerk in December 1877 and was promoted to corporal on January 1, 1878. He was elevated to sergeant on January 21, 1878 and became the acting company quartermaster sergeant in April 1878. He served as the company clerk and in charge of the company kitchen from August 1878 to June 1879. While in the kitchen he lacerated his right hand and thumb on August 23, 1878.[163]

Senn was diagnosed with acute diarrhea on September 17, 1878, not a good illness to have as a cook. He reported ill with bronchitis on December 31, 1878. On June 1, 1879 Senn was diagnosed with rheumatism.[164]

Senn was acquitted of General Court Martial charges in August 1879 of advising a soldier to desert; Major Marcus Reno served as the President of the Court in the proceedings.[165] Senn later became the company cook and repaired telegraph lines from September to December of 1879. Senn served as the post clerk at Fort Meade from February to June of 1880. On September 22, 1880 he was discharged at Fort Meade, Dakota Territory as a private of fair character, but it remains unknown as to where he went later and what happened to him.[166]

• • •

By 1933, the last veteran of Company M had passed from the scene. But the country had moved on without them long before.

Grave of Private Joseph Bates (also known as Joseph C. Murphy); he is buried at the Bear Butte Cemetery in Sturgis, SD.

Grave of Colonel Frederick Benteen; he is buried at Arlington National Cemetery, VA.

Grave of Private Frank Braun (also known as Frank Brown); Braun died of his wounds at Fort Abraham Lincoln on October 4, 1876 and was buried there. He was later reinterred at the Custer Battlefield National Cemetery, MT.

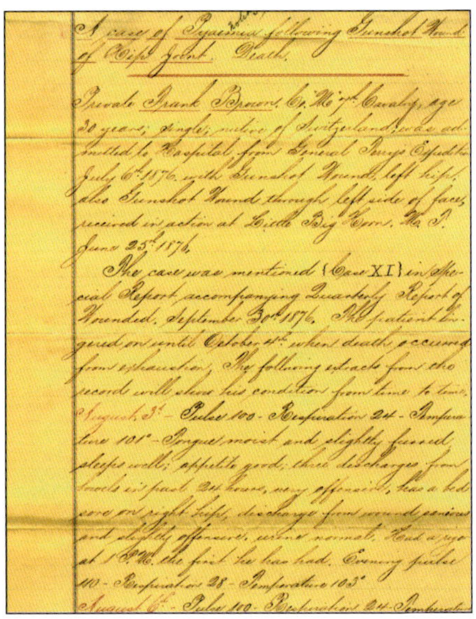

A case of Pyaemia following Gunshot Wound of Hip Joint. Death.

Private Frank Brown, Co. M 7th Cavalry, age 30 years, single, native of Switzerland, was admitted to Hospital from General Terry's Expedition July 6th 1876, with Gunshot Wound, left hip, also Gunshot Wound through left side of face, received in action at Little Big Horn, M. T. June 25th 1876.

The case was mentioned (Case XI) in special Report accompanying Quarterly Report of Wounded, September 30th 1876. The patient lingered on until October 4th when death occurred from exhaustion. The following extracts from the record will show his condition from time to time.

August 3rd - Pulse 100 - Respiration 24 - Temperature 101° - Tongue moist and slightly furred, sleeps well; appetite good; three discharges from bowels in past 24 hours, very offensive, has a bed sore on right hip, discharge from wound copious and slightly offensive, urine normal. Had a rigor at 1 P.M. the first he has had. Evening pulse 110 - Respiration 28 - Temperature 103°

August [illegible] - Pulse 100 - Respiration 24 - Temperat[illegible]

Medical Report on Private Frank Braun. Front page, shown here, indicates that Braun had a high fever in early August 1876, five weeks after he was wounded and two months before he died. *Photo courtesy of the National Museum of Health and Medicine, Armed Forces Institute of Pathology.*

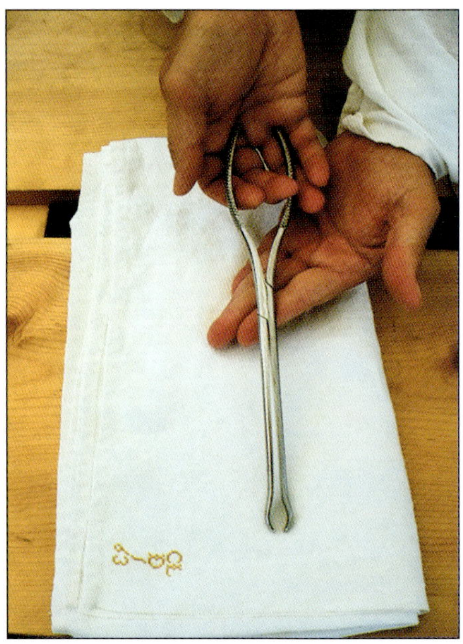

Long bullet forceps. A surgical tool of this nature was probably used by Dr. J.V.D. Middleton, the post surgeon at Fort Abraham Lincoln, who probed the wound of Private Frank Braun before Braun died of infection.

Grave of Sergeant Patrick Carey; he is buried at the U.S. Soldiers' Home in Washington, DC.

Grave of Private James W. Darcy, also known as James Wilber; he is buried at the U.S. Soldiers' Home in Washington, DC.

Grave of Captain Thomas H. French; he is buried at Holy Rood Cemetery in Washington, DC.

Grave of Captain Thomas H. French.

Jean Baptiste Gallenne (center, at rear) in middle age. He is surrounded by his family, including his mother-in-law on the left. Photo was taken probably in the early/mid 1890s. *Photo courtesy Bob and Edward Connor, great-grandsons of Jean Gallenne.*

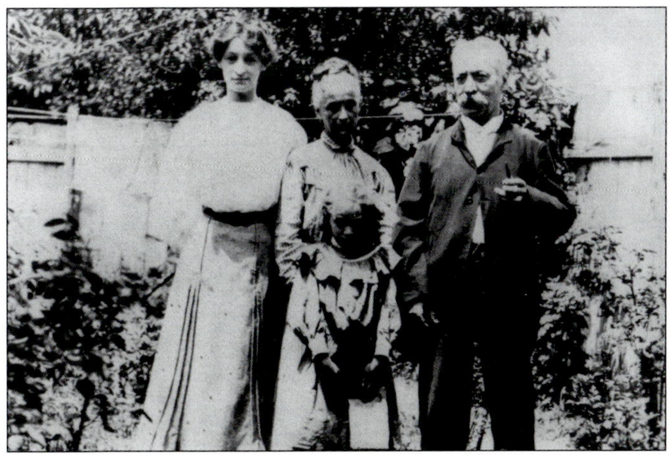

Jean Baptiste Gallenne (right) in his older years. He is next to his wife Josephine, and two of his daughters, Isabelle and Louisa. Note the cane in Jean's right hand, which assisted him walking with his wooden leg. Photo appears to be from about 1908. *Photo courtesy Bob and Edward Connor, great-grandsons of Jean Gallenne.*

First Lieutenant Charles C. "Count No-Account" DeRudio; his later complaint led to the court-martial of Captain Thomas H. French in 1879. French despised DeRudio, once writing: "That thing knows no more of the fight than any washer-woman in Chicago. He was not in it. Before the first shot was fired he was in the bushes, and stayed there." *Photo courtesy of the Little Bighorn Battlefield National Monument.*

Grave of Private Jean B. Gallenne; he is buried at the Mt. Olivet Cemetery in Washington, DC.

Grave of Private George Heid; he is buried at the Custer Battlefield National Cemetery, MT.

Grave of Private Charles Kavanaugh; he is buried at the U.S. Soldiers' Home in Washington, DC.

Grave of Lieutenant Colonel Edward Mathey; he is buried at Arlington National Cemetery, VA.

Grave of Private Daniel Mahoney; he is buried at the U.S. Soldiers' Home in Washington, DC. Inscription is almost illegible.

Grave of Sergeant First Class John McGlone; he is buried at the U.S. Soldiers' Home in Washington, DC.

Grave of Private Hugh N. Moore; he is buried at the U.S. Soldiers' Home in Washington, DC.

Grave of Private Daniel J. Newell; he is buried at the Bear Butte Cemetery in Sturgis, SD.

Forensic sculpture of Sergeant Miles O'Hara. Archaeologists used this technique to attempt to identify remains found at an L-shaped entrenchment near the Company H position on Reno Hill. Historic accounts indicate that O'Hara was killed in the valley, but forensics opens the possibility that he was wounded there and may have later been buried on Reno Hill. *Photo courtesy of the Little Bighorn Battlefield National Monument.*

Edward Pigford in his older years as a coal miner, about 1932. *Photo courtesy of the Newberry Library.*

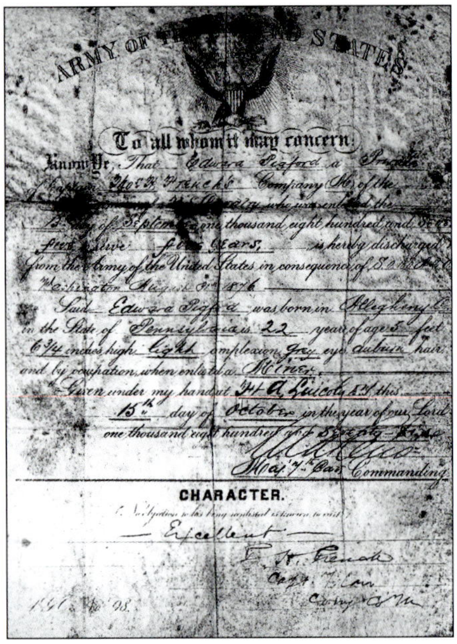

Private Edward Pigford's discharge certificate dated October 15, 1876, signed by Major Marcus Reno and Captain Thomas French. Pigford's character was rated as "excellent." *Photo courtesy of the Newberry Library.*

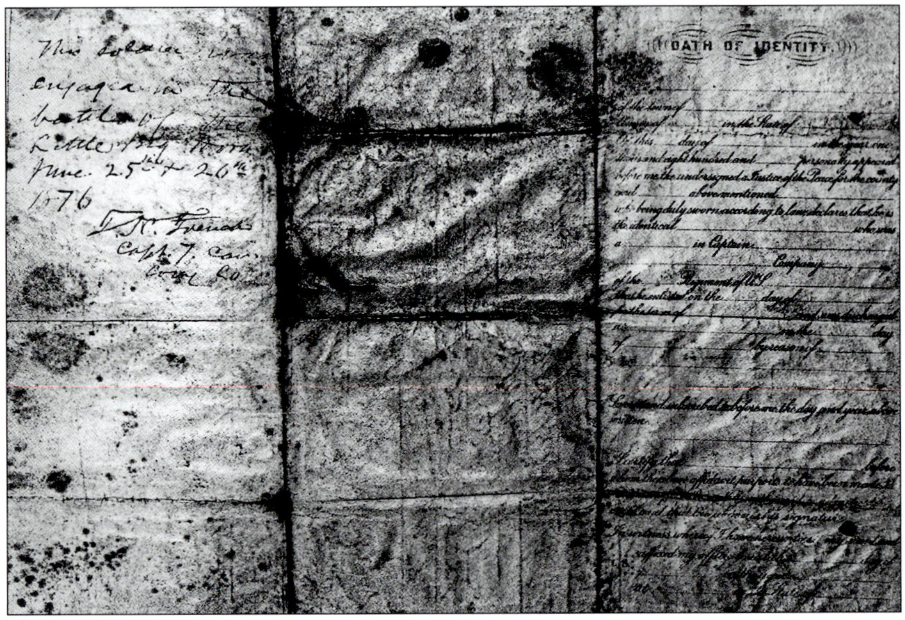

Reverse side of Private Edward Pigford's discharge. On the left, Captain Thomas French wrote: "This soldier was engaged in the Battle of the Little Big Horn, June 25, 1876." Center section has faint annotations regarding back pay and right section was unused. *Photo courtesy of the Newberry Library.*

Grave of Private Edward Pigford; he is buried at Dravosburg, PA. There do not appear to be any relatives buried near him.

Grave of Major Marcus A. Reno; he is buried at the Custer Battlefield National Cemetery, MT. In 1966 the family of Marcus Reno made an official application for reinstatement into the army, which would have overridden the court-martial verdict. An Army Correction Board agreed and Reno's remains were reburied with full military honors in September 1967.

Grave of Private Roman Rutten; he is buried at the National Cemetery at Fort Leavenworth, KS.

A cavalryman first takes care of his horse; First Sergeant John Ryan about 1920. *Photo courtesy of the Little Bighorn Battlefield National Monument.*

First Sergeant John Ryan sitting tall in the saddle; photo taken about 1920, when Ryan was 75 years old. *Photo courtesy of the Little Bighorn Battlefield National Monument.*

First Sergeant John Ryan showing how he held the reins of his horse while lying on the ground trying to get some sleep; photo taken about 1920. *Photo courtesy of the Little Bighorn Battlefield National Monument.*

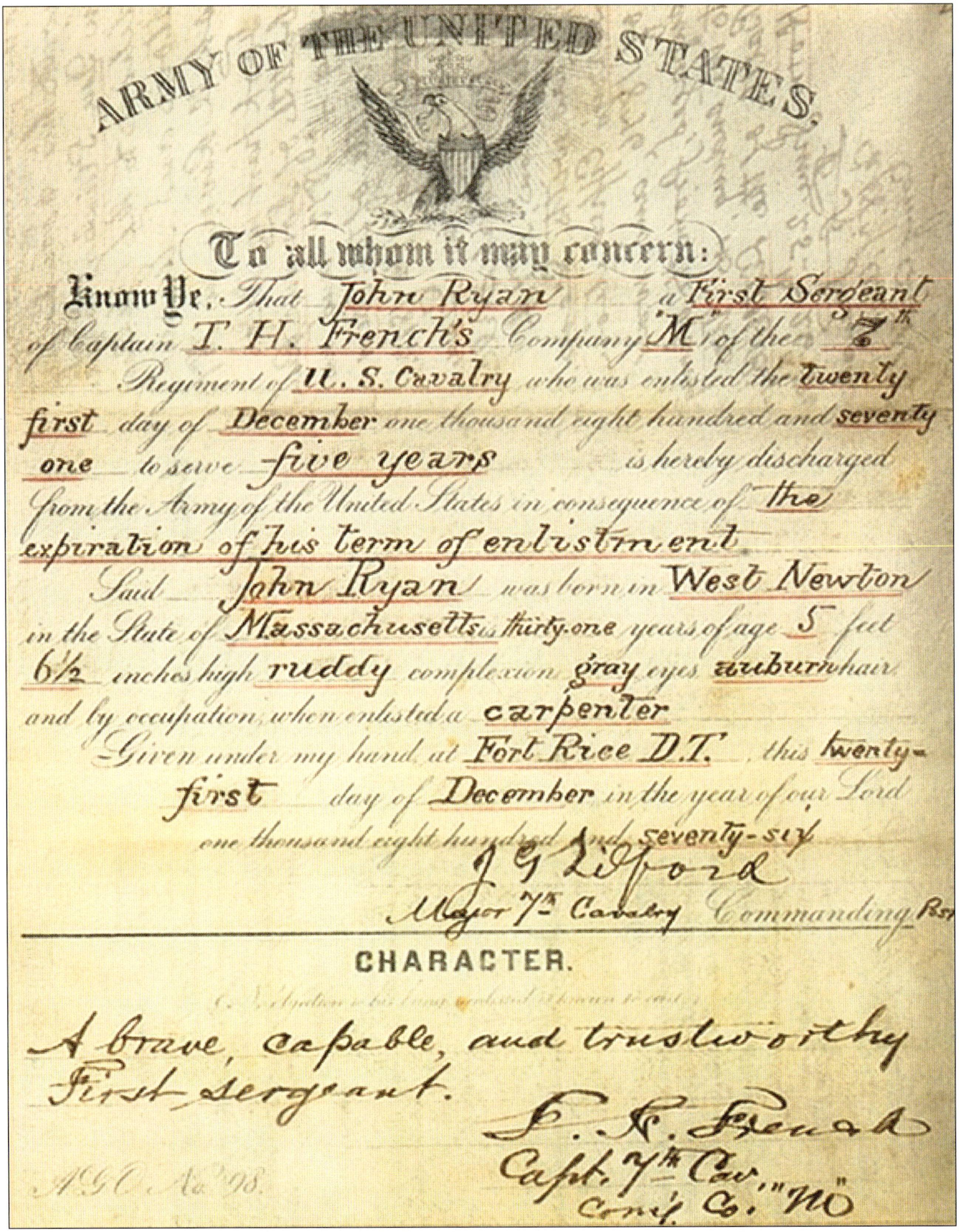

ARMY OF THE UNITED STATES.

To all whom it may concern:

Know Ye, That John Ryan a First Sergeant of Captain T. H. French's Company "M" of the 7th Regiment of U. S. Cavalry who was enlisted the twenty first day of December one thousand eight hundred and seventy one to serve five years is hereby discharged from the Army of the United States in consequence of the expiration of his term of enlistment.

Said John Ryan was born in West Newton in the State of Massachusetts is thirty-one years of age 5 feet 6½ inches high ruddy complexion gray eyes auburn hair and by occupation, when enlisted a carpenter

Given under my hand at Fort Rice D.T. this twenty-first day of December in the year of our Lord one thousand eight hundred and seventy-six

J G Tilford
Major 7th Cavalry Commanding Post

CHARACTER.

A brave, capable, and trustworthy First Sergeant.

T. H. French
Capt. 7th Cav.
Comd. Co. "M"

A.G.O. No. 98.

Discharge certificate for First Sergeant John Ryan dated December 21, 1876, signed by Major Joseph Tilford and Captain Thomas French. At the bottom, Captain Thomas French characterized his service as: "A brave, capable, and trustworthy First Sergeant."

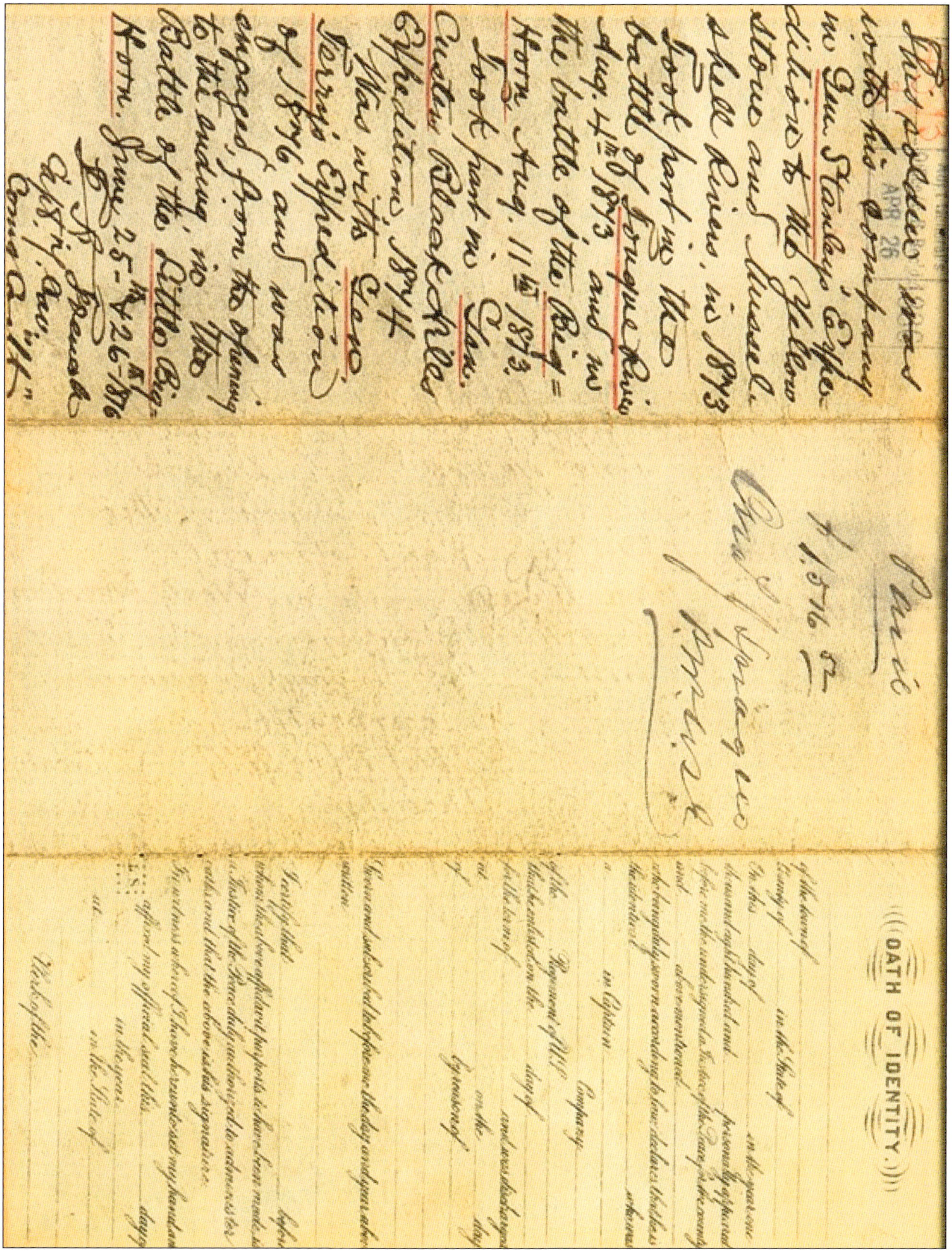
This soldier was with his company in Gen. Stanley's Expedition to the Yellowstone and Mussel Shell River, in 1873. Took part in the battle of Tongue River Aug. 4th 1873 and in the battle of the Big Horn Aug. 11th 1873. Took part in Gen. Custer's Black Hills Expedition 1874. Was with Gen. Terry's Expedition of 1876 and was engaged from the opening to the ending in the Battle of the Little Big Horn June 25th & 26th 1876.
T. H. French
Capt. 7 Cav.
Comd Co. "M."

Paid
$1,076 [illegible]
[illegible]

OATH OF IDENTITY.

Reverse side of First Sergeant Ryan's discharge. On the left, Captain French has listed all the campaigns in which Ryan participated while with Company M of the 7th Cavalry.

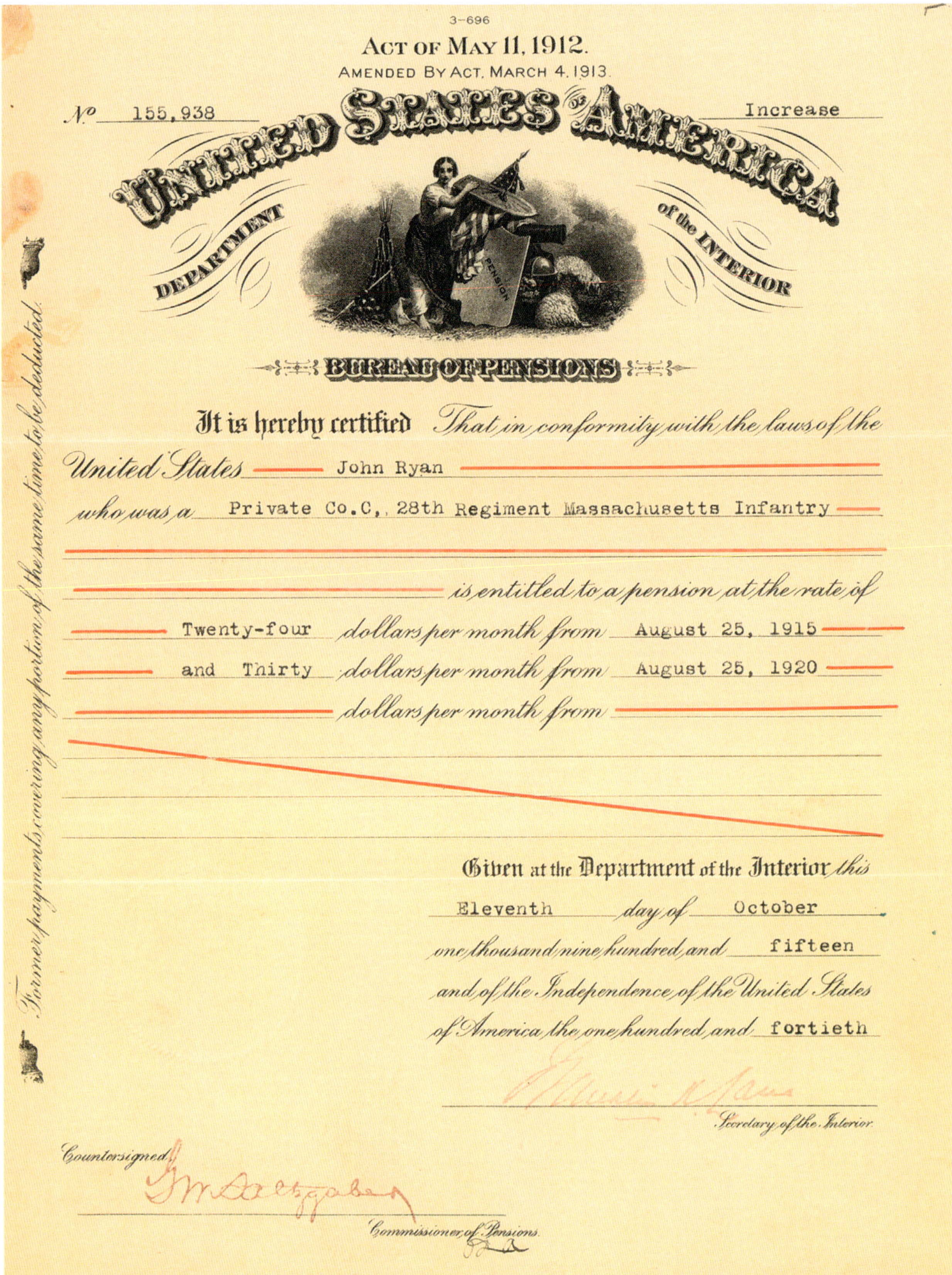
3-696

ACT OF MAY 11, 1912.
AMENDED BY ACT, MARCH 4, 1913.

No 155,938 Increase

UNITED STATES OF AMERICA
DEPARTMENT OF THE INTERIOR
PENSION
BUREAU OF PENSIONS

It is hereby certified That in conformity with the laws of the United States John Ryan who was a Private Co. C., 28th Regiment Massachusetts Infantry is entitled to a pension at the rate of Twenty-four dollars per month from August 25, 1915 and Thirty dollars per month from August 25, 1920 dollars per month from

Given at the Department of the Interior this Eleventh day of October one thousand nine hundred and fifteen and of the Independence of the United States of America the one hundred and fortieth

Secretary of the Interior.

Countersigned, Commissioner of Pensions.

Former payments covering any portion of the same time to be deducted.

Bureau of Pensions document to John Ryan dated October 11, 1915. It states that beginning that August his monthly pension would be $24 a month, which would increase to $30 a month in 1920. Enlisted men had to fight for pension increases.

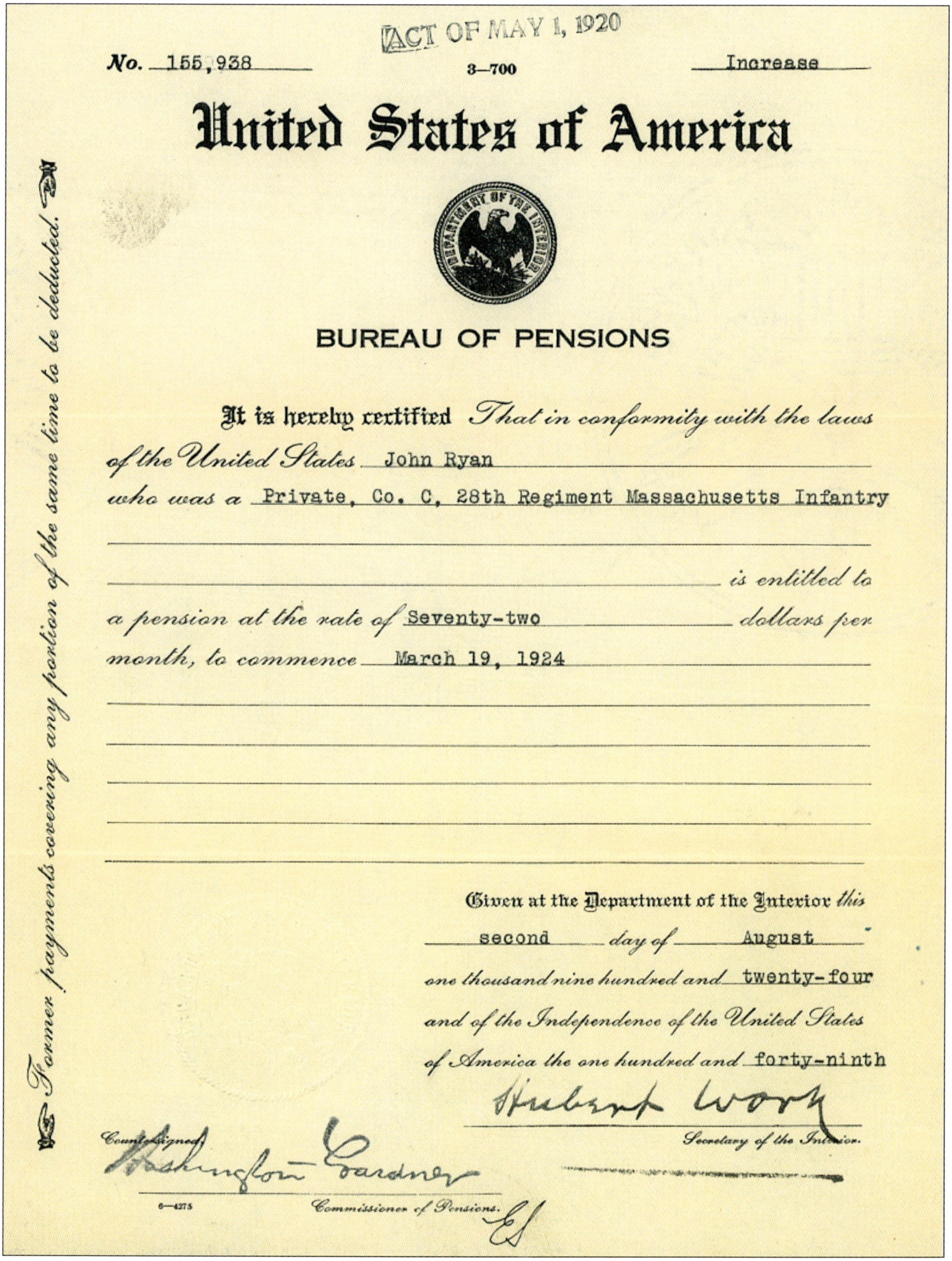

ACT OF MAY 1, 1920

No. 155,938 3—700 Increase

United States of America

BUREAU OF PENSIONS

It is hereby certified That in conformity with the laws of the United States John Ryan who was a Private, Co. C, 28th Regiment Massachusetts Infantry is entitled to a pension at the rate of Seventy-two dollars per month, to commence March 19, 1924

Given at the Department of the Interior this second day of August one thousand nine hundred and twenty-four and of the Independence of the United States of America the one hundred and forty-ninth

Hubert Work
Secretary of the Interior.

Countersigned,
Washington Gardner
Commissioner of Pensions.

6—4275

Former payments covering any portion of the same time to be deducted.

Bureau of Pensions document to John Ryan dated August 2, 1924, stating that Ryan would begin to receive a pension of $72 a month. Pension is denoted for Ryan's Civil War service in Company C of the 28th Regiment of Massachusetts Infantry.

Invalid Division 3-2310

I.C. No. 155,938

John Ryan

Co. C, 28" Mass. Inf.

DEPARTMENT OF THE INTERIOR
BUREAU OF PENSIONS
WASHINGTON

W.J.M.

Aug.11,1924

Mr. John Ryan,
29 Auburndale ave,
West Newton, Mass.

Sir:

Your claim for increase under section 2, act of May 1, 1920, filed June 7, 1924, has been allowed at the rate of $72 per month from March 19, 1924.

The evidence on file fails to show that you required the regular aid and attendance of another person prior to that date.

Respectfully,

Hays Haymaker
Commissioner.

Bureau of Pensions letter to John Ryan dated August 11, 1924. Document informs Ryan that his $72 a month pension will not be effective prior to March 19, 1924. Again, there is no mention of his Company M, 7th Cavalry service.

Grave of First Sergeant John Ryan. His service in the Civil War is shown as is his tenure in Company M.

Second gravestone for John Ryan. This lists his service in the 31st Massachusetts Infantry Regiment in the Civil War.

Grave of General Philip Sheridan; he is buried at Arlington National Cemetery, VA.

Grave of General William T. Sherman; he is buried at Calvary Cemetery in St. Louis, MO.

Sherman once remarked that "War is Hell." Sherman, too, experienced great pain during the Civil War. In 1863 his nine-year-old- son, Willie, nicknamed "the Little Sergeant" by the troops, visited the general in Tennessee, but unfortunately died from typhoid fever. He is buried in the Sherman family plot in St. Louis.

Grave of Private John "Big Fritz" Sivertsen; he is buried at the U.S. Soldiers' Home in Washington, DC.

Grave of Private Frank W. Sniffin, the trooper who saved Company M's colors; he is buried at the Chattanooga National Cemetery, TN.

Reverse side of Private Frank Sniffin's gravestone. In military cemeteries the name of the spouse is sometimes engraved in the reverse of the headstone. In this case Sniffin's wife did not die until 1959, eighty-three years after the battle.

Grave of Private Levi Thornberry; he is buried at Watertown, OH. Metal commemoration plate is relatively new.

Stone tombstone of Levi Thornberry. Both gravestones are adjacent to each other. Watertown is in the hill country in southeastern Ohio.

Grave of Private George "Cully" Weaver; he is buried at Fort Meade, SD in the Post Cemetery. Workers were re-laying tombstones in the small cemetery on the day in June 2009 when this photo was taken.

Grave of Sergeant Henry C. Weihe (also known as Charles White); he is buried at Fort Meade, SD in the Post Cemetery.

Conclusion

"Then too, for many a lonely old man who had little else to show for his service to his country but lingering wounds, broken health, and a paltry pension, there was a rich, warm glow from within that money could not buy nor fame replace. It was the sweet satisfaction that he had, indeed 'seen stirring times,' a golden dawning that he had not only been a part of, but had played a prominent role in, one of the most romantic dramas the world had ever known – the winning of the West."[1]

Company M performed admirably at the Little Bighorn. Led by an outstanding company commander and first sergeant, the troops fought well in the valley and later on Reno Hill. In the valley, Company M's disciplined withdrawal from the skirmish line to the timber line – after Company A and G withdrew in a hurry, leaving Captain French's company to hold the line by itself – certainly saved the company from possible destruction and may well have saved Reno's entire detachment from an even more serious defeat in the timber than what actually happened. Had Company M broken and run, it is quite conceivable that the warriors may have been able to pursue the company right into the timber and overrun both Company A and G, which had still not organized a defense.

Had this occurred and Reno's detachment been annihilated or so depleted as to be combat ineffective, it raises another question of what would have happened to Captain Frederick Benteen's battalion – and Company B with the pack train – as they approached the battlefield. Could Benteen with only four companies have held any piece of terrain that day against the combined warrior force? Would General Alfred Terry two days later have found three "Last Stand" sites: Calhoun Ridge/Custer Hill with Custer's dead, the valley timber with the deceased of Marcus Reno's battalion, and perhaps Sharpshooter Ridge or Weir Point with the bodies of Frederick Benteen and the four remaining companies of the 7th Cavalry Regiment?

On Reno Hill, Company M played a major role in successfully counterattacking warriors that had moved dangerously close to the exposed positions of Company H. Had Company H been overrun, the entire Reno Hill defensive works would have been compromised and possibly overrun, with disastrous results for the remnants of the regiment. Several Company M troopers served in the dangerous role of water carriers; although none received Medals of Honor, several certainly deserved the award.

Twelve troopers in Company M were killed in action at the Little Bighorn, with Second Lieutenant James Sturgis (assigned on paper to Company M) a thirteenth, when he died with Custer's wing. One Company M trooper died of his wounds several months later. Ten other men in the company were wounded during the fighting but survived. This study concludes that almost all of the wounds to Company M soldiers were caused by gunshots and not arrows; Private Klotzbucher may have been the sole exception. Having said that, we simply do not know exactly what happened to Private George Smith, who rode his uncontrollable horse into the Indian village at the start of the fight. Concerning the mounts, Walter Camp later concluded that Company M had 19 horses killed at the battle or put out of their misery afterward.[2]

Assessing casualties on the warriors inflicted by Company M is a far more difficult task because we cannot verify Indian casualties with any certainty. General William Sherman estimated in his report to the Secretary of War that between 40 and 100 warriors perished. Some white sources argue that the Indians carried their dead away so the army would never know the true extent of their losses, but Dr. Thomas Marquis asserted that the Indians would only transfer their dead as far as was necessary to locate a suitable burial place.[3]

Indian estimates of the total casualties vary greatly. Blackfeet Lakota Chief Kill Eagle estimated that 16 warriors were killed in action and 400 were wounded. Lakota Chief Red Horse asserted that 136 Indians were killed and 160 were wounded. Horned Horse seemed to believe that 58 warriors died and 60 were wounded. Hunkpapa Chief Crow King stated that 30 to 50 Indians died, but that a much larger number of wounded braves died later. Oglala Chief Low Dog thought that 38 warriors died on the field of battle, but that "a great many" that were wounded, died afterward. The wife of Spotted Horn Bull asserted that only 22 braves died at the Little Bighorn. Chief Gall of the Hunkpapas said that 43 warriors died in the fight and that nearly as many later succumbed to their wounds. Minneconjou warrior Feather Earring told General Hugh Scott in 1919 that 16 warriors were killed outright but that there were "a terrible number" of wounded.[4]

A Cheyenne survivor also provided estimates on the number of Indian casualties. Two Moons said that 39 Lakota and seven Northern Cheyenne, a total of 46, warriors were killed and about 100 were wounded. Arapahoe warrior Waterman stated that 12 warriors were killed and that "there were many wounded." Another Arapahoe, Left Hand, stated that "only a few Sioux and Northern Cheyenne" were killed.[5]

Given the disparity between sources, but considering that each generally falls within a certain range, combined with the expected lethality of the large-caliber cavalry weapons, this study concludes that about 100 warriors died on the actual field of battle or as a direct

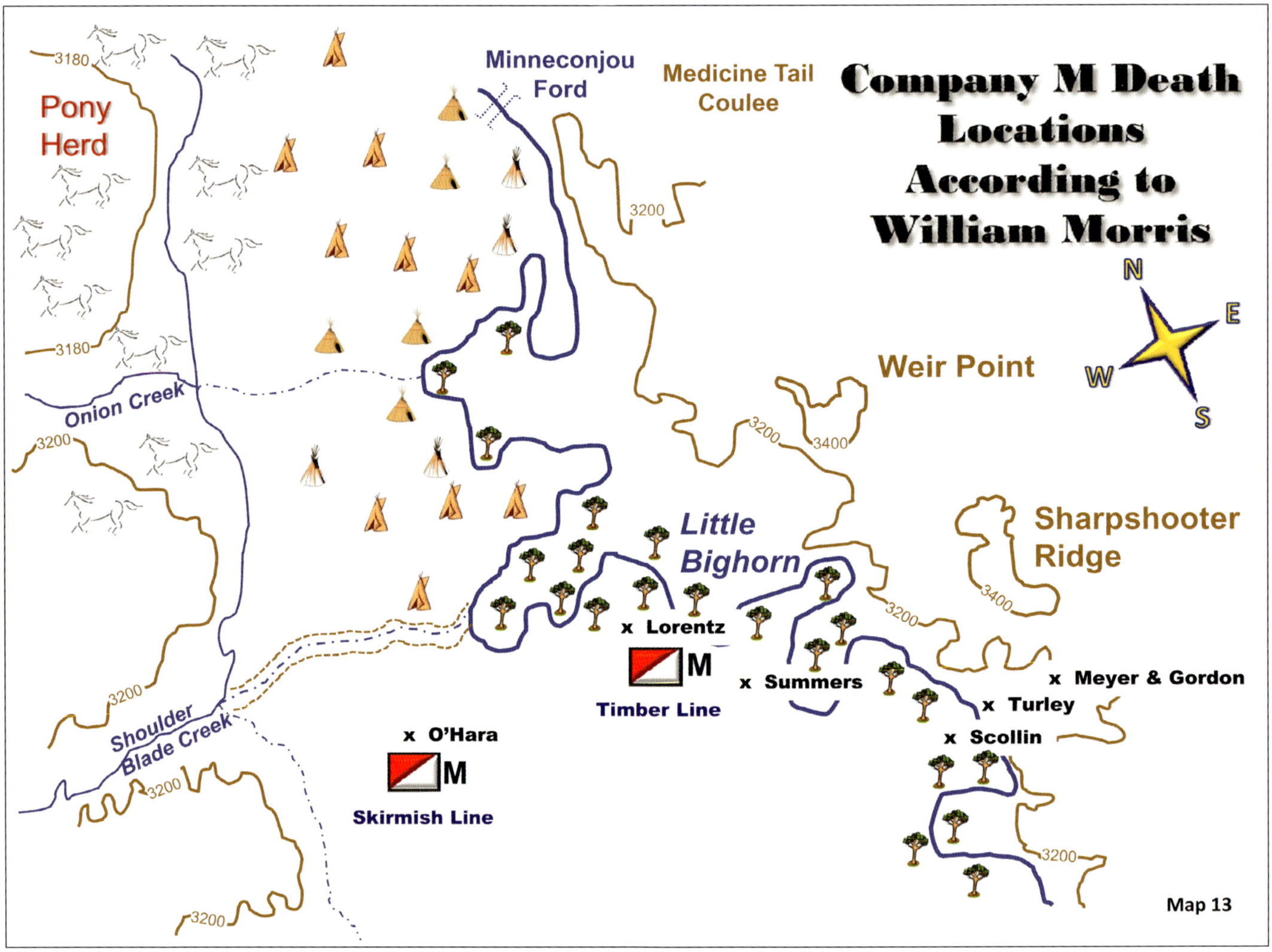

result of their wounds, perhaps several days to a week later.[i] With this figure in mind, we can turn to an estimate of the fatalities inflicted by Company M. For this, the only starting point is found in post-battle memoirs or accounts of survivors – we simply do not know how many warriors those men, who did not survive, killed before they went down, nor do we know which surviving cavalrymen shot warriors unless they mentioned doing so or unless some other survivor witnessed the act.

With those parameters, this study has concluded that Company M probably accounted for 12 warrior fatalities; seven by Captain Thomas French, three by First Sergeant John Ryan and two by Private Edward Pigford. The number could obviously have been larger; Captain French stated in a later letter that he killed 21 warriors, but this was probably too high a figure. Private Pigford was known to exaggerate on occasion, but his accounts of two warriors killed could be correct. My feeling on Ryan is that with such an excellent weapon as an 1874 Sharps with a telescopic sight, he could have shot and killed more than three warriors, although he never claimed to have done so nor have other eyewitnesses confirmed a larger total.

If we assume that 100 warriors died overall, the 12 credited by this study for just one of the dozen companies of the 7th Cavalry Regiment would seem within possibility. But bravery on the field of battle was not just about shooting the enemy. This study has noted that 10 Company M troopers deserved the award of the Medal of Honor, given the standards of the award at the time. Captain Thomas H. French led his unit to safety from the valley fight through hostile lines; conducted a counterattack on Reno Hill; and moved exposed and under enemy fire to defensive positions to fix weapons – any single act should have resulted in the award. First Sergeant John Ryan rescued a wounded soldier under enemy fire on Reno Hill and showed conspicuous gallantry as a sharpshooter. Sergeant Charles Weihe led several soldiers out of the timber to safety after they had been cut off. Private James W. Severs recovered a supply mule under enemy fire, an act similar to that of another soldier who received the Medal of Honor. Private James W. Darcy (James Wilber), Private James Weeks and Private William C. Slaper carried water under

[i] In the Dr. Kenneth Hammer Special Collection at the University of Wisconsin-Whitewater Library, Box 2, 7th Cavalry Muster Rolls Folder, there is a list of named Indian warriors at the battle that includes tribe, sub-group (when known), location of fighting and, where known, casualty status. The list shows the following warriors killed in action (KIA) at the valley fighting or at Reno Hill: Bear with Horns, Hunkpapa, KIA valley; Big Design, Oglala, KIA valley; Breech Cloth, Lakota, KIA Reno Hill; Chased by Owls, Two Kettle, KIA valley; Deed, Sans Arc, KIA valley; Dog Backbone, Minneconjou, KIA Reno Hill; Eagle Hat, Sans Arc, KIA Reno Hill; Flying Charge, Blackfeet, KIA valley; High Eagle, Lakota, KIA valley; Long Robe, Sans Arc, KIA Reno Hill; Old Man, Cheyenne, KIA valley; Roman Nose, Cheyenne, KIA valley; Swift Bear, Hunkpapa, KIA valley; Three Bear, Minneconjou, KIA valley; Two Bear, Sans Arc, KIA valley; White Bull, Lakota, KIA valley; White Eagle, Oglala, KIA valley; and Young Black Moon, Hunkpapa, KIA valley. Northern Cheyenne warrior Wooden Leg added the following casualties: Hump Nose, KIA west side of valley; Whirlwind, KIA east side of valley.

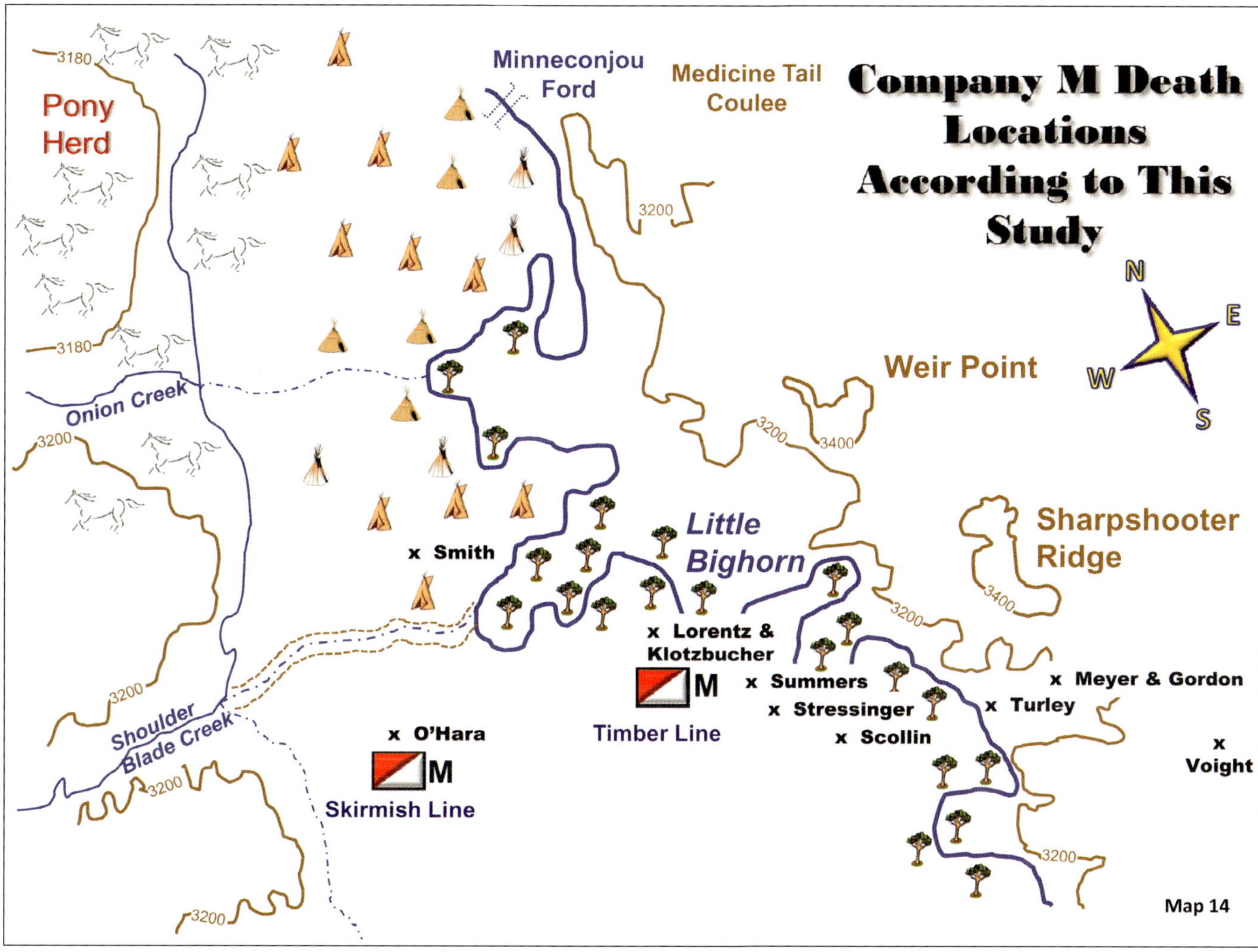

enemy fire to wounded comrades. Private Frank Sniffin saved the company colors. Private John H. Meier valiantly, but unsuccessfully, attempted to save Second Lieutenant Hodgson by the river; Private Rollins Thorpe attempted the same manner of rescue of Corporal Henry Cody – his effort also met with no success. All these troopers should have received the Medal of Honor for their acts of bravery.

Another trooper showed great courage at the moment of his death. While his exact identity cannot be concluded, this study believes that either Private George Lorentz or Private Henry Klotzbucher fought to the end at the Company M location in the timber, where a scrap of uniform, a button and several expended cartridges were found in 1995 by Jason Pitsch, the owner of the land at the time. Professional archaeologists should search this vicinity and if human bone fragments are subsequently discovered, the Little Bighorn National Monument authorities should erect an "Unknown Soldier" stone marker at the site.

Providing a wealth of personal battle observations in numerous post-war accounts that have assisted students of the battle to this day, the absence of any Company M witnesses at the Reno Court of Inquiry in 1879 contributed to an incomplete accounting of events in that official proceeding.

Some post-battle accounts often bemoan the inexperience of the 7th Cavalry soldiers – many of whom came from working class backgrounds, with a large number being first-generation immigrants, possessing low levels of education and inadequate mounted and marksmanship training. But the men of Company M were more than demographic statistics; and they certainly did not consider themselves under-educated or disadvantaged. They were buddies: nicknamed "Tucker," "Paddy," "Barney," "Patsy," "Bounce," "Cully," "Harrison," "Snopsy," "Tinker Bill," "Dan," "Frank," "Frenchy," "Henry," "Crazy Jim," "Big Fritz," "Sandy," "Bill," "Jim," "Jack," "Joe," "Tom" and "Happy Jack," when the going got tough at the Little Bighorn, they fought for each other – a fine example of what an outnumbered, but cohesive unit under good non-commissioned officers could accomplish under heavy enemy fire.

The same could not be said of many of the commissioned officers in the fight. If we are to believe Sergeant White's diary – and there is no reason that we should not, as it was never meant to be published – almost every officer but Captain Thomas French, Second Lieutenant Luther Hare and Second Lieutenant Charles Varnum performed poorly during the fight in the valley, either through the effects of alcohol, inexperience or cowardice.

The troopers of Company M were no saints themselves. The 58 Company M men who participated in the fight racked up a total of at least 62 courts martial during their years of service. "Snopsy" Meier appears to have led the way with at least six convictions; Frank Sniffin had five; Hugh N. Moore and Charles "Bounce" Fischer each were convicted by a court martial four times; even Captain Thomas French was convicted at a General Court Martial, while First Sergeant John Ryan ran afoul of a Garrison Court Martial.

But the story of Company M was neither one solely of glory nor of saints and sinners. The later years of many of the Company M troopers – as well as other 7th Cavalry Regiment Little Bighorn survivors – were hard and their deaths often lonely and under depressing situations. At age 33, Private "Jim" Weeks was shot and killed in a fight with a fellow Company M trooper. Captain Thomas H. French died of alcoholism or lead poisoning at age 39, two years after he departed the army under a cloud. Private Daniel Mahoney – whose brother was killed with Custer – died at the Soldiers' Home, at age 33, of tuberculosis, diarrhea and exhaustion, a soldier broken in body before his time. Six months later, Private Charles Kavanaugh coughed his own lungs out and died of tuberculosis at the U.S. Soldiers Home at age 45. Private Hobart Ryder probably committed suicide. Private Joseph Bates (also known as Joseph C. Murphy) did, in fact, commit suicide – by drinking a component of insecticide, at age 56.

Harsh conditions did not end at the death of the trooper in many cases. The government allowed the families for those men killed in action just 30 days to vacate their quarters at Fort Abraham Lincoln and Fort Rice. There were no immediate monetary death benefits for the families.[6] In some instances, the surviving next of kin of the heroes of Company M received as little as $4 a month in military pensions. Such was the case with the mother of Private Jacob Gebhart (James Tanner) – who began receiving the pension in 1890 – and she had lost her husband in the Civil War as well.[7] Other next of kin received nothing at all, such as the father of Private Henry Voight, who was killed at the battle. In 1880 his father applied for his son's pension, but the request was denied as it was determined that he had not been dependent on his son for support.[8]

• • •

Some of the veterans of the Little Bighorn attended various reunions at the old battlefield, while others corresponded with former comrades and their families. Today, several of the gravestones of these men in federal cemeteries such as the Soldiers' Home in Washington, D.C. have become almost unreadable due to the affects of weather over so many years since they died.

The country could have done better than that for the men at the Little Bighorn, but in many respects, since those hot days in Montana, the nation has wanted to forget what happened on June 25 and 26, 1876 and just go on to the future.

But not everyone moved on; the Little Bighorn has asserted its strange magnetic hold on our imaginations ever since.

In his first novel, *A Garden of Sand*, Earl Thompson wrote of Depression-era Kansas in the 1930s. At one point in the story, he described the inside of a truck-stop, where a young man often fantasizes about doing something bigger with his life than his friends – being a part of something bigger than himself, maybe working for the Western Union. Above the jukebox in the old café was an Anheuser-Busch Brewing Company print depicting *Custer's Last Stand*, at which point Thompson's story continues, describing the Americana masterpiece:[9]

> "It was a great picture with ponies wild-eyed and frothing in the dust of battle, ridden by howling Indians in warpaint, dropping, dragging, dying like flies all over it. And Custer, his hair like golden flypapers, golden mustachios, great white hat, fringed buckskin jacket, supported dying troopers around his knees, his pearl-handled six-guns blazing, mowing down Indians as if they were wheat. That dusty golden land was of the world and the boy knew. He lived where Indians had walked. Where buffalo grazed. *Listen!* For the silent step. He could look at the picture for hours. Nuts to Western Union! When he grew up, he was going with the cavalry."

United States Scout insignia. Insignia such as this became prevalent after the Little Bighorn to serve as a morale-booster and to avoid fratricide of troopers firing at friendly warriors. One of Custer's scouts was shot by a Company M trooper at the Little Bighorn, but fortunately survived. Insignia measures 2.67" wide and 1.51" high.

***Right*: Grave of Colonel Richard I. Dodge.** Dodge once said: "The Government and the Indian are each too poor to afford to waste more than ten cartridges a month on drill, and no man ever became an expert marksman on that allowance." After the Little Bighorn, the army put more emphasis on marksmanship training. Dodge is buried in Section 1 of the Arlington National Cemetery.

***Below*: Custer's Last Fight**. Poster by Anheuser Busch Brewing Association in 1896. *Photo courtesy of Wes Cowan Auctions.*

EPILOGUE

"The color o' the skin ain't so damned important. Ain't nothin' about bones scattered over the plains to tell which was red and which was white."[1]

While the Battle of the Little Bighorn may have been the most significant event in the post-Civil War U.S. campaigns against the Plains tribes, the final result of that unequal campaign was never in doubt. One researcher has concluded that in the mid-1800s the Lakota may have numbered 20,000 people. On the other side, there were at least 40,000,000 Euro-Americans in the United States. Those numbers do not even begin to address the disparity in technology and equipment.[2] It would only be a matter of time before one culture gained ascendency over the other; one was not necessarily better than the other – they were just different. Or were they? Historian Charles M. Robinson, perhaps, said it best in his work *A Good Year to Die: The Story of the Great Sioux War*:[3]

> "The tragedy of the war is that despite their many cultural differences, the Indians and whites were so much alike. With few exceptions, the Indians were neither noble mystics nor savages. They were people. In particular, the thoughts, dreams, and problems of the young Indians strike a chord in today's young people throughout the world. Many younger warriors lived at home with their parents. They had household chores, which they tried to duck. They were not necessarily obedient if something distracted them. They found the girls from the next camp more fascinating than those from their own. They stayed out too late. They got into trouble."

• • •

The army was able to halt the decline in its strength because of the defeat. Cavalry companies were increased in authorized strength to 100 men per unit. Secretary of War James D. Cameron pushed a congressional resolution to temporarily increase the army's end-strength from 25,000 to 27,500 for the duration of the fighting. After he had come to grips with the 7th Cavalry's defeat, General William Sherman remarked to Lieutenant General Philip Sheridan on July 22, 1876:[4]

> "We must not have another massacre like Custer's and Congress is now in session willing to give us all we want."

The army finally listened to the protestations of Colonel Richard Dodge and others concerning marksmanship and other training. Washington concluded that a recruit could not just be dressed, taught to march and burdened with fatigue duties. Marksmanship training increased, so much so that a decade after the Little Bighorn the United States Army was producing some of the finest military marksmen in the world. Recruit training improved as well. Although the food still left something to be desired, recruits started to learn the fundamentals of actually riding a horse, not just caring for it.

• • •

Those changes did not ease the pain of the survivors or the families of the dead. In 1878, "Mamie" Sturgis, the wife of Colonel Samuel Sturgis and the mother of Second Lieutenant James Sturgis – the Company M lieutenant detailed to Company E for the campaign – demanded to visit the battlefield to search for her missing son, whose remains had never been found. Out of respect for the family, the army authorized Colonel Nelson Miles to escort the grieving mother to the battlefield.[i] They were accompanied by a battalion of Miles' 5th Infantry Regiment. Just before Mrs. Sturgis arrived at the battlefield, a detail of soldiers built a stone cairn and placed a hasty wooden marker on the site, bearing the name "Lt. Sturgis." The marker convinced "Mamie" of her son's actual death; but many survivors believed he had been first captured and then tortured to death.[5]

The popular "Jack" Sturgis was sorely missed by his comrades as well. After his death, his chair at the bachelor officer's mess was always left vacant at Fort Abraham Lincoln.[6]

Francis Gibson, who commanded Company M for many years in the 1880s, later selected a spot where he wanted to be buried at Arlington Cemetery, along with his brother-in-law Donald McIntosh; he picked a location in the cemetery close to Fort Myer:[7]

[i] Nelson A. Miles was one of the most distinguished army generals during the Indian Wars. Born August 8, 1839 in Westminster, Massachusetts, he volunteered for the Union Army in 1861. Miles fought at Antietam, Fredericksburg, Chancellorsville and Appomattox; he was wounded four times. A recipient of the Medal of Honor, Miles was ultimately promoted to brevet major general. After the conflict he became a colonel in the Regular Army. Fighting in frontier conflicts from the Nez Percé in Montana to the pursuit of Geronimo and his Apache bands in Arizona, Miles later fought in the Spanish-American War. In 1895 he was named Commanding General of the United States Army. He fought in Cuba during that conflict and also personally led the invasion of Puerto Rico, landing at Guánica. General Miles retired in 1903. Nelson Miles died on May 15, 1925 of a heart attack in Washington, D.C. He is buried at Arlington National Cemetery in the Miles Mausoleum in Section 3.

"Because Donald and I will always be within sound of the trumpet calls we loved."

• • •

Company M soldiered on. In 1890, some 14 years after the Battle of the Little Bighorn, the army reorganized the structure of all its cavalry regiments. Part of this reorganization was the elimination of Company L and Company M from each cavalry regiment. After the units were inactivated – termed "skeletonized" – the men from these companies were then distributed to the remaining ten companies of the regiment. First Sergeant Emil Walker of Company M was selected by the other men to write a letter to the company commander expressing the profound sorrow the men of the company were feeling. First Sergeant Walker chose to write a letter to his captain with his own thoughts:[8]

> "We might be separated, but the comradeship among the members will not cease and we dread the day, when we have to leave our quarters, where we have lived in harmony for a long time...We have never broken our reputation and the day we lay aside the letter 'M' our record as a 'model troop' will always remain and the members will always try and hold on to it."

Well said, First Sergeant; well said.

50th Anniversary parade in 1926. Private William C. Slaper (hidden) is carrying American flag. Even at this late date, some warriors were reluctant to attend the ceremony for fear that the whites might try and exact revenge. *Photo courtesy of the Little Bighorn Battlefield National Monument.*

Dedication plaque commemorating the officers of the 7th Cavalry who fell at: the Washita River on November 27, 1868; the Little Bighorn on June 25, 1876; and Bear Paw Mountain on September 30, 1877. Plaque is located at the Old Post Chapel at Fort Leavenworth, KS. Photo taken in 2010.

Battlefield marker for Lieutenant Donald McIntosh near the tree line position. McIntosh's body was later transferred to Arlington National Cemetery. Bullet marks on the stone attest to some continued friction between some Native Americans and whites in the area, but generally relations are good. Photo taken in 2010.

Battlefield marker for Isaiah Dorman, a former slave and interpreter for the 7th Cavalry. Dorman was the only black known to be at the fight. Married to a Lakota woman, he was a friend of Company M's Roman Rutten. Some sources state that as Dorman lay mortally wounded, Sitting Bull gave him a drink of water, but his body had been horribly mutilated when found two days later. Black troopers made a name for themselves as "Buffalo Soldiers" in the all-black 9th and 10th Cavalry Regiments that fought with distinction all along the frontier. Photo taken in 2010.

Battlefield marker for Sans Arc Lakota warrior Long Road (*Cankuhanska*) on Reno Hill. One historian believes that Long Road may have been killed by Company M's Private Edward Pigford. Photo taken in 2010. In recent years battlefield historians have begun the painstaking work of providing the Lakota and Northern Cheyenne warrior view of the battle, although work concerning the valley fight has lagged behind that of the Custer battlefield and Reno-Benteen Hill.

Battlefield marker for the trusty horses of the 7th Cavalry that died at the battlefield. Marker is on the backside on "Last Stand Hill." Grizzled veteran troopers were known to weep after the loss of a trusted equine companion. Photo taken in 2010.

Dedication plaque commemorating some of the officers who fell in the 7th Cavalry campaigns. Plaque is located at the Old Post Chapel at Fort Leavenworth, KS. Officer losses were well-remembered on the frontier; unfortunately most enlisted casualties were not. Photo taken in 2010.

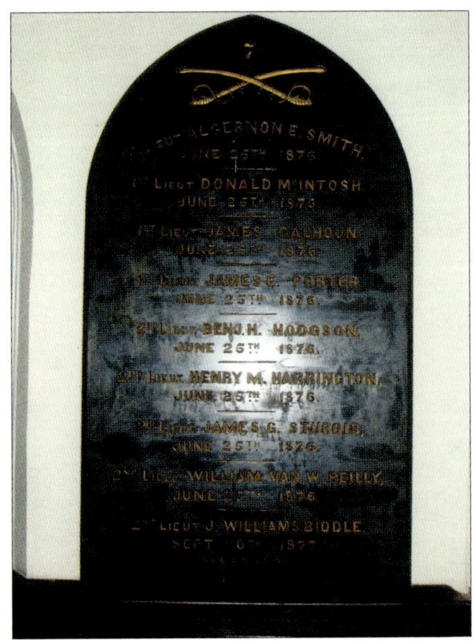

Second dedication plaque commemorating some of the officers who fell in the 7th Cavalry campaigns. Plaque is located at the Old Post Chapel at Fort Leavenworth, KS. Photo taken in 2010.

APPENDICES

Appendix 1
Company M Little Bighorn Battle Roster

CPT Thomas H. "Tucker" French (Company Commander) **[CW] [V2] (MB) {7}**
1LT Edward G. "Bible-Thumper" Mathey (detached to command the pack train) **[V3]**
2LT James G. "Jack" Sturgis (detached with Company E) **(KIA)**
1SG John "Paddy" Ryan (Company First Sergeant) **[CW] [V3] (RS) {3}**
SGT Patrick "Patsy" Carey **(WIA) [V2] (MB) *(RT)***
SGT John McGlone **[V2] (PT)**
SGT Miles O'Hara **(KIA) [V2] (AG)**
SGT Henry C. Weihe [aka Charles White] (First Duty Sergeant) **(WIA) [V2] (AG) *(RT)***
CPL Henry M. Cody [aka Henry Scollin] **(KIA) (AG)**
CPL William Lalor **[V2] (MB)**
CPL Frederick Stressinger **(KIA) [V2] (MB)**
Trumpeter Charles "Bounce" Fischer **(MB)**
Trumpeter Henry C. Weaver **[CW] (MB)**
Saddler John "Jack" Donahoe **[V2] (PT)**
Farrier William D. "Tinker Bill" Meyer **(KIA) [V2] (MB)**
Farrier George "Cully" Weaver **(MB)**
PVT Joseph "Joe" Bates [aka Joseph Murphy] **(MB)**
PVT Frank Braun **(DOW) [R] (AG)**
PVT Morris Cain **[R] (MB)**
PVT James W. Darcy [aka James Wilber] **(WIA) [R] (RS)**
PVT Henry H. "Harrison" Davis **[CW] [V3] (PT)**
PVT Jean B. "Frenchy" Gallenne **(AG) *(H/H)***
PVT Jacob H. Gebhart [aka James J. Tanner] **(DOW) [R]**
PVT Bernard "Barney" Golden **(MB)**
PVT Henry "Tom" Gordon **(KIA) [V2] (AG)**
PVT George Heid **(MB)**
PVT Charles Kavanaugh **[CW] (MB)**
PVT Henry Klotzbucher (Company Clerk) **(KIA) (MB)**
PVT George Lorentz **(KIA) [V2] (MB)**
PVT Daniel Mahoney **[R] (MB)**
PVT John H. "Snopsy" Meier **(WIA) (AG)**
PVT Hugh N. Moore **[V2] (MB)**
PVT William E. "Bill" Morris **(WIA) [R] (RS)**
PVT Francis "Frank" Neely **(AG)**
PVT Daniel J. "Dan" Newell **(WIA) (AG) *(T/B)***
PVT Edward D. Pigford **(WIA) [R] (MB) {2}**
PVT William E. Robinson (detached service as an assistant to Dr. Henry Porter)
PVT Roman "Henry" Rutten **(WIA) [V2] (RS)**
PVT Hobart Ryder **(RS)**
PVT William W. Rye **[R] (MB)**
PVT John Seamans **[R] (MB)**
PVT Robert Senn **[R] (MB)**
PVT James W. "Crazy Jim" Severs **[V2] (MB)**
PVT John "Big Fritz" Sivertsen **[V2] (MB) *(RT) (T/B)***
PVT William C. "Bill" Slaper **[R] (MB)**
PVT George E. Smith **(KIA) [R] (MB)**
PVT Frank W. Sniffin (Company Color Bearer) **[R] (MB)**
PVT Frank Stratton **[R] (MB)**
PVT David "Sandy" Summers **(KIA) (MB) *(H/H)***
PVT Levi M. Thornberry **[R] (MB)**
PVT Rollins L. "Robert" Thorpe **[R] (AG)**
PVT Henry J. "Jim" Turley **(KIA) [V2] (AG)**
PVT Thomas B. "Happy Jack" Varner **(WIA) [R] (MB)**
PVT Henry C. Voight **(KIA) (MB)**
PVT James "Jim" Weeks **[R] (MB)**
PVT John V. Whisten **(MB)**
PVT Charles T. Wiedman **(WIA) [R] (MB)**
PVT Charles H. Williams **(MB)**

Not Present at the Little Bighorn
SGT William Capes (Powder River Camp)
PVT John Dolan (Powder River Camp)
PVT James McCormick (Powder River Camp)
Wagoner Joseph Ricketts (Powder River Camp)
PVT Walter Sterland (Powder River Camp)
PVT Ferdinand Widmayer (Powder River Camp)
Farrier William Wood (Fort Rice)
PVT John Zametzer (Fort Rice)

Legend:

CPT=Captain; 1LT=First Lieutenant; 2LT=Second Lieutenant; 1SG=First Sergeant; SGT=Sergeant; CPL=Corporal; PVT=Private

KIA= killed in action; **WIA**=wounded in action; **DOW**=died of wounds; **CW**=Civil War veteran; **V1**=Battle of Washita veteran; **V2**=fought Indians on 1873 Yellowstone expedition; **V3**=veteran of both Washita and Yellowstone campaigns; **R**=recruit (less than nine months service); **AG**=on advance guard mission; **RS**=on 1SG Ryan's timber scout mission; **MB**=with main body in valley; **PT**=detailed to pack train; ***RT***=remained in timber during retreat; ***H/H***=believed to have been a horse-holder; ***T/B***=trained as a blacksmith

{2, 3, 7} = estimated number of enemy warriors that the trooper shot & killed during the entire battle

Opposite
***Top*: Northeastern corner of Fort Abraham Lincoln in 1875.** Missouri River is to the left. Wooden one-story buildings above the tents are horse stables. Two larger buildings facing right with multiple chimneys are enlisted barracks. Photo appears to be from 1875; during that year Company M was stationed twenty miles south at Fort Rice. For in-depth information on Fort Lincoln, see Schiffer Books, *Fort Abraham Lincoln Dakota Territory*, by Lee Chambers. *Photo courtesy of the Little Bighorn Battlefield National Monument.*

***Bottom*: Southwestern corner of Fort Abraham Lincoln in 1875.** Row of seven large houses is "Officers' Row," where the commissioned officers lived. George Custer's house is the fourth from the right and has five chimneys. It appears that Custer's field tent may be set up behind his quarters, perhaps drying. Longest building is the quartermaster headquarters; just to the right of it is another long building, which is the commissary. *Photo courtesy of the Little Bighorn Battlefield National Monument.*

Appendix 2
Causes of Victory and Defeat

In the main body of this work I have tried to avoid inserting any of my personal opinions concerning the causes of victory – for the Indian warriors – and defeat for Lieutenant Colonel Custer and the 7th Cavalry Regiment. Since I am frequently asked my opinion on these issues, I will take this small appendix and offer my own views on causation and responsibility for better or worse.

The overwhelming reasons that the Lakota and Northern Cheyenne warriors defeated the 7th Cavalry were that the warriors were well-led, highly-motivated, well-equipped with repeating firearms, were fighting with interior lines on terrain advantageous to their tactics and disadvantageous to cavalry tactics, and that there were significantly more warriors than cavalrymen.[i]

The significant reasons leading to the 7th Cavalry's defeat – and Custer's personal demise with over 200 of the soldiers with him – was that the 7th Cavalry was unable to engage the enemy simultaneously with the entire regiment (which led to a situation of being defeated in detail), the command climate was polluted by several officers who worked at cross purposes to that of their commander, there were a substantial number of soldiers in the regiment who were "green" and relatively untrained, over 100 men assigned on paper to the regiment were not available to go on the complete campaign, the marksmanship level in the regiment – except for a few key leaders – appears to have been poor, the regimental leaders failed to appreciate the difficult nature of the terrain, and the scheme of maneuver occurred in such a manner that the element of complete surprise – a key factor in achieving previous victories over the Indians – was unattainable.

A famous saying is that "victory has a thousand fathers, while defeat is an orphan." Having said that, in this defeat, I believe we can lay the component causes of Custer's demise at the feet of specific individuals. The following is my attempt to affix that responsibility, based in part on my experiences as the Inspector General for the United States Army Europe – and the preparation I received to perform that mission – as well as general tactical experiences in six battalions during my years in the service. I would feel much more comfortable analyzing this event if I had finished thirty-four years in the army in 1909 and was making this assessment then, rather than in 2009. Over the years, concepts change, roles of officers and non-commissioned are retooled and training improves, but we can often become prisoners of our own recent experience when going back and analyzing an engagement that long ago; hopefully we can avoid this.

I believe there are seven general reasons for the defeat of the 7th Cavalry Regiment at the Little Bighorn.

The 7th Cavalry was unable to engage the enemy simultaneously with the entire regiment.

Responsibility: George Custer, Marcus Reno and Frederick Benteen. Custer made the plan, which relied on Benteen accomplishing his scout to the left quickly – and then returning to assist either Reno or Custer – and with Reno pressing home the attack on the village proper in the Little Bighorn valley, while Custer attacked the village from the east or north. However, Reno did not have the nerve, or understanding of his commander's overall scheme, to continue the attack or – failing that – to remain in the timber, tying down enemy forces. In the worst interpretation of events, Benteen disobeyed Custer's orders; in the most-favorable analysis, Benteen dawdled; either way, he was never in a position to timely reinforce Reno in his attack in the valley (arriving at Reno Hill minutes after Reno's force did) or to assist Custer at all.

Custer should have known his subordinates' capabilities and tendencies better before he put a captain with an attitude in charge of a semi-independent mission or a timid major in command of a mission that depended on his personal élan in the attack. Additionally, by assuming command of the right wing (Companies C, E, F, I and L), Custer effectively lost command of the entire regiment, as he had put himself in a position where he could not command the actions of all his companies.

He would have been much better served letting Yates or Keogh command the right wing, while Custer remained somewhere on or near Weir Point with a corps of messengers he could dispatch with changing orders – where he could have seen much of Reno's valley fight as well as the right wing advance. Custer expected that his subordinates would carry out their orders vigorously and faithfully – and may have even hoped they would do so imaginatively and even exceed his expectations, but in this he clearly overestimated them. Having said that, Reno and Benteen did not do Custer any favors in the way they conducted their operations, so all share responsibility for this failure.

The command climate was polluted by several officers, who worked at cross purposes to that of their commander.

Responsibility: George Custer.
Captain Frederick Benteen was a capable officer with a corrosive attitude that was highly disruptive to the regiment over a number of years; in military jargon, Benteen's conduct disrupted unity of command. Major Marcus Reno was less capable, displayed little initiative, and had almost no experience fighting Indians. Custer knew the limitations of both men. Equally as important, George Custer had close mentors at high levels of the army. At the beginning of 1876, when the operational battle plan was devised to throw three independent columns at the Indians that spring, Custer should have gone to Lieutenant General Philip H. Sheridan, the author of that plan and commander of the Department of the Missouri, and demanded that both Major Reno and Captain Benteen be assigned to other organizations before the campaign commenced.

Custer did not request this, even though there were competent replacements available; Major Joseph Tilford – a competent officer assigned to the regiment – was on-hand as commander of Fort Rice; Tilford had served in the field with Custer in 1874. Custer requested another officer, Major Lewis Merrill,[ii] return to the regiment for the campaign, but this did not occur.[1] Captain Michael Sheridan, General Phil Sheridan's brother and at the time his aide-de-camp, was also assigned to Company L of the 7th Cavalry on paper and General Sheridan could have re-assigned him back to the regiment for the

[i] Eminent historian John Gray estimated that there were 2,150 warriors available for the battle.

[ii] Major Lewis Merrill may not have been of much help had he reported for duty in the campaign. Born in New Berlin, Pennsylvania on October 28, 1834 he graduated from West Point in 1855. During the Civil War Merrill served on various anti-partisan operations. He was assigned to the 7th Cavalry from November 27, 1868 to May 21, 1886, but seems to have been uninterested in front line duty. Merrill was promoted to major on December 14, 1868, with an effective date of November 27, 1868. He was appointed to the grade of lieutenant colonel on January 21, 1891 (with an effective date of rank of January 9, 1886.) Reno categorized Merrill as a "notorious coward and shirk" while Benteen summarized his thoughts of Merrill in one word, a "chump." Merrill retired in 1886. He died in Philadelphia on February 27, 1896. He is buried at Arlington National Cemetery in Section 2.

expedition without a problem. Captains Owen Hale, Charles Ilsley and John Tourtellotte were also absent and should have been asked to return to the regiment.

While acquiring officers detached from the regiment required outside assistance, the assignment of officers within the regiment was Custer's purview. Of the thirty officers present at the battle on June 25, eleven (37 percent) were not with their assigned commands. In Company M, both lieutenants were absent, one with the pack train and the other with Company E. We can only assume the effects that the troopers' unfamiliarity with these eleven officers had on their performance, but it probably was not a positive situation.

A substantial number of soldiers in the regiment were "green" and relatively untrained.

Responsibility: George Custer, Marcus Reno, all company commanders and company first sergeants.

Custer was the commander and as such was responsible for everything his unit did or failed to do. However, leading up to the campaign Custer was frequently away from the regiment, and during those periods Major Marcus Reno was in temporary command. For example, Custer was absent from the regiment in 1876 from January 1 to March 11, when he returned for only eight days. On March 20 Custer departed for Washington D.C. to testify before Congress; he did not return until May 11, just six days before the expedition began. *Thus, in 1876, with the exception of fourteen days, Major Marcus Reno was in charge of the regiment for a four-and-a-half-month period – the preparation phase to get the unit ready for the expedition.*[iii] Reno and the company commanders and first sergeants needed to conduct a significant period of training to get the new soldiers up to snuff. Whatever they did implement, it was not enough, as evidenced by some of the actions of the new soldiers in combat.[iv]

Over 100 men assigned on paper to the regiment were not available to go on the complete campaign.

Responsibility: George Custer, Marcus Reno, Alfred Terry and Phil Sheridan.

Custer in Washington and Reno from Fort Abraham Lincoln should have contacted General Terry and General Sheridan and demanded that the regiment's men – especially twelve commissioned officers – on detached duty be returned to the regiment in time to train with the unit before going on the expedition. There is another aspect to this problem; about one hundred recruits had to begin the expedition on foot, in the hope that additional horses would be procured at the Yellowstone River.

In Custer's absence during the months before the expedition began, Reno should have submitted reports concerning the lack of availability of these mounts and if he did requisition additional horses, Terry – as the commander of the Department of Dakota – and Sheridan should have gotten involved and procured the horses for the regiment. Although Reno did alert the department on February 9, 1876 of the horse shortage, it does not appear that he followed up on the request.[2] Additionally, Terry should have more closely monitored Reno, knowing that Custer was away and could not adequately supervise the preparations of the regiment. Terry finally freed up 17 horses, when he directed that the band would not go on the final part of the campaign, but that wasn't enough and thus some men had to remain on the Yellowstone as they had no mounts – leaving the regiment under-strength on the day of battle.

The general marksmanship level in the regiment – except for a few key leaders – appears to have been poor.

Responsibility: George Custer, all company commanders and company first sergeants, and Henry J. Nowlan (regimental quartermaster.)

Custer and his chain of command needed to scour the Military Department of the Dakota for every round they could find before the expedition and scrounge up enough carbine ammunition to conduct adequate training. One hundred rounds of ammunition per man would have done the trick. The chain of command could have gone to Fort Bennett and other posts in the region that were not involved in the campaign, called in a few old favors, and probably could have found the ammunition.

They didn't, and most battle testimony later related that very few Indians at the Little Bighorn were killed by cavalry gunfire. Custer seemed to think that maneuver could win the day, and while maneuver was indeed crucial to success in mounted actions of the time, delivering overwhelming, effective fire – after this maneuver had brought about an advantage – was also important. The Indians had no deterrence coming in their direction in the form of braves dropping out of the saddle at an alarming rate. If the attacker senses he is not receiving losses, there is no reason to slow or stop an attack. The .45 caliber Springfield carbine was an excellent weapon, and while there were a few instances of improper extraction during the battle, the weapon provided the cavalry with significant standoff capability.[3] And there was no denying that the Springfield's massive, soft lead bullet could drop an enemy in his tracks at several hundred yards and fatally wound Indian ponies as well.[v] This wasn't just a 7th Cavalry Regiment problem, however; at the Rosebud fight a week earlier, George Crook's men fired 25,000 rounds, killing just 36 and wounding only 63 warriors for their trouble![4]

The level of marksmanship was further hurt by what appears to be a lack of fire control on the part of many cavalry leaders, who may have fallen into the trap of concentrating on their own engagements with the enemy, rather than direct effective firing on the part of their entire unit – sort of a target-fixation syndrome that led them to ignore what was going on around them due to their overriding focus on personally killing the enemy.

[iii] Emphasis is by the author.

[iv] There is evidence that the chain of command did not inform company commanders and first sergeants about the impending operation for several months in 1876. First Sergeant Ryan later stated that in the spring of 1876 there were rumors of an impending campaign against the Indians. The regimental leadership should have confirmed that information with these senior non-commissioned officers early on, precisely so that they would conduct a period of more intense training for the men. Source: Sandy Barnard, editor, *Ten Years with Custer: A 7th Cavalryman's Memoirs*, Terre Haute, IN: AST Press, 2001, 260.

[v] The muzzle velocity of the .45 caliber 1873 Springfield carbine using cartridges with 55 grains of powder was 1,150 feet per second; the muzzle velocity of the .45 caliber 1873 Springfield rifle using the more powerful cartridges filled with 70 grains of powder was 1,350 feet per second. This compared to the Indian-used Model 1873 .44/40 Winchester with a muzzle velocity of 1,245 feet per second, and the 1860 .44 Henry with a muzzle velocity of 1,124 feet per second. However, concerning stopping power, a more accurate measurement is muzzle energy, measured in foot-pounds. In this category the four weapons produced the following muzzle energy: .45/70 1873 Springfield rifle, 1,525 foot-pounds; .45/55 1873 Springfield carbine, 930 foot-pounds, Model 1873 .44/40 Winchester, 688 foot-pounds; and the 1860 .44 Henry, 568 foot-pounds. Source: Douglas C. McChristian, *The U.S. Army in the West: 1870-1880*, Norman, OK: University of Oklahoma Press, 1995, 113. The Colt .45 revolver fired a 255-grain bullet at a muzzle velocity of over 800 feet per second, which translated to a muzzle energy of over 400 foot-pounds. Source: Garry James, "Custer's Last Gun," *Guns & Ammo*, InterMedia Outdoors Inc, December 2009, 65-66.

The regimental leaders failed to appreciate the difficult nature of the terrain.

Responsibility: George Custer, Marcus Reno, Frederick Benteen, George Yates and Myles Keogh.

Maps do not do justice to the actual terrain at the Little Bighorn. Cross-river movement is restricted based on steep riverbanks at potential crossing sites and high bluffs that limit even approaching the river. Vantage points from which to see the extent of the Indian village were few. On the eastern side of the river – away from the bluffs – fairly flat, gently undulating terrain – seen from a distance – promised ideal mobility for mounted cavalry. But up close this terrain was criss-crossed with gullies that actually provided cover and concealment for approaching dismounted warriors, and limits cavalry mobility.

In 1876, there were no detailed topographical maps of the region; the army generally knew where the rivers and major tributaries were (but not potential difficulties at crossing sites), and even the scouts had but rudimentary knowledge of the distances involved.[5] Thus, Custer's first understanding of the terrain would be his last.

Once the cavalry got into this terrain east of the Little Bighorn, there was little possibility for escape should momentum swing to the enemy; even with binoculars, when Custer reached Weir Point and looked at the final battlefield, he would have been unable to see the subtle folds in the ground that made what first appeared to be good "cavalry country" a veritable deathtrap; most army issue field glasses of the era were designed with straight-through optics that provided only a magnification of 2.5 to four power. Had Custer waited to attack until the next day, he might have been able to get some officers within visual distance of the battlefield at daybreak and modified his plans accordingly. But he thought he couldn't wait to attack, and the terrain "surprised" the cavalry leaders with its complexity.

The scheme of maneuver occurred in such a manner that the element of complete surprise – a key factor in achieving previous victories over the Indians – was unattainable.

Responsibility: George Custer.

Custer's earlier victories, especially at the Washita in 1868, had attained surprise by attacking early in the morning, and it was Custer's plan to move closer to the village on June 25, but not launch the attack until dawn on June 26. However, events on the morning of June 25 led Custer to believe that the village was aware of the presence of the cavalry and that if he did not attack immediately, the village would move quickly to avoid capture. Thus, Custer advanced his attack timetable, but attacking at midday, when most of the Indians were awake, was far different than attacking at first light, when almost all would be asleep. While some Indians were indeed initially surprised by the attacks of Reno – in the valley – and Custer on the bluff, the warriors quickly overcame their temporary psychological shock and mounted an effective counterattack, which doomed Custer.

Small water ditch coming off bench land west of the skirmish line fighting. Such small obstacles often could not be seen until the last second and made the overall area poorly-suited to offensive cavalry operations.

Minneconjou Ford; view looks east across the Little Bighorn from the Indian village location. At no time in the battle could Company M troopers see this important point. Terrain is deceptive; from a distance it appears to be gently rolling, but actually has many small ravines and gullies where warriors could hide. Custer did not realize this until it was too late.

Minneconjou Ford looking upstream (south). High bluffs on the left limited crossing sites on the Little Bighorn, effectively separating the regiment.

Minneconjou Ford looking downstream (north). Custer's force went in this direction, but warriors pursued them across the river from here. Again, bluffs along the river limited crossing sites.

Battlefield marker for famed guide "Lonesome Charlie" Reynolds. Reynolds was killed during the fighting in the valley and served alongside Company M. Custer should have listened to "Lonesome Charlie" before attacking such a large gathering of warriors, as many of the scouts saw signs that this group of warriors was too large to attack in the middle of the day.

View of 1873 Springfield carbine sight in the "down" position. In this "down" mode, which was standard for cavalrymen, the sight could be set in one-hundred yard increments to a maximum of 500 yards. Shown here, the sight is set at 100 yards. Note: the sight mounting screws are of the slotted variety, a variant introduced after the Little Bighorn, but the sighting mechanism is that of the 1873 carbine used at the battle.

***Right*: A second view of the 1873 Springfield carbine sight in the "down" position.** Shown here, the sight is set for 400 yards, which raises the rear sight notch at the front of the mechanism. To maintain a correct sight picture, the shooter then raises the front of the barrel as the range increases. Failure to adjust the sight as the warriors moved closer would almost certainly guarantee a miss.

View of the 1873 Springfield carbine sight in the "up" position. In this mode, which generally required a more-veteran trooper, the moveable leaf sight could be set in one-hundred yard increments from 600 to a maximum of 1,200 yards. Now the sight is set for 600 yards. Very few cavalrymen could use the sight in this manner, while mounted.

A second view of the 1873 Springfield carbine sight in the "up" position. Now the leaf sight is set for 1,000 yards. Only a very few cavalrymen could hit their targets at this range. In fact, many troopers in Company M – and the entire regiment – had very little marksmanship training at all.

***Top left:* .45/55 cartridge from 1873 Springfield carbine from the Company M position in the timberline.** This cartridge was found in 1994.

***Top center:* same cartridge; note knife mark on rim where soldier dug it out of the chamber after firing.**

***Top right:* same cartridge; red arrow points to a second knife mark that was not as deep.** Private William "Bill" Morris later recalled that his carbine jammed during the valley fighting after he fired 25-30 rounds. It is not possible to say if this cartridge came from Morris' weapon.

***Right:* same cartridge; red arrow points to knife mark.** Soldiers recalled that Captain Thomas French picked out jammed cartridges from weapons on Reno Hill, but there are no accounts that he did so earlier in the timberline.

Appendix 3
Battlefield Artifacts for the Valley Fight at the Little Bighorn

Some of the conclusions of this book are based on battlefield artifacts from the fighting in the valley on June 25, 1876. While I have not personally located artifacts on the battlefield, many others have. As early as Michael Sheridan's mission to the Little Bighorn in 1877, there has been evidence of relic hunting at the Little Bighorn.[1] As the Little Bighorn Battlefield National Monument Resources Management Plan states:[2]

> "Relics of the battle have been of interest to the general public since the end of the battle. Such artifacts were first collected immediately after the battle. Prior to the establishment of the monument, relic collecting was a favorite past-time within the park boundaries as well as across the entire battlefield and associated Native American campsite. Relic collecting continues to be a favorite past time on adjacent private lands. One collector has published his interpretation of the battle from his personal findings."

We can get supporting observations by the grand lady herself, Elizabeth Custer, who once wrote:[3]

> "I have received many letters in the past twelve years, describing articles that were reported to have come from the Indians who captured them of the 25th of June, but investigation has proved that none of the supposed trophies were what they had been represented to those purchasing them."

Not only have battlefield artifacts been taken from the scene of the fighting, others have been added over time. Army expeditions visited the battlefield to clean up remains and escort visitors and undoubtedly some post-battle material left during these later visits became mixed with actual evidence from the days of the fighting. There is at least anecdotal evidence that one superintendent of the battlefield actually "salted" the Custer battlefield with some expended rounds and fired bullets in hopes of generating enthusiasm from battlefield visitors, undoubtedly with a long-term hope that more visitors would come and see "his" battlefield in the future.

Let us unequivocally state upfront: It is illegal to look for and take any battlefield relic on public lands or Indian land under the provisions of the Federal Archaeological Resources Protection Act. In fact, it's a felony. So relics from the Custer fight (Calhoun Hill, Custer Hill, etc.) and Reno-Benteen Area (Reno Hill), all within the Little Bighorn National Monument, should be avoided. These two areas are not contiguous, but are connected by the battlefield road. The land between the two battle areas is owned by the Crow Indian Tribe, so finding artifacts along the road is out. However, at one point, much of the land on the Little Bighorn valley floor – where Reno and his detachment began the fighting – was privately owned, some by Native Americans, and some by whites. Now much of that land is under the supervision of the Custer Battlefield Preservation Committee. So it would be against some law to look for artifacts on land administered by the Preservation Committee, unless they gave you permission to do so.

Legal restrictions are but one hurdle. Whenever the use is made of battlefield artifacts that were found on private land, there can be a social price to be paid for such an undertaking. National Park Service archaeologist Doug Scott, an eminent expert on the battle, was reported to have been "beside himself" when he found out that the items were being unearthed in the valley, stating:[4]

> "We're missing the part of the battle that tells us how the warriors and the soldiers all got there."

So for artifacts found in the valley floor during the limited time that land was privately owned, the researcher is faced with the dilemma of whether or not to base research on legally-obtained, but perhaps academically-shunned, artifacts. Perhaps it is more accurate to say archaeologically-shunned artifacts. Most private artifact seekers find items with metal detectors, put them in a container and take them home, which results in a loss of important data concerning artifact location, condition, surrounding terrain and so forth – all the bread and butter of trained archaeologists.

For this work, I chose what I believe to be the best practical ground. Doug Scott, Richard Fox and a host of others did a magnificent job of painstakingly uncovering evidence on the Custer battlefield and Reno-Benteen Hill beginning in 1984. Due to a variety of conditions beyond their control they have not been able to do the same outstanding work in the valley, and with economic conditions being what they are, a task of this magnitude may be years, if not decades, away.

However, in my opinion, the private landowner in this case at that time, Jason Pitsch, did the next best thing. During the 1990s he spent years combing much of his land armed with a metal detector. But he went a step further and for that he deserves our thanks. He also went armed with topographic maps and aerial photographs. On these, he located his position, assigned a serial number to each artifact and fastidiously plotted the location of each item. Using his maps and sophisticated topographic software, I was able to pinpoint these locations with a high degree of accuracy and base some conclusions accordingly. One day, trained forensic examiners may be able to look at Jason's finds – or my modest artifact photographs in this work – and make even more precise conclusions, not only of the valley fight, but also – for example – to determine if cartridges found in the valley have matches with cartridges found on Custer Hill.

We will never know how many artifacts would have been washed away, trampled flat by livestock or had other misfortunes had they not been found in the 1990s, but rather lay dormant until sometime in the nebulous future when a bonded archaeological team unearthed them – if that indeed were ever to occur at all. But Mr. Pitsch found, and in my opinion may have saved, thousands of pieces of information concerning that fight on the afternoon of June 25, 1876. It would be foolish not to attempt to use his findings to add to the body of knowledge we have about the fight just because he does not have a degree in advanced archaeology or that he might not have followed all the procedures laid down by the Society of American Archaeology.

I have used but a few of Jason Pitsch's findings to illustrate information about Company M. They are shown in this appendix, along with the location in which they were found to the most exact coordinates I could determine. I hope that they might help in some small way researchers who come after me.

.45/55 cartridge fired from a Model 1873 Springfield carbine; cartridge was found in 1996 at the Company M initial skirmish line at (45° 31' 12.232" N, 107° 24' 49.762" W).

"An ounce of lead!" .45 caliber bullet from a Springfield carbine; bullet was found impacted in the low hills just west of the Hunkpapa camp along the Little Bighorn (45° 31' 21.412" N, 107° 25' 29.783" W). When Reno attacked, this was one of the first positions to which the warriors went. It is not known which company fired this round, although Company M was the closest in range to where the bullet impacted. Bullet measures 1.06" long and is .45" in diameter; it actually weighs just under an ounce at 0.919 ounces.

Nose view of the same .45 caliber bullet found in the low hills west of the Hunkpapa camp.

.50/70 cartridge fired from a Model 1870 Springfield rifle; cartridge was found in 1999 at the Company M position in the timberline (45° 31' 23.653" N, 107° 24' 19.940" W). The 1.79"long cartridge could have been fired by Captain Thomas H. French, who is the only member of Company M known to have carried this type of weapon at the battle. Jason Pitsch found a total of seven of these cartridges at this position.

Base view of same .45/55 cartridge fired from a Model 1873 Springfield carbine at the Company M initial skirmish line; note firing pin mark.

.50 caliber bullet fired from a .50/70 cartridge that landed at the Hunkpapa camp (45°31'44.365" N, 107°24' 57.235" W). Bullet was probably fired by a 7th Cavalry Indian scout on the left flank of the skirmish line. Bullet was found in 1995; it weighs 1.012 ounces.

Nose view of the same .50 caliber bullet.

Base view of same .50/70 cartridge fired from a Model 1870 Springfield rifle at the Company M position in the timberline; note indentation caused by firing pin strike.

A .44 caliber round ball found behind the initial skirmish line between Company A and Company G (45° 31' 18.121" N, 107° 24' 37.838" W). It was found in 1994; Jason Pitsch concluded that it was fired by a Model 1860 Colt percussion revolver. Bullet weighs 0.329 ounces. Only the warriors seem to have had such weapons at the Little Bighorn; in fact only about a dozen bullets for this type of weapon have been found at the Custer battle site. Northern Cheyenne warrior Wooden Leg later said he owned a revolver of this type and fired four rounds in the valley fight. He described his weapon: "My cap-and-ball six shooter was my warring weapon. I had plenty of caps, powder and lead for it. I had a bullet mold to make its bullets from the lead. I kept the bullets and the caps in two small tin boxes. The powder I carried in a horn swung by a thong from my shoulder. For the gun I had a good scabbard. This was fastened to my leather belt." Future forensic examination could show this was one of the rounds fired by Wooden Leg given the paucity of 1860 Colts at the battle.

Unfired .50/70 round available for use in .50 caliber Springfield rifles and carbines, as well as a variety of other weapons. The round was often called the "Big Fifty." It is 2.25" long and was popular with buffalo hunters. This particular round was not found at the Little Bighorn.

.45/55 cartridge fired from an 1873 Springfield carbine; cartridge was found in 1998 at the Company M position in the timberline (45° 31' 23.352" N, 107° 24' 16.359" W).

.45/70 cartridge fired from an 1874 Sharps rifle; the 2.105 in. long cartridge was found in 1995 at the Company M timberline position at (45° 31' 22.662" N, 107° 24' 19.363" W); First Sergeant John Ryan was the only soldier in Company M known to have this type of weapon at the battle. Scout "Lonesome Charlie" Reynolds and interpreter Isaiah Dorman also carried Sharps and may have fired this round from the Company M location as well.

Base view of same .45/70 cartridge fired from an 1874 Sharps rifle at the Company M timberline position; note firing pin mark and how it shows a drag on the cartridge base as the breech block moves, causing a unique forensic signature.

Base view of same .45/55 cartridge fired from an 1873 Springfield carbine at the Company M position in the timberline; note firing pin mark. In many ammunition photographs exact color was sacrificed to gain contrast and resolution, sometimes going to black and white in difficult shots.

A lucky penny belonging to a Company M trooper? This 1865 U.S. penny was found in 1997 at the Company M timberline position at (45° 31' 23.034" N, 107° 24' 19.557" W).

Reverse side of an 1865 U.S. penny found at the Company M timberline position.

A .45 caliber Model 1873 Colt "Peacemaker" cartridge; the cartridge was found in 1991 at the Company M timberline position (45° 31' 22.898" N, 107° 24' 16.141" W); it is 1.29" long.

Base view of same .45 caliber cartridge; note firing pin mark in the center of the cartridge.

Eagle pattern 4/5" cavalry uniform button found in 1997 at the Company M timberline position (45° 31' 23.720" N, 107° 24' 16.732" W).

A .44 caliber bullet fired from an Indian-owned repeating rifle; bullet was found in 1995 at the rear of the Company M timberline position (45° 31' 23.650" N, 107° 24' 8.166" W) near the Little Bighorn River. Between one-third and one-half of the warriors at the Little Bighorn carried a firearm. Bullet measures 0.59" long and 0.44" in diameter; it weighs 0.462 ounces.

A .44 Henry-made cartridge fired from an Indian-owned repeating rifle; cartridge was found at a warrior flanking position on the bench-land plateau just west/southwest of the Company M initial skirmish line position (45° 30' 58.552" N, 107° 25' 1.162" W).

Base view of the same .44 caliber cartridge; it was fired from a Winchester or Henry repeating rifle; cartridge was found in 1994.

.50 caliber bullet fired from an Indian-owned .50/70 rifle; bullet was found at Company M's position in the timberline (45° 31' 23.387" N, 107° 24' 19.460" W) in 1995. Bullet measures 0.85" long and .50" in diameter; it weighs 0.969 ounces.

Base view of the same .50 caliber bullet from the Company M timberline position.

Nose view of the same .50 caliber bullet from the Company M timberline position.

Complete .45/55 Model 1873 Springfield Carbine round; the round was found between the Company A and Company M position in the timberline (45° 31' 25.755" N, 107° 24' 20.230" W) in 1993. It measures 2.65" long.

Unfired .45/70 round available for use in .45 caliber Springfield Rifles and Carbines, as well as a variety of other .45 caliber weapons. This particular round was not found at the Little Bighorn.

Iron arrowhead found in 1992 in the Company M timberline position at (45° 31' 24.101" N, 107° 24' 17.724" W). Tip of arrowhead (closest to small hole) is broken. The opposite end would be affixed to the arrow shaft. It appears to be made of hoop iron and is 2.7" long and .93" wide at its widest point. Warriors sharpened these on both sides. Troopers shot with a war arrow had to have the arrow removed quickly, before the sinew fastening the arrowhead to the shaft loosened and allowed the shaft to pull free – leaving the head still imbedded in the wound.

Reverse side of iron arrowhead found at the Company M timberline position. Private Henry Klotzbucher of Company M may have been killed by an arrow shot into his stomach.

Spencer bullet found near the Retreat Crossing site on the Little Bighorn River (45° 31' 17.822" N, 107° 23' 15.316" W).

Another view of a Spencer bullet found in 1992 near the Retreat Crossing site. Flat part is the bullet base. The bullet weighs 0.818 ounces.

Unfired Model 1860 Spencer carbine 56/56 round. These weapons were in the hands of the warriors, although this particular round did not come from the Little Bighorn. The 56/56 bullet weighed 0.80 ounces, with a muzzle velocity of 1,200 feet/second and hit with a force of 1,125 foot-pounds at the muzzle, making it ineffective past short range. It is 1.63" long.

Unfired Model 1865 Spencer carbine 56/50 round. These carbines were also used by some warriors at the Little Bighorn, although this particular round was not found there. The bullet weighed the same as the 56/56 but had a slightly higher velocity and corresponding energy. Dark blotches on case are examples of verdigris weathering often found on copper. Such material could cause cartridge to experience extraction problems.

Unfired Henry .44 caliber repeating rifle round. This cartridge could be fired in either a Henry or a Winchester repeating rifle, both of which could put out a stream of fire at close range compared to the single shot carbine the cavalrymen had. This particular round was not found at the Little Bighorn. It is 1.335" long.

Unfired Model 1873 Colt .45 revolver round. The Colt was a close-defense weapon, sighted for 25 yards. Its 860 feet/second muzzle velocity and 420 foot-pounds of energy at the muzzle made it a decent man-stopper at that range or closer. The overall length of the round is 1.60". The Colt round was too long to function in the Schofield revolver. This particular round was not found at the Little Bighorn.

Unfired Schofield caliber .45 revolver round, designed for the Smith & Wesson Model 3 revolver, but also used in the Model 1873 Colt .45 revolver. The overall length of the round is 1.43". This particular round was not found at the Little Bighorn.

Tin cavalry trouser button; button was found with cavalry uniform piece of cloth.

Reverse side of cavalry trouser button. No thread or material was attached to the button when found.

Cavalry uniform piece. Dark-blue cloth, identified as linen cotton, measures about 2.75" high and 4.65" wide at greatest point and shows two sewn seams; it is likely part of a privately purchased uniform shirt. This artifact was found at the Company M position in the timberline (45° 21' 22.415" N, 107° 24' 20.835" W) at the same location as the trouser button and .45/55 cartridge.

Reverse view of cavalry uniform piece. Some edge portions appear to have sustained a degree of fire damage; warriors set fire to the tall grass in the timberline to drive troopers out, but the blaze did not fully take hold. Wes Cowan, owner of Cowan's Auctions, and an acknowledged expert of the period, examined the cloth and offered two opinions; first, it is possible for this amount of cloth to have survived from the battle until today in this condition – and second, that forensic archaeologists should examine the surrounding area for human bones.

A .45/55 cartridge fired from an 1873 Springfield carbine. Cartridge was found with trouser button and uniform piece in 1995. Given the proximity of the three items, the location could mark where a Company M trooper was killed in the timberline and later buried at the spot.

Base view of the same .45/55 cartridge fired from an 1873 Springfield carbine. If this location marked the "Last Stand" for one cavalry trooper, it is likely that warriors then took the soldier's weapons and ammunition and perhaps used them later in the battle.

Doing archaeology by the book. Uncovering a .45/55 cartridge on Reno-Benteen Hill in 2004 during official excavations. *Photo courtesy of John Doerner.*

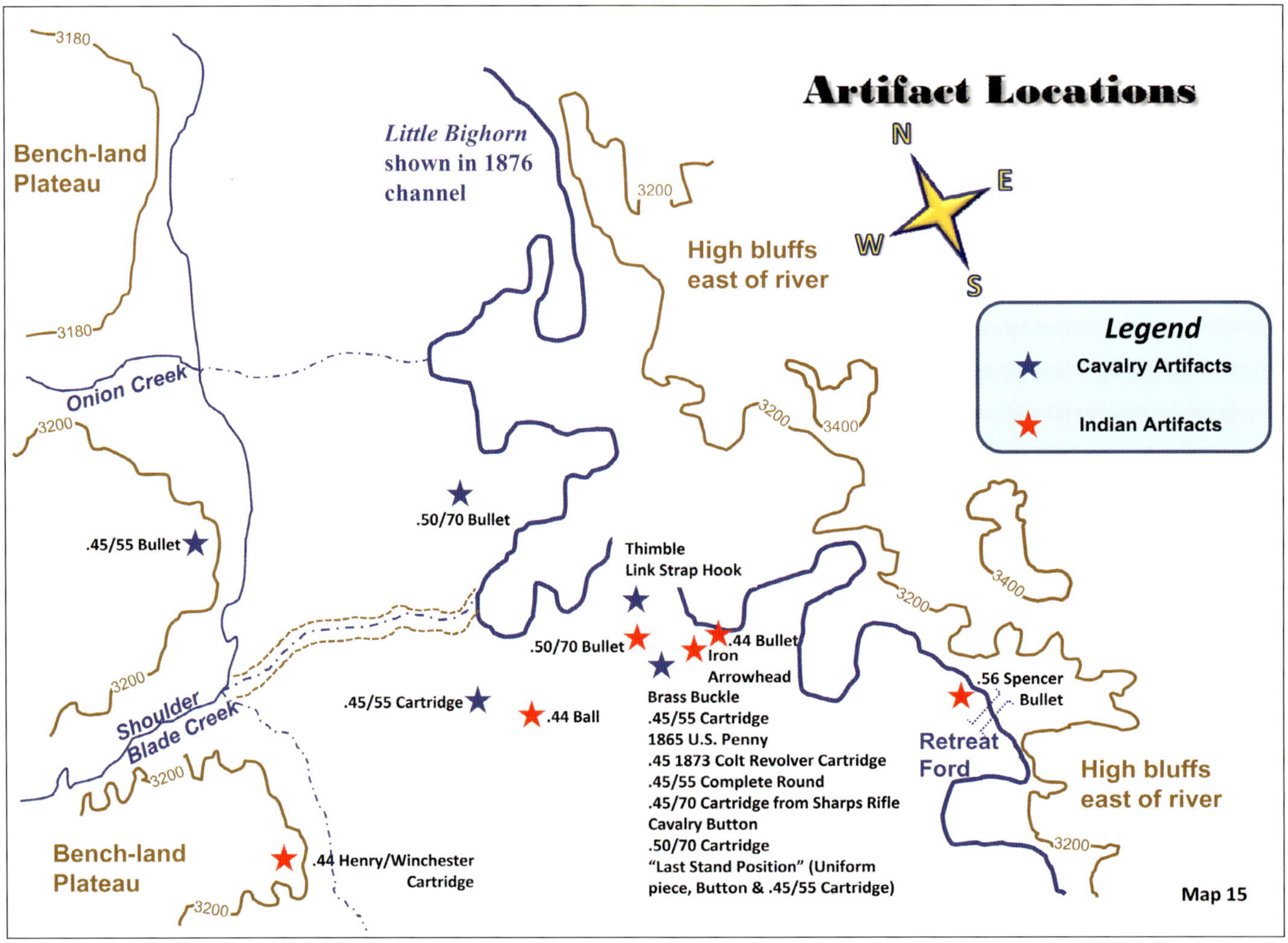

Endnotes

Dedication

[1] Quotation attributed to General Dwight Eisenhower.

[2] Larry Sklenar, *To Hell with Honor; Custer and the Little Bighorn*, Norman, OK: University of Oklahoma Press, 2003, 6, 67.

[3] Jeremy Agnew, *Life of a Soldier on the Western Frontier*, Missoula, MT: Mountain Press Publishing Company, 2008, 116.

[4] Larry Sklenar, *To Hell with Honor; Custer and the Little Bighorn*, Norman, OK: University of Oklahoma Press, 2003, 261-262.

Preface

[1] Glendolin D. Wagner, *Old Neutriment*, New York: Sol Lewis, 1973, 144.

[2] Nathaniel Philbrick, *The Last Stand: Custer, Sitting Bull, and the Battle of the Little Bighorn*, New York: The Penguin Group, 2010, xv.

[3] Paul Andrew Hutton, *The Custer Reader*, Lincoln, NE: University of Nebraska Press, 1993, 542.

[4] Jeremy Agnew, *Life of a Soldier on the Western Frontier*, Missoula, MT: Mountain Press Publishing Company, 2008, 11.

[5] Dippie, Brian W. *Nomad: George A. Custer in Turf, Field, and Farm*, Austin, TX: University of Texas Press, 1980, xi.

[6] Charles M. Robinson, *A Good Year to Die: The Story of the Great Sioux War*, New York: Random House, 1995, 34; and Nathaniel Philbrick, *The Last Stand: Custer, Sitting Bull, and the Battle of the Little Bighorn*, New York: The Penguin Group, 2010, 172.

[7] Larry Sklenar, *To Hell with Honor; Custer and the Little Bighorn*, Norman, OK: University of Oklahoma Press, 2003, 20.

[8] Brian W. Dippie, *Custer's Last Stand: The Anatomy of an American Myth*, Lincoln, NE: University of Nebraska Press, 1976, 1.

[9] Tim Mulligan, "Custer and the Little Bighorn: A Needed Perspective," *Research Review: The Journal of the Little Bighorn Associates,* Volume 23, Number 2, Summer 2009, Rockville, MD: The Little Bighorn Associates, 18. Article reprinted from the Spring 1973 *Research Review*.

[10] Arthur Koenig, *Authentic History of the Indian Campaign Which Culminated in Custer's Last Battle, June 25, 1876*, St. Louis, MO: Anheuser Busch, 12.

Introduction

[1] Quotation attributed to Richard Marcinko, former U.S. Navy SEAL and author.

[2] Douglas D. Scott, P. Willey and Melissa A. Connor, *They Died with Custer: Soldiers Bones from the Battle of the Little Bighorn*, Norman, OK: University of Oklahoma Press, 38.

[3] Don Rickey, Jr., *Forty Miles a Day on Beans and Hay*, Norman, OK: University of Oklahoma Press, 1972, 77, 124-125.

[4] Edgar I. Stewart, *Custer's Luck*, Norman, OK: University of Oklahoma Press, 1980, 172; and Gregory Michno, *The Mystery of E Troop: Custer's Gray Horse Company at the Little Bighorn*, Missoula, Montana: Mountain Press Publishing Company, 1994, 199.

[5] Walter M. Camp, "Field Notes," Lilly Library, Indiana University, Bloomington, IN., Box 2, Folder 11 – Little Bighorn, Part 3.

[6] Larry Sklenar, *To Hell with Honor; Custer and the Little Bighorn*, Norman, OK: University of Oklahoma Press, 2003, 84.

[7] Larry Sklenar, *To Hell with Honor; Custer and the Little Bighorn*, Norman, OK: University of Oklahoma Press, 2003, 117.

[8] Larry Sklenar, *To Hell with Honor; Custer and the Little Bighorn*, Norman, OK: University of Oklahoma Press, 2003, 124.

[9] Nathaniel Philbrick, *The Last Stand: Custer, Sitting Bull, and the Battle of the Little Bighorn*, New York: The Penguin Group, 2010, 73.

[10] Larry Sklenar, *To Hell with Honor; Custer and the Little Bighorn*, Norman, OK: University of Oklahoma Press, 2003, 183.

[11] James Willert, *Little Big Horn Diary: Chronicle of the 1876 Indian War*, El Segundo, CA: Upton and Sons, 1997, 302.

[12] Gregory Michno, *The Mystery of E Troop: Custer's Gray Horse Company at the Little Bighorn*, Missoula, Montana: Mountain Press Publishing Company, 1994, 294.

[13] Ronald H. Nichols, editor, *Men with Custer: Biographies of the 7th Cavalry*, Hardin, MT: Custer Battlefield Historical and Museum Association, 2000, 349-350.

[14] Kenneth Hammer, *Custer in '76: Walter Camp's Notes on the Custer Fight*, Provo, UT: Brigham Young University, 1976, 1-3.

[15] C. Lee Noyes, "Was There A Timber Fight?" Indianapolis, IN: Indianapolis Little Bighorn Symposium, September 12, 2009.

[16] Kenneth Hammer, *Custer in '76: Walter Camp's Notes on the Custer Fight*, Provo, UT: Brigham Young University, 1976, 2-3.

[17] Walter M. Camp, "Field Notes," Lilly Library, Indiana University, Bloomington, IN., Box 2, Folder 9 – Little Bighorn, Part 1.

[18] C. Lee Noyes, "Was There A Timber Fight?" Indianapolis, IN: Indianapolis Little Bighorn Symposium, September 12, 2009.

Chapter One: Company M History

[1] Douglas C. McChristian, *The U.S. Army in the West: 1870-1880*, Norman, OK: University of Oklahoma Press, 1995, 5.

[2] Gregory Michno, *The Mystery of E Troop: Custer's Gray Horse Company at the Little Bighorn*, Missoula, Montana: Mountain Press Publishing Company, 1994, 1.

[3] Jeremy Agnew, *Life of a Soldier on the Western Frontier*, Missoula, MT: Mountain Press Publishing Company, 2008, 13, 177.

[4] Larry Sklenar, *To Hell with Honor; Custer and the Little Bighorn*, Norman, OK: University of Oklahoma Press, 2003, 5.

[5] Jeremy Agnew, *Life of a Soldier on the Western Frontier*, Missoula, MT: Mountain Press Publishing Company, 2008, 85.

[6] James Donovan, *A Terrible Glory: Custer and the Little Bighorn – the Last Great Battle of the American West*, New York: Little, Brown and Company, 2008, 90-91.

[7] Kevin Adams, *Class and Race in the Frontier Army: Military Life in the West,* 1870-1890, Norman, OK: University of Oklahoma Press, 2009, 13.

[8] Larry D. Underwood, *The Custer Fight: and Other Tales of the Old West*, Lincoln, NE: Media Publishing, 1989, 8.

[9] Charles K. Mills, *Rosters from 7th U.S. Cavalry campaigns, 1866-1896*, Mattituck, NY: J.M. Carroll and Company, 1983, 2.

[10] Kenneth Hammer, *Custer in '76: Walter Camp's Notes on the Custer Fight*, Provo, UT: Brigham Young University, 1976, 138.

[11] Marc E. Kollbaum, *Gateway to the West: The History of Jefferson Barracks from 1826 – 1894*, Volume 1, St. Louis, MO: Friends of Jefferson Barracks, 202.

[12] Melbourne C. Chandler, *Of Garry Owen in Glory: The History of the 7th Cavalry*, Annandale, VA: Turnpike Press, 1960, 2, 3, 345, 355; Ernest L. Reedstrom, *Bugles, Banners & War Bonnets*, Caldwell, ID: The Caxton Printers, 1977, 22; and Steve Arnold, "Cooke's scrawled note: Last word from doomed command," *Greasy Grass Magazine*, Volume 14, May 1998, Hardin, MT: Custer Battlefield Historical & Museum Association, 21.

[13] Sandy Barnard, editor, *Ten Years with Custer: A 7th Cavalryman's Memoirs*, Terre Haute, IN: AST Press, 2001, 17; Roger L. Williams, *Military Register of Custer's Last Command*, Norman, OK: The Arthur H. Clark Company, 2009, 36; and Muster Rolls – 7th U.S. Cavalry, Company L-M, 1866-1884, Company M Muster Roll dated December 31, 1866, Microfilm Roll #5 at the Little Bighorn National Monument Archive.

[14] Melbourne C. Chandler, *Of Garry Owen in Glory: The History of the 7th Cavalry*, Annandale, VA: Turnpike Press, 1960, 3-5; Ernest L. Reedstrom, *Bugles, Banners & War Bonnets*, Caldwell, ID: The Caxton Printers, 1977, 22; and Thom Hatch, *The Custer Companion: A Comprehensive Guide to the Life of George Armstrong Custer and the Plains Indian Wars*, Mechanicsburg, PA: The Stackpole Company, 2002, 42.

[15] Sandy Barnard, *Custer's First Sergeant John Ryan*, Terre Haute, IN: AST Press, 1996, 103.

[16] Steve Arnold, "Cooke's scrawled note: Last word from doomed command," *Greasy Grass Magazine*, Volume 14, May 1998, Hardin, MT: Custer Battlefield Historical & Museum Association, 21.

[17] Muster Rolls – 7th U.S. Cavalry, Company L-M, 1866-1884, Company M Muster Roll dated February 28, 1867, Microfilm Roll #5 at the Little Bighorn National Monument Archive.

[18] Muster Rolls – 7th U.S. Cavalry, Company L-M, 1866-1884, Company M Muster Roll dated April 30, 1867, Microfilm Roll #5 at the Little Bighorn National Monument Archive.

[19] Melbourne C. Chandler, *Of Garry Owen in Glory: The History of the 7th Cavalry*, Annandale, VA: Turnpike Press, 1960, 3-5; and Ernest L. Reedstrom, *Bugles, Banners & War Bonnets*, Caldwell, ID: The Caxton Printers, 1977, 22.

[20] Brian W. Dippie, *Nomad: George A. Custer in Turf, Field, and Farm*, Austin, TX: University of Texas Press, 1980, 4.

[21] Muster Rolls – 7th U.S. Cavalry, Company L-M, 1866-1884, Company M Muster Roll dated June 30, 1867, Microfilm Roll #5 at the Little Bighorn National Monument Archive.

[22] Melbourne C. Chandler, *Of Garry Owen in Glory: The History of the 7th Cavalry*, Annandale, VA: Turnpike Press, 1960, 3-5; and Sandy Barnard, editor, *Ten Years with Custer: A 7th Cavalryman's Memoirs*, Terre Haute, IN: AST Press, 2001, 38.

[23] Melbourne C. Chandler, *Of Garry Owen in Glory: The History of the 7th Cavalry*, Annandale, VA: Turnpike Press, 1960, 3-5; Thom Hatch, *The Custer Companion: A Comprehensive Guide to the Life of George Armstrong Custer and the Plains Indian Wars*, Mechanicsburg, PA: The Stackpole Company, 2002, 59, 72; Charles K. Hofling, *Custer and the Little Big Horn: A Psychobiographical Inquiry*, Detroit, MI: Wayne State University Press, 1981, 68; and Larry D. Underwood, *The Custer Fight: and Other Tales of the Old West*, Lincoln, NE: Media Publishing, 1989, 10.

[24] Muster Rolls – 7th U.S. Cavalry, Company L-M, 1866-1884, Company M Muster Roll dated August 31, 1867, October 31, 1867 and December 31, 1867, Microfilm Roll #5 at the Little Bighorn National Monument Archive.

[25] Sandy Barnard, editor, *Ten Years with Custer: A 7th Cavalryman's Memoirs*, Terre Haute, IN: AST Press, 2001, 65; and Larry D. Underwood, *The Custer Fight: and Other Tales of the Old West*, Lincoln, NE: Media Publishing, 1989, 10.

[26] Gregory Michno, *The Mystery of E Troop: Custer's Gray Horse Company at the Little Bighorn*, Missoula, Montana: Mountain Press Publishing Company, 1994, 9, 10.

[27] Melbourne C. Chandler, *Of Garry Owen in Glory: The History of the 7th Cavalry*, Annandale, VA: Turnpike Press, 1960, 8-28.

[28] James Donovan, *A Terrible Glory: Custer and the Little Bighorn – the Last Great Battle of the American West*, New York: Little, Brown and Company, 2008, 60.

[29] Gregory Michno, *The Mystery of E Troop: Custer's Gray Horse Company at the Little Bighorn*, Missoula, Montana: Mountain Press Publishing Company, 1994, 10.

[30] Melbourne C. Chandler, *Of Garry Owen in Glory: The History of the 7th Cavalry*, Annandale, VA: Turnpike Press, 1960, 12-28, 345; Thom Hatch, *The Custer Companion: A Comprehensive Guide to the Life of George Armstrong Custer and the Plains Indian Wars*, Mechanicsburg, PA: The Stackpole Company, 2002, 76-78, 93-94; and James Donovan, *A Terrible Glory: Custer and the Little Bighorn – the Last Great Battle of the American West*, New York: Little, Brown and Company, 2008, 62.

[31] Charles K. Mills, *Rosters from 7th U.S. Cavalry campaigns, 1866-1896*, Mattituck, NY: J.M. Carroll and Company, 1983, 3.

[32] Melbourne C. Chandler, *Of Garry Owen in Glory: The History of the 7th Cavalry*, Annandale, VA: Turnpike Press, 1960, 12-28, 345;

Thom Hatch, *The Custer Companion: A Comprehensive Guide to the Life of George Armstrong Custer and the Plains Indian Wars*, Mechanicsburg, PA: The Stackpole Company, 2002, 76-78, 93-94; James Donovan, *A Terrible Glory: Custer and the Little Bighorn – the Last Great Battle of the American West*, New York: Little, Brown and Company, 2008, 62; and Colonel W.A. Graham, *The Custer Myth: A Source Book of Custeriana*, Mechanicsburg, PA: Stackpole Books, 2000, 202.

[33] Thom Hatch, *The Custer Companion: A Comprehensive Guide to the Life of George Armstrong Custer and the Plains Indian Wars*, Mechanicsburg, PA: The Stackpole Company, 2002, 76-78, 93-94; and Larry Sklenar, *To Hell with Honor; Custer and the Little Bighorn*, Norman, OK: University of Oklahoma Press, 2003, 35.

[34] Brian W. Dippie, *Custer's Last Stand: The Anatomy of an American Myth*, Lincoln, NE: University of Nebraska Press, 1976, 5.

[35] Sandy Barnard, editor, *Ten Years with Custer: A 7th Cavalryman's Memoirs*, Terre Haute, IN: AST Press, 2001, 77.

[36] Sandy Barnard, editor, *Ten Years with Custer: A 7th Cavalryman's Memoirs*, Terre Haute, IN: AST Press, 2001, 78.

[37] Melbourne C. Chandler, *Of Garry Owen in Glory: The History of the 7th Cavalry*, Annandale, VA: Turnpike Press, 1960, 24-25; Ernest L. Reedstrom, *Bugles, Banners & War Bonnets*, Caldwell, ID: The Caxton Printers, 1977, 65; James Donovan, *A Terrible Glory: Custer and the Little Bighorn – the Last Great Battle of the American West*, New York: Little, Brown and Company, 2008, 64; and Sandy Barnard, editor, *Ten Years with Custer: A 7th Cavalryman's Memoirs*, Terre Haute, IN: AST Press, 2001, 85.

[38] Melbourne C. Chandler, *Of Garry Owen in Glory: The History of the 7th Cavalry*, Annandale, VA: Turnpike Press, 1960, 24-25.

[39] Don Rickey, Jr., *Forty Miles a Day on Beans and Hay*, Norman, OK: University of Oklahoma Press, 1972, 267.

[40] Don Rickey, Jr., *Forty Miles a Day on Beans and Hay*, Norman, OK: University of Oklahoma Press, 1972, 132.

[41] Muster Rolls – 7th U.S. Cavalry, Company L-M, 1866-1884, Company M Muster Roll dated February 29, 1868, April 30, 1868, June 30, 1868, August 31, 1868, October 31, 1868 and December 31, 1868, Microfilm Roll #5 at the Little Bighorn National Monument Archive.

[42] Kevin Adams, *Class and Race in the Frontier Army: Military Life in the West*, 1870-1890, Norman, OK: University of Oklahoma Press, 2009, 12.

[43] Melbourne C. Chandler, *Of Garry Owen in Glory: The History of the 7th Cavalry*, Annandale, VA: Turnpike Press, 1960, 28-31; and Larry Sklenar, *To Hell with Honor; Custer and the Little Bighorn*, Norman, OK: University of Oklahoma Press, 2003, 49.

[44] Paul L. Hedron, *The Great Sioux War 1876-77*, Helena, MT: Montana Historical Society Press, 1991, 91. This information came from Paul Andrew Hutton's "Phil Sheridan's Frontier" in Hedron's work.

[45] Kenneth Hammer, *Custer in '76: Walter Camp's Notes on the Custer Fight*, Provo, UT: Brigham Young University, 1976, 30.

[46] Kenneth Hammer, *Custer in '76: Walter Camp's Notes on the Custer Fight*, Provo, UT: Brigham Young University, 1976, 30.

[47] Sandy Barnard, *Custer's First Sergeant John Ryan*, Terre Haute, IN: AST Press, 1996, 132.

[48] Muster Rolls – 7th U.S. Cavalry, Company L-M, 1866-1884, Company M Muster Roll dated February 28, 1869, April 30, 1869, June 30, 1869, August 31, 1869, October 31, 1869 and December 31, 1869, Microfilm Roll #5 at the Little Bighorn National Monument Archive.

[49] Melbourne C. Chandler, *Of Garry Owen in Glory: The History of the 7th Cavalry*, Annandale, VA: Turnpike Press, 1960, 34-35; and Sandy Barnard, *Custer's First Sergeant John Ryan*, Terre Haute, IN: AST Press, 1996, 132-133.

[50] Muster Rolls – 7th U.S. Cavalry, Company L-M, 1866-1884, Company M Muster Roll dated February 28, 1870, April 30, 1870, June 30, 1870, August 31, 1870, October 31, 1870 and December 31, 1870, Microfilm Roll #5 at the Little Bighorn National Monument Archive.

[51] National Archives and Records Administration, Washington, D.C., Records Group 94, Records of the Adjutant General's Office – Army, Carded Medical Records Regular Army, 1821-1884, Entry 529 (Unit 7), David Gordon – Box 406 (Gallene-Graham).

[52] Sandy Barnard, editor, *Ten Years with Custer: A 7th Cavalryman's Memoirs*, Terre Haute, IN: AST Press, 2001, 121-124; and Ernest L. Reedstrom, *Bugles, Banners & War Bonnets*, Caldwell, ID: The Caxton Printers, 1977, 180.

[53] Sandy Barnard, editor, *Ten Years with Custer: A 7th Cavalryman's Memoirs*, Terre Haute, IN: AST Press, 2001, 121-124; and Ernest L. Reedstrom, *Bugles, Banners & War Bonnets*, Caldwell, ID: The Caxton Printers, 1977, 180.

[54] Melbourne C. Chandler, *Of Garry Owen in Glory: The History of the 7th Cavalry*, Annandale, VA: Turnpike Press, 1960, 35-37; and Ernest L. Reedstrom, *Bugles, Banners & War Bonnets*, Caldwell, ID: The Caxton Printers, 1977, 22.

[55] Larry D. Underwood, *The Custer Fight: and Other Tales of the Old West*, Lincoln, NE: Media Publishing, 1989, 13.

[56] Muster Rolls – 7th U.S. Cavalry, Company L-M, 1866-1884, Company M Muster Roll dated February 28, 1871, April 30, 1871, June 30, 1871, August 31, 1871, October 31, 1871 and December 31, 1871, Microfilm Roll #5 at the Little Bighorn National Monument Archive.

[57] Melbourne C. Chandler, *Of Garry Owen in Glory: The History of the 7th Cavalry*, Annandale, VA: Turnpike Press, 1960, 37-38; and Larry Sklenar, *To Hell with Honor; Custer and the Little Bighorn*, Norman, OK: University of Oklahoma Press, 2003, 5.

[58] Muster Rolls – 7th U.S. Cavalry, Company L-M, 1866-1884, Company M Muster Roll dated February 29, 1872, April 30, 1872, June 30, 1872, August 31, 1872, October 31, 1872 and December 31, 1872, Microfilm Roll #5 at the Little Bighorn National Monument Archive.

[59] Larry D. Underwood, *The Custer Fight: and Other Tales of the Old West*, Lincoln, NE: Media Publishing, 1989, 14.

[60] Roger Darling, *Custer's Seventh Cavalry Comes to Dakota*, El Segundo, CA: Upton and Sons, 1989, 46-47.

[61] Charles K. Mills, *Rosters from 7th U.S. Cavalry campaigns, 1866-1896*, Mattituck, NY: J.M. Carroll and Company, 1983, 6; and Kenneth Hammer, *Custer in '76: Walter Camp's Notes on the Custer Fight*, Provo, UT: Brigham Young University, 1976, 182.

[62] Melbourne C. Chandler, *Of Garry Owen in Glory: The History of the 7th Cavalry*, Annandale, VA: Turnpike Press, 1960, 38-40; Dennis Clark, "Private Roman Rutten: Custer's Tailor," 15th Annual Symposium, Custer Battlefield Historical & Museum Association, held at Hardin, MT on June 22, 2001, 34; James Donovan, *A Terrible Glory: Custer and the Little Bighorn – the Last Great Battle of the American West*, New York: Little, Brown and Company, 2008, 81; and Sandy Barnard, editor, *Ten Years with Custer: A 7th Cavalryman's Memoirs*, Terre Haute, IN: AST Press, 2001, 163.

[63] Barry Johnson, *A Captain of Chivalric Courage: Thomas H. French, 7th Cavalry*, The Brand Book, Vol. 25, Numbers 1&2, London: The English Westerners' Society, 1987, 10.

[64] "The Last Summons: Death of Captain French," *The Leavenworth Times*, Leavenworth, Kansas, March 28, 1882.

[65] Sandy Barnard, editor, *Ten Years with Custer: A 7th Cavalryman's Memoirs*, Terre Haute, IN: AST Press, 2001, 178.

[66] Barry Johnson, *A Captain of Chivalric Courage: Thomas H. French, 7th Cavalry*, The Brand Book, Vol. 25, Numbers 1&2, London: The English Westerners' Society, 1987, 11 and 20.

[67] Sandy Barnard, *Custer's First Sergeant John Ryan*, Terre Haute, IN: AST Press, 1996, 158.

[68] Muster Rolls – 7th U.S. Cavalry, Company L-M, 1866-1884, Company M Muster Roll dated February 28, 1873, April 30, 1873, June 30, 1873, August 31, 1873, October 31, 1873 and December 31, 1873, Microfilm Roll #5 at the Little Bighorn National Monument Archive.

[69] National Archives and Records Administration, Washington, D.C., Microfilm Publication M-617, "Returns from U.S. Military Posts, 1800-1916, Fort Rice, North Dakota," Roll 1007.

[70] Charles K. Mills, *Rosters from 7th U.S. Cavalry campaigns, 1866-1896*, Mattituck, NY: J.M. Carroll and Company, 1983, 11.

[71] Letter from George A. Custer to Joseph A. Tilford, Fort Lincoln, Dakota Territory, June 26, 1874. Letter is from the Raab Collection gallery with provenance to the Tilford family.

[72] James Calhoun, *With Custer in '74: James Calhoun's Diary of the Black Hills Expedition*, Provo, UT: Brigham Young University Press, 1979, 19.

[73] Nathaniel Philbrick, *The Last Stand: Custer, Sitting Bull, and the Battle of the Little Bighorn*, New York: The Penguin Group, 2010, 54; and Charles Windolph, *I Fought with Custer: The Story of Sergeant Windolph, Last Survivor of the Battle of the Little Big Horn*, edited by Frazier Hunt and Robert Hunt, New York: Charles Scribner's Sons, 1947, 40.

[74] James Welch, *Killing Custer: The Battle of the Little Bighorn and the Fate of the Plains Indians*, New York: W.W. Norton & Company, 1994, 84; and James Calhoun, *With Custer in '74: James Calhoun's Diary of the Black Hills Expedition*, Provo, UT: Brigham Young University Press, 1979, 60.

[75] John Carroll, *The Sunshine Magazine Articles*, Bryan, TX: Privately Published, 1979, 4-5.

[76] James Calhoun, *With Custer in '74: James Calhoun's Diary of the Black Hills Expedition*, Provo, UT: Brigham Young University Press, 1979, 49-51.

[77] Melbourne C. Chandler, *Of Garry Owen in Glory: The History of the 7th Cavalry*, Annandale, VA: Turnpike Press, 1960, 41-43; Douglas D. Scott, P. Willey and Melissa A. Connor, *They Died with Custer: Soldiers Bones from the Battle of the Little Bighorn*, Norman, OK: University of Oklahoma Press, 288; Barry Johnson, *A Captain of Chivalric Courage: Thomas H. French, 7th Cavalry*, The Brand Book, Vol. 25, Numbers 1&2, London: The English Westerners' Society, 1987, 11 and 20; and John Gray, *Centennial Campaign: The Sioux War of 1876*, Fort Collins, CO: The Old Army Press, 1976, 17.

[78] Muster Rolls – 7th U.S. Cavalry, Company L-M, 1866-1884, Company M Muster Roll dated February 28, 1874, April 30, 1874, June 30, 1874, August 31, 1874, October 31, 1874 and December 31, 1874, Microfilm Roll #5 at the Little Bighorn National Monument Archive.

[79] National Archives and Records Administration, Washington, D.C., Microfilm Publication M-617, "Returns from U.S. Military Posts, 1800-1916, Fort Rice, North Dakota," Roll 1007.

[80] Melbourne C. Chandler, *Of Garry Owen in Glory: The History of the 7th Cavalry*, Annandale, VA: Turnpike Press, 1960, 43-45; and Douglas D. Scott, P. Willey and Melissa A. Connor, *They Died with Custer: Soldiers Bones from the Battle of the Little Bighorn*, Norman, OK: University of Oklahoma Press, 288.

[81] Katherine Gibson Fougera, *With Custer's Cavalry*, Caldwell, ID: The Caxton Printers, 1940, 234.

[82] Special Orders No. 131, Headquarters, Fort Rice, Dakota Territory, dated October 6, 1875, Records Group 393, Records of U. S. Army Continental Commands, 1821-1920, Part V, Military Installations, Fort Rice, North Dakota, Entry 6.

[83] Letter, Headquarters, Fort Rice, Dakota Territory to 7th Cavalry Regimental Quartermaster, dated September 5, 1875 and Letter, Headquarters, Fort Rice, Dakota Territory to Assistant Adjutant General, Department of Dakota, dated November 20, 1875, Records Group 393, Records of U.S. Army Continental Commands, 1821-1920, Part V, Military Installations, Fort Rice, South Dakota, Entry 1.

[84] Special Orders No. 137, Headquarters, Fort Rice, Dakota Territory, dated October 17, 1875, Records Group 393, Records of U.S. Army Continental Commands, 1821-1920, Part V, Military Installations, Fort Rice, North Dakota, Entry 6.

[85] Special Orders No. 138, Headquarters, Fort Rice, Dakota Territory, dated October 19, 1875, Records Group 393, Records of U. S. Army Continental Commands, 1821-1920, Part V, Military Installations, Fort Rice, North Dakota, Entry 6.

[86] Special Orders No. 160, Headquarters, Fort Rice, Dakota Territory, dated November 18, 1875, Records Group 393, Records of U. S. Army Continental Commands, 1821-1920, Part V, Military Installations, Fort Rice, North Dakota, Entry 6.

[87] Garrison Circular, Headquarters, Fort Rice, Dakota Territory, dated November 15, 1875, Records Group 393, Records of U. S. Army Continental Commands, 1821-1920, Part V, Military Installations, Fort Rice, North Dakota, Entry 5.

[88] James Donovan, *A Terrible Glory: Custer and the Little Bighorn – the Last Great Battle of the American West*, New York: Little, Brown and Company, 2008, 424.

[89] John Gray, *Centennial Campaign: The Sioux War of 1876*, Fort Collins, CO: The Old Army Press, 1976, 86.

[90] Roger L. Williams, *Military Register of Custer's Last Command*, Norman, OK: The Arthur H. Clark Company, 2009, 389.

[91] Post Orders No. 28, Headquarters, Fort Rice, Dakota Territory, dated March 23, 1876, Records Group 393, Records of U. S. Army Continental Commands, 1821-1920, Part V, Military Installations, Fort Rice, North Dakota, Entry 5.

[92] Post Orders No. 28, Headquarters, Fort Rice, Dakota Territory, dated March 23, 1876, Records Group 393, Records of U. S. Army Continental Commands, 1821-1920, Part V, Military Installations, Fort Rice, North Dakota, Entry 5.

[93] Sandy Barnard, editor, *Ten Years with Custer: A 7th Cavalryman's Memoirs*, Terre Haute, IN: AST Press, 2001, 264.

[94] Gregory Michno, *The Mystery of E Troop: Custer's Gray Horse Company at the Little Bighorn*, Missoula, Montana: Mountain Press Publishing Company, 1994, 278.

[95] George A. Custer, "Life on the Plains," *The Galaxy*, Volume XVII, January 1874 to June 1874, New York: Sheldon & Company, 1874, June 1874, 767.

[96] Alexander Rose, *American Rifle: A Biography*, New York: Delacorte Press, 2008, 155-156.

[97] Thomas Goodrich, *Scalp Dance: Indian Warfare on the High Plains, 1865-1879*, Mechanicsburg, PA: Stackpole Books, 1997, x.

[98] Charles M. Robinson, *A Good Year to Die: The Story of the Great Sioux War*, New York: Random House, 1995, xxv. Comment was made in a letter written in 1868.

[99] Nathaniel Philbrick, *The Last Stand: Custer, Sitting Bull, and the Battle of the Little Bighorn*, New York: The Penguin Group, 2010, 9.

[100] Alexander Rose, *American Rifle: A Biography*, New York: Delacorte Press, 2008, 155-156.

[101] John Gray, *Centennial Campaign: The Sioux War of 1876*, Fort Collins, CO: The Old Army Press, 1976, 9, 23; Nathaniel Philbrick, *The Last Stand: Custer, Sitting Bull, and the Battle of the Little Bighorn*, New York: The Penguin Group, 2010, 110; and James Welch, *Killing Custer: The Battle of the Little Bighorn and the Fate of the Plains Indians*, New York: W.W. Norton & Company, 1994, 90.

[102] James Welch, *Killing Custer: The Battle of the Little Bighorn and the Fate of the Plains Indians*, New York: W.W. Norton & Company, 1994, 84.

[103] John Gray, *Centennial Campaign: The Sioux War of 1876*, Fort Collins, CO: The Old Army Press, 1976, 9, 23.

[104] James Donovan, *A Terrible Glory: Custer and the Little Bighorn – the Last Great Battle of the American West*, New York: Little, Brown and Company, 2008, 10, 97.

[105] John Gray, *Centennial Campaign: The Sioux War of 1876*, Fort Collins, CO: The Old Army Press, 1976, 27-31.

[106] Paul L. Hedron, *The Great Sioux War 1876-77*, Helena, MT: Montana Historical Society Press, 1991, 30. This information came from Mark H. Brown's "A New Focus on the Sioux War" in Hedron's work.

[107] James Donovan, *A Terrible Glory: Custer and the Little Bighorn – the Last Great Battle of the American West*, New York: Little, Brown and Company, 2008, 96.

[108] John Gray, *Centennial Campaign: The Sioux War of 1876*, Fort Collins, CO: The Old Army Press, 1976, 34-39.

[109] John Gray, *Centennial Campaign: The Sioux War of 1876*, Fort Collins, CO: The Old Army Press, 1976, 39-43, 87; and James Donovan, *A Terrible Glory: Custer and the Little Bighorn – the Last Great Battle of the American West*, New York: Little, Brown and Company, 2008, 99.

[110] Arthur Koenig, *Authentic History of the Indian Campaign Which Culminated in Custer's Last Battle, June 25, 1876*, St. Louis, MO: Anheuser Busch, 2.

[111] Charles M. Robinson, *A Good Year to Die: The Story of the Great Sioux War*, New York: Random House, 1995, 106.

[112] John Gray, *Centennial Campaign: The Sioux War of 1876*, Fort Collins, CO: The Old Army Press, 1976, 39-43, 87; and James Donovan, *A Terrible Glory: Custer and the Little Bighorn – the Last Great Battle of the American West*, New York: Little, Brown and Company, 2008, 119. Reno would fire the best Ree interpreter in the country, Frederic F. Gerard, on May 6, but Custer persuaded Gerard to join the expedition when he returned from Washington. Isaiah Dorman, a Lakota interpreter, was not hired until May 15; he was a former slave from New Orleans and was married to a Lakota woman named Visible.

[113] James Donovan, *A Terrible Glory: Custer and the Little Bighorn – the Last Great Battle of the American West*, New York: Little, Brown and Company, 2008, 105, 120-121, 139.

[114] Edgar I. Stewart, *Custer's Luck*, Norman, OK: University of Oklahoma Press, 1980, 177.

[115] James Donovan, *A Terrible Glory: Custer and the Little Bighorn – the Last Great Battle of the American West*, New York: Little, Brown and Company, 2008, 422.

[116] Kevin Adams, *Class and Race in the Frontier Army: Military Life in the West,* 1870-1890, Norman, OK: University of Oklahoma Press, 2009, 19.

[117] Letter, Headquarters, Fort Rice, Dakota Territory to Assistant Adjutant General, Department of Dakota, dated February 25, 1876, Records Group 393, Records of U.S. Army Continental Commands, 1821-1920, Part V, Military Installations, Fort Rice, South Dakota, Entry 1.

[118] Bill Yenne, *Indian Wars: The Campaign for the American West*, Yardley, PA: Westholme Publishing, 2006, 179.

[119] James Donovan, *A Terrible Glory: Custer and the Little Bighorn – the Last Great Battle of the American West*, New York: Little, Brown and Company, 2008, 107; Larry D. Underwood, *The Custer Fight: and Other Tales of the Old West*, Lincoln, NE: Media *Publishing, 1989, 16*; and John Koster, "Fulcrum to Disaster," *Wild West Magazine*, Volume 23, No. 1, Leesburg, VA, June 2010, 58.

[120] Bill Yenne, *Indian Wars: The Campaign for the American West*, Yardley, PA: Westholme Publishing, 2006, 180.

[121] John Gray, *Centennial Campaign: The Sioux War of 1876*, Fort Collins, CO: The Old Army Press, 1976, 42-68; and James Donovan, *A Terrible Glory: Custer and the Little Bighorn – the Last Great Battle of the American West*, New York: Little, Brown and Company, 2008, 111.

[122] James Donovan, *A Terrible Glory: Custer and the Little Bighorn – the Last Great Battle of the American West*, New York: Little, Brown and Company, 2008, 113; and Larry D. Underwood, *The Custer Fight: and Other Tales of the Old West*, Lincoln, NE: Media Publishing, 1989, 17.

[123] John Gray, *Centennial Campaign: The Sioux War of 1876*, Fort Collins, CO: The Old Army Press, 1976, 68-72, 89; and James Donovan, *A Terrible Glory: Custer and the Little Bighorn – the Last Great Battle of the American West*, New York: Little, Brown and Company, 2008, 112.

Chapter Two: Company Organization and Leadership

[1] Glendolin D. Wagner, *Old Neutriment*, New York: Sol Lewis, 1973, 49-50.

[2] Kenneth Hammer, *Custer in '76: Walter Camp's Notes on the Custer Fight*, Provo, UT: Brigham Young University, 1976, 140; and Sandy Barnard, editor, *Ten Years with Custer: A 7th Cavalryman's Memoirs*, Terre Haute, IN: AST Press, 2001, 261.

[3] Thomas B. Marquis, *Keep the Last Bullet for Yourself*, Algonac, MI: Reference Publications, 1985, 48.

[4] Kenneth Hammer, *Custer in '76: Walter Camp's Notes on the Custer Fight*, Provo, UT: Brigham Young University, 1976, 140; and Sandy Barnard, editor, *Ten Years with Custer: A 7th Cavalryman's Memoirs*, Terre Haute, IN: AST Press, 2001, 261.

[5] Don Rickey, Jr., *Forty Miles a Day on Beans and Hay*, Norman, OK: University of Oklahoma Press, 1972, 33-35; and Douglas C. McChristian, *The U.S. Army in the West: 1870-1880*, Norman, OK: University of Oklahoma Press, 1995, 38.

[6] Richard G. Hardorff, editor, *On the Little Bighorn with Walter Camp; A Collection of Walter Mason Camp's Letters, Notes and opinions on Custer's Last Fight*, El Segundo, CA: Upton & Sons Publishers, 2002, 12. Comment came in a letter from Daniel A. Knipe to Walter Camp.

[7] Douglas C. McChristian, *The U.S. Army in the West: 1870-1880*, Norman, OK: University of Oklahoma Press, 1995, 69.

[8] Don Rickey, Jr., *Forty Miles a Day on Beans and Hay*, Norman, OK: University of Oklahoma Press, 1972, 39-40, 117.

[9] Marc E. Kollbaum, *Gateway to the West: The History of Jefferson Barracks from 1826 – 1894*, Volume 1, St. Louis, MO: Friends of Jefferson Barracks, 244.

[10] Don Rickey, Jr., *Forty Miles a Day on Beans and Hay*, Norman, OK: University of Oklahoma Press, 1972, 40; and Jeremy Agnew, *Life of a Soldier on the Western Frontier*, Missoula, MT: Mountain Press Publishing Company, 2008, 123.

[11] Don Rickey, Jr., *Forty Miles a Day on Beans and Hay*, Norman, OK: University of Oklahoma Press, 1972, 96.

[12] Jeremy Agnew, *Life of a Soldier on the Western Frontier*, Missoula, MT: Mountain Press Publishing Company, 2008, 128.

[13] Earle Alonzo Brininstool, *Troopers with Custer: Incidents of the Battle of the Little Big Horn*, Harrisburg, PA: The Stackpole Company, 1952, 39.

[14] Don Rickey, Jr., *Forty Miles a Day on Beans and Hay*, Norman, OK: University of Oklahoma Press, 1972, 57; and James Donovan, *A Terrible Glory: Custer and the Little Bighorn – the Last Great Battle of the American West*, New York: Little, Brown and Company, 2008, 123.

[15] Robert J. Kershaw, *Red Sabbath: The Battle of Little Bighorn*, Surrey, England: Ian Allan Publishing, 2005, 36.

[16] James Donovan, *A Terrible Glory: Custer and the Little Bighorn – the Last Great Battle of the American West*, New York: Little, Brown and Company, 2008, 440; Nathaniel Philbrick, *The Last Stand: Custer, Sitting Bull, and the Battle of the Little Bighorn*, New York: The Penguin Group, 2010, 174; and William O. Taylor, *With Custer on the Little Bighorn*, New York: Viking, 1996.

[17] United States Army, *Cavalry Tactics* (Reprint), New York: D. Appleton and Company, 1874, 133.

[18] Don Rickey, Jr., *Forty Miles a Day on Beans and Hay*, Norman, OK: University of Oklahoma Press, 1972, 51; and Ernest L. Reedstrom, *Bugles, Banners & War Bonnets*, Caldwell, ID: The Caxton Printers, 1977, 223.

[19] James Donovan, *A Terrible Glory: Custer and the Little Bighorn – the Last Great Battle of the American West*, New York: Little, Brown and Company, 2008, 121.

[20] Sandy Barnard, "A 7th Cavalryman speaks out," *Greasy Grass Magazine*, Volume 21, May 2005, Hardin, MT: Custer Battlefield Historical & Museum Association, 28.

[21] Al Johnson, "The Preparation at Fort Abraham Lincoln," Billings, MT: 2009 Little Bighorn Associates 36th Annual Conference, June 23, 2009.

[22] Joe Poyer and Craig Riesch, *The .45-70 Springfield*, Tustin, CA: North Cape Publications, 2006, 12.

[23] United States Army, *Cavalry Tactics* (Reprint), New York: D. Appleton and Company, 1874, 67.

[24] Greg Michno, "Battle of Little Bighorn: Were the Weapons the Deciding Factor?" *Wild West*, Leesburg, VA: Weider History Group, June 1998.

[25] United States Army, *Cavalry Tactics* (Reprint), New York: D. Appleton and Company, 1874, 70.

[26] Laudie J. Chorne, *Following the Custer Trail of 1876*, Bismarck, ND: Trails West Publishing, 2001, 4.

[27] United States Army, *Cavalry Tactics* (Reprint), New York: D. Appleton and Company, 1874, 70.

[28] United States Army, *Cavalry Tactics* (Reprint), New York: D. Appleton and Company, 1874, 71.

[29] Thomas Goodrich, *Scalp Dance: Indian Warfare on the High Plains, 1865-1879*, Mechanicsburg, PA: Stackpole Books, 1997, 170.

[30] James Donovan, *A Terrible Glory: Custer and the Little Bighorn – the Last Great Battle of the American West*, New York: Little, Brown and Company, 2008, 121, 422.

[31] James Donovan, *A Terrible Glory: Custer and the Little Bighorn – the Last Great Battle of the American West*, New York: Little, Brown and Company, 2008, 422.

[32] Don Rickey, Jr., *Forty Miles a Day on Beans and Hay*, Norman, OK: University of Oklahoma Press, 1972, 275.

[33] United States Army, *Cavalry Tactics* (Reprint), New York: D. Appleton and Company, 1874, 200.

[34] United States Army, *Cavalry Tactics* (Reprint), New York: D. Appleton and Company, 1874, 72.

[35] Don Rickey, Jr., *Forty Miles a Day on Beans and Hay*, Norman, OK: University of Oklahoma Press, 1972, 100.

[36] Pamphlet 45, University of Wisconsin at Whitewater Special Collection of Dr. Kenneth Hammer: Hammer, Kenneth M. "The Springfield Carbine on the Western Frontier," 6.

[37] Edgar I. Stewart, *Custer's Luck*, Norman, OK: University of Oklahoma Press, 1980, 177.

[38] Bruce R. Liddic, *Vanishing Victory: Custer's Final March*, El Segundo, CA: Upton & Sons, Publishers, 2004, 69.

[39] Alexander Rose, *American Rifle: A Biography*, New York: Delacorte Press, 2008, 168, 179-180.

[40] Dušan P. Farrington, *Arming & Equipping the U.S. Cavalry 1865-1902*, Lincoln, RI: Andrew Mowbray Publishers, 2004, 16, 24, 26, 29, 75, 76, 77-78.

[41] Dušan P. Farrington, *Arming & Equipping the U.S. Cavalry 1865-1902*, Lincoln, RI: Andrew Mowbray Publishers, 2004, 145-148.

[42] Laudie J. Chorne, *Following the Custer Trail of 1876*, Bismarck, ND: Trails West Publishing, 2001, 5.

[43] Don Rickey, Jr., *Forty Miles a Day on Beans and Hay*, Norman, OK: University of Oklahoma Press, 1972, 250.

[44] Ami Frank Mulford, *Fighting Indians in the 7th U.S. Cavalry*, Corning, NY: Paul Lindsley Mulford, 1879, 19.

[45] Katherine Gibson Fougera, *With Custer's Cavalry*, Caldwell, ID: The Caxton Printers, 1940, 111. The author was the daughter of Lieutenant Francis Gibson; she published the memoirs of her mother who had heard the remark by Captain Thomas French.

[46] Letter, Post Surgeon, Fort Rice, Dakota Territory to Post Adjutant, dated October 31, 1875, Records Group 393, Records of U.S. Army Continental Commands, 1821-1920, Part V, Military Installations, Fort Rice, South Dakota, Entry 4.

[47] John Carroll, editor, *A Seventh Cavalry Scrapbook*, Volume 1, "Memories of the Battle of the Little Big Horn," by Daniel Newell, Bryan, TX: Privately Published, 1978, 20. Newell's comments may have initially been made in a letter to General E.S. Godfrey in 1926, while Newell lived in Sturgis, SD.

[48] Kevin Adams, *Class and Race in the Frontier Army: Military Life in the West,* 1870-1890, Norman, OK: University of Oklahoma Press, 2009, 68.

[49] Don Rickey, Jr., *Forty Miles a Day on Beans and Hay*, Norman, OK: University of Oklahoma Press, 1972, 58.

[50] Charles M. Robinson, *A Good Year to Die: The Story of the Great Sioux War*, New York: Random House, 1995, 188.

[51] Ami Frank Mulford, *Fighting Indians in the 7th U.S. Cavalry*, Corning, NY: Paul Lindsley Mulford, 1879, 104-105.

[52] Kenneth Hammer, *Custer in '76: Walter Camp's Notes on the Custer Fight*, Provo, UT: Brigham Young University, 1976, 140.

[53] National Archives and Records Administration, Washington, D.C., Records Group 94, Records of the Adjutant General's Office – Army, Carded Medical Records Regular Army, 1821-1884, Entry 529 (Unit 7), George Weaver – Box 425 (Volkmann-Weller).

[54] Ronald H. Nichols, editor, *Men with Custer: Biographies of the 7th Cavalry*, Hardin, MT: Custer Battlefield Historical and Museum Association, 2000, 347; and Roger L. Williams, *Military Register of Custer's Last Command*, Norman, OK: The Arthur H. Clark Company, 2009, 303.

[55] Barry Johnson, *A Captain of Chivalric Courage: Thomas H. French, 7th Cavalry*, The Brand Book, Vol. 25, Numbers 1&2, London: The English Westerners' Society, 1987, 2-4; and Eugene L. Meyer, "Tracking a Custer Indian Fighter," *The Washington Post*, March 27, 1980, A1.

[56] Barry Johnson, *A Captain of Chivalric Courage: Thomas H. French, 7th Cavalry*, The Brand Book, Vol. 25, Numbers 1&2, London: The English Westerners' Society, 1987, 5.

[57] Barry Johnson, *A Captain of Chivalric Courage: Thomas H. French, 7th Cavalry*, The Brand Book, Vol. 25, Numbers 1&2, London: The English Westerners' Society, 1987, 4-6.

[58] Barry Johnson, *A Captain of Chivalric Courage: Thomas H. French, 7th Cavalry*, The Brand Book, Vol. 25, Numbers 1&2, London: The English Westerners' Society, 1987, 7.

[59] Thom Hatch, *The Custer Companion: A Comprehensive Guide to the Life of George Armstrong Custer and the Plains Indian Wars*, Mechanicsburg, PA: The Stackpole Company, 2002, 121-122; and Barry Johnson, *A Captain of Chivalric Courage: Thomas H. French, 7th Cavalry*, The Brand Book, Vol. 25, Numbers 1&2, London: The English Westerners' Society, 1987, 6-7.

[60] Sandy Barnard, editor, *Ten Years with Custer: A 7th Cavalryman's Memoirs*, Terre Haute, IN: AST Press, 2001, 198.

[61] Bob Snelson, *Death of a Myth: Seventh Cavalry at the Little Bighorn*, Snelsonbooks.com, 2005, 10; and Hal Herring, *Famous Firearms of the Old West*, Guilford, CN: Morris Book Publishing, 2008, 36.

[62] Evan S. Connell, *Son of the Morning Star: Custer and the Little Bighorn*, San Francisco, CA: North Point Press, 1984, 289; Barry Johnson, *A Captain of Chivalric Courage: Thomas H. French, 7th Cavalry*, The Brand Book, Vol. 25, Numbers 1&2, London: The English Westerners' Society, 1987, 12.

[63] Sandy Barnard, editor, *Ten Years with Custer: A 7th Cavalryman's Memoirs*, Terre Haute, IN: AST Press, 2001, 255.

[64] Letter, Headquarters, Fort Rice, Dakota Territory to Assistant Adjutant General, Department of Dakota, dated September 1, 1875, Records Group 393, Records of U.S. Army Continental Commands, 1821-1920, Part V, Military Installations, Fort Rice, South Dakota, Entry 1.

[65] National Archives and Records Administration, Washington, D.C., Records Group 94, Records of the Adjutant General's Office – Army, Carded Medical Records Regular Army, 1821-1884, Entry 529 (Unit 7), Thomas H. French – Box 405 (Fish-Gaffney).

[66] Discussions with Olga MacLean, former Drug and Alcohol Counselor for the U.S. Army at Frankfurt and Mannheim, Germany, June 2010.

[67] National Archives and Records Administration, Washington, D.C., Records Group 94, Records of the Adjutant General's Office – Army, Carded Medical Records Regular Army, 1821-1884, Entry 529 (Unit 7), Thomas H. French – Box 405 (Fish-Gaffney).

[68] Katherine Gibson Fougera, *With Custer's Cavalry*, Caldwell, ID: The Caxton Printers, 1940, 198.

[69] Special Orders No. 137, Headquarters, Fort Rice, Dakota Territory, dated October 17, 1875, Records Group 393, Records of U. S. Army Continental Commands, 1821-1920, Part V, Military Installations, Fort Rice, North Dakota, Entry 6.

[70] Special Orders No. 137, Headquarters, Fort Rice, Dakota Territory, dated October 17, 1875, Records Group 393, Records of U. S. Army Continental Commands, 1821-1920, Part V, Military Installations, Fort Rice, North Dakota, Entry 6.

[71] National Archives and Records Administration, Washington, D.C., Records Group 94, Records of the Adjutant General's Office – Army, Carded Medical Records Regular Army, 1821-1884, Entry 529 (Unit 7), John Ryan – Box 420 (Roeder-Schneider).

[72] Special Orders No. 41, Headquarters, Fort Rice, Dakota Territory, dated April 16, 1876, Records Group 393, Records of U. S. Army Continental Commands, 1821-1920, Part V, Military Installations, Fort Rice, North Dakota, Entry 6.

[73] Special Orders No. 37, Headquarters, 7th Cavalry, Fort Abraham Lincoln, Dakota Territory, dated May 9, 1876, Records Group 393, Records of U. S. Army Continental Commands, 1821-1920, Military Installations, Fort Abraham Lincoln, North Dakota, Entry 5.

[74] Bob Snelson, *Death of a Myth: Seventh Cavalry at the Little Bighorn*, Snelsonbooks.com, 2005, 10; Sandy Barnard, *Custer's First Sergeant John Ryan*, Terre Haute, IN: AST Press, 1996, 191; Sam Fadala, *The Complete Blackpowder Handbook*, Iola, WI: DBI Books, 1996, 209; and discussion with John Doerner, Chief Historian Little Bighorn of the Little Bighorn Battlefield National Monument, at the battlefield archives, May 10-12, 2010.

[75] Bob Snelson, *Death of a Myth: Seventh Cavalry at the Little Bighorn*, Snelsonbooks.com, 2005, 10; Sandy Barnard, *Custer's First Sergeant John Ryan*, Terre Haute, IN: AST Press, 1996, 191; Sam Fadala, *The Complete Blackpowder Handbook*, Iola, WI: DBI Books, 1996, 209; and discussion with John Doerner, Chief Historian Little Bighorn of the Little Bighorn Battlefield National Monument, at the battlefield archives, May 10-12, 2010.

[76] Ronald H. Nichols, editor, *Men with Custer: Biographies of the 7th Cavalry*, Hardin, MT: Custer Battlefield Historical and Museum Association, 2000, 51; and Roger L. Williams, *Military Register of Custer's Last Command*, Norman, OK: The Arthur H. Clark Company, 2009, 64.

[77] Ronald H. Nichols, editor, *Men with Custer: Biographies of the 7th Cavalry*, Hardin, MT: Custer Battlefield Historical and Museum Association, 2000, 217; and Roger L. Williams, *Military Register of Custer's Last Command*, Norman, OK: The Arthur H. Clark Company, 2009, 202.

[78] Ronald H. Nichols, editor, *Men with Custer: Biographies of the 7th Cavalry*, Hardin, MT: Custer Battlefield Historical and Museum Association, 2000, 251; Kenneth Hammer, *Men with Custer; the Working Copy*, 2009, 202; Roger L. Williams, *Military Register of Custer's Last Command*, Norman, OK: The Arthur H. Clark

Company, 2009, 237; and Dr. Kenneth Hammer Special Collection at the University of Wisconsin-Whitewater Library, Box 4, Widows and Children Folder.

[79] National Archives and Records Administration, Washington, D.C., Records Group 94, Records of the Adjutant General's Office – Army, Carded Medical Records Regular Army, 1821-1884, Entry 529 (Unit 7), Charles White (Henry Weihe) – Box 426 (Wemster-Winter).

[80] Ronald H. Nichols, editor, *Men with Custer: Biographies of the 7th Cavalry*, Hardin, MT: Custer Battlefield Historical and Museum Association, 2000, 349-350; Sandy Barnard, editor, *Ten Years with Custer: A 7th Cavalryman's Memoirs*, Terre Haute, IN: AST Press, 2001, 262; and Roger L. Williams, *Military Register of Custer's Last Command*, Norman, OK: The Arthur H. Clark Company, 2009, 304, 316.

[81] Ronald H. Nichols, editor, *Men with Custer: Biographies of the 7th Cavalry*, Hardin, MT: Custer Battlefield Historical and Museum Association, 2000, 58; Kenneth Hammer, *Men with Custer; the Working Copy*, 2009, 232; Roger L. Williams, *Military Register of Custer's Last Command*, Norman, OK: The Arthur H. Clark Company, 2009, 68; and Muster Rolls – 7th U.S. Cavalry, Company L-M, 1866-1884, Company M Muster Roll dated February 28, 1875, April 30, 1875, June 30, 1875, August 31, 1875, October 31, 1875 and December 31, 1875, Microfilm Roll #5 at the Little Bighorn National Monument Archive.

[82] Ronald H. Nichols, editor, *Men with Custer: Biographies of the 7th Cavalry*, Hardin, MT: Custer Battlefield Historical and Museum Association, 2000, 186; Roger L. Williams, *Military Register of Custer's Last Command*, Norman, OK: The Arthur H. Clark Company, 2009, 186; and National Archives and Records Administration, Washington, D.C., Records Group 94, Records of the Adjutant General's Office – Army, Carded Medical Records Regular Army, 1821-1884, Entry 529 (Unit 7), William Lalor – Box 411 (Keogh-Lawrence).

[83] Garrison Orders No. 3, Headquarters, Fort Rice, Dakota Territory, dated February 5, 1875, Records Group 393, Records of U. S. Army Continental Commands, 1821-1920, Part V, Military Installations, Fort Rice, North Dakota, Entry 5.

[84] Ronald H. Nichols, editor, *Men with Custer: Biographies of the 7th Cavalry*, Hardin, MT: Custer Battlefield Historical and Museum Association, 2000, 319; Roger L. Williams, *Military Register of Custer's Last Command*, Norman, OK: The Arthur H. Clark Company, 2009, 279; and Garrison Orders No. 7, Headquarters, Fort Rice, Dakota Territory, dated April 13, 1875, Records Group 393, Records of U. S. Army Continental Commands, 1821-1920, Part V, Military Installations, Fort Rice, North Dakota, Entry 5.

[85] Ronald H. Nichols, editor, *Men with Custer: Biographies of the 7th Cavalry*, Hardin, MT: Custer Battlefield Historical and Museum Association, 2000, 15. Previously known as Joseph C. Murphy; committed suicide on September 13, 1893 at Sturgis, SD.

[86] Ronald H. Nichols, editor, *Men with Custer: Biographies of the 7th Cavalry*, Hardin, MT: Custer Battlefield Historical and Museum Association, 2000, 15; Roger L. Williams, *Military Register of Custer's Last Command*, Norman, OK: The Arthur H. Clark Company, 2009, 36; and Letter from Captain Charles E. Morse, 16th Infantry Regiment, Headquarters, Post Lebanon, Kentucky, December 19, 1873 to Commanding Officer, 7th Cavalry stating that Joseph Bates had been apprehended for desertion. Letter is found in the alphabetical digital files on 7th Cavalry personnel at the Little Big Horn Battlefield National Monument Archives.

[87] Ronald H. Nichols, editor, *Men with Custer: Biographies of the 7th Cavalry*, Hardin, MT: Custer Battlefield Historical and Museum Association, 2000, 78-79; and Roger L. Williams, *Military Register of Custer's Last Command*, Norman, OK: The Arthur H. Clark Company, 2009, 106.

[88] Douglas D. Scott, P. Willey and Melissa A. Connor, *They Died with Custer: Soldiers Bones from the Battle of the Little Bighorn*, Norman, OK: University of Oklahoma Press, 288; and National Archives and Records Administration, Washington, D.C., Records Group 94, Records of the Adjutant General's Office – Army, Carded Medical Records Regular Army, 1821-1884, Entry 529 (Unit 7), Henry Davis – Box 402 (Creedon-Denny).

[89] Ronald H. Nichols, editor, *Men with Custer: Biographies of the 7th Cavalry*, Hardin, MT: Custer Battlefield Historical and Museum Association, 2000, 78-79; Sandy Barnard, editor, *Ten Years with Custer: A 7th Cavalryman's Memoirs*, Terre Haute, IN: AST Press, 2001, 130; and Garrison Orders No. 71, Headquarters, Fort Rice, Dakota Territory, dated October 1, 1874, Records Group 393, Records of U. S. Army Continental Commands, 1821-1920, Part V, Military Installations, Fort Rice, North Dakota, Entry 5. Another source indicates that Davis was born in Fayette City, Pennsylvania.

[90] Sandy Barnard, editor, *Ten Years with Custer: A 7th Cavalryman's Memoirs*, Terre Haute, IN: AST Press, 2001, 263.

[91] National Archives and Records Administration, Washington, D.C., Records Group 153, Records of the Office of the Judge Advocate General – Army, Court-Martial Case Files, 1809-1894, Private Henry C. Weaver – Case # QQ-619; Headquarters Department of Dakota, General Court-Martial Orders, St. Paul, MN, May 9, 1878.

[92] Colonel William Winthrop, *Military Law and Precedents*, Volume 1 and 2, Boston: Little, Brown and Company, 1896, 13-15, 64.

[93] Colonel William Winthrop, *Military Law and Precedents*, Volume 1 and 2, Boston: Little, Brown and Company, 1896, 745.

[94] Colonel William Winthrop, *Military Law and Precedents*, Volume 1 and 2, Boston: Little, Brown and Company, 1896, 173.

[95] Colonel William Winthrop, *Military Law and Precedents*, Volume 1 and 2, Boston: Little, Brown and Company, 1896, 263, 269.

[96] Colonel William Winthrop, *Military Law and Precedents*, Volume 1 and 2, Boston: Little, Brown and Company, 1896, 295.

[97] Colonel William Winthrop, *Military Law and Precedents*, Volume 1 and 2, Boston: Little, Brown and Company, 1896, 13-15, 64.

[98] Colonel William Winthrop, *Military Law and Precedents*, Volume 1 and 2, Boston: Little, Brown and Company, 1896, 746.

[99] Colonel William Winthrop, *Military Law and Precedents*, Volume 1 and 2, Boston: Little, Brown and Company, 1896, 244.

[100] Colonel William Winthrop, *Military Law and Precedents*, Volume 1 and 2, Boston: Little, Brown and Company, 1896, 752.

[101] Colonel William Winthrop, *Military Law and Precedents*, Volume 1 and 2, Boston: Little, Brown and Company, 1896, 756.

[102] Douglas D. Scott, P. Willey and Melissa A. Connor, *They Died with Custer: Soldiers Bones from the Battle of the Little Bighorn*, Norman, OK: University of Oklahoma Press, 57.

[103] Sandy Barnard, *Custer's First Sergeant John Ryan*, Terre Haute, IN: AST Press, 1996, 170. Ryan made the comment in 1922 in a letter to W.A. Falconer of Bismarck, ND.

[104] Kenneth Hammer, *Custer in '76: Walter Camp's Notes on the Custer Fight*, Provo, UT: Brigham Young University, 1976, 68.

[105] Sandy Barnard, editor, *Ten Years with Custer: A 7th Cavalryman's Memoirs*, Terre Haute, IN: AST Press, 2001, 258.

[106] Ronald H. Nichols, editor, *Men with Custer: Biographies of the 7th Cavalry*, Hardin, MT: Custer Battlefield Historical and Museum Association, 2000, 46; and Roger L. Williams, *Military Register of Custer's Last Command*, Norman, OK: The Arthur H. Clark Company, 2009, 62.

[107] James Donovan, *A Terrible Glory: Custer and the Little Bighorn – the Last Great Battle of the American West*, New York: Little, Brown and Company, 2008, 120.

[108] Letter from the Adjutant General's Office, Washington, dated September 21, 1868 to Commanding Officer, 7th U.S. Cavalry inquiring about the dispositions of several deserters including Charles Kavanaugh of Company G. Letter is found in the alphabetical digital files on 7th Cavalry personnel.

[109] Ronald H. Nichols, editor, *Men with Custer: Biographies of the 7th Cavalry*, Hardin, MT: Custer Battlefield Historical and Museum Association, 2000, 171-172; and Roger L. Williams, *Military Register of Custer's Last Command*, Norman, OK: The Arthur H. Clark Company, 2009, 173.

[110] Garrison Orders No. 2, Headquarters, Fort Rice, Dakota Territory, dated January 16, 1876, Records Group 393, Records of U. S. Army Continental Commands, 1821-1920, Part V, Military Installations, Fort Rice, North Dakota, Entry 5.

[111] Sandy Barnard, editor, *Ten Years with Custer: A 7th Cavalryman's Memoirs*, Terre Haute, IN: AST Press, 2001, 261, 263; and Roger L. Williams, *Military Register of Custer's Last Command*, Norman, OK: The Arthur H. Clark Company, 2009, 173.

[112] Sandy Barnard, editor, *Ten Years with Custer: A 7th Cavalryman's Memoirs*, Terre Haute, IN: AST Press, 2001, 263.

[113] James Donovan, *A Terrible Glory: Custer and the Little Bighorn – the Last Great Battle of the American West*, New York: Little, Brown and Company, 2008, 470-471.

[114] Robert C. Kain, *In the Valley of the Little Bighorn: The 7th and the Sioux*, Newfane, VT: Self-published, 1969, xviii. This volume has personal notes and observations from Colonel Edward M. Offley, United States Cavalry, retired.

[115] Edgar I. Stewart, *Custer's Luck*, Norman, OK: University of Oklahoma Press, 1980, 173.

[116] Kevin Adams, *Class and Race in the Frontier Army: Military Life in the West,* 1870-1890, Norman, OK: University of Oklahoma Press, 2009, 144.

[117] Ernest L. Reedstrom, *Bugles, Banners & War Bonnets*, Caldwell, ID: The Caxton Printers, 1977, 176.

[118] Douglas D. Scott, P. Willey and Melissa A. Connor, *They Died with Custer: Soldiers Bones from the Battle of the Little Bighorn*, Norman, OK: University of Oklahoma Press, 65.

[119] National Archives and Records Administration, Washington, D.C., Records Group 94, Records of the Adjutant General's Office – Army, Carded Medical Records Regular Army, 1821-1884, Entry 529 (Unit 7), Rollins Thorpe – Box 424 (Tempes-Vigny).

[120] Ronald H. Nichols, editor, *Men with Custer: Biographies of the 7th Cavalry*, Hardin, MT: Custer Battlefield Historical and Museum Association, 2000, 51, 330; and Roger L. Williams, *Military Register of Custer's Last Command*, Norman, OK: The Arthur H. Clark Company, 2009, 290. One source says that Private William E. Morris was possibly just over 14 when he enlisted but this study has not been able to verify that claim.

[121] Douglas D. Scott, P. Willey and Melissa A. Connor, *They Died with Custer: Soldiers Bones from the Battle of the Little Bighorn*, Norman, OK: University of Oklahoma Press, 72; and Larry Sklenar, *To Hell with Honor; Custer and the Little Bighorn*, Norman, OK: University of Oklahoma Press, 2003, 89; Don Rickey, Jr., *Forty Miles a Day on Beans and Hay*, Norman, OK: University of Oklahoma Press, 1972, 220-221; C. Lee Noyes, "A Question of Arms: Ordnance "Causes" and Consequences of the Little Bighorn," 11th Annual Symposium, Custer Battlefield Historical & Museum Association, held at Hardin, MT on June 27, 1997, 54; Ernest L. Reedstrom, *Bugles, Banners & War Bonnets*, Caldwell, ID: The Caxton Printers, 1977, 216; James Donovan, *A Terrible Glory: Custer and the Little Bighorn – the Last Great Battle of the American West*, New York: Little, Brown and Company, 2008, 443; William O. Taylor, *With Custer on the Little Bighorn*, New York: Viking, 1996, 156; and Pamphlet 54, University of Wisconsin at Whitewater Special Collection of Dr. Kenneth Hammer: Hutchins, James S. "The Cavalry Campaign Outfit at the Little Bighorn," *Military Collector and Historian*, Winter 1956, 94, 96.

[122] Dušan P. Farrington, *Arming & Equipping the U.S. Cavalry 1865-1902*, Lincoln, RI: Andrew Mowbray Publishers, 2004, 183.

[123] Charles M. Robinson, *A Good Year to Die: The Story of the Great Sioux War*, New York: Random House, 1995, 8.

[124] James Donovan, *A Terrible Glory: Custer and the Little Bighorn – the Last Great Battle of the American West*, New York: Little, Brown and Company, 2008, 26, 75.

[125] Nathaniel Philbrick, *The Last Stand: Custer, Sitting Bull, and the Battle of the Little Bighorn*, New York: The Penguin Group, 2010, 38; and Arlington Cemetery Website, www.arlingtoncemetery.net.

[126] James Donovan, *A Terrible Glory: Custer and the Little Bighorn – the Last Great Battle of the American West*, New York: Little, Brown and Company, 2008, 56-57.

[127] Lorna Thackeray, "Haunted by history: Tragedy followed Bighorn battle survivors," *Billings Gazette*, Billings, MT: June 21, 2009.

[128] James Donovan, *A Terrible Glory: Custer and the Little Bighorn – the Last Great Battle of the American West*, New York: Little, Brown and Company, 2008, 56-57, 61, 92, 125; Thomas Goodrich, *Scalp Dance: Indian Warfare on the High Plains, 1865-1879*, Mechanicsburg, PA: Stackpole Books, 1997, 40; Walter M. Camp, "Field Notes," Lilly Library, Indiana University, Bloomington, IN., Box 5, Folder 11, Envelope 64 – Includes recollections of Walter Sterland; Nathaniel Philbrick, *The Last Stand: Custer, Sitting Bull, and the Battle of the Little Bighorn*, New York: The Penguin Group, 2010, 129; and Glenwood J. Swanson, *G. A. Custer: His Life and Times*, Agua Dulce, CA: Swanson Productions, 2004, 111.

[129] John Carroll, *Ten Years with Custer among the American Indians and Other Writings by John Ryan*, Bryan, TX: Privately Published, 1980, 79.

[130] Sandy Barnard, editor, *Ten Years with Custer: A 7th Cavalryman's Memoirs*, Terre Haute, IN: AST Press, 2001, 256.

[131] Kevin Adams, *Class and Race in the Frontier Army: Military Life in the West, 1870-1890,* Norman, OK: University of Oklahoma Press, 2009, 7.

[132] Ernest L. Reedstrom, *Bugles, Banners & War Bonnets*, Caldwell, ID: The Caxton Printers, 1977, 174.

Chapter Three: The March from Hell

[1] Glendolin D. Wagner, *Old Neutriment*, New York: Sol Lewis, 1973, 131.

[2] William O. Taylor, *With Custer on the Little Bighorn*, New York: Viking, 1996, 179.

[3] Ronald H. Nichols, editor, *Men with Custer: Biographies of the 7th Cavalry*, Hardin, MT: Custer Battlefield Historical and Museum Association, 362, 367.

[4] Ron Nichols, "Command Decision – 1876 Style: How did Custer organize his regiment?" *Greasy Grass Magazine*, Volume 21, May 2005, Hardin, MT: Custer Battlefield Historical & Museum Association, 5.

[5] Naval Oceanography Portal, *Complete Sun and Moon Data for One Day: U.S. Cities and Towns*, http://www.usno.navy.mil/USNO/astronomical-applications/data-services/rs-one-day-us

[6] Al Johnson, "The Preparation at Fort Abraham Lincoln," Billings, MT: 2009 Little Bighorn Associates 36th Annual Conference, June 23, 2009.

[7] Orin G. Libby, editor, *The Arikara Narrative of Custer's Campaign and the Battle of the Little Bighorn*, Norman, OK: University of Oklahoma Press, 1998, 26.

[8] Pamphlet 43, University of Wisconsin at Whitewater Special Collection of Dr. Kenneth Hammer: Hammer, Kenneth M. "Custer's Valiant Soldiers."

[9] Laudie J. Chorne, *Following the Custer Trail of 1876*, Bismarck, ND: Trails West Publishing, 2001, 10, 11, 15; James Donovan, *A Terrible Glory: Custer and the Little Bighorn – the Last Great Battle of the American West*, New York: Little, Brown and Company, 2008, 133; and Sandy Barnard, editor, *Ten Years with Custer: A 7th Cavalryman's Memoirs*, Terre Haute, IN: AST Press, 2001, 22.

[10] Laudie J. Chorne, *Following the Custer Trail of 1876*, Bismarck, ND: Trails West Publishing, 2001, 15, 73.

[11] Walter M. Camp, "Field Notes," Lilly Library, Indiana University, Bloomington, IN., Box 5, Folder 11, Envelope 64 – Includes recollections of Walter Sterland.

[12] Laudie J. Chorne, *Following the Custer Trail of 1876*, Bismarck, ND: Trails West Publishing, 2001, 12; and Nathaniel Philbrick, *The Last Stand: Custer, Sitting Bull, and the Battle of the Little Bighorn*, New York: The Penguin Group, 2010, 10.

[13] Douglas D. Scott, P. Willey and Melissa A. Connor, *They Died with Custer: Soldiers Bones from the Battle of the Little Bighorn*, Norman, OK: University of Oklahoma Press, 298-299; and Shannon Marjorie Vihlene, *Custer's Last Drag: An Examination of Tobacco Use Among the Seventh Cavalry during the Nineteenth Century*, Master of Arts in Anthropology (Forensic Anthropology) Thesis, Missoula, MT: The University of Montana, 2008, 29.

[14] Larry Sklenar, *To Hell with Honor; Custer and the Little Bighorn*, Norman, OK: University of Oklahoma Press, 2003, 68.

[15] Roger L. Williams, *Military Register of Custer's Last Command*, Norman, OK: The Arthur H. Clark Company, 2009, 214, 387.

[16] Laudie J. Chorne, *Following the Custer Trail of 1876*, Bismarck, ND: Trails West Publishing, 2001, 25, 46.

[17] Laudie J. Chorne, *Following the Custer Trail of 1876*, Bismarck, ND: Trails West Publishing, 2001, 17.

[18] Laudie J. Chorne, *Following the Custer Trail of 1876*, Bismarck, ND: Trails West Publishing, 2001, 19.

[19] Walter M. Camp, "Field Notes," Lilly Library, Indiana University, Bloomington, IN., Box 2, Folder 10 – Little Bighorn, Part 2.

[20] Ernest L. Reedstrom, *Bugles, Banners & War Bonnets*, Caldwell, ID: The Caxton Printers, 1977, 216-217.

[21] John Carroll, *The Sunshine Magazine Articles*, Bryan, TX: Privately Published, 1979, 6.

[22] Edgar I. Stewart, *Custer's Luck*, Norman, OK: University of Oklahoma Press, 1980, 211.

[23] Laudie J. Chorne, *Following the Custer Trail of 1876*, Bismarck, ND: Trails West Publishing, 2001, 21.

[24] Naval Oceanography Portal, *Complete Sun and Moon Data for One Day: U.S. Cities and Towns*, http://www.usno.navy.mil/USNO/astronomical-applications/data-services/rs-one-day-us

[25] Laudie J. Chorne, *Following the Custer Trail of 1876*, Bismarck, ND: Trails West Publishing, 2001, 25, 28.

[26] Laudie J. Chorne, *Following the Custer Trail of 1876*, Bismarck, ND: Trails West Publishing, 2001, 30, 33.

[27] Nathaniel Philbrick, *The Last Stand: Custer, Sitting Bull, and the Battle of the Little Bighorn*, New York: The Penguin Group, 2010, 36.

[28] Laudie J. Chorne, *Following the Custer Trail of 1876*, Bismarck, ND: Trails West Publishing, 2001, 37.

[29] Laudie J. Chorne, *Following the Custer Trail of 1876*, Bismarck, ND: Trails West Publishing, 2001, 40, 42.

[30] Laudie J. Chorne, *Following the Custer Trail of 1876*, Bismarck, ND: Trails West Publishing, 2001, 44, 45, 48.

[31] Orin G. Libby, editor, *The Arikara Narrative of Custer's Campaign and the Battle of the Little Bighorn*, Norman, OK: University of Oklahoma Press, 1998, 61.

[32] National Archives and Records Administration, Washington, D.C., Records Group 94, Records of the Adjutant General's Office – Army, Carded Medical Records Regular Army, 1821-1884, Entry 529 (Unit 7), David Summers – Box 423 (Starl-Taylor).

[33] Laudie J. Chorne, *Following the Custer Trail of 1876*, Bismarck, ND: Trails West Publishing, 2001, 50, 53, 54.

[34] "Songs of the Seventh Cavalry," CD, Bismarck, ND: *The Bismarck Tribune*.

[35] Charles Windolph, *I Fought with Custer: The Story of Sergeant Windolph, Last Survivor of the Battle of the Little Big Horn*, edited by Frazier Hunt and Robert Hunt, New York: Charles Scribner's Sons, 1947, 38.

[36] National Archives and Records Administration, Washington, D.C., Records Group 94, Records of the Adjutant General's Office – Army, Carded Medical Records Regular Army, 1821-1884, Entry 529 (Unit 7), David Summers – Box 423 (Starl-Taylor).

[37] Laudie J. Chorne, *Following the Custer Trail of 1876*, Bismarck, ND: Trails West Publishing, 2001, 56-60; Nathaniel Philbrick, *The Last Stand: Custer, Sitting Bull, and the Battle of the Little Bighorn*, New York: The Penguin Group, 2010, 37; and Edgar I. Stewart, *Custer's Luck*, Norman, OK: University of Oklahoma Press, 1980, 213.

[38] Laudie J. Chorne, *Following the Custer Trail of 1876*, Bismarck, ND: Trails West Publishing, 2001, 56-60.

[39] Jeremy Agnew, *Life of a Soldier on the Western Frontier*, Missoula, MT: Mountain Press Publishing Company, 2008, 39.

[40] National Archives and Records Administration, Washington, D.C., Records Group 94, Records of the Adjutant General's Office – Army, Carded Medical Records Regular Army, 1821-1884, Entry 529 (Unit 7), David Summers – Box 423 (Starl-Taylor).

[41] Laudie J. Chorne, *Following the Custer Trail of 1876*, Bismarck, ND: Trails West Publishing, 2001, 62, 63, 66.

[42] National Archives and Records Administration, Washington, D.C., Records Group 94, Records of the Adjutant General's Office – Army, Carded Medical Records Regular Army, 1821-1884, Entry 529 (Unit 7), David Summers – Box 423 (Starl-Taylor).

[43] National Archives and Records Administration, Washington, D.C., Records Group 94, Records of the Adjutant General's Office – Army, Carded Medical Records Regular Army, 1821-1884, Entry 529 (Unit 7), George Weaver – Box 425 (Volkmann-Weller).

[44] Laudie J. Chorne, *Following the Custer Trail of 1876*, Bismarck, ND: Trails West Publishing, 2001, 68, 71, 73.

[45] National Archives and Records Administration, Washington, D.C., Records Group 94, Records of the Adjutant General's Office – Army, Carded Medical Records Regular Army, 1821-1884, Entry 529 (Unit 7), David Summers – Box 423 (Starl-Taylor).

[46] National Archives and Records Administration, Washington, D.C., Records Group 94, Records of the Adjutant General's Office – Army, Carded Medical Records Regular Army, 1821-1884, Entry 529 (Unit 7), Charles Wiedman (filed under Weidman) – Box 425 (Volkmann-Weller).

[47] Laudie J. Chorne, *Following the Custer Trail of 1876*, Bismarck, ND: Trails West Publishing, 2001, 76, 79; and Edgar I. Stewart, *Custer's Luck*, Norman, OK: University of Oklahoma Press, 1980, 216.

[48] James Donovan, *A Terrible Glory: Custer and the Little Bighorn – the Last Great Battle of the American West*, New York: Little, Brown and Company, 2008, 142.

[49] National Archives and Records Administration, Washington, D.C., Records Group 94, Records of the Adjutant General's Office – Army, Carded Medical Records Regular Army, 1821-1884, Entry 529 (Unit 7), David Summers – Box 423 (Starl-Taylor).

[50] Laudie J. Chorne, *Following the Custer Trail of 1876*, Bismarck, ND: Trails West Publishing, 2001, 82, 84, 85.

[51] William O. Taylor, *With Custer on the Little Bighorn*, New York: Viking, 1996, 21.

[52] Laudie J. Chorne, *Following the Custer Trail of 1876*, Bismarck, ND: Trails West Publishing, 2001, 82, 84, 85.

[53] National Archives and Records Administration, Washington, D.C., Records Group 94, Records of the Adjutant General's Office – Army, Carded Medical Records Regular Army, 1821-1884, Entry 529 (Unit 7), David Summers – Box 423 (Starl-Taylor).

[54] Laudie J. Chorne, *Following the Custer Trail of 1876*, Bismarck, ND: Trails West Publishing, 2001, 86-90.

[55] James Willert, *Little Big Horn Diary: Chronicle of the 1876 Indian War*, El Segundo, CA: Upton and Sons, 1997, 62.

[56] National Archives and Records Administration, Washington, D.C., Records Group 94, Records of the Adjutant General's Office – Army, Carded Medical Records Regular Army, 1821-1884, Entry 529 (Unit 7), David Summers – Box 423 (Starl-Taylor).

[57] Edgar I. Stewart, *Custer's Luck*, Norman, OK: University of Oklahoma Press, 1980, 217.

[58] Laudie J. Chorne, *Following the Custer Trail of 1876*, Bismarck, ND: Trails West Publishing, 2001, 91-95; Jeremy Agnew, *Life of a Soldier on the Western Frontier*, Missoula, MT: Mountain Press Publishing Company, 2008, 129; and Edgar I. Stewart, *Custer's Luck*, Norman, OK: University of Oklahoma Press, 1980, 217.

[59] John Carroll, *The Sunshine Magazine Articles*, Bryan, TX: Privately Published, 1979, 6.

[60] John Gray, *Centennial Campaign: The Sioux War of 1876*, Fort Collins, CO: The Old Army Press, 1976, 94-95.

[61] Earle Alonzo Brininstool, *Troopers with Custer: Incidents of the Battle of the Little Big Horn*, Harrisburg, PA: The Stackpole Company, 1952, 5.

[62] National Archives and Records Administration, Washington, D.C., Records Group 94, Records of the Adjutant General's Office – Army, Carded Medical Records Regular Army, 1821-1884, Entry 529 (Unit 7), David Summers – Box 423 (Starl-Taylor).

[63] Laudie J. Chorne, *Following the Custer Trail of 1876*, Bismarck, ND: Trails West Publishing, 2001, 97-100.

[64] National Archives and Records Administration, Washington, D.C., Records Group 94, Records of the Adjutant General's Office – Army, Carded Medical Records Regular Army, 1821-1884, Entry 529 (Unit 7), David Summers – Box 423 (Starl-Taylor).

[65] Laudie J. Chorne, *Following the Custer Trail of 1876*, Bismarck, ND: Trails West Publishing, 2001, 101-106.

[66] National Archives and Records Administration, Washington, D.C., Records Group 94, Records of the Adjutant General's Office – Army, Carded Medical Records Regular Army, 1821-1884, Entry 529 (Unit 7), David Summers – Box 423 (Starl-Taylor).

[67] Laudie J. Chorne, *Following the Custer Trail of 1876*, Bismarck, ND: Trails West Publishing, 2001, 101-106.

[68] Orin G. Libby, editor, *The Arikara Narrative of Custer's Campaign and the Battle of the Little Bighorn*, Norman, OK: University of Oklahoma Press, 1998, 67.

[69] National Archives and Records Administration, Washington, D.C., Records Group 94, Records of the Adjutant General's Office – Army, Carded Medical Records Regular Army, 1821-1884, Entry 529 (Unit 7), David Summers – Box 423 (Starl-Taylor).

[70] Laudie J. Chorne, *Following the Custer Trail of 1876*, Bismarck, ND: Trails West Publishing, 2001, 109-111; and Sandy Barnard, editor, *Ten Years with Custer: A 7th Cavalryman's Memoirs*, Terre Haute, IN: AST Press, 2001, 24.

[71] National Archives and Records Administration, Washington, D.C., Records Group 94, Records of the Adjutant General's Office – Army, Carded Medical Records Regular Army, 1821-1884, Entry 529 (Unit 7), David Summers – Box 423 (Starl-Taylor).

[72] Laudie J. Chorne, *Following the Custer Trail of 1876*, Bismarck, ND: Trails West Publishing, 2001, 112-118; and John Gray, *Centennial Campaign: The Sioux War of 1876*, Fort Collins, CO: The Old Army Press, 1976, 102.

[73] Glendolin D. Wagner, *Old Neutriment*, New York: Sol Lewis, 1973, 129.

[74] National Archives and Records Administration, Washington, D.C., Records Group 94, Records of the Adjutant General's Office – Army, Carded Medical Records Regular Army, 1821-1884, Entry 529 (Unit 7), David Summers – Box 423 (Starl-Taylor).

[75] Laudie J. Chorne, *Following the Custer Trail of 1876*, Bismarck, ND: Trails West Publishing, 2001, 119-121; and Sandy Barnard, editor, *Ten Years with Custer: A 7th Cavalryman's Memoirs*, Terre Haute, IN: AST Press, 2001, 24.

[76] National Archives and Records Administration, Washington, D.C., Records Group 94, Records of the Adjutant General's Office – Army, Carded Medical Records Regular Army, 1821-1884, Entry 529 (Unit 7), David Summers – Box 423 (Starl-Taylor).

[77] Nathaniel Philbrick, *The Last Stand: Custer, Sitting Bull, and the Battle of the Little Bighorn*, New York: The Penguin Group, 2010, 45.

[78] Laudie J. Chorne, *Following the Custer Trail of 1876*, Bismarck, ND: Trails West Publishing, 2001, 122-124.

[79] Laudie J. Chorne, *Following the Custer Trail of 1876*, Bismarck, ND: Trails West Publishing, 2001, 125-129; James Donovan, *A Terrible Glory: Custer and the Little Bighorn – the Last Great Battle of the American West*, New York: Little, Brown and Company, 2008, 118; and Naval Oceanography Portal, *Complete Sun and Moon Data for One Day: U.S. Cities and Towns*, http://www.usno.navy.mil/USNO/astronomical-applications/data-services/rs-one-day-us.

[80] Laudie J. Chorne, *Following the Custer Trail of 1876*, Bismarck, ND: Trails West Publishing, 2001, 130-133; Nathaniel Philbrick, *The Last Stand: Custer, Sitting Bull, and the Battle of the Little Bighorn*, New York: The Penguin Group, 2010, 126; and William O. Taylor, *With Custer on the Little Bighorn*, New York: Viking, 1996, 23.

[81] Glendolin D. Wagner, *Old Neutriment*, New York: Sol Lewis, 1973, 130.

[82] National Archives and Records Administration, Washington, D.C., Records Group 94, Records of the Adjutant General's Office – Army, Carded Medical Records Regular Army, 1821-1884, Entry 529 (Unit 7), David Summers – Box 423 (Starl-Taylor).

[83] Laudie J. Chorne, *Following the Custer Trail of 1876*, Bismarck, ND: Trails West Publishing, 2001, 134-139.

[84] National Archives and Records Administration, Washington, D.C., Records Group 94, Records of the Adjutant General's Office – Army, Carded Medical Records Regular Army, 1821-1884, Entry 529 (Unit 7), David Summers – Box 423 (Starl-Taylor).

[85] Laudie J. Chorne, *Following the Custer Trail of 1876*, Bismarck, ND: Trails West Publishing, 2001, 140-142.

[86] Thomas Goodrich, *Scalp Dance: Indian Warfare on the High Plains, 1865-1879*, Mechanicsburg, PA: Stackpole Books, 1997, 40.

[87] Charles M. Robinson, *A Good Year to Die: The Story of the Great Sioux War*, New York: Random House, 1995, xxv.

[88] National Archives and Records Administration, Washington, D.C., Records Group 94, Records of the Adjutant General's Office – Army, Carded Medical Records Regular Army, 1821-1884, Entry 529 (Unit 7), David Summers – Box 423 (Starl-Taylor).

[89] James Donovan, *A Terrible Glory: Custer and the Little Bighorn – the Last Great Battle of the American West*, New York: Little, Brown and Company, 2008, 162; and Charles M. Robinson, *A Good Year to Die: The Story of the Great Sioux War*, New York: Random House, 1995, 67.

[90] Larry Sklenar, *To Hell with Honor; Custer and the Little Bighorn*, Norman, OK: University of Oklahoma Press, 2003, 71-72; Thomas M. Heski, "Camp Powell: The Powder River Supply Depot," 15th Annual Symposium, Custer Battlefield Historical & Museum Association, held at Hardin, MT on June 22, 2001, 5; and James Donovan, *A Terrible Glory: Custer and the Little Bighorn – the Last Great Battle of the American West*, New York: Little, Brown and Company, 2008, 162.

[91] Thomas M. Heski, "Camp Powell: The Powder River Supply Depot," 15th Annual Symposium, Custer Battlefield Historical & Museum Association held at Hardin, MT on June 22, 2001, 5, 10 and 11.

[92] Sandy Barnard, editor, *Ten Years with Custer: A 7th Cavalryman's Memoirs*, Terre Haute, IN: AST Press, 2001, 28.

[93] Laudie J. Chorne, *Following the Custer Trail of 1876*, Bismarck, ND: Trails West Publishing, 2001, 148.

[94] Laudie J. Chorne, *Following the Custer Trail of 1876*, Bismarck, ND: Trails West Publishing, 2001, 149-153; and James Donovan, *A Terrible Glory: Custer and the Little Bighorn – the Last Great Battle of the American West*, New York: Little, Brown and Company, 2008, 165.

[95] Orin G. Libby, editor, *The Arikara Narrative of Custer's Campaign and the Battle of the Little Bighorn*, Norman, OK: University of Oklahoma Press, 1998, 207.

[96] Glendolin D. Wagner, *Old Neutriment*, New York: Sol Lewis, 1973, 91.

[97] Nathaniel Philbrick, *The Last Stand: Custer, Sitting Bull, and the Battle of the Little Bighorn*, New York: The Penguin Group, 2010, 2-3; and Edgar I. Stewart, *Custer's Luck*, Norman, OK: University of Oklahoma Press, 1980, 223.

[98] Nathaniel Philbrick, *The Last Stand: Custer, Sitting Bull, and the Battle of the Little Bighorn*, New York: The Penguin Group, 2010, 2-3; and Edgar I. Stewart, *Custer's Luck*, Norman, OK: University of Oklahoma Press, 1980, 223. The *Far West* sank near St. Charles, Missouri after hitting a pile of submerged trees on October 30, 1883.

[99] Laudie J. Chorne, *Following the Custer Trail of 1876*, Bismarck, ND: Trails West Publishing, 2001, 154-156.

[100] *History Channel Magazine*, "Custer's Selenium Factor," New York, November/December 2005, 8.

[101] Laudie J. Chorne, *Following the Custer Trail of 1876*, Bismarck, ND: Trails West Publishing, 2001, 157-158.

[102] Ronald H. Nichols, editor, *Men with Custer: Biographies of the 7th Cavalry*, Hardin, MT: Custer Battlefield Historical and Museum Association, 50, 211-212, 278, 316, 357.

[103] Kenneth Hammer, "Recalling the Little Bighorn: Stories Told by 7th Cavalry Survivors," *Greasy Grass Magazine*, Volume 24, May 2008, Hardin, MT: Custer Battlefield Historical & Museum Association, 39.

[104] Roger L. Williams, *Military Register of Custer's Last Command*, Norman, OK: The Arthur H. Clark Company, 2009, 64.

[105] Roger L. Williams, *Military Register of Custer's Last Command*, Norman, OK: The Arthur H. Clark Company, 2009, 110.

[106] Roger L. Williams, *Military Register of Custer's Last Command*, Norman, OK: The Arthur H. Clark Company, 2009, 110.

[107] Roger L. Williams, *Military Register of Custer's Last Command*, Norman, OK: The Arthur H. Clark Company, 2009, 199.

[108] Roger L. Williams, *Military Register of Custer's Last Command*, Norman, OK: The Arthur H. Clark Company, 2009, 253-254.

[109] Roger L. Williams, *Military Register of Custer's Last Command*, Norman, OK: The Arthur H. Clark Company, 2009, 277 and 285; and Special Orders No. 147, Headquarters, Fort Rice, Dakota Territory, dated October 30, 1875, Records Group 393, Records of U. S. Army Continental Commands, 1821-1920, Part V, Military Installations, Fort Rice, North Dakota, Entry 6.

[110] Roger L. Williams, *Military Register of Custer's Last Command*, Norman, OK: The Arthur H. Clark Company, 2009, 308; and Garrison Orders No. 77, Headquarters, Fort Rice, Dakota Territory, dated December 5, 1874, Records Group 393, Records of U. S. Army Continental Commands, 1821-1920, Part V, Military Installations, Fort Rice, North Dakota, Entry 5.

[111] "Epworth's History is in God's Time," *Epworth United Methodist Church Newsletter*, Palmyra, NJ: Epworth UMC, September 2007.

[112] "Epworth's History is in God's Time," *Epworth United Methodist Church Newsletter*, Palmyra, NJ: Epworth UMC, September 2007.

[113] Roger L. Williams, *Military Register of Custer's Last Command*, Norman, OK: The Arthur H. Clark Company, 2009, 310; and Post Orders No. 97, Headquarters, Fort Rice, Dakota Territory, dated July 28, 1876, Records Group 393, Records of U. S. Army Continental Commands, 1821-1920, Part V, Military Installations, Fort Rice, North Dakota, Entry 5.

[114] Roger L. Williams, *Military Register of Custer's Last Command*, Norman, OK: The Arthur H. Clark Company, 2009, 320.

[115] Larry Sklenar, *To Hell with Honor; Custer and the Little Bighorn*, Norman, OK: University of Oklahoma Press, 2003, 73-74.

[116] Larry Sklenar, *To Hell with Honor; Custer and the Little Bighorn*, Norman, OK: University of Oklahoma Press, 2003, 74-75; Laudie J. Chorne, *Following the Custer Trail of 1876*, Bismarck, ND: Trails West Publishing, 2001, 159-162; and James Donovan, *A Terrible Glory: Custer and the Little Bighorn – the Last Great Battle of the American West*, New York: Little, Brown and Company, 2008, 166.

[117] Laudie J. Chorne, *Following the Custer Trail of 1876*, Bismarck, ND: Trails West Publishing, 2001, 163.

[118] Laudie J. Chorne, *Following the Custer Trail of 1876*, Bismarck, ND: Trails West Publishing, 2001, 163-166.

[119] Laudie J. Chorne, *Following the Custer Trail of 1876*, Bismarck, ND: Trails West Publishing, 2001, 167; John Gray, *Centennial Campaign: The Sioux War of 1876*, Fort Collins, CO: The Old Army Press, 1976, 123; and Arthur C. Unger, *The ABCs of Custer's Last Stand: Arrogance, Betrayal and Cowardice*, El Segundo, CA: Upton & Sons Publishers, 2004, 6.

[120] Laudie J. Chorne, *Following the Custer Trail of 1876*, Bismarck, ND: Trails West Publishing, 2001, 168-169.

[121] Orin G. Libby, editor, *The Arikara Narrative of Custer's Campaign and the Battle of the Little Bighorn*, Norman, OK: University of Oklahoma Press, 1998, 72.

[122] Kenneth Hammer, *Custer in '76: Walter Camp's Notes on the Custer Fight*, Provo, UT: Brigham Young University, 1976, 123.

[123] Laudie J. Chorne, *Following the Custer Trail of 1876*, Bismarck, ND: Trails West Publishing, 2001, 170-173; and James Donovan, *A Terrible Glory: Custer and the Little Bighorn – the Last Great Battle of the American West*, New York: Little, Brown and Company, 2008, 165, 167.

[124] Larry Sklenar, *To Hell with Honor; Custer and the Little Bighorn*, Norman, OK: University of Oklahoma Press, 2003, 74-75.

[125] United States Army, *Cavalry Tactics* (Reprint), New York: D. Appleton and Company, 1874, 468.

[126] Naval Oceanography Portal, *Complete Sun and Moon Data for One Day: U.S. Cities and Towns*, http://www.usno.navy.mil/USNO/astronomical-applications/data-services/rs-one-day-us.

[127] Laudie J. Chorne, *Following the Custer Trail of 1876*, Bismarck, ND: Trails West Publishing, 2001, 174-177.

[128] Naval Oceanography Portal, *Complete Sun and Moon Data for One Day: U.S. Cities and Towns*, http://www.usno.navy.mil/USNO/astronomical-applications/data-services/rs-one-day-us.

[129] Bill Yenne, *Indian Wars: The Campaign for the American West*, Yardley, PA: Westholme Publishing, 2006, 190.

[130] Kenneth Hammer, *Custer in '76: Walter Camp's Notes on the Custer Fight*, Provo, UT: Brigham Young University, 1976, 229.

[131] Nathaniel Philbrick, *The Last Stand: Custer, Sitting Bull, and the Battle of the Little Bighorn*, New York: The Penguin Group, 2010, 95.

[132] Email discussions with Dennis K. "DK" Clark, author of "Private Roman Rutten: Custer's Tailor," 15th Annual Symposium, Custer Battlefield Historical & Museum Association, October 2009.

[133] Naval Oceanography Portal, *Complete Sun and Moon Data for One Day: U.S. Cities and Towns*, http://www.usno.navy.mil/USNO/astronomical-applications/data-services/rs-one-day-us.

[134] Laudie J. Chorne, *Following the Custer Trail of 1876*, Bismarck, ND: Trails West Publishing, 2001, 182; James Donovan, *A Terrible Glory: Custer and the Little Bighorn – the Last Great Battle of the American West*, New York: Little, Brown and Company, 2008, 176-177; and Thomas B. Marquis, *Keep the Last Bullet for Yourself*, Algonac, MI: Reference Publications, 1985, 89.

[135] Jeremy Agnew, *Life of a Soldier on the Western Frontier*, Missoula, MT: Mountain Press Publishing Company, 2008, 191.

[136] Ernest L. Reedstrom, *Bugles, Banners & War Bonnets*, Caldwell, ID: The Caxton Printers, 1977, 195.

[137] Laudie J. Chorne, *Following the Custer Trail of 1876*, Bismarck, ND: Trails West Publishing, 2001, 183-184.

[138] Lorna Thackeray, "Haunted by history: Tragedy followed Bighorn battle survivors," *Billings Gazette*, Billings, MT: June 21, 2009.

[139] James Donovan, *A Terrible Glory: Custer and the Little Bighorn – the Last Great Battle of the American West*, New York: Little, Brown and Company, 2008, 177.

Chapter Four: Company M at the Little Bighorn Battle Summary

[1] John Carroll, editor, *A Seventh Cavalry Scrapbook*, Volume 1, "Memories of the Battle of the Little Big Horn," by Daniel Newell, Bryan, TX: Privately Published, 1978, 20.

[2] Naval Oceanography Portal, *Complete Sun and Moon Data for One Day: U.S. Cities and Towns*, http://www.usno.navy.mil/USNO/astronomical-applications/data-services/rs-one-day-us.

[3] Kenneth Hammer, *Custer in '76: Walter Camp's Notes on the Custer Fight*, Provo, UT: Brigham Young University, 1976, 138.

[4] Email discussions with Dennis K. "DK" Clark, author of "Private Roman Rutten: Custer's Tailor," 15th Annual Symposium, Custer Battlefield Historical & Museum Association, October 2009.

[5] John Gray, *Centennial Campaign: The Sioux War of 1876*, Fort Collins, CO: The Old Army Press, 1976, 272.

[6] Edgar I. Stewart, *Custer's Luck*, Norman, OK: University of Oklahoma Press, 1980, 253.

[7] James Donovan, *A Terrible Glory: Custer and the Little Bighorn – the Last Great Battle of the American West*, New York: Little, Brown and Company, 2008, 192.

[8] Kenneth Hammer, *Custer in '76: Walter Camp's Notes on the Custer Fight*, Provo, UT: Brigham Young University, 1976, 135.

[9] Gregory Michno, *The Mystery of E Troop: Custer's Gray Horse Company at the Little Bighorn*, Missoula, Montana: Mountain Press Publishing Company, 1994, 11; and email discussions with Dennis K. "DK" Clark, author of "Private Roman Rutten: Custer's Tailor," 15th Annual Symposium, Custer Battlefield Historical & Museum Association, October 2009.

[10] Roger L. Williams, *Military Register of Custer's Last Command*, Norman, OK: The Arthur H. Clark Company, 2009, 389.

[11] Charles Windolph, *I Fought with Custer: The Story of Sergeant Windolph, Last Survivor of the Battle of the Little Big Horn*, edited by Frazier Hunt and Robert Hunt, New York: Charles Scribner's Sons, 1947, 9.

[12] United States Army, *Cavalry Tactics* (Reprint), New York: D. Appleton and Company, 1874, 457.

[13] Charles M. Robinson, *A Good Year to Die: The Story of the Great Sioux War*, New York: Random House, 1995, 108; and Charles Windolph, *I Fought with Custer: The Story of Sergeant Windolph, Last Survivor of the Battle of the Little Big Horn*, edited by Frazier Hunt and Robert Hunt, New York: Charles Scribner's Sons, 1947, 56.

[14] Letter, Captain Thomas French, Company M, to Post Adjutant, dated January 4, 1876, Records Group 393, Records of U.S. Army Continental Commands, 1821-1920, Part V, Military Installations, Fort Rice, South Dakota, Entry 4.

[15] Laudie J. Chorne, *Following the Custer Trail of 1876*, Bismarck, ND: Trails West Publishing, 2001, 63; email discussions with Dennis K. "DK" Clark, author of "Private Roman Rutten: Custer's Tailor," 15th Annual Symposium, Custer Battlefield Historical & Museum Association, October 2009; and Walter Mason Camp, *Walter M. Camp's Little Bighorn Rosters*, annotated by Richard G. Hardoff, Spokane, WA: Arthur H. Clark Company, 2002, 195.

[16] Nathaniel Philbrick, *The Last Stand: Custer, Sitting Bull, and the Battle of the Little Bighorn*, New York: The Penguin Group, 2010, 39.

[17] Glendolin D. Wagner, *Old Neutriment*, New York: Sol Lewis, 1973, 140-141.

[18] Larry Sklenar, *To Hell with Honor; Custer and the Little Bighorn*, Norman, OK: University of Oklahoma Press, 2003, 87. The remark was made in an immediate post-battle letter on July 5, 1876 to Reverend Father Genin.

[19] Ronald H. Nichols, editor, *Men with Custer: Biographies of the 7th Cavalry*, Hardin, MT: Custer Battlefield Historical and Museum Association, 2000, 111; and Roger L. Williams, *Military Register of Custer's Last Command*, Norman, OK: The Arthur H. Clark Company, 2009, 133, 142; and email discussions with Bob and Edward Connor, great-grandsons of Private Jean Baptiste Gallenne, July 2010.

[20] National Archives and Records Administration, Washington, D.C., Records Group 94, Records of the Adjutant General's Office – Army, Carded Medical Records Regular Army, 1821-1884, Entry 529 (Unit 7), Jean Gallenne – Box 406 (Gallene-Graham).

[21] Garrison Orders No. 9, Headquarters, Fort Rice, Dakota Territory, dated April 29, 1875, Records Group 393, Records of U. S. Army Continental Commands, 1821-1920, Part V, Military Installations, Fort Rice, North Dakota, Entry 5.

[22] Don Rickey, Jr., *Forty Miles a Day on Beans and Hay*, Norman, OK: University of Oklahoma Press, 1972, 265.

[23] Arthur C. Unger, *The ABCs of Custer's Last Stand: Arrogance, Betrayal and Cowardice*, El Segundo, CA: Upton & Sons Publishers, 2004, 8.

[24] Don Rickey, Jr., *Forty Miles a Day on Beans and Hay*, Norman, OK: University of Oklahoma Press, 1972, 266; Al Johnson, "The Preparation at Fort Abraham Lincoln," Billings, MT: 2009 Little Bighorn Associates 36th Annual Conference, June 23, 2009; and Ernest L. Reedstrom, *Bugles, Banners & War Bonnets*, Caldwell, ID: The Caxton Printers, 1977, 195.

[25] Larry Sklenar, *To Hell with Honor; Custer and the Little Bighorn*, Norman, OK: University of Oklahoma Press, 2003, 92-93.

[26] Larry Sklenar, *To Hell with Honor; Custer and the Little Bighorn*, Norman, OK: University of Oklahoma Press, 2003, 93; and James Donovan, *A Terrible Glory: Custer and the Little Bighorn – the Last Great Battle of the American West*, New York: Little, Brown and Company, 2008, 194.

[27] Naval Oceanography Portal, *Complete Sun and Moon Data for One Day: U.S. Cities and Towns*, http://www.usno.navy.mil/USNO/astronomical-applications/data-services/rs-one-day-us.

[28] Naval Oceanography Portal, *Complete Sun and Moon Data for One Day: U.S. Cities and Towns*, http://www.usno.navy.mil/USNO/astronomical-applications/data-services/rs-one-day-us.

[29] Larry Sklenar, *To Hell with Honor; Custer and the Little Bighorn*, Norman, OK: University of Oklahoma Press, 2003, 95; James Donovan, *A Terrible Glory: Custer and the Little Bighorn – the Last Great Battle of the American West*, New York: Little, Brown and Company, 2008, 195; and William O. Taylor, *With Custer on the Little Bighorn*, New York: Viking, 1996, 27.

[30] James Donovan, *A Terrible Glory: Custer and the Little Bighorn – the Last Great Battle of the American West*, New York: Little, Brown and Company, 2008, 195.

[31] Larry Sklenar, *To Hell with Honor; Custer and the Little Bighorn*, Norman, OK: University of Oklahoma Press, 2003, 95.

[32] Louis A. DiMarco, *War Horse: A History of the Military Horse and Rider*, Yardley, PA: Westholme Press, 2008, 284.

[33] United States Army, *Cavalry Tactics* (Reprint), New York: D. Appleton and Company, 1874, 465.

[34] Charles M. Robinson, *A Good Year to Die: The Story of the Great Sioux War*, New York: Random House, 1995, 189.

[35] Sandy Barnard, editor, *Ten Years with Custer: A 7th Cavalryman's Memoirs*, Terre Haute, IN: AST Press, 2001, 205.

[36] United States Army, *Cavalry Tactics* (Reprint), New York: D. Appleton and Company, 1874, 474.

[37] Nathaniel Philbrick, *The Last Stand: Custer, Sitting Bull, and the Battle of the Little Bighorn*, New York: The Penguin Group, 2010, 140.

[38] Nathaniel Philbrick, *The Last Stand: Custer, Sitting Bull, and the Battle of the Little Bighorn*, New York: The Penguin Group, 2010, 42.

[39] Ernest L. Reedstrom, *Bugles, Banners & War Bonnets*, Caldwell, ID: The Caxton Printers, 1977, 209.

[40] Louis A. DiMarco, *War Horse: A History of the Military Horse and Rider*, Yardley, PA: Westholme Press, 2008, 288.

[41] James Donovan, *A Terrible Glory: Custer and the Little Bighorn – the Last Great Battle of the American West*, New York: Little, Brown and Company, 2008, 178.

[42] Nathaniel Philbrick, *The Last Stand: Custer, Sitting Bull, and the Battle of the Little Bighorn*, New York: The Penguin Group, 2010, 121.

[43] Naval Oceanography Portal, *Complete Sun and Moon Data for One Day: U.S. Cities and Towns*, http://www.usno.navy.mil/USNO/astronomical-applications/data-services/rs-one-day-us.

[44] Bruce R. Liddic, *Vanishing Victory: Custer's Final March*, El Segundo, CA: Upton & Sons, Publishers, 2004, 13.

[45] Walter M. Camp, "Field Notes," Lilly Library, Indiana University, Bloomington, IN., Box 2, Folder 10 – Little Bighorn, Part 2.

[46] James Donovan, *A Terrible Glory: Custer and the Little Bighorn – the Last Great Battle of the American West*, New York: Little, Brown and Company, 2008, 197.

[47] William O. Taylor, *With Custer on the Little Bighorn*, New York: Viking, 1996, 30.

[48] Email discussions with Dennis K. "DK" Clark, author of "Private Roman Rutten: Custer's Tailor," 15th Annual Symposium, Custer Battlefield Historical & Museum Association, October 2009; and Elwood L. Nye, *Marching with Custer: a day-to-day evaluation of the uses, abuses, and conditions of the animals on the ill-fated expedition of 1876*, Glendale, CA: Arthur H. Clark Company, 1964, 27.

[49] Edgar I. Stewart, *Custer's Luck*, Norman, OK: University of Oklahoma Press, 1980, 265.

[50] Naval Oceanography Portal, *Complete Sun and Moon Data for One Day: U.S. Cities and Towns*, http://www.usno.navy.mil/USNO/astronomical-applications/data-services/rs-one-day-us.

[51] C. Lee. Noyes, "The Valley Fight: The Enlisted Man's Perspective," 20th Annual Symposium, Custer Battlefield Historical & Museum Association, held at Hardin, MT on June 23, 2006, 50; and John Gray, *Centennial Campaign: The Sioux War of 1876*, Fort Collins, CO: The Old Army Press, 1976, 162.

[52] Naval Oceanography Portal, *Complete Sun and Moon Data for One Day: U.S. Cities and Towns*, http://www.usno.navy.mil/USNO/astronomical-applications/data-services/rs-one-day-us.

[53] Thomas M. Heski, "Night March, Halt and Reconnaissance, and Preparation for Battle, 18th Annual Symposium, Custer Battlefield Historical & Museum Association, held at Hardin, MT on June 25, 2004, 55; James Donovan, *A Terrible Glory: Custer and the Little Bighorn – the Last Great Battle of the American West*, New York: Little, Brown and Company, 2008, 191; and Kenneth Hammer, *Custer in '76: Walter Camp's Notes on the Custer Fight*, Provo, UT: Brigham Young University, 1976, 78.

[54] Tom Heski, "The Journey from Fort Abraham Lincoln to the Little Big Horn," Billings, MT: 2009 Little Bighorn Associates 36th Annual Conference, June 23, 2009.

[55] Larry Sklenar, *To Hell with Honor; Custer and the Little Bighorn*, Norman, OK: University of Oklahoma Press, 2003, 119.

[56] Ronald H. Nichols, editor, *Men with Custer: Biographies of the 7th Cavalry*, Hardin, MT: Custer Battlefield Historical and Museum Association, 2000, 208-209; James V. Schneider, *Behind Custer at the Little Big Horn: The Story of Lieutenant Edward Mathey and the Packtrain*, Fort Wayne, IN: Privately Published, 1980; Roger L. Williams, *Military Register of Custer's Last Command*, Norman, OK: The Arthur H. Clark Company, 2009, 214-215; "Un Bisontin entre bisons et Indiens," *L'Est Républicain* (Besancon, France), June 25, 2006; and James B. Klokner, *The Officer Corps of Custer's Seventh Cavalry 1866-1876*, Atglen, PA: Schiffer Publishing, 2007, 78-79.

[57] Ronald H. Nichols, editor, *Men with Custer: Biographies of the 7th Cavalry*, Hardin, MT: Custer Battlefield Historical and Museum Association, 2000, 208-209; James V. Schneider, *Behind Custer at the Little Big Horn: The Story of Lieutenant Edward Mathey and the Packtrain*, Fort Wayne, IN: Privately Published, 1980; and Roger L. Williams, *Military Register of Custer's Last Command*, Norman, OK: The Arthur H. Clark Company, 2009, 214-215.

[58] National Archives and Records Administration, Washington, D.C., Records Group 94, Records of the Adjutant General's Office – Army, Carded Medical Records Regular Army, 1821-1884, Entry 529 (Unit 7), Edward Mathey – Box 408 (Mackey-McCarthey).

[59] Katherine Gibson Fougera, *With Custer's Cavalry*, Caldwell, ID: The Caxton Printers, 1940, 123.

[60] Ronald H. Nichols, editor, *Men with Custer: Biographies of the 7th Cavalry*, Hardin, MT: Custer Battlefield Historical and Museum Association, 2000, 208-209; James V. Schneider, *Behind Custer at the Little Big Horn: The Story of Lieutenant Edward Mathey and the Packtrain*, Fort Wayne, IN: Privately Published, 1980; "Un Bisontin entre bisons et Indiens," *L'Est Républicain* (Besancon, France), June 25, 2006; and Roger L. Williams, *Military Register of Custer's Last Command*, Norman, OK: The Arthur H. Clark Company, 2009, 214-215.

[61] Special Orders No. 135 and 147, Headquarters, Fort Rice, Dakota Territory, dated October 12, 1875 and October 23, 1875, Records Group 393, Records of U. S. Army Continental Commands, 1821-1920, Part V, Military Installations, Fort Rice, North Dakota, Entry 6.

[62] Walter Mason Camp, *Walter M. Camp's Little Bighorn Rosters*, annotated by Richard G. Hardoff, Spokane, WA: Arthur H. Clark Company, 2002, 195.

[63] Walter M. Camp, "Field Notes," Lilly Library, Indiana University, Bloomington, IN., Box 2, Folder 9 – Little Bighorn, Part 1.

[64] Richard G. Hardorff, editor, *On the Little Bighorn with Walter Camp; A Collection of Walter Mason Camp's Letters, Notes and opinions on Custer's Last Fight*, El Segundo, CA: Upton & Sons Publishers, 2002, 75. Comment made in a letter from Charles Varnum to Walter Camp.

[65] James Donovan, *A Terrible Glory: Custer and the Little Bighorn – the Last Great Battle of the American West*, New York: Little, Brown and Company, 2008, 197, 201.

[66] Bruce R. Liddic, *Vanishing Victory: Custer's Final March*, El Segundo, CA: Upton & Sons, Publishers, 2004, 23.

[67] Charles M. Robinson, *A Good Year to Die: The Story of the Great Sioux War*, New York: Random House, 1995, xxvii; and Email discussions with Dennis K. "DK" Clark, author of "Private Roman Rutten: Custer's Tailor," 15th Annual Symposium, Custer Battlefield Historical & Museum Association, October 2009.

[68] Thomas M. Heski, "Night March, Halt and Reconnaissance, and Preparation for Battle, 18th Annual Symposium, Custer Battlefield Historical & Museum Association, held at Hardin, MT on June 25, 2004, 63; and James Donovan, *A Terrible Glory: Custer and the Little Bighorn – the Last Great Battle of the American West*, New York: Little, Brown and Company, 2008, 204.

[69] Edgar I. Stewart, *Custer's Luck*, Norman, OK: University of Oklahoma Press, 1980, 270.

[70] Sandy Barnard, editor, *Ten Years with Custer: A 7th Cavalryman's Memoirs*, Terre Haute, IN: AST Press, 2001, 289.

[71] Naval Oceanography Portal, *Complete Sun and Moon Data for One Day: U.S. Cities and Towns*, http://www.usno.navy.mil/USNO/astronomical-applications/data-services/rs-one-day-us.

[72] James Donovan, *A Terrible Glory: Custer and the Little Bighorn – the Last Great Battle of the American West*, New York: Little, Brown and Company, 2008, 201.

[73] Thomas M. Heski, "Night March, Halt and Reconnaissance, and Preparation for Battle, 18th Annual Symposium, Custer Battlefield Historical & Museum Association, held at Hardin, MT on June 25, 2004, 64.

[74] Ronald H. Nichols, editor, *Men with Custer: Biographies of the 7th Cavalry*, Hardin, MT: Custer Battlefield Historical and Museum Association, 2000, 306; Earle Alonzo Brininstool, *Troopers with Custer: Incidents of the Battle of the Little Big Horn*, Harrisburg, PA: The Stackpole Company, 1952, 36; and Roger L. Williams, *Military Register of Custer's Last Command*, Norman, OK: The Arthur H. Clark Company, 2009, 273.

[75] Kevin Adams, *Class and Race in the Frontier Army: Military Life in the West,* 1870-1890, Norman, OK: University of Oklahoma Press, 2009, 118.

[76] Ronald H. Nichols, editor, *Men with Custer: Biographies of the 7th Cavalry*, Hardin, MT: Custer Battlefield Historical and Museum Association, 2000, 306; and Roger L. Williams, *Military Register of Custer's Last Command*, Norman, OK: The Arthur H. Clark Company, 2009, 273.

[77] Robert S. Ellison, "Walter M. Camp Papers," WH1702, Western History Collection, The Denver Public Library, Denver, CO., File Folder 35, Correspondence from William Morris to Major A.B. Ostrander; letter dated March 26, 1927.

[78] Thomas M. Heski, "Night March, Halt and Reconnaissance, and Preparation for Battle, 18th Annual Symposium, Custer Battlefield Historical & Museum Association, held at Hardin, MT on June 25, 2004, 64; and James Donovan, *A Terrible Glory: Custer and the Little Bighorn – the Last Great Battle of the American West*, New York: Little, Brown and Company, 2008, 205.

[79] Sandy Barnard, *Custer's First Sergeant John Ryan*, Terre Haute, IN: AST Press, 1996, 175; and Larry Sklenar, *To Hell with Honor; Custer and the Little Bighorn*, Norman, OK: University of Oklahoma Press, 2003, 103, 111.

[80] Larry Sklenar, *To Hell with Honor; Custer and the Little Bighorn*, Norman, OK: University of Oklahoma Press, 2003, 111.

[81] John Gray, *Centennial Campaign: The Sioux War of 1876*, Fort Collins, CO: The Old Army Press, 1976, 166.

[82] James Donovan, *A Terrible Glory: Custer and the Little Bighorn – the Last Great Battle of the American West*, New York: Little, Brown and Company, 2008, 210.

[83] James Donovan, *A Terrible Glory: Custer and the Little Bighorn – the Last Great Battle of the American West*, New York: Little, Brown and Company, 2008, 210.

[84] William O. Taylor, *With Custer on the Little Bighorn*, New York: Viking, 1996, 37.

[85] James Donovan, *A Terrible Glory: Custer and the Little Bighorn – the Last Great Battle of the American West*, New York: Little, Brown and Company, 2008, 210, 211, 213.

[86] Edgar I. Stewart, *Custer's Luck*, Norman, OK: University of Oklahoma Press, 1980, 281.

[87] Roger L. Williams, *Military Register of Custer's Last Command*, Norman, OK: The Arthur H. Clark Company, 2009, 385, 394.

[88] Roger L. Williams, *Military Register of Custer's Last Command*, Norman, OK: The Arthur H. Clark Company, 2009, 395.

[89] Email discussions with Dennis K. "DK" Clark, author of "Private Roman Rutten: Custer's Tailor," 15th Annual Symposium, Custer Battlefield Historical & Museum Association, October 2009.

[90] Larry Sklenar, *To Hell with Honor; Custer and the Little Bighorn*, Norman, OK: University of Oklahoma Press, 2003, 119.

[91] Ronald H. Nichols, editor, *Men with Custer: Biographies of the 7th Cavalry*, Hardin, MT: Custer Battlefield Historical and Museum Association, 2000, 87; Douglas D. Scott, P. Willey and Melissa A. Connor, *They Died with Custer: Soldiers Bones from the Battle of the Little Bighorn*, Norman, OK: University of Oklahoma Press, 288; William O. Taylor, *With Custer on the Little Bighorn*, New York: Viking, 1996, 182; Walter Mason Camp, *Walter M. Camp's Little Bighorn Rosters*, annotated by Richard G. Hardoff, Spokane, WA: Arthur H. Clark Company, 2002, 198, and Roger L. Williams, *Military Register of Custer's Last Command*, Norman, OK: The Arthur H. Clark Company, 2009, 110.

[92] Garrison Orders No. 18, Headquarters, Fort Rice, Dakota Territory, dated June 12, 1875, Records Group 393, Records of U. S. Army Continental Commands, 1821-1920, Part V, Military Installations, Fort Rice, North Dakota, Entry 5.

[93] Garrison Orders No. 2, Headquarters, Fort Rice, Dakota Territory, dated January 16, 1876, Records Group 393, Records of U. S. Army Continental Commands, 1821-1920, Part V, Military Installations, Fort Rice, North Dakota, Entry 5.

[94] Edgar I. Stewart, *Custer's Luck*, Norman, OK: University of Oklahoma Press, 1980, 281.

[95] Larry Sklenar, *To Hell with Honor; Custer and the Little Bighorn*, Norman, OK: University of Oklahoma Press, 2003, 114-115; James Donovan, *A Terrible Glory: Custer and the Little Bighorn – the Last Great Battle of the American West*, New York: Little, Brown and Company, 2008, 203; Bruce R. Liddic, *Vanishing Victory: Custer's Final March*, El Segundo, CA: Upton & Sons, Publishers, 2004, 31; and Edgar I. Stewart, *Custer's Luck*, Norman, OK: University of Oklahoma Press, 1980, 316.

[96] Jack Pennington, *The Battle of the Little Bighorn: A Comprehensive Study*, El Segundo, CA: Upton & Sons, Publishers, 2001, 13-14.

[97] Kenneth Hammer, *Custer in '76: Walter Camp's Notes on the Custer Fight*, Provo, UT: Brigham Young University, 1976, 68.

[98] Larry Sklenar, *To Hell with Honor; Custer and the Little Bighorn*, Norman, OK: University of Oklahoma Press, 2003, 106.

[99] Earle Alonzo Brininstool, *Troopers with Custer: Incidents of the Battle of the Little Big Horn*, Harrisburg, PA: The Stackpole Company, 1952, 76.

[100] John Gray, *Centennial Campaign: The Sioux War of 1876*, Fort Collins, CO: The Old Army Press, 1976, 248.

[101] James Welch, *Killing Custer: The Battle of the Little Bighorn and the Fate of the Plains Indians*, New York: W.W. Norton & Company, 1994, 149.

[102] John Gray, *Centennial Campaign: The Sioux War of 1876*, Fort Collins, CO: The Old Army Press, 1976, 256-257.

[103] Larry Sklenar, *To Hell with Honor; Custer and the Little Bighorn*, Norman, OK: University of Oklahoma Press, 2003, 131.

[104] Larry Sklenar, *To Hell with Honor; Custer and the Little Bighorn*, Norman, OK: University of Oklahoma Press, 2003, 146; and Nathaniel Philbrick, *The Last Stand: Custer, Sitting Bull, and the Battle of the Little Bighorn*, New York: The Penguin Group, 2010, 157.

[105] John Gray, *Centennial Campaign: The Sioux War of 1876*, Fort Collins, CO: The Old Army Press, 1976, 266-267.

[106] James Donovan, *A Terrible Glory: Custer and the Little Bighorn – the Last Great Battle of the American West*, New York: Little, Brown and Company, 2008, 215.

[107] James Donovan, *A Terrible Glory: Custer and the Little Bighorn – the Last Great Battle of the American West*, New York: Little, Brown and Company, 2008, 216.

[108] "William E. Morris, Jurist, Dead at 75," *New York Times*, New York: November 27, 1933, 17.

[109] Douglas Paul Westfall, *Letters from the Field: Wallace at the Little Big Horn*, Orange, CA: The Paragon Agency, 1997, 22.

[110] C. Lee. Noyes, "The Valley Fight: The Enlisted Man's Perspective," 20th Annual Symposium, Custer Battlefield Historical & Museum Association, held at Hardin, MT on June 23, 2006, 50.

[111] Don Rickey, Jr., *Forty Miles a Day on Beans and Hay*, Norman, OK: University of Oklahoma Press, 1972, 275.

[112] Bruce R. Liddic, *Vanishing Victory: Custer's Final March*, El Segundo, CA: Upton & Sons, Publishers, 2004, 60.

[113] John Carroll, editor, *A Seventh Cavalry Scrapbook*, Volume 1, "Memories of the Battle of the Little Big Horn," by Daniel Newell, Bryan, TX: Privately Published, 1978, 19.

[114] Walter Mason Camp, *Walter M. Camp's Little Bighorn Rosters*, annotated by Richard G. Hardoff, Spokane, WA: Arthur H. Clark Company, 2002, 202.

[115] Don Rickey, Jr., *Forty Miles a Day on Beans and Hay*, Norman, OK: University of Oklahoma Press, 1972, 276.

[116] Kenneth Hammer, *Custer in '76: Walter Camp's Notes on the Custer Fight*, Provo, UT: Brigham Young University, 1976, 65; and Jeremy Agnew, *Life of a Soldier on the Western Frontier*, Missoula, MT: Mountain Press Publishing Company, 2008, 114. In Plains Indian sign language the sign for "wolf" was the same as that for "scout."

[117] Michael Donahue, *Drawing Battle Lines: The Map Testimony of Custer's Last Fight*, El Segundo, CA: Upton & Sons Publishers, 2008, xix.

[118] James Willert, *Little Big Horn Diary: Chronicle of the 1876 Indian War*, El Segundo, CA: Upton and Sons, 1997, 273.

[119] Jack Pennington, *The Battle of the Little Bighorn: A Comprehensive Study*, El Segundo, CA: Upton & Sons, Publishers, 2001, 28. It was originally cited as coming from *Hardin (Montana) Gazette*, June 22, 1923.

[120] Robert Earle Forrest, "Fighting with Custer: Two Men Who Were with Gallant General Custer at Little Bighorn Battle Are Still Living," *Morning Observer*, Washington, PA: October 8, 1932.

[121] Edgar I. Stewart, *Custer's Luck*, Norman, OK: University of Oklahoma Press, 1980, 347.

[122] Larry Sklenar, *To Hell with Honor; Custer and the Little Bighorn*, Norman, OK: University of Oklahoma Press, 2003, 151.

[123] Walter M. Camp, "Field Notes," Lilly Library, Indiana University, Bloomington, IN., Box 2, Folder 11 – Little Bighorn, Part 3; Kenneth Hammer, *Custer in '76: Walter Camp's Notes on the Custer Fight*, Provo, UT: Brigham Young University, 1976, 182.

[124] William O. Taylor, *With Custer on the Little Bighorn*, New York: Viking, 1996, 37, 151; and Edgar I. Stewart, *Custer's Luck*, Norman, OK: University of Oklahoma Press, 1980, 306-307, 312-313.

[125] Nathaniel Philbrick, *The Last Stand: Custer, Sitting Bull, and the Battle of the Little Bighorn*, New York: The Penguin Group, 2010, 213.

[126] Edgar I. Stewart, *Custer's Luck*, Norman, OK: University of Oklahoma Press, 1980, 306-307; and Orin G. Libby, editor, *The Arikara Narrative of Custer's Campaign and the Battle of the Little Bighorn*, Norman, OK: University of Oklahoma Press, 1998, 125.

[127] William O. Taylor, *With Custer on the Little Bighorn*, New York: Viking, 1996, 37, 151.

[128] Nathaniel Philbrick, *The Last Stand: Custer, Sitting Bull, and the Battle of the Little Bighorn*, New York: The Penguin Group, 2010, 168.

[129] Edgar I. Stewart, *Custer's Luck*, Norman, OK: University of Oklahoma Press, 1980, 312-313; and Joseph M. Marshall, *The Day the World Ended at Little Bighorn: A Lakota History*, New York: Viking, 2003, 24.

[130] Edgar I. Stewart, *Custer's Luck*, Norman, OK: University of Oklahoma Press, 1980, 313.

[131] Larry Sklenar, *To Hell with Honor; Custer and the Little Bighorn*, Norman, OK: University of Oklahoma Press, 2003, 162.

[132] C. Lee Noyes, "Was There A Timber Fight?" Indianapolis, IN: Indianapolis Little Bighorn Symposium, September 12, 2009; Walter M. Camp, "Field Notes," Lilly Library, Indiana University, Bloomington, IN., Box 5, Folder 11, Envelope 64 – Includes recollections of Walter Sterland; and Robert S. Ellison, "Walter M. Camp Papers," WH1702, Western History Collection, The Denver Public Library, Denver, CO., File Folder 45, Walter Camp Research; letter from William Morris to Walter M. Camp dated November 18, 1908.

[133] Jeremy Agnew, *Life of a Soldier on the Western Frontier*, Missoula, MT: Mountain Press Publishing Company, 2008, 182.

[134] Larry Sklenar, *To Hell with Honor; Custer and the Little Bighorn*, Norman, OK: University of Oklahoma Press, 2003, 162; and J.W. Vaughn, *Indian Fights: New Facts on Seven Encounters*, Norman, OK: University of Oklahoma Press, 1966, 146; and James Donovan, *A Terrible Glory: Custer and the Little Bighorn – the Last Great Battle of the American West*, New York: Little, Brown and Company, 2008, 190, 217.

[135] John Carroll, *The Sunshine Magazine Articles*, Bryan, TX: Privately Published, 1979, 9.

[136] John Carroll, *The Sunshine Magazine Articles*, Bryan, TX: Privately Published, 1979, 9.

[137] Email discussions with Dennis K. "DK" Clark, author of "Private Roman Rutten: Custer's Tailor," 15th Annual Symposium, Custer Battlefield Historical & Museum Association, October 2009.

[138] Dale Schoenberger, "Custer's Scouts," *Montana Western History*, Volume XVI, No. 2, Spring 1966, 43.

[139] Email discussions with Dennis K. "DK" Clark, author of "Private Roman Rutten: Custer's Tailor," 15th Annual Symposium, Custer Battlefield Historical & Museum Association, October 2009.

[140] Larry Sklenar, *To Hell with Honor; Custer and the Little Bighorn*, Norman, OK: University of Oklahoma Press, 2003, 162; and James Donovan, *A Terrible Glory: Custer and the Little Bighorn – the Last Great Battle of the American West*, New York: Little, Brown and Company, 2008, 439.

[141] Joseph M. Marshall, *The Day the World Ended at Little Bighorn: A Lakota History*, New York: Viking, 2003, 26; and Richard G. Hardorff, *Cheyenne Memories of the Custer Fight*, Lincoln, NE: University of Nebraska Press (Bison Press), 1998, 42.

[142] Guy Gibbon, *The Sioux: the Dakota and Lakota Nations*, Malden, MA: Blackwell Publishing, 2003, 128.

[143] Charles M. Robinson, *A Good Year to Die: The Story of the Great Sioux War*, New York: Random House, 1995, 8.

[144] Thomas B. Marquis, *Keep the Last Bullet for Yourself*, Algonac, MI: Reference Publications, 1985, 58.

[145] Thomas B. Marquis, *A Warrior Who Fought Custer*, Minneapolis, MN: The Midwest Company, 1931, 211-212.

[146] Guy Gibbon, *The Sioux: the Dakota and Lakota Nations*, Malden, MA: Blackwell Publishing, 2003, 129.

[147] Edgar I. Stewart, *Custer's Luck*, Norman, OK: University of Oklahoma Press, 1980, 307-309; and Joseph M. Marshall, *The Day the World Ended at Little Bighorn: A Lakota History*, New York: Viking, 2003, 26.

[148] Larry Sklenar, *To Hell with Honor; Custer and the Little Bighorn*, Norman, OK: University of Oklahoma Press, 2003, 162-163.

[149] C. Lee Noyes, "Was There A Timber Fight?" Indianapolis, IN: Indianapolis Little Bighorn Symposium, September 12, 2009; James Donovan, *A Terrible Glory: Custer and the Little Bighorn – the Last*

Great Battle of the American West, New York: Little, Brown and Company, 2008, 439; and Edgar I. Stewart, *Custer's Luck*, Norman, OK: University of Oklahoma Press, 1980, 343.

[150] Jean B. Gallenne, "The Fatal Day: A Soldier's Journal," St. Paul (MN) *Pioneer Press*, January 16, 1879.

[151] Kenneth Hammer, *Custer in '76: Walter Camp's Notes on the Custer Fight*, Provo, UT: Brigham Young University, 1976, 65, 111; James Donovan, *A Terrible Glory: Custer and the Little Bighorn – the Last Great Battle of the American West*, New York: Little, Brown and Company, 2008, 233.

[152] Bruce R. Liddic, *Vanishing Victory: Custer's Final March*, El Segundo, CA: Upton & Sons, Publishers, 2004, 14.

[153] Charles Windolph, *I Fought with Custer: The Story of Sergeant Windolph, Last Survivor of the Battle of the Little Big Horn*, edited by Frazier Hunt and Robert Hunt, New York: Charles Scribner's Sons, 1947, 80.

[154] Cyrus T. Brady, *Indian Fights and Fighters*, New York: Doubleday, Page & Company, 1909, 402. Morris' comments to Brady came in the form of a letter from Haven, Maine, and were dated September 21, 1904.

[155] C. Lee Noyes, "Was There A Timber Fight?" Indianapolis, IN: Indianapolis Little Bighorn Symposium, September 12, 2009.

[156] Kenneth Hammer, *Custer in '76: Walter Camp's Notes on the Custer Fight*, Provo, UT: Brigham Young University, 1976, 148.

[157] C. Lee Noyes, "The Valley Fight: The Enlisted Man's Perspective," 20th Annual Symposium, Custer Battlefield Historical & Museum Association, held at Hardin, MT on June 23, 2006, 40.

[158] Bruce R. Liddic, *Vanishing Victory: Custer's Final March*, El Segundo, CA: Upton & Sons, Publishers, 2004, 62.

[159] James Donovan, *A Terrible Glory: Custer and the Little Bighorn – the Last Great Battle of the American West*, New York: Little, Brown and Company, 2008, 186, 221.

[160] John Carroll, editor, *A Seventh Cavalry Scrapbook*, Volume 1, "Memories of the Battle of the Little Big Horn," by Daniel Newell, Bryan, TX: Privately Published, 1978, 19.

[161] James Donovan, *A Terrible Glory: Custer and the Little Bighorn – the Last Great Battle of the American West*, New York: Little, Brown and Company, 2008, 221.

[162] Larry Sklenar, *To Hell with Honor; Custer and the Little Bighorn*, Norman, OK: University of Oklahoma Press, 2003, 167-168; and James Donovan, *A Terrible Glory: Custer and the Little Bighorn – the Last Great Battle of the American West*, New York: Little, Brown and Company, 2008, 220.

[163] Edgar I. Stewart, *Custer's Luck*, Norman, OK: University of Oklahoma Press, 1980, 344, 349.

[164] James Donovan, *A Terrible Glory: Custer and the Little Bighorn – the Last Great Battle of the American West*, New York: Little, Brown and Company, 2008, 228, 232; and Bruce R. Liddic, *Vanishing Victory: Custer's Final March*, El Segundo, CA: Upton & Sons, Publishers, 2004, 63.

[165] Bruce R. Liddic, *Vanishing Victory: Custer's Final March*, El Segundo, CA: Upton & Sons, Publishers, 2004, 63; James Welch, *Killing Custer: The Battle of the Little Bighorn and the Fate of the Plains Indians*, New York: W.W. Norton & Company, 1994, 153-154; and Thomas B. Marquis, *A Warrior Who Fought Custer*, Minneapolis, MN: The Midwest Company, 1931, 214.

[166] Email discussions with Dennis K. "DK" Clark, author of "Private Roman Rutten: Custer's Tailor," 15th Annual Symposium, Custer Battlefield Historical & Museum Association, October 2009; Nathaniel Philbrick, *The Last Stand: Custer, Sitting Bull, and the Battle of the Little Bighorn*, New York: The Penguin Group, 2010, 178; and Henry and Don Weibert, *Sixty-six Years in Custer's Shadow*, Billings, MT: Falcon Press, 1985, 22.

[167] Ronald H. Nichols, editor, *Men with Custer: Biographies of the 7th Cavalry*, Hardin, MT: Custer Battlefield Historical and Museum Association, 2000, 311, 101.

[168] Ronald H. Nichols, editor, *Men with Custer: Biographies of the 7th Cavalry*, Hardin, MT: Custer Battlefield Historical and Museum Association, 2000, 311; and Roger L. Williams, *Military Register of Custer's Last Command*, Norman, OK: The Arthur H. Clark Company, 2009, 275.

[169] Garrison Orders No. 34, Headquarters, Fort Rice, Dakota Territory, dated November 6, 1875, Records Group 393, Records of U. S. Army Continental Commands, 1821-1920, Part V, Military Installations, Fort Rice, North Dakota, Entry 5.

[170] Garrison Orders No. 4, Headquarters, Fort Rice, Dakota Territory, dated February 2, 1876, Records Group 393, Records of U. S. Army Continental Commands, 1821-1920, Part V, Military Installations, Fort Rice, North Dakota, Entry 5.

[171] Ronald H. Nichols, editor, *Men with Custer: Biographies of the 7th Cavalry*, Hardin, MT: Custer Battlefield Historical and Museum Association, 2000, 101; and Roger L. Williams, *Military Register of Custer's Last Command*, Norman, OK: The Arthur H. Clark Company, 2009, 147-148.

[172] National Archives and Records Administration, Washington, D.C., Records Group 153, Records of the Office of the Judge Advocate General – Army, Court-Martial Case Files, 1809-1894, Trumpeter Charles Fischer – Case # PP-5461. Headquarters Department of Dakota, General Court-Martial Orders #57, St. Paul, MN, December 28, 1876.

[173] Ronald H. Nichols, editor, *Men with Custer: Biographies of the 7th Cavalry*, Hardin, MT: Custer Battlefield Historical and Museum Association, 2000, 348; and Roger L. Williams, *Military Register of Custer's Last Command*, Norman, OK: The Arthur H. Clark Company, 2009, 303.

[174] Sandy Barnard, editor, *Ten Years with Custer: A 7th Cavalryman's Memoirs*, Terre Haute, IN: AST Press, 2001, 291.

[175] Larry Sklenar, *To Hell with Honor; Custer and the Little Bighorn*, Norman, OK: University of Oklahoma Press, 2003, 170.

[176] Earle Alonzo Brininstool, *Troopers with Custer: Incidents of the Battle of the Little Big Horn*, Harrisburg, PA: The Stackpole Company, 1952, 48.

[177] Thomas B. Marquis, *Keep the Last Bullet for Yourself*, Algonac, MI: Reference Publications, 1985, 159.

[178] Bruce R. Liddic, *Vanishing Victory: Custer's Final March*, El Segundo, CA: Upton & Sons, Publishers, 2004, 61.

[179] Ronald H. Nichols, editor, *Men with Custer: Biographies of the 7th Cavalry*, Hardin, MT: Custer Battlefield Historical and Museum Association, 2000, 308; and Roger L. Williams, *Military Register of Custer's Last Command*, Norman, OK: The Arthur H. Clark Company, 2009, 274.

[180] Garrison Orders No. 2, Headquarters, Fort Rice, Dakota Territory, dated January 16, 1876, Records Group 393, Records of U. S. Army Continental Commands, 1821-1920, Part V, Military Installations, Fort Rice, North Dakota, Entry 5.

[181] Gregory Michno, *The Mystery of E Troop: Custer's Gray Horse Company at the Little Bighorn*, Missoula, Montana: Mountain Press Publishing Company, 1994, 129.

[182] Robert S. Ellison, "Walter M. Camp Papers," WH1702, Western History Collection, The Denver Public Library, Denver, CO., File Folder 45, Walter Camp Research; letter from William Morris to Walter M. Camp dated November 18, 1908.

[183] Edgar I. Stewart, *Custer's Luck*, Norman, OK: University of Oklahoma Press, 1980, 354.

[184] United States Army, *Cavalry Tactics* (Reprint), New York: D. Appleton and Company, 1874, 243; and Richard A. Fox, *Archaeology, History, and Custer's Last Battle*, Norman, OK: University of Oklahoma Press, 1993, 43.

[185] Kenneth Hammer, *Custer in '76: Walter Camp's Notes on the Custer Fight*, Provo, UT: Brigham Young University, 1976, 66, 112; Larry Sklenar, *To Hell with Honor; Custer and the Little Bighorn*, Norman, OK: University of Oklahoma Press, 2003, 171, 173; and Richard G. Hardorff, *Cheyenne Memories of the Custer Fight*, Lincoln, NE: University of Nebraska Press (Bison Press), 1998, 39.

[186] Bruce R. Liddic, *Vanishing Victory: Custer's Final March*, El Segundo, CA: Upton & Sons, Publishers, 2004, 67; Sandy Barnard, *Custer's First Sergeant John Ryan*, Terre Haute, IN: AST Press, 1996, 178; Richard G. Hardorff, *Cheyenne Memories of the Custer Fight*, Lincoln, NE: University of Nebraska Press (Bison Press), 1998, 39; and Robert C. Kain, *In the Valley of the Little Bighorn: The 7th and the Sioux*, Newfane, VT: Self-published, 1969, 36. This volume has personal notes and observations from Colonel Edward M. Offley, United States Cavalry, retired.

[187] Edgar I. Stewart, *Custer's Luck*, Norman, OK: University of Oklahoma Press, 1980, 351.

[188] Larry Sklenar, *To Hell with Honor; Custer and the Little Bighorn*, Norman, OK: University of Oklahoma Press, 2003, 172; and Orin G. Libby, editor, *The Arikara Narrative of Custer's Campaign and the Battle of the Little Bighorn*, Norman, OK: University of Oklahoma Press, 1998, 122.

[189] Richard G. Hardorff, *Cheyenne Memories of the Custer Fight*, Lincoln, NE: University of Nebraska Press (Bison Press), 1998, 46.

[190] Edgar I. Stewart, *Custer's Luck*, Norman, OK: University of Oklahoma Press, 1980, 349.

[191] Joseph M. Marshall, *The Day the World Ended at Little Bighorn: A Lakota History*, New York: Viking, 2003, 26.

[192] Richard A. Fox, *Archaeology, History, and Custer's Last Battle*, Norman, OK: University of Oklahoma Press, 1993, 45.

[193] Discussion with John Doerner, Chief Historian Little Bighorn of the Little Bighorn Battlefield National Monument, conducted at the battlefield archives, May 10-12, 2010.

[194] J.W. Vaughn, *Indian Fights: New Facts on Seven Encounters*, Norman, OK: University of Oklahoma Press, 1966, 146; James Donovan, *A Terrible Glory: Custer and the Little Bighorn – the Last Great Battle of the American West*, New York: Little, Brown and Company, 2008, 230; and William O. Taylor, *With Custer on the Little Bighorn*, New York: Viking, 1996, 37.

[195] Jean B. Gallenne, "The Fatal Day: A Soldier's Journal," St. Paul (MN) *Pioneer Press*, January 16, 1879.

[196] Joseph M. Marshall III, *The Day the World Ended at Little Bighorn: A Lakota History*, New York: Viking, 2003, 101.

[197] Bruce R. Liddic, *Vanishing Victory: Custer's Final March*, El Segundo, CA: Upton & Sons, Publishers, 2004, 61.

[198] Dennis Clark, "Private Roman Rutten: Custer's Tailor," 15th Annual Symposium, Custer Battlefield Historical & Museum Association, held at Hardin, MT on June 22, 2001, 36-37; and Kenneth Hammer, *Custer in '76: Walter Camp's Notes on the Custer Fight*, Provo, UT: Brigham Young University, 1976, 118.

[199] Walter M. Camp, "Field Notes," Lilly Library, Indiana University, Bloomington, IN., Box 2, Folder 11 – Little Bighorn, Part 3.

[200] Larry Sklenar, *To Hell with Honor; Custer and the Little Bighorn*, Norman, OK: University of Oklahoma Press, 2003, 174.

[201] Ronald H. Nichols, editor, *Men with Custer: Biographies of the 7th Cavalry*, Hardin, MT: Custer Battlefield Historical and Museum Association, 2000, 226-227. It was originally cited as coming from Daniel Newell in "The Story of the Bighorn Campaign of 1876," *The Sunshine Magazine*, September 1930.

[202] Ronald H. Nichols, editor, *Men with Custer: Biographies of the 7th Cavalry*, Hardin, MT: Custer Battlefield Historical and Museum Association, 2000, 335. It was originally cited in the *Billings (Montana) Gazette*, June 25, 1923.

[203] Ronald H. Nichols, editor, *Men with Custer: Biographies of the 7th Cavalry*, Hardin, MT: Custer Battlefield Historical and Museum Association, 2000, 335; Douglas D. Scott, P. Willey and Melissa A. Connor, *They Died with Custer: Soldiers Bones from the Battle of the Little Bighorn*, Norman, OK: University of Oklahoma Press, 287; and Roger L. Williams, *Military Register of Custer's Last Command*, Norman, OK: The Arthur H. Clark Company, 2009, 291.

[204] Garrison Orders No. 24, Headquarters, Fort Rice, Dakota Territory, dated July 28, 1875, Records Group 393, Records of U. S. Army Continental Commands, 1821-1920, Part V, Military Installations, Fort Rice, North Dakota, Entry 5.

[205] Melbourne C. Chandler, *Of Garry Owen in Glory: The History of the 7th Cavalry*, Annandale, VA: Turnpike Press, 1960, 69.

[206] Melbourne C. Chandler, *Of Garry Owen in Glory: The History of the 7th Cavalry*, Annandale, VA: Turnpike Press, 1960, 69.

[207] Ronald H. Nichols, editor, *Men with Custer: Biographies of the 7th Cavalry*, Hardin, MT: Custer Battlefield Historical and Museum Association, 2000, 305; Kenneth Hammer, *Custer in '76: Walter Camp's Notes on the Custer Fight*, Provo, UT: Brigham Young University, 1976, 141; Walter Mason Camp, *Walter M. Camp's Little Bighorn Rosters*, annotated by Richard G. Hardoff, Spokane, WA: Arthur H. Clark Company, 2002, 205; Special Orders No. 132, Headquarters, Fort Rice, Dakota Territory, dated October 8, 1875, Records Group 393, Records of U. S. Army Continental Commands, 1821-1920, Part V, Military Installations, Fort Rice, North Dakota, Entry 6; and Roger L. Williams, *Military Register of Custer's Last Command*, Norman, OK: The Arthur H. Clark Company, 2009, 273.

[208] Cyrus T. Brady, *Indian Fights and Fighters*, New York: Doubleday, Page & Company, 1909, 402. Morris' comments to Brady came in the form of a letter from Haven, Maine, and were dated September 21, 1904.

[209] Neil C. Mangum, editor, "Reno's Battalion in the Battle of the Little Big Horn," G*reasy Grass Magazine*, Volume 2, May 1986, Hardin, MT: Custer Battlefield Historical & Museum Association, 5.

[210] Sandy Barnard, editor, *Ten Years with Custer: A 7th Cavalryman's Memoirs*, Terre Haute, IN: AST Press, 2001, 293; and Larry Sklenar, *To Hell with Honor; Custer and the Little Bighorn*, Norman, OK: University of Oklahoma Press, 2003, 175.

[211] Richard A. Fox, *Archaeology, History, and Custer's Last Battle*, Norman, OK: University of Oklahoma Press, 1993, 43.

[212] Joe Poyer and Craig Riesch, *The .45-70 Springfield*, Tustin, CA: North Cape Publications, 2006, 118.

[213] J.W. Vaughn, *Indian Fights: New Facts on Seven Encounters*, Norman, OK: University of Oklahoma Press, 1966, 146.

[214] Dale Schoenberger, "Custer's Scouts," *Montana Western History*, Volume XVI, No. 2, Spring 1966, 44.

[215] Dale Schoenberger, "Custer's Scouts," *Montana Western History*, Volume XVI, No. 2, Spring 1966, 45.

[216] James Donovan, *A Terrible Glory: Custer and the Little Bighorn – the Last Great Battle of the American West*, New York: Little, Brown and Company, 2008, 232.

[217] "Official Transcript of the Court Martial of Captain Thomas H. French," Fort Abraham Lincoln, Dakota Territory, January 1879, page 161.

[218] Larry Sklenar, *To Hell with Honor; Custer and the Little Bighorn*, Norman, OK: University of Oklahoma Press, 2003, 174.

[219] C. Lee. Noyes, "The Valley Fight: The Enlisted Man's Perspective," 20th Annual Symposium, Custer Battlefield Historical & Museum Association, held at Hardin, MT on June 23, 2006, 52.

[220] Nathaniel Philbrick, *The Last Stand: Custer, Sitting Bull, and the Battle of the Little Bighorn*, New York: The Penguin Group, 2010, 178.

[221] Ronald H. Nichols, editor, *Men with Custer: Biographies of the 7th Cavalry*, Hardin, MT: Custer Battlefield Historical and Museum Association, 2000, 291; Roger L. Williams, *Military Register of Custer's Last Command*, Norman, OK: The Arthur H. Clark Company, 2009, 259; Walter Mason Camp, *Walter M. Camp's Little Bighorn Rosters*, annotated by Richard G. Hardoff, Spokane, WA: Arthur H. Clark Company, 2002, 204; and Garrison Orders No. 8, Headquarters, Fort Rice, Dakota Territory, dated April 24, 1875, Records Group 393, Records of U. S. Army Continental Commands, 1821-1920, Part V, Military Installations, Fort Rice, North Dakota, Entry 5.

[222] Kenneth Hammer, *Custer in '76: Walter Camp's Notes on the Custer Fight*, Provo, UT: Brigham Young University, 1976, 131.

[223] Ronald H. Nichols, editor, *Men with Custer: Biographies of the 7th Cavalry*, Hardin, MT: Custer Battlefield Historical and Museum Association, 2000, 235-236; Sandy Barnard, *Custer's First Sergeant John Ryan*, Terre Haute, IN: AST Press, 1996, 180; and Roger L. Williams, *Military Register of Custer's Last Command*, Norman, OK: The Arthur H. Clark Company, 2009, 222.

[224] Sandy Barnard, editor, *Ten Years with Custer: A 7th Cavalryman's Memoirs*, Terre Haute, IN: AST Press, 2001, 259-261; and Letter, Headquarters, Fort Rice, Dakota Territory to Assistant Adjutant General, Department of Dakota, dated March 4, 1876, Records Group 393, Records of U.S. Army Continental Commands, 1821-1920, Part V, Military Installations, Fort Rice, South Dakota, Entry 1.

[225] Post Orders No. 34, Headquarters, Fort Rice, Dakota Territory, dated April 5, 1876, Records Group 393, Records of U. S. Army Continental Commands, 1821-1920, Part V, Military Installations, Fort Rice, North Dakota, Entry 5.

[226] Walter Mason Camp, *Walter M. Camp's Little Bighorn Rosters*, annotated by Richard G. Hardoff, Spokane, WA: Arthur H. Clark Company, 2002, 202.

[227] Larry D. Underwood, *The Custer Fight: and Other Tales of the Old West*, Lincoln, NE: Media Publishing, 1989, 37-43; and Glendolin D. Wagner, *Old Neutriment*, New York: Sol Lewis, 1973, 234.

[228] Larry D. Underwood, *The Custer Fight: and Other Tales of the Old West*, Lincoln, NE: Media Publishing, 1989, 45.

[229] Kenneth Hammer, *Custer in '76: Walter Camp's Notes on the Custer Fight*, Provo, UT: Brigham Young University, 1976, 106. Observation was made later by Private Thomas F. O'Neill of Company G in an interview with Walter Camp in 1919.

[230] Don Rickey, Jr., *Forty Miles a Day on Beans and Hay*, Norman, OK: University of Oklahoma Press, 1972, 275, 288.

[231] Bruce R. Liddic, *Vanishing Victory: Custer's Final March*, El Segundo, CA: Upton & Sons, Publishers, 2004, 68 and 72.

[232] Edgar I. Stewart, *Custer's Luck*, Norman, OK: University of Oklahoma Press, 1980, 356; and Kenneth Hammer, *Custer in '76: Walter Camp's Notes on the Custer Fight*, Provo, UT: Brigham Young University, 1976, 222 and 232.

[233] Greg Michno, "Battle of Little Bighorn: Were the Weapons the Deciding Factor?" *Wild West*, Leesburg, VA: Weider History Group, June 1998.

[234] Kenneth Hammer, *Custer in '76: Walter Camp's Notes on the Custer Fight*, Provo, UT: Brigham Young University, 1976, 143; and Larry Sklenar, *To Hell with Honor; Custer and the Little Bighorn*, Norman, OK: University of Oklahoma Press, 2003, 177.

[235] John Carroll, editor, *A Seventh Cavalry Scrapbook*, Volume 1, "Memories of the Battle of the Little Big Horn," by Daniel Newell, Bryan, TX: Privately Published, 1978, 19.

[236] Larry Sklenar, *To Hell with Honor; Custer and the Little Bighorn*, Norman, OK: University of Oklahoma Press, 2003, 184-185, 240; and Bruce R. Liddic, *Vanishing Victory: Custer's Final March*, El Segundo, CA: Upton & Sons, Publishers, 2004, 73.

[237] Kenneth Hammer, *Custer in '76: Walter Camp's Notes on the Custer Fight*, Provo, UT: Brigham Young University, 1976, 107, 118, 143; and Larry D. Underwood, *The Custer Fight: and Other Tales of the Old West*, Lincoln, NE: Media Publishing, 1989, 43.

[238] Gregory F. Michno, *Lakota Noon: The Indian Narrative of Custer's Defeat*, Missoula, MT: Mountain Press Publishing Company, 2007, 41, 73.

[239] Thomas B. Marquis, *Keep the Last Bullet for Yourself*, Algonac, MI: Reference Publications, 1985, 132.

[240] Alexander Rose, *American Rifle: A Biography*, New York: Delacorte Press, 2008, 175.

[241] Richard Hook, *Warriors at the Little Bighorn 1876*, Osprey Men at Arms Series #408, Oxford, England: Osprey Publishing, 2004, 11; and Douglas C. McChristian, *The U.S. Army in the West: 1870-1880*, Norman, OK: University of Oklahoma Press, 1995, 32-33.

[242] Robert J. Kershaw, *Red Sabbath: The Battle of Little Bighorn*, Surrey, England: Ian Allan Publishing, 2005, 142; and Joseph M. Marshall, *The Day the World Ended at Little Bighorn: A Lakota History*, New York: Viking, 2003, 29.

[243] Thomas B. Marquis, *Keep the Last Bullet for Yourself*, Algonac, MI: Reference Publications, 1985, 137.

[244] Reginald and Gladys Laubin, *American Indian Archery*, Norman, OK: University of Oklahoma Press, 1980, 6-7, 115-116.

[245] Richard Hook, *Warriors at the Little Bighorn 1876*, Osprey Men at Arms Series #408, Oxford, England: Osprey Publishing, 2004, 12.

[246] Reginald and Gladys Laubin, *American Indian Archery*, Norman, OK: University of Oklahoma Press, 1980, 142.

[247] C. Lee Noyes, "Was There A Timber Fight?" Indianapolis, IN: Indianapolis Little Bighorn Symposium, September 12, 2009.

[248] Edgar I. Stewart, *Custer's Luck*, Norman, OK: University of Oklahoma Press, 1980, 356; and Bruce R. Liddic, *Vanishing Victory: Custer's Final March*, El Segundo, CA: Upton & Sons, Publishers, 2004, 72.

[249] J.W. Vaughn, *Indian Fights: New Facts on Seven Encounters*, Norman, OK: University of Oklahoma Press, 1966, 147.

[250] James Donovan, *A Terrible Glory: Custer and the Little Bighorn – the Last Great Battle of the American West*, New York: Little, Brown and Company, 2008, 236.

[251] James Donovan, *A Terrible Glory: Custer and the Little Bighorn – the Last Great Battle of the American West*, New York: Little, Brown and Company, 2008, 236.

[252] Barry Johnson, *A Captain of Chivalric Courage: Thomas H. French, 7th Cavalry*, The Brand Book, Vol. 25, Numbers 1&2, London: The English Westerners' Society, 1987, 16. Moore's comments were made at the court-martial of Captain French in January 1879.

[253] Ronald H. Nichols, editor, *Men with Custer: Biographies of the 7th Cavalry*, Hardin, MT: Custer Battlefield Historical and Museum Association, 2000, 234; Douglas D. Scott, P. Willey and Melissa A. Connor, *They Died with Custer: Soldiers Bones from the Battle of the Little Bighorn*, Norman, OK: University of Oklahoma Press, 288; and Roger L. Williams, *Military Register of Custer's Last Command*, Norman, OK: The Arthur H. Clark Company, 2009, 221.

[254] Bruce R. Liddic, *Vanishing Victory: Custer's Final March*, El Segundo, CA: Upton & Sons, Publishers, 2004, 73.

[255] John Carroll, editor, *A Seventh Cavalry Scrapbook*, Volume 1, "Memories of the Battle of the Little Big Horn," by Daniel Newell, Bryan, TX: Privately Published, 1978, 20.

[256] James Donovan, *A Terrible Glory: Custer and the Little Bighorn – the Last Great Battle of the American West*, New York: Little, Brown and Company, 2008, 235-236.

[257] Larry Sklenar, *To Hell with Honor; Custer and the Little Bighorn*, Norman, OK: University of Oklahoma Press, 2003, 182, 184.

[258] Bruce R. Liddic, *Vanishing Victory: Custer's Final March*, El Segundo, CA: Upton & Sons, Publishers, 2004, 73.

[259] James Donovan, *A Terrible Glory: Custer and the Little Bighorn – the Last Great Battle of the American West*, New York: Little, Brown and Company, 2008, 237.

[260] C. Lee Noyes, "Was There A Timber Fight?" Indianapolis, IN: Indianapolis Little Bighorn Symposium, September 12, 2009.

[261] Bruce R. Liddic, *Vanishing Victory: Custer's Final March*, El Segundo, CA: Upton & Sons, Publishers, 2004, 73.

[262] *The Teepee Book, A Monthly Periodical*, Reprint of Volume 2, #4 (April 1916) to Volume 2, #12 (December 1916), New York: Sol Lewis, 1974, Part 2:580.

[263] "Official Transcript of the Court Martial of Captain Thomas H. French," Fort Abraham Lincoln, Dakota Territory, January 1879, page 161.

[264] Richard G. Hardorff, *Cheyenne Memories of the Custer Fight*, Lincoln, NE: University of Nebraska Press (Bison Press), 1998, 46.

[265] Nathaniel Philbrick, *The Last Stand: Custer, Sitting Bull, and the Battle of the Little Bighorn*, New York: The Penguin Group, 2010, 184 and 186.

[266] Larry Sklenar, *To Hell with Honor; Custer and the Little Bighorn*, Norman, OK: University of Oklahoma Press, 2003, 244.

[267] Sandy Barnard, editor, *Ten Years with Custer: A 7th Cavalryman's Memoirs*, Terre Haute, IN: AST Press, 2001, 293.

[268] Evan S. Connell, *Son of the Morning Star: Custer and the Little Bighorn*, San Francisco, CA: North Point Press, 1984, 8.

[269] Ronald H. Nichols, editor, *Men with Custer: Biographies of the 7th Cavalry*, Hardin, MT: Custer Battlefield Historical and Museum Association, 2000, 198; and Roger L. Williams, *Military Register of Custer's Last Command*, Norman, OK: The Arthur H. Clark Company, 2009, 192.

[270] Post Orders No. 14, Headquarters, Fort Rice, Dakota Territory, dated February 6, 1876, Records Group 393, Records of U. S. Army Continental Commands, 1821-1920, Part V, Military Installations, Fort Rice, North Dakota, Entry 6.

[271] John Gray, *Centennial Campaign: The Sioux War of 1876*, Fort Collins, CO: The Old Army Press, 1976, 276.

[272] L.G. Walker, Jr., *Dr. Henry R. Porter: The Surgeon Who Survived Little Bighorn*, Jefferson, NC: McFarland & Company, Inc., 2008, 56.

[273] C. Lee. Noyes, "The Valley Fight: The Enlisted Man's Perspective," 20th Annual Symposium, Custer Battlefield Historical & Museum Association, held at Hardin, MT on June 23, 2006, 38.

[274] Bruce R. Liddic, *Vanishing Victory: Custer's Final March*, El Segundo, CA: Upton & Sons, Publishers, 2004, 75.

[275] C. Lee. Noyes, "The Valley Fight: The Enlisted Man's Perspective," 20th Annual Symposium, Custer Battlefield Historical & Museum Association, held at Hardin, MT on June 23, 2006, 40.

[276] Bruce R. Liddic, *Vanishing Victory: Custer's Final March*, El Segundo, CA: Upton & Sons, Publishers, 2004, 76; and Richard Collin, "Custer's Favorite Scout," *Greasy Grass Magazine*, Volume 13, May 1997, Hardin, MT: Custer Battlefield Historical & Museum Association, 8.

[277] Larry D. Underwood, *The Custer Fight: and Other Tales of the Old West*, Lincoln, NE: Media Publishing, 1989, 46.

[278] John Carroll, editor, *A Seventh Cavalry Scrapbook*, Volume 1, "Memories of the Battle of the Little Big Horn," by Daniel Newell, Bryan, TX: Privately Published, 1978, 20.

[279] John Carroll, editor, *A Seventh Cavalry Scrapbook*, Volume 1, "Memories of the Battle of the Little Big Horn," by Daniel Newell, Bryan, TX: Privately Published, 1978, 20; and John Carroll, *The Sunshine Magazine Articles*, Bryan, TX: Privately Published, 1979, 10.

[280] Gregory F. Michno, *Lakota Noon: The Indian Narrative of Custer's Defeat*, Missoula, MT: Mountain Press Publishing Company, 2007, 87.

[281] Email discussions with Brian Spatola, Collections Manager, Anatomical Division and Michael Rhode, Archivist, Otis Historical Archives, National Museum of Health and Medicine, Armed Forces Institute of Pathology, concerning the medical aspects of the death of Private Frank Braun of Company M, November 2009.

[282] Ronald H. Nichols, editor, *Men with Custer: Biographies of the 7th Cavalry*, Hardin, MT: Custer Battlefield Historical and Museum Association, 2000, 33; Roger L. Williams, *Military Register of Custer's Last Command*, Norman, OK: The Arthur H. Clark Company, 2009, 46; and National Archives and Records Administration, Washington, D.C., Records Group 94, Records of the Adjutant General's Office – Army, Carded Medical Records Regular Army, 1821-1884, Entry 529 (Unit 7), Frank Braun (Brown) – Box 398 (Blush-Brown, J.).

[283] Earle Alonzo Brininstool, *Troopers with Custer: Incidents of the Battle of the Little Big Horn*, Harrisburg, PA: The Stackpole Company, 1952, 51. The 7th Cavalry survivors found the body of Henry Klotzbucher after the battle; he apparently had not been discovered by the Indians and his body was not mutilated.

[284] James Donovan, *A Terrible Glory: Custer and the Little Bighorn – the Last Great Battle of the American West*, New York: Little, Brown and Company, 2008, 241.

[285] Don Rickey, Jr., *Forty Miles a Day on Beans and Hay*, Norman, OK: University of Oklahoma Press, 1972, 325.

[286] Ronald H. Nichols, editor, *Men with Custer: Biographies of the 7th Cavalry*, Hardin, MT: Custer Battlefield Historical and Museum Association, 2000, 182; Don Rickey, Jr., *Forty Miles a Day on Beans and Hay*, Norman, OK: University of Oklahoma Press, 1972, 71; and Roger L. Williams, *Military Register of Custer's Last Command*, Norman, OK: The Arthur H. Clark Company, 2009, 179.

[287] Douglas D. Scott, P. Willey and Melissa A. Connor, *They Died with Custer: Soldiers Bones from the Battle of the Little Bighorn*, Norman, OK: University of Oklahoma Press, 287; Larry Sklenar, *To Hell with Honor; Custer and the Little Bighorn*, Norman, OK: University of Oklahoma Press, 2003, 65; Jeremy Agnew, *Life of a Soldier on the Western Frontier*, Missoula, MT: Mountain Press Publishing Company, 2008, 151; Roger L. Williams, *Military Register of Custer's Last Command*, Norman, OK: The Arthur H. Clark Company, 2009, 179; and National Archives and Records Administration, Washington, D.C., Records Group 94, Records of the Adjutant General's Office – Army, Carded Medical Records Regular Army, 1821-1884, Entry 529 (Unit 7), Henry Klotzbucher – Box 411 (Keogh-Lawrence).

[288] Post Orders No. 31, Headquarters, Fort Rice, Dakota Territory, dated March 31, 1876, Records Group 393, Records of U. S. Army Continental Commands, 1821-1920, Part V, Military Installations, Fort Rice, North Dakota, Entry 6.

[289] National Archives and Records Administration, Washington, D.C., Records Group 94, Records of the Adjutant General's Office – Army, Carded Medical Records Regular Army, 1821-1884, Entry 529 (Unit 7), Frank Neely – Box 411 (L. Moore-Neilson).

[290] Ronald H. Nichols, editor, *Men with Custer: Biographies of the 7th Cavalry*, Hardin, MT: Custer Battlefield Historical and Museum Association, 2000, 244; Sandy Barnard, editor, *Ten Years with Custer: A 7th Cavalryman's Memoirs*, Terre Haute, IN: AST Press, 2001, 130; and Roger L. Williams, *Military Register of Custer's Last Command*, Norman, OK: The Arthur H. Clark Company, 2009, 232; and Muster Rolls – 7th U.S. Cavalry, Company L-M, 1866-1884, Company M Muster Roll dated June 30, 1873 and December 31, 1873, Microfilm Roll #5 at the Little Bighorn National Monument Archive.

[291] Douglas D. Scott, P. Willey and Melissa A. Connor, *They Died with Custer: Soldiers Bones from the Battle of the Little Bighorn*, Norman, OK: University of Oklahoma Press, 288; and Roger L. Williams, *Military Register of Custer's Last Command*, Norman, OK: The Arthur H. Clark Company, 2009, 232.

[292] C. Lee Noyes, "Was There A Timber Fight?" Indianapolis, IN: Indianapolis Little Bighorn Symposium, September 12, 2009.

[293] C. Lee Noyes, "Was There A Timber Fight?" Indianapolis, IN: Indianapolis Little Bighorn Symposium, September 12, 2009; and Nathaniel Philbrick, *The Last Stand: Custer, Sitting Bull, and the Battle of the Little Bighorn*, New York: The Penguin Group, 2010, 191.

[294] Gregory F. Michno, *Lakota Noon: The Indian Narrative of Custer's Defeat*, Missoula, MT: Mountain Press Publishing Company, 2007, 25, 81.

[295] Gregory F. Michno, *Lakota Noon: The Indian Narrative of Custer's Defeat*, Missoula, MT: Mountain Press Publishing Company, 2007, 24.

[296] Colonel W.A. Graham, *The Custer Myth: A Source Book of Custeriana*, Mechanicsburg, PA: Stackpole Books, 2000, 341.

[297] Larry Sklenar, *To Hell with Honor; Custer and the Little Bighorn*, Norman, OK: University of Oklahoma Press, 2003, 253.

[298] Thomas B. Marquis, *A Warrior Who Fought Custer*, Minneapolis, MN: The Midwest Company, 1931, 221; and Gregory F. Michno, *Lakota Noon: The Indian Narrative of Custer's Defeat*, Missoula, MT: Mountain Press Publishing Company, 2007, 35.

[299] C. Lee. Noyes, "The Valley Fight: The Enlisted Man's Perspective," 20th Annual Symposium, Custer Battlefield Historical & Museum Association, held at Hardin, MT on June 23, 2006, 52.

[300] "Official Transcript of the Court Martial of Captain Thomas H. French," Fort Abraham Lincoln, Dakota Territory, January 1879, 161-162.

[301] Edgar I. Stewart, *Custer's Luck*, Norman, OK: University of Oklahoma Press, 1980, 367.

[302] Ronald H. Nichols, editor, *Men with Custer: Biographies of the 7th Cavalry*, Hardin, MT: Custer Battlefield Historical and Museum Association, 2000, 58, 245. It was originally cited as coming from Daniel Newell in "The Story of the Bighorn Campaign of 1876," *The Sunshine Magazine*, September 1930. Cody's body was later found severely mutilated. Information on Newell's shooting came from, C. Lee Noyes, "Was There A Timber Fight?" Indianapolis, IN: Indianapolis Little Bighorn Symposium, September 12, 2009.

[303] Walter M. Camp, "Field Notes," Lilly Library, Indiana University, Bloomington, IN., Box 6, Folder 7, Envelope 82 – Includes recollections of William Morris.

[304] Walter M. Camp, "Field Notes," Lilly Library, Indiana University, Bloomington, IN., Box 6, Folder 7, Envelope 82 – Includes recollections of William Morris.

[305] Larry Sklenar, *To Hell with Honor; Custer and the Little Bighorn*, Norman, OK: University of Oklahoma Press, 2003, 252.

[306] John Carroll, editor, *A Seventh Cavalry Scrapbook*, Volume 1, "Memories of the Battle of the Little Big Horn," by Daniel Newell, Bryan, TX: Privately Published, 1978, 20; and John Carroll, *The Sunshine Magazine Articles*, Bryan, TX: Privately Published, 1979, 11.

[307] Ronald H. Nichols, editor, *Men with Custer: Biographies of the 7th Cavalry*, Hardin, MT: Custer Battlefield Historical and Museum Association, 2000, 291; and Richard G. Hardorff, editor, *On the Little Bighorn with Walter Camp; A Collection of Walter Mason Camp's Letters, Notes and opinions on Custer's Last Fight*, El Segundo, CA: Upton & Sons Publishers, 2002, 192.

[308] Jean B. Gallenne, "The Fatal Day: A Soldier's Journal," St. Paul (MN) *Pioneer Press*, January 16, 1879.

[309] National Archives and Records Administration, Washington, D.C., Records Group 94, Records of the Adjutant General's Office – Army, Carded Medical Records Regular Army, 1821-1884, Entry 529 (Unit 7), Daniel Newell – Box 417 (Nelau-O'Sullivan).

[310] Ronald H. Nichols, editor, *Men with Custer: Biographies of the 7th Cavalry*, Hardin, MT: Custer Battlefield Historical and Museum Association, 2000, 245; and John Carroll, editor, *A Seventh Cavalry Scrapbook*, Volume 1, "Memories of the Battle of the Little Big Horn," by Daniel Newell, Bryan, TX: Privately Published, 1978, 20.

[311] Douglas D. Scott, P. Willey and Melissa A. Connor, *They Died with Custer: Soldiers Bones from the Battle of the Little Bighorn*, Norman, OK: University of Oklahoma Press, 288; Roger L. Williams, *Military Register of Custer's Last Command*, Norman, OK: The Arthur H. Clark Company, 2009, 233; and National Archives and Records Administration, Washington, D.C., Records Group 94, Records of the Adjutant General's Office – Army, Carded Medical Records Regular Army, 1821-1884, Entry 529 (Unit 7), Daniel Newell – Box 417 (Nelau-O'Sullivan).

[312] Garrison Orders No. 17, Headquarters, Fort Rice, Dakota Territory, dated June 6, 1875, Records Group 393, Records of U. S. Army Continental Commands, 1821-1920, Part V, Military Installations, Fort Rice, North Dakota, Entry 5.

[313] Garrison Orders No. 18, Headquarters, Fort Rice, Dakota Territory, dated June 12, 1875, Records Group 393, Records of U. S. Army Continental Commands, 1821-1920, Part V, Military Installations, Fort Rice, North Dakota, Entry 5.

[314] Roger L. Williams, *Military Register of Custer's Last Command*, Norman, OK: The Arthur H. Clark Company, 2009, 211.

[315] Ronald H. Nichols, editor, *Men with Custer: Biographies of the 7th Cavalry*, Hardin, MT: Custer Battlefield Historical and Museum Association, 2000, 203; Roger L. Williams, *Military Register of Custer's Last Command*, Norman, OK: The Arthur H. Clark Company, 2009, 211; and Walter Mason Camp, *Walter M. Camp's Little Bighorn Rosters*, annotated by Richard G. Hardoff, Spokane, WA: Arthur H. Clark Company, 2002, 201.

[316] Ronald H. Nichols, editor, *Men with Custer: Biographies of the 7th Cavalry*, Hardin, MT: Custer Battlefield Historical and Museum Association, 2000, 319, 324; and Roger L. Williams, *Military Register of Custer's Last Command*, Norman, OK: The Arthur H. Clark Company, 2009, 281.

[317] Kenneth Hammer, *Custer in '76: Walter Camp's Notes on the Custer Fight*, Provo, UT: Brigham Young University, 1976, 66.

[318] Nathaniel Philbrick, *The Last Stand: Custer, Sitting Bull, and the Battle of the Little Bighorn*, New York: The Penguin Group, 2010, 192.

[319] Bruce R. Liddic, *Vanishing Victory: Custer's Final March*, El Segundo, CA: Upton & Sons, Publishers, 2004, 94.

[320] Kenneth Hammer, *Custer in '76: Walter Camp's Notes on the Custer Fight*, Provo, UT: Brigham Young University, 1976, 141; and Richard G. Hardorff, editor, *On the Little Bighorn with Walter Camp; A Collection of Walter Mason Camp's Letters, Notes and opinions on Custer's Last Fight*, El Segundo, CA: Upton & Sons Publishers, 2002, 19.

[321] Cyrus T. Brady, *Indian Fights and Fighters*, New York: Doubleday, Page & Company, 1909, 403. Morris' comments to Brady came in the form of a letter from Haven, Maine, and were dated September 21, 1904.

[322] *The Teepee Book, A Monthly Periodical*, Reprint of Volume 2, #4 (April 1916) to Volume 2, #12 (December 1916), New York: Sol Lewis, 1974, Part 2:580.

[323] Kenneth Hammer, *Custer in '76: Walter Camp's Notes on the Custer Fight*, Provo, UT: Brigham Young University, 1976, 224-225.

[324] Kenneth Hammer, *Custer in '76: Walter Camp's Notes on the Custer Fight*, Provo, UT: Brigham Young University, 1976, 225.

[325] Ronald H. Nichols, editor, *Men with Custer: Biographies of the 7th Cavalry*, Hardin, MT: Custer Battlefield Historical and Museum Association, 2000, 262; and Roger L. Williams, *Military Register of Custer's Last Command*, Norman, OK: The Arthur H. Clark Company, 2009, 215.

[326] Douglas D. Scott, P. Willey and Melissa A. Connor, *They Died with Custer: Soldiers Bones from the Battle of the Little Bighorn*, Norman, OK: University of Oklahoma Press, 288, 289; and John Carroll, *Ten Years with Custer Among the American Indians and Other Writings by John Ryan*, Bryan, TX: Privately Published, 1980, 196.

[327] Ronald H. Nichols, editor, *Men with Custer: Biographies of the 7th Cavalry*, Hardin, MT: Custer Battlefield Historical and Museum Association, 2000, 262; Robert Earle Forrest, "Fighting with Custer: Two Men Who Were with Gallant General Custer at Little Bighorn Battle Are Still Living," *Morning Observer*, Washington, PA: October 1932; and Roger L. Williams, *Military Register of Custer's Last Command*, Norman, OK: The Arthur H. Clark Company, 2009, 243.

[328] Robert Earle Forrest, "Fighting with Custer: Two Men Who Were with Gallant General Custer at Little Bighorn Battle Are Still Living," *Morning Observer*, Washington, PA: October 1932.

[329] Bruce R. Liddic, *Vanishing Victory: Custer's Final March*, El Segundo, CA: Upton & Sons, Publishers, 2004, 78.

[330] Kenneth Hammer, *Custer in '76: Walter Camp's Notes on the Custer Fight*, Provo, UT: Brigham Young University, 1976, 119; and Dennis Clark, "Private Roman Rutten: Custer's Tailor," 15th Annual Symposium, Custer Battlefield Historical & Museum Association, held at Hardin, MT on June 22, 2001, 36-37.

[331] Kenneth Hammer, *Custer in '76: Walter Camp's Notes on the Custer Fight*, Provo, UT: Brigham Young University, 1976, 119; and Don Rickey, Jr., *Forty Miles a Day on Beans and Hay*, Norman, OK: University of Oklahoma Press, 1972, 316.

[332] Larry Sklenar, *To Hell with Honor; Custer and the Little Bighorn*, Norman, OK: University of Oklahoma Press, 2003, 252; and Walter M. Camp, "Field Notes," Lilly Library, Indiana University, Bloomington, IN., Box 2, Folder 11 – Little Bighorn, Part 3.

[333] Larry Sklenar, *To Hell with Honor; Custer and the Little Bighorn*, Norman, OK: University of Oklahoma Press, 2003, 254; and James Donovan, *A Terrible Glory: Custer and the Little Bighorn – the Last Great Battle of the American West*, New York: Little, Brown and Company, 2008, 240.

[334] Dennis Clark, "Private Roman Rutten: Custer's Tailor," 15th Annual Symposium, Custer Battlefield Historical & Museum Association, held at Hardin, MT on June 22, 2001, 33.

[335] National Archives and Records Administration, Washington, D.C., Records Group 94, Records of the Adjutant General's Office – Army, Carded Medical Records Regular Army, 1821-1884, Entry 529 (Unit 7), Roman Rutten – Box 420 (Roeder-Schneider).

[336] Ronald H. Nichols, editor, *Men with Custer: Biographies of the 7th Cavalry*, Hardin, MT: Custer Battlefield Historical and Museum Association, 2000, 287-288; Dennis Clark, "Private Roman Rutten: Custer's Tailor," 15th Annual Symposium, Custer Battlefield Historical & Museum Association, held at Hardin, MT on June 22, 2001, 33-34; Larry Sklenar, *To Hell with Honor; Custer and the Little Bighorn*, Norman, OK: University of Oklahoma Press, 2003, 63; and Roger L. Williams, *Military Register of Custer's Last Command*, Norman, OK: The Arthur H. Clark Company, 2009, 257.

[337] Jeremy Agnew, *Life of a Soldier on the Western Frontier*, Missoula, MT: Mountain Press Publishing Company, 2008, 122.

[338] Larry Sklenar, *To Hell with Honor; Custer and the Little Bighorn*, Norman, OK: University of Oklahoma Press, 2003, 255; and Kenneth Hammer, *Custer in '76: Walter Camp's Notes on the Custer Fight*, Provo, UT: Brigham Young University, 1976, 119.

[339] James Donovan, *A Terrible Glory: Custer and the Little Bighorn – the Last Great Battle of the American West*, New York: Little, Brown and Company, 2008, 245-246.

[340] Evan S. Connell, *Son of the Morning Star: Custer and the Little Bighorn*, San Francisco, CA: North Point Press, 1984, 5.

[341] Cyrus T. Brady, *Indian Fights and Fighters*, New York: Doubleday, Page & Company, 1909, 405. Morris' comments to

Brady came in the form of a letter from Haven, Maine, and were dated September 21, 1904.

[342] Committee in Charge of the Commemoration Exercises Fifty Years Later, *The Teepee Book*, Sheridan, WY: The Miles Company, 1926, 47.

[343] Bruce R. Liddic, *Vanishing Victory: Custer's Final March*, El Segundo, CA: Upton & Sons, Publishers, 2004, 94 and 128.

[344] Edgar I. Stewart, *Custer's Luck*, Norman, OK: University of Oklahoma Press, 1980, 372.

[345] Bruce R. Liddic, *Vanishing Victory: Custer's Final March*, El Segundo, CA: Upton & Sons, Publishers, 2004, 95; and Thomas B. Marquis, *Keep the Last Bullet for Yourself*, Algonac, MI: Reference Publications, 1985, 112.

[346] Ronald H. Nichols, editor, *Men with Custer: Biographies of the 7th Cavalry*, Hardin, MT: Custer Battlefield Historical and Museum Association, 2000, 77-78; and Roger L. Williams, *Military Register of Custer's Last Command*, Norman, OK: The Arthur H. Clark Company, 2009, 105.

[347] Cyrus T. Brady, *Indian Fights and Fighters*, New York: Doubleday, Page & Company, 1909, 403; and Nathaniel Philbrick, *The Last Stand: Custer, Sitting Bull, and the Battle of the Little Bighorn*, New York: The Penguin Group, 2010, 195. Morris' comments to Brady came in the form of a letter from Haven, Maine, and were dated September 21, 1904.

[348] Walter Mason Camp, *Walter M. Camp's Little Bighorn Rosters*, annotated by Richard G. Hardoff, Spokane, WA: Arthur H. Clark Company, 2002, 212.

[349] Garrison Orders No. 3, Headquarters, Fort Rice, Dakota Territory, dated January 25, 1876, Records Group 393, Records of U. S. Army Continental Commands, 1821-1920, Part V, Military Installations, Fort Rice, North Dakota, Entry 5.

[350] Ronald H. Nichols, editor, *Men with Custer: Biographies of the 7th Cavalry*, Hardin, MT: Custer Battlefield Historical and Museum Association, 2000, 291.

[351] Earle Alonzo Brininstool, *Troopers with Custer: Incidents of the Battle of the Little Big Horn*, Harrisburg, PA: The Stackpole Company, 1952, 52.

[352] James Donovan, *A Terrible Glory: Custer and the Little Bighorn – the Last Great Battle of the American West*, New York: Little, Brown and Company, 2008, 245.

[353] Sandy Barnard, editor, *Ten Years with Custer: A 7th Cavalryman's Memoirs*, Terre Haute, IN: AST Press, 2001, 161.

[354] Robert Earle Forrest, "Fighting with Custer: Two Men Who Were with Gallant General Custer at Little Bighorn Battle Are Still Living," *Morning Observer*, Washington, PA: October 1932.

[355] Ronald H. Nichols, editor, *Men with Custer: Biographies of the 7th Cavalry*, Hardin, MT: Custer Battlefield Historical and Museum Association, 2000, 226-227. It was originally cited as coming from Daniel Newell in "The Story of the Bighorn Campaign of 1876," *The Sunshine Magazine*, September 1930.

[356] Orin G. Libby, editor, *The Arikara Narrative of Custer's Campaign and the Battle of the Little Bighorn*, Norman, OK: University of Oklahoma Press, 1998, 124.

[357] Kenneth Hammer, *Custer in '76: Walter Camp's Notes on the Custer Fight*, Provo, UT: Brigham Young University, 1976, 143.

[358] Robert Earle Forrest, "Fighting with Custer: Two Men Who Were with Gallant General Custer at Little Bighorn Battle Are Still Living," *Morning Observer*, Washington, PA: October 6, 1932.

[359] Garrison Orders No. 2, Headquarters, Fort Rice, Dakota Territory, dated January 16, 1876, Records Group 393, Records of U. S. Army Continental Commands, 1821-1920, Part V, Military Installations, Fort Rice, North Dakota, Entry 5.

[360] Ronald H. Nichols, editor, *Men with Custer: Biographies of the 7th Cavalry*, Hardin, MT: Custer Battlefield Historical and Museum Association, 2000, 229; Sandy Barnard, editor, *Ten Years with Custer: A 7th Cavalryman's Memoirs*, Terre Haute, IN: AST Press, 2001, 193; Roger L. Williams, *Military Register of Custer's Last Command*, Norman, OK: The Arthur H. Clark Company, 2009, 217; and Dr. Kenneth Hammer Special Collection at the University of Wisconsin-Whitewater Library, Box 2, Miscellaneous Papers, "Custer's Pittsburg Followers," *The Pittsburg Leader*, July 8, 1876, reprint.

[361] Bruce R. Liddic, *Vanishing Victory: Custer's Final March*, El Segundo, CA: Upton & Sons, Publishers, 2004, 95.

[362] Edgar I. Stewart, *Custer's Luck*, Norman, OK: University of Oklahoma Press, 1980, 377.

[363] Bruce R. Liddic, *Vanishing Victory: Custer's Final March*, El Segundo, CA: Upton & Sons, Publishers, 2004, 96.

[364] Ronald H. Nichols, editor, *Men with Custer: Biographies of the 7th Cavalry*, Hardin, MT: Custer Battlefield Historical and Museum Association, 2000, 126, 229, 235; and Nathaniel Philbrick, *The Last Stand: Custer, Sitting Bull, and the Battle of the Little Bighorn*, New York: The Penguin Group, 2010, 194-195.

[365] Don Rickey, Jr., *Forty Miles a Day on Beans and Hay*, Norman, OK: University of Oklahoma Press, 1972, 299; and James Donovan, *A Terrible Glory: Custer and the Little Bighorn – the Last Great Battle of the American West*, New York: Little, Brown and Company, 2008, 247.

[366] Thomas Goodrich, *Scalp Dance: Indian Warfare on the High Plains, 1865-1879*, Mechanicsburg, PA: Stackpole Books, 1997, 246.

[367] Ronald H. Nichols, editor, *Men with Custer: Biographies of the 7th Cavalry*, Hardin, MT: Custer Battlefield Historical and Museum Association, 2000, 126; and Roger L. Williams, *Military Register of Custer's Last Command*, Norman, OK: The Arthur H. Clark Company, 2009, 138.

[368] Nathaniel Philbrick, *The Last Stand: Custer, Sitting Bull, and the Battle of the Little Bighorn*, New York: The Penguin Group, 2010, 195.

[369] William O. Taylor, *With Custer on the Little Bighorn*, New York: Viking, 1996, 42-44.

[370] Nathaniel Philbrick, *The Last Stand: Custer, Sitting Bull, and the Battle of the Little Bighorn*, New York: The Penguin Group, 2010, 377.

[371] Walter M. Camp, "Field Notes," Lilly Library, Indiana University, Bloomington, IN., Box 2, Folder 9 – Little Bighorn, Part 1.

[372] Earle Alonzo Brininstool, *Troopers with Custer: Incidents of the Battle of the Little Big Horn*, Harrisburg, PA: The Stackpole Company, 1952, 52.

[373] Walter M. Camp, "Field Notes," Lilly Library, Indiana University, Bloomington, IN., Box 2, Folder 11 – Little Bighorn, Part 3.

[374] Bill Yenne, *Indian Wars: The Campaign for the American West*, Yardley, PA: Westholme Publishing, 2006, 200.

[375] Larry Sklenar, *To Hell with Honor; Custer and the Little Bighorn*, Norman, OK: University of Oklahoma Press, 2003, 299.

[376] William O. Taylor, *With Custer on the Little Bighorn*, New York: Viking, 1996, 48.

[377] Larry Sklenar, *To Hell with Honor; Custer and the Little Bighorn*, Norman, OK: University of Oklahoma Press, 2003, 296-297; and James Donovan, *A Terrible Glory: Custer and the Little Bighorn – the Last Great Battle of the American West*, New York: Little, Brown and Company, 2008, 259.

[378] *The Teepee Book, A Monthly Periodical*, Reprint of Volume 2, #4 (April 1916) to Volume 2, #12 (December 1916), New York: Sol Lewis, 1974, Part 2:581.

[379] Richard G. Hardorff, *Hokahey! A Good Day to Die!* Lincoln, NE: University of Nebraska Press, 1999, 52.

[380] Richard G. Hardorff, *Hokahey! A Good Day to Die!* Lincoln, NE: University of Nebraska Press, 1999, 52.

[381] Nathaniel Philbrick, *The Last Stand: Custer, Sitting Bull, and the Battle of the Little Bighorn*, New York: The Penguin Group, 2010, 200.

[382] Jean B. Gallenne, "The Fatal Day: A Soldier's Journal," St. Paul (MN) *Pioneer Press*, January 16, 1879.

[383] Larry Sklenar, *To Hell with Honor; Custer and the Little Bighorn*, Norman, OK: University of Oklahoma Press, 2003, 296-297; and James Donovan, *A Terrible Glory: Custer and the Little Bighorn – the Last Great Battle of the American West*, New York: Little, Brown and Company, 2008, 259.

[384] Barry Johnson, *A Captain of Chivalric Courage: Thomas H. French, 7th Cavalry*, The Brand Book, Vol. 25, Numbers 1&2, London: The English Westerners' Society, 1987, 14.

[385] Bruce R. Liddic, *Vanishing Victory: Custer's Final March*, El Segundo, CA: Upton & Sons, Publishers, 2004, 129.

[386] Bruce R. Liddic, *Vanishing Victory: Custer's Final March*, El Segundo, CA: Upton & Sons, Publishers, 2004, 167.

[387] Larry Sklenar, *To Hell with Honor; Custer and the Little Bighorn*, Norman, OK: University of Oklahoma Press, 2003, 301.

[388] Larry Sklenar, *To Hell with Honor; Custer and the Little Bighorn*, Norman, OK: University of Oklahoma Press, 2003, 307.

[389] Kenneth Hammer, *Custer in '76: Walter Camp's Notes on the Custer Fight*, Provo, UT: Brigham Young University, 1976, 56; James Donovan, *A Terrible Glory: Custer and the Little Bighorn – the Last Great Battle of the American West*, New York: Little, Brown and Company, 2008, 279; and Bruce R. Liddic, *Vanishing Victory: Custer's Final March*, El Segundo, CA: Upton & Sons, Publishers, 2004, 129.

[390] Larry Sklenar, *To Hell with Honor; Custer and the Little Bighorn*, Norman, OK: University of Oklahoma Press, 2003, 307.

[391] Nathaniel Philbrick, *The Last Stand: Custer, Sitting Bull, and the Battle of the Little Bighorn*, New York: The Penguin Group, 2010, 225.

[392] Robert Earle Forrest, "Fighting with Custer: Two Men Who Were with Gallant General Custer at Little Bighorn Battle Are Still Living," *Morning Observer*, Washington, PA: October 1932.

[393] Larry Sklenar, *To Hell with Honor; Custer and the Little Bighorn*, Norman, OK: University of Oklahoma Press, 2003, 310.

[394] John Carroll, editor, *A Seventh Cavalry Scrapbook*, Volume 2, "The Sioux Campaign and the Last Battle of General Custer," by General C.A. Woodruff, Bryan, TX: Privately Published, 1978, 17. Woodruff's remarks were originally made in a speech given at the Commonwealth Club in San Francisco on October 5, 1912.

[395] Bruce R. Liddic, *Vanishing Victory: Custer's Final March*, El Segundo, CA: Upton & Sons, Publishers, 2004, 131.

[396] Pamphlet 23, University of Wisconsin at Whitewater Special Collection of Dr. Kenneth Hammer: Edgerly, Winfield S. "Narrative on the March of the 7th Cavalry from the Yellowstone River to Sitting Bull's Camp," 5-6.

[397] Bruce R. Liddic, *Vanishing Victory: Custer's Final March*, El Segundo, CA: Upton & Sons, Publishers, 2004, 134.

[398] Pamphlet 23, University of Wisconsin at Whitewater Special Collection of Dr. Kenneth Hammer: Edgerly, Winfield S. "Narrative on the March of the 7th Cavalry from the Yellowstone River to Sitting Bull's Camp," 5-6.

[399] Sandy Barnard, editor, *Ten Years with Custer: A 7th Cavalryman's Memoirs*, Terre Haute, IN: AST Press, 2001, 306.

[400] Walter M. Camp, "Field Notes," Lilly Library, Indiana University, Bloomington, IN., Box 2, Folder 11 – Little Bighorn, Part 3.

[401] Don L. Weibert, *Custer, Cases & Cartridges: The Weibert Collection Analyzed*, Billings, MT: D. Weibert, 1989, Reno Hill artifacts map.

[402] Edgar I. Stewart, *Custer's Luck*, Norman, OK: University of Oklahoma Press, 1980, 412; and Charles M. Robinson, *A Good Year to Die: The Story of the Great Sioux War*, New York: Random House, 1995, 202.

[403] Walter M. Camp, "Field Notes," Lilly Library, Indiana University, Bloomington, IN., Box 2, Folder 11 – Little Bighorn, Part 3.

[404] Henry and Don Weibert, *Sixty-six Years in Custer's Shadow*, Billings, MT: Falcon Press, 1985, 33.

[405] Larry Sklenar, *To Hell with Honor; Custer and the Little Bighorn*, Norman, OK: University of Oklahoma Press, 2003, 313; Bruce R. Liddic, *Vanishing Victory: Custer's Final March*, El Segundo, CA: Upton & Sons, Publishers, 2004, 168-169; and James Donovan, *A Terrible Glory: Custer and the Little Bighorn – the Last Great Battle of the American West*, New York: Little, Brown and Company, 2008, 281.

[406] Don L. Weibert, *Custer, Cases & Cartridges: The Weibert Collection Analyzed*, Billings, MT: D. Weibert, 1989, 185.

[407] Ronald H. Nichols, editor, *Men with Custer: Biographies of the 7th Cavalry*, Hardin, MT: Custer Battlefield Historical and Museum Association, 2000, 349. It was originally cited as coming from Daniel Newell in "The Story of the Bighorn Campaign of 1876," *The Sunshine Magazine*, September 1930.

[408] National Archives and Records Administration, Washington, D.C., Records Group 153, Records of the Office of the Judge Advocate General – Army, Court-Martial Case Files, 1809-1894, Trumpeter Charles Fischer – Case # PP-5461. Headquarters Department of Dakota, General Court-Martial Orders #57, St. Paul, MN, December 28, 1876.

[409] Kenneth Hammer, *Custer in '76: Walter Camp's Notes on the Custer Fight*, Provo, UT: Brigham Young University, 1976, 124.

[410] Ronald H. Nichols, editor, *Men with Custer: Biographies of the 7th Cavalry*, Hardin, MT: Custer Battlefield Historical and Museum Association, 2000, 280; Roger L. Williams, *Military Register of Custer's Last Command*, Norman, OK: The Arthur H. Clark Company, 2009, 254; and Walter Mason Camp, *Walter M. Camp's Little Bighorn Rosters*, annotated by Richard G. Hardoff, Spokane, WA: Arthur H. Clark Company, 2002, 203.

[411] Dr. Kenneth Hammer Special Collection at the University of Wisconsin-Whitewater Library, Box 4, Casualties Folder, draft "Wounded Casualties in the Little Bighorn River Fight," by Kenneth Hammer and Vern Smalley.

[412] Ronald H. Nichols, editor, *Men with Custer: Biographies of the 7th Cavalry*, Hardin, MT: Custer Battlefield Historical and Museum Association, 2000, 287, 337; Dennis Clark, "Private Roman Rutten: Custer's Tailor," 15th Annual Symposium, Custer Battlefield Historical & Museum Association, held at Hardin, MT on June 22, 2001, 39; and Roger L. Williams, *Military Register of Custer's Last Command*, Norman, OK: The Arthur H. Clark Company, 2009, 258.

[413] Ronald H. Nichols, editor, *Men with Custer: Biographies of the 7th Cavalry*, Hardin, MT: Custer Battlefield Historical and Museum Association, 2000, 337; and Roger L. Williams, *Military Register of Custer's Last Command*, Norman, OK: The Arthur H. Clark Company, 2009, 295.

[414] National Archives and Records Administration, Washington, D.C., Records Group 94, Records of the Adjutant General's Office – Army, Carded Medical Records Regular Army, 1821-1884, Entry 529 (Unit 7), Thomas Varner – Box 424 (Tempes-Vigny).

[415] National Archives and Records Administration, Washington, D.C., Records Group 94, Records of the Adjutant General's Office – Army, Carded Medical Records Regular Army, 1821-1884, Entry 529 (Unit 7), Charles Wiedman (filed under Weidman) – Box 425 (Volkmann-Weller).

[416] Ronald H. Nichols, editor, *Men with Custer: Biographies of the 7th Cavalry*, Hardin, MT: Custer Battlefield Historical and Museum Association, 2000, 299. It was originally cited as coming from *Billings (Montana) Gazette*, June 25, 1923.

[417] Kenneth Hammer, *Custer in '76: Walter Camp's Notes on the Custer Fight*, Provo, UT: Brigham Young University, 1976, 136; and Bruce R. Liddic, *Vanishing Victory: Custer's Final March*, El Segundo, CA: Upton & Sons, Publishers, 2004, 168.

[418] Ronald H. Nichols, editor, *Men with Custer: Biographies of the 7th Cavalry*, Hardin, MT: Custer Battlefield Historical and Museum Association, 2000, 340; and Roger L. Williams, *Military Register of Custer's Last Command*, Norman, OK: The Arthur H. Clark Company, 2009, 296-297.

[419] Post Orders No. 171, Headquarters, Fort Rice, Dakota Territory, dated December 11, 1875, Records Group 393, Records of U. S. Army Continental Commands, 1821-1920, Part V, Military Installations, Fort Rice, North Dakota, Entry 6.

[420] Sandy Barnard, editor, *Ten Years with Custer: A 7th Cavalryman's Memoirs*, Terre Haute, IN: AST Press, 2001, 266.

[421] Pamphlet 23, University of Wisconsin at Whitewater Special Collection of Dr. Kenneth Hammer: Edgerly, Winfield S. "Narrative on the March of the 7th Cavalry from the Yellowstone River to Sitting Bull's Camp," 9.

[422] Robert Earle Forrest, "Fighting with Custer: Two Men Who Were with Gallant General Custer at Little Bighorn Battle Are Still Living," *Morning Observer*, Washington, PA: October 8, 1932.

[423] Gregory Michno, *The Mystery of E Troop: Custer's Gray Horse Company at the Little Bighorn*, Missoula, Montana: Mountain Press Publishing Company, 1994, 281; and Naval Oceanography Portal, *Complete Sun and Moon Data for One Day: U.S. Cities and Towns*, http://www.usno.navy.mil/USNO/astronomical-applications/data-services/rs-one-day-us.

[424] "The Little Horn Massacre," *New York Times*, July 7, 1876, 1.

[425] Peter Panzeri, *Little Big Horn 1876: Custer's Last Stand*, Osprey Campaign #39, Oxford, England: Osprey Publishing, 1995, 81; Bruce R. Liddic, *Vanishing Victory: Custer's Final March*, El Segundo, CA: Upton & Sons, Publishers, 2004, 169; James Donovan, *A Terrible Glory: Custer and the Little Bighorn – the Last Great Battle of the American West*, New York: Little, Brown and Company, 2008, 290; and Charles M. Robinson, *A Good Year to Die: The Story of the Great Sioux War*, New York: Random House, 1995, 201.

[426] William O. Taylor, *With Custer on the Little Bighorn*, New York: Viking, 1996, 52-53.

[427] Naval Oceanography Portal, *Complete Sun and Moon Data for One Day: U.S. Cities and Towns*, http://www.usno.navy.mil/USNO/astronomical-applications/data-services/rs-one-day-us.

[428] Kenneth Hammer, *Men with Custer; the Working Copy*, 2009, 190. Hammer sourced the comment to Neil Mangum's article "Reno's Battalion in the Battle of the Little Bighorn," from the 1985 *Greasy Grass* magazine.

[429] Walter M. Camp, "Field Notes," Lilly Library, Indiana University, Bloomington, IN., Box 2, Folder 11 – Little Bighorn, Part 3.

[430] William O. Taylor, *With Custer on the Little Bighorn*, New York: Viking, 1996, 54.

[431] Don Rickey, Jr., *Forty Miles a Day on Beans and Hay*, Norman, OK: University of Oklahoma Press, 1972, 324-325.

[432] Naval Oceanography Portal, *Complete Sun and Moon Data for One Day: U.S. Cities and Towns*, http://www.usno.navy.mil/USNO/astronomical-applications/data-services/rs-one-day-us.

[433] Nathaniel Philbrick, *The Last Stand: Custer, Sitting Bull, and the Battle of the Little Bighorn*, New York: The Penguin Group, 2010, 237.

[434] Larry Sklenar, *To Hell with Honor; Custer and the Little Bighorn*, Norman, OK: University of Oklahoma Press, 2003, 315.

[435] Kenneth Hammer, *Custer in '76: Walter Camp's Notes on the Custer Fight*, Provo, UT: Brigham Young University, 1976, 144.

[436] Richard G. Hardorff, *Hokahey! A Good Day to Die!* Lincoln, NE: University of Nebraska Press, 1999, 89.

[437] Robert Earle Forrest, "Fighting with Custer: Two Men Who Were with Gallant General Custer at Little Bighorn Battle Are Still Living," *Morning Observer*, Washington, PA: October 1932.

[438] Larry Sklenar, *To Hell with Honor; Custer and the Little Bighorn*, Norman, OK: University of Oklahoma Press, 2003, 316.

[439] Glendolin D. Wagner, *Old Neutriment*, New York: Sol Lewis, 1973, 162.

[440] Walter M. Camp, "Field Notes," Lilly Library, Indiana University, Bloomington, IN., Box 2, Folder 9 – Little Bighorn, Part 1, Camp interview with George W. Wylie.

[441] *The Teepee Book, A Monthly Periodical*, Reprint of Volume 2, #4 (April 1916) to Volume 2, #12 (December 1916), New York: Sol Lewis, 1974, Part 2:581.

[442] Earle Alonzo Brininstool, *Troopers with Custer: Incidents of the Battle of the Little Big Horn*, Harrisburg, PA: The Stackpole Company, 1952, 116; Henry and Don Weibert, *Sixty-six Years in Custer's Shadow*, Billings, MT: Falcon Press, 1985, 34; and Ronald H. Nichols, editor, *Men with Custer: Biographies of the 7th Cavalry*, Hardin, MT: Custer Battlefield Historical and Museum Association, 2000, 115. It was originally cited as coming from Daniel Newell in "The Story of the Bighorn Campaign of 1876," *The Sunshine Magazine*, September 1930.

[443] William O. Taylor, *With Custer on the Little Bighorn*, New York: Viking, 1996, 59; and Edgar I. Stewart, *Custer's Luck*, Norman, OK: University of Oklahoma Press, 1980, 425. Cheyenne warrior Wooden Leg later claimed that he had killed Tanner but this claim appears to be unverifiable.

[444] Ronald H. Nichols, editor, *Men with Custer: Biographies of the 7th Cavalry*, Hardin, MT: Custer Battlefield Historical and Museum Association, 2000, 114-115; Nathaniel Philbrick, *The Last Stand: Custer, Sitting Bull, and the Battle of the Little Bighorn*, New York: The Penguin Group, 2010, 242; and Roger L. Williams, *Military Register of Custer's Last Command*, Norman, OK: The Arthur H. Clark Company, 2009, 134, 142. Gebhart was originally buried on the battlefield but his body was reinterred in 1903 in the Custer Battlefield National Cemetery.

[445] Charles M. Robinson, *A Good Year to Die: The Story of the Great Sioux War*, New York: Random House, 1995, 203.

[446] Barry Johnson, *A Captain of Chivalric Courage: Thomas H. French, 7th Cavalry*, The Brand Book, Vol. 25, Numbers 1&2, London: The English Westerners' Society, 1987, 16.

[447] John Carroll, editor, *The Court Martial of Captain Thomas H. French; or Why Captain French Did Not Testify at the Reno Court of Inquiry*, Bryan, TX: Privately Published, 1974, 72-73. This testimony came at the court-martial of Captain French.

[448] Edgar I. Stewart, *Custer's Luck*, Norman, OK: University of Oklahoma Press, 1980, 424; and Walter M. Camp, "Field Notes," Lilly Library, Indiana University, Bloomington, IN., Box 2, Folder 11 – Little Bighorn, Part 3.

[449] Ronald H. Nichols, editor, *Men with Custer: Biographies of the 7th Cavalry*, Hardin, MT: Custer Battlefield Historical and Museum Association, 2000, 33; Melbourne C. Chandler, *Of Garry Owen in Glory: The History of the 7th Cavalry*, Annandale, VA: Turnpike Press, 1960, 70; and Roger L. Williams, *Military Register of Custer's Last Command*, Norman, OK: The Arthur H. Clark Company, 2009, 105.

[450] "Reno-Benteen Entrenchment Trail," *Little Bighorn Battlefield Guidebook*, Western National Parks Association, 2002, 7.

[451] Nathaniel Philbrick, *The Last Stand: Custer, Sitting Bull, and the Battle of the Little Bighorn*, New York: The Penguin Group, 2010, 244.

[452] William O. Taylor, *With Custer on the Little Bighorn*, New York: Viking, 1996, 167.

[453] Kenneth Hammer, *Custer in '76: Walter Camp's Notes on the Custer Fight*, Provo, UT: Brigham Young University, 1976, 144.

[454] Robert Earle Forrest, "Fighting with Custer: Two Men Who Were with Gallant General Custer at Little Bighorn Battle Are Still Living," *Morning Observer*, Washington, PA: October 8, 1932.

[455] Charles M. Robinson, *A Good Year to Die: The Story of the Great Sioux War*, New York: Random House, 1995, 201.

[456] Royal G. Jackson, "An Oral History of the Battle of Little Bighorn from the Perspective of the Northern Cheyenne Descendants," University of Wyoming National Park Research Center, Winter 1987 (Contract CX 1200-4-A037), 55. Copy is at the Little Bighorn Battlefield National Monument Archives.

[457] Sandy Barnard, editor, *Ten Years with Custer: A 7th Cavalryman's Memoirs*, Terre Haute, IN: AST Press, 2001, 300.

[458] Glendolin D. Wagner, *Old Neutriment*, New York: Sol Lewis, 1973, 169-170.

[459] Henry and Don Weibert, *Sixty-six Years in Custer's Shadow*, Billings, MT: Falcon Press, 1985, 32; and Sandy Barnard, *Custer's First Sergeant John Ryan*, Terre Haute, IN: AST Press, 1996, 193.

[460] Don Rickey, Jr., *Forty Miles a Day on Beans and Hay*, Norman, OK: University of Oklahoma Press, 1972, 101.

[461] Ronald H. Nichols, editor, *Men with Custer: Biographies of the 7th Cavalry*, Hardin, MT: Custer Battlefield Historical and Museum Association, 2000, 297; and Roger L. Williams, *Military Register of Custer's Last Command*, Norman, OK: The Arthur H. Clark Company, 2009, 268.

[462] Garrison Orders No. 2, Headquarters, Fort Rice, Dakota Territory, dated January 16, 1876, Records Group 393, Records of U. S. Army Continental Commands, 1821-1920, Part V, Military Installations, Fort Rice, North Dakota, Entry 5.

[463] Ronald H. Nichols, editor, *Men with Custer: Biographies of the 7th Cavalry*, Hardin, MT: Custer Battlefield Historical and Museum Association, 2000, 298; and Roger L. Williams, *Military Register of Custer's Last Command*, Norman, OK: The Arthur H. Clark Company, 2009, 269.

[464] National Archives and Records Administration, Washington, D.C., Records Group 94, Records of the Adjutant General's Office – Army, Carded Medical Records Regular Army, 1821-1884, Entry 529 (Unit 7), Robert Senn – Box 421 (Scholl-Simius).

[465] Ronald H. Nichols, editor, *Men with Custer: Biographies of the 7th Cavalry*, Hardin, MT: Custer Battlefield Historical and Museum Association, 2000, 319; and Roger L. Williams, *Military Register of Custer's Last Command*, Norman, OK: The Arthur H. Clark Company, 2009, 278.

[466] Ronald H. Nichols, editor, *Men with Custer: Biographies of the 7th Cavalry*, Hardin, MT: Custer Battlefield Historical and Museum Association, 2000, 330; Roger L. Williams, *Military Register of Custer's Last Command*, Norman, OK: The Arthur H. Clark Company, 2009, 289; and National Archives and Records Administration, Washington, D.C., Records Group 94, Records of the Adjutant General's Office – Army, Carded Medical Records Regular Army, 1821-1884, Entry 529 (Unit 7), Levi Thornberry – Box 424 (Tempes-Vigny).

[467] Ronald H. Nichols, editor, *Men with Custer: Biographies of the 7th Cavalry*, Hardin, MT: Custer Battlefield Historical and Museum Association, 2000, 123; Douglas D. Scott, P. Willey and Melissa A. Connor, *They Died with Custer: Soldiers Bones from the Battle of the Little Bighorn*, Norman, OK: University of Oklahoma Press, 288; and Roger L. Williams, *Military Register of Custer's Last Command*, Norman, OK: The Arthur H. Clark Company, 2009, 137-138.

[468] Garrison Orders No. 1, Headquarters, Fort Rice, Dakota Territory, dated January 5, 1876, Records Group 393, Records of U. S. Army Continental Commands, 1821-1920, Part V, Military Installations, Fort Rice, North Dakota, Entry 5.

[469] Ronald H. Nichols, editor, *Men with Custer: Biographies of the 7th Cavalry*, Hardin, MT: Custer Battlefield Historical and Museum Association, 2000, 145; Muster Rolls – 7th U.S. Cavalry, Company L-M, 1866-1884, Company M Muster Roll dated April 30, 1874, Microfilm Roll #5 at the Little Bighorn National Monument Archive; National Archives and Records Administration, Washington, D.C., Records Group 94, Records of the Adjutant General's Office – Army, Carded Medical Records Regular Army, 1821-1884, Entry 529 (Unit 7), George Heid – Box 408 (Harryman-Hoefig); and Garrison Orders No. 5, Headquarters, Fort Rice, Dakota Territory, dated March 9, 1875, Records Group 393, Records of U. S. Army Continental Commands, 1821-1920, Part V, Military Installations, Fort Rice, North Dakota, Entry 5.

[470] Ronald H. Nichols, editor, *Men with Custer: Biographies of the 7th Cavalry*, Hardin, MT: Custer Battlefield Historical and Museum Association, 2000, 354; Roger L. Williams, *Military Register of Custer's Last Command*, Norman, OK: The Arthur H. Clark Company, 2009, 306.

[471] Ronald H. Nichols, editor, *Men with Custer: Biographies of the 7th Cavalry*, Hardin, MT: Custer Battlefield Historical and Museum Association, 2000, 359; and Roger L. Williams, *Military Register of Custer's Last Command*, Norman, OK: The Arthur H. Clark Company, 2009, 309.

[472] National Archives and Records Administration, Washington, D.C., Records Group 94, Records of the Adjutant General's Office – Army, Carded Medical Records Regular Army, 1821-1884, Entry 529 (Unit 7), Charles Williams – Box 426 (Wemster-Winter).

[473] Larry Sklenar, *To Hell with Honor; Custer and the Little Bighorn*, Norman, OK: University of Oklahoma Press, 2003, 319; Nathaniel Philbrick, *The Last Stand: Custer, Sitting Bull, and the Battle of the Little Bighorn*, New York: The Penguin Group, 2010, 249; and Thomas B. Marquis, *Keep the Last Bullet for Yourself*, Algonac, MI: Reference Publications, 1985, 170.

[474] Larry Sklenar, *To Hell with Honor; Custer and the Little Bighorn*, Norman, OK: University of Oklahoma Press, 2003, 320; and Bruce R. Liddic, *Vanishing Victory: Custer's Final March*, El Segundo, CA: Upton & Sons, Publishers, 2004, 179.

[475] Godfrey, Edward Settle. *The field diary of Lt. Edward Settle Godfrey, commanding Co. K, 7th Cavalry Regiment under Lt. Colonel George Armstrong Custer in the Sioux encounter at the Battle of the Little Big Horn, covering the period from May 17, 1876 when the expedition commanded by Brigadier General Alfred H. Terry left Ft. Abraham Lincoln, Bismarck Dakota Territory until the return of the battered regiment a few days after September 24, 1876, to the same place*, Portland, OR: Champoeg Press, 1957, 17.

[476] Naval Oceanography Portal, *Complete Sun and Moon Data for One Day: U.S. Cities and Towns*, http://www.usno.navy.mil/USNO/astronomical-applications/data-services/rs-one-day-us.

[477] James Donovan, *A Terrible Glory: Custer and the Little Bighorn – the Last Great Battle of the American West*, New York: Little, Brown and Company, 2008, 298.

[478] Naval Oceanography Portal, *Complete Sun and Moon Data for One Day: U.S. Cities and Towns*, http://www.usno.navy.mil/USNO/astronomical-applications/data-services/rs-one-day-us.

[479] William O. Taylor, *With Custer on the Little Bighorn*, New York: Viking, 1996, 61; and Muster Rolls – 7th U.S. Cavalry, Company L-M, 1866-1884, Company M Muster Roll dated June 30, 1876, Microfilm Roll #5 at the Little Bighorn National Monument Archive.

[480] Kenneth Hammer, *Custer in '76: Walter Camp's Notes on the Custer Fight*, Provo, UT: Brigham Young University, 1976, 236.

[481] Henry and Don Weibert, *Sixty-six Years in Custer's Shadow*, Billings, MT: Falcon Press, 1985, 39.

[482] Don Rickey, Jr., *Forty Miles a Day on Beans and Hay*, Norman, OK: University of Oklahoma Press, 1972, 314.

[483] Gregory Michno, *The Mystery of E Troop: Custer's Gray Horse Company at the Little Bighorn*, Missoula, Montana: Mountain Press Publishing Company, 1994, 40.

[484] William O. Taylor, *With Custer on the Little Bighorn*, New York: Viking, 1996, 76; Sandy Barnard, *Custer's First Sergeant John Ryan*, Terre Haute, IN: AST Press, 1996, 195.

[485] Sandy Barnard, editor, *Ten Years with Custer: A 7th Cavalryman's Memoirs*, Terre Haute, IN: AST Press, 2001, 212; and Sandy Barnard, *Custer's First Sergeant John Ryan*, Terre Haute, IN: AST Press, 1996, 196.

[486] Gregory Michno, *The Mystery of E Troop: Custer's Gray Horse Company at the Little Bighorn*, Missoula, Montana: Mountain Press Publishing Company, 1994, 41, 286.

[487] Robert Earle Forrest, "Fighting with Custer: Two Men Who Were with Gallant General Custer at Little Bighorn Battle Are Still Living," *Morning Observer*, Washington, PA: October 10, 1932.

[488] Ronald H. Nichols, editor, *Men with Custer: Biographies of the 7th Cavalry*, Hardin, MT: Custer Battlefield Historical and Museum Association, 2000, 79; and Barry Johnson, *A Captain of Chivalric Courage: Thomas H. French, 7th Cavalry*, The Brand Book, Vol. 25, Numbers 1&2, London: The English Westerners' Society, 1987, 16.

[489] William O. Taylor, *With Custer on the Little Bighorn*, New York: Viking, 1996, 77; and Letter from John Ryan to Walter Camp, West Newton, Massachusetts, February 26, 1910. Copy of the letter is in the Little Bighorn Battlefield National Monument Archive, Item #11743.

[490] Gregory Michno, *The Mystery of E Troop: Custer's Gray Horse Company at the Little Bighorn*, Missoula, Montana: Mountain Press Publishing Company, 1994, 40, 141.

[491] Evan S. Connell, *Son of the Morning Star: Custer and the Little Bighorn*, San Francisco, CA: North Point Press, 1984, 6; and Kenneth Hammer, *Men with Custer; the Working Copy*, 2009, 232.

[492] Walter M. Camp, "Field Notes," Lilly Library, Indiana University, Bloomington, IN., Box 5, Folder 11, Envelope 64 – Includes recollections of Walter Sterland; and Letter from John Ryan to Walter Camp, West Newton, Massachusetts, April 7, 1920. Copy of the letter is in the Little Bighorn Battlefield National Monument Archive, Item #11744-A.

[493] Earle Alonzo Brininstool, *Troopers with Custer: Incidents of the Battle of the Little Big Horn*, Harrisburg, PA: The Stackpole Company, 1952, 65.

[494] Earle Alonzo Brininstool, *Troopers with Custer: Incidents of the Battle of the Little Big Horn*, Harrisburg, PA: The Stackpole Company, 1952, 65.

[495] Larry D. Underwood, *The Custer Fight: and Other Tales of the Old West*, Lincoln, NE: Media Publishing, 1989, 46.

[496] Charles M. Robinson, *A Good Year to Die: The Story of the Great Sioux War*, New York: Random House, 1995, 182.

[497] William O. Taylor, *With Custer on the Little Bighorn*, New York: Viking, 1996, 182; and Nathaniel Philbrick, *The Last Stand: Custer, Sitting Bull, and the Battle of the Little Bighorn*, New York: The Penguin Group, 2010, 242.

[498] Richard G. Hardorff, editor, *On the Little Bighorn with Walter Camp; A Collection of Walter Mason Camp's Letters, Notes and opinions on Custer's Last Fight*, El Segundo, CA: Upton & Sons Publishers, 2002, 67. Comment made to Walter Camp.

[499] Roger L. Williams, *Military Register of Custer's Last Command*, Norman, OK: The Arthur H. Clark Company, 2009, 393.

[500] Pamphlet 42, University of Wisconsin at Whitewater Special Collection of Dr. Kenneth Hammer: Hammer, Kenneth M. "Custer's Valiant Men," 9; and John Koster, "Captain Grant Marsh Was King of the Missouri River," *Wild West Magazine*, Volume 23, No. 1, Leesburg, VA, June 2010, 22-23.

[501] Nathaniel Philbrick, *The Last Stand: Custer, Sitting Bull, and the Battle of the Little Bighorn*, New York: The Penguin Group, 2010, 283.

Chapter Five: Accounts of Bravery in Company M at the Little Bighorn

[1] Sandy Barnard, editor, *Ten Years with Custer: A 7th Cavalryman's Memoirs*, Terre Haute, IN: AST Press, 2001, 298.

[2] Kenneth Hammer, *Custer in '76: Walter Camp's Notes on the Custer Fight*, Provo, UT: Brigham Young University, 1976, 115.

[3] Earle Alonzo Brininstool, *Troopers with Custer: Incidents of the Battle of the Little Big Horn*, Harrisburg, PA: The Stackpole Company, 1952, 59. Weeks was killed on August 26, 1877 in an altercation with Bernard Golden, another Company M soldier.

[4] Ronald H. Nichols, editor, *Men with Custer: Biographies of the 7th Cavalry*, Hardin, MT: Custer Battlefield Historical and Museum Association, 2000, 349; Roger L. Williams, *Military Register of Custer's Last Command*, Norman, OK: The Arthur H. Clark Company, 2009, 304; and Walter Mason Camp, *Walter M. Camp's Little Bighorn Rosters*, annotated by Richard G. Hardoff, Spokane, WA: Arthur H. Clark Company, 2002, 207.

[5] Ronald H. Nichols, editor, *Men with Custer: Biographies of the 7th Cavalry*, Hardin, MT: Custer Battlefield Historical and Museum Association, 2000, 299. It was originally cited as coming from Daniel Newell in "The Story of the Bighorn Campaign of 1876," *The Sunshine Magazine*, September 1930.

[6] Ronald H. Nichols, editor, *Men with Custer: Biographies of the 7th Cavalry*, Hardin, MT: Custer Battlefield Historical and Museum Association, 2000, 298-299; Don Rickey, Jr., *Forty Miles a Day on Beans and Hay*, Norman, OK: University of Oklahoma Press, 1972, 52; Laudie J. Chorne, *Following the Custer Trail of 1876*, Bismarck, ND: Trails West Publishing, 2001, 66; and Roger L. Williams, *Military Register of Custer's Last Command*, Norman, OK: The Arthur H. Clark Company, 2009, 269.

[7] Garrison Orders No. 67 and Garrison Orders No. 74, Headquarters, Fort Rice, Dakota Territory, dated September 22, 1874 and November 3, 1875, Records Group 393, Records of U. S. Army Continental Commands, 1821-1920, Part V, Military Installations, Fort Rice, North Dakota, Entry 5.

[8] James Donovan, *A Terrible Glory: Custer and the Little Bighorn – the Last Great Battle of the American West*, New York: Little, Brown and Company, 2008, 248.

[9] James Donovan, *A Terrible Glory: Custer and the Little Bighorn – the Last Great Battle of the American West*, New York: Little, Brown and Company, 2008, 248.

[10] Bruce R. Liddic, *Vanishing Victory: Custer's Final March*, El Segundo, CA: Upton & Sons, Publishers, 2004, 137.

[11] Ronald H. Nichols, editor, *Men with Custer: Biographies of the 7th Cavalry*, Hardin, MT: Custer Battlefield Historical and Museum Association, 2000, 109. It was originally cited as coming from Daniel Newell in "The Story of the Bighorn Campaign of 1876," *The Sunshine Magazine*, September 1930.

[12] Colonel W.A. Graham, *The Custer Myth: A Source Book of Custeriana*, Mechanicsburg, PA: Stackpole Books, 2000, 61; and Committee in Charge of the Commemoration Exercises Fifty Years Later, *The Teepee Book*, Sheridan, WY: The Miles Company, 1926, 55.

[13] Colonel W.A. Graham, *The Custer Myth: A Source Book of Custeriana*, Mechanicsburg, PA: Stackpole Books, 2000, 61.

[14] Kenneth Hammer, *Custer in '76: Walter Camp's Notes on the Custer Fight*, Provo, UT: Brigham Young University, 1976, 142.

[15] "Official Transcript of the Court Martial of Captain Thomas H. French," Fort Abraham Lincoln, Dakota Territory, January 1879, 161-162.

[16] Sandy Barnard, editor, *Ten Years with Custer: A 7th Cavalryman's Memoirs*, Terre Haute, IN: AST Press, 2001, 298.

[17] James B. Klokner, *The Officer Corps of Custer's Seventh Cavalry 1866-1876*, Atglen, PA: Schiffer Publishing, 2007, 61.

[18] Earle Alonzo Brininstool, *Troopers with Custer: Incidents of the Battle of the Little Big Horn*, Harrisburg, PA: The Stackpole Company, 1952, 53.

[19] Sandy Barnard, editor, *Ten Years with Custer: A 7th Cavalryman's Memoirs*, Terre Haute, IN: AST Press, 2001, 300.

[20] National Archives and Records Administration, Washington, D.C., Records Group 153, Records of the Office of the Judge Advocate General – Army, Court-Martial Case Files, 1809-1894, Sergeant Charles White – Case # QQ-1418. Headquarters Department of Dakota, General Court-Martial Orders #100, St. Paul, MN, September 25, 1879.

Chapter Six Company Ms Exclusion from Bravery Awards

[1] Eugene L. Meyer, "Tracking a Custer Indian Fighter," *The Washington Post*, March 27, 1980, A1.

[2] Don Rickey, Jr., *Forty Miles a Day on Beans and Hay*, Norman, OK: University of Oklahoma Press, 1972, 309.

[3] Cyrus T. Brady, *Indian Fights and Fighters*, New York: Doubleday, Page & Company, 1909, 404-405. Morris' comments to Brady came in the form of a letter from Haven, Maine, and were dated September 21, 1904.

[4] Eugene L. Meyer, "Tracking a Custer Indian Fighter," *The Washington Post*, March 27, 1980, A1.

[5] Bruce R. Liddic, *Vanishing Victory: Custer's Final March*, El Segundo, CA: Upton & Sons, Publishers, 2004, 178.

[6] Roger L. Williams, *Military Register of Custer's Last Command*, Norman, OK: The Arthur H. Clark Company, 2009, 216, 290.

[7] Larry Sklenar, "Medals for Custer's Men," *Montana: The Magazine of Western History*, Helena, MT: Montana Historical Society, Volume 50, Winter 2000, 61.

[8] Larry Sklenar, "Medals for Custer's Men," *Montana: The Magazine of Western History*, Helena: MT: Montana Historical Society, Volume 50, Winter 2000, 61.

[9] Charles Windolph, *I Fought with Custer: The Story of Sergeant Windolph, Last Survivor of the Battle of the Little Big Horn*, edited by Frazier Hunt and Robert Hunt, New York: Charles Scribner's Sons, 1947, 105.

[10] Don Rickey, Jr., *Forty Miles a Day on Beans and Hay*, Norman, OK: University of Oklahoma Press, 1972, 311. To say that Ryan disliked Benteen would be an understatement. Shortly before the 1876 expedition began, after Ryan was reinstated as company First Sergeant after Benteen, as acting post commander, had ordered that he be reduced in rank, Ryan did the following:

"The tents [in camp] were strung out in regimental line with a certain interval between the different squadrons to allow the companies to march through to the river to water their horses. We rode our horses from the picket line down through those intervals to the Missouri River. It was quite dusty around this camp at the time and in going to water one day, while in charge of my company, I rode pretty close to my former post commander's [Benteen's] tent. I also started the horses on the trot and gave him the benefit of a shower of dust."

Source: Sandy Barnard, editor, *Ten Years with Custer: A 7th Cavalryman's Memoirs*, Terre Haute, IN: AST Press, 2001, 266.

[11] Robert Barr Smith, "Benteen: Between a Rock and a Hard Place," *Wild West Magazine*, Volume 23, No. 1, Leesburg, VA, June 2010, 34.

[12] Michael L. Wyman, and Rocky L. Boyd, "Towards an Understanding of Peter Thompson and His Accounts of the Battle

of the Little Big Horn," 18th Annual Symposium, Custer Battlefield Historical & Museum Association, held at Hardin, MT on June 25, 2004, 51.

Chapter Seven: Company M's Absence at the 1879 Marcus Reno Inquiry

[1] James Donovan, *A Terrible Glory: Custer and the Little Bighorn – the Last Great Battle of the American West*, New York: Little, Brown and Company, 2008, 472. Quotation came from Captain Robert G. Carter.

[2] "The Reno Court, Fact or Fiction," Jim Donovan, Billings, MT: 2009 Little Bighorn Associates 36th Annual Conference, June 23, 2009; and Colonel W.A. Graham, *The Custer Myth: A Source Book of Custeriana*, Mechanicsburg, PA: Stackpole Books, 2000, 152.

[3] Glenwood J. Swanson, *G. A. Custer: His Life and Times*, Agua Dulce, CA: Swanson Productions, 2004, 141.

[4] "The Reno Court, Fact or Fiction," Jim Donovan, Billings, MT: 2009 Little Bighorn Associates 36th Annual Conference, June 23, 2009.

[5] Jack Pennington, *The Battle of the Little Bighorn: A Comprehensive Study*, El Segundo, CA: Upton & Sons, Publishers, 2001, 353.

[6] James Donovan, *A Terrible Glory: Custer and the Little Bighorn – the Last Great Battle of the American West*, New York: Little, Brown and Company, 2008, 480.

[7] Jack Pennington, *The Battle of the Little Bighorn: A Comprehensive Study*, El Segundo, CA: Upton & Sons, Publishers, 2001, 34.

[8] Jack Pennington, *The Battle of the Little Bighorn: A Comprehensive Study*, El Segundo, CA: Upton & Sons, Publishers, 2001, 34.

[9] Larry Sklenar, *To Hell with Honor; Custer and the Little Bighorn*, Norman, OK: University of Oklahoma Press, 2003, 21.

[10] "The Reno Court, Fact or Fiction," Jim Donovan, Billings, MT: 2009 Little Bighorn Associates 36th Annual Conference, June 23, 2009.

[11] Robert S. Ellison, "Walter M. Camp Papers," WH1702, Western History Collection, The Denver Public Library, Denver, CO., notes of private diary of Charles White [real name Henry Charles Weihe], contemporaneously written by him and loaned three years after White's death in 1906 by his widow Jennie W. Weihe to Walter Camp.

[12] James Donovan, *A Terrible Glory: Custer and the Little Bighorn – the Last Great Battle of the American West*, New York: Little, Brown and Company, 2008, 238.

[13] "Testifying About Major Reno," *New York Times*, New York: January 19, 1879, 1.

[14] Robert S. Ellison, "Walter M. Camp Papers," WH1702, Western History Collection, The Denver Public Library, Denver, CO., notes of private diary of Charles White [real name Henry Charles Weihe], contemporaneously written by him and loaned three years after White's death in 1906 by his widow Jennie W. Weihe to Walter Camp.

[15] Robert S. Ellison, "Walter M. Camp Papers," WH1702, Western History Collection, The Denver Public Library, Denver, CO., notes of private diary of Charles White [real name Henry Charles Weihe], contemporaneously written by him and loaned three years after White's death in 1906 by his widow Jennie W. Weihe to Walter Camp.

[16] Robert S. Ellison, "Walter M. Camp Papers," WH1702, Western History Collection, The Denver Public Library, Denver, CO., notes of private diary of Charles White [real name Henry Charles Weihe], contemporaneously written by him and loaned three years after White's death in 1906 by his widow Jennie W. Weihe to Walter Camp.

[17] Nathaniel Philbrick, *The Last Stand: Custer, Sitting Bull, and the Battle of the Little Bighorn*, New York: The Penguin Group, 2010, 301.

[18] Robert S. Ellison, "Walter M. Camp Papers," WH1702, Western History Collection, The Denver Public Library, Denver, CO., notes of private diary of Charles White [real name Henry Charles Weihe], contemporaneously written by him and loaned three years after White's death in 1906 by his widow Jennie W. Weihe to Walter Camp.

[19] Walter M. Camp, "Field Notes," Lilly Library, Indiana University, Bloomington, IN., Box 2, Folder 9 – Little Bighorn, Part 1.

Chapter Eight: Post Battle Accounts of Company M Participants at the Little Bighorn

[1] Dr. James Lederle, *To Gaze into the Eyes of Hell*, Indiana: Innovative Ventures Group, 2009, 71.

[2] Ronald H. Nichols, editor, *Men with Custer: Biographies of the 7th Cavalry*, Hardin, MT: Custer Battlefield Historical and Museum Association, 2000, 111.

[3] Sandy Barnard, editor, *Ten Years with Custer: A 7th Cavalryman's Memoirs*, Terre Haute, IN: AST Press, 2001, xiv.

[4] Sandy Barnard, *Custer's First Sergeant John Ryan*, Terre Haute, IN: AST Press, 1996, 157.

[5] Robert S. Ellison, "Walter M. Camp Papers," WH1702, Western History Collection, The Denver Public Library, Denver, CO., File Folder 45, Walter Camp Research; letter from William Morris to Walter M. Camp dated November 18, 1908.

[6] Cyrus T. Brady, *Indian Fights and Fighters*, New York: Doubleday, Page & Company, 1909, 402.

[7] Kenneth Hammer, "Recalling the Little Bighorn: Stories Told by 7th Cavalry Survivors," *Greasy Grass Magazine*, Volume 24, May 2008, Hardin, MT: Custer Battlefield Historical & Museum Association, 40.

[8] Douglas W. Ellison, "Mystery along Rosebud Creek," *Greasy Grass Magazine*, Volume 17, May 2001, Hardin, MT: Custer Battlefield Historical & Museum Association, 22.

[9] C. Lee Noyes, "Was There A Timber Fight?" Indianapolis, IN: Indianapolis Little Bighorn Symposium, September 12, 2009.

[10] Kenneth Hammer, "Recalling the Little Bighorn: Stories Told by 7th Cavalry Survivors," *Greasy Grass Magazine*, Volume 24, May 2008, Hardin, MT: Custer Battlefield Historical & Museum Association, 39; and Roger L. Williams, *Military Register of Custer's Last Command*, Norman, OK: The Arthur H. Clark Company, 2009, 115.

[11] Barry Johnson, *A Captain of Chivalric Courage: Thomas H. French, 7th Cavalry*, The Brand Book, Vol. 25, Numbers 1&2, London: The English Westerners' Society, 1987, 17.

[12] C. Lee Noyes, "Was There A Timber Fight?" Indianapolis, IN: Indianapolis Little Bighorn Symposium, September 12, 2009.

[13] Kenneth Hammer, *Custer in '76: Walter Camp's Notes on the Custer Fight*, Provo, UT: Brigham Young University, 1976, 143.

[14] Walter M. Camp, "Field Notes," Lilly Library, Indiana University, Bloomington, IN., Box 2, Folder 11 – Little Bighorn, Part 3.

Chapter Nine: Old Soldiers Never Die They Just Fade Away

[1] Lorna Thackeray, "Cavalry men's lives come to troubled ends," *Billings Gazette*, Billings, MT: June 21, 2009.

[2] Post Orders No. 164, Headquarters, Fort Rice, Dakota Territory, dated November 27, 1876, Records Group 393, Records of U. S. Army Continental Commands, 1821-1920, Part V, Military Installations, Fort Rice, North Dakota, Entry 5.

[3] Don Rickey, Jr., *Forty Miles a Day on Beans and Hay*, Norman, OK: University of Oklahoma Press, 1972, 341-342.

[4] Gregory Michno, *The Mystery of E Troop: Custer's Gray Horse Company at the Little Bighorn*, Missoula, Montana: Mountain Press Publishing Company, 1994, 288.

[5] Ronald H. Nichols, editor, *Men with Custer: Biographies of the 7th Cavalry*, Hardin, MT: Custer Battlefield Historical and Museum Association, 2000, 33; Wayne R. Gutowsky, *Burial Sites of the Survivors of the Little Big Horn Battle*, unpublished manuscript, 5; and Email discussions with Brian Spatola, Collections Manager, Anatomical Division and Michael Rhode, Archivist, Otis Historical Archives, National Museum of Health and Medicine, Armed Forces Institute of Pathology, concerning the medical aspects of the death of Private Frank Braun of Company M, November 2009.

[6] Ronald H. Nichols, editor, *Men with Custer: Biographies of the 7th Cavalry*, Hardin, MT: Custer Battlefield Historical and Museum Association, 2000, 349; and Roger L. Williams, *Military Register of Custer's Last Command*, Norman, OK: The Arthur H. Clark Company, 2009, 138, 304.

[7] Letter from Captain Thomas French, Camp on Rosebud Creek, Montana, August 6, 1876, to the Assistant Adjutant General of the Department of the Dakota, requesting he be allowed to purchase an iron-gray horse for $110.

[8] Nathaniel Philbrick, *The Last Stand: Custer, Sitting Bull, and the Battle of the Little Bighorn*, New York: The Penguin Group, 2010, 286.

[9] National Archives and Records Administration, Washington, D.C., Records Group 94, Records of the Adjutant General's Office – Army, Carded Medical Records Regular Army, 1821-1884, Entry 529 (Unit 7), Thomas H. French – Box 405 (Fish-Gaffney).

[10] Barry Johnson, *A Captain of Chivalric Courage: Thomas H. French, 7th Cavalry*, The Brand Book, Vol. 25, Numbers 1&2, London: The English Westerners' Society, 1987, 25-26.

[11] Barry Johnson, *A Captain of Chivalric Courage: Thomas H. French, 7th Cavalry*, The Brand Book, Vol. 25, Numbers 1&2, London: The English Westerners' Society, 1987, 26.

[12] Barry Johnson, *A Captain of Chivalric Courage: Thomas H. French, 7th Cavalry*, The Brand Book, Vol. 25, Numbers 1&2, London: The English Westerners' Society, 1987, 49.

[13] Dusan P. Farrington, *Arming & Equipping the U.S. Cavalry 1865-1902*, Lincoln, RI: Andrew Mowbray Publishers, 2004, 199.

[14] National Archives and Records Administration, Washington, D.C., Records Group 94, Records of the Adjutant General's Office – Army, Carded Medical Records Regular Army, 1821-1884, Entry 529 (Unit 7), Thomas H. French – Box 405 (Fish-Gaffney); and discussions with Olga MacLean, former Drug and Alcohol Counselor for the U.S. Army at Frankfurt and Mannheim, Germany, June 2010.

[15] National Archives and Records Administration, Washington, D.C., Records Group 153, Records of the Office of the Judge Advocate General – Army, Court-Martial Case Files, 1809-1894, P Corporal Hobart Ryder – Case # QQ-1361. Headquarters Department of Dakota, General Court-Martial Orders #96, St. Paul, MN, September 10, 1879.

[16] Barry Johnson, *A Captain of Chivalric Courage: Thomas H. French, 7th Cavalry*, The Brand Book, Vol. 25, Numbers 1&2, London: The English Westerners' Society, 1987, 26-28.

[17] Barry Johnson, *A Captain of Chivalric Courage: Thomas H. French, 7th Cavalry*, The Brand Book, Vol. 25, Numbers 1&2, London: The English Westerners' Society, 1987, 25-41.

[18] John Carroll, editor, *The Court Martial of Captain Thomas H. French; or Why Captain French Did Not Testify at the Reno Court of Inquiry*, Bryan, TX: Privately Published, 1974, 103.

[19] John Carroll, editor, *The Court Martial of Captain Thomas H. French; or Why Captain French Did Not Testify at the Reno Court of Inquiry*, Bryan, TX: Privately Published, 1974, 103.

[20] John Carroll, editor, *The Court Martial of Captain Thomas H. French; or Why Captain French Did Not Testify at the Reno Court of Inquiry*, Bryan, TX: Privately Published, 1974, 103-104.

[21] Barry Johnson, *A Captain of Chivalric Courage: Thomas H. French, 7th Cavalry*, The Brand Book, Vol. 25, Numbers 1&2, London: The English Westerners' Society, 1987, 44.

[22] Barry Johnson, *A Captain of Chivalric Courage: Thomas H. French, 7th Cavalry*, The Brand Book, Vol. 25, Numbers 1&2, London: The English Westerners' Society, 1987, 44; and email discussions with Dennis K. "DK" Clark, author of "Private Roman Rutten: Custer's Tailor," 15th Annual Symposium, Custer Battlefield Historical & Museum Association, October 2009.

[23] Pamphlet 28, University of Wisconsin at Whitewater Special Collection of Dr. Kenneth Hammer: French, Thomas H. "Letter of Capt. French to the Mother of Lieut. W. W. Cooke, 1880," 1.

[24] Barry Johnson, *A Captain of Chivalric Courage: Thomas H. French, 7th Cavalry*, The Brand Book, Vol. 25, Numbers 1&2, London: The English Westerners' Society, 1987, 47; and Pamphlet 28, University of Wisconsin at Whitewater Special Collection of Dr. Kenneth Hammer: French, Thomas H. "Letter of Capt. French to the Mother of Lieut. W. W. Cooke, 1880."

[25] Ronald H. Nichols, editor, *Men with Custer: Biographies of the 7th Cavalry*, Hardin, MT: Custer Battlefield Historical and Museum Association, 2000, 110; Wayne R. Gutowsky, *Burial Sites of the Survivors of the Little Big Horn Battle*, unpublished manuscript, 5; Eugene L. Meyer, "Tracking a Custer Indian Fighter," *The Washington Post*, March 27, 1980, A1; and email discussions with Dennis K. "DK" Clark, author of "Private Roman Rutten: Custer's Tailor," 15th Annual Symposium, Custer Battlefield Historical & Museum Association, October 2009.

[26] "The Last Summons: Death of Captain French," *The Leavenworth Times*, Leavenworth, Kansas, March 28, 1882.

[27] Ronald H. Nichols, editor, *Men with Custer: Biographies of the 7th Cavalry*, Hardin, MT: Custer Battlefield Historical and Museum Association, 2000, 203; Wayne R. Gutowsky, *Burial Sites of the Survivors of the Little Big Horn Battle*, unpublished manuscript, 4; Roger L. Williams, *Military Register of Custer's Last Command*, Norman, OK: The Arthur H. Clark Company, 2009, 211; and Walter Mason Camp, *Walter M. Camp's Little Bighorn Rosters*, annotated by Richard G. Hardoff, Spokane, WA: Arthur H. Clark Company, 2002, 201.

[28] Email discussions with Sheila Abarr, Public Affairs Specialist, Armed Forces Retirement Home in Washington, DC, November 2009.

[29] Email discussions with Sheila Abarr, Public Affairs Specialist, Armed Forces Retirement Home in Washington, DC, November 2009.

[30] Ronald H. Nichols, editor, *Men with Custer: Biographies of the 7th Cavalry*, Hardin, MT: Custer Battlefield Historical and Museum Association, 2000, 171-172; Wayne R. Gutowsky, *Burial Sites of the Survivors of the Little Big Horn Battle*, unpublished manuscript, 4; Roger L. Williams, *Military Register of Custer's Last Command*, Norman, OK: The Arthur H. Clark Company, 2009, 173; and National Archives and Records Administration, Washington, D.C., Records Group 94, Records of the Adjutant General's Office – Army, Carded Medical Records Regular Army, 1821-1884, Entry 529 (Unit 3), Charles Kavanaugh – Box 190 (W. Johnson-Kielhaver.)

[31] National Archives and Records Administration, Washington, D.C., Records Group 94, Records of the Adjutant General's Office – Army, Carded Medical Records Regular Army, 1821-1884, Entry 529 (Unit 7), George Weaver – Box 425 (Volkmann-Weller).

[32] Records Group 393, Records of U. S. Army Continental Commands, 1821-1920, Military Installations, Fort Meade, South Dakota (298), Entry 24 – Register of Patients, Volume 2; 28 and 36.

[33] Ronald H. Nichols, editor, *Men with Custer: Biographies of the 7th Cavalry*, Hardin, MT: Custer Battlefield Historical and Museum Association, 2000, 348; Wayne R. Gutowsky, *Burial Sites of the Survivors of the Little Big Horn Battle*, unpublished manuscript, 12; and Roger L. Williams, *Military Register of Custer's Last Command*, Norman, OK: The Arthur H. Clark Company, 2009, 303.

[34] Ronald H. Nichols, editor, *Men with Custer: Biographies of the 7th Cavalry*, Hardin, MT: Custer Battlefield Historical and Museum Association, 2000, 145; Wayne R. Gutowsky, *Burial Sites of the Survivors of the Little Big Horn Battle*, unpublished manuscript, 5; and Roger L. Williams, *Military Register of Custer's Last Command*, Norman, OK: The Arthur H. Clark Company, 2009, 152-153.

[35] Ronald H. Nichols, editor, *Men with Custer: Biographies of the 7th Cavalry*, Hardin, MT: Custer Battlefield Historical and Museum Association, 2000, 15; Wayne R. Gutowsky, *Burial Sites of the Survivors of the Little Big Horn Battle*, unpublished manuscript, 12; and Roger L. Williams, *Military Register of Custer's Last Command*, Norman, OK: The Arthur H. Clark Company, 2009, 36.

[36] Ronald H. Nichols, editor, *Men with Custer: Biographies of the 7th Cavalry*, Hardin, MT: Custer Battlefield Historical and Museum Association, 2000, 15; Wayne R. Gutowsky, *Burial Sites of the Survivors of the Little Big Horn Battle*, unpublished manuscript, 12; and Roger L. Williams, *Military Register of Custer's Last Command*, Norman, OK: The Arthur H. Clark Company, 2009, 36.

[37] National Archives and Records Administration, Washington, D.C., Records Group 153, Records of the Office of the Judge Advocate General – Army, Court-Martial Case Files, 1809-1894, Sergeant Patrick Carey – Case # QQ-1465. Headquarters, Department of Dakota, St. Paul, MN; General Court-Martial Orders No. 120, November 18, 1879.

[38] National Archives and Records Administration, Washington, D.C., Records Group 153, Records of the Office of the Judge Advocate General – Army, Court-Martial Case Files, 1809-1894, Sergeant Patrick Carey – Case # QQ-1465. Captain Thomas French, Sworn Statement, Fort Meade, Dakota Territory, November 11, 1879.

[39] National Archives and Records Administration, Washington, D.C., Records Group 153, Records of the Office of the Judge Advocate General – Army, Court-Martial Case Files, 1809-1894, Sergeant Patrick Carey – Case # QQ-1465; Sergeant Patrick Carey, Statement, Fort Meade, Dakota Territory, November 11, 1879.

[40] Ronald H. Nichols, editor, *Men with Custer: Biographies of the 7th Cavalry*, Hardin, MT: Custer Battlefield Historical and Museum Association, 2000, 51; Wayne R. Gutowsky, *Burial Sites of the Survivors of the Little Big Horn Battle*, unpublished manuscript, 4; and Roger L. Williams, *Military Register of Custer's Last Command*, Norman, OK: The Arthur H. Clark Company, 2009, 64.

[41] National Archives and Records Administration, Washington, D.C., Records Group 153, Records of the Office of the Judge Advocate General – Army, Court-Martial Case Files, 1809-1894, Sergeant Hugh N. Moore – Case # QQ-603; Captain Thomas French Statement, Fort Abraham Lincoln, Dakota Territory, January 12, 1878.

[42] National Archives and Records Administration, Washington, D.C., Records Group 153, Records of the Office of the Judge Advocate General – Army, Court-Martial Case Files, 1809-1894, Sergeant Hugh N. Moore – Case # QQ-603. Headquarters Department of Dakota, General Court-Martial Orders #21, St. Paul, MN, March 21, 1878.

[43] Ronald H. Nichols, editor, *Men with Custer: Biographies of the 7th Cavalry*, Hardin, MT: Custer Battlefield Historical and Museum Association, 2000, 234; Wayne R. Gutowsky, *Burial Sites of the Survivors of the Little Big Horn Battle*, unpublished manuscript, 4; Barry Johnson, *A Captain of Chivalric Courage: Thomas H. French, 7th Cavalry*, The Brand Book, Vol. 25, Numbers 1&2, London: The English Westerners' Society, 1987, 40; and Roger L. Williams, *Military Register of Custer's Last Command*, Norman, OK: The Arthur H. Clark Company, 2009, 221.

[44] National Archives and Records Administration, Washington, D.C., Records Group 153, Records of the Office of the Judge Advocate General – Army, Court-Martial Case Files, 1809-1894, Sergeant Hugh N. Moore – Case # QQ-2851. Headquarters Department of Dakota, General Court-Martial Orders #169, Fort Snelling, MN, December 28, 1881.

[45] National Archives and Records Administration, Washington, D.C., Records Group 153, Records of the Office of the Judge Advocate General – Army, Court-Martial Case Files, 1809-1894, Sergeant Hugh N. Moore – Case # QQ-4224. Headquarters Department of Dakota, General Court-Martial Orders #161, St. Paul, MN, October 16, 1883.

[46] Records Group 393, Records of U. S. Army Continental Commands, 1821-1920, Military Installations, Fort Meade, South Dakota (298), Entry 24 – Register of Patients, Volume 1; 145.

[47] Roger L. Williams, *Military Register of Custer's Last Command*, Norman, OK: The Arthur H. Clark Company, 2009, 221; and Records Group 393, Records of U. S. Army Continental Commands, 1821-1920, Military Installations, Fort Meade, South Dakota (298), Entry 24 – Register of Patients, Volume 2; 123 and 138.

[48] National Archives and Records Administration, Washington, D.C., Records Group 153, Records of the Office of the Judge Advocate General – Army, Court-Martial Case Files, 1809-1894, Private Hugh N. Moore – Case # RR-2826. Headquarters Department of Dakota, General Court-Martial Orders #33, St. Paul, MN, December 26, 1887.

[49] Roger L. Williams, *Military Register of Custer's Last Command*, Norman, OK: The Arthur H. Clark Company, 2009, 221.

[50] Ronald H. Nichols, editor, *Men with Custer: Biographies of the 7th Cavalry*, Hardin, MT: Custer Battlefield Historical and Museum Association, 2000, 234; Wayne R. Gutowsky, *Burial Sites of the Survivors of the Little Big Horn Battle*, unpublished manuscript, 4; Barry Johnson, *A Captain of Chivalric Courage: Thomas H. French, 7th Cavalry*, The Brand Book, Vol. 25, Numbers 1&2, London: The English Westerners' Society, 1987, 40; and Roger L. Williams, *Military Register of Custer's Last Command*, Norman, OK: The Arthur H. Clark Company, 2009, 221.

[51] National Archives and Records Administration, Washington, D.C., Records Group 94, Records of the Adjutant General's Office – Army, Carded Medical Records Regular Army, 1821-1884, Entry 529 (Unit 7), Levi Thornberry – Box 424 (Tempes-Vigny).

[52] Ronald H. Nichols, editor, *Men with Custer: Biographies of the 7th Cavalry*, Hardin, MT: Custer Battlefield Historical and Museum Association, 2000, 330; Wayne R. Gutowsky, *Burial Sites of the Survivors of the Little Big Horn Battle*, unpublished manuscript, 11; and Roger L. Williams, *Military Register of Custer's Last Command*, Norman, OK: The Arthur H. Clark Company, 2009, 289.

[53] National Archives and Records Administration, Washington, D.C., Records Group 94, Records of the Adjutant General's Office – Army, Carded Medical Records Regular Army, 1821-1884, Entry 529 (Unit 7), Henry Davis – Box 402 (Creedon-Denny).

[54] Ronald H. Nichols, editor, *Men with Custer: Biographies of the 7th Cavalry*, Hardin, MT: Custer Battlefield Historical and Museum Association, 2000, 79-80; and Roger L. Williams, *Military Register of Custer's Last Command*, Norman, OK: The Arthur H. Clark Company, 2009, 106.

[55] Records Group 393, Records of U.S. Army Continental Commands, 1821-1920, Military Installations, Fort Meade, South Dakota (298), Entry 24 – Register of Patients, Volume 1; 13, 59, 103 and 123.

[56] Records Group 393, Records of U.S. Army Continental Commands, 1821-1920, Military Installations, Fort Meade, South Dakota (298), Entry 24 – Register of Patients, Volume 1; 191, 223, 237, 305, 353 and Volume 2; 18.

[57] Records Group 393, Records of U.S. Army Continental Commands, 1821-1920, Military Installations, Fort Meade, South Dakota (298), Entry 24 – Register of Patients, Volume 2; 43, 54 and 106.

[58] Ronald H. Nichols, editor, *Men with Custer: Biographies of the 7th Cavalry*, Hardin, MT: Custer Battlefield Historical and Museum Association, 2000, 87; William O. Taylor, *With Custer on the Little Bighorn*, New York: Viking, 1996, 182; and Roger L. Williams, *Military Register of Custer's Last Command*, Norman, OK: The Arthur H. Clark Company, 2009, 110 .

[59] Ronald H. Nichols, editor, *Men with Custer: Biographies of the 7th Cavalry*, Hardin, MT: Custer Battlefield Historical and Museum Association, 2000, 46; and Roger L. Williams, *Military Register of Custer's Last Command*, Norman, OK: The Arthur H. Clark Company, 2009, 62 and 79.

[60] National Archives and Records Administration, Washington, D.C., Records Group 94, Records of the Adjutant General's Office – Army, Carded Medical Records Regular Army, 1821-1884, Entry 529 (Unit 7), Charles White (Henry Weihe) – Box 426 (Wemster-Winter).

[61] Ronald H. Nichols, editor, *Men with Custer: Biographies of the 7th Cavalry*, Hardin, MT: Custer Battlefield Historical and Museum Association, 2000, 349-350; Wayne R. Gutowsky, *Burial Sites of the Survivors of the Little Big Horn Battle*, unpublished manuscript, 12; Sandy Barnard, *Custer's First Sergeant John Ryan*, Terre Haute, IN: AST Press, 1996, 204; Sandy Barnard, editor, *Ten Years with Custer: A 7th Cavalryman's Memoirs*, Terre Haute, IN: AST Press, 2001, 216; Barry Johnson, *A Captain of Chivalric Courage: Thomas H. French, 7th Cavalry*, The Brand Book, Vol. 25, Numbers 1&2, London: The English Westerners' Society, 1987, 40; and Roger L. Williams, *Military Register of Custer's Last Command*, Norman, OK: The Arthur H. Clark Company, 2009, 304.

[62] National Archives and Records Administration, Washington, D.C., Records Group 94, Records of the Adjutant General's Office – Army, Carded Medical Records Regular Army, 1821-1884, Entry 529 (Unit 7), Charles White (Henry Weihe) – Box 426 (Wemster-Winter).

[63] National Archives and Records Administration, Washington, D.C., Records Group 94, Records of the Adjutant General's Office – Army, Carded Medical Records Regular Army, 1821-1884, Entry 529 (Unit 7), Charles White (Henry Weihe) – Box 426 (Wemster-Winter).

[64] National Archives and Records Administration, Washington, D.C., Records Group 153, Records of the Office of the Judge Advocate General – Army, Court-Martial Case Files, 1809-1894, Sergeant Charles White – Case # QQ-1418. Headquarters Department of Dakota, General Court-Martial Orders #100, St. Paul, MN, September 25, 1879.

[65] National Archives and Records Administration, Washington, D.C., Records Group 153, Records of the Office of the Judge Advocate General – Army, Court-Martial Case Files, 1809-1894, Sergeant Charles White – Case # QQ-1418. Headquarters Department of Dakota, General Court-Martial Orders #100, St. Paul, MN, September 25, 1879.

[66] National Archives and Records Administration, Washington, D.C., Records Group 153, Records of the Office of the Judge Advocate General – Army, Court-Martial Case Files, 1809-1894, Sergeant Charles White – Case # QQ-1418. Headquarters Department of Dakota, General Court-Martial Orders #100, St. Paul, MN, September 25, 1879.

[67] National Archives and Records Administration, Washington, D.C., Records Group 94, Records of the Adjutant General's Office – Army, Carded Medical Records Regular Army, 1821-1884, Entry 529 (Unit 7), Charles White (Henry Weihe) – Box 426 (Wemster-Winter).

[68] Roger L. Williams, *Military Register of Custer's Last Command*, Norman, OK: The Arthur H. Clark Company, 2009, 304.

[69] Ronald H. Nichols, editor, *Men with Custer: Biographies of the 7th Cavalry*, Hardin, MT: Custer Battlefield Historical and Museum Association, 2000, 349-350; Wayne R. Gutowsky, *Burial Sites of the Survivors of the Little Big Horn Battle*, unpublished manuscript, 12; Sandy Barnard, *Custer's First Sergeant John Ryan*, Terre Haute, IN: AST Press, 1996, 204; Sandy Barnard, editor, *Ten Years with Custer: A 7th Cavalryman's Memoirs*, Terre Haute, IN: AST Press, 2001, 216; Barry Johnson, *A Captain of Chivalric Courage: Thomas H. French, 7th Cavalry*, The Brand Book, Vol. 25, Numbers 1&2, London: The English Westerners' Society, 1987, 40; and Roger L. Williams, *Military Register of Custer's Last Command*, Norman, OK: The Arthur H. Clark Company, 2009, 304.

[70] National Archives and Records Administration, Washington, D.C., Records Group 94, Records of the Adjutant General's Office – Army, Carded Medical Records Regular Army, 1821-1884, Entry 529 (Unit 7), Frank Neely – Box 411 (L. Moore-Neilson).

[71] Ronald H. Nichols, editor, *Men with Custer: Biographies of the 7th Cavalry*, Hardin, MT: Custer Battlefield Historical and Museum Association, 2000, 244; Roger L. Williams, *Military Register of Custer's Last Command*, Norman, OK: The Arthur H. Clark Company, 2009, 232; and National Archives and Records Administration, Washington, D.C., Records Group 94, Records of the Adjutant General's Office – Army, Carded Medical Records Regular Army, 1821-1884, Entry 529 (Unit 6), Frank Neely – Box 383 (Naughton-Oliver).

[72] Ronald H. Nichols, editor, *Men with Custer: Biographies of the 7th Cavalry*, Hardin, MT: Custer Battlefield Historical and Museum Association, 2000, 244; and Roger L. Williams, *Military Register of Custer's Last Command*, Norman, OK: The Arthur H. Clark Company, 2009, 232.

[73] Kenneth Hammer, *Men with Custer; the Working Copy*, 2009, 197.

[74] Records Group 94, Records of the Adjutant General's Office – Reports of Surgeons Accompanying Expeditions, Entry 624 (Box 1), Letter from Surgeon Tilton to the Surgeon General, October 26, 1877.

[75] Email discussions with Bob and Edward Connor, great-grandsons of Private Jean Baptiste Gallenne, July 2010.

[76] National Archives and Records Administration, Washington, D.C., Records Group 94, Records of the Adjutant General's Office – Army, Carded Medical Records Regular Army, 1821-1884, Entry 529 (Unit 7), Jean Gallenne – Box 406 (Gallene-Graham).

[77] Email discussions with Bob and Edward Connor, great-grandsons of Private Jean Baptiste Gallenne, July 2010; and Genealogy website www.ceangail.com.

[78] Ronald H. Nichols, editor, *Men with Custer: Biographies of the 7th Cavalry*, Hardin, MT: Custer Battlefield Historical and Museum Association, 2000, 111; Jean B. Gallenne, "The Fatal Day: A Soldier's Journal," St. Paul (MN) *Pioneer Press*, January 16, 1879; and Roger L. Williams, *Military Register of Custer's Last Command*, Norman, OK: The Arthur H. Clark Company, 2009, 133.

[79] Email discussions with Bob and Edward Connor, great-grandsons of Private Jean Baptiste Gallenne, July 2010; and Genealogy website www.ceangail.com.

[80] Ronald H. Nichols, editor, *Men with Custer: Biographies of the 7th Cavalry*, Hardin, MT: Custer Battlefield Historical and Museum Association, 2000, 298-299; Lorna Thackeray, "Haunted by history: Tragedy followed Bighorn battle survivors," *Billings Gazette*, Billings, MT: June 21, 2009; and Roger L. Williams, *Military Register of Custer's Last Command*, Norman, OK: The Arthur H. Clark Company, 2009, 269-270.

[81] National Archives and Records Administration, Washington, D.C., Records Group 153, Records of the Office of the Judge Advocate General – Army, Court-Martial Case Files, 1809-1894, Private John Whisten – Case # PP-5461. Headquarters Department of Dakota, General Court-Martial Orders #57, St. Paul, MN, December 28, 1876.

[82] National Archives and Records Administration, Washington, D.C., Records Group 153, Records of the Office of the Judge Advocate General – Army, Court-Martial Case Files, 1809-1894, Private John Whisten – Case # PP-5461. Headquarters Department of Dakota, General Court-Martial Orders #57, St. Paul, MN, December 28, 1876.

[83] National Archives and Records Administration, Washington, D.C., Records Group 94, Records of the Adjutant General's Office – Army, Carded Medical Records Regular Army, 1821-1884, Entry 529 (Unit 7), John Whisten – Box 426 (Wemster-Winter).

[84] Ronald H. Nichols, editor, *Men with Custer: Biographies of the 7th Cavalry*, Hardin, MT: Custer Battlefield Historical and Museum Association, 2000, 354-355; Wayne R. Gutowsky, *Burial Sites of the Survivors of the Little Big Horn Battle*, unpublished manuscript, 5; and Roger L. Williams, *Military Register of Custer's Last Command*, Norman, OK: The Arthur H. Clark Company, 2009, 306.

[85] Ronald H. Nichols, editor, *Men with Custer: Biographies of the 7th Cavalry*, Hardin, MT: Custer Battlefield Historical and Museum Association, 2000, 209; and Dr. Kenneth Hammer Special Collection at the University of Wisconsin-Whitewater Library, Box 4, Widows and Children Folder.

[86] National Archives and Records Administration, Washington, D.C., Records Group 94, Records of the Adjutant General's Office – Army, Carded Medical Records Regular Army, 1821-1884, Entry 529 (Unit 7), Edward Mathey – Box 408 (Mackey-McCarthey).

[87] Ronald H. Nichols, editor, *Men with Custer: Biographies of the 7th Cavalry*, Hardin, MT: Custer Battlefield Historical and Museum Association, 2000, 209; Dr. Kenneth Hammer Special Collection at the University of Wisconsin-Whitewater Library, Box 4, Widows and Children Folder and Wayne R. Gutowsky, *Burial Sites of the Survivors of the Little Big Horn Battle*, unpublished manuscript, 4.

[88] Post Orders No. 97, Headquarters, Fort Rice, Dakota Territory, dated July 28, 1876, Records Group 393, Records of U. S. Army Continental Commands, 1821-1920, Part V, Military Installations, Fort Rice, North Dakota, Entry 5.

[89] Records Group 393, Records of U.S. Army Continental Commands, 1821-1920, Part V, Military Installations, Fort Meade, South Dakota, Entry 24 – Register of Patients, Volume 1; 209.

[90] National Archives and Records Administration, Washington, D.C., Records Group 153, Records of the Office of the Judge Advocate General – Army, Court-Martial Case Files, 1809-1894, Sergeant John H. Meier – Case # RR-2319. Headquarters Department of Dakota, General Court-Martial Orders #2, St. Paul, MN, February 14, 1887; including Captain Francis M. Gibson Statement.

[91] National Archives and Records Administration, Washington, D.C., Records Group 153, Records of the Office of the Judge Advocate General – Army, Court-Martial Case Files, 1809-1894, Sergeant John H. Meier – Case # RR-2319. Headquarters Department of Dakota, General Court-Martial Orders #2, St. Paul, MN, February 14, 1887.

[92] Records Group 393, Records of U.S. Army Continental Commands, 1821-1920, Part V, Military Installations, Fort Meade, South Dakota, Entry 24 – Register of Patients, Volume 2; 108.

[93] National Archives and Records Administration, Washington, D.C., Records Group 153, Records of the Office of the Judge Advocate General – Army, Court-Martial Case Files, 1809-1894, Private John H. Meier – Case # RR-3698. Headquarters Department of the Missouri, General Court-Martial Orders #35, Fort Leavenworth, KS, August 26, 1889.

[94] National Archives and Records Administration, Washington, D.C., Records Group 153, Records of the Office of the Judge Advocate General – Army, Court-Martial Case Files, 1809-1894, Private John H. Meier – Case # RR-3698. Headquarters Department of the Missouri, General Court-Martial Orders #35, Fort Leavenworth, KS, August 26, 1889.

[95] Roger L. Williams, *Military Register of Custer's Last Command*, Norman, OK: The Arthur H. Clark Company, 2009, 215-216.

[96] Ronald H. Nichols, editor, *Men with Custer: Biographies of the 7th Cavalry*, Hardin, MT: Custer Battlefield Historical and Museum Association, 2000, 226; and Wayne R. Gutowsky, *Burial Sites of the Survivors of the Little Big Horn Battle*, unpublished manuscript, 14.

[97] Ronald H. Nichols, editor, *Men with Custer: Biographies of the 7th Cavalry*, Hardin, MT: Custer Battlefield Historical and Museum Association, 2000, 77-78; Wayne R. Gutowsky, *Burial Sites of the Survivors of the Little Big Horn Battle*, unpublished manuscript, 4; and Roger L. Williams, *Military Register of Custer's Last Command*, Norman, OK: The Arthur H. Clark Company, 2009, 105.

[98] Ronald H. Nichols, editor, *Men with Custer: Biographies of the 7th Cavalry*, Hardin, MT: Custer Battlefield Historical and Museum Association, 2000, 217; and Roger L. Williams, *Military Register of Custer's Last Command*, Norman, OK: The Arthur H. Clark Company, 2009, 202.

[99] National Archives and Records Administration, Washington, D.C., Records Group 153, Records of the Office of the Judge Advocate General – Army, Court-Martial Case Files, 1809-1894, Corporal John McGlone – Case # RR-1047. Headquarters Department of the East, Governor's Island, New York City, General Court-Martial Orders #92, April 15, 1885.

[100] Ronald H. Nichols, editor, *Men with Custer: Biographies of the 7th Cavalry*, Hardin, MT: Custer Battlefield Historical and Museum Association, 2000, 217; Wayne R. Gutowsky, *Burial Sites of the Survivors of the Little Big Horn Battle*, unpublished manuscript, 4; and Roger L. Williams, *Military Register of Custer's Last Command*, Norman, OK: The Arthur H. Clark Company, 2009, 202.

[101] National Archives and Records Administration, Washington, D.C., Records Group 94, Records of the Adjutant General's Office – Army, Carded Medical Records Regular Army, 1821-1884, Entry 529 (Unit 7), Charles Wiedman (filed under Weidman) – Box 425 (Volkmann-Weller).

[102] Ronald H. Nichols, editor, *Men with Custer: Biographies of the 7th Cavalry*, Hardin, MT: Custer Battlefield Historical and Museum Association, 2000, 358; Wayne R. Gutowsky, *Burial Sites of the Survivors of the Little Big Horn Battle*, unpublished manuscript, 5; and Roger L. Williams, *Military Register of Custer's Last Command*, Norman, OK: The Arthur H. Clark Company, 2009, 308.

[103] National Archives and Records Administration, Washington, D.C., Records Group 94, Records of the Adjutant General's Office – Army, Carded Medical Records Regular Army, 1821-1884, Entry 529 (Unit 7), Roman Rutten – Box 420 (Roeder-Schneider).

[104] National Archives and Records Administration, Washington, D.C., Records Group 94, Records of the Adjutant General's Office – Army, Carded Medical Records Regular Army, 1821-1884, Entry 529 (Unit 7), Roman Rutten – Box 420 (Roeder-Schneider).

[105] Records Group 393, Records of U.S. Army Continental Commands, 1821-1920, Military Installations, Fort Meade, South Dakota (298), Entry 24 – Register of Patients, Volume 1; 133 and Volume 2; 18, 42 and 99.

[106] Email discussions with Dennis K. "DK" Clark, author of "Private Roman Rutten: Custer's Tailor," 15th Annual Symposium, Custer Battlefield Historical & Museum Association, October 2009.

[107] Ronald H. Nichols, editor, *Men with Custer: Biographies of the 7th Cavalry*, Hardin, MT: Custer Battlefield Historical and Museum Association, 2000, 287-288; Wayne R. Gutowsky, *Burial Sites of the Survivors of the Little Big Horn Battle*, unpublished manuscript, 6; and Dennis Clark, "Private Roman Rutten: Custer's Tailor," 15th Annual Symposium, Custer Battlefield Historical & Museum Association, held at Hardin, MT on June 22, 2001, 42-43.

[108] Ronald H. Nichols, editor, *Men with Custer: Biographies of the 7th Cavalry*, Hardin, MT: Custer Battlefield Historical and Museum Association, 2000, 305; Wayne R. Gutowsky, *Burial Sites of the Survivors of the Little Big Horn Battle*, unpublished manuscript, 4; Richard G. Hardorff, editor, *On the Little Bighorn with Walter Camp; A Collection of Walter Mason Camp's Letters, Notes and opinions on Custer's Last Fight*, El Segundo, CA: Upton & Sons Publishers, 2002, 128; and Roger L. Williams, *Military Register of Custer's Last Command*, Norman, OK: The Arthur H. Clark Company, 2009, 273.

[109] Gregory Michno, *The Mystery of E Troop: Custer's Gray Horse Company at the Little Bighorn*, Missoula, Montana: Mountain Press Publishing Company, 1994, 140.

[110] Ronald H. Nichols, editor, *Men with Custer: Biographies of the 7th Cavalry*, Hardin, MT: Custer Battlefield Historical and Museum Association, 2000, 289; Wayne R. Gutowsky, *Burial Sites of the Survivors of the Little Big Horn Battle*, unpublished manuscript, 8; Sandy Barnard, *Custer's First Sergeant John Ryan*, Terre Haute, IN: AST Press, 1996, 206; Sandy Barnard, editor, *Ten Years with Custer: A 7th Cavalryman's Memoirs*, Terre Haute, IN: AST Press, 2001, 7; United States of America Bureau of Pensions Letter to John Ryan dated October 11, 1915; and United States of America Bureau of Pensions Letter to John Ryan dated August 11, 1924.

[111] National Archives and Records Administration, Washington, D.C., Records Group 94, Records of the Adjutant General's Office – Army, Carded Medical Records Regular Army, 1821-1884, Entry 529 (Unit 7), William Robinson – Box 419 (Radigando-Roche).

[112] Ronald H. Nichols, editor, *Men with Custer: Biographies of the 7th Cavalry*, Hardin, MT: Custer Battlefield Historical and Museum Association, 2000, 280; and Wayne R. Gutowsky, *Burial Sites of the Survivors of the Little Big Horn Battle*, unpublished manuscript, 14.

[113] Roger L. Williams, *Military Register of Custer's Last Command*, Norman, OK: The Arthur H. Clark Company, 2009, 275.

[114] National Archives and Records Administration, Washington, D.C., Records Group 153, Records of the Office of the Judge Advocate General – Army, Court-Martial Case Files, 1809-1894, Corporal Frank Sniffin – Case # QQ-2687. Headquarters Department of Dakota, General Court-Martial Orders #118, Fort Snelling, MN, September 17, 1881.

[115] National Archives and Records Administration, Washington, D.C., Records Group 153, Records of the Office of the Judge Advocate General – Army, Court-Martial Case Files, 1809-1894, Corporal Frank Sniffin – Case # QQ-3230. Headquarters Department of Dakota, General Court-Martial Orders #118, Fort Snelling, MN, June 12, 1882.

[116] National Archives and Records Administration, Washington, D.C., Records Group 94, Records of the Adjutant General's Office – Army, Carded Medical Records Regular Army, 1821-1884, Entry 529 (Unit 7), Frank Sniffin – Box 422 (Skillmano-Staunton).

[117] National Archives and Records Administration, Washington, D.C., Records Group 153, Records of the Office of the Judge Advocate General – Army, Court-Martial Case Files, 1809-1894, Corporal Frank Sniffin – Case # RR-367. Headquarters Department of Dakota, General Court-Martial Orders #78, Fort Snelling, MN, June 5, 1884.

[118] Records Group 393, Records of U.S. Army Continental Commands, 1821-1920, Part V, Military Installations, Fort Meade, South Dakota, Entry 24 – Register of Patients, Volume 1; 155.

[119] Roger L. Williams, *Military Register of Custer's Last Command*, Norman, OK: The Arthur H. Clark Company, 2009, 275.

[120] Ronald H. Nichols, editor, *Men with Custer: Biographies of the 7th Cavalry*, Hardin, MT: Custer Battlefield Historical and Museum Association, 2000, 311; Wayne R. Gutowsky, *Burial Sites of the Survivors of the Little Big Horn Battle*, unpublished manuscript, 13; Kenneth Hammer, *Men with Custer; the Working Copy*, 2009, 245; and Roger L. Williams, *Military Register of Custer's Last Command*, Norman, OK: The Arthur H. Clark Company, 2009, 275.

[121] Robert Earle Forrest, "Fighting with Custer: Two Men Who Were with Gallant General Custer at Little Bighorn Battle Are Still Living," *Morning Observer*, Washington, PA: October 1932.

[122] Ronald H. Nichols, editor, *Men with Custer: Biographies of the 7th Cavalry*, Hardin, MT: Custer Battlefield Historical and Museum Association, 2000, 262; and Wayne R. Gutowsky, *Burial Sites of the Survivors of the Little Big Horn Battle*, unpublished manuscript, 12.

[123] Post Orders No. 119, Headquarters, Fort Rice, Dakota Territory, dated September 9, 1876, Records Group 393, Records of U. S. Army Continental Commands, 1821-1920, Part V, Military Installations, Fort Rice, North Dakota, Entry 5.

[124] National Archives and Records Administration, Washington, D.C., Records Group 94, Records of the Adjutant General's Office – Army, Carded Medical Records Regular Army, 1821-1884, Entry 529 (Unit 7), Daniel Newell – Box 417 (Nelau-O'Sullivan).

[125] National Archives and Records Administration, Washington, D.C., Records Group 94, Records of the Adjutant General's Office – Army, Carded Medical Records Regular Army, 1821-1884, Entry 529 (Unit 7), Daniel Newell – Box 417 (Nelau-O'Sullivan).

[126] John Carroll, *The Sunshine Magazine Articles*, Bryan, TX: Privately Published, 1979, 15.

[127] Ronald H. Nichols, editor, *Men with Custer: Biographies of the 7th Cavalry*, Hardin, MT: Custer Battlefield Historical and Museum Association, 2000, 245; Wayne R. Gutowsky, *Burial Sites of the Survivors of the Little Big Horn Battle*, unpublished manuscript, 12; John Carroll, editor, *A Seventh Cavalry Scrapbook*, Volume 1, "Memories of the Battle of the Little Big Horn," by Daniel Newell, Bryan, TX: Privately Published, 1978, 20; Dr. Kenneth Hammer Special Collection at the University of Wisconsin-Whitewater Library, Box 4, Widows and Children Folder and Roger L. Williams, *Military Register of Custer's Last Command*, Norman, OK: The Arthur H. Clark Company, 2009, 233.

[128] Ronald H. Nichols, editor, *Men with Custer: Biographies of the 7th Cavalry*, Hardin, MT: Custer Battlefield Historical and Museum Association, 2000, 306; Wayne R. Gutowsky, *Burial Sites of the Survivors of the Little Big Horn Battle*, unpublished manuscript, 5; Earle Alonzo Brininstool, *Troopers with Custer: Incidents of the Battle of the Little Big Horn*, Harrisburg, PA: The Stackpole Company, 1952, 39, 64; and Roger L. Williams, *Military Register of Custer's Last Command*, Norman, OK: The Arthur H. Clark Company, 2009, 273.

[129] Kenneth Hammer, *Custer in '76: Walter Camp's Notes on the Custer Fight*, Provo, UT: Brigham Young University, 1976, 131.

[130] National Archives and Records Administration, Washington, D.C., Records Group 94, Records of the Adjutant General's Office – Army, Carded Medical Records Regular Army, 1821-1884, Entry 529 (Unit 7), William Morris – Box 411 (L. Moore-Neilson).

[131] Neil C. Mangum, editor, "Reno's Battalion in the Battle of the Little Big Horn," *Greasy Grass Magazine*, Volume 2, May 1986, Hardin, MT: Custer Battlefield Historical & Museum Association, 3.

[132] National Archives and Records Administration, Washington, D.C., Records Group 94, Records of the Adjutant General's Office – Army, Carded Medical Records Regular Army, 1821-1884, Entry 529 (Unit 7), William Morris – Box 411 (L. Moore-Neilson).

[133] National Archives and Records Administration, Washington, D.C., Records Group 94, Records of the Adjutant General's Office – Army, Carded Medical Records Regular Army, 1821-1884, Entry 529 (Unit 7), William Morris – Box 411 (L. Moore-Neilson).

[134] Ronald H. Nichols, editor, *Men with Custer: Biographies of the 7th Cavalry*, Hardin, MT: Custer Battlefield Historical and Museum Association, 2000, 235-236; Don Rickey, Jr., *Forty Miles a Day on Beans and Hay*, Norman, OK: University of Oklahoma Press, 1972, 344; "William E. Morris, Jurist, Dead at 75," *New York Times*, New York: November 27, 1933, 17; and Roger L. Williams, *Military Register of Custer's Last Command*, Norman, OK: The Arthur H. Clark Company, 2009, 222.

[135] Ronald H. Nichols, editor, *Men with Custer: Biographies of the 7th Cavalry*, Hardin, MT: Custer Battlefield Historical and Museum Association, 2000, 235-236; Don Rickey, Jr., *Forty Miles a Day on Beans and Hay*, Norman, OK: University of Oklahoma Press, 1972, 344; Dr. Kenneth Hammer Special Collection at the University of Wisconsin-Whitewater Library, Box 4, Widows and Children Folder; "William E. Morris, Jurist, Dead at 75," *New York Times*, New York: November 27, 1933, 17; and File #133, William E. Morris; includes Bureau of Pensions Questionnaire, October 30, 1923, Washington, located at the Little Big Horn Battlefield National Monument Archives (White Swan Library), Crow Agency, Montana.

[136] Ronald H. Nichols, editor, *Men with Custer: Biographies of the 7th Cavalry*, Hardin, MT: Custer Battlefield Historical and Museum Association, 2000, 186; National Archives and Records Administration, Washington, D.C., Records Group 153, Records of the Office of the Judge Advocate General – Army, Court-Martial Case Files, 1809-1894, Sergeant Charles White – Case # QQ-1418. Headquarters Department of Dakota, General Court-Martial Orders #100, St. Paul, MN, September 25, 1879; and Roger L. Williams, *Military Register of Custer's Last Command*, Norman, OK: The Arthur H. Clark Company, 2009, 186.

[137] Roger L. Williams, *Military Register of Custer's Last Command*, Norman, OK: The Arthur H. Clark Company, 2009, 290, 293.

[138] National Archives and Records Administration, Washington, D.C., Records Group 94, Records of the Adjutant General's Office – Army, Carded Medical Records Regular Army, 1821-1884, Entry 529 (Unit 7), Bernard Golden – Box 406 (Gallene-Graham).

[139] Ronald H. Nichols, editor, *Men with Custer: Biographies of the 7th Cavalry*, Hardin, MT: Custer Battlefield Historical and Museum Association, 2000, 123, 349; Roger L. Williams, *Military Register of Custer's Last Command*, Norman, OK: The Arthur H. Clark Company, 2009, 137-138; and Letter from Roman Rutten to John Ryan, Leavenworth, Kansas, April 9, 1911. A copy of the letter is in the Little Big Horn Battlefield National Monument Archive, c.3622, A.19.

[140] National Archives and Records Administration, Washington, D.C., Records Group 153, Records of the Office of the Judge Advocate General – Army, Court-Martial Case Files, 1809-1894, Trumpeter Charles Fischer – Case # PP-5461. Headquarters Department of Dakota, General Court-Martial Orders #57, St. Paul, MN, December 28, 1876.

[141] Ronald H. Nichols, editor, *Men with Custer: Biographies of the 7th Cavalry*, Hardin, MT: Custer Battlefield Historical and Museum Association, 2000, 101; Sandy Barnard, *Custer's First Sergeant John Ryan*, Terre Haute, IN: AST Press, 1996, 202-203; and Roger L. Williams, *Military Register of Custer's Last Command*, Norman, OK: The Arthur H. Clark Company, 2009, 147-148.

[142] Roger L. Williams, *Military Register of Custer's Last Command*, Norman, OK: The Arthur H. Clark Company, 2009, 309.

[143] National Archives and Records Administration, Washington, D.C., Records Group 94, Records of the Adjutant General's Office – Army, Carded Medical Records Regular Army, 1821-1884, Entry 529 (Unit 7), Charles Williams – Box 426 (Wemster-Winter).

[144] Ronald H. Nichols, editor, *Men with Custer: Biographies of the 7th Cavalry*, Hardin, MT: Custer Battlefield Historical and Museum Association, 2000, 359; and Roger L. Williams, *Military Register of Custer's Last Command*, Norman, OK: The Arthur H. Clark Company, 2009, 309.

[145] National Archives and Records Administration, Washington, D.C., Records Group 153, Records of the Office of the Judge Advocate General – Army, Court-Martial Case Files, 1809-1894, Private Henry C. Weaver – Case # QQ-619. Headquarters Department of Dakota, General Court-Martial Orders, St. Paul, MN, May 9, 1878.

[146] National Archives and Records Administration, Washington, D.C., Records Group 153, Records of the Office of the Judge Advocate General – Army, Court-Martial Case Files, 1809-1894, Private Henry C. Weaver – Case # QQ-1044. Headquarters Department of Dakota, General Court-Martial Orders #3, St. Paul, MN, January 15, 1879.

[147] National Archives and Records Administration, Washington, D.C., Records Group 153, Records of the Office of the Judge Advocate General – Army, Court-Martial Case Files, 1809-1894, Private Henry C. Weaver – Case # QQ-1044; Private Henry C. Weaver Statement.

[148] Ronald H. Nichols, editor, *Men with Custer: Biographies of the 7th Cavalry*, Hardin, MT: Custer Battlefield Historical and Museum Association, 2000, 348; and Roger L. Williams, *Military Register of Custer's Last Command*, Norman, OK: The Arthur H. Clark Company, 2009, 303.

[149] National Archives and Records Administration, Washington, D.C., Records Group 153, Records of the Office of the Judge Advocate General – Army, Court-Martial Case Files, 1809-1894, Sergeant Charles White – Case # QQ-1418. Headquarters Department of Dakota, General Court-Martial Orders #100, St. Paul, MN, September 25, 1879.

[150] Ronald H. Nichols, editor, *Men with Custer: Biographies of the 7th Cavalry*, Hardin, MT: Custer Battlefield Historical and Museum Association, 2000, 337; Roger L. Williams, *Military Register of Custer's Last Command*, Norman, OK: The Arthur H. Clark Company, 2009, 295.

[151] Ronald H. Nichols, editor, *Men with Custer: Biographies of the 7th Cavalry*, Hardin, MT: Custer Battlefield Historical and Museum Association, 2000, 291; and Roger L. Williams, *Military Register of Custer's Last Command*, Norman, OK: The Arthur H. Clark Company, 2009, 259.

[152] National Archives and Records Administration, Washington, D.C., Records Group 94, Records of the Adjutant General's Office – Army, Carded Medical Records Regular Army, 1821-1884, Entry 529 (Unit 7), John Seamans – Box 421 (Scholl-Simius).

[153] Ronald H. Nichols, editor, *Men with Custer: Biographies of the 7th Cavalry*, Hardin, MT: Custer Battlefield Historical and Museum Association, 2000, 297; and Roger L. Williams, *Military Register of Custer's Last Command*, Norman, OK: The Arthur H. Clark Company, 2009, 268.

[154] National Archives and Records Administration, Washington, D.C., Records Group 153, Records of the Office of the Judge Advocate General – Army, Court-Martial Case Files, 1809-1894, Private Frank Stratton – Case # QQ-109; Private Frank Stratton Statement.

[155] National Archives and Records Administration, Washington, D.C., Records Group 153, Records of the Office of the Judge Advocate General – Army, Court-Martial Case Files, 1809-1894, Private Frank Stratton – Case # QQ-109. Headquarters, Department of Dakota, General Court-Martial Orders #8, St. Paul, MN, February 27, 1877.

[156] Ronald H. Nichols, editor, *Men with Custer: Biographies of the 7th Cavalry*, Hardin, MT: Custer Battlefield Historical and Museum Association, 2000, 319; and Roger L. Williams, *Military Register of Custer's Last Command*, Norman, OK: The Arthur H. Clark Company, 2009, 278.

[157] Ronald H. Nichols, editor, *Men with Custer: Biographies of the 7th Cavalry*, Hardin, MT: Custer Battlefield Historical and Museum Association, 2000, 291; Barry Johnson, *A Captain of Chivalric Courage: Thomas H. French, 7th Cavalry*, The Brand Book, Vol. 25, Numbers 1&2, London: The English Westerners' Society, 1987, 40; William O. Taylor, *With Custer on the Little Bighorn*, New York: Viking, 1996, 182; Box 4, Casualties Folder, draft "Wounded Casualties in the Little Bighorn River Fight," by Kenneth Hammer and Vern Smalley; Roger L. Williams, *Military Register of Custer's Last Command*, Norman, OK: The Arthur H. Clark Company, 2009, 259; and John Gray, *Centennial Campaign: The Sioux War of 1876*, Fort Collins, CO: The Old Army Press, 1976, 281.

[158] National Archives and Records Administration, Washington, D.C., Records Group 153, Records of the Office of the Judge Advocate General – Army, Court-Martial Case Files, 1809-1894, Corporal Hobart Ryder – Case # QQ-1361. Headquarters Department of Dakota, General Court-Martial Orders #96, St. Paul, MN, September 10, 1879; Corporal Hobart Ryder Statement.

[159] National Archives and Records Administration, Washington, D.C., Records Group 153, Records of the Office of the Judge Advocate General – Army, Court-Martial Case Files, 1809-1894, Corporal Hobart Ryder – Case # QQ-1361. Headquarters Department of Dakota, General Court-Martial Orders #96, St. Paul, MN, September 10, 1879.

[160] National Archives and Records Administration, Washington, D.C., Records Group 94, Records of the Adjutant General's Office – Army, Carded Medical Records Regular Army, 1821-1884, Entry 529 (Unit 7), Hobart Ryder – Box 420 (Roeder-Schneider).

[161] Ronald H. Nichols, editor, *Men with Custer: Biographies of the 7th Cavalry*, Hardin, MT: Custer Battlefield Historical and Museum Association, 2000, 291; William O. Taylor, *With Custer on the Little Bighorn*, New York: Viking, 1996, 182; Roger L. Williams, *Military Register of Custer's Last Command*, Norman, OK: The Arthur H. Clark Company, 2009, 259; and John Gray, *Centennial Campaign: The Sioux War of 1876*, Fort Collins, CO: The Old Army Press, 1976, 281.

[162] National Archives and Records Administration, Washington, D.C., Records Group 94, Records of the Adjutant General's Office – Army, Carded Medical Records Regular Army, 1821-1884, Entry 529 (Unit 7), Robert Senn – Box 421 (Scholl-Simius).

[163] National Archives and Records Administration, Washington, D.C., Records Group 94, Records of the Adjutant General's Office

– Army, Carded Medical Records Regular Army, 1821-1884, Entry 529 (Unit 7), Robert Senn – Box 421 (Scholl-Simius).

[164] National Archives and Records Administration, Washington, D.C., Records Group 94, Records of the Adjutant General's Office – Army, Carded Medical Records Regular Army, 1821-1884, Entry 529 (Unit 7), Robert Senn – Box 421 (Scholl-Simius).

[165] National Archives and Records Administration, Washington, D.C., Records Group 153, Records of the Office of the Judge Advocate General – Army, Court-Martial Case Files, 1809-1894, Private Robert Senn – Case # QQ-1361. Headquarters Department of Dakota, General Court-Martial Orders #96, St. Paul, MN, September 10, 1879.

[166] Ronald H. Nichols, editor, *Men with Custer: Biographies of the 7th Cavalry*, Hardin, MT: Custer Battlefield Historical and Museum Association, 2000, 298; and Roger L. Williams, *Military Register of Custer's Last Command*, Norman, OK: The Arthur H. Clark Company, 2009, 269.

Conclusion

[1] Thomas Goodrich, *Scalp Dance: Indian Warfare on the High Plains, 1865-1879*, Mechanicsburg, PA: Stackpole Books, 1997, 310.

[2] Walter M. Camp, "Field Notes," Lilly Library, Indiana University, Bloomington, IN., Box 2, Folder 9 – Little Bighorn, Part 1.

[3] Larry Sklenar, *To Hell with Honor; Custer and the Little Bighorn*, Norman, OK: University of Oklahoma Press, 2003, 328; and Thomas B. Marquis, *Keep the Last Bullet for Yourself*, Algonac, MI: Reference Publications, 1985, 167-169.

[4] Colonel W.A. Graham, *The Custer Myth: A Source Book of Custeriana*, Mechanicsburg, PA: Stackpole Books, 2000, 52, 60, 63, 76, 78, 87, 91 and 98.

[5] Colonel W.A. Graham, *The Custer Myth: A Source Book of Custeriana*, Mechanicsburg, PA: Stackpole Books, 2000, 103, 110, 112.

[6] Lorna Thackeray, "Haunted by history: Tragedy followed Bighorn battle survivors," *Billings Gazette*, Billings, MT: June 21, 2009.

[7] Kenneth Hammer, *Men with Custer; the Working Copy*, 2009, 254; and Roger L. Williams, *Military Register of Custer's Last Command*, Norman, OK: The Arthur H. Clark Company, 2009, 134.

[8] Roger L. Williams, *Military Register of Custer's Last Command*, Norman, OK: The Arthur H. Clark Company, 2009, 296.

[9] Brian W. Dippie, *Custer's Last Stand: The Anatomy of an American Myth*, Lincoln, NE: University of Nebraska Press, 1976, 53.

Epilogue

[1] Glendolin D. Wagner, *Old Neutriment*, New York: Sol Lewis, 1973, 83.

[2] Joseph M. Marshall, *The Day the World Ended at Little Bighorn: A Lakota History*, New York: Viking, 2003, 19.

[3] Charles M. Robinson, *A Good Year to Die: The Story of the Great Sioux War*, New York: Random House, 1995, xxx-xxxi.

[4] Charles M. Robinson, *A Good Year to Die: The Story of the Great Sioux War*, New York: Random House, 1995, 225, 237.

[5] Gregory Michno, *The Mystery of E Troop: Custer's Gray Horse Company at the Little Bighorn*, Missoula, Montana: Mountain Press Publishing Company, 1994, 203.

[6] Katherine Gibson Fougera, *With Custer's Cavalry*, Caldwell, ID: The Caxton Printers, 1940, 234.

[7] Katherine Gibson Fougera, *With Custer's Cavalry*, Caldwell, ID: The Caxton Printers, 1940, 284.

[8] Don Rickey, Jr., *Forty Miles a Day on Beans and Hay*, Norman, OK: University of Oklahoma Press, 1972, 78.

Appendix 2: Causes of Victory and Defeat

[1] Edgar I. Stewart, *Custer's Luck*, Norman, OK: University of Oklahoma Press, 1980, 177.

[2] Roger L. Williams, *Military Register of Custer's Last Command*, Norman, OK: The Arthur H. Clark Company, 2009, 389.

[3] Major Reno wrote a letter to the Army Chief of Ordnance, Brigadier General Stephen Vincent Benet, on July 11, 1876 concerning extraction issues. In the letter, Reno claimed that six of the 380 carbines in his command had become unserviceable when the breech block had failed to close properly, with the result that the head of the cartridge was torn off when the weapon was fired. That equates to a 1.5% carbine failure rate, but this may not have counted the carbine extraction problems that Captain French fixed during the fight. Nor would it have accounted for those carbines belonging to the troops that went with Custer and were picked up by the Indians. Having said that, the numbers do not support significant extraction problems – unless you look at it from the individual trooper's point of view, where if his carbine becomes unfireable, it is a 100% failure. Source: C. Lee Noyes, "A Question of Arms: Ordnance "Causes" and Consequences of the Little Bighorn," 11th Annual Symposium, Custer Battlefield Historical & Museum Association, held at Hardin, MT on June 27, 1997, 38.

[4] Alexander Rose, *American Rifle: A Biography*, New York: Delacorte Press, 2008, 192.

[5] Edgar I. Stewart, *Custer's Luck*, Norman, OK: University of Oklahoma Press, 1980, 179.

Appendix 3: Battlefield Artifacts for the Valley Fight at the Little Bighorn

[1] Charles E. Rankin, *Legacy: New Perspectives on the Battle of the Little Bighorn*, Helena, MT: Montana Historical Society Press, 1996, 197.

[2] Darrell Cook, *Little Bighorn Battlefield National Monument Resources Management Plan*, Little Bighorn Battlefield National Monument, MT: July 9, 2007, 11.

[3] John S. duMont, *Custer Battle Guns*, Fort Collins, CO: The Old Army Press, 1974, 87.

[4] Brigid Schulte, "Unearthed War Relics See Battle Again: Archaeologists Decry History Buffs' Digs," *The Washington Post*, April 16, 2006, A-01.

Bibliography

Primary Source Documents

Denver Public Library, Denver, Colorado.

Ellison, Robert S. "Walter M. Camp Papers," WH1702, Western History Collection

File Folder 35, Correspondence from William Morris to Major A.B. Ostrander; letter dated March 26, 1927.

File Folder 45, Walter Camp Research; notes of private diary of Charles White [Henry Charles Weihe], contemporaneously written by him and loaned three years after White's death in 1906 by his widow Jennie W. Weihe to Walter M. Camp.

File Folder 45, Walter Camp Research; letter from William Morris to Walter M. Camp dated November 18, 1908.

Lilly Library, Indiana University, Bloomington, Indiana.

Camp, Walter M. "Field Notes,"

Box 1, Folder 5 – Rosters for US Cavalry, 7th Regiment, Companies G-M

Box 2, Folder 9 – Little Bighorn, Part 1

Box 2, Folder 10 – Little Bighorn, Part 2

Box 2, Folder 11 – Little Bighorn, Part 3

Box 5, Folder 11, Envelope 64 – Includes recollections of Walter Sterland

Box 6, Folder 7, Envelope 82 – Includes recollections of William Morris

Little Big Horn Battlefield National Monument Archives (White Swan Library), Crow Agency, Montana.

File #133, William E. Morris; includes Bureau of Pensions Questionnaire, October 30, 1923, Washington.

Jackson, Royal G. "An Oral History of the Battle of Little Bighorn from the Perspective of the Northern Cheyenne Descendants," University of Wyoming National Park Research Center, Winter 1987 (Contract CX 1200-4-A037).

Letter from the Adjutant Generals Office, Washington to Commanding Officer, 7th U.S. Cavalry, dated September 21, 1868. Letter inquires about the dispositions of several deserters, including Charles Kavanaugh of Company G; letter is found in the alphabetical digital files on 7th Cavalry personnel at the museum.

Letter from Captain Thomas French, Camp on Rosebud Creek, Montana to the Assistant Adjutant General of the Department of the Dakota, dated August 6, 1876. Letter requests that he be allowed to purchase an iron-gray horse for $110; letter is found in the alphabetical digital files on 7th Cavalry personnel at the museum.

Letter from Captain Charles E. Morse, 16th Infantry Regiment, Headquarters, Post: Lebanon, Kentucky, December 19, 1873 to Commanding Officer, 7th Cavalry. Letter states that Joseph Bates had been apprehended for desertion; letter is found in the alphabetical digital files on 7th Cavalry personnel at the museum.

Letter from Roman Rutten to John Ryan, Leavenworth, Kansas, April 9, 1911. Copy of the letter is in the Little Big Horn Battlefield National Monument Archive, c.3622, A.19.

Letter from John Ryan to Walter Camp, West Newton, Massachusetts, February 26, 1910. Copy of the letter is in the Little Bighorn Battlefield National Monument Archive, Item #11743.

Letter from John Ryan to Walter Camp, West Newton, Massachusetts, April 7, 1920. Copy of the letter is in the Little Bighorn Battlefield National Monument Archive, Item #11744-A.

Muster Rolls – 7th U.S. Cavalry, Company L-M, 1866-1884, Microfilm Roll #5 at the Little Bighorn National Monument Archive.

General Court Martial, Orders No. 19, "Official Transcript of the Court Martial of Captain Thomas H. French," Fort Abraham Lincoln, Dakota Territory, January 1879, Headquarters of the Army, Adjutant General's Office, Washington, March 26, 1879. Copy is labelled File #157.

National Archives and Records Administration, Washington, D.C.

Microfilm Publication M-617, "Returns from U.S. Military Posts, 1800-1916, Fort Rice, North Dakota," Roll 1007.

Records Group 94, Records of the Adjutant General's Office – Army, Carded Medical Records Regular Army, 1821-1884, Entry 529 (Unit 3).

Charles Kavanaugh – Box 190 (W. Johnson-Kielhaver)

Records Group 94, Records of the Adjutant General's Office – Army, Carded Medical Records Regular Army, 1821-1884, Entry 529 (Unit 6).

Frank Neely – Box 383 (Naughton-Oliver)

Records Group 94, Records of the Adjutant General's Office – Army, Carded Medical Records Regular Army, 1821-1884, Entry 529 (Unit 7).

Frank Brown (Braun) – Box 398 (Blush-J. Brown)
Henry Davis – Box 402 (Creedon-Denny)
Thomas H. French – Box 405 (Fish-Gaffney)
Jean Gallenne – Box 406 (Gallene-Graham)
Bernard Golden – Box 406 (Gallene-Graham)
Henry Gordon – Box 406 (Gallene-Graham)
George Heid – Box 408 (Harryman-Hoefig)
Henry Klotzbucher – Box 411 (Keogh-Lawrence)
William Lalor – Box 411 (Keogh-Lawrence)
Edward Mathey – Box 413 (Mackey-McCarthey)
William Morris – Box 416 (L. Moore-Neilson)
Frank Neely – Box 416 (L. Moore-Neilson)
Daniel Newell – Box 417 (Nelau-O'Sullivan)
William Robinson – Box 419 (Radigando-Roche
Roman Rutten – Box 420 (Roeder-Schneider)
John Ryan – Box 420 (Roeder-Schneider)
Hobart Ryder – Box 420 (Roeder-Schneider)
John Seamans – Box 421 (Scholl-Simius)
Robert Senn – Box 421 (Scholl-Simius)
Frank Sniffin – Box 422 (Skillmano-Staunton)
David Summers – Box 423 (Starl-Taylor)
Levi Thornberry – Box 424 (Tempes-Vigny)
Rollins Thorpe – Box 424 (Tempes-Vigny)
Thomas Varner – Box 424 (Tempes-Vigny)
George Weaver – Box 425 (Volkmann-Weller)
Charles Wiedman (filed under Weidman) – Box 425 (Volkmann-Weller)
John Whisten – Box 426 (Wemster-Winter)
Charles White (Henry Weihe) – Box 426 (Wemster-Winter)
Charles Williams – Box 426 (Wemster-Winter)

Records Group 94, Records of the Adjutant General's Office – Reports of Surgeons Accompanying Expeditions, Entry 624 (Box 1), Letter from Surgeon Tilton to the Surgeon General, October 26, 1877.

Records Group 153, Records of the Office of the Judge Advocate General – Army, Court Martial Case Files, 1809-1894.

Sergeant Patrick Carey – Case# QQ-603.
Sergeant Patrick Carey – Case# QQ-1465.
Private Charles Fischer – Case# PP-5461.
Captain Thomas H. French – Case# QQ-994.
Corporal John McGlone – Case# RR-1047.
Sergeant John H. Meier – Case# RR-2319.
Private John H. Meier – Case# RR-3698.
Sergeant Hugh N. Moore – Case# QQ-603.
Sergeant Hugh N. Moore – Case# QQ-2851.
Private Hugh N. Moore – Case# QQ-4224.
Private Hugh N. Moore – Case# RR-2826.
Corporal Hobart Ryder – Case# QQ-1361.
Private Robert Senn – Case# QQ-1361.
Corporal Frank Sniffin – Case# QQ-2687.
Sergeant Frank Sniffin – Case# QQ-3230.
Private Frank Sniffin – Case# RR-367.
Private Frank Stratton – Case# QQ-109.
Private Henry C. Weaver – Case#619.
Private Henry C. Weaver – Case# QQ-1044.
Private John Whisten – Case# PP-5461.
First Sergeant Charles White – Case# QQ-1418.

Records Group 393, Records of U. S. Army Continental Commands, 1821-1920, Part V, Military Installations, Fort Abraham Lincoln, North Dakota, Entry 5 – Special Orders.

Special Orders No. 37, Headquarters, 7th Cavalry, Fort Abraham Lincoln, Dakota Territory, dated May 9, 1876.

Records Group 393, Records of U. S. Army Continental Commands, 1821-1920, Part V, Military Installations, Fort Meade, South Dakota, Entry 24 – Register of Patients, Volume 1 and 2.

Records Group 393, Records of U.S. Army Continental Commands, 1821-1920, Part V, Military Installations, Fort Rice, South Dakota, Entry 1 – Letters and Endorsements.

Letter, Headquarters, Fort Rice, Dakota Territory to Assistant Adjutant General, Department of Dakota, dated September 1, 1875.

Letter, Headquarters, Fort Rice, Dakota Territory to the 7th Cavalry Regimental Quartermaster, dated September 5, 1875.

Letter, Headquarters, Fort Rice, Dakota Territory to the Assistant Adjutant General, Department of Dakota, dated November 20, 1875.

Letter, Headquarters, Fort Rice, Dakota Territory to the Assistant Adjutant General, Department of Dakota, dated February 25, 1876.

Letter, Headquarters, Fort Rice, Dakota Territory to the Assistant Adjutant General, Department of Dakota, dated March 4, 1876.

Records Group 393, Records of U.S. Army Continental Commands, 1821-1920, Part V, Military Installations, Fort Rice, South Dakota, Entry 4 – Letters and Telegrams Received.

Letter, Post Surgeon, Fort Rice, Dakota Territory to Post Adjutant, dated October 31, 1875.

Letter, Headquarters, Fort Rice, Dakota Territory to Captain Thomas French, Company M, dated December 1, 1875.

Letter, Captain Thomas French, Company M to Post Adjutant, Fort Rice, Dakota Territory, dated January 4, 1876.

Records Group 393, Records of U.S. Army Continental Commands, 1821-1920, Part V, Military Installations, Fort Rice, South Dakota, Entry 5 – General Orders and Circulars.

Garrison Orders No. 67, Headquarters, Fort Rice, Dakota Territory, dated September 22, 1874.

Garrison Orders No. 71, Headquarters, Fort Rice, Dakota Territory, dated October 1, 1874.

Garrison Orders No. 74, Headquarters, Fort Rice, Dakota Territory, dated November 3, 1874.

Garrison Orders No. 77, Headquarters, Fort Rice, Dakota Territory, dated December 5, 1874.

Garrison Orders No. 3, Headquarters, Fort Rice, Dakota Territory, dated February 5, 1875.

Garrison Orders No. 5, Headquarters, Fort Rice, Dakota Territory, dated March 9, 1875.

Garrison Orders No. 7, Headquarters, Fort Rice, Dakota Territory, dated April 13, 1875.

Garrison Orders No. 8, Headquarters, Fort Rice, Dakota Territory, dated April 24, 1875.

Garrison Orders No. 9, Headquarters, Fort Rice, Dakota Territory, dated April 29, 1875.

Garrison Orders No. 17, Headquarters, Fort Rice, Dakota Territory, dated June 6, 1875.

Garrison Orders No. 18, Headquarters, Fort Rice, Dakota Territory, dated June 12, 1875.

Garrison Orders No. 24, Headquarters, Fort Rice, Dakota Territory, dated July 28, 1875.

Garrison Orders No. 34, Headquarters, Fort Rice, Dakota Territory, dated November 6, 1875.

Garrison Circular, Headquarters, Fort Rice, Dakota Territory, dated November 15, 1875.

Garrison Orders No. 1, Headquarters, Fort Rice, Dakota Territory, dated January 5, 1876.

Garrison Orders No. 2, Headquarters, Fort Rice, Dakota Territory, dated January 16, 1876.

Garrison Orders No. 3, Headquarters, Fort Rice, Dakota Territory, dated January 25, 1876.

Garrison Orders No. 4, Headquarters, Fort Rice, Dakota Territory, dated February 2, 1876.

Post Orders No. 28, Headquarters, Fort Rice, Dakota Territory, dated March 23, 1876.

Post Orders No. 34, Headquarters, Fort Rice, Dakota Territory, dated April 5, 1876.

Post Orders No. 41, Headquarters, Fort Rice, Dakota Territory, dated April 16, 1876.

Post Orders No. 119, Headquarters, Fort Rice, Dakota Territory, dated September 9, 1876.

Post Orders No. 164, Headquarters, Fort Rice, Dakota Territory, dated November 27, 1876.

Records Group 393, Records of U. S. Army Continental Commands, 1821-1920, Part V, Military Installations, Fort Rice, North Dakota, Entry 6 – Special Orders.

Special Orders No. 131, Headquarters, Fort Rice, Dakota Territory, dated October 6, 1875.

Special Orders No. 132, Headquarters, Fort Rice, Dakota Territory, dated October 9, 1875.

Special Orders No. 135, Headquarters, Fort Rice, Dakota Territory, dated October 12, 1875.

Special Orders No. 137, Headquarters, Fort Rice, Dakota Territory, dated October 17, 1875.

Special Orders No. 138, Headquarters, Fort Rice, Dakota Territory, dated October 23, 1875.

Special Orders No. 141, Headquarters, Fort Rice, Dakota Territory, dated October 23, 1875.

Special Orders No. 147, Headquarters, Fort Rice, Dakota Territory, dated October 30, 1875.

Special Orders No. 160, Headquarters, Fort Rice, Dakota Territory, dated November 18, 1875.

Post Orders No. 171, Headquarters, Fort Rice, Dakota Territory, dated December 11, 1875.

Post Orders No. 14, Headquarters, Fort Rice, Dakota Territory, dated February 6, 1876.

Post Orders No. 31, Headquarters, Fort Rice, Dakota Territory, dated March 31, 1876.

Special Orders No. 41, Headquarters, Fort Rice, Dakota Territory, dated April 16, 1876.

Privately Owned Documents

Letter from George A. Custer to Joseph A. Tilford, Fort Lincoln, Dakota Territory, dated June 26, 1874. (Letter is from the Raab Collection gallery with provenance to the Tilford family.)

Letter from John Ryan to Thomas S. Norwood, Littlestown, PA, dated January 19, 1922. (Letter in the possession of Joanne Codi of Coatesville, PA [cyclist@verizon.net])

United States of America Bureau of Pensions Letters to John Ryan; correspondence dated October 11, 1915 and August 11, 1924. (Author's collection)

United States Army Discharge for First Sergeant John Ryan, 7th Cavalry; discharge dated December 21, 1876. (Author's collection)

Secondary Source Documents

Books

Adams, Kevin. *Class and Race in the Frontier Army: Military Life in the West, 1870-1890,* Norman, OK: University of Oklahoma Press, 2009.

Agnew, Jeremy. *Life of a Soldier on the Western Frontier*, Missoula, MT: Mountain Press Publishing Company, 2008.

Barnard, Sandy. *Custer's First Sergeant John Ryan*, Terre Haute, IN: AST Press, 1996.

Barnard, Sandy. *Digging Into Custer's Last Stand*, Terre Haute, IN: AST Press, 2003.

Barnard, Sandy, editor. *Ten Years with Custer: A 7th Cavalryman's Memoirs*, Terre Haute, IN: AST Press, 2001.

Bourke, John G. *On the Border with Crook*, New York: C. Scribner's Sons, 1891.

Brady, Cyrus T. *Indian Fights and Fighters*, New York: Doubleday, Page & Company, 1909.

Brininstool, Earle Alonzo. *Troopers with Custer: Incidents of the Battle of the Little Big Horn*, Harrisburg, PA: The Stackpole Company, 1952.

Calhoun, James. *With Custer in '74: James Calhoun's Diary of the Black Hills Expedition*, edited by Lawrence A. Frost, Provo, UT: Brigham Young University Press, 1979.

Camp, Walter Mason. *Walter M. Camp's Little Bighorn Rosters*, annotated by Richard G. Hardoff, Spokane, WA: Arthur H. Clark Company, 2002.

Carroll, John, editor. *A Seventh Cavalry Scrapbook*, Volume 1, "Memories of the Battle of the Little Big Horn," by Daniel Newell, Bryan, TX: Privately Published, 1978.

Carroll, John, editor. *A Seventh Cavalry Scrapbook*, Volume 2, "A General Godfrey Letter," by E.S. Godfrey, Bryan, TX: Privately Published, 1978.

Carroll, John, editor. *A Seventh Cavalry Scrapbook*, Volume 2, "The Sioux Campaign and the Last Battle of General Custer," by General C.A. Woodruff, Bryan, TX: Privately Published, 1978.

Carroll, John. *Ten Years with Custer Among the American Indians and Other Writings by John Ryan*, Bryan, TX: Privately Published, 1980.

Carroll, John, editor. *The Court Martial of Captain Thomas H. French; or Why Captain French Did Not Testify at the Reno Court of Inquiry*, Bryan, TX: Privately Published, 1974.

Carroll, John. *The Sunshine Magazine Articles*, Bryan, TX: Privately Published, 1979.

Chambers, Lee. *Fort Abraham Lincoln Dakota Territory*, Atglen, PA: Schiffer Publishing, 2008.

Chandler, Melbourne C. *Of Garry Owen in Glory: The History of the 7th Cavalry*, Annandale, VA: Turnpike Press, 1960.

Chorne, Laudie J. *Following the Custer Trail of 1876*, Bismarck, ND: Trails West Publishing, 2001.

Committee in Charge of the Commemoration Exercises Fifty Years Later, *The Teepee Book*, Sheridan, WY: The Miles Company, 1926.

Connell, Evan S. *Son of the Morning Star: Custer and the Little Bighorn*, San Francisco, CA: North Point Press, 1984.

Custer, George A. *My Life on the Plains*, New York: Promontory Press, 1995.

Darling, Roger. *Custer's Seventh Cavalry Comes to Dakota*, El Segundo, CA: Upton and Sons, 1989.

DeBarthe, Joe. *The Life and Adventures of Frank Grouard, Chief of Scouts, U.S.A.*, St. Joseph, MO: Combe Printing Company, 1894.

DiMarco, Louis A. *War Horse: A History of the Military Horse and Rider*, Yardley, PA: Westholme Press, 2008.

Dippie, Brian W. *Custer's Last Stand: The Anatomy of an American Myth*, Lincoln, NE: University of Nebraska Press, 1976.

Dippie, Brian W. *Nomad: George A. Custer in Turf, Field, and Farm*, Austin, TX: University of Texas Press, 1980.

Donahue, Michael. *Drawing Battle Lines: The Map Testimony of Custer's Last Fight*, El Segundo, CA: Upton & Sons Publishers, 2008.

Donovan, James. *A Terrible Glory: Custer and the Little Bighorn – the Last Great Battle of the American West*, New York: Little, Brown and Company, 2008.

Fadala, Sam. *The Complete Blackpowder Handbook*, Iola, WI: DBI Books, 1996.

Farrington, Dusan P. *Arming & Equipping the U.S. Cavalry 1865-1902*, Lincoln, RI: Andrew Mowbray Publishers, 2004.

Finerty, John F. *War-path and Bivouac: the Big Horn and Yellowstone Expedition*, Chicago, IL: R.R. Donnelley & Sons Company, 1955.

Fougera, Katherine Gibson. *With Custer's Cavalry*, Caldwell, ID: The Caxton Printers, 1940.

Fox, Richard A. *Archaeology, History, and Custer's Last Battle*, Norman, OK: University of Oklahoma Press, 1993.

Gibbon, Guy. *The Sioux: the Dakota and Lakota Nations*, Malden, MA: Blackwell Publishing, 2003.

Godfrey, Edward Settle. *The field diary of Lt. Edward Settle Godfrey, commanding Co. K, 7th Cavalry Regiment under Lt. Colonel George Armstrong Custer in the Sioux encounter at the Battle of the Little Big Horn, covering the period from May 17, 1876 when the expedition commanded by Brigadier General Alfred H. Terry left Ft. Abraham Lincoln, Bismarck Dakota Territory until the return of the battered regiment a few days after September 24, 1876, to the same place*, Portland, OR: Champoeg Press, 1957.

Goodrich, Thomas. *Scalp Dance: Indian Warfare on the High Plains, 1865-1879*, Mechanicsburg, PA: Stackpole Books, 1997.

Grafe, Ernest and Paul Horsted. *Exploring with Custer: The 1874 Black Kills Expedition*, Custer, SD: Golden Valley Press, 2005.

Graham, Colonel W.A. *The Custer Myth: A Source Book of Custeriana*, Mechanicsburg, PA: Stackpole Books, 2000.

Gray, John S. *Centennial Campaign: The Sioux War of 1876*, Fort Collins, CO: The Old Army Press, 1976.

Hammer, Kenneth. *Custer in '76: Walter Camp's Notes on the Custer Fight*, Provo, UT: Brigham Young University, 1976.

Hardorff, Richard G. *Cheyenne Memories of the Custer Fight*, Lincoln, NE: University of Nebraska Press (Bison Press), 1998.

Hardorff, Richard G. *Hokahey! A Good Day to Die!* Lincoln, NE: University of Nebraska Press, 1999.

Hardorff, Richard G., editor. *On the Little Bighorn with Walter Camp; A Collection of Walter Mason Camp's Letters, Notes and opinions on Custer's Last Fight*, El Segundo, CA: Upton & Sons Publishers, 2002.

Hatch, Thom. *The Custer Companion: A Comprehensive Guide to the Life of George Armstrong Custer and the Plains Indian Wars*, Mechanicsburg, PA: The Stackpole Company, 2002.

Hedron, Paul L. *Traveler's Guide to the Great Sioux War*, Helena, MT: Montana Historical Society Press, 1996.

Hedron, Paul L. *The Great Sioux War 1876-77*, Helena, MT: Montana Historical Society Press, 1991.

Herring, Hal. *Famous Firearms of the Old West*, Guilford, CN: Morris Book Publishing, 2008.

Hofling, Charles K. *Custer and the Little Big Horn: A Psychobiographical Inquiry*, Detroit, MI: Wayne State University Press, 1981.

Hook, Richard. *Warriors at the Little Bighorn 1876*, Osprey Men at Arms Series #408, Oxford, England: Osprey Publishing, 2004.

Hutton, Paul Andrew. *The Custer Reader*, Lincoln, NE: University of Nebraska Press, 1993.

Johnson, Barry. *A Captain of Chivalric Courage: Thomas H. French, 7th Cavalry*, The Brand Book, Vol. 25, Numbers 1&2, London: The English Westerners' Society, 1987.

Kain, Robert C. *In the Valley of the Little Bighorn: The 7th and the Sioux*, Newfane, VT: Self-published, 1969. This volume has personal notes and observations from Colonel Edward M. Offley, United States Cavalry, retired.

Kershaw, Robert J. *Red Sabbath: The Battle of Little Bighorn*, Surrey, England: Ian Allan Publishing, 2005.

Klokner, James B. *The Officer Corps of Custer's Seventh Cavalry 1866-1876*, Atglen, PA: Schiffer Publishing, 2007.

Koenig, Arthur. *Authentic History of the Indian Campaign Which Culminated in Custer's Last Battle, June 25, 1876*, St. Louis, MO: Anheuser Busch.

Kollbaum, Marc E. *Gateway to the West: The History of Jefferson Barracks from 1826 – 1894*, Volume 1, St. Louis, MO: Friends of Jefferson Barracks.

Koster, John. *Custer Survivor: The End of a Myth, the Beginning of a Legend*, Palisades, NY: History Publishing Company LLC, 2010.

Laubin, Reginald and Gladys. *American Indian Archery*, Norman, OK: University of Oklahoma Press, 1980.

Lederle, Dr. James. *To Gaze into the Eyes of Hell*, Indiana: Innovative Ventures Group, 2009.

Libby, Orin G., editor. *The Arikara Narrative of Custer's Campaign and the Battle of the Little Bighorn*, Norman, OK: University of Oklahoma Press, 1998.

Liddic, Bruce R. *Vanishing Victory: Custer's Final March*, El Segundo, CA: Upton & Sons, Publishers, 2004.

Marquis, Thomas B. *Keep the Last Bullet for Yourself*, Algonac, MI: Reference Publications, 1985.

Marquis, Thomas B. *A Warrior Who Fought Custer*, Minneapolis, MN: The Midwest Company, 1931.

Marshall, Joseph M. *The Day the World Ended at Little Bighorn: A Lakota History*, New York: Viking, 2003.

McChristian, Douglas C. *The U.S. Army in the West: 1870-1880*, Norman, OK: University of Oklahoma Press, 1995.

Michno, Gregory F. *Lakota Noon: The Indian Narrative of Custer's Defeat*, Missoula, MT: Mountain Press Publishing Company, 2007.

Michno, Gregory F. *The Mystery of E Troop: Custer's Gray Horse Company at the Little Bighorn*, Missoula, MT: Mountain Press Publishing Company, 1994.

Mills, Charles K. *Harvest of Barren Regrets: The Army Career of Frederick William Benteen, 1834-1898*, Glendale, CA: The Arthur H. Clark Company, 1985.

Mills, Charles K. *Rosters from 7th U.S. Cavalry campaigns, 1866-1896*, Mattituck, NY: J.M. Carroll and Company, 1983.

Mulford, Ami Frank. *Fighting Indians in the 7th U.S. Cavalry*, Corning, NY: Paul Lindsley Mulford, 1879.

Nichols, Ronald H., editor. *Men with Custer: Biographies of the 7th Cavalry*, Hardin, MT: Custer Battlefield Historical and Museum Association, 2000.

Nye, Elwood L. *Marching with Custer: a day-to-day evaluation of the uses, abuses, and conditions of the animals on the ill-fated expedition of 1876*, Glendale, CA: Arthur H. Clark Company, 1964.

Olejniczak, *Julian M. Register of Graduates and Former Cadets of the United States Military Academy West Point New York, 2000*, West Point, NY: Association of Graduates USMA, 2000.

Overfield, Loyd J. *The Little Bighorn, 1876: the official communications, documents and reports, with rosters of the officers and troops of the campaign*, Glendale, CA: A.H. Clark Company, 1971.

Panzeri, Peter. *Little Big Horn 1876: Custer's Last Stand*, Osprey Campaign #39, Oxford, England: Osprey Publishing, 1995.

Pennington, Jack. *The Battle of the Little Bighorn: A Comprehensive Study*, El Segundo, CA: Upton & Sons, Publishers, 2001.

Philbrick, Nathaniel. *The Last Stand: Custer, Sitting Bull, and the Battle of the Little Bighorn*, New York: The Penguin Group, 2010.

Poyer, Joe and Craig Riesch. *The .45-70 Springfield*, Tustin, CA: North Cape Publications, 2006.

Reedstrom, Ernest L. *Bugles, Banners & War Bonnets*, Caldwell, ID: The Caxton Printers, 1977.

Remsburg, John E. *Charley Reynolds, Soldier, Hunter, Scout and Guide*, Reprint of The Potter Weekly Kansan, Potter, KS, 1914-1915.

"Reno-Benteen Entrenchment Trail," Little Bighorn Battlefield Guidebook, Western National Parks Association, 2002.

Rickey, Don. *Forty Miles a Day on Beans and Hay*, Norman, OK: University of Oklahoma Press, 1972.

Robinson, Charles M. *A Good Year to Die: The Story of the Great Sioux War*, New York: Random House, 1995.

Rose, Alexander. *American Rifle: A Biography*, New York: Delacorte Press, 2008.

Schneider, James V. *Behind Custer at the Little Big Horn: The Story of Lieutenant Edward Mathey and the Packtrain*, Fort Wayne, IN: Privately Published, 1980.

Scott, Douglas D., Richard A. Fox, Jr. and Melissa A. Connor, *Archaeological Perspectives on the Battle of the Little Bighorn*, Norman, OK: University of Oklahoma Press, 1989.

Scott, Douglas D., P. Willey and Melissa A. Connor, *They Died with Custer: Soldiers Bones from the Battle of the Little Bighorn*, Norman, OK: University of Oklahoma Press.

Sklenar, Larry. *To Hell with Honor; Custer and the Little Bighorn*, Norman, OK: University of Oklahoma Press, 2003.

Snelson, Bob. *Death of a Myth: Seventh Cavalry at the Little Bighorn*, Snelsonbooks.com, 2005.

Stands in Timber, John and Margot Liberty. *Cheyenne Memories*, Lincoln, NE: University of Nebraska Press, 1967.

Stewart, Edgar I. *Custer's Luck*, Norman, OK: University of Oklahoma Press, 1980.

Swanson, Glenwood J. *G. A. Custer: His Life and Times*, Agua Dulce, CA: Swanson Productions, 2004.

Tate, Michael L. *The Frontier Army in the Settlement of the West*, Norman, OK: University of Oklahoma Press, 1999.

Taylor, William O. *With Custer on the Little Bighorn*, New York: Viking, 1996.

The Teepee Book, A Monthly Periodical, Reprint of Volume 2, #4 (April 1916) to Volume 2, #12 (December 1916), New York: Sol Lewis, 1974.

Underwood, Larry D. *The Custer Fight: and Other Tales of the Old West*, Lincoln, NE: Media Publishing, 1989.

Unger, Arthur C. *The ABCs of Custer's Last Stand: Arrogance, Betrayal and Cowardice*, El Segundo, CA: Upton & Sons Publishers, 2004.

United States Army, *Cavalry Tactics* (Reprint), New York: D. Appleton and Company, 1874.

Urwin, Gregory J.W. *The United States Cavalry: An Illustrated History*, Poole, England: Blandford Press, 1983.

Utley, Robert M. *Life in Custer's Cavalry: Diaries and Letters of Albert and Jennie Barnitz*, 1867-1868, New Haven, CN: Yale University Press, 1977.

Vaughn, J.W. *Indian Fights: New Facts on Seven Encounters*, Norman, OK: University of Oklahoma Press, 1966.

Wagner, Glendolin Damon. *Old Neutriment*, New York: Sol Lewis, 1973.

Walker, L.G. Jr. *Dr. Henry R. Porter: The Surgeon Who Survived Little Bighorn*, Jefferson, NC: McFarland & Company, Inc., 2008.

Weibert, Don L. *Custer, Cases & Cartridges: The Weibert Collection Analyzed*, Billings, MT: D. Weibert, 1989.

Weibert, Henry and Don L. *Sixty-six Years in Custer's Shadow*, Billings, MT: Falcon Press, 1985.

Welch, James. *Killing Custer: The Battle of the Little Bighorn and the Fate of the Plains Indians*, New York: W.W. Norton & Company, 1994.

Westfall, Douglas Paul. *Letters from the Field: Wallace at the Little Big Horn*, Orange, CA: The Paragon Agency, 1997.

Willert, James. *Little Big Horn Diary: Chronicle of the 1876 Indian War*, El Segundo, CA: Upton and Sons, 1997.

Williams, Roger L. *Military Register of Custer's Last Command*, Norman, OK: The Arthur H. Clark Company, 2009.

Windolph, Charles. *I Fought with Custer: The Story of Sergeant Windolph, Last Survivor of the Battle of the Little Big Horn*, edited by Frazier Hunt and Robert Hunt, New York: Charles Scribner's Sons, 1947.

Winthrop, Colonel William. *Military Law and Precedents*, Volume 1 and 2, Boston: Little, Brown and Company, 1896.

Yenne, Bill. *Indian Wars: The Campaign for the American West*, Yardley, PA: Westholme Publishing, 2006.

Newspaper Articles

"Custer Trooper a Suicide," *New York Times*, November 8, 1925.

Forrest, Robert Earle. "Fighting with Custer: Two Men Who Were with Gallant General Custer at Little Bighorn Battle Are Still Living," *Morning Observer*, Washington, PA: October 1932.

Gallenne, Jean B. "The Fatal Day: A Soldier's Journal," *St. Paul and Minneapolis Pioneer Press*, January 16, 1879.

"General Custer's Last Fight," *New York Times*, July 9, 1876.

Meyer, Eugene L. "Tracking a Custer Indian Fighter," *The Washington Post*, March 27, 1980.

Schulte, Brigid. "Unearthed War Relics See Battle Again: Archaeologists Decry History Buffs' Digs," *The Washington Post*, April 16, 2006.

"Testifying About Major Reno," *New York Times*, New York: January 19, 1879.

Thackeray, Lorna. "Cavalry men's lives come to troubled ends," *Billings Gazette*, Billings, MT: June 21, 2009.

Thackeray, Lorna. "Haunted by history: Tragedy followed Bighorn battle survivors," *Billings Gazette*, Billings, MT: June 21, 2009.

"The Indian Slaughter," *New York Times*, July 8, 1876.

"The Last Summons: Death of Captain French," *The Leavenworth Times*, Leavenworth, Kansas, March 28, 1882.

"The Little Horn Massacre," *New York Times*, July 7, 1876.

"Un Bisontin entre bisons et Indiens," *L'Est Républicain* (Besancon, France), June 25, 2006.

"William E. Morris, Jurist, Dead at 75," *New York Times*, New York: November 27, 1933.

Periodical Articles

Army and Navy Journal, "Recent Deaths," April 1, 1882.

Arnold, Steve. "Cooke's scrawled note: Last word from doomed command," *Greasy Grass Magazine*, Volume 14, May 1998, Hardin, MT: Custer Battlefield Historical & Museum Association.

Barnard, Sandy. "A 7th Cavalryman speaks out," *Greasy Grass Magazine*, Volume 21, May 2005, Hardin, MT: Custer Battlefield Historical & Museum Association.

Barnard, Sandy. "Pvt. Sivertsen's Horse: Victim of the Little Big Horn," *Greasy Grass Magazine*, Volume 12, May 1996, Hardin, MT: Custer Battlefield Historical & Museum Association.

Clark, Dennis. "Private Roman Rutten: Custer's Tailor," 15th Annual Symposium, Custer Battlefield Historical & Museum Association, held at Hardin, MT on June 22, 2001.

Collin, Richard. "Custer's Favorite Scout," *Greasy Grass Magazine*, Volume 13, May 1997, Hardin, MT: Custer Battlefield Historical & Museum Association.

Custer, George A. "Life on the Plains," *The Galaxy*, Volume XVII, January 1874 to June 1874, New York: Sheldon & Company, 1874.

Doerner, John A. "The Boys of '76: Seventh Cavalry Letters and Recollections of the 1876 Sioux Campaign," Cave Creek, AZ: *True West Magazine*, May/June 2001.

Ellison, Douglas W. "Mystery along Rosebud Creek," *Greasy Grass Magazine*, Volume 17, May 2001, Hardin, MT: Custer Battlefield Historical & Museum Association.

"Epworth's History is in God's Time," *Epworth United Methodist Church Newsletter*, Palmyra, NJ: Epworth UMC, September 2007.

Godfrey, Edward Settle. *After the Custer Battle*, Historical Reprints, Sources of Northwest History No. 29, Missoula, MT: Frontier and Midland, 1939.

Hammer, Kenneth. "Recalling the Little Bighorn: Stories Told by 7th Cavalry Survivors," *Greasy Grass Magazine*, Volume 24, May 2008, Hardin, MT: Custer Battlefield Historical & Museum Association.

Heski, Thomas M. "Camp Powell: The Powder River Supply Depot," 15th Annual Symposium, Custer Battlefield Historical & Museum Association, held at Hardin, MT on June 22, 2001.

Heski, Thomas M. "Night March, Halt and Reconnaissance, and Preparation for Battle, 18th Annual Symposium, Custer Battlefield Historical & Museum Association, held at Hardin, MT on June 25, 2004.

History Channel Magazine, "Custer's Selenium Factor," New York, November/December 2005.

James, Garry. "Custer's Last Gun," *Guns & Ammo*, InterMedia Outdoors Inc, December 2009.

Koster, John. "Captain Grant Marsh Was King of the Missouri River," *Wild West Magazine*, Volume 23, No. 1, Leesburg, VA, June 2010.

Koster, John. "Fulcrum to Disaster," *Wild West Magazine*, Volume 23, No. 1, Leesburg, VA, June 2010.

Leinicke, Kris. *The Indian guns of the Little Big Horn*, Rock Island, IL: Rock Island Arsenal Historical Society, 1988.

Mangum, Neil C., editor. "Reno's Battalion in the Battle of the Little Big Horn," *Greasy Grass Magazine*, Volume 2, May 1986, Hardin, MT: Custer Battlefield Historical & Museum Association.

Michno, Greg. "Battle of Little Bighorn: Were the Weapons the Deciding Factor?" *Wild West*, Leesburg, VA: Weider History Group, June 1998.

Mulligan, Tim. "Custer and the Little Bighorn: A Needed Perspective," *Research Review: The Journal of the Little Bighorn Associates,* Volume 23, Number 2, Summer 2009, Rockville, MD: The Little Bighorn Associates. The article was reprinted from the Spring 1973 *Research Review*.

Nichols, Ron. "Command Decision – 1876 Style: How did Custer organize his regiment?" *Greasy Grass Magazine*, Volume 21, May 2005, Hardin, MT: Custer Battlefield Historical & Museum Association.

Noyes, C. Lee. "A Question of Arms: Ordnance "Causes" and Consequences of the Little Bighorn," 11th Annual Symposium, Custer Battlefield Historical & Museum Association, held at Hardin, MT on June 27, 1997.

Noyes, C. Lee. "The Valley Fight: The Enlisted Man's Perspective," 20th Annual Symposium, Custer Battlefield Historical & Museum Association, held at Hardin, MT on June 23, 2006.

Pitsch, Jason and Keith T. Werts, "The Reno Valley Fight: Assessing river and land changes," *Greasy Grass Magazine*, Volume 23, May 2007, Hardin, MT: Custer Battlefield Historical & Museum Association.

Schoenberger, Dale. "Custer's Scouts," *Montana Western History*, Volume XVI, No. 2, Spring 1966.

Sklenar, Larry. "Medals for Custer's Men," *Montana: The Magazine of Western History*, Helena, MT: Montana Historical Society, Volume 50, Winter 2000.

Smith, Robert Barr. "Benteen: Between a Rock and a Hard Place," *Wild West Magazine*, Volume 23, No. 1, Leesburg, VA, June 2010.

Wyman, Michael L. and Rocky L. Boyd. "Towards an Understanding of Peter Thompson and His Accounts of the Battle of the Little Big Horn," 18th Annual Symposium, Custer Battlefield Historical & Museum Association, held at Hardin, MT on June 25, 2004.

Presentations

"The Battle," Michael Kouri, Billings, MT: 2009 Little Bighorn Associates 36th Annual Conference, June 23, 2009.

"The Journey from Fort Abraham Lincoln to the Little Big Horn," Tom Heski, Billings, MT: 2009 Little Bighorn Associates 36th Annual Conference, June 23, 2009.

"The Preparation at Fort Abraham Lincoln," Al Johnson, Billings, MT: 2009 Little Bighorn Associates 36th Annual Conference, June 23, 2009.

"The Reno Court, Fact or Fiction," Jim Donovan, Billings, MT: 2009 Little Bighorn Associates 36th Annual Conference, June 23, 2009.

"The Size of the Indian Village and Squaw Creek," Michael N. Donahue, Billings, MT: 2009 Little Bighorn Associates 36th Annual Conference, June 23, 2009.

"Was There A Timber Fight?" C. Lee Noyes, Indianapolis, IN: Indianapolis Little Bighorn Symposium, September 12, 2009.

Correspondence and Discussions

Discussion with Lou DiMarco, author of *War Horse*, conducted at Leavenworth, KS, on May 15, 2010.

Discussion with John Doerner, Chief Historian Little Bighorn of the Little Bighorn Battlefield National Monument, conducted at the battlefield archives, May 10-12, 2010.

Discussions with Olga MacLean, former Drug and Alcohol Counselor for the U.S. Army at Frankfurt and Mannheim, Germany, June 2010.

Discussion with Dianne Tokach, great-great-granddaughter of Yellow Eyes, a Hunkpapa woman who was at the Little Bighorn on the day of the battle, conducted at Fort Abraham Lincoln, ND, May 8, 2010.

Email discussions with Sheila Abarr, Public Affairs Specialist, Armed Forces Retirement Home in Washington, D.C., November 2009.

Email discussions with Dennis K. (DK) Clark, author of "Private Roman Rutten: Custer's Tailor," 15th Annual Symposium, Custer Battlefield Historical & Museum Association, October-November 2009.

Email discussions with Bob and Edward Connor, great-grandsons of Private Jean Baptiste Gallenne, July 2010.

Email discussions with Lee C. Noyes, author of "The Valley Fight: The Enlisted Man's Perspective," 20th Annual Symposium, Custer Battlefield Historical & Museum Association, September-November 2009.

Email discussions with Brian Spatola, Collections Manager, Anatomical Division and Michael Rhode, Archivist, Otis Historical Archives, National Museum of Health and Medicine, Armed Forces Institute of Pathology, concerning the medical aspects of the death of Private Frank Braun of Company M, November 2009.

Unpublished Sources

Arlington Cemetery Website, www.arlingtoncemetery.net.

Genealogy Website, www.ceangail.com.

Gutowsky, Wayne R. *Burial Sites of the Survivors of the Little Big Horn Battle*.

Naval Oceanography Portal. *Complete Sun and Moon Data for One Day: U.S. Cities and Towns*. http://www.usno.navy.mil/USNO/astronomical-applications/data-services/rs-one-day-us.

Vihlene, Shannon Marjorie. *Custer's Last Drag: An Examination of Tobacco Use Among the Seventh Cavalry during the Nineteenth Century*, Master of Arts in Anthropology (Forensic Anthropology) Thesis, Missoula, MT: The University of Montana, 2008.

Special Collections

University of Wisconsin at Whitewater Library

Dr. Kenneth Hammer, noted Little Bighorn historian, donated his private papers to the University of Wisconsin at Whitewater Library in 2009. For many years, Dr. Hammer was a professor of Economic History at the university. Much of the collection has been divided into what the library has classified as pamphlets. These include:

Pamphlet 23, University of Wisconsin at Whitewater Special Collection of Dr. Kenneth Hammer: Edgerly, Winfield S. "Narrative on the March of the 7th Cavalry from the Yellowstone River to Sitting Bull's Camp."

Pamphlet 28, University of Wisconsin at Whitewater Special Collection of Dr. Kenneth Hammer: French, Thomas H. "Letter of Capt. French to the Mother of Lieut. W. W. Cooke, 1880."

Pamphlet 42, University of Wisconsin at Whitewater Special Collection of Dr. Kenneth Hammer: Hammer, Kenneth M. "Custer's Valiant Men."

Pamphlet 43, University of Wisconsin at Whitewater Special Collection of Dr. Kenneth Hammer: Hammer, Kenneth M. "Custer's Valiant Soldiers."

Pamphlet 45, University of Wisconsin at Whitewater Special Collection of Dr. Kenneth Hammer: Hammer, Kenneth M. "The Springfield Carbine on the Western Frontier."

Pamphlet 54, University of Wisconsin at Whitewater Special Collection of Dr. Kenneth Hammer: Hutchins, James S. "The Cavalry Campaign Outfit at the Little Bighorn," *Military Collector and Historian*, Winter 1956.

Other papers from Dr. Hammer are contained in four large cardboard storage boxes, each box containing several dozen un-numbered, but titled, folders, each folder containing letters, clipped articles, and notes. For this study, the following folders were especially helpful:

Box 2, 7th Cavalry Muster Rolls File Folder. This folder contains a list of 7th Cavalry soldiers and a list of Indian warriors at the battle.

Box 2, Miscellaneous Papers Folder. Among many things, there is information on 7th Cavalry soldiers from Pennsylvania.

Box 4, Widows and Children Folder.

Additionally, in this special collection is an annotated update by Dr. Hammer, titled *Men with Custer; the Working Copy*, 2009.

INDEX

7th Cavalry Army Personnel

7th Cavalry Civilian Personnel

7th Cavalry U.S. Indian Scouts

Warriors

U.S. Army Personnel

U.S. Civilians

Foreign Civilians

Index Abbreviations: PVT (Private), CPL (Corporal), SGT (Sergeant), 1SG (First Sergeant), 2LT (Second Lieutenant), 1LT (First Lieutenant), CPT (Captain), MAJ (Major), LTC (Lieutenant Colonel), COL (Colonel), BG (Brigadier General), MG (Major General), LTG (Lieutenant General), GEN (General).

f/n = in the footnotes